**HOLOCAUST**
Mothers &
Daughters

# HBI SERIES ON JEWISH WOMEN

SHULAMIT REINHARZ, General Editor

SYLVIA BARACK FISHMAN, Associate Editor

The HBI Series on Jewish Women, created by the Hadassah-Brandeis Institute, publishes a wide range of books by and about Jewish women in diverse contexts and time periods. Of interest to scholars and the educated public, the HBI Series on Jewish Women fills major gaps in Jewish Studies and in Women and Gender Studies as well as their intersection.

The HBI Series on Jewish Women is supported by a generous gift from Dr. Laura S. Schor.

For the complete list of books that are available in this series, please see www.upne.com

Federica K. Clementi, *Holocaust Mothers and Daughters: Family, History, and Trauma*

Elana Maryles Sztokman and Chaya Rosenfeld Gorsetman, *Educating in the Divine Image: Gender Issues in Orthodox Jewish Day Schools*

Ilana Szobel, *A Poetics of Trauma: The Work of Dahlia Ravikovitch*

Susan M. Weiss and Netty C. Gross-Horowitz, *Marriage and Divorce in the Jewish State: Israel's Civil War*

Ronit Irshai, *Fertility and Jewish Law: Feminist Perspectives on Orthodox Responsa Literature*

Elana Maryles Sztokman, *The Men's Section: Orthodox Jewish Men in an Egalitarian World*

Sharon Faye Koren, *Forsaken: The Menstruant in Medieval Jewish Mysticism*

Sonja M. Hedgepeth and Rochelle G. Saidel, editors, *Sexual Violence against Jewish Women during the Holocaust*

Julia R. Lieberman, editor, *Sephardi Family Life in the Early Modern Diaspora*

Derek Rubin, editor, *Promised Lands: New Jewish American Fiction on Longing and Belonging*

Carol K. Ingall, editor, *The Women Who Reconstructed American Jewish Education: 1910–1965*

Gaby Brimmer and Elena Poniatowska, *Gaby Brimmer: An Autobiography in Three Voices*

Harriet Hartman and Moshe Hartman, *Gender and American Jews: Patterns in Work, Education, and Family in Contemporary Life*

Dvora E. Weisberg, *Levirate Marriage and the Family in Ancient Judaism*

Ellen M. Umansky and Dianne Ashton, editors, *Four Centuries of Jewish Women's Spirituality: A Sourcebook*

## THE TAUBER INSTITUTE SERIES FOR
## THE STUDY OF EUROPEAN JEWRY

JEHUDA REINHARZ, General Editor
SYLVIA FUKS FRIED, Associate Editor
EUGENE R. SHEPPARD, Associate Editor

The Tauber Institute Series is dedicated to publishing compelling and innovative approaches to the study of modern European Jewish history, thought, culture, and society. The series features scholarly works related to the Enlightenment, modern Judaism and the struggle for emancipation, the rise of nationalism and the spread of antisemitism, the Holocaust and its aftermath, as well as the contemporary Jewish experience. The series is published under the auspices of the Tauber Institute for the Study of European Jewry—established by a gift to Brandeis University from Dr. Laszlo N. Tauber—and is supported, in part, by the Tauber Foundation and the Valya and Robert Shapiro Endowment.

For the complete list of books that are available in this series, please see www.upne.com

FEDERICA K. CLEMENTI

# HOLOCAUST
# Mothers &
# Daughters

## FAMILY, HISTORY, AND TRAUMA

BRANDEIS UNIVERSITY PRESS
WALTHAM, MASSACHUSETTS

BRANDEIS UNIVERSITY PRESS
An imprint of University Press of New England
www.upne.com
© 2013 Brandeis University
All rights reserved
Manufactured in the United States of America
Designed by Eric M. Brooks
Typeset in Quadraat and DIN Next by Passumpsic Publishing

University Press of New England is a member of the
Green Press Initiative. The paper used in this book meets
their minimum requirement for recycled paper.

Library of Congress Cataloging-in-Publication Data
Clementi, Federica K., author.
Holocaust mothers and daughters: family, history, and trauma /
Federica K. Clementi.
    pages  cm. — (HBI series on Jewish women)
Includes bibliographical references and index.
ISBN 978-1-61168-475-9 (cloth: alk. paper) —
ISBN 978-1-61168-476-6 (pbk.: alk. paper) —
ISBN 978-1-61168-477-3 (ebook)
1. Jewish women in the Holocaust—Biography. 2. Mothers and daughters.
3. Jewish children in the Holocaust—Biography. 4. Holocaust, Jewish (1939–
1945)—Psychological aspects. 5. Holocaust, Jewish (1939-1945)—Moral and
ethical aspects. 6. Jewish Women—Violence against—Europe—History—
20th century. 7. World War, 1939-1945—Atrocities—Moral and ethical
aspects. 8. Psychic trauma in literature. I. Title.
D804.47.C54   2013
940.53'18082—dc23      2013024057

5 4 3 2 1

To the eight-year-old girl,
deported from Berlin with her parents,
who never returned

# CONTENTS

# FOREWORD
Shulamit Reinharz

Immediately after World War II, published writing about the Holocaust (in Hebrew, *Shoah*) was scarce. But as time passed, a multitude of analyses and personal testimonies appeared, creating a virtual flood of attempts to document, bear witness, and understand the Shoah. This first transition—from relative silence to an ocean of writing—became a sea change for Holocaust studies.

A second sea change, as documented by the Hadassah-Brandeis Institute (HBI), occurred in the 1990s when researchers began to ask questions about Jews and gender within the Holocaust context. A new flood of literature ensued, with works by Judith Baumel, Lenore Weitzman, Dalia Ofer, Rochelle Saidel and many others. In 2010, the HBI published *Sexual Violence against Jewish Women during the Holocaust*, edited by Sonja M. Hedgepeth and Rochelle G. Saidel. It was that anthology, I believe, that initiated serious discussion of a new incendiary topic: the sexual violation of Jewish women during the Holocaust.

Prior to that book's publication, the notion of Jewish women being raped by Nazis, for example, was unmentioned and nearly preposterous. After all, Nazis portrayed Jewish women as disgusting, dirty characters. Sexual congress with them, therefore, would debilitate the glorious Aryan race. The notion that not only Nazis but also Jewish men and gentile rescuers might rape Jewish girls and women was also unthinkable. And yet, Hedgepeth and Saidel produced incontrovertible documentation that such crimes did actually occur, repeatedly. In fact, Hedgepeth and Saidel demonstrated that accounts of rape were part of Jewish women's taped testimonies in various survivor collections, and yet somehow this material was not recognized, named or analyzed.

It is possible that 2013 will be seen as another sea change in Holocaust research. With the publication of this new book, Federica K. Clementi's *Holocaust Mothers and Daughters: Family, History, and Trauma*, we are now able to recognize, name, and analyze yet another dimension of the Holocaust experience: the mother-daughter relationship. Until now, writing harsh critical perspectives on relationships within the Jewish family was taboo. The pain of Holocaust memories and survivors' children's desires to protect parents who were victimized kept many from admitting that some (all?) families were less than perfect. And even if a survivor knew that, as human beings, their parents had flaws, their children were not going to be the ones to announce that fact. Clementi's book may be the first to question the idealization of the Jewish mother-daughter relationship during and after the War.

Using a psychoanalytic lens to view Jewish children's development under Nazi rule, Clementi explains that because girls' adolescence is always fraught with ambivalence, hostility, hatred, and rebellion, we will find these emotions in mother-daughter relations during and after the Holocaust. Clementi uses the term "compulsory enmity" to describe this classic Freudian dualism. As she writes, "[T]he Shoah does not allow for [an] exception to the psychic script that demands the mother-daughter story end in conflict." This strong statement declares that not even Holocaust forces before, during, and after those years were sufficiently powerful to destroy normal patterns of psychosexual development.

Clementi develops this monumental idea by a close reading of six memoirs, recounted in six major chapters, each one devoted to a different memoir/diary writer and representing a different facet of the mother-daughter relationship. While Clementi's theoretical orientation is deeply psychoanalytic, she does not limit herself to psychoanalytic theory. In fact, in the introduction to the book, she explains that her first chapters "are interpreted primarily through the analytic lens of philosophy and child psychology." Indeed, her mastery of these fields and their literatures is impressive and profound, as she carries out a truly interdisciplinary treatment of each memoir.

Clementi situates the final three chapters of her book in cultural history. In these she discusses memoirs of Kindertransport refugees, second-generation daughters, and artists who perished in the Holocaust. Clementi invokes the HBI's mission when she places her work at the intersection of Jews and gender on an international scale. She draws heavily on survivor accounts written in languages other than English or Hebrew, including Italian, German, and French. Her doing so may remind readers that English speakers have written much of what they have read about the Holocaust.

Clementi parses the mother-daughter experience into six categories, thereby revealing underlying differences and emphases. Thus, memoirs can be divided into those that describe

 (1) dying in Auschwitz with the mother;
 (2) witnessing the mother's death in Auschwitz;
 (3) surviving Auschwitz with the mother;
 (4) surviving in hiding with the mother;

(5) mothers and women organizing the children's rescue abroad; and
(6) being born to mother-survivors.

In parallel, the material on which the book is based consists of six memoirs likely to be unfamiliar to the English reading audience (except for the Anne Frank diary). Along with a straightforward presentation of the gist of the text, Clementi submits each of these memoirs to intense and sophisticated literary criticism.

The first memoir is by Edith Bruck, a Hungarian-born, Italian-language writer and poet. The second, by Ruth Klüger, illuminates the dynamics of a mother and daughter who survived Auschwitz together. Another chapter deals with the case of children in hiding with their mother, both of whom are being mothered in turn by a rescuing non-Jewish family. Illustrating this dynamic is Sarah Kofman's complex story of her life that includes her biological mother as well as a "second mother—the Christian woman who saved her life." For Sarah, one woman becomes the representation of death, while the other, (ironically named) Mémé, becomes the strong, life-sustaining mother. A taxing ambivalence grows from these roots: daughters who both love and hate their mothers; who want both to grow up and stay little; who want both to remain childless and become parents; who want both to remember and forget; and who want both to embrace feminism and to hide in the seductive/destructive arms of patriarchy.

The fourth memoir, Milena Roth's *Lifesaving Letters*, recounting her experiences as a child survivor brought to England on the Kindertransport, displays the classic time lag between the experience of the Holocaust and the ability to write about it. This chapter is an example of the generalization that it "took almost half a century for the children to overcome their survivor's guilt and begin to tell their experiences" (with some exceptions). Clementi claims that because of this gulf, "the plight of these children did not figure as part of the Holocaust story." In the fifth chapter, Clementi reaches forward into the second generation and deals with children of survivors, drawing on Helena Janeczek's *Lessons of Darkness* (published in Italian). Born in Munich after the war, Janeczek lives today in Italy where she has become a "successful writer and intellectual literary figure."

As Clementi tells us, her book ends, "almost counterintuitively, with the case of Anne Frank." Frank's iconic work "epitomizes many of the themes that emerge from the [other] mother-daughter models." Clementi was compelled to include the now ubiquitous memoir because, as she writes, Anne Frank is first and foremost a rebellious daughter, "a brilliant young writer who is struggling to overcome her adolescent conflict with her mother while at the same time striving to survive a most brutal attack against her own person, her family, and hence the very same mother against whom she struggles." In the Anne Frank chapter, as in others, Clementi reestablishes an understanding of the meaning of writing memoirs for each of these women (including the girl, Anne). Writing, Clementi claims, expresses and creates an abiding ironic contradiction. Anne both rebels against her mother and tries to help her survive; she allows her to die and keeps her alive in the perpetually reread memoir. This ironic contradiction is embodied in the act of writing about one's experience in the Holocaust. It is like the contradiction writing Amalek's name so that one can cross it out. As Clementi points out, "the act of writing or producing any art in times of extreme, life-threatening circumstances [is] a courageous strategy for psychic, ideological, moral and even physical resistance to annihilation." By recording these events, each woman forces us to re-enter them in endless perpetuity. Thus, we might conclude that both psychosexual development and artistic creation are processes that are affected by, but not inevitably crushed by the Holocaust.

Clementi explains in the chapters described above, in concert with a detailed opening chapter, such highly charged and challenging concepts as the literary apostrophe, postmemory, and traumatic realism, among others. She is particularly interested in *apostrophe*, a term that refers to an author's act of addressing someone even if that "someone" is an inanimate object or idea. An apostrophe shows us an author in conversation or declamation with a third party, the addressee.

Federica K. Clementi's skill in this volume rests on her ability to apply highly sophisticated theory to illuminate women's memoirs, while also introducing surprisingly simple concrete ideas. Examples are her study of Anne Frank's use of humor as well as Janeczek's references to food (and food control, as in anorexia) and language (the continuous switching of languages). Clementi also introduces frequently overlooked frameworks in Holocaust literature, such as class, religiosity, and patriarchy. Nazism, she reminds us, includes many things, one of which is a male-dominated conception of history. With this in mind, she argues, we must reach the conclusion that the Holocaust is part of "a history of oppression rather than a freak explosion of bottled-up political sentiments and resentments." Clementi's fresh eye allows her to see in these women's memoirs "a strong distrust of those patriarchal tenets that sustain the Western sociocultural system."

Although strongly feminist in her analysis, Clementi takes an essentialist cultural view concerning the psychological differences between men and women, a difference she sees confirmed in the work of such Holocaust historians as

Marion Kaplan and Judith Baumel. She points out that Primo Levi reinforced this vision when he wrote, "I felt guilty of being a man because men had built Auschwitz."

Gender difference is not, however, the major analytic tool of *Holocaust Mothers and Daughters*. After all, Clementi does not offer a comparative analysis of men's and women's thoughts, reactions and experiences during the Holocaust. Rather, her book can be thought of as extending Mary Catherine Bateson's *Composing a Life*; it puts an end to being ignored. In so doing, Clementi's emphasis on women's writing against patriarchy produces an ironic and abiding dilemma: "How can one attack patriarchy without attacking the Jewish father?"

Every account of the Holocaust, every Jewish family's dinner table discussion, every book, tells a unique story about this unfathomable crime. It is the task of the researcher to find commonalities, patterns, and differences among the unique parts. Federica K. Clementi has done that task admirably, using the tools of literary criticism, feminism, and psychoanalysis to find the essential tropes, the key phenomena that shaped her authors' very beings. Clementi's analysis enhances our understanding of the myriad personal testimonies that survivors continue to tell, like the one told to me by a grandmother on a kibbutz 30 years ago. This woman wanted me to know that she had stood in line with her mother at Auschwitz, shuffling forward toward Mengele. A soldier shoved her mother to the left to die, while she, the daughter, was able to go to the right and work, at least temporarily. At the split second of separation, the mother squeezed her daughter's arm gently. For the daughter, this squeeze was at once a kiss, a life lesson, a goodbye—a promise that her mother would always somehow be with her. The squeeze sustained this woman throughout her life, she told me. Her relationship with her mother was frozen in time.

# ACKNOWLEDGEMENTS

I could never say it better than Virginia Woolf: "Anyone moderately familiar with the rigours of composition will not need to be told the story in detail; how she wrote and it seemed good; read and it seemed vile; corrected and tore up; cut out; put in; was in ecstasy; in despair; had her good nights and bad mornings; snatched at ideas and lost them; saw her book plain before her and it vanished; acted her people's parts as she ate; mouthed them as she walked; now cried; now laughed; vacillated between this style and that; now preferred the heroic and pompous; next the plain and simple; now the vales of Tempe; then the fields of Kent or Cornwall; and could not decide whether she was the divinest genius or the greatest fool in the world." I took the liberty of changing Woolf's narrating subject into a woman, but as it's a quote from *Orlando*, I think she wouldn't have minded my small manipulation.

Even the greatest fool in the world can take on the impossible task of writing a book when help comes to her from the capable hands of wonderful, ingenious people. Many friends, institutions, and specialists have supported, escorted, and protected me in the course of writing this book.

Friends: Thank you, Nancy K. Miller and Sandy Petrey (my much loved mentors), Stan Dubinsky, Drue Barker, Michal Rubin (the therapist and the *hazzan*, the ear and the voice), Laurie Weber, Philippe Lees (the French in my head), Jean-Luc Nancy, Jimmie Killingsworth, Giulia Guarnieri, Debra Rae Cohen, Scott Trafton, Yael Feldman, Paula Feldman, Paweł Piasecki, Sara Schwebel, and William Rivers. Each of you knows what for, and each bit of help meant everything to me. In a subcategory of his own, alone and unmatched, stands Chris Holcomb, who channeled all his support, belief, strength, patience, love, encouragement, and trust into me and my project.

Institutions: This book would not have been possible without the generous support of the University of South Carolina (USC), its Jewish Studies Program, its Department of English Language and Literature, its Women's and Gender Studies Program, and the Dean's Office through its commitment to faculty and research. My heartfelt thanks also go to the National Foundation for Jewish

Culture, the Blanksteen Family Fund for Jewish Studies, the Josephine Abney Fund for Women's and Gender Studies, the US Holocaust Memorial Museum, the Kindertransport Association, and the staff of USC Columbia Cooper Library (Mark Volmer and Amber Gibbs, you are two angels), and USC Beaufort North.

Specialists: These are the people immoderately familiar "with the rigours of composition" who have believed in the promise of my manuscript and have nurtured it into its present form with their expertise, intelligence, knowledge, preparedness. Thank you, Matthew Seidel and Jeanne Ferris, for your editorial brilliance. A truly special thank-you goes to Phyllis Deutsch, editor-in-chief at the University Press of New England, for her unwavering support, expert guidance, and superlative professionalism (all of the above enveloped in her incomparable warmth). Lastly, I owe a great debt of gratitude to the anonymous readers of my manuscript, whose comments and excellent suggestions pointed me in all the right directions. I am forever indebted to all of you.

# HOLOCAUST
## Mothers &
## Daughters

# INTRODUCTION
## Remember What Amalek Did to You

The mother is the faceless figure of a *figurant*, an extra. She gives rise to all the figures by losing herself in the background of the scene like an anonymous persona. Everything comes back to her, beginning with life; everything addresses and destines itself to her. She survives on the condition of remaining at bottom.

 **JACQUES DERRIDA**, *The Ear of the Other*

In *Against the Apocalypse*, David G. Roskies shares the following personal story:

> Not long ago . . . I visited one of my mother's Israeli friends, Regina, and brought a fountain pen as a gift. Regina, who studied with Eisenstein in Moscow and is the first professor of film history at an Israeli university, tested the pen just as her father had taught her to do in Bialystok before World War I: she wrote the word "Amalek," and then crossed it out. Here was a lapsed daughter of her people heeding the ancient call of Deuteronomy: "Remember what Amalek did to you on your journey, after you left Egypt . . . You shall blot out the memory of Amalek from under heaven. Do not forget!" (25:17, 19).[1]

Of the numerous biblical injunctions to "remember," this one quoted from Deuteronomy by Roskies is to me the most intriguing and profound. Its historical referent is an incident, reported in Exodus, in which Amalek led his seminomadic tribe in a particularly savage and cowardly raid against the Israelites, then in flight from Egypt, attacking their temporary encampment and massacring those incapable of defending themselves—the women and children, the old and infirm. Thus Amalek, a progenitor of Haman, became the symbol of pure evil for the Jews and an enemy not only to Israel but to God, who pledged to annihilate his nation.

But how is one to never forget to forget him? I am fascinated by the idea that we must write his story in order to *unwrite* him from history. Thus the act of writing, so meaningful in the eternal Jewish quest for deciphering history, is both capable of creation and its opposite. This way, remembering for the Jews is established as the act of charging the perpetrators for their guilt while

1

blotting out the qualities they embody, the unethical message their dreadful and murderous stories carry. To wipe out the "memory" (*zekher*, *zikaron*, meaning remembrance) of Amalek means to wipe out his "name" (also *zekher*). The connection existing between a man (*zakhar*, denoting male in Hebrew), his name, and the memory that carries into his genealogical line is the central concern of chapter 25 in Deuteronomy, which deals with the rules of levirate—according to which a brother-in-law is obliged to take his sister-in-law as his wife, should she be widowed, and devote their first-born son to the memory of the deceased husband and brother by naming the child after him.[2] Within this brief chapter, as Roskies reminds us, the fateful name of Amalek suddenly reappears: it is in the context of illustrating what God abhors (that is, fraud and deceit) and how such abominable crimes should be dealt with (that is, by blotting out forever the memory of their perpetrators). Thanks to the way in which Deuteronomy frames Amalek's story, his symbolic meaning becomes manifest: we write "Amalek" in order to preempt his posterity (the continuation of his "name"). But blotting out the memory has to do with annihilating the lineage of evil, certainly not with forgetting its effects. "Do not forget!" We must remember to write his name in order to blot it out, and in the act of blotting it out, we etch it all the deeper into our personal and collective consciousness. A distant relative of that ancient injunction, and a product of twentieth-century history, is the post-Holocaust mantra "Never again!" In order to assure that the Holocaust is never repeated, we make sure to repeat its story over and over again in as many variations and different media as possible: "Never again" in history, but "forever and ever" in the Jewish mind.

Although men have been the patrons of the written records of Jewish history throughout the millennia, from the middle of the twentieth century onward, women have picked up the pen and contributed their viewpoints to the archives of Jewish collective memory with an unprecedented engagement. The Holocaust has been retold equally devotedly by men and women alike. Legions of women stepped into the place of disappeared fathers, brothers, or husbands and assumed the responsibility of writing Jewish history, of remembering what "Amalek" did to them personally and collectively. In so doing, women have allowed new, unexpected nuances to emerge from within the all-encompassing Jewish fold, whose dominant voice has traditionally understood itself as male.

The appearance of women's voices within the Jewish canon on such a large scale has many interesting consequences and developments. The testimony of women has made it apparent that mass historical experiences cannot be looked at only through the flattening lens of cumulative history. Instead, we need to attend to the heterogeneity that is always embedded in such large-scale events.

By paying attention to the subtleties of women's accounts (regardless of the medium in which they are expressed), we have learned that women experience war and genocide differently from men. More than that, we now know that differences in social class, age, degrees of religiosity and assimilation, sexual and linguistic identities, nationalities, and geographical locations of the victims shape each one's experience and memory. Although these distinguishing factors made no difference to the Nazis in terms of their extermination plans (sooner or later, every Jew was going to be annihilated), they could significantly affect the way the victims experienced the genocide, and whether they succumbed to it or were able to resist it and survive (the outsized role that chance and luck played in survival notwithstanding). As the historian Judith Baumel has brilliantly said, reformulating the 1960s feminist motto "the personal is political," "the personal was lethal" during the Holocaust.[3] Baumel's 1998 *Double Jeopardy* pays an invaluable scholarly tribute to the variety, multifacetedness, and multilayeredness of the Holocaust experience through the lens of gender by interlacing analyses of both Jewish and non-Jewish contributions and collaborations in the fight against or resistance to Nazism and Fascism. She is also among the first scholars to have brought into the mix the distinctiveness of ultra-Orthodox women's experiences, which, due to our widespread inability to "[break] their linguistic and cultural codes, scholars have often found it easier to ignore . . . or to treat . . . marginally."[4] A good example of a historical blind spot with gender-relevant implications is explored by Rochelle Saidel in *The Jewish Women of Ravensbrück Concentration Camp*, where she unveils the horrors that occurred in a single death camp. Because of postwar Eastern bloc politics, the camp had been left grossly understudied for decades, despite the fact that during the war, it had gas chambers of its own and one of the highest murder rates among all concentration camps (second only to Auschwitz-Birkenau). Predictably, and in line with party ideology, the Soviets programmatically minimized the Jewish identity of the prisoners there. However, the distinguishing feature of Ravensbrück was not the Jewishness of its prisoners but the fact that it had been designated as a women's camp, and therefore, the majority of its prisoners (one of whom was American-born Gemma LaGuardia Gluck, sister of New York City Mayor Fiorello LaGuardia) and victims were women and children. According to Saidel, for a very long time this fact was "ignored in memorial exhibits, monuments, and publications in the United States."[5]

According to Joan Ringelheim, thirty years ago no one would have thought to apply feminist theory to the Shoah. "The connection between genocide and gender," she writes, "has been difficult to conceive for some; for others, it has been difficult to construct."[6] The insistence on gender individualization within the uniform category of victims—a uniformity that is often strictly maintained in order to simplify the ethical divide between the two main camps of any genocidal story, victims and victimizers—still causes some anxiety. Some still fear that gendering the Holocaust would detract from, not add to, our understanding of the catastrophe because it would spuriously entangle us in the dialectics of ideology (read, feminist ideology). Others fear that the intent behind an inclusive and particularized reading of the human experience is to create a hierarchy of sufferance, not a more complex portrait of this sufferance. However, in considering the earlier groundbreaking works of Ringelheim, Carol Rittner, John Roth, Vera Laska, and Marion Kaplan and the more recent scholarship on the subject (by Nechama Tec, Elizabeth Baer, Myrna Goldenberg, Sara Horowitz, Phyllis Lassner, Anna Reading, and others),[7] it seems to me that the most compelling and successful argument is the one in favor of focusing on gender and the minutiae of intimate family portraits as a productive, not detractive, way to observe the devastating effects of the genocide. The focus on the singular, personal, and domestic allows us to trace the genocide's rippling impacts on the daily lives of its victims. As Lenore Weitzman and Dalia Ofer argue in their momentous edited volume *Women in the Holocaust*, it is precisely "the details of everyday life—the portrait of a woman who saved her single ration of bread for her children, or that of a man who volunteered for forced labor because his wages were promised to his family—that restore individuality and humanity to the victims."[8] My research aligns itself with this current in Jewish studies. Throughout the last three decades of research, feminist scholars have brought to the fore how the Nazis' treatment of their victims differed depending on gender and how Jewish men and women experienced the Nazi war against them in unique ways. The present volume hopes to contribute to this strand of feminist theory by observing that women have also written differently than men about their Shoah experiences.

In *Women's Holocaust Writing*, Lillian Kremer takes fictional and historical texts by men and women and compares their treatment of the same topics. For instance, she offers an interesting example of how stories about children in the ghettos are narrated by different genders: "Male historians and novelists often celebrate the heroism of children as major actors in smuggling operations to supplement the meager supply of food in the ghettos . . . [while i]n ghetto representations by women writers, the focus is unrelentingly maintained on the children's victimization, starvation, illness, subjection to lethal injection, or deportation to the death camps."[9] Although *Holocaust Mothers and Daughters* carries forward the work started by Kremer, it also shifts the terms of the inquiry by focusing exclusively on autobiographical texts, mostly memoirs, from several countries and in several different languages, and examining only the testimony of those women who were directly touched by the Shoah and those who experienced its aftershocks (that is, the second generation). Most importantly, I focus on one central topic whose treatment, I argue, is handled in gender-specific terms in both male and female war writings: the mother. The Jewish mother-daughter bond is the articulatory hinge on which my analysis swings. From the incredibly vast bibliography available, I chose texts that make central to the life of a Jewish daughter the presence, influence, example, and love of a "Holocaust mother." These authors experienced the genocide with or through their victim-mother, and in looking back at their formative childhood years, they understood the maternal genealogy (biological and adoptive) as the foundational root of their identities as women, Jews, and (when it applies) survivors.

The inspiration for *Holocaust Mothers and Daughters* came from my experience in the classroom teaching Shoah literature to college students. The comments during class discussions showed clearly that the readings offered by my conventional assignments (Primo Levi's *If This Is a Man*, Elie Wiesel's *Night*, and Tadeusz Borowski's Auschwitz chronicles) were teaching students a lot about the horrors of life in Auschwitz but very little about life outside of Auschwitz at the time, or about the Jewish experience in Europe at large. I decided therefore to make room in the syllabus for less prominent wartime texts—specifically, women's memoirs—and students were very responsive to the new perspectives these had to offer. At that point I began to think comparatively of women's and men's Shoah writing. To give a quick example, if we take two comparable Italian postwar classics, Levi's *If This Is a Man*[10] and Natalia Ginzburg's *Family Sayings*[11] the gendered differences to which I am referring become apparent. *If This Is a Man* begins at the time of deportation and ends with the liberation of the camps: this strict temporal bracketing contributes to the impression that Auschwitz was indeed a freak parenthesis—a historical bubble, a suspension outside of time and space—rather than part of a longer historical development. Levi lingers neither over the fate of his family members nor over the details of his adult life in Turin before the war. The text opens with the story of his capture by the Fascist Militia in 1943, not for being a Jew but for fighting with the partisans. Once he reveals his Jewish identity, Levi is immediately sent to the camps. All this is covered in a one-page preamble. Levi skips any portraiture of family life before the war; in general, canonic Shoah autobiographies rarely linger over such details, and when they do, they draw family portraits in quite a stylized or idealized manner. Zoë Waxman has pointed out that the tendency to idealize memories of the prewar past can also be understood "as an attempt to emphasize how much was destroyed by the Nazis, and to show that the Holocaust constitutes more than just the suffering endured in the ghettos or concentration camps, or in hiding; it means the obliteration of individual histories."[12] As I will show later, Wiesel's *Night* is a prime example of such a stylized account. Ginzburg's *Family Sayings*, in contrast, is a text of Jewish memory where family life and national history intersect in ways that do not end up overwhelming the personal in its treatment of the communal. In her memoir we receive an unforgettable portrayal of one Italian Jewish family from long before the war, a portrayal that emphasizes the importance of domestic bonds, daily routines, and the family's "language" (made up of funny proverbs, personal linguistic quirks, regional inflections, and so on) in which Ginzburg locates identity.[13] *Family Sayings* is not only a war story but an immortal homage to the quirks and humor, weaknesses and resourcefulness, little tyrannies and subversive anticonformism of the memoirist's mother and father. Unlike Levi, Ginzburg survived in hiding with her children (her husband, Leone Ginzburg, was tortured to death by the Nazis in Rome) and was not deported to Auschwitz, which certainly explains the moments of relative levity in her narrative; spared the camps as she was, such levity was still possible. Nevertheless, there is great value in integrating the vision of events that Levi's memoir offers with parallel perspectives decribing the domestic life that is often obscured in masculine narratives such as his.

Even more so than postwar memoirs, wartime diaries enhance our understanding of the history by juxtaposing viewpoints that vary greatly depending on the location, gender, social status, and age of the writers. The genre of the personal diary or journal is particularly well suited to present details of domestic life. In her analysis of dozens of published and unpublished Holocaust diaries, Alexandra Garbarini notices that diarists "possessed a keen sense of the historicity of their experiences and wrote in their dual capacity as victims and witnesses. Some were concerned with recording the history of their families, in particular, rather than with contributing to Jewish history or European history or human history, in general."[14] For instance, a comparison between Emanuel Ringelblum's and Hélène Berr's journals helps illustrate the wide range of purposes that Garbarini identifies and also proves that the differences in the scopes of diaries were inflected by the gender of the diarists. Through the pages of Ringelblum's journal, we peek into the bestial, anarchic, corrupt hell of the Warsaw Ghetto, witnessing the apocalyptic fate of tens of thousands of people and the destruction of an entire community through the words of someone who had set for himself the task of leaving behind a record of what the perpetrators wished to conceal from history. Ringelblum was a social activist, a historian, and a prominent international figure in Jewish public affairs. In writing his journal and leading the underground operation Oyneg Shabes,[15] which sought to document Jewish life in the ghetto under occupation in a secret archive, he was keenly aware of his historical role as chronicler of his community's fate, aware that his words might be the only remaining testament for future generations of what had been done to the Jews—men, women, and children; the old and the young—by the Nazis. As chronicler of his community, Ringelblum did not overlook women. With these lines, his journal famously pays tribute to the role of women during the crisis: "Future historians will have to devote a whole separate chapter to the Jewish Woman in wartime. She holds a prominent place in the history of the Jews. Thanks to her courage and endurance, thousands of families are able to withstand these awful times. Lately, we are noticing an interesting development: in some Komitety Domowe [House Committees], women are stepping forward to replace men who, emaciated and exhausted, are leaving the jobs they've held until now. There are some Komitety Domowe entirely run by women."[16] Contemporaneously, many unknown Jewish men and women all over Europe were also recording their daily experiences under German occupation in personal journals, sometimes just to keep themselves from sinking into despair. One of these was Hélène Berr, a woman in her early twenties from the Parisian petite bourgeoisie who was a talented violinist and a lover of English language and poetry (she was getting her degree in English from the Sorbonne). Her journal, which was published only in 2008, chronicles the way victims clung to daily routines as a way of holding onto a quickly dissolving normalcy.[17] For Berr, these routines—meeting friends, playing violin with her chamber group, visiting her family's country house—took place within the sophisticated yet increasingly circumscribed boundaries of her private Parisian world.

We follow the rather sheltered Berr as she journeys from incomprehension to a full awareness of the enormity of the situation. The journal, particularly the first part, is very self-centered: the writer holds onto her reassuring routines with a youthful insouciance due not only to her age but also to an honest ignorance of political events. Naiveté permeates this first part of her text, until the situation becomes so obviously hopeless that any subconscious effort to deny reality collapses and the despairing Hélène uses her diary to consciously record the horror she witnesses around her. In this way, what begins as a sort of *journal intime* gradually turns into a more intentional historical testimony. "They are separating mothers and children," writes Berr with mounting panic. "I note down the facts . . . in order not to forget them, because one *must* not forget. In Miss Monsaingeon's neighborhood, an entire family—father, mother and five children—have killed themselves with gas to escape the roundup. A woman jumped out of a window. They say that several policemen have been shot for having warned people to run away . . . What are the long-term consequences of this thing that happened the night before last?"[18] Eventually, Berr started volunteering with a local organization to help Jewish children whose parents had been deported. However, despite her work, she had no way of knowing with absolute certainty what was in store for French Jews. She was deported east with her parents on March 27, 1944, when she was twenty-three; none of them returned.[19]

The events she witnessed were but one version of the horrors that were occurring everywhere in Nazi-occupied Europe. Like Ringelblum's chronicle, Berr's journal shows us how people were taken away, suffered, shared their grief intimately with family and friends in their homes, despaired, fled, or took their lives. We also learn of small acts of solidarity from the Christian world. However, Berr did not fashion her journal with the same powerful conviction that sustained Ringelblum—that one day a simple diary would be a monument to the disappeared, an indictment of a history that erased so many victims. In Berr's writings, we sense instead the despair of women who are helpless once the men in their lives are rounded up and taken away, as her father was. Berr is particularly shocked by the fate of the mothers and young children around her to whom she cannot be of any support. She gives us a portrait of the terror that the lack of reliable information produces in the victims, especially women. Moreover, Berr does not position herself or her diary as a bridge between the chaotic experience of the victims and a posterity that will remember and honor their struggles; rather, her perspective is a very personal one, and she is alone in her efforts to figure out each move. Her father, Raymond Berr, seems to be at a complete loss (weakened and traumatized as he is after his brief detention and release from Drancy), and her mother and her connections are of no help. Ringelblum's account is more impersonal. If, as some scholars felt, "Ringelblum went too far in his attempt to write himself out of his *ghetto* narratives,"[20] Berr put herself, her story, and her sentiments at the very center of her narrative. Ringelblum's and Berr's are two versions of the same story: one is delivered by an authoritative and influential leader, the other by an inexpert and private voice. As Ringelblum reminds us, women played an important role in all aspects of Jewish life during the war; however, very few women held positions of power or visibility comparable to his, largely because such preeminence would have had to be established before the war.

The history and timing of the publication of these two victims' documents reveal something about the perception the world at large had of their roles as witnesses. Of the dozens of people who had earnestly collaborated with Ringelblum to assemble the secret archive, only three were alive after the war. Of these, the former secretary of the Oyneg Shabes, Hersz Wasser, led the recovery operation that rescued two-thirds of the hidden archive in 1946 and 1950.[21] Berr's journal, as explained in a postscript to the text by Mariette Job, the daughter of the diarist's sister, was typed up after the war by an employee of the Établissements Kuhlmann, the prestigious company Hélène's father had directed. It was in this format that it circulated for decades among the members of the Berr family. In the early 1990s, Job decided to locate the original manuscript, and she found it in 1994 with the help of those who had been close to her aunt during her lifetime. With the permission of her family, Job donated it to the Centre de Documentation Juive Contemporaine in Paris in 2002, and it is now on display at the Mémorial de la Shoah, together with a detailed history of the Berr family. And yet for sixty-three years, this document had survived not as a crucial historical record but as a family's private and intimate treasure. As Kassow points out, "had he survived, Ringelblum would have been the first to insist that Holocaust historiography consider not only the perpetrators and the bystanders but also the silenced voices of the victims. To hear those voices requires an understanding of who they were before the war."[22] In this respect, Berr's diary is quite powerful because of the insights it gives us into the cultural milieu and everyday life of Jews before their annihilation; it is, in sum, exactly the kind of invaluable documentation of Jewish life that Ringelblum himself appreciated and was hoping to save from erasure. Taken together, both diarists deepen our vision of the events: Ringelblum, the social activist and leader who speaks for all those who cannot,[23] and Berr, an unknown woman who, though she can only speak for herself, still helps us see the larger story through her own narrow perspective.

Feminist scholarship has helped us recognize that in the literature and autobiographies of women, the domestic stage is central in peacetime and wartime alike. I couldn't help notice that the same remains true for Shoah memoirs, and hence a desire was born in me to write a book that analyzes the Jewish domestic stage from a female perspective under the alternately deforming and informing pressure of genocide. As feminist analysis has proven time and again, it is in the writing of women that we can best uncover the intimate details of family life because of the domestic origins of women's literary worlds—the female domain historically being the house, not the agora (the public space). Women's narratives center on everyday rituals, domestic geographies, and the quotidian familial details usually removed from traditional male narratives. In women's domestic perspectives, the truth of personal history enriches, reevaluates, and ultimately questions the Truth of History. Hence, "the Jewish historical experience of ordinary women," which was traditionally "subsumed in that of the Jewish community as a whole," and "(like all histories) has been told from the vantage point of Jewish men," finally finds room to emerge.[24] Turning to the gender specificity of memory, I challenge the widespread practice of studies in Shoah literature to focus "primarily on the writings of men, whose perspectives have been taken as representative of the experience of all Holocaust victims," as Marlene Heinemann puts it.[25] It is still the norm that the writings of male witnesses outnumber those of women in practically every Holocaust school curriculum and in most anthologies. For instance, in Lawrence Langer's important volume on Holocaust cultural production, *Art from the Ashes*, the only woman to appear in the section devoted to firsthand witnessing is Charlotte Delbo, a Christian; in the chapter "Journals and Diaries," there are no excerpts from Anne Frank's or other women's diaries; and, finally, had the section on painters not been limited to those imprisoned in Terezín, it could have been enriched by the inclusion of Charlotte Salomon, who remains unmentioned there and elsewhere in the volume.[26] Only four women (one of whom was not Jewish) are featured in a volume that includes thirty men.

There are stark differences between the style of women survivor writers and their male counterparts. The former are more likely to recount the memories of domestic life and the complex child-parent relationships therein by presenting their own childhood perspective on events; furthermore, female writers tend not to follow the long-standing tradition of talking about victims of injustice in highly idealized terms. The key example of this is the figure of the mother. Women often don't hide the fact that "hating" their mothers, even during the Holocaust, was as much a part of their relationship as depending on them for life and survival. Therefore, I decided to gather the voices of a group of women who have, in their Shoah-inflected writings, highlighted their difficult relations with their mothers so as to examine how they described these relationships despite or because of—through and beyond—the impact of the genocide. What I make visible is the courageous act of portraying the complex, ambiguous, and sometimes unbearable side of a girl's love for and inextricable bond with her mother—and vice versa—under the extreme conditions of a great historical upheaval.

In literary criticism as much as in psychoanalytic theory, there is a gap on the subject of the mother-daughter relationship, which tends either to take on the perspective of the mother or to be subsumed under the broader mother-child rubric. Caroline Eliacheff and Nathalie Heinich—a French psychoanalyst and sociologist, respectively—have pointed out: "We can't rely on established theories [on the mother-daughter topic] . . . Despite the fact that it is a very engaging subject for those who are invested in it, it is strangely very little studied: an overabundance of studies about maternity, filiation, femininity or female sexuality is contrasted with . . . the almost complete absence of analyses, especially psychoanalytical, of mother-daughter relations."[27] However, there is no lack of literature on the "Jewish mother": the stereotype, the myth, the fiction. Oppressive and limiting representations in popular culture cast her either as an insupportable kvetcher—that is, a chronically smothering, over-protective complainer (a staple of Jewish humor, from Eastern Europe to West Hollywood)—or as the epitome of female sainthood, representing an idealized and unrecoverable past (the lost *Yiddishkeit*). Both views, however contrasting, are the products of male imagination; Jewish mothers in Jewish men's works appear to be either portrayed in archetypal terms or not portrayed at all.

Many American feminist scholars—including Joyce Antler, Sylvia Barack Fishman, Donna Bassin, Margaret Honey, Meryle Mahrer Kaplan, Janet Burstein, Adalgisa Giorgio, and Marianne Hirsch—have engaged in important critical reformulations of the maternal figure (Jewish and non-Jewish) in our culture.[28] All of these authors have played a fundamental role in the creation of a counternarrative for mothers and daughters, especially as it pertains to American and American-Jewish culture. *Holocaust Mothers and Daughters* pushes the bounds of our inquiry into the Jewish mother-daughter plot by daring to touch on the sensitive topic of Shoah memory and victimhood.

The Shoah offers an important observation point from which to study mother-child dynamics. The fates of young children and those of their mothers are never so tightly knitted together as they are in times of war. Typically, children and the elderly remain under the care of women once men leave for the front, but genocide is a collateral war that primarily targets women as the reproductive source of the people designated for annihilation. As Mary Felstiner notes, "genocide is the act of putting women and children first."[29] Women who entered the concentration camps with children or pregnant were automatically selected for the gas chambers, regardless of their ability to work (a default fate spared to men). "When a Jewish child is born, or when a woman comes to the camp with a child already," Josef Mengele, known as the Angel of Death of Auschwitz-Birkenau, is reported to have said, "I don't know what to do with the child . . . It would not be humanitarian to send a child to the ovens without permitting the mother to be there to witness the child's death. That is why I send the mother and the child to the gas ovens together."[30]

As mentioned above, the most read, translated, and studied (in schools and universities) Shoah writers still largely remain Elie Wiesel, Primo Levi, and Tadeusz Borowski, joined relatively recently by Art Spiegelman, the author of *Maus*. These writers are taken as the Holocaust's most authoritative voices. (Anne Frank holds an uncontested place as the most iconic Holocaust victim, but her diary is rarely treated as a serious work of literature in its own right.) Yet in Wiesel's autobiographical novel *Night*, for instance, the word "mother" makes its first appearance in the text only after we have met the father, the village people, and other secondary characters. The mother's presence exhausts itself in a couple of epigraphic lines. In 1943, with the deportations of the Jews well under way, all we are told is that "my mother was beginning to think it was high time to find an appropriate match for Hilda," her daughter; and when the Germans start arresting the Jews of Sighet, throwing the entire village in a panic, Wiesel notes: "As for my mother, she went on attending [to] the many chores in the house."[31] We see her twice more before she disappears forever in Birkenau, including a fleeting glimpse of her silently walking to her death holding the youngest of her daughters by the hand.[32] There is no further description of her in Wiesel's book.

Likewise, in reading Spiegelman's *Maus*—a work that undeniably made history for its groundbreaking use of comics to represent the Shoah—one is struck by the graphic and textual marginality of women, particularly the mother's side of the story. Spiegelman's mother, Anja, had survived the camps and later committed suicide without leaving a note. She had apparently left a written record of her memories for her son to read one day, but after her death, her husband, Vladek, the central protagonist of *Maus*, burned all of his wife's diaries. "Anja's missing diaries exemplify the marginality of women's experience in constructing a master narrative of the Nazi genocide," writes Sara Horowitz in regard to the mother's absent story, which I believe to be a textual and psychological black hole in *Maus*. Horowitz adds: "Only at the end of the volume does Vladek reveal that after Anja's death, in an attempt to 'make order' with *his* memories, he burned her notebooks and no longer recalls what she had written . . . In the absence of her own words . . . Anja's story is recoverable only through the reconstruction of Vladek's and Art's memories."[33] By the time Anja took her own life in 1968, however, her son was twenty, old enough to have known more about her than what appears in his text. Had she never mentioned her Shoah past in front of the son? Had he never asked her what had happened to her during the Shoah? The frustrating question remains: what truths did her diaries reveal that Vladek could not allow his son to know? Vladek's disturbing violation of his late wife's voice is hard to come to terms with.

In sum, the widespread tendency of Shoah literature is either to strongly stylize the portraits of the victims or limit the treatment of their trials to the bare minimum. Domestic conflict is often downplayed, denied, or removed in order to keep the narrative focus exclusively on the apodictic distinction between good and evil, victims and victimizers. This tendency may reflect a fear on the part of the witnesses that admitting the flaws of the dead could distract—or, worse, detract—from their innocence as victims. As the British author Anne Karpf has pointedly noted in her marvelous text *The War After* (a mixture of autobiography, memoir, historical reportage, and biography), "it's hard to speak about Holocaust survivors in anything but a reverent tone or without turning their suffering into a sacrament. People expect of them abnormally high standards of behaviour, as if a dehumanizing experience might somehow dignify and elevate, and along with the loss of their worldly goods they should also have lost all worldliness."[34] It often proves too difficult for Holocaust survivors to talk about the victims in any terms other than romanticized ones. Characters in Shoah memoirs then risk remaining one-dimensional; their status of victims eclipses their complex and multifaceted identities.[35] This reverential attitude is picked up by popular culture's representations of the Shoah, which, more often than not, offer quite uncomplicated portraits of victims or victimizers. One case in point is the award-winning film *Schindler's List*—a must see in every Holocaust curriculum—in which the victims are universally surrounded by an aura of saintliness that works at subconsciously eliciting the viewer's pity for their innocence rather than depicting their humanity.[36] This way of understanding victimhood, so deeply rooted in our Western imaginary, is the heritage of our millennia-old culture that elevates all martyrs to the status of saints and that, therefore, implicitly makes only saints the object of martyrdom. I find it crucial, especially in the classroom, to elaborate on the perniciousness of such logic and to remind students that genocide is a crime independent of the personal qualities of its victims.

In contrast to these idealizing tendencies, I gather in this book a group of female Shoah writers who place the mother (often an unlikable mother) and the domestic world at the very core of their texts. I then analyze, through a number of theoretical lenses, the way in which these mothers are ushered onto the historical scene as simultaneously heroic and unbearable protagonists, victims and victimizers, half-crazed women yet life-saving forces, their daughters' inexorable nemeses but also the origin and raison d'être of their art or writing. The portrayals of mothers in the present work are not easy to assimilate for readers accustomed to highly idealized representations of the martyrs of injustice. Mothers in this literature have a history (genealogy) and a story (personal and communal). They may be difficult, oppressive, impossible mothers, but they are also visible mothers.

The daughters' critical judgment of their mothers in this literature is novel and subversive because it inserts itself disruptively within the frame of the Shoah and the Jewish discourse on memorialization. These daughters resist the temptation to paint an elegiac portrait of their mothers (adoptive in some cases); rather, they are severely critical of them, highlighting conflict more than heroism, resentment rather than trust, normalcy rather than exceptionality. This is surprising, especially when we consider that the fate of these girls was inextricably intertwined with that of their mothers, biological or not, in whose sole care they were left once the fathers had been killed, deported, or separated from them in the concentration camps. I claim that in remembering the anger and conflicts they felt as children and in staging them as an important component of their textual reconstructions of their personal history and the communal history of the Jews in the Shoah, the authors studied here grant (albeit, in some cases, posthumously) their mothers and themselves an existence outside the genocide, beside and despite that "unholy situation."[37]

This book contributes to our knowledge and remembrance of the past through a study of daughters' texts steeped in the experience of genocide. I use the term "daughters" because the writers treated in this book actually speak as daughters and not merely as Jewish women. Their works use the figure of the mother as their central articulatory element.[38] These texts exist because the daughters' need to have a dialogue with and about their mothers exists.

My analysis of these texts reveals how Jewish patriarchy, patriarchy in toto, and antisemitism were all simultaneously at work in challenging and shaping the way in which women reacted to the imminent danger, as well as the way in which the maternal is seen, conceived of, and experienced by Jewish girls and, consequently, represented in their literature. Furthermore, the objective historical circumstances of the Shoah are complemented by the psychic dynamics at work in the way a daughter relates to her mother, dynamics that are articulated around compulsory enmity rather than alliance and that become all the more problematic when removed from the normality of everyday life and thrown into the chaos of life-threatening, extraordinary events. The simultaneous analysis of both these planes, historical and familial dynamics, in the mother-daughter plot (and in the Jewish daughter's identity) is the new contribution offered by the present study.

In the texts I select, the Shoah does not allow for a pause in or exception to the psychic script that demands the mother-daughter story end in conflict. This script allows for the symbolic order to stand unchallenged by ensuring conflict among women and the misrecognition or rejection of one's maternal origins, what Amber Jacobs has described as the uninstitutionalized law of matricide. She elaborates:

Oedipal structuration radically denies the daughter a symbolically mediated relation to her mother. Psychoanalytic feminist research has repeatedly described the ubiquitous pathological organizations operating within the mother-daughter relation. Clinical accounts of the symptoms specific to the mother-daughter relation tend to describe the psychosexual difficulties in this relation as resulting from collapsed identifications, lack of boundaries, and murderous and suicidal phantasies . . . Separation-individuation between mother and daughter seems to be an area of acute difficulty leading to (at best) a flight to the father and an acceptance of his law as an inevitable defense and escape route from a psychically dangerous symbiotic fusion with the mother.[39]

Although patricide is "legislated" and clearly present to the mind via the Oedipus complex, the failure to acknowledge the disappearance or murder of the mother (the original act of matricide that I address in the epilogue) causes the story of women to be constantly retold within the frame of the father's discourse, a frame that forecloses the daughter's loyalty to her female kin and her self-recognition as her mother's daughter (not only her father's). But it is the symbolic order itself that produces a daughter's need to escape the mother. Jacobs continues: "The daughter . . . is cut off from her origin and sequestered in a position in the patriarchal economy that denies her the possibility of achieving a sexed subject position outside the powerful structure of phallic binarism . . . So long as there is no possibility of giving symbolic expression to the mother-daughter relation, the latter will inevitably remain an area of pathology."[40] Despite the Shoah, the pathological mother-daughter relation is manifested without exception in the experiences of the daughters I examine here. However, I claim that by placing the normality of this conflictual relation at center stage even in the midst of the utter abnormality of the historical situation, these daughters end up exposing the fact that they, like their mothers before them, are limited by the patriarchal frame in what they can represent and how they understand their own history as women. The patriarchal symbolic configuration (in psychological terms) or the patriarchal power-relation structuration (in historical terms) set them up as victims. But when the daughters pick up their pens—that is, when they symbolically gain control of the phallic scepter—in order to reclaim a place in the culture of the father by writing down their war memories and speaking for and to the mother, they finally reaffirm and reappropriate the maternal origination that is otherwise programmatically left unexplored or unproblematized.

Whereas in her seminal work on the war retold through children's eyes, Sue Vice compares novels narrated in the child's voice, the books I present here are autobiographical texts written in an adult voice that tries to recuperate and reconnect to its childhood perspective (the only exception being the narrator in Anne Frank's diary, as I will discuss later). As Vice points out, the characteristic constants in the way children relate and experience the unfolding of incomprehensible and traumatic events include "defamiliarization; errors of fact and perception; attention to detail at the expense of context; loss of affect; indefinite or divided temporality; irony of various kinds; the confusion of developmental with historical events; charged relations between author, narrator and protagonist; and age-specific concerns with the nature of writing and memory."[41] However, given the highly self-conscious nature of these writings, the voice of the adult author intervenes to adjust, amend, correct, or question the impressions of the evoked child. My argument is that it is at the interface between the consciousness of the author's voice and that of the child evoked from memory that the pathological mother-daughter relation (part and parcel of the patriarchal script) is sabotaged by these daughters: that is, this occurs at the generative interface between remembering and writing, between witnessing and creating.

## THE AUTHORS

Each chapter in this work is centered on the analysis of one author while also drawing parallels between her and other writers, either contemporaries or predecessors. These analyses draw on several theoretical formulations that help ground my main claims. The first three chapters are based on a close reading of three autobiographical texts, which are interpreted primarily through the analytical lenses of philosophy (chapter 1), psychoanalysis (chapter 2), and child psychology (chapter 3). The last three chapters are broader in scope and thus allow for a more extensive discussion of historical contexts, drawing numerous parallels among the principal texts and other comparable works by Kindertransport refugees (chapter 4), second-generation daughters (chapter 5) and artists who perished in the Holocaust (chapter 6 and the epilogue). Some of the featured authors are relatively unfamiliar to the North American audience. Therefore, I want to briefly introduce here the writers to whom each chapter is devoted and highlight some of the similarities among them as well as the threads that tie the chapters together.

First, a brief word about the organizing principle of this work. World War II and the genocide of the Jews have birthed myriad different stories with many common features but also with many unique variations. I thought it productive, therefore, to identify six broad master plots within the larger frame of the Shoah experience. Consequently, I created six chapters that explore, through literature, each permutation and its effects on the mother-daughter relationship according to the variable circumstances within the larger historical context. The six scenarios presented in the chapters are: dying in Auschwitz with the mother; witnessing the mother's death in Auschwitz; surviving Auschwitz with the mother; surviving in hiding with the mother; surviving by being sent abroad as refugees (and never being reunited with the mothers and fathers who remained in Europe and were killed); and being born to survivor mothers.

This volume opens with Edith Bruck, a Hungarian-born, Italian-language writer and poet. After the war and a short stay in Israel, she emigrated to Rome, where she still resides. For thirty years she worked in Italian television and published numerous novels and poems, all permeated by her inescapable experience of Auschwitz where, at the age of eleven, she witnessed her mother's murder. The translation of two of her texts into English (*Who Loves You Like This* in 2001 and *Letter to My Mother* in 2006) has recently introduced Bruck to a larger international audience. Two of her poems appeared in 1992 in *A Book of Women Poets from Antiquity to Now*.[42] Prior to the present analysis, only the Italian cultural studies scholar Adalgisa Giorgio devoted significant analytical attention to Bruck's writings, to her literary legacy in Italy and within the larger Shoah canon, and to the mother-daughter relation framed by the trauma of Auschwitz in her work.[43] The starting point of my analysis was dictated by the titles and structures that Bruck chose for her most famous books. The theme of letters and letter writing seems to be the leitmotif that connects them all: *Lettera alla madre* (Letter to My Mother), *Signora Auschwitz* (Mrs. Auschwitz), and *Lettera da Francoforte* (Letter from Frankfurt).[44] The letter is a form that always assumes an interpellation, a call to an addressee. In Bruck's case, the addressee of her Shoah writings is, explicitly or implicitly, her dead mother, with whom she strives to keep an imaginary conversation alive. The maternal apostrophe—the halting call with which the daughter calls out to the mother and urges "Listen!"—is a returning figure in Bruck's prose and poetry. I thus interlace the use of the fictional letter and the dialogue with the dead in Bruck's literature with a philosophical reflection on the rhetorical figure of the apostrophe and of prosopopoeia. Irene Kacandes has examined the precious and indeed "capacious concept" of the apostrophe, pointing out that the ancient rhetoricians Cicero and Demosthenes had located the power of the apostrophe in its being "both double and duplicitous . . . because it is mobilized to provoke reaction—though not verbal reply—in those who hear it, not in those to whom it is explicitly addressed."[45] Bruck's injunction to listen to what she has to say, I claim, is intended for the dead in absentia and therefore ends up eliciting a response (or demanding one) from the living—from us, the readers, the ultimate receivers of her missives to the mother. Bruck's undeliverable letter and her call, "Listen, Mother!" are the epitaphs on the mother's tomb, epitaphs that mark the mother's and daughter's victimhood at the hand not only of the Nazis in Auschwitz but also, as I show, of the Jewish and patriarchal culture that oppressed them through religion, social hierarchies, and violence.

For chapter 2, I chose Ruth Klüger's story as the model plot for a mother and daughter who survive Auschwitz together. Klüger first wrote her memoir in German under the title *weiter leben: Eine Jugend*; a decade later, she rewrote a new version of it in English and published it as *Still Alive: A Holocaust Girlhood Remembered*.[46] Ever since, Klüger has received much attention from scholars both in Europe and America. Her memoir provided one of the two central testimonial texts (together with Charlotte Delbo's) that Michael Rothberg used to develop his intriguing theory of traumatic realism.[47] Klüger conflicted identity as a German Austrian and a Jewish German has been explored by Pascale Bos, whose studies of memoirs such as Klüger's and Grete Weil's has explored these narratives' power to "explicitly problematize memory and the limits of language and of imagination in the face of the Holocaust."[48] A more critical assessment of Klüger's text appears in Jerry Schuchalter's *Poetry and Truth*, a work that raises important questions of genre for German-language Shoah survivors' writings.[49]

Klüger was born in Vienna. After her father escaped from Austria early on, when it was assumed that only men were in danger, she remained alone with her mother, with whom she was deported to Theresienstadt, Auschwitz, and eventually other camps, all of which they survived together. Her father was captured in southern France and deported east, where he was murdered. After the war, mother and daughter resettled in the United States, where Klüger became a college professor of German literature. What prompted Klüger to write her story was a near-death experience, this time unrelated to the Shoah. During a summer stay in Germany as director of her American university's Education Abroad Program in 1988, she was run over by a sixteen-year-old boy on a bicycle, and she ended up fighting for her life in a hospital in Göttingen. Klüger came to view this fight as a metaphor for a much bigger combat she was carrying on (almost half a century after the fact) with the entire Germanic nation and its past: "I want to push him [the biker] away with both arms outstretched, but he is on top of me, bike and all. Germany, Deutschland, a moment like hand-to-hand combat . . . Why this struggle . . . why did I return?"[50] While she was recovering in the hospital, memories that she had kept at bay for decades rushed back to her. She then began to write her "difficult" memoir in German, confident that her mother, Alma Hirschel, would never learn of it because, by then an old lady in America, she refused to take notice of all things German. However, *weiter leben* became an immediate literary sensation; it was promptly made widely available in translation all over Europe and Japan. A family friend who had learned about the book's success through a cousin in Switzerland told Alma about it. Making an exception to her rule, Alma picked up her daughter's German text and "easily found all the passages that were critical of her and was badly hurt. All her neighbors, she said, now knew she was a bad mother."[51] Alma had a point. Her daughter had written a memoir that was not simply a story of Shoah survival, exile, and emigration, but also the story of her emotionally complex relationship with a mother who was both a proto-feminist model and a patriarchal mother: a heroic, determined, brave, strong woman who was simultaneously an overcritical, pathologically suspicious, neurotic parent. In 2001 Klüger's memoir first appeared in America, not as a literal translation but as a new version of the previous memoir, a "parallel book" as she calls it.[52] Caroline Schaumann analyzed the differences between the two texts, the most glaring of which is found in the two versions of the epilogue. The German book ends in Göttingen—memorably, the town from where Heinrich Heine's classic *Harzreise* takes off—as Klüger recounts how the idea of writing the memoir came to her; *Still Alive* ends in Irvine, California, a place that, at last, Klüger can safely call home. *Still Alive* fills us in on what happened after the publication of the German version, and some of the new developments in part affect and alter even the telling of the episodes from the past that the two books have in common. Schaumann's comparison shows that not only have Klüger's memories of the past altered over time, but so have the contexts within which these memories are stored and discussed (discourses on the Holocaust in Europe and America, school curricula, etc.). Schaumann remarks: "Nowadays, discussions of the Holocaust in both Germany and the United States focus on entirely different issues than they did in earlier decades. For instance, one might think of psychiatrists' diagnoses of the 'survivor syndrome' in the 1950s, of the Eichmann trial and the ensuing 'banality of evil' discourse in the 1960s, of the increased attention to Holocaust studies following the TV miniseries 'Holocaust' in the 1970s, of the Historians' Debate in the 1980s, of the emergence of research on women in the Holocaust in the late 1980s, of the intentionalist-functionalist dispute and the Americanization of the Holocaust in the 1990s, and of the increasing attention to second-generation Holocaust representation in the 2000s." Therefore, as Schaumann poignantly concludes, Klüger's two versions of one memory, "*weiter leben* and *Still Alive*, are as much a mirror of their places as of their time."[53]

*Still Alive* is not simply the English version of *weiter leben* but an Americanized version of it. Schaumann points out that "in Klüger's two texts, the Holocaust is conceptualized and verbalized for two different audiences, a German and an American one. Instead of calling for universal lessons, Klüger engages each audience in a dialogue about the Holocaust that is based on the shared experiences of each culture."[54] In the years that elapsed between the publication of the two books, more pieces of information about her past began to reach Klüger from various sources (including friends, readers, and colleagues), confirming, contradicting, reshaping, or simply filling in the voids in her own narrative. Klüger had to fit them all together. The puzzle of memory holds more than one solution; its pieces change each time we set out to combine them. Klüger's two textual variations exemplarily demonstrate the shifting nature of memory. To give an example, the most crucial new piece of information that forced Klüger to revise a "memory" that she had created and kept safe in her mind for decades concerned the death of her father. She had always believed that he had been gassed in Auschwitz, but thanks to a Frenchwoman who got in touch with her after reading *weiter leben*, Klüger found out that her father had in fact been transported farther east to the Baltic States and may have died in transport. Such new facts are introduced in *Still Alive*, which is further complicated and enriched by this enhanced knowledge and by the change in life circumstances that occurred between the writing of the two books: Klüger's newfound fame allowed (or perhaps forced) the intensification of her dialogue with Germany, the site of her difficult past, and with European people who had their own mixed feelings about national histories and Klüger's personal story; she became a grandmother; and, most important, she lost her mother, who died in her bed, surrounded by her children, grandchildren, and great-grandchildren in 2000. My study will focus on the English edition of Klüger's survival story because it is in this text that the shared journey of a mother and daughter comes full circle. Not by chance, while *weiter leben* had been dedicated to "den Göttinger Freunden" (to my friends in Göttingen), *Still Alive* is dedicated to the memory of Alma Hirschel, Klüger's mother.

What is of particular relevance to my project is that *weiter leben* and *Still Alive* are more than just about the memory of the Shoah. If they were, then Alma would not have taken the text so much to heart, nor would Klüger have tried to conceal its existence from her and delayed its publication in English for so long. Through Klüger's work, the daughter engages in a fight not only with her Germanic past but also with her mother. The daughter's memories are split into two—those in which she is a victim alongside her mother and those in which she and her mother inhabit two separate, warring camps. Schuchalter is not totally inaccurate when he declares, not without some acrimony on his own part, that "*weiter leben* is suffused with the bile of its narrator and this bile, combined with vitriol, molds the entire work, raising doubts about how reliable the entire autobiography is." He goes on to characterize Klüger's work as full of an "unbridled animus towards the most outrageous of regimes—the tyranny of the maternal."[55] However, what Schuchalter finds questionable, I find inceptive; and I argue that the daughter's anger, rather than nullifying her testimony, reveals new truths about both maternal and historical tyrannies.

We must also consider that Still Alive, because of its new audience and the chronological gap that separates it from weiter leben, has what Schaumann calls a more "compassionate quality": "Although the incidents of motherly abuse narrated in weiter leben also appear in Still Alive, Klüger's rage seems to have been tempered, her voice softened."[56] Schaumann rightly points out the difference for Klüger between Göttingen, and Europe in general, and America, and California in particular: the latter is home to Klüger, the place she has spent the longest period of her life, established a successful career, brought up her children, and cultivated long-lasting friendships. The fact that Göttingen was the place where she discovered a voice with which to tell the story that had remained buried for forty years and where, because of the circumstances of her hospitalization, she found herself having to deal intimately with German people, to depend on their generosity and help, explains why the book—born out of this important, perhaps cathartic, encounter—should be dedicated to her friends in that town. However, the fact that the revised book of memory, Still Alive, was written from home, from a place of safety that had lost its estranging exilic quality, does not completely explain why it should be dedicated to Alma. I suggest that Klüger had an important insight between weiter leben and Still Alive, between the Göttingen hospital and the campus of the University of California, Irvine, a new recognition by the Jewish daughter of the mother's position in her life and of her own position with the mother in history. And as this particular recognition is the trail that Holocaust Mothers and Daughters follows, the maternal reconciliation envisioned by Still Alive determined my choice to work with the English text. Furthermore, it is Still Alive, not weiter leben, that gives us the mother-daughter story in its entirety. Finally, and most importantly, Still Alive displays significant shifts in the author's style stemming from the physical loss of the mother, shifts that are important for this study.

Specifically, my analysis centers on how Klüger transplants the classic fairy-tale modes of narration—which entail the construction of a "wicked (step)mother" type—into her childhood vision of the surrounding world. Not surprisingly for a German-language author brought up in the volk-enamored culture of Goethe, the Grimm brothers, and E. T. A. Hoffmann, Klüger embeds in Still Alive numerous references to mythical figures, guardian angels, and fairy tales. To illustrate her narrative technique and its larger implications, I read her story through the theoretical frame of Bruno Bettelheim's psychoanalytical understanding of fairy tales. Through this frame, I am able to reveal the symbolic language and narrative strategies through which the psychic world of children—in particular, the Holocaust child—evoked in *Still Alive* is formed. At the same time, I offer a critique of Bettelheim and the patriarchal system that his reading of fables supports, a system that I claim Klüger's conscious manipulations of the enchanted mirror of her memoir aim at exposing. Fairy tales reward the girl who remains meek and submissive to the patriarchal regime (marriage with the prince) and punishes (in quite horrific ways) the powerful woman (witch or stepmother), who is set up as the perennial antagonist of other, less powerful women (innocent maidens and stepdaughters). These stories are supposed to help children make sense of their identity and grow up into well-socialized adults. Through Klüger's case, I demonstrate how these narrative motifs do not help a Jewish girl make sense of her identity or cope with the destructive forces of the Holocaust. In the end, Klüger's text exposes these fairy-tale lessons as utterly misogynistic, coercive, and potentially murderous. They might enrich our imagination and cultural patrimony, but they also poison our sense of self and our perception of reality, and—most insidiously of all—they undermine a daughter's loyalty toward her mother.

Next, to illustrate the case of children in hiding with their mothers, I feature the story of Sarah Kofman, which takes place in Nazi-occupied Paris and is retold in her memoir *Rue Ordener, Rue Labat*.[57] The exceptionality of her story arises from the disruptive appearance of a second mother—the Christian woman who saved her life. The eight-year-old Sarah and her mother had fled to this woman's apartment just minutes before a nighttime roundup conducted by the French police helped consign thousands of foreign and French Jews to German control. Kofman's father had already been deported and, unbeknown to his family, was about to be brutally murdered in Auschwitz. Claire Chemitre (referred to in the memoir as Mémé), the French woman who harbored and saved the lives of Sarah and her mother, developed a profound attachment to the girl and did everything in her power—successfully—to alienate Kofman from her biological mother. A war over the affection of the child between the adult women, the girl's two mothers, ensued and persisted for the rest of Kofman's teenage years. I argue that for the young girl, falling in love with Mémé signified, subconsciously, the recuperation of a symbolic father: Mémé takes total control over her protégées—the mother must accept her rule or risk death, while Sarah follows Mémé's lead, which distances her from her mother; Mémé replaces the lost father as family protector, breadwinner and lawgiver, while at the same time she represents the majority culture, the triumphant Christian world in which the girl could have a safer present and a guaranteed future (were it not for her Jewish identity which, with Mémé's collaboration, she'll work to erase).

Through an impulse of self-preservation, the girl thus falls under the spell of this new, stronger, "winning" mother. This impulse requires the sacrifice of the Jewish mother and the roots she represents, roots that paradoxically include the Jewish Shoah father whom Mémé had come to both replace and preserve.

"Kofman's texts," writes Kathryn Robson in her discussion of *Rue Ordener, Rue Labat*, "reiterate an irresolvable tension between the need to remember and the will to forget, between the story of the child who survived and the father who did not."[58] I would reverse the terms posited in the quote from Robson and suggest that for Kofman, as perhaps for all Shoah memoirists discussed in this volume, it is rather the need to forget (in order to live on) that fights against the will to remember (in order not to betray the dead), and that Kofman's specific struggle is not between the divergent fates of child and father but the inner struggle of the surviving daughter to overcome an intolerable sense of guilt. The daughter is capable of keeping the father "alive" (through Mémé's symbolic substitution for him) only at the cost of sacrificing the mother (the Jewish past). I offer an interpretation of *Rue Ordener, Rue Labat* as a confession, as a book of public penance and of intimate sacrifice(s): Kofman's auto-da-fé.

We owe to Alice Jardine an important interview conducted with Kofman and published in English in 1991.[59] However, only since her death in 1994 has Kofman's intellectual legacy begun to be seriously examined by some of the most important contemporary analysts, such as Kelly Oliver, Tina Chanter, and her life-long friend and colleague, Jean-Luc Nancy.[60] A volume was released in 2007 that collected excerpts from Sarah Kohman's longer works and, most importantly, her autobiographical short pieces.[61] So far, only seven of her twenty-five scholarly texts on the thought and legacy of some of the illustrious fathers of Western civilization have been translated into English.

Chapter 4 takes up the stories of the Kindertransport refugees, who remained the least studied and discussed casualties of the Holocaust until the 1990s. It is to these victims that Milena Roth's extraordinary memoir, *Lifesaving Letters*, the central focus of my analysis, calls attention.[62] In 1938, after long internal political negotiations, the British government allowed about 10,000 Jewish children from Central Europe to enter Great Britain. Left behind in countries occupied by the Nazis, most of their families were unable to obtain similar entry visas and, as a result, were murdered. The orphaned refugees speedily assimilated into their new environment. Their host families, the British school system, and British society at large aided in this assimilation, partly owing to the country's Victorian monocultural ideal of Englishness as well as a remaining antisemitism, which did not encourage Jewish children to retain their cultural heritage. For the most part, it took almost half a century for the children (Kinder) to overcome their survivor's guilt and begin to tell their experiences (the exception being Lore Segal, who published an autobiographical Kindertransport novel in 1964).[63] For a long time, the plight of these children did not figure as part of the Holocaust story because the circumstances of their survival seemed to delegitimize the Kinders' experience in the Shoah. Therefore, I thought it relevant for my study to briefly survey the history of the Kindertransports and highlight two of their relevant aspects that, ironically, are in diametric opposition to each other. On the one hand, as scholarship on the subject by Tony Kushner, Bryan Cheyette, David Cesarani, Phyllis Lassner, and Richard Bolchover among others has already demonstrated,[64] a specific brand of British antisemitism existed that represented an obstacle before and after the war for Jewish refugees, whose successful integration and assimilation tacitly required a total erasure of their past. On the other hand, Great Britain distinguished itself by accepting refugees who were being denied access visas by other free nations, and it was the unprecedented involvement of women at all levels of the bureaucracy who made this rescue operation possible and successful. Roth's memoir permits a fascinating examination of both of these aspects—British antisemitism and the colonization of the foreign subject, together with the antifascist stand of an entire nation that allowed the survival of a small yet vital portion of the Shoah victims.

After surveying many memoirs and stories of Kindertransport refugees, I couldn't help noticing that they all have one compelling aspect in common: the relevance of objects in the lives of these exiles. The fleeing children had been allowed to carry no more than two suitcases, and these contained the only material things that would remain of their European past after the war. I call these "memory objects" (objets de mémoire, a permutation of Pierre Nora's concept of lieux de mémoire[65]), and I propose that they are sites that make it possible to trace specifically feminine ways of bonding and memory making. These were objects from the house, simple objects with domestic roots: a teddy bear, a family Bible, a pillowcase, a special blanket, a father's belt, a mother's piece of jewelry. Often it was the mothers who chose the objects and most likely packed them as well—in a panicked rush, heartbroken or numbed by fear. In the chapter on the Kindertransport, I raise the question of whether the domestic, and therefore feminine and maternal, character of these memory objects has been and remains an obstacle to their representation and presence in Holocaust museums and other memorialization sites (all of which are strongly informed by a patriarchal, masculine conception of memory and history). As Reading has demonstrated, the main Holocaust museums in the West have only recently started to find an appropriate collocation for women's specific experiences in their exhibits, thanks to the direct involvement and expertise of feminist historians such as

Ringelheim and Marion Kaplan.[66] Most Shoah memorial sites, however, are still greatly lacking in this regard.

On top of these material or maternal connections, I look at Roth's *Lifesaving Letters* from other perspectives. Hers is another story of a double motherhood, but it is of a very different kind from Kofman's. In Kofman's case, two mothers existed simultaneously and tore apart the daughter's loyalties and sense of self, but Roth's British savior, Doris Campbell, never replaced the biological mother in the heart of the refugee girl. Roth's narrative is shared between the first-person voice of the daughter and the first-person voice of the Holocaust mother, through the reproduction in the text of the letters that her mother, Anna Rothová, exchanged with her British friend Doris, who eventually saved Roth's life. Anna kept writing to Doris up until her deportation to Theresienstadt; she was later sent to Auschwitz, from where she and her husband, along with their extended families, never returned. As in Kofman's case, here again we have a young Jewish girl's forced assimilation into a Christian environment that requires that she demonstrate gratitude and forgetfulness. We also see the culturally bridging figure of a second mother. Unlike Mémé, however, Doris Campbell—that "benevolent" woman with a "strange sadistic undertow, the punishing Victorianism, with which they'd all been brought up"[67]—never became a mother to Roth in the emotional sense of the word because of her detached and cold character. This disposition made Roth feel unwelcomed and lacking in some essential qualities, set apart for being a foreigner, a Jew, and a stranger.

To be sure, there is no lack of memoirs written by these former child refugees. Yet only in recent years has scholarship caught up with this aspect of the war, and some crucial studies have finally analyzed both the historical context and the testimonies of the Kindierstransport. In 2004 the journal *Shofar* devoted an entire issue to the Kindertransport rescue operation. Phillys Lassner dedicated a large section of *Anglo-Jewish Women Writing the Holocaust* to the analysis of this chapter in British and Jewish history through a literary perspective. And Iris Guske, Vera Fast, and Ann Byers have written three recent monographs devoted to the Kindertransport.[68]

Next, in chapter 5, I delve into the experience of Holocaust survivors' children, the Shoah's second generation, who lived through the aftershocks of the catastrophe. The post-Holocaust mother-daughter relationship that I take as paradigmatic is found in the memoir *Lezioni di tenebra* (Lessons of darkness), by Helena Janeczek.[69] Janeczek was born in Munich, where her Polish Jewish parents had relocated after the war, but she now lives in Italy, where she became a successful writer and leading intellectual figure. Her memoir recalls her experience as a Jew brought up in postwar democratic Germany; it explores her multilayered identity together with the relationship between exile and language in present-day multicultural Europe; and, finally, it explores the ethical and humanizing role that collective and personal memory, particularly Jewish memory, can still play in European society.

To better understand the mechanics of such memory, I turn to the work on postmemory by Hirsch. She coined the interesting, and by now canonic, neologism "postmemory" in the late 1990s, and in a recent book, she revisits the term and describes it thusly: "'Postmemory' describes the relationship that the 'generation after' bears to the personal, collective, and cultural trauma of those who came before—to experiences they 'remember' only by means of the stories, images, and behaviors among which they grew up. But these experiences were transmitted to them so deeply, and affectively as to *seem* to constitute memories in their own right."[70] The field of postmemory studies has seen an incredible proliferation of scholarly works in the last two decades that tackle the issue of inherited trauma from a number of disciplinary angles—in particular, the literary, sociological, and psychoanalytical ones. Significant work on the subject has been produced by the Israeli psychotherapist Dina Wardi, who specializes in the therapeutic treatment of children of survivors.[71] Alan Berger has devoted an important volume *Children of Job* to what is now referred to as second-generation literature.[72] Scholars have not yet reached a consensus as to whether children of victims and children of perpetrators should be grouped together in one camp (of asymmetrical yet analogous relations), or whether the term "inherited trauma" (the stress being on trauma) can be justifiably applied to both groups.[73] During the last fifteen years in America and Israel, Efraim Sicher, Dan Bar-On, Helen Epstein, Geoffrey Hartman, and numerous others have interwoven academic research and personal experience—as Jewish secondhand victims themselves—to contribute to the formation of an indispensable corpus of historical and personal considerations on the inheritance of trauma and the long-term effects of genocide(s) on the human mind and on our social systems.[74]

Through a comparison of Janeczek's work with some of the best-known postwar memoirs by women born or raised in America, England, or Canada, my study showcases the problematic and ambiguous nature of the identity-making processes that marked the experience of postwar European Jewish women. The strongly conflicted and deeply moving mother-daughter relationship in Janeczek's memoir is contextualized in the historical and philosophical framework of Jewish exile and diaspora in Europe. I read this relationship through two pivotal tropes of the diasporic or migrant experience: food and language. Janeczek's text exemplifies the complexities of both. As a young girl, she suffered from eating disorders and other pathologies due to her low self-esteem and poor self-image, which her memoir clearly relates to the tyrannical, controlling, and smothering attitude of her mother. *Lezioni di tenebra* is a study of both the mother's damaged psyche and the effects of these damages on the daughter. In particular, Janeczek reflects on the way the expressions of love, anger, or fear of the mother appear through her choice of language—the way in which she switches from German to Polish, Yiddish, or even Italian or French depending on the mood she wishes to express or the lessons she intends to impart to her daughter. Janeczek receives from her mother the Shoah's "lessons of darkness" that persecute instead of teaching anything and that leave an insatiable void in the survivors' lives and in the lives of their children as well.

My book ends, almost counterintuitively, with the case of Anne Frank. Frank's autobiographical epistolary (meant to be published after the war as a memoir of a young girl in hiding) is unusual when compared with the other memoirs, but it epitomizes many of the themes that emerge from the previous Jewish mother-daughter models. The famous diary boasts unique features of its own that could not be left unexplored in a discussion about the mother-daughter bond as defined by the Shoah tragedy. Frank is the rebellious daughter who writes about (and against) family, against the war, against the patriarchal world she intuits will hinder her dreams of independence one day (a day that never came for her), and who, like her mother, perishes in a concentration camp. She is the writer without hindsight, her chronicle perpetually stuck in a present tense that knows no future. Here we encounter a brilliant young writer who is struggling to overcome her adolescent conflict with her mother while at the same time striving to survive a most brutal attack against her person, her family, and hence the very same mother against whom she struggles. We are left with a phenomenal description of a Jewish family in times of extraordinary hardship from the pen of an artist who is a blooming woman. Frank's writings (her diary and *Tales from the Secret Annex*)[75] squarely belong in the canon of Holocaust witnessing. They are also centered on the family, in particular the conflict between daughter and mother—a conflict that the aspiring writer knows how to connect to and distinguish from the effects of the contingent historical upheaval. In this closing chapter, I show how the famous mother-daughter conflict and father-daughter worship in the diary is not as clear-cut as it is usually understood to be. Instead, I claim that the creative act of life writing, even for such a young author in the midst of adolescent turmoil and war, allows Frank to gain a new understanding of herself and of the Other. It is through writing that she slowly begins to look beyond the bad mother of the Oedipus complex and discover a new horizon—a different, productive rather than destructive, mother-daughter bond. I also show how the reader's propensity to take the negative descriptions that the girl gives of her mother at face value has influenced the way Edith Frank was viewed by friends and critics after the war. Many used unflattering terms that they uncritically took from the mouth of Anne the icon (the child martyr, not the complex writer), whose legacy they were trying to safeguard.

Building on the trailblazing work of Rachel Brenner and Denise De Costa,[76] my chapter on Anne Frank interprets the act of writing or producing any art in times of extreme, life-threatening circumstances as a courageous strategy for psychic, ideological, moral, and even physical resistance to annihilation. Esther "Etty" Hillesum, Hélène Berr, Simone Weil, Charlotte Salomon, Anne Frank, and scores of other victims engendered a host of cultural responses and went on creating art despite art's utter impotence, despite the incongruity of making art amidst the annihilation of a people and a civilization. Yet to disregard, as some do, these last testaments on the grounds that annihilation triumphed over creation, or that these writers did not survive the events they described, seems to me an act of expropriation that strips the victims of their subjectivities.

Indebted as it is to the strictly psychoanalytical reading of Frank's diary by Katherine Dalsimer,[77] my study turns to one particular aspect of Frank's art that has not been analyzed before but that is as ancient as the human community, an aspect that is usually associated with men but that is a significant characteristic of the diary: humor. Aristotle defined wit as "cultured insolence"[78] because since times immemorial it has been used to ridicule those in power and because, ultimately, it is laughter that bonds together the oppressed and enables them to attack and even defeat tyrants (at least, in the eyes of history). Frank did not defeat her murderers, but she left embedded in her interrupted book this very potent quality. And, as I show using Sigmund Freud's theories on humor and narcissism,[79] humor allows the teenage girl to reconnect with her parents and bridge the gulf that seems to separate her from her mother; to begin to see herself as part of the larger world beyond the basic family circle; and, lastly, to hold on to a humanist conception of society and history—one that, as Langer has cynically though correctly pointed out, did not save her, but without which, I believe, life for her would have been inconceivable.[80] It is through the evaluation of humor in Frank's worldview and narrative voice that I propose a different understanding of the famous conflict between her and her mother.

## CHARGING PATRIARCHY

By sustaining their focus on mothers and their personal and domestic stories, the women featured in Holocaust Mothers and Daughters foreground the fact that the Shoah did not happen in a vacuum. The implementation of the Holocaust came after years of growing antisemitism in Germany, which in turn had accrued over centuries of Judeophobia in Christian Europe. From a women's perspective, however, I venture to say that being targeted as Jews by this genocide was one more expression (the most extreme) of patriarchy's oppressive attitude toward them, neither a recent invention nor one specific to the Nazis: Jewish women were oppressed as Jews and as women. The war happened within the patriarchal mind-set of Europe—imperialistic, hegemonic, and controlling. As the literary historian Gill Plain writes, "The act and idea of war itself . . . [represent] both the self-destructive impulse of a patriarchal society and the ultimate achievement of its competitive rationale."[81] Western patriarchal society marginalizes the voices of women, children, and those who do not fit into the dominant categories— Jewish and non-Jewish; Judaism, as part of the same sociocultural system, has functioned in much the same way.[82] From a Jewish woman's perspective, the war collapsed into one phenomenon various strata of domination and persecution: the antisemitism of a portion of Christian society, the specific targeting of women by genocide, and the universal threat of war (which traditionally leaves women defenseless and uses them as spoils for the victors). In such a context, the varying degrees of a Jewish woman's religious orthodoxy, her assimilation into a given culture, and her subordination to or relative independence from certain power structures could determine her chances of survival. Bruck, for instance, shows us a portrait of an utterly impotent mother whose blind religiosity and crippling poverty, together with her geographical isolation and lack of community support, worked in concert to prevent her escape. She was in no position to get up-to-date information about political events, and she probably would not have considered it her place to do so (politics and world affairs being the business of men); and her dependence on her husband's guidance (despite his constantly being away in search of work) reduced the chances that she might have been able to take some kind of action before it was too late. To be sure, no one was prepared enough for the apocalypse that was about to unfold, but certain factors made women less prepared than men. Klüger poignantly remarks: "The catastrophe seemed to have come out of the blue sky, even though, with hindsight, everyone recited the forewarnings with relish. Politics was not meant to be a feminine domain, and in my mother's Czech finishing school they didn't teach the girls how to read a newspaper critically any more than they instructed them on how to delouse the heads of children."[83] Auschwitz is understood by the writers I present here as one of the many products (undoubtedly the most monstrous) of the oppression produced by male-dominated history, a history that often sacrifices women. The writers I discuss explicitly connect their mothers' state of semipermanent hysteria, paranoia, neurotic anxiety, and fear for their children's safety to very concrete sociohistorical roots, and these roots only pierce through the Shoah—they do not begin or end with it.

From the numerous existing Jewish memoirs, journals, and other records produced during and after the war, there emerges a picture of mothers as usually quicker to panic but also more likely to take seriously the mounting threat of Nazism and Fascism than their husbands were. These husbands generally tried to minimize the danger, keep calm, and not show fear, probably so as not to scare the people in their charge. Historians confirm this impression. "Gender made a difference in deciding between fight and flight," writes Marion Kaplan. "In the early years, Jewish women were more sensitive to discrimination, more eager to leave Germany, more willing to face uncertainty abroad than discrimination and ostracism at home . . . We see anxious but highly energetic women, taking note of the political and social environment and strategizing ways of responding."[84] Judith Baumel writes: "Jewish women often sensed the need for emigration long before their male counterparts, possibly because of their closer contact with grassroots anti-Semitism, their lack of business and political ties and their family-oriented identity which heightened their perceptions of the changes in Germany . . . For many, the decision to leave [Germany was taken] by the women of the family."[85] For instance, the former maid of the Frank family in Frankfurt reported this anecdote in a postwar interview with Ernst Schnabel: "It must have been 1929 . . . at lunch, I asked Mr. Frank who these brownshirts [Hitler's storm troops] were. And, you know, Mr. Frank just laughed and tried to make a joke of the whole thing, and although it wasn't very much of a laugh and not much of a joke, he did try. But Mrs. Frank looked up from her plate, she did, and she fixed her eyes on us and said: 'We'll find out soon enough who they are, Kati.' And that was no joke, and it wasn't said like a joke."[86] Apparently, "Jewish women," as Baumel points out, "perceived the far-reaching implications of Nazism faster than their male counterparts and were less likely to indulge in self-deception regarding its temporary nature."[87] Klüger recalls an episode (similar to the one that took place in the Frank's household) in which her father brings home the new German currency with which the Nazis had replaced the Austrian one and explains the new money while doing a hilarious imitation of the invaders' pronunciation (different from the Austrian variation). "In brief, we had fun," Klüger writes. "My mother indicated that this was scandalously childish behavior in desperate times. I didn't understand what she meant and wondered if she was right . . . or if she was being a spoilsport."[88] Although women were rightly scared by the desperate times, their worries could easily be dismissed by the surrounding world as expressions of female overexcitability or feebleness. Fear, being culturally understood as unheroic, is also categorized as female, shameful, or hysterical. Fear is actually a healthy mechanism of self-preservation, although women's panic is often scorned, deflated, or altogether dismissed.[89] In her graphic autobiography, Charlotte Salomon (who was gassed in Auschwitz at the age of twenty-six) depicts with love and sympathy a grandmother who was looked at as a typical oversensitive nineteenth-century woman, a rich and sophisticated Berliner with feeble nerves whose fears were paternalistically shushed by a distant and supercilious husband. As soon as Hitler came to power in 1933, the grandmother had forced her husband to escape Berlin and move to the Côte d'Azur, where Salomon eventually joins them in the false hope that they will all be safe in southern France. Salomon portrays the grandmother as she was in the late 1930s, in France, curled up by the radio listening to a report on the "terrible excesses against Jews in Germany." The caption to this illustration reads: "Mrs. Knarre [the pseudonym Salomon uses for her grandmother] spends all her time sitting by the radio," and a dialogue between her and her husband follows: "*Grandmother:* 'Oh Dear, what times we live in—will I ever see "her" [Charlotte] again?' *Grandfather:* 'Don't upset yourself, it won't help matters. I believe in Providence–and what is to be will be' . . . *Grandmother:* 'She [Charlotte] must come here as quickly as possible!'"[90] Although the grandmother has her way, and Salomon is sent to them by her worried parents, this is not enough to calm the grandmother's shaken nerves or to reassure her that from now on everything will be fine. She seems to understand better than the others the horror that is about to reach them. "Old Mrs. Knarre tries to hang herself in the bathroom. The awful pain that has pursued her throughout her life but had been kept somewhat in abeyance seems to have resurfaced into full consciousness as a result of the raging war," writes Salomon, "and she feels her sharp intellect and self-control . . . breaking up against a greater force."[91] The grandfather, despite having already experienced many deaths by suicide in the family, unwisely dismisses his wife's attempt: "It seems to be only a passing attack."[92] However, the grandmother's agitated response to the doom facing them isn't a passing instance of *Weltschmerz*. She tries again almost immediately, and this time she succeeds in killing herself.

*Holocaust Mothers and Daughters* underscores the value of understanding the Holocaust as an integrated part of a history of oppression rather than as a freak explosion of bottled-up sentiments and resentments on the part of (any) one nation or people against another. The writers discussed in the book focus our attention on the tentacular reach of oppression beyond Auschwitz, and in spite of it. As an adult intellectual in the 1970s and 80s—a woman with an impressive publishing record and a position at the very center of the postmodern current as a peer and friend of Jacques Derrida, Gilles Deleuze, Jean-François Lyotard, and

Jean-Luc Nancy—Kofman felt isolated and insufficiently recognized because of the sexist French academic system that kept her on the margins for a long time. "I'm a university professor but only a *maître de conferences* [untenured professor]," she lamented in an interview, "in spite of my nineteen books—this must be kept in mind."[93] And in a footnote in that published interview, she wrote: "This year, the Université de Paris I—Pantheon—Sorbonne once again refused to promote me to professor. The 'scandalous injustice' of this refusal led to a unanimous protest on the part of all the famous contemporary philosophers and the entire French press."[94] Eventually, a couple of years before her death, Kofman was made a full professor.[95] Klüger has also complained about the racial and sexual prejudices, as well as the not-so-veiled signs of suspicion and even contempt that she experienced early in her academic career as she was trying to establish herself as Germanist in America.[96]

For the Jews, the Shoah was a universalizing force, in the sense that all of them without distinction were victims of it. Life before and after the war was, by contrast, dominated by all sorts of *distinguos*, as Bruck makes sure to point out repeatedly in her works. Bruck's many autobiographical books and poems talk about how both parents and their children had to endure many forms of humiliation and degradation, not only from the antisemitic world surrounding them but also from wealthier Jews. Her father was a pariah in both the Christian and Jewish world. Bruck's autobiographical stories and poems portray an ineffectual father and a desperate mother left alone, battling poverty and dejection and faced with the challenge of raising her many children by herself in a small village on the easternmost frontiers of Hungary. She was a patriarchal mother, instilling in her daughters lessons she herself had been taught: to be good wives, not to sin, to keep a Jewish home, and to abstain from desiring anything more. However, the most pernicious form of oppression, according to Bruck, was her mother's unflinching religiosity. The mother in Bruck's writings is portrayed as utterly subjugated to God and the consequent hierarchies of male rulers: father or husband, king or rabbi. In her daughter's perception, she was a victim of them all long before the Nazis came to deliver the last and fatal blow against her. In the autobiographical *Lettera*, the narrator talks of an uncle who sexually molested her when she was a child (we are left to wonder whether this is fiction or part of the author's life experience, or something that happened to her sisters or people she knew);[97] after Auschwitz, one of Bruck's husbands physically and mentally abused her; and in Israel, a stranger raped her. Her foreignness and poverty remained a crushing force in her life for a long time. She faced anti-semitism in the Hungary of her childhood as well as in postwar, contemporary

Italy; today, she still feels somewhat isolated and unwelcome, both in the Christian world (her books constantly take up the issue of her nonbelonging) and in the infamously hermetic Italian Jewish community (one very different from the Ashkenazi world of her mother). In an interview in Rome in 2007, she told me: "A foreigner remains a stranger for the rest of his life. I will never be considered 'one of them' by the Italian Jews, never!"

The author who more than any other delves into the position of women in the patriarchal world before and after the war is Klüger. Rather than shaping her memoir to fit within the confines of the Auschwitz parenthesis, Klüger emphasizes the tensions that worked against women in society regardless of the Nazis. In fact, of the five parts into which *Still Alive* is divided, only one deals specifically with the conditions of internment in the camps. Compelling sections of *Still Alive* braid the ever-present Holocaust shadow together with the masculinist world of Judaism, "which reduces its daughters to helpmeets of men and circumscribes their spiritual life within the confines of domestic functions," sardonically concluding that "recipes for gefilte fish are no recipe for coping with the Holocaust."[98] Klüger denounces the attitudes of Americans (both Jewish and non-Jewish) toward Shoah survivors, especially women survivors, who after the war, she explains, had to justify themselves for having lived when so many Jewish men did not: "I felt inferior, saw myself through the eyes of others . . . [A]t a time when women were constantly put in their supposed place, it was natural for a young refugee to question her own value. In my family the women had survived, not the men. And that meant that the more valuable human beings had lost their lives."[99]

While still in Germany after the war, waiting for a visa to emigrate to the United States, Klüger started to attend school again, where she was wounded by the contemptuous remark of a teacher who claimed that girls have no sense of honor. Klüger writes: "While Germans had to revise their judgment of Jews, however reluctantly and sporadically, they didn't even try to revise their Nazi-bred contempt for women."[100] Once in the safety of America, Klüger makes it crystal clear that though the survivors were finally free from Auschwitz, they were still in a world not very different from the one they had known before the war. From a woman's perspective, in what way had society truly changed from the 1930s to the mid- or late 1940s? "The return to peace," Sheila Meintjes, Anu Pillay and Meredeth Turshen point out, "is invariably conceptualized as a return to the gender status quo irrespective of the nontraditional roles assumed by women during the conflict."[101] In America, for instance, the postwar era tried to reestablish the role of women as goddesses of the home, striving to push them out of the workforce to make room for the men who had returned from the front and to stabilize society on the pillars of the patriarchal family model. "War must be seen," Plain insists, "not as the demise but as the rebirth of patriarchy. Between 1930 and 1950 the cycle comes full circle from the decadence of the old, through the apocalypse of war, to the birth of the new. The new, however, is not different; it does not represent change. It is instead the infant patriarchy, nurtured on the breast of women's wartime labour—a breast which it must inevitably reject. In the new era of the 1950s women are safely back in the home, stabilizing the shaken male ego, and effectively marginalised from the concerns of the symbolic order." [102]

In the literature presented here, we encounter a strong distrust of those patriarchal tenets that sustain the Western sociocultural system. Before the war, Jewish fathers were part of (and therefore complicit with) the old patriarchal system; during the war, they became victims of the new order that the Nazis' and Fascists' ideology was shaping. In either position, though, the fathers were of no help to their daughters: either they were supporting a male status quo that oppressed women, or because of historical circumstances they were incapable of protecting the women in their care. In *Still Alive* we read:

> I had spent my life among women, and this didn't change in New York. In my family, in the camps, and even after the war, men had been at the periphery of my life. It was true that from that periphery they called the shots because they had the power, and my mother never ceased to assure me that a woman needed to marry someone who'd provide for her. But her own example was different. From the beginning of the Hitler period until the time I left her, she was without a husband. Before and after she was a wife. But I knew her in the postwar time as a working woman, and under the Nazis her men had been powerless and had perished. [103]

The writers in my study had fathers who either died in the war or remained ineffectual figures after it. The fathers of Bruck, Kofman, Klüger, and Roth never returned. Janeczek's father survived, but he shrank away (sadly and quietly) from the lives of his wife and daughter and is largely absent from his daughter's postwar memoir. Frank's is the exceptional case in that everybody in the family died except her father, who became a kind of receptacle for all the other victims' stories, as well as the steward of his daughter's legacy. He turned his life into an act of continuous witnessing of the tragic lot of those he loved but could not save.

These, of course, were Jewish fathers, whose role inside the family and the world at large had been injured and altered by hatred and genocide. As we know, both men and women shared tribulations and heroisms, victories and unimaginable losses, during the six-year-long conflict. Many women played a role in the war as partisans, discreet saboteurs, spies, good Samaritans who risked their lives to hide the Jews, parachutists, and volunteer nurses.[104] Baumel notes: "As in the case of German-Jewish women, Jewish mothers in occupied Poland were usually the driving force in trying to find havens for their children. Through former neighbors, the underground movements and even the Church, mothers in ghettos made contact with people willing to hide their children . . . Here too, gentile Polish women were instrumental in saving these children . . . Nannies and household maids were often devoted to their families and saved them, or at least their children, where possible."[105] Roth's and Kofman's mothers are perfect examples of women who organized the rescue of their children against impossible odds. Anna Rothová, Roth's mother, understood the gravity of the situation immediately after the annexation of the Sudetenland by Nazi Germany. She had traveled to England in her youth before getting married, and the bonds she had formed and maintained with women there meant the difference between life and death to her only daughter. Rothová had obtained a visa for herself to escape Czechoslovakia, but she had chosen to stay behind, unwilling to leave her husband in Europe by himself. Kofman's mother, Fineza, had been able to connect to the underground resistance, and the partisans helped her place all her children with various French saviors across the countryside. She also found an ideal haven for herself and her daughter in downtown Paris, the heart of Nazi-occupied France, in the apartment of Mémé. Fineza Kofman was an observant Jew, the wife of a Polish rabbi, and she knew little French. She was a devout executioner of her husband's desires in the home, yet, as I will show in chapter 3, in her daughter's memoir we glimpse small acts of decisiveness and even rebellion that provide two insights into the mother's situation. On the one hand, she was endowed with remarkable practical sense and wisdom; on the other hand, these qualities could be nullified at any time by the power of her husband, whose decisions would invariably outweigh her objections. Rabbi Kofman practically gave himself up for arrest in the hope that his self-sacrifice would spare his family. But this was a gross miscalculation. His wife intuited this and opposed her husband's decision, but her logic was overridden by the rabbi's will to do as he saw fit, with dire consequences.

In both Roth's and Kofman's stories, the place of honor is occupied by two Christian women who selflessly opened their houses to persecuted Jews. These female figures enrich the mother-daughter plot examined here by presenting alternative scenarios of a double motherhood and split loyalties on the part of the daughter. During the war, such rescuers constituted a tiny minority, and thus their courage was all the more extraordinary. Doris Campbell was a strong woman who had decided to take action and obtained the acquiescence of her husband, who as a rule delegated all domestic decisions to his "bossy" wife. Mémé, in contrast, was not married; she demonstrated her total independence by defying her family's insistence that she not risk her own, and everybody else's, life to shelter two Jews in her apartment. Wives and mothers like Doris Campbell, Mémé, Anna Rothová, and Alma Klüger clearly break the rule of the patriarchal system that forbids women to take matters into their own hands or decide what to do for themselves.[106]

Frank displays a similar independence, though her case is an anomalous one. Young and inexperienced as she may have been, the walled-in girl in the attic had begun to develop a clear sense of the world's expectations and demands on her as a woman. She responds to the pressures from the surrounding world with heightened affirmations of independence, rebellion, and self-reliance. Quickly falling out of love with Peter, she chooses to be a writer rather than the sentimental heroine of the secret annex romance. She is perceived by the other people in the hiding place as a spoiled brat at best, at worst a seditious element to be reined in before it is too late. The characters of Petronella van Daan (Auguste van Pels), her husband (Hermann van Pels), and later Dr. Dussel (Fritz Pfeffer) are there to speak for the controlling forces of the outside world that the author is preparing herself to combat after the war. She rightly foresees that her desire to be independent and pursue a career of her choosing will not be greeted enthusiastically by the outside world, even after the defeat of the Nazis.[107] "You know way too much about things you're not supposed to," begins one of the many harangues from Mrs. van Daan and Dr. Dussel: "You've been brought up all wrong . . . You'd better hurry if you want to catch a husband or fall in love." To this, Frank adds the following insightful comment: "They apparently believe that good child-rearing includes trying to pit me against my parents."[108] From her teenage perspective, she is able to glimpse the problematic nature of gender and power imbalances even within her terrifyingly constricted daily world: "One of the many questions that have often bothered me is why women have been, and still are, thought to be so inferior to men. It's easy to say it's unfair, but that's not enough for me; I'd really like to know the reason for this great injustice!"[109] Of course, she lacks the hindsight that is available to the other survivors writers included here, who use their adult understanding of these difficult and oppressive dynamics to put into focus, examine, and critique their childhood circumstances decades later. In revisiting their childhood selves from a distanced perspective, they make sense of their relationships with their mothers much better than the girl in the Amsterdam attic could with her restricted vision. The most compelling suggestion that comes out of these self-examining texts (Frank's diary among them) is that larger changes must occur in our sociocultural and sociosymbolic systems to ensure that "never again" apply not only to the Nazis and the Holocaust but also to the societal conditions that made both these aberrant phenomena possible: to wit, gender imbalance and inequality of all kinds.

## "ODE TO A FOUNTAIN PEN" : CAN WOMEN'S WRITING WORK AGAINST OBLIVION?

Imbedded in women's autobiographical writings—even those concentrated on the communal trauma of a genocide that unites all victims, as Shoah stories do—are traces of those tensions that arise in women's lives each time a woman attempts to carve out a space (artistic, occupational, political, and so forth) for herself in society and let her experiences emerge. It is relevant, for example, that—at some point and with varying degrees of emphasis—all the women discussed in this book mention that their desire to write or to achieve a better place in life had been discouraged, thwarted, or ridiculed by someone around them. Bruck, Kofman, and Klüger battled against their mothers' open aversion to their artistic propensities from a very young age. Janeczek's mother does not appreciate her daughter's desire to be a writer and makes sure to control her by interfering with her work, telling her what to delete and what to include in her manuscript (see chapter 5). In *Tales from the Secret Annex*, we read of an argument that exploded among the people in hiding when Anne and Margot Frank angered the van Pels and Dr. Pfeffer for wasting their time reading and writing rather than occupying themselves with more feminine chores. "It'd be better for the children [Anne and Margot]," Frank reports Hermann van Pels (nicknamed Mr. van Daan in the diary and *Tales*) as saying, "if they helped out . . . instead of sitting around all day with their noses in a book. Girls don't need that much education anyway!"[110] Roth practically had to suppress any aspirations to rise in British society because as a foreigner, an orphaned girl, a Jew, and a former refugee, she was given to feel that she should keep a low profile and be grateful for what had already been given to her, rather than asking for more. Her mother had ardently wished to go to college, but she had been marked from birth as the child who would help out in the family's trade; similarly, Roth's grandmother had been taken out of school to work as seamstress, helping to support the family and her brother's studies so that he could become a doctor. Bruck laments that her mother perceived her desire to write poetry as almost sinful and would not listen to her when she recited or read aloud to her mother. Klüger admits that her mother "considered [her] career an embarrassment" and that "my father's generation didn't pay much attention to small children. My mother claims that he was crazy about me, but that's like staging and then retouching a family photo. I know better."[111]

Mothers coming of age in the harsh, competitive, unsentimental world of early-twentieth-century bourgeois Europe—a world marred by a Victorian conception of human relations that, if stifling for everyone, was particularly so for girls—were as a result often cruel and oppressive themselves. For example, Roth writes of her English adoptive mother: "Doris actually wished me to fail and forecast my downfall daily . . . She couldn't bear anyone to have any success she had not had herself. This extended to her own daughter, *but not to her two sons*."[112]

In this literature, there is no evading the struggle with one's gender and one's national, religious, and social identity. These writers' acts of witnessing display a different conception of victimhood, history, and Judaism, one that places them in a unique category that breaks the bounds of other preconceived rubrics we traditionally use—such as Jew, survivor, and woman. These Jewish mothers and daughters embody a compromise with a tradition that would rather ignore the historical woman and her experience while honoring her as a discursive symbol or valuing her only for her reproductive indispensability. These women strategize to keep themselves and their children alive, and they fight for their rights both in the inimical Christian world and in the limiting Jewish one. The daughters who become writers of their own history are already an exception—if not also a threat—to the récit that Jewish and non-Jewish traditions have constructed of and about themselves. Also in these autobiographical texts, we find authors who, as Suzette Henke writes in her book on the therapeutic power of women's autobiographical practices, attempt "to fashion an enabling discourse of testimony and self-revelation . . . Women daring to name themselves, to articulate their personal histories in diary, memoir, and fictional form, reinscribe the claims of feminine desire onto the text of a traditionally patriarchal culture. In so doing, they begin to celebrate a semiotic discourse and a maternal subculture that has always generated experimental modes of feminine self-invention."[113]

Of course, the question remains: How can one attack patriarchy without attacking the Jewish father, the victim of the Nazi extermination plan? How are we to split our loyalty between ideology (history) and biology (family)? The writings of these survivor daughters (and survivors' daughters) are marked by intolerable pain at various levels: rehashing traumatic losses and experiences; returning to the "place" (trauma) of one's utter impotence and vulnerability, unable to affect the past and yet compelled to make that terror visible to others; and evoking the dead to bear witness to their victimhood while resisting the temptation to deny one's ambiguous feelings toward them, which can prove acutely painful. Writing is not exactly, *pace* Henke, a healing process in these Shoah autobiographies. Henke uses the term "scriptotherapy" to describe the healing power of autobiographical writings about traumatic experience. "Autobiography could so effectively mimic the scene of psychoanalysis," she argues, that "life-writing might provide a therapeutic alternative for victims of severe anxiety."[114] However, I would argue that in these texts there is also a resistance to therapy insofar as it promises a cure and a dia-gnosis (knowledge, from *diagignoskein*, or to know thoroughly). Representations of genocide must be configured in ways that hinder catharsis: representationality is disempowered in that it is no longer capable of generating knowledge. I detect in the testimonies of these daughters a resistance to catharsis and to healing, and this resistance operates through admitting the mother into the text. I do not disagree with Henke or other scholars who rightly detect in diaristic or autobiographical writing a positive impact on the life and psyche of the writer, especially those disempowered by society. I simply suggest that the extraordinariness of the Holocaust may challenge our understanding of the human psychic relation to artistic creation. Concerning diaries written by the victims during the war, Garbarini poignantly offers the following observation:

> The experiences that Jews had undergone by that time [the second and harshest phase—and the final years—of the Holocaust] attenuated the therapeutic function of writing . . . Indeed, Jews who were writing diaries during the latter years of the war struggled with the relationship between their experiences and the representation of their experiences much as survivors and scholars would after the war . . . They, too, considered their diaries representations that transformed their experiences into the symbolic order of language, or narrative, and this realization made some diarists uneasy. Instead of a window that rendered their experiences plainly visible to others, they perceived their writing to be distanced from their experiences. Yet rather than open up a self-affirming space, the distancing reinforced their feelings of isolation from the outside world. They feared their experiences were ultimately incommunicable and would remain, therefore, incomprehensible.[115]

Garbarini's assessment is equally valid for all the writers I examine here. A prerequisite for healing in Henke's scenario is the idea of telling or writing one's story to an absent listener who is imagined as validating and sympathetic. Often, Shoah victims' writings, and certainly the postwar texts discussed here, do not seek such an alliance with the reader, though they do invest the reader with the heavy burden of accepting their testimony, the injunction to hear and remember. These texts do not aim to reproduce the dynamics of the psychoanalytical session; rather, they mimic the dynamics of the mother-daughter relationship. Bruck's imagined interlocutor is her mother, who represents neither a validating nor a sympathetic ear to the daughter's anger. The fictional dialogue is not between the wounded author and a messianic Other, but between the wounded daughter and a mother whose very appearance in the dialogue guarantees that the wound, reopened by remembrance, will never heal. The wound of memory remains open.

What particularly touches me in the quote from Roskies with which this introduction opened is the mention of a fountain pen, the one he brings as a present to his mother's friend, Regina. Roskies ends his anecdote about Regina with these words: "A quarter century of Yiddish secular life in Vilna followed by another quarter century of professional success in communist Poland had done nothing to dim what Regina had learned about memory from an ultraorthodox father in Bialystok. Memory is an aggressive act."[116] With the fountain pen, a woman duplicates the tradition passed down by her father, simultaneously making that patriarchal tradition her own and inserting herself into it. As Bella Brodzki aptly reminds us, "to appropriate by means of the word has been a divine privilege rarely accorded women."[117] As if to highlight this appropriation, two of the authors treated in this book explicitly mention a deep connection to their fountain pens. Kofman begins her war memoir with these words: "A fountain pen, that's all I have left of [my father] . . . [I]t lies on my desk before my eyes, it compels me to write, to write."[118] Fifty-two years earlier, under the heading "Ode to My Fountain Pen," Frank had written the following enthusiastic words in her diary: "My fountain pen was always one of my most prized possessions; I valued it highly . . . Me, Anne Frank, the proud owner of a fountain pen."[119] Kofman's fountain pen, standing in for the disappeared father, compels the daughter to go on writing about victimhood and about a past she feels obligated to make known. Frank's fountain pen disappears one day when it accidentally gets mixed together with scraps of food wrapped in some old newspapers and is thrown into the burning stove. The owner works through the pain of her loss by penning these words that, for us today, vibrate with tragic irony:

I'm left with one consolation, small though it may be: my fountain pen was cremated, just as I would like to be someday!

*Yours, Anne.*[120]

Two broken fountain pens; two victims; two struggles against oblivion deploying a different kind of Jewish memory—a feminine memory that has no claim over Jewish ritual or history but that works, from its marginal position, at challenging both.

Etymologically, *zakhar* (Hebrew for "male") and *zekher* (Hebrew for "memory") are related "as we might expect of a patriarchal society," explains Amos Funkenstein, "in which 'nation,' 'community,' or 'assembly,' is always exclusive of women. The male alone (*zakhar*) constitutes the memory (*zekher*)." Personal memory is, according to Funkenstein, the act of drawing out of a cultural collective repository the necessary linguistic signs and codes to instantiate it. Yet he also observes that "the analogy between language and memory is not seamless."[121] Hence, though daughters can write themselves into history only through the instrument of the father, I claim that they succeed in delivering themselves from the place of forgetfulness assigned to them within the symbolic order by invoking the mother as an instrument of memory.

Carmel Finnan has examined how identity is constructed in the *now* of writing through the crucial continuity that memory (as much as history) assumes between past and present.[122] Traditionally, memory has been the underdog of historical exploration; personal memory has been kept either out of the empirical examination altogether or relegated to an extremely marginal position. "History and memory," writes David Myers, "have often been cast in dialectical opposition to one another, the former connoting the quest for objective knowledge of what actually happened in the past and the latter marking the subjective use of the past to sustain a vision of individual or collective identity."[123] However, Shoah autobiographies have helped elevate the historical importance of personal memory and of the victims' perspective on trauma. As Michael Rothberg notes, "autobiography and history supplement each other without bringing forth the totality of the event."[124] Indeed, the Shoah writer needs history as much as history needs the Shoah writer. In women's autobiography, the home, as an intimate domestic and maternal space, is revealed in its strategic public function as a political and historical location as much as a psychic one. The process of self-representation in these texts is not limited to history, but it makes central the complex and ambiguous configuration of personal memory and psychic history.

In the process of writing this book, I discovered a different way of conceiving of historical and familial restoration, of honoring the memory of the Other—of, in sum, loving the mother. I learned that it is possible to retool an archetype (the Jewish mother), turning it inside out so as to reveal hidden seams whose strength resides in their ambiguous, intricate, and interrelated nature. These hidden patterns in the mother-daughter plot are ultimately, for a daughter's art, generative articulations.

ART SPIEGELMAN, *Maus: A Survivor's Tale* (New York: Pantheon, 1996), 147.

# CHAPTER 1

# EDITH BRUCK'S DEAD LETTERS

No one pushes his way through here, certainly not someone with
a message from a dead man. But you sit at your window and dream
of that message when evening comes.

 **FRANZ KAFKA**, "An Imperial Message"

With these words, Samuel Taylor Coleridge immortalized the horror a person feels at being interrupted in the course of his serene life by someone who forces on him an awful truth, a story the untroubled man does not want to hear and resents for having nothing to do with him:

> He holds him with his skinny hand,
> "There was a ship," quoth he.
> "Hold off! unhand me, grey-beard loon!"
> Eftsoons his hand dropt he.[1]

Not unlike the Ancient Mariner of Coleridge's poem, the Shoah witness carries a story that, besides being an unfathomable tale, must also be forced onto its listeners: it's a story no one volunteers to hear.

In *Il Sistema periodico*, Primo Levi recalls his first months after the liberation: "The things I saw and suffered were burning inside of me; I felt closer to the dead than to the living, and I felt guilty of being a man because men had built Auschwitz and Auschwitz had swallowed millions of human beings, among whom many were my friends, including a woman very dear to my heart. I thought that telling all of this could purify me, and I felt like Coleridge's Ancient Marnier, who waylays the wedding guests on their way to the feast and inflicts on them the story of his misfortune."[2] The writer and poet Edith Bruck, Levi's good friend, had a similar outlook. After years of going from school to school, from one TV show to the next, repeating her Holocaust survival story to crowds of anonymous people, she also began to doubt the efficacy of imposing such testimony on those who form a merely passing, and often passive, audience to a narration. No matter how sympathetic and sincerely touched these audiences were, Bruck felt, they were being charged with a message from the dead that they would rather do without. Children especially ended up more confused than enlightened by this elderly lady's visits to their classrooms; a young member of such an audience once addressed Bruck as "Mrs. Auschwitz." Bruck writes: "Often . . . I felt as if I were talking into a void, a desert, despite the hundreds of heads in front of me that all looked the same."[3] Feeling, as did Levi, that she was like someone from the land of the dead who harasses the living with a horror-filled narration, Bruck for a long time stopped accepting invitations for public appearances and kept to herself, choosing instead to write in her sun-drenched apartment by the Spanish Steps in Rome, where today she still sits at her small desk with typewriter, paper, her indispensable cigarettes, and sepia photographs of her martyrs lining the walls.

Born in 1932 in the small town of Tiszakarad, Hungary, Bruck and her seven siblings grew up in conditions of extreme poverty (two of the children died before the war). Her mother, a strict Orthodox woman, strove to maintain the household and feed and clothe the children with the little her husband was able to procure for the family through his unstable work. For the most part he was absent and not interested in what went on at home, but the main cause of tension between him and his wife was due to the fact that he wasn't a believer and did not share her unfaltering love of God. Tiszakarad, an agricultural village that today is close to the border with Slovakia and Ukraine, was not a *shtetl*, and there were few Jews living there. Antisemitism was a constant threat, and hunger and isolation were just as dangerous. When the war broke out and the Nazis, helped by the local police, hunted down Hungarian Jews, Tiszakarad's remoteness did not safeguard Bruck's family. They were seized early one morning in 1944 and herded onto a cattle train headed for the ghetto of Satoraljaulhely before the final transfer to Auschwitz. Once there, the eleven-year-old Edith and her mother were immediately selected for extermination. The SS selection panel distributed victims into two lines: to the left, those destined to die; to the right, those (temporarily) spared. Edith and her mother, among numberless others, stood on the left, unaware of the sentence that had just been pronounced on them. Bruck reports the events of that day at Auschwitz, the last with her mother, in two different ways. In her memoir she writes:

> I was holding on to my mom's arm with all my strength. Suddenly, I realized that a soldier was pushing me toward the right and was kind of whispering, "To the right, to the right!"
>     I resisted. My mother got down on her knees and implored the soldier in German: "Leave me my baby girl, leave her to me, don't bring her away!" she

said. But the soldier shoved her aside with his rifle and wouldn't stop hitting me until I moved to the right-hand line.[4]

And years later, in the autobiographical *Lettera alla madre*, she writes:

"Obey! Obey!" you screamed while letting go of my hand, of my body, to the point of pushing me away from you into the hands of the soldier, toward his fury that was forcing me to the other side, in a direction opposite to yours.[5]

However, rather than two contradictory memories, these seem to be two moments in a single hellish scene of despair and utter confusion: perhaps, first the mother had understandably wanted to keep her daughter, but once she found out what would have happened to both of them had they stayed together, she began to push the frightened and uncomprehending child away from her. The image of a mother on her knees begging to remain with her daughter mixed with the one of a mother violently detaching the daughter from herself is the last memory, or impression, Bruck has of her mother, Sarah; the latter was gassed the same day. Bruck's uncles, aunts, cousins, friends, a brother, and both parents were all murdered. Bruck and her sister Eliz survived Auschwitz, Dachau, Christianstadt, and Bergen-Belsen together; two older sisters, Marta and Leila, spent the war in hiding; and one brother, Peter, was interned with their father and witnessed his death in Dachau.

Bruck's adversities did not end at Auschwitz. Once back from the camp, she was reunited with her sisters, who in the meantime had started families of their own and could not take on the economic, as well as emotional, burden of their younger sister, a suvivor of the camps. Still a teenager, she moved to Palestine, where she found even less support and sympathy. Palestine was coping with the absorption of thousands of survivors like Bruck, and she was too young, too damaged, and too lonely to enter yet another race for survival and win it. By the age of twenty, she had already been married three times, twice to possessive and abusive men; she had repeatedly been sexually assaulted, including by a cousin who then forced her to have an abortion and tried to push her to commit suicide; and, while in Israel, at the age of seventeen, she had been raped. She left Israel in the early 1950s and returned to Europe. Her choice of a new homeland deviated from the standard postwar migration path, which took the largest number of refugees to the United States and Canada; instead, Bruck moved to Italy. She landed in that small nation, itself in shambles after the war and whose people were mostly very poor and indifferent to her Jewishness and survival story. But there were Jews in Italy, and many of those who had survived the Holocaust felt the urgent need to record their experiences as soon as they were liberated, often while still recovering in the hospitals or even while traveling on the trains that brought them back home from the camps. However, it took a long time before the facts began to penetrate widely into the personal and national consciousness of Italy. As Manuela Consonni explains in her essay on Shoah memoirs written in Italy between 1945 and 1947, this early Shoah-witnessing literary production received very little acknowledgment, which "evidently reflect[ed], if not a lack of interest, certainly the problematic attitude of an entire society. Everywhere—not only in Italy—the attention from the beginning, the participation, the awareness of individuals and the collective consciousness of society to the survivors' story, neither fulfilled expectations of survivors nor measured up to the magnitude of events."[6] I would add that Italy manifested a particularly strong tendency of its own to subsume, and make disappear, the Holocaust under rubrics far more pressing for the ideological agenda du jour (the solemnization of antifascist resistance, left-wing party politics, and so forth), an urgency felt less strongly in countries less imbricated than Italy with Nazism and Fascism during the prewar and war years.[7] Today, Bruck lives in Rome with her husband, the documentary film director Nelo Risi. Bruck is the name of her third husband, a name she still uses and which has forever replaced her original surname (Steinschreiber).

Bruck's numerous literary works repeatedly tell the story of the traumatic events that shaped her life and tormented her existence. With one exception— her 1997 *Il silenzio degli amanti*, which she ended up disavowing[8]—Bruck's *oeuvre* is always autobiographical and grows from the dark humus of tragedy and inescapable trauma. As Adalgisa Giorgio points out, "if the Shoah representation must be faithful to the truth, the autobiographical origin of Edith Bruck's works guarantees their moral and artistic credibility."[9] Bruck's pain often expresses itself through this psychically wounded woman's apostrophes to an unresponsive universe—unresponsive because it is entirely identified with the unreachable mother. Hers is a literature that brings into focus the communicative breakdown after the Holocaust and the traumatized mind's struggle to overcome a deep melancholia that, for Bruck, constantly threatens to end art and life.

Bruck's autobiographical texts—*Lettera alla madre* (*Letter to My Mother*), *Signora Auschwitz* (*Mrs. Auschwitz*), and *Lettera da Francoforte* (*Letter from Frankfurt*)[10]— reveal a literature clearly dominated by the idea of conversation and correspondence. The addressee of *Lettera alla madre* no longer exists, and neither do all the apostrophized characters in her poems dedicated to the dead of Auschwitz. Yet these undeliverable messages answer the daughter's desire to maintain a dialogue, however illusory, with the Auschwitz victims. In the present chapter, I attend to the symptom of melancholia as it relates to a Holocaust mother, and I examine Bruck's fictitious letter to her, as well as the intrinsically rhetorical figure of the apostrophe that sustains it, as a strategic way for the traumatized daughter to dramatize the unjust fate of her family so that the reader (the indirect addressee) can bear witness to it. Furthermore, I intend to show that this imaginary dialogue with the dead, which appears in both her prose and poetry, is Bruck's way of not letting go of them and of her mother specifically, because the spectral presence of the mother helps the writer herself to stay alive.

Through poetic or fictional apostrophe, a writer achieves the task of calling the inanimate to order, of forging presence out of absence, of arousing understanding where not even listening is possible. Like centuries of poets before her, Bruck uses her medium to inspirit things as well as memories. The magic power of the artistic utterance recreates worlds that are no longer there, no longer visible. Things not uttered end up disappearing or being forgotten. Naming things renders them present, at least symbolically. Judaism in particular crafts a special understanding between Creator and the created as it relates to the power of the word (*logos*) to call things into being, and the biblical writers exalted the evocative force of the apostrophe at pivotal moments throughout the text. Most notable is "Hear, oh Israel!" the injunction of the *Shemah Israel* that summons the Jews to accept a poetic incarnation to become a people. But the times when the Hebrew God still apostrophized his chosen ones are over; God has withdrawn from his creation, and Man now—from the periphery of a self-intelligent universe, imprisoned in the strict parameters of time and space—struggles to fill the void left by the silent divinity. Pious people, Bruck's mother among them, keep up the conversation with God through their prayers, a kind of missive to a silent recipient. An author such as Bruck fills the void with her creative power, an art composed of missives, or calls, to a silent mother. Her conversation is not with *the* Creator but with *her* creator, her mother. Like the biblical *auctor*, an author apostrophizes in order to "will a state of affairs, to attempt to call it into being by asking inanimate objects to bend themselves to [his] desire," Jonathan Culler writes. "In these terms the function of apostrophe would be to make the objects of the universe potentially responsive forces . . . The apostrophizing poet identifies his universe as a world of sentient forces."[11] Using the figure of the apostrophe ("Listen Mother!"), Bruck desperately attempts to make silence respond to her call. In this chapter, I will analyze the implications of such a message, which has no hope of arriving at its intended destination. Bruck's apostrophe, by assuming the *fiat*-like power of the *logos*, responds to the subversive need of the artist to upset the cosmic hierarchy and dethrone the center as incapable or unwilling of speaking by itself. In the process, Bruck highlights how vital the mother-daughter dialogue is to her own survival.

I will also appropriate some of Paul de Man's formulations about the poetical apostrophe, conscious though I am that he applied his critique of history to an era far removed in context and content from my study of Bruck. De Man famously rediscovered and redressed the figure of the apostrophe as monumentalized by the Romantics. Through his deconstruction of William Wordsworth's "Essays on Epitaphs," de Man was able to subvert our understanding of the autobiographical project as one no longer depending on reference (the author's life) the way "a photograph depends on its subject or a (realistic) picture on its model" but as something that "may itself produce and determine life."[12] Bruck's Shoah prose and poetry—a dialogue with the dead—gives new meaning and relevance to the rhetorical figure of the apostrophe, and interestingly, as I will show, this rhetoric allows her to utterly recast an ancient figure dear to all poets: the muse. Like an epitaph, Bruck's invocation to the mother apostrophizes the Holocaust victims in an attempt to exhume them from the mass graveyard of Jewish twentieth-century history. Furthermore, as I intend to highlight, her autobiographical project can be understood, following de Man's formulation, as one that is not simply referential but that shapes and determines her own life as a survivor.

Commenting on Wordsworth's statement that the "naked name" on a gravestone is a permanent text before the sun's eyes, de Man explains: "The sun becomes the eye that *reads* the text of the epitaph . . . At this point, it can be said of 'the language of the senseless stone' that it acquires a 'voice,' the *speaking* stone counterbalancing the *seeing* sun. The system [of metaphors] passes from sun to eye to language as name and as voice."[13] What is especially germane to my argument in de Man's interpretation is his idea that the figure that holds Wordsworth's intricate structure of metaphors in place is the prosopopeia:

> the fiction of an apostrophe to an absent, deceased, or voiceless entity, which posits the possibility of the latter's reply and confers upon it the power of speech. Voice assumes mouth, eye, and finally face, a chain that is manifest in the etymology of the trope's name, *prosopon poien*, to confer a mask or a face (*prosopon*). Prosopopeia is the trope of autobiography, by which one's name . . . is made as intelligible and memorable as a face. Our topic deals with the giving and taking away of faces, with the face and deface, *figure*, figuration and disfiguration.[14]

Of course, de Man's reading of Wordsworth's epitaphs ends up shaping a text quite different from Wordsworth's reading of epitaphs.[15] Following de Man's important theorization of autobiographical acts and their relation to history, I argue that in turning the elegiac apostrophe of poets into an accusatory call that recasts her muse (the mother) as a hardened, oppressed, and defeated woman, Bruck de-faces herself to confer voice, mouth, and eyes on "the naked name" of the mother, thereby saving the mother from being buried under the text of history. The daughter thus succeeds in revealing to us, the readers of the epitaph, the mother's history, humanity, and unacceptable death.

## UNDER MOTHER, GOD, AND MENGELE

When Bruck submitted her manuscript of *Lettera alla madre* to a publisher, the book was so short and unusual that the editor asked her to add something to it to make it financially feasible for the publishing house to produce. Thus *Lettera* became a tripartite text, a work more hybrid than originally intended. It is composed of the title chapter (the book Bruck originally submitted to the publisher), which was conceived of as a long, uninterrupted letter from a Holocaust survivor daughter to her victim mother, followed by "Tracce" (traces), a first-person narrative—which is further divided into two sections—about a daughter's trip to Germany, almost half a century after the facts, to gather clues about her father's death in Dachau. Despite the generic and stylistic switches throughout this new text, it is clear that the reader is being led by the same voice from one part of the book to the next. The speaking "I" of *Lettera* and "Tracce" is Bruck's alterego and is recognizable as the narrator of both stories. The three sections recount three different stages in the life of the same female survivor. However, Bruck can tell only the first part, the one exclusively about her mother, in the form of a (fictitious or imagined) dialogue.

In the process of reconstructing her mother as a presence in *Lettera*, Bruck alternates between describing scenes of daily life before the war and recounting the moment of being separated from her mother at Auschwitz. In both the descriptions of normal life and the description of the dramatic upheaval, a particularly harsh portrait of motherhood emerges. In his essay about epitaphs, Wordsworth ironically mused: "When a Stranger has walked around a Country Church-yard and glanced his eye over so many brief chronicles, as the tombstones usually contain, of faithful wives, tender husbands, dutiful children, and good men of all classes; he will be tempted to exclaim in the language of one of the characters of a modern Tale, in a similar situation, 'Where are all the *bad* people buried?'"[16] Bruck, in contrast, does not allow her mother's martyrdom to influence the kind of epitaph she composes. Her filial memories include moments of love and caring but also recount her mother's faults and weaknesses; she makes sure not to sugarcoat the complexity of the mother-daughter bond, and of women's historical situation in general, throughout her literature. "How many times you blamed me for being born!" Bruck has her narrative alterego rail, and adds: "You should have caressed me to make me stronger. Maybe even my body would be healthier today if you had kissed me everywhere the way I had seen mothers do with their naked baby daughters after the bath. You never kissed my tummy, my little feet, my sex, my buttocks."[17] In her memoir, we read: "I can't say that mine was a serene and happy family; our misery grew day after day and with it also our arguments. We would fight over anything. My mother was thirty-nine but looked as if she were much older because she had only a few teeth left, and her face was beautiful but full of pain. She always wore a foulard on her head in the Jewish Orthodox fashion, and when she was not yelling [at us] she was praying."[18] The lacerating sadness of the maternal loss stands side by side with an analysis of the embittered woman Bruck had known before her mother was turned into a sacred symbol of martyrdom, one of the faceless six million, and whose victimization had deep roots in a much broader and ancient oppression that cannot be diagnosed exclusively in terms of Nazi evil.

Bruck's mother had an unhappy and frustrated relationship with her husband and their many children. In a humble house surrounded by fields and unpaved roads, she struggled to make ends meet, unsupported by her husband whom, as Bruck implies, she loved but whose failings (a lack of religious faith and an inability to provide for the family) had profoundly embittered her. They were poor and at times went hungry for days. The children were sent to school only until they were old enough to find work to help support the family. Edith, like her alter-ego Katia in Lettera, dreamed of a different life, fantasizing about a glamorous future in the big city and experimenting with writing poetry: "Remember when I announced that I had written a poem for you which you wouldn't even bother to read or pay attention to as I read it out loud?" (Lettera, 80). In her memory, Bruck sees herself as a child always reaching for her mother, asking her questions, and bothering her during her prayers by trying to secure her undivided attention (for which she would be punished each time). In Signora Auschwitz, Bruck recalls how angry her questions, especially the ones about God, used to make her mother, who as a consequence would send her to school without food for three days (and that food, the author tells us, was always meager to begin with). But the worst punishment, Bruck says, was that her mother "would stop talking to me . . . I became invisible to her resentful eyes full of pain for and against me . . . Those three days of punishment were the longest of my short childhood."[19] The daughter's artistic inclination, her inquisitive mind, and her need for attention and affection were not appreciated; instead, they irritated and unsettled a mother faced with so many other more pragmatic concerns. "You did not listen to me, everything was more important than I was for you," the writer of the letter to the dead mother declares (Lettera, 78). In a conversation with me, Bruck said that these types of arguments rehearsed in Lettera were very much part of her interactions with her mother in real life, too. Bruck remembers very vividly her mother's disapprobation of everything she did, chose, or said. In particular, her resistance to her mother's extreme religiosity was felt by the mother as a sign of amorality, an unpardonable flaw. Giorgio rightly points out that the use of characters that hide the identity of real people from Bruck's life behind pseudonyms or other literary traits helps shield the writer from the deep suffering that remembering causes, and it is also an effective way to respect the victims' modesty and privacy.[20] Another description of the mother reads: "There was something evil in your silence. Something dangerous . . . You did not love me anymore: in fact, it would have been better if I hadn't been born. You held me responsible for all your troubles as mother, wife, and Jew" (Lettera, 36). Assessing her mother's incapacity for sentimentality and forgiveness, the writer scathingly remarks: "I bet you anything that even Mengele's mother forgave her son . . . while I, instead, would no longer be your daughter as soon as I did something wrong, told a small lie, a dirty word, a point of view different from yours, or for doubting God. Because I laughed too much, because anything would make me cry, because I broke the leg of one of our old chairs. It took even less for you to reject me, it took nothing. You would tell me that your womb gave birth to an extraneous daughter" (Lettera, 63–64). Much like Ruth Klüger and Sarah Kofman, Bruck portrays a superstitious, often cold, and—at moments—even cruel, mother, one who had fits of jealousy at the daughter's affection for her father. As did Kofman's mother, Bruck's had faith in divine justice, a power rejected by her daughter and one that the daughter ends up lumping together with her Auschwitz experience. "My mother," Bruck writes of the days in the ghetto before their transfer to Auschwitz, "shaved her head, the way in which she should have done, according to our faith, the day she married. She said that God was now punishing us because when she got married she had not cut her hair and that now she had no intention of passing into the next world with long hair: we were all bound to be punished even in Purgatory."[21] Mother and God often exchange roles in Bruck's reanimations: both are guilty of not loving enough; of being too inscrutable, controlling, judgmental, and unreliable; and of never being there when the daughter most needs them. Both are creators and destroyers of life with a complete power over the daughter, just—as Bruck eerily implies—like Mengele in Auschwitz: "How I long to hear you say that I was wrong . . . not to believe in the magic wand of God, who, if he exists, is probably a kind of Mengele of the heavens" (Lettera, 20).

Although aware of the tremendous impact that the death camp parenthesis had on her life, Bruck composes a larger picture that includes a pre-Shoah world, one whose importance in her development is not mitigated by the enormity of the later catastrophe. Like other authors featured in this book, she strives to recompose herself rather than merely composing memories of the Holocaust—that is, she seeks a memory that is not exclusively defined by remembering the Shoah. Her humble origins and her family's poverty leave very little room in the portrait she sketches of her childhood years for pre-Shoah idylls (unlike Elie Wiesel's highly romanticized *shtetl* atmospheres in *Night*, for instance). Even if Bruck, as she herself says, has assimilated the lesson that the martyrs of Auschwitz are untouchable, almost saints (*Lettera*, 47), she can't bring herself to forget the injustices she suffered, the unfair humiliations, the adults' misbehaviors.

Bruck speaks of the "sacred dead of Auschwitz" on the one hand, while on the other she makes sure to desacralize them. The daughter cannot vent her rage, cannot be sacrilegious and angry, disrespectful or impertinent, or even ambivalent and faithful to the complexity of their relationship as long as the mother is elevated to the status of sacred symbol. "Oh my, forgive me, a million times forgive me, you are a sacred dead, an untouchable martyr; this is true but you are also my mother. And to my mother I have the right to say everything," Bruck writes (*Lettera* 47). She makes full use of the authorial power implicit in all apostrophes; the daughter both grants a voice to the mother but also has "the power to take it away from her."[22] *Lettera* opens with the mother peremptorily demanding obedience from the daughter and closes with the daughter demanding obedience from the mother: "Obey! Obey!" the mother yells at her child in Auschwitz (*Lettera*, 8), and "for once, you obey me!" yells the adult daughter at her mother at the end of her letter to her (*Lettera*, 94). Hence, the daughter's writing can be an act of vengeance: "You can't tell me anything unless I let you talk" (*Lettera*, 8). However, in several more tender moments, Bruck uses her power to pay loving tribute to a mother capable of producing little daily miracles that kept her children alive against all odds. She tells stories of her mother conjuring a Shabbat dinner out of an empty pantry; baking bread despite the scarcity of flour; and, most movingly, producing a ribbon out of thin air with which she adorned little Edith's short hair while they were being carried away on a cattle train to Auschwitz.[23] In another novel, *Lettera da Francoforte*—in which, once again, we encounter many real characters from Bruck's life and plenty of autobiographical references—the narrator highlights a similar admiration for her Auschwitz victim mother: "Particularly during the High Holidays, according to which my mother kept track of months and seasons, she was always able to make something special to put on the table from our nonexistent stores, like a wizard."[24] And in her bilingual collection of poems, she recalls:

Mia madre era una santa
faceva dei miracoli

nella dispensa vuota
trovava sempre qualcosa.[25]

My mother was a saint
she worked miracles
in the empty cupboard
she could always find something.

This loving representation, however, is often countered by bitterer ones. "What were our last years at home if not the antechamber of Auschwitz?" she asks the phantom of the mother (*Lettera*, 88). Nor does she romanticize the relationship she would have had with her mother had they both survived the concentration camps. "How would you have lived the aftermath, mama?" she asks: "I would have kept fighting with you. Would we have fought all the time? You would have never approved of anything I did, yet I would have done it all the same but suffering twice as much for it. You would have probably stopped talking to me, just like when I was little" (*Lettera*, 35). And again: "Knowing myself, mama, even though I had been a slave-child, I would have ended up rebelling against your omnipotent will the way I rebelled against your orders when I was a young girl" (*Lettera*, 60). The humanity of both victims and survivors is established in this literature through a blunt and often painful exaltation of the conflicts between mother and daughter. Sacralization of the dead martyrs would only serve to separate mother and daughter; the daughter longs instead for proximity. Bruck needs the real mother with whom she fought, and with whom she keeps fighting in her imagination and texts, in order to nourish the fiction that her textual self and the mother's phantom are alive and together. Bruck declares to her mother that "only death will sever the umbilical cord" that binds them (*Lettera*, 47). Whose death? The umbilical cord that ties together mother and child is at once a symbol of their original bond and of their physical and emotional separation. In Bruck's case, the umbilical cord becomes a metaphor for the birth-death event that truly conjoins them: Auschwitz. There the daughter was granted life, and there the mother lost hers. In this liminal area, accessed through poetry and narrative, daughter and mother are both alive and die over and over again.

An elderly lady today, Bruck suffers from all sorts of medical conditions. Many of her ailments stem from the hunger she experienced and the blows she suffered during her internment in the camps, and many others are psychosomatic expressions of trauma. In particular, she complains about stomach problems and nausea, which apparently worsen each time she gives an interview or visits a school and must talk to students about the Shoah. She finds it harder and harder to capture the listeners' interest. However, not writing or talking about her experience is not an option, as she compares the knowledge she carries inside her to a malignant creature that she must try to expel. In *Signora Auschwitz* we read: "Between trips [to give her public testimonial talks], I kept thinking about the newly conceived novel meant to liberate me, and I kept ending up in this or that hospital or clinic where they . . . [searched] for the organic cause of those pains that tormented me without reprieve . . . Doctors could not know or even suspect of the monster inside of me. Possibly, I myself did not want to get rid of it, maybe because only that way I could keep my dead, all the dead, alive?"[26] Writing is this melancholic daughter's answer to an impossible life: the alternative to suicide or, rather, its aesthetic sublimation.

Bruck's dialogue with her mother, metaphorical and illusory, is nonetheless experienced as real by the speaking I. Her survival strategy consists of reviving the mother in language; however, all the artistic utterance can do (language always being purely symbolic) is reproduce the mother's absence. Without this dialogue, the mother would not only be lost a second time, but the daughter would vanish as well: "And if I forget you, I forget myself. I'll be around as long as you'll be around, and you'll be around as long as I'll be around" (*Lettera*, 47). And because writing about her mother means talking about the Shoah, the daughter is forced, despite the physical and emotional pain, to keep bearing oral and written witness to what happened to all Jews: "With the passage of time, the only thing that has become stronger is my need for my mother, for her faith, to feel her closer to me . . . My mother, whom I fear even now that she's dead, would not forgive me, I believe, if I actually stopped keeping her alive through my testimonial stories, if I no longer talked about her who perhaps was turned into a bar of soap, a lamp shade, or fertilizer."[27]

In her writing, Bruck invokes a conception of the womb as a place of death, a tomb. When death is stirred up by memory, the belly quite literally responds to the writer's invocation with hurtful spasms and pangs: this somatization torments the author who is reminded, each time she writes or talks about Auschwitz, of the malignant creature it seeded in her:

La solitudine è profonda
un ventre materno buio e silenzioso
tutto è ovattato
i rumori giungono da lontano
il passato come corda ombelicale nutre
tutto è perfetto
come la vita non nata
come la morte mai conosciuta.[28]

My solitude is deep
a maternal womb that is dark and quiet
muffled
sounds arrive from afar
the past nourishes like an umbilical cord
everything is perfect
like unborn life
like death not experienced.

That death-filled past from which the author claims to receive her nourishment includes one scene in which the eyes of death come to rest on her womb, permanently turning it from a symbol of peace into one of horror. One day in the camp, a group of young women were brought in front of Josef Mengele, as possible subjects of his sadistic experiments. Bruck was among them. This episode returns in *Lettera*, and the narrator describes the moment when the "doctor," considering his doomed candidates, rested his eyes for a few moments on her abdomen: "So I saw him, he was there, and I held my stomach and my belly with all my strength telling myself that he won't see me, he can't see me, may his cursed eyes fall on someone else" (*Lettera*, 47). It is through scenes like these that Bruck conceives of her womb not as a "dark and quiet" sanctum but as carrying the malignant creature Auschwitz planted there, which perhaps explains her anxiety about having children of her own. She fears that "children are often vampires" (*Lettera*, 63); certainly, the *Shoah child* she permanently carries is. "I never had children, as you know," the daughter imagines telling her mother, "how could I have brought someone into this world after the way you died? I have always aborted them, mama. Here is another reason to be repudiated" (*Lettera*, 32). And again: "It is for the best that I never had to explain everything to my children. Perhaps this is exactly why I never had them" (*Lettera*, 18). Regardless of whether literal or metaphorical, womb, maternity, and death are the agony to which this Shoah author is chained: "Had I had a daughter, perhaps she'd be like Sara [her niece], beautiful Sara who sucked Auschwitz milk and in whose splendid eyes there is a kind of resistance, a hostility toward life, the same you could find in a great Italian writer, my friend who recently committed suicide" (*Lettera*, 32–33). Auschwitz infects the notion of procreation. Even her niece Sara has sucked through her mother's milk the awareness of the lives senselessly and brutally lost: of the 1.5 million children who were murdered; of Bruck's mother; of Primo Levi (the "friend who recently committed suicide"). As Bruck says of the creative and self-annihilating process of writing, "There remains no trace of myself on the typescript" (*Lettera*, 32). In *Lettera*, the long unfinished letter—

like an umbilical cord—holds together the fractured identity of the survivor by paradoxically making the irremediable separation that results from Auschwitz's personal and communal trauma into a connecting thread between mother and daughter.

"Sometimes, without apparent reason, I feel incredibly happy," the daughter tells her mother. "Sometimes, when I feel the most lonely, a black wave overwhelms me . . . in those moments, like my friend, the writer who committed suicide, I think that there is no hope, that there's never been and there'll never be hope" (Lettera, 71). In Bruck's works, we recognize both a fundamental and a successive mourning at play: the former goes back to the primary loss of "the Thing" at birth (la Chose, in Lacan's terminology, or the cause of desire), and the latter is rooted in subsequent traumatic loss. The onda nera (black wave) that Bruck laments and faces repeatedly has much in common with the notion of the "black sun" developed by the French psychoanalytical theorist Julia Kristeva. In her book about melancholia in life and art evocatively entitled Soleil Noir (Black sun), Kristeva diagnosed the extreme sadness felt by the depressed mind as rooted in the loss of the mother. I want to borrow Kristeva's question about her depressed patients and redirect it toward Bruck: "Where does this black sun come from?"[29] I would say that in Bruck's poetics, her black sun's eerie galaxy is death, and its ruling planet is the mother. As I will show later in the chapter, Kristeva understands melancholia as a form of living death. For Bruck, this living death begins with the irremediable separation of mother and daughter at birth, continues when her mother urges her to enter a different sorting line during the Selektion in Auschwitz, and only partially reaches a conclusion with her mother's death in the camp:

> You were guilty, if one can call it guilt, only with us, your children, completely subdued to your will until the end, when you told me: "Go! Obey! Go! Move away, do as your mother tells you!" and I obeyed. And for this I am alive. And I am happy to be alive. With inexpressible pain, you gave birth to me a second time. (Lettera, 92)

Ever since that tragic episode at Auschwitz, creation for this survivor artist is tinged with a sickness. The creation of such sickening autobiographical stories and poems is a technique through which Bruck expels an undesired presence within herself, a kind of creative abortion: "I thought, I deluded myself, that with every new book a piece of the child-monster conceived in Auschwitz would finally come out. Perhaps this is why I never loved my books, never opened them once they saw the light, though I hoped they would not remain orphans but find adoptive parents."[30] Maternity is the axis around which Auschwitz, writing, and sickness revolve in Bruck's work. Death, which is often associated with her mother, is infectious, sickening the author and her imagination without reprieve.

Bruck's apostrophic dialogue with the lost mother recasts daughterhood, as much as her own unfulfilled motherhood, as a matter of death, self-erasure, and suicide on the part of the apostrophizing voice. No rhetorical tool is more effective at making the dead live again than the lyrical apostrophe, by which poets re-present the absent by bringing the evoked "Thou" back into a dialogue from which they were excluded by death. Barbara Johnson analyzes the effect of the apostrophe in women's poetry on abortion, observing that this calling of the dead expels the speaker into a state of otherness. She concludes that "each [abortion poem] exists, finally, because a child does not."[31] Abortion poems are thematically about a life that has been lost, but Johnson's analysis suggests that this premise might be deceptive, for "the life that is lost may be someone else's."[32] Bruck's *Lettera* and Shoah poems exemplify the terms of the deception that Johnson discovers in abortion poetry—that is, the life of the living is what is wasted, destroyed, lost when one witnesses the death or murder of the Other. Performing in language the death of the Other, the living poet invokes her own death. The resuscitation of the dead allows the living to express their death wish.

It is her own death that Bruck the author constantly stages and that she sees incarnated in the ghost of the mother, who uncannily literalizes the trope of the voice from the other world. Here, since it is a daughter writing a letter to the murdered mother, we witness an interesting twist: the daughter gives life back to the mother, rebirths her mother because her own life (literary as well as biological) would be imperiled by the mother's absence. Literature makes the encounter between the living and dead possible, and Bruck stages this encounter in the womb—her inner graveyard. She demands that the mother feel her heart as if she were still in her womb. "Don't you feel me in your womb?" she asks her mother, "Can't you feel my heart beat? If you can't feel me, then there's nothing you can feel anymore" (*Lettera*, 47). (The Italian verb *sentire* means to feel, to hear, and to heed all at once.)

Even a writing that sickens the author and that symbolically stages an abortion (the death of the daughter, the stillbirth of her books, and so on) is preferable to its alternative. Without writing, Bruck suggests more than once, she would choose death. Suicide is always an attractive option that promises the end of the unbearable middle position inhabited by the survivor: neither completely belonging among the living nor having a place among the dead. When Bruck's friend, Levi, reached the point where he could no longer write a book (or feared he couldn't), he let go of his life. Bruck reports a conversation with him not long before he died, in which Levi had exclaimed: "Can you imagine? . . . I don't know if I'll ever write another book" (*Lettera*, 71). About Levi's death, Bruck asks herself: "From what phantom was he fleeing in the hope, perhaps, of surviving once again? And he did survive again. He made it. He is alive" (*Lettera*, 72). This paradoxical declaration can be understood in light of a particular spiritual technique that Bruck adopts to deal with the world of dead people surrounding her and through which she maintains the illusion of resurrecting them: "I never thought him dead. When I pronounce his name, it is the name of a living man, just like when I read him, his books are more alive than ever. Only when I look at one of his many photographs from when he was still alive can I see that he is dead" (*Lettera*, 72). All names, therefore, are names of living people. There is no such thing as a name referring to a thing that is not. A name allows itself to be called: the sine qua non of an apostrophe. Not surprisingly, Bruck always expresses doubts about the existence of a God who, in Judaism, indeed has no name, cannot be called, and will reunite with his creation only after the right composition of his name's letters is deciphered. This, however, is a job requiring too much piety, and piety is alien to Bruck's world. Perhaps this realization has allowed her to neutralize God and any residual fears of him: "Unlike you, mother, I am not afraid of God. I fear only human beings" (*Lettera*, 74).

### THE LETTER OF DESTINATION

In *The Post Card*, his convoluted psychoanalysis of the history and technology of the dispatch (*envoi*) and the address, Jacques Derrida entertains the possibility of readdressing language so that the message about untellable experiences could be carried and manifested. The central concern of Derrida's philosophical inquiry here is the question of whether communication in the "postal era" (the logocentric era)—and with it literature, the humanities, identity, and knowledge—is destined to end. "The end of a postal epoch is doubtless also the end of literature," writes Derrida.[33] Of crucial relevance here is the book's first section, "Envois" (almost an epistolary autobiography),[34] in which a man who signs himself J. D. writes postcard-length letters (with various blanks, suspensions, and deletions) to a female lover whose answers, if they exist, are not revealed to us. The inspiration behind this book was a thirteenth-century illustration by Matthew Paris showing Socrates seated in the act of writing, with Plato standing behind him and pointing his finger toward the written page. Interestingly, it was Culler, one of Derrida's most famous disciples, who showed Paris's postcard to Derrida in Oxford, or who delivered the letter, so to speak.[35] In his book, Derrida calls the address by the German word *Geschick*, which means "fate" or "lot" (after all, Paris's postcard had been taken from a fortune-telling book) and which shares its root with the German verb *schicken*, meaning "to send." Hence in a typical Derridean wordplay, the envoi ends up conforming to destiny. According to Derrida, the fascinating role reversal figured in Paris's image, where Socrates, who has never written, is now writing while the writer, Plato, is dictating to him what to write, upends the history of philosophy and its destination in a way that is relevant to our discussion about the apostrophe and the catastrophe of communication: "The letters shuttle between this apostrophe (the turning aside of discourse in a singular address) and the catastrophe (literally: an overturning) of destination which has already turned the address aside from itself. The singular address divides, fragments, goes astray, and, like a misdelivered post card, lays itself open to anyone's reading," writes Peggy Kamuf of Derrida's method in *The Post Card*.[36] In one of the letters that make up *The Post Card*, Derrida connects the problem of identity to the question of the envoi and its technologies, a problem certainly applicable to Bruck, whose destiny and identity are entangled in her one-way correspondence with her dead mother, an endless self-destination. Derrida writes:

> Thus I have lost my life writing in order to give this song a chance, unless it were in order to let it silence itself, by itself. You understand that whoever writes must indeed ask himself what it is asked of him to write, and then he writes under the dictation of some addressee . . . Thereby everything is corrupted, there is only the mirror, no more image, they [Plato and Socrates] no longer see each other, no longer destine each other, nothing more.[37]

In the scenario described by Derrida, Plato makes Socrates write, and in Bruck's *Lettera* and poetry, the daughter demands that her dead mother write. Through the catastrophe (overturning) of destination that occurs as she addresses her messages, we can say that Bruck's dream ends up matching Plato's, which is "to make Socrates write, and to make him write what he wants, his last command, *his will*."[38] In fact, the daughter tells her mother: "I will let you say what I already know, I will let you repeat what I heard from your mouth until the last moment, your last word, it is *your will*" (*Lettera*, 8, emphasis added). Bruck writes under the mother's dictation, which, in turn, composes the daughter's (auto)biographical text: the story of their anger, oppression, reciprocity, and death.

In Paris's illustration, Socrates holds a pen in one hand and an eraser in the other, with which he undoes the destiny (destination) of the text even as he creates it. With this double gesture, Socrates determines not only his own destiny but the destinies of those who will continue his text in the future. Bruck's mother, a ghost, functions in much the same way. "Socrates turns his *back* to plato [sic], who has made him write whatever he wanted while pretending to receive it from him," explains Derrida, while admiring the Oxford postcard that, like all postcards, has the fantastic quality of being always open, never sealed: "even if in an envelope, they are made to circulate like an open but illegible letter."[39] I will explore the function of Bruck's prosopopeia at length soon, but suffice it to say here that through the apostrophe (which calls the mother into being) and the prosopopeia (which ventriloquizes her), Bruck makes her mother assume the Socratic position from the card, makes her mother sit at the desk and compose the story of her life and death—a story that will be accessible to us only through the daughter's version. Most importantly for our purposes, the postcard, the text that dictates itself to the sender or writer, holds, as Derrida puts it, "a kind of personal message, a secret between us, the secret of reproduction":[40] the reproduction of Socrates into Plato? Plato and Socrates are linked by a chain of inheritance, even when this chain is reversed. But there is also reproduction of Plato into Derrida, the receiver of Paris's postcard. The phantom woman with whom J. D. conducts a one-sided conversation, and whose answers to J. D.'s posts we never read, is the rhetorical ghost that bridges the distance between writer and reader. The same goes for mother and daughter in Bruck's "undestined" or misdelivered letter. Between us (the unintended receivers of the message) and the sender there stands a martyred mother. In Bruck's as well as in Derrida's letters, the secret that the mute ghost guards is that someone is invoking death and suicide through the act of writing—a writing that is illegible, invisible, and without *Geschick*. "Watch closely," Derrida adjures his mute addressee, "while Socrates signs his death sentence."[41]

It is through the act of writing that Bruck is able to keep on living. However, her writing is a form of suicide. Death occurs in each act of writing, in each and every text. Derrida says in a "letter" dated June 6, 1977, that "a young student (very handsome) thought he could provoke me and, I think, seduce me a bit by asking me why I didn't kill myself." With perfect Socratic irony, Derrida "sends" the question back to the questioner: "And what proves to you, I said to him . . . , that I do not do so, and more than once."[42] With each postcard, with each text, the beginning and end of the *auctor*'s word, the beginning and end of the writer, is repeated. The same question, if put to Bruck, would produce a similar answer put to us in return. She does live and die each time she (re)produces a text about the death of the mother. Or better yet, each time her story forces her to write (dictates itself to her), it also forces her to revisit death, her own included. If, as I mentioned, writing sustains life for Bruck, I should also point out that only a specific kind of writing allows her to stay alive: the personal letter, the autobiographical apostrophe, the retelling of variations of her Shoah story. And where could such a story end? The story gains force in its telling rather than in its conclusion, and it is forever on its way to an unreachable destination. Presence is thus ensured by absence, and, to prove it, the writer must send a letter whose impossible arrival extends the distance between addresser and intended addressee and to which no answer will be returned. "The condition for it to arrive," says Derrida of his envoi or *carte de l'adestination*, "is that it ends up and even that it begins by not arriving."[43] But someone will receive the letter and know that the writer lives.

In turning the addressee of her letter into the dictating voice of the letter itself, Bruck recasts the role of the muse in her literary deliverance. The classical muse—epitomized by Homer's still vibrating "Mênin aeide thea Pêlêïadeô Achilêos" (Sing, o goddess, the anger of Achilles!)—is the woman who inspires, the light that comes to shine through the poet to illuminate the reader and reflect glory back on the muse herself. The Shoah muse, however, was stripped naked, branded, and murdered in Auschwitz. In the ancient world, Hesiod reminds us, the daughters of Mnemosyne (Memory) were nine, but were collectively referred to as the muse. Bruck's dark muse is a similar amalgam, a single persona and a composite of six million.

Bruck's mother is the doleful, sinister, dark muse created by the Holocaust. The survivor strives to convey a story that only those who perished in Auschwitz could tell. She needs this muse, and vice versa. This muse's presence does not elevate the artist as it did in classical times; rather, it compels her to live on. Bruck's muse is an unhappy, distant, resentful woman, yet only she, not the father, can fill this indispensable position: "I am torturing myself, yes, I am. And I write. I write to you because you are my mother" (*Lettera*, 66). Bruck's muse can be imagined and lived only through the mother's body. Despite the fact that Bruck loved her father ("I liked him so much. Once I grew up I would have married him" [*Lettera*, 67]), the powerless and absent man was no muse for the letter-writing daughter:

> I could have turned to papa as well but I must confess it never crossed my mind. I don't think he would have had the patience to listen to me; at times he didn't even know my name! He didn't quarrel with me like you did. He didn't say anything to me. He didn't talk. He was mute. Impotent. He didn't even chat with God like you used to. He was alone. He didn't talk to anybody. He was the loneliest man I've ever known. (*Lettera*, 67)

In order to be able to face Auschwitz (and its dehumanizing harshness), the daughter must face the mother (and her very human weaknesses).[44] Inspired by Levi's Dantesque reconstruction of Auschwitz, Giorgio Agamben imagined the architecture of the concentration camp as a gyre at whose center resides the all-devouring head of the Gorgon, the sight of which turns the onlooker into stone, into a nonhuman. The Gorgon represents the nonnegotiable impossibility of seeing. The Gorgon—for whom the Greeks would never use the word face, *prósōpon*—is the apostrophe from which the survivor cannot turn away.[45] Bruck cannot turn away from the Gorgon, because the blindness the monster inflicts is the condition for any acts of witnessing. Thus blinded, the daughter must align her sight with that of her mother in order to face the unseeable and witness for those erased from language, for those who are outside of speech. The survivor poet summons a muse who doesn't help the artist develop or illuminate her work; rather, this muse consumes the voice of the artist who invokes her and only increases her blindness. And in the blind spot of history that is the Shoah, mother and daughter exist together: "Perhaps my letter to you is only an instrument to write about Auschwitz, but you and Auschwitz are inseparable" (*Lettera*, 66).

## APOSTROPHE

"Mother" is a primary word for Bruck in the sense used by the Viennese philosopher Martin Buber in reference to the Man-God encounter. "Primary words," Buber explains, "do not signify things, but they intimate relations. Primary words do not describe something that might exist independently of them, but being spoken they bring about existence . . . If *Thou* is said, the *I* of the combination *I-Thou* is said along with it . . . The primary word *I-Thou* can only be spoken with the whole being."[46] Through his philosophy, Buber found a way to temper the fear and trembling of existentialism with the warmth and promises of Hassidism—a solution foreclosed to Bruck after her Auschwitz experience. Buber was able to live through the first half of the twentieth century and still keep God in place at the center of his philosophical vision by focusing on the potential, rather than the loss, that meaningful communication still holds for the future of humanity. He expounded his ideas on the necessity of reciprocity in one of the most influential texts of modern Jewish thought, *I and Thou* (first published in German as *Ich und Du* in 1923). Interestingly, Buber saw in the *I-Thou* relationship the roots of art itself: "A man is faced by a form which desires to be made through him into a work [of art]. This form is no offspring of his soul, but is an appearance that steps up to it and demands of it the effective power. The man is concerned with an act of his being. If he carries it through, if he speaks the primary word out of his being to the form which appears, then the effective power streams out, and the work arises."[47] Buber's concept can be reformulated to illustrate the reciprocity of Bruck's mother-daughter dyad. "When a primary word is spoken the speaker enters the word and takes his stand in it," Buber writes,[48] and Bruck echoes this I-Thou symbiosis (a relationship that knows no past tense but that is constantly in the present) by way of asserting time and again that she is the personification of her mother, especially in the most agonizing moments, such as when she is writing her books. She constantly embodies and disembodies the conjured ghost: she is her but is also radically separate from and other than her. Buber notes that the act of artistic creation "includes a sacrifice and a risk"—both of which are felt in Bruck's writing at every turn. "This," Buber explains, "is the sacrifice: the endless possibility that is offered up on the altar of the form. For everything . . . must be obliterated . . . The exclusiveness of what is facing it demands that it be so. This is the risk: the primary word can only be spoken with the whole being. He who gives himself to it may withhold nothing of himself. The work does not suffer me . . . to turn aside and relax in the world of It; but it commands. If I do not serve it aright it is broken, or it breaks me."[49] In a rather mystical and exultant passage (almost at the threshold of a neopantheism) that nonetheless resonates with the Shoah mother-daughter encounter Bruck tries to reanimate in her text, Buber affirms: "If test is made of its objectivity the form is certainly not 'there.' Yet what is actually so much present as it is? And the relation in which I stand to it is real, for it affects me, as I affect it."[50] There is no isolation between mother and daughter; their union (a type of I-Thou encounter in the daughter's text) transcends and at the same time guarantees each one's radical separation, caused by birth or by death.

For Bruck, the mother is the midpoint between origin and goal, similar to the concept of the biblical God as defined by Buber in Israel and the World: a mobile midpoint, not pinned down in time but perceivable at any given time, the "voice which from earliest beginnings has been speaking in the direction of the goal."[51] The apostrophe to her dead mother allows Bruck to make a similar shift from historical to ahistorical time. In fact, the address to the dead, Culler remarks, points to the fact that "something once present has been lost or attenuated; this loss can be narrated but the temporal sequence is irreversible, like time itself. Apostrophes displace this irreversible structure by removing the opposition between presence and absence from empirical time and locating it in a discursive time."[52] The ineluctable gap between the now of writing and the now of the event, and the daughter's mediating role in bridging this gap, is perfectly exemplified in the poem "L'uguaglianza padre! Az egyenlöség, apa!" (Equality Father!), in which Bruck, herself a ghost, visits the ghost of her father in Dachau. To meet the father's specter, the daughter must also assume the form of one; only as a ghost can she enter his territory. Speaking from a distance, the poetic voice calls and incites the father to keep going, not to give in to impossible circumstances. She reminds him that his lifelong experience of the world's injustice and violence should have made him strong enough to endure the concentration camp. The daughter thus tries to affect the unchangeable course of history. But the father can't hear her, and, as we know, he did not endure. After describing the full gamut of humiliations he had to suffer in life (long before Dachau)—poor and rejected by all communities, both Jewish and non-Jewish—the daughter offers herself to him in reparation: "Take me father! / I will give you pleasure not children, / love not duties, / love not reproaches, / love that was unknown to you / and only imagined by me, hurry / it is time for the Apocalypse! / Let us commit the mortal sin / to deserve our death."[53] The daughter returns to the dead to repair something irrevocably broken. Incest is no longer taboo. The horrors of the Shoah make such social taboos irrelevant. The true horror is not incest but Auschwitz. On closer inspection, behind the incestuous proposal there is a more important reparatory arrangement: "So you turn to me! You don't recognize me, / I am older and have firm breasts / soft pure pubic hair / like that of mother when they brought her to you / in marriage. Take me father!"[54] The scene draws on a memory from Dachau in which the daughter and her father briefly saw each other in the obscenity of their emaciated nudities, their vulnerability and proximity to an unjustifiable death. However, the ghost also represents the poet at the present time of her poetic vision, a vision in which she courageously offers up her adult body. Confirming Culler's observation quoted earlier, empirical and discursive time collapse into each other.

In this poem, the function of the daughter's ghost is to offer up a different version of womanhood, wifehood, and sexual experience to both her father and her mother. In *Lettera*, Bruck portrays the marital position of the mother as one of pure reproductive organ, rather than lover and partner to her husband: "You [mother] did not make love out of love, though you loved father, but out of duty. We were born out of divine will, as if we were God's children, and not yours and father's. It was as if papa had had nothing to do with it, as if God himself had impregnated you" (*Lettera*, 8). In the ghastly yet "magical" space of her poem "L'uguaglianza padre!," the daughter's incestuous proposal aims at fixing the imbalance between the sexes evident in her own private, familial history. It also seeks to symbolically repay her father (via her own sensuous generosity) for all the times doors had been shut in his face and richer men had refused him help. Bruck conceives of the Shoah as an integral part of a violent history of oppression, of which Auschwitz is a disproportionate yet consequent result. She repeatedly describes both of her parents as victims of a civilization rife with social injustice. The ethical system in which parents of the Shoah generation strongly believed is under attack in Bruck's writing. In fact, as Bruck declares in another poem apostrophizing her brother, life was just as painful as death for those people whom she encounters in her trespassing as a poet and mediator ("My dear brother . . . life is no more fair than was your death").[55] In another poem, she attacks the patriarchal world order that her parents' generation thought imperative to pass down to their children: "They are growing up like savages you [Mother] used to say / without God / without a proper father / without bread / without education / without future / poor daughters. / If you'll be honest and obedient / good and pure / you'll find someone / that won't care about the dowry / . . . if you won't be squeamish / and won't expect to choose / since you cannot afford it."[56] And about the old-fashioned style of parenting she also wrote in Lettera: "When on earth would a father talk or play with his children back then!" (63).

The daughter's text is the account book of life, which, like God, she holds in her hands during the final judgment. There is a trial constantly in session in Bruck's literary memory, and in this court, the daughter holds the mother accountable for her mistakes too: "You did not listen to me, everything was more important than I was for you"; "How many times you flung it in my face that I was born"; "Did you ever caress me? I really can't remember you doing it" (Lettera, 78, 59, 63). However, the adult narrator knows all too well that her mother was just one in a countless line of mothers from the lower classes beaten down by misery and centuries-old oppression, a type of person neither unique nor generalizable. Along with her merciless criticism, Bruck also reconstructs an image of her, and her protagonist's, mother as a "lioness,"[57] acknowledging with love and gratitude the ethical fiber she passed on to her daughter that proved essential to her survival in Auschwitz and afterwards. Bruck recognizes several times that both the mother and daughter reconstructed in her book were destined to victimhood not only by the Nazis but by a long history inimical to them, poor and at the margins as they were: "Mothers who are poor are harsh . . . and bad too . . . The child of the poor grows up surrounded by screams, physical violence, and with a shortage of love" (Lettera, 61); "the peasant life wasn't good, it was harsh . . . Peasants were turned into savages by their labor. . . . they took it out on their children, on their animals, always fighting among themselves" (Lettera, 22); and "You were the daughter-mother of a culture convinced that all there is to children is feeding them" (Lettera, 63). The apostrophe "You, Mother!" collapses the time of writing into the time of remembered trauma. In the time of writing, a woman, looks at the life of another woman, her mother, and understands both of their histories in context; she forgives, justifies, and reconciles with her mother. In the time of remembered trauma, a young daughter—angry, terrified, and uncomprehending—still tries to fix, set straight, and even prevent a painful, irrevocable history amid her mother's reproaches, cries, and impotence. The American sociologist Kai Erikson describes the workings of trauma in vivid terms: "Something alien breaks in on you, smashing through whatever barriers your mind has set up as a line of defense. It invades you, takes you over, becomes a dominating feature of your interior landscape . . . and in the process threatens to drain you and leave you empty."[58] Bruck wills just such an alien invasion to create an experience that mediates and reconciles through the use of apostrophe and the hallucination of an impossible dialogue; the "invasion" reanimates the inanimate and nonexistent and bridges past and future. It also connects the solitary victim to the outside world, which she feels compelled to summon to listen to her story. Behind each command of "Listen!" hides the appeal of "Let me talk," through which the survivor speaker both requests and asserts her right to living.

W. H. Auden once said that "poetry makes nothing happen," or rather something happens, and it is the survival itself of poetry: "it survives, / A way of happening, a mouth."[59] Bruck's apostrophes to the dead are key to the survival of writing and to the survival of the poet.

### PROSOPOPEIA

To transform absence into presence, Bruck must fluidly inhabit the territories of life and the space of death (the inner site of trauma) so that she may speak to and for the dead. The space where this encounter takes shape is the work of art. As I suggested earlier, the mother-daughter relationship here seems to reflect Buber's generative I-Thou one; however, as Buber suggests, the moment this relation is spoken into art—that is, the moment it is given form—the Thou inevitably turns into an It and, like all objects, is lost again. Or rather, it is always lost because it was always radically separate from I. Buber says that "this is the exalted melancholy of our fate, that every Thou in our world must become an It . . . In the work of art, realization in one sense means loss of reality in another."[60] The daughter writer's melancholia consists of just such a double-edged sword; she must give birth to her texts about her mother, but the cost of this production is the repetition of a traumatic loss.

This loss also occurs at the level of language, within the text itself. In his "Shelley Disfigured" and "Autobiography as De-Facement" (which claims that "autobiography" is the mode of all writing),[61] de Man claims that the text produces figures and disfigures them at the same time. Bruck's letter to the Holocaust mother restores the name and the voice of the dead and the living into a text: but because it is a voice grounded in death (communicability having died at Auschwitz), it paradoxically erases the letter even as it composes it. This ironic movement, or defacement as de Man calls it, creates the mother as it erases her and creates the daughter as it simultaneously denies her existence. She cannot be daughter to a mother who is not. She cannot be witness to an event (death) she did not participate in.

In the space of the text, mother and daughter are both different and the same; as they write or read each other, they originate meaning and make their identities possible. To create the complicated scene of the daughter looking at the mother looking at the daughter, Bruck must use prosopopeia, a figurative incarnation by means of language—or, as de Man says, "the fiction of an apostrophe to an absent, deceased, or voiceless entity, which posits the possibility of the latter's reply and confers upon it the power of speech."[62] De Man identifies in prosopopeia the mask of autobiography, the trope that makes one's name "as intelligible and memorable as a face."[63] In Bruck's dialectics between mother and daughter, and between history and language, a displacement is at work, and the prosopopeia enables this displacement by supplying the mask or face (*prosopon*) that the author wears and through which she speaks. The feminist scholar Susan Gubar has also engaged in an important theorization of prosopopeia. In particular, she was committed to championing poets like Sylvia Plath,[64] who adopted the rhetorical *tekhnē* of personification (*prosopopoei*) in order to speak about their personal suffering through a performative identification with the victims of human catastrophes like the Holocaust, despite having had no direct involvement with the events. Rather than being an impudent affront to the memory of the dead, Gubar posits, poetic incarnation is the fundamental response of art, and poetry in particular, to the historical and ethical questions raised by the disappearance of millions. In other words, it is art's way of creating a space of mourning for the millions who have no graveyard. The use of "prosopopoeia allows the authors who manipulate it to summon the posthumous voice, to conceive of subjectivity enduring beyond the concentration camp, and thereby to suggest that the anguish of the Shoah does not, and will not, dissipate, Gubar writes.[65] But she also clarifies that "such a shocking re-animation of the dead cannot be equated with the traditional elegiac attempt to bring a particularly cherished person back into living memory, to assert the dead person's immortality, or to envision some union with the dead in a place elsewhere."[66] In other words, the Romantic trope of life as a journey interrupted but not ended by death is no longer viable in Shoah poetry or narrative. Examining several poems by Jewish and non-Jewish authors, Gubar observes that all poets are in fact aware of the ultimate inauthenticity of their attempts at speaking for or speaking as the dead. She identifies the place where this recognition (the failure of language itself) is made manifest in the trope of the death mask that underlies any prosopopeia. Gubar remarks that "even those poets who strenuously decrease their distance from the 'deathmask' disclose an awareness of the inescapable inauthenticity at the core of their undertaking." Furthermore, following de Man, she concludes: "Bestowing presence onto the absent dead is inherently oxymoronic."[67] Thinking of Bruck's personal writing and the death mask she wears to allow the absent to speak, I suggest that while autobiography has traditionally functioned as the genre capable of restoring selfhood and of creating a coherent, meaningful, and stable universe, Holocaust memory has disabled this function. In so doing, however, it has revealed the paradoxically productive failures that constitute all autobiographical attempts to construct the self: language (always figurative) both creates the face (figure) and disfigures it as the text unfolds.

Gubar does disagree with one idea that de Man puts forth—specifically, his postulation that "by making the dead speak, the symmetrical structure of the trope implies, by the same token, that the living are struck dumb, frozen in their own death."[68] According to Gubar, if I understand her correctly, it is the poetic capacity for heteropathic identification that invalidates de Man's proposition. "Heteropathic identification" is the term coined by Kaja Silverman for an identification that maintains alterity while simultaneously succeeding in sharing the Other's position—of disadvantage, pain, oppression, marginality.[69] (Its opposite is idiopathic identification, which entails the devouring of the Other into one's subjectivity, assimilating it to death, so to speak, so that the Other is utterly interiorized into one and vanishes.) My view, however, is that these two positions are not mutually exclusive: how could the living be struck dumb and remain speechless if not through a process of deep heteropathic identification? To signify would mean to break that important distance between the reader and what stands before his or her eyes.[70] The reader's muteness is the condition for seeing—the gaze, being the motor of the ethical move toward the Other—and muteness is not, I believe, rooted in apathy, but rather in heteropathy.

To return to Wordsworth and his history of the epitaph, de Man argues that Wordsworth's Essays revealed to the poet a stance from which to compose his own hyperbolic epitaph or autobiography; Wordsworth succeeded in moving "without compromise, from death or life to life and death" by collapsing the distinction between them, by annulling the and/or dichotomy.[71] Likewise, Bruck's poetics achieves this collapsing of opposites and allows the unimaginable to happen: while affirming death, it eliminates the radical distance between presence and absence. Wordsworth's poetic act uses all the available rhetorical tools to accomplish this fabulous spiritual leap; Bruck's melancholia, as I will show later, demands of her language the exact opposite—an extreme aesthetic impoverishment, a sonority close to silence. For Bruck, language stands in for the loss of the mother, who is at once declared to be lost through language and simultaneously recovered through language. Kristeva claims that the true melancholic cannot be an artist because those affected by melancholia lack the connection to the metaphorical. "Melancholia," according to Kristeva, "ends up in asymbolia, in loss of meaning: if I am no longer capable of translating or metaphorizing, I become silent and die."[72] The melancholic, unlike the artist, has no recourse to the beneficent palliative of the symbolic and the metaphorical: the melancholic is a literal creature. The truly depressive subject is trapped in the cage of an extreme sadness that followed the loss of what Kristeva calls the "unnamed Thing"—that originary attachment the depressed mind feels has been taken away and that "an *invocation* might point out, but no word could signify."[73] The ideas of naming (bestowing on the postwar children the names of the dead) and namelessness (the unmarked mass graves, the tattooed numbers that replaced names, and so forth), so relevant to Shoah memoirs, returns, this time in a psychoanalytic framework. Contrary to Kristeva's clinical conclusions, I will argue that Bruck, the artist afflicted by a radical melancholia, is able to overcome melancholia through art despite the unsymbolizable loss she experienced at Auschwitz.

Adalgisa Giorgio notes that the letter represents the daughter's way "to make amends for her mother's death and to express her love for her, while begging her forgiveness and requesting her blessing for her life."[74] However, I would argue that the impossibility of an answer to this missive guarantees, in turn, that forgiveness shall never be granted. This impossibility is the center of Bruck's intellectual world and is a theme running throughout her *oeuvre*. Giorgio claims that "appeasement with her mother comes to signify appeasement with herself as a woman, a Jew, and also as a writer."[75] I believe instead that it is precisely the failure of appeasement that the text affirms, and the text is lacerated by this failure. *Lettera* has no narrative closure; it just ends with three ellipsis points in the middle of an unfinished sentence from the kaddish, the mourner's prayer. The story does not reach a natural conclusion because it tells the story not of a meaningfully lived life but of a senseless death: a story stripped of epiphany, catharsis, denouement, and conclusion. Can Bruck forgive? And who is to be forgiven? Is it possible to forgive patriarchy and the culture of violence that created not only Auschwitz but also an oppressed mother who could love only through anger? I canot answer these questions on Bruck's behalf. Reflecting on Dostoyevsky, Kristeva suggests that the aesthetic act shakes the writer out of his or her depressive state of inaction and becomes an act of forgiveness.[76] But in Bruck's case, isn't the aesthetic act one of anger (her rage against her mother, against Auschwitz, against the injustices her family had to suffer even before the war) that allows the artist to shake off her apathetic desperation that might lead to suicide? Bruck refuses the closure that a pardon would afford because such forgiveness might preclude the continuation of a dialogue (though exercised in writing) that alone guarantees her existence. Not by chance, *Lettera* ends with an ellipsis that cuts short the chance of a happy ending just as it seems as if the final judgment and reconciliation were near, thereby guaranteeing that a new text (another piece of her Shoah story) will have to be produced.

Kristeva revisits some of her own conclusions on melancholy in real-life patients when she turns to examine melancholy in literature. She attempts to demonstrate that art (via the allegorization of the imagination) can triumph over melancholia. But Kristeva, always very much invested in Christian iconography and symbology, is interested in proving the possibility of cathartic resurrection (albeit only in art). I believe that unlike the prison of melancholia that allows the hostage to peek through its bars at the outside world in which the disconnected (depressed) person has lost all interest, the prison of trauma is an isolation cell with no bars, only thick, padded walls. One is certainly melancholy and depressed in this space as well, but one has no direct way to reach out to a world one yearns to be part of as usual—but to which usual access is denied by the experience of extreme terror that haunts the traumatized mind. Of interest for my analysis here is the fact that Kristeva's study of melancholia considers it a form of living death—similar, therefore, to my understanding of Bruck's traumatized state. "I live a living death," writes Kristeva, speaking for the depressed patient (and hence putting on the patient's mask). "My flesh is wounded, bleeding, cadaverized [. . .] [T]ime has been erased or bloated, absorbed into sorrow . . . Absent from other people's meaning, alien, accidental with respect to naïve happiness, I owe a supreme, metaphysical lucidity to my depression."[77] Although Kristeva theorizes that sadness is the melancholic's survival strategy—the depressive person remains attached to his or her unsymbolizable sadness and thus remains attached to life—I claim that Bruck's melancholia does not cling to a fetishized sadness but to art, to writing. Therefore, her obsessive attachment to writing exclusively about her Shoah memory allows her to counteract the pull of death while remaining deeply enmeshed in the humus of death.

### READING AS ANSWERING

Interpreting Friedrich Hölderlin's *Wein und Brot*, de Man concludes that Romantic poetry's apostrophe ultimately fails to manifest the longed-for epiphany, fails to "materialize" what it is calling forth. The crux of this failure resides in language itself. In our everyday use of language, according to de Man, "words are exchanged and put to a variety of tasks, but they are not supposed to originate anew; on the contrary, one wants them to be as well-known, as 'common' as possible, to make certain that they will obtain for us what we want to obtain. They are used as established signs to confirm that something is recognized as being the same as before; and re-cognition excludes pure origination. But in poetic language words are not used as signs, not even as names, but in order to *name*."[78] What is the Shoah survivor naming, calling, and thus originating but death itself? The calling of ghosts flings open the door to their tombs. If it is an epiphany that the daughter's apostrophe expects to conjure, the epiphany will fail. The magic word that Bruck uses in the hope of bringing about the longed-for epiphany is "mother," a word destined to fail because, as de Man writes, it "is pure origination."[79] Ultimately, Bruck's texts repeatedly reproduce the impossibility of this epiphany (the encounter with her dead, the representation of her trauma). As the numerous quotes offered throughout this chapter show, Bruck's Italian sheds its proverbial adjectival richness, her poetry and prose consisting of very short clauses. Direct and spare, Bruck's language attempts to express her complex feelings and unimaginable memories in the most telegraphic manner. It is the language of the depressed, "repetitive and monotone," as Kristeva describes it: "Faced with the impossibility of concatenating, they [the depressed persons] utter sentences that are interrupted, exhausted, come to a standstill . . . A repetitive rhythm, a monotonous melody emerge and dominate the broken logical sequences, changing them into recurring, obsessive litanies."[80] Deprived of its literary beauty, Italian becomes but a means to an end: recognition. To make sure that the memory of the past, when the mother and father were alive, is still intact, Bruck repeats her telegraphic messages over and over with similar rhythms and in similar forms throughout all her books.

Bruck lives her emotional and psychic life on the threshold between language and silence. But how can we achieve silence without renouncing testimony? Without dying a second time? Bruck finds an ingenious compromise to this *pilpul*: she writes an undestined letter, one that the intended addressee will never receive. The addresser will imagine and fantasize about the answers of the addressee, but these responses are only projections of the daughter's illusion. Jewish mystical tradition teaches us that the Word is One, but one within which all letters are contained and destined to an interminable creation. For Bruck's pious Jewish mother, words existed to be combined in ever more sorrowful prayers, the ultimate apostrophes inviting God to join in a conversation from which he has withdrawn. To the godless daughter, words and the letters (meaning both the alphabet and her missives) that carry them are empty graves that echo her solitude, loss, and desperation. If in the beginning was the Word, in the end, a barbaric twentieth century gives forth only silence.

To a certain extent, Bruck recuperates the Romantic conception of the relationship between language and its referents, a relationship that de Man explains in these terms: "Poetic language seems to originate in the desire to draw closer and closer to the ontological status of the object, and its growth and development are determined by this inclination."[81] At times the evocation is so intense, the demands of consciousness so obliterating, that it seems impossible to distinguish between literality and mimesis. The fiction of address, "Sta Viator!" (Pause, traveler!), de Man argues, "thus acquires a sinister connotation that is not only the prefiguration of one's own mortality but of our actual entry into the frozen world of the dead."[82] In Bruck's case, the apostrophe to the mother and the other dead figures becomes uncanny and makes the reader uncomfortable because of the frozen space of death into which it drags us. In this mother-daughter dialogue from which I, as the reader, am excluded, what is my role? What does this impossible mother-daughter correspondence do to and expect of a reader? Reading such a text, such apostrophes destined to someone other than me as the reader, creates a state of uneasiness in the unintended recipients who receive the message. Culler notes that apostrophes in Romantic poetry "may complicate and disrupt the circuit of communication, raising questions about who is the addressee, but above all they are embarrassing: embarrassing to me and to you."[83] I claim that in Bruck's Lettera, the reader is discomfited ("embarrassed") by the fact that he or she is drawn into the drama of the mother by the daughter's missives, which—lacking any correlation in the real world—turn any receiver of her message into its addressee. Bruck's Lettera is delivered into our hands, and we realize that it is not addressed to us. We become more than eavesdroppers; we become witnesses. As Derrida explains to his "invisible" interlocutor in The Post Card, "one kills someone by addressing a letter to him that is not destined to him, and thereby declaring one's love or even one's hatred. And I kill you at every moment, but I love you. And you can no longer doubt it, even if I destroy everything with the most amorous patience (as do you, moreover), beginning with myself."[84] So are we also witnesses to a murder? If we follow Derrida's conjecture, Bruck kills the mother—that is, she makes her mother die again each time she rehearses the story of her death in literature, and each time her books meant for the mother reach not her but unintended addressees, the daughter's readers. By killing, of course, is meant the failure to make the mother reappear, to actually give her back the life that was brutally taken from her as well as making the extent of the trauma they both lived representable. At the same time, by writing about this act of brutality perpetrated against the mother, the daughter succeeds in forcing the reader to see, to become aware of the crime committed. We are called through such a mistaken delivery to be part of Bruck's painful universe.

If de Man can say of Wordsworth's self-composed epitaph that "an unlettered stone [tombstone] would leave the sun suspended in nothingness,"[85] we can see how for Bruck, an unlettered book would leave the memoirist suspended in nothingness. Bruck is compelled to call out "Mother!" even though she is conscious that this invocation will reach someone else. It is the reader who assumes the interlocutionary position, and by indirectly witnessing the apostrophe, the reader witnesses the injustice committed against these victims and its immitigable aftereffects.

In her analysis of abortion poetry, Johnson writes: "The absent, dead, or inanimate entity addressed is thereby made present, animate, and anthropomorphic. Apostrophe is a form of ventriloquism through which the speaker throws voice, life, and human form into the addressee, turning its silence into mute responsiveness."[86] Bruck's misdelivery ensures that someone alive will react to her message, that the reader will listen to a stranger's story of suffering and death. The frozen silence of the mother in response to the daughter's invocation draws us into the traumatic dimension from which the author is speaking. There is more than sheer emotional participation in this apostrophe. Bruck's apostrophe affects us not just emotionally but also in a way closer to the original rhetorical goal of the ancient orators who first used it. As Irene Kacandes points out, Cicero and Demosthenes located the power of the apostrophe in its being "both double and duplicitous . . . because it is mobilized to provoke reaction—though not verbal reply—in those who hear it, not in those to whom it is explicitly addressed."[87] Not surprisingly, the classical rhetoricians especially valued the apostrophe's power in the court of law, where it signified "the act of an orator turning away from his normal audience—the judge(s)—to address another, whether adversary, a specific member of the jury, someone absent or dead, or even an abstract concept or inanimate object."[88] Bruck's injunction to listen to her story, I claim, is intended for the dead in absentia and therefore ends up eliciting a response (or demanding one) from the living—the readers, the audience that receives the message.

Kacandes has coined a new theoretical term, "talk fiction," to describe and analyze the widespread attempt by many authors of twentieth-century literature to animate (inspirit) a communication with an absent, unseen, or even nonexistent interlocutor—fiction as a conversation in which the reader is called on to participate. Although Bruck's texts would not squarely fit into the "talk fiction" rubric, Kacandes's conclusions about the apostrophic talk mode, and in particular what she calls "narrative apostrophe," are nevertheless relevant here: "In narrative witnessing, the construction of the message takes center stage; speaker and listener as witness and cowitness must orient toward exchange so that a story of the trauma can flow. Narrative apostrophes draw attention to the mechanisms of orientation to exchange by putting into question the issue of who is involved."[89] The reader of Bruck's apostrophic Shoah texts is a respondent to the text in the sense developed by Kacandes, who with this term distinguishes those who are hearers of an apostrophic call but are not its addressees.[90] Bruck's apostrophe institutes an ethics of presence, whereby we are summoned to respond. The dead have a claim on us, and Bruck does not allow us to ignore it. The respondent must inevitably react—in our case not verbally, but ethically—to the encounter with the calling voice.

Again turning to classical rhetoric, we see that Quintilian argues in favor of the apostrophe and against the pedantic rhetoricians who forbid its use. He underlines the ornamental and pragmatic usefulness of the apostrophe in the context of forensic oratory and explains that the apostrophe "consists in the diversion of our address from the judge, [it] is wonderfully stirring, whether we attack our adversary . . . or turn to make some invocation . . . or to entreaty that will bring odium on our opponents."[91] I want to propose that by turning away from us (the listening audience) and toward the mother (the unresponsive addressee), Bruck makes us aware of the witness's radical absence, of her tragic life and of their (lost) relationship. The magic of language (which finally reinstates the name of the Thing through the explicit call "Mother!") animates the events of the past before the audience's eyes. We witness, albeit from an empathic distance, what happened: a mother (and with her, life itself for the speaking daughter, the speaking gravestone) has disappeared. We are brought to mourn for the mother with her daughter, becoming the necessary minyan that allows the daughter to express her kaddish in art.

"'Not even a kaddish?' you complain" (Lettera, 70), Bruck writes, and "You want . . . a kaddish, a prayer that was never pronounced by a daughter for her mother" (Lettera, 93). However, the real kaddish, the prayer the daughter imagines the mother demands of her, is resisted by the text. To recite the actual mourner's prayer would mean to let go of her mother, to allow closure, as well as to address a prayer to God—and these are sacrifices the daughter is not willing or able to make. As in so much of Shoah testimonial literature, the kaddish becomes the crux of the daughter's critique of Judaism and gender. The ritualization of death through the recitation of a kaddish brings to the fore the voicelessness of these daughters, female survivors. They cannot say a kaddish because they are women (only a minyan of men can utter it); they cannot address their prayers to any specific place because there is no grave for the victims; and they cannot recite the prayer because they have lost sight of the God who demands that these words be uttered, and hence the *logoi* (words, grammar, letters, as well as signification) he embodies. The message implied in the ancient Aramaic prayer thus remains undeliverable or illegible. Ruth Klüger writes in her Shoah memoir:

> I keep wanting to celebrate [father] in some way, to find or invent an appropriate way of mourning, some ceremony for him. And yet celebrations and ceremonies are not my thing. I suspect them of mendacity, and often they strike me as ridiculous. Nor would I know where to start. In the Jewish tradition only men say the *Kaddish*, the prayer for the dead. (Who is keeping you from saying any prayer you please? my friends ask. But it wouldn't count, couldn't be part of a prescribed communal ritual, so what would be the point?) . . . If it were different, if I could mourn my ghosts in some accepted public way, like saying *Kaddish* for my father, I'd have a friendlier attitude towards this religion, which reduces its daughters to helpmeets of men and circumscribes their spiritual life within the confines of domestic functions.[92]

Faced with the impossibility of pronouncing the formal one, a text composed of memories and unsent letters become the new kaddish for many Shoah women authors, not only Bruck.

In principle, Bruck's text is the final blessing of the living over the memory of the dead. However, *Lettera*'s endlessness indicates that the daughter is not willing or ready to let go. She can only assuage her sadness at being alive by making her life resonate with death. This is the living daughter's role: to incarnate the memory of her dead mother, to become her memory in the sense of both remembering her mother and voicing her mother's memories. In a letter to Richard Woodhouse, John Keats described a poet as "the most unpoetical of any thing in existence, because he has no identity . . . continually . . . filling some other Body."[93] In order to "fill" the mother's body, the daughter has to momentarily die in the text by plunging herself down among ghosts to bring a light that will illuminate them and make them present to the reader: "I am somewhere else too when I am writing. Just like you were with God, I am with you and I chase away my cats, I even push away my friends, the people I love. I forget all about eating, drinking, telephoning people. I forget my back pain" (*Lettera*, 87). Just like her mother, who when she prayed forgot about everything else, (*Lettera*, 87) the daughter mystically reaches a different state of being when visiting her past in writing.

In describing the state of mind of chronically melancholic patients, Kristeva points out that a form of mysticism arises in the depressed psyche and turns on their otherwise inactive belief. "I have assumed depressed persons to be atheistic," Kristeva ponders. "Nevertheless, and although atheistic, those in despair are mystics—adhering to the preobject, not believing in Thou, but mute and steadfast devotees of their own inexpressible container. It is to this fringe of strangeness that they devote their tears and jouissance."[94] Bruck has chosen writing as a form of religiosity, a form she senses her mother will not approve of: "Writing is my religion . . . Forgive me" (Lettera, 24). This devoted type of writing establishes Thou, unlike what Kristeva observed in her patients, as the only logic precondition of I, a Thou that eerily bonds the I to both death and creation: "I owe the illness of writing to you [Mother], and to Auschwitz, where you let me go, or to be precise where you pushed me away yelling that I had to obey a guy who was hitting me with his rifle" (Lettera, 78). According to Kristeva, the drama of the psychotic child is: "If I don't agree to lose my mother, I could neither imagine nor name her." Kristeva continues: "'But no, I have found her again in signs, or rather since I consent to lose her I have not lost her (that is the negation), I can recover her in language.'"[95] Language denies absence and hence loss, and this is why a denial of language's denial (denegation, in Kristeva's terms) is necessary. A suspension of this negative in language allows for this spectral encounter with the ghosts. Bruck annuls the denial like Kristeva's depressed patients, who "nostalgically fall back on the real object (the Thing) of their loss, which is just what they do not manage to lose, to which they remain painfully riveted."[96]

We can say that for Bruck the kaddish, Judaism, and the mother's God and the fixed identity he represents have nothing to do with that umbilical cord that still binds daughter and mother together. The kaddish's masculinity, canonicity, and homogeneity are what ultimately separate the mother and her dogmatic religiosity from the daughter's antidogmatic creativity and disbelief in everything but the magic of her words and the ghosts they animate (whom she knows are a fiction, but in whom she chooses to believe—testing Kristeva's idea of denegation) and the anger they allow her to expel. Yet despite her resistance to her mother's tradition, the daughter reaches out for the prayer book. Neither the book nor the kaddish will be finished, and Lettera ends with these words:

Pretend that you are my daughter and I your mother. No, don't worry. The kaddish is yours, come on give me a push. Up and down, up and down, faster, higher, faster, faster, nearer to God, mama! Nearer! I want Him too to hear my kaddish:

*"Yit'gadal v'yit'kadash sh'mei raba; b'al'ma di v'ra khir'utei, v'yam'likh mal'khutei b'chayeikhon uv'yomeikhon, uv'chayei d'khol beit Yis'ra'eil Ba'agala uviz'man kariv v'im'ru amen . . ."* (Lettera, 95)

## POST SCRIPTUM

Curiously, the daughter's apostrophization of an unresponsive mother in Bruck has an illustrious precedent in another unhappy Jewish child, who also poured all his angst and anger into an undeliverable letter to a flawed yet beloved parent: Franz Kafka. Kafka wrote letters all his life. His correspondence with friends and family was so abundant, especially when compared with the scarcity of his literary production, that scholars consider it a vital part of his output. But Kafka's most revealing letter may be one that found no destination: his 1919 *Brief an den Vater* (*Letter to His Father*). "I could be grateful to you for everything only as a beggar is, and could never show it by doing the right things," Kafka writes.[97] Never intended to be delivered, Kafka's missive also bears the filial injunction, "Listen Father!," which—like Bruck's to the mother—remains unheard. These two Jewish authors, positioned one at the beginning and the other at the end of the 1900s, frame the past century through the story of their critical relationship with their parents, a story that can be told only in an undeliverable letter. Ironically, the English editions of both works chose to "misaddress" these books, translating them respectively as *Letter to His Father* and *Letter to My Mother*, thereby disregarding the lack of possessive pronouns in the German and Italian originals (a literal translation would have been "Letter to the Father" and "Letter to the Mother"), which quite tellingly universalized the terms of the messages.

For obvious reasons, Bruck's text has at its core the Shoah and literature's relation to it. Kafka's sensitivity and imagination may have allowed him to sense the drama in store for the human race, but that became for Bruck a nightmarish reality. Though he would never read it, Kafka's father was still alive when his son composed his missive. It was the father's explicit request that compelled Kafka to write—"Dearest Father, You asked me recently why I maintain that I am afraid of you . . . I now try to give you an answer in writing"[98]—but it was the mother's silence and unresponsiveness, even when she was still alive, that compelled the daughter to respond: "If you had listened to me to the end only once, maybe I wouldn't be writing to you now."[99] All differences aside, however, the two letters, and the two authors who penned them, suggest a philosophical and spiritual involvement with and a profound concern for the fate of communication, and more specifically for parent-child correspondence and the dynamic between a creator and his or her creation. From their different perspectives, both Kafka's and Bruck's works engage with the issue of representability in language. Experience becomes incommunicable when it cannot be expressed within the envelope of our common signifiers—when, in other words, it is located outside of language. Such is the case with dreams or nightmares, of course, but also with subconscious fears (as in Kafka's case) and with trauma (as in Bruck's). Between these poles, twentieth-century literature posits two sets of letters: Kafka's to a deadly patriarch, and Bruck's to a dead mother.

Kafka also left us a marvelous parable—"An Imperial Message"—that serves as a paradigm of what Kamuf calls the catastrophe of destination.[100] The story begins as follows: "The Emperor—so they say—has sent a message, directly from his death bed, to you alone, his pathetic subject, a tiny shadow which has taken refuge at the furthest distance from the imperial sun. He ordered the herald to kneel down beside his bed and whispered the message in his ear."[101] The message remains unknown to the reader, subverting the expectation that, in literature, the reader will always receive the message—even one that is not intended for him. Here the reader is cut out of the secret by Kafka's uncanny parable. The emperor dies, the message does not arrive, and the addresser's death forecloses any chance of reproducing its contents. This parable short-circuits communication and reality. The reader will receive an open letter, as illegible as Derrida's postcard, whose message is being written as it is being read, one that is without end or beginning (for the reader). The story continues: "But the crowd is so huge; its dwelling places are infinite. If there were an open field, how he [the messenger] would fly along, and soon you would hear the marvelous pounding of his fist on your door. But instead of that, how futile are all his efforts. He is still forcing his way through the private rooms of the inner-most palace. Never will he win his way through."[102] The fact that the message is from a dead person nullifies its destiny (which is also the emperor's destina-tion) altogether: "No one pushes his way through here, certainly not someone with a message from a dead man," writes Kafka.[103] Indeed, who wants to heed the message of a dead man? Similarly, the absence of replies from Bruck's ad-dressee, the mother, speaks to the central message of her dead communication: the injustice of a mother's death leaves the daughter without answers, and the mother's infinite silence is the dead letter (*lettera morta*) that finds no post in history.

To "address" etymologically means "to make straight" (from *ad directiare*) —that is, to make spoken words arrive directly at the intended addressee. Bruck's apostrophes lead straight to a single origination point: the forced and violent physical detachment from her mother's embrace in Auschwitz as they were lined up for the final selection. There, mother, God, and daughter were all present and all sacrificed. The daughter's traumatized psyche is trapped at that specific point, and it is from this psychic bound that the adult survivor silently awaits what she knows will never come: "I could describe my present state as that of a traveler waiting at a station, from which no train arrives or departs" (*Lettera*, 109). Which train station is this? Perhaps the same one Charlotte Delbo has written of in the opening of her war memoir:

> They do not know there is no arriving in this station.
> They expect the worse—not the unthinkable. . .
> The station is not a railroad station. It is the end of the line. They stare, distressed by the surrounding desolation.[104]

Kafka ends his parable about the message from the dead emperor with a scene as melancholic as Delbo's or Bruck's: "No one pushes his way through here, certainly not someone with a message from a dead man. But you sit at your window and dream of that message when evening comes."[105] As she grows older, beset by pain and fear, Bruck too awaits an answer from her silent interlocutor that never comes. We, the readers, detain a post in history and are thus mistakenly delivered the letter intended for the ghosts of Auschwitz. Therefore, we are also called to action by an apostrophe turned away from us: we must decipher an unreadable message.

Naturally things cannot in reality fit together the way the evidence does in my letter; life is more than a Chinese puzzle. But . . . in my opinion something has been achieved which so closely approximates the truth that it might reassure us both a little and make our living and our dying easier.

**FRANZ KAFKA**, *Letter to His Father*

# CHAPTER 2

# *LUPUS IN FABULA*
## The End of the Fairy Tale in Ruth Klüger's Mother-Daughter Shoah Plot

All great storytellers have in common the freedom with which they move up and

down the rungs of their experience as on a ladder. A ladder extending downward to

the interior of the earth and disappearing into the clouds is the image for a collective

experience to which even the deepest shock of every individual experience, death,

constitutes no impediment or barrier.

 **WALTER BENJAMIN**, *Illuminations*

In the summer of 1943, the Dutch intellectual Etty Hillesum wrote a letter to Han Wegerif and other friends from her temporary imprisonment in Westerbork, noting: "One should be able to write fairy tales here." Referring to the misery and human squalor in that place, she added: "One would have to be a very great poet indeed to describe them; perhaps in about ten years I might get somewhat near it."[1] Hillesum could not have known what we who have lived to look back at those barbaric times are well aware of: For one thing, she would be murdered in Auschwitz four months later, at the age of twenty-nine, and would not live the extra ten years she assumed it would take her to find the right words to describe the circumstances of that grotesque place. For another, she didn't know that poets and other artists would attempt to represent the irrepresent-ability of such horrors and the twilight of morality by using a mode of narration not dissimilar from that of fairy tales. As Hillesum realized, although it sounded strange, "if you wanted to convey something of Westerbork life [and by extension of life in the camps] you could do it best in that form."[2] Fairy tales possess a special language so psychically powerful that since time immemorial societies have used them to channel with particular efficacy messages from the dark abysses of our human subconscious, as well as to make sense of the past or express their ethos. Through repetition, the value of these stories is reinforced in time, and the messages they contain gain in cultural power. Residing as they do at the intersection of personal psychology and culture, fairy tales partake of the formation of both.[3] They influence the psychology of the child and the adult alike as much as they reflect and represent it; they are a cultural product inalienably connected to the context from which they arose; and they end up shaping, as all art does, the identikit of a culture. Individual fantasy and collective imagination lock eyes in search of reciprocal legitimization on the magical and untrustworthy terrain of folk and fairy mythology. In his seminal *When Dreams Come True*, Jack Zipes explains that "both the oral and the literary forms of the fairy tale are grounded in history: they emanate from specific struggles to humanize bestial and barbaric forces, which have terrorized our minds and communities in concrete ways, threatening to destroy free will and human compassion. The fairy tale sets out to conquer this concrete terror through metaphors."[4] Shoah memoirs, which are also grounded in history, set out to conquer this terror in much the same way: via a metaphorical (mimetic) retelling of each survivor's story. Even the Shoah teller is at bottom a storyteller. And history retold has the potential to become myth, while myth has the power to keep history—or, better, its lessons—alive.

Walter Benjamin once wrote: "The storyteller takes what he tells from experience—his own or that reported by others. And he in turn makes it the experience of those who are listening to his tale."[5] Just as myths and folk stories are organized around recognizable structures that give form to their dark content, preexisting structures and time-tested narrative devices can, through language and imagery, help the Shoah teller write about that which resists expression. For example, in *Night*, Elie Wiesel is able to reconstruct the scenes of his youth just before the apocalyptic climax (the deportations to the camps) by tapping into an old Yiddish storytelling repertoire of legendary topoi. He gives us characters such as Moishe the Beadle, a figure who is at once the fool and the savant of the village of Sighet, Wiesel's home *shtetl*, and a Chagallesque *luftmensch* who has witnessed what others do not even begin to suspect—the Nazis committing mass murder in the East—and is not believed when he warns the village. The disbelieving crowds, the *schlemiel* who is *no fool*, the pious mother, and the tzaddik father are the stock characters that populate the universe of this fable. The description of the nights the child Eliezer spends with Moishe the Beadle, his spiritual mentor, in the candle-lit *shtibl*, decoding the secrets of the Zohar until dawn, are drenched in the atmosphere that is born out of the Yiddish literary tradition of S. Ansky, Sholem Asch, Mendele Mocher Sforim, Der Nister, and others. As in the mythical and *shtetl* literary tradition, the cycle of life—or rather, here, the cycle of death—is inextricably linked with the cycles of nature in *Night*. "Spring 1944," we read. "Splendid news from the Russian Front . . . The trees were in bloom. It was a year like so many others, with its spring, its engagements, its weddings, and its births." But of course, instead, it turns into a season of death, arrests, deportations, and crimes. It was springtime, it was Passover: "The weather was sublime. My mother was busy in the kitchen."[6] The Jews of Sighet had been already relocated to the ghetto, where, regardless of the impending doom, a couple of weeks before Shavuot, they could still enjoy a carefree stroll.[7] The expulsion from the prewar paradise will happen on Shabbat: the Jewish day of rest and joy turns into a day of frantic packing and tears. To describe the hecatomb (the deportation, the journey in the cattle cars, the arrival at the camp), the narrator repeatedly uses the image of the night, symbolically enshrouding everything in the darkness that had fallen over the Jews' lives. We are told of a crazed woman on the train to Auschwitz, a Jewish Cassandra, who has visions of their destinies ahead: "Fire! I see a fire! I see a fire!"[8] Thus *Night* brings into post-Shoah literature echoes of those three main submetaphors on which, according to Dan Miron, Hebrew and Yiddish *shtetl* literature have traditionally stood: exodus, pseudomessianic visits, and fire.[9]

Unlike folk tales and old yarns, however, the Shoah is not an instructive source yielding positive messages, and when a happy ending does occur (as when a victim survives), it cannot be inscribed within the fairy-tale framework of the triumph of good over evil. Yet Hillesum was right: there are many ways in which the techniques of fairy tales can be applied to the retelling of an experience as unlike a fairy tale as Auschwitz. Both folk tales and Shoah memoirs rely on the ability of the human mind to perceive what is read or heard as unreal (either too fantastical or too horrible to comprehend) but not necessarily untrue. We perceive a folk tale as something abstract yet also "part of our own experience," as Cristina Bacchilega writes.[10] Using a similar strategy from folk tales, but under the sign of tragedy, a Shoah memoir demands of the reader a suspension of disbelief. In particular, Shoah memoirs that focus on the childhood years of the writer share certain characteristics with the plot patterns of traditional fairy tales. The memoirs reflect on life from a vanished personal and collective past and show its connection to the present and the future, drawing its trajectories in terms of a continuum. Like the folk tales analyzed by Vladimir Prop,[11] the Shoah narrative also has plots with functions that differ from story to story, but within the same story there are several plot paths that rarely reach their end with the resolution of one single crisis. Northrop Frye reminds us that a central characteristic of folk tales is their abstract story patterns.[12] The arbitrariness and implausibility of the events of the Holocaust force its stories toward such abstraction, enshrouding most Shoah tales in a disturbing aura of unworldliness, as if they were suspended in an ahistorical moment, a sort of vacuum sealed off from this world. The fact that many Holocaust memoirs begin at the time of deportation and end around the time of liberation from the camps further contributes to these narrations' aura of atemporality by bracketing off the experience from what came before and after it.

The world of a fairy tale is insular, perfectly self-contained. Once good has triumphed over evil, things remain frozen in time, happy from then on. War memoirs, and childhood war memoirs in particular, are often told in this self-contained way. When a Shoah story is retold so as to exclude the life of the protagonist(s) before and after the war, it runs the risk of creating the false impression that the protagonist's life has reached an optimum stage (survival) and that he or she can go on living happily ever after. However, studies on posttraumatic stress disorder, along with the suicide rate among survivors and other psychopathologies arising in genocide escapees, show the opposite to be true. For the survivor, the Shoah story does not end with the liberation from the death camps. He or she never shakes free from the trauma. Auschwitz didn't just end.

In this chapter, I examine Ruth Klüger's *Still Alive*, a memoir illustrating the experience of a mother and daughter surviving Auschwitz together.[13] This text explicitly addresses the complex question of how to tell a child's story of survival without making it sound like a fairy-tale triumph of good over evil, even though such a structure could handle the events with narrative efficiency. I propose we look at how, from the perspective of the Shoah teller herself, particularly one who revisits her childhood, the structure of fairy tales can help make (at least narrative) sense of the unimaginable. It helps to tell the unspeakable. If we take the way in which fairy tales tackle the ambiguities of identity, the perception of reality, the formation of a self, the unconscious and its symbolic language, and the moral division between right and wrong, it becomes apparent how compatible the Shoah story is with the fairy-tale plot: a good and innocent child is born in an inimical world; she has to undergo exceptional trials; and in the end, aided by her own ingenuity, providential intermediaries, or luck, she prevails and becomes a new person, the successful and individuated adult. After all, as Bruno Bettelheim once said, "like Snow White, each child in his development must repeat the history of man, real or imagined."[14] However, I will show how Klüger uses her own memories as a Shoah child and Auschwitz survivor to demonstrate the pernicious allure of such a narrative. Furthermore, I will explore how, through her personal story as reflected in the mirror of her memoir, Klüger exposes the numerous myths that have shaped her psyche since childhood—including the film *Snow White*, from which, as we will see, she learns a very dramatic life lesson; the Viennese legend of Drunken August that she knew from her schooldays; the antisemitic tales depicting an infectious Other that surrounded her as a child; and Jewish stories about bitter herbs and the parting of the sea, which were also part of the repertoire of tales she grew up with.

Though Klüger warns us that there is no solace to be found in the fairy-tale ending of her autobiographical journey, the narrated conflicts (pivotal in the girl's identity formation) follow and repeat a universal pattern from which millennia of folk stories about human impulses have drawn their material.

We have been trained by our Western literary tradition—from Augustine's foundational *Confessions* onward—to expect from autobiographies truths that are recognizable and undisputable. The reader hopes to learn something from them, to gain some sort of illumination. We perceive autobiographies as transparent reflections of the self: they are mirrors that reflect an author and his or her life, as well as a version of the world of which we ourselves are a part. We look into an autobiography in order to see our own image integrated into the larger human picture. Canonic autobiographies, which Sidonie Smith rightly calls the androcentric genre par excellence,[15] establish the speaker as a universal model in whom readers can see their own foibles and tribulations and in whose triumphs they recognize an ideal to strive for. In their influential text on women's autobiographies, Bella Brodzki and Celeste Schenck explain:

> "The (masculine) tradition of autobiography . . . had taken as its first premise the mirroring capacity of the autobiographer: *his* universality, *his* representativeness, *his* role as spokesman for the community. But only a critical ideology that reifies a unified, transcendent self can expect to see in the mirror of autobiography a self whose depths can be plumbed, whose heart can be discovered, and whose essence can be definitively known. No mirror of *her* era, the female autobiographer takes as a given that selfhood is mediated: her invisibility results from her lack of a tradition, her marginality in male-dominated culture, her fragmentation—social and political as well as psychic."[16]

Klüger's awareness of the social and historical construction of the autobiographical self makes her text a particularly compelling postmodern work of memory. In this Shoah autobiography, the first-person narrator posits herself as precisely the opposite of an exemplary universal model; on the contrary, the uniqueness of her experience and its anti-exemplarity puts into question the viability of Shoah autobiography itself. Just as Shoah memoirs disable the work of autobiography (the work of constructing a coherent self), so do they disable the work of fairy tales (the work of imparting clear lessons and happy endings) while still functioning like fairy tales.[17] As I will show, Klüger questions the authority of her text, the faithfulness of the reflection produced by the mirror of memory. Since I began this chapter by talking about fairy tales, any association between fairy tales and mirrors inevitably conjures up the story of Snow

White,[18] which is central to my discussion of Klüger's memoir. More than any other fairy tale, Snow White's story represents the conflict in a mother-daughter relationship that is defined and limited, as Sandra Gilbert and Susan Gubar famously decreed, by that "transparent enclosure" into which, as women in a fiercely patriarchal world, they "both have been locked: a magic looking glass, an enchanted and enchanting glass coffin."[19] I would therefore argue that if autobiographies are metaphorically thought of as mirrors, then they are in fact "enchanted" mirrors that do not simply reflect the truth as a fixed, frozen, objective state but that answer differently depending on who's interrogating them, and that reflect different images depending on which subject is looking into their surface. These are mirrors that allow us to look not only backward but also forward and inward. I argue that Klüger's most important contribution to the genre is her questioning the veracity, and hence the authority, of this powerful mirror. In doing so, I highlight two important issues raised by this text: whose purposes do its reflections serve, and what role does patriarchy play in the way Klüger frames her mother-daughter story?

Although Zipes remains the scholar who more than anybody else over the last few decades has helped us understand how magic spells are formulated and sustained in culture through fairy tales, my study is also greatly informed by the feminist approach to the genre proposed by Bacchilega in her seminal *Postmodern Fairly Tales*. Discussing the cultural construct of women, Bacchilega takes the example of Snow White, who is artfully constructed as a "natural woman," and this construction encourages "thinking of her and other stereotypical heroines in pre-cultural, unchangeable terms. By showcasing 'women' and making them disappear at the same time, the fairy tale . . . transforms us/them into man-made constructs of 'Woman.'"[20] I will use this position as the backdrop for my inquiry into Shoah autobiography: if autobiography is a genre or mirror with its own mechanisms or magic spells, it too can make essentialized categories such as Woman and Victim disappear. Klüger intuits this danger and in response tries to break the spell by writing a memoir in which she continuously shifts frames of reference and undercuts the reliability of all speakers, including the authoritative voice of the writer who is holding the mirror to her past. This chapter maintains that, although Klüger's autobiography is a Shoah memoir (and therefore simultaneously the least fantastic and most unimaginable of stories), it can be read as a feminist and postmodern fairy tale that rearticulates the repetition implied in performative discourse and unearths the "unexploited or forgotten possibilities"[21] in the repetition of a known story such as the Holocaust.

Furthermore, what Klüger's memoir makes evident is the fact that the unimaginable happens in fairy tales, as it does, surprisingly often—for better and for worse—in history as well.

## GROWING UP AUSTRIAN

Mitteleuropa: a single word, ambitious and imposing, used to describe an entire era and a seemingly limitless place, a luxuriant cultural atmosphere and a stagnant political climate. It is a German word, but it incontestably belongs to Austria. It conjures up images of a fossilized mammoth of an empire, an empire whose ruling classes were erased by history and that was defunct long before it actually came to an end. Mitteleuropa, or Central Europe, was an assortment of nations clustered around the Danube and its tributaries like leaves on the branches of an ancient tree: Hungary, Romania, Bohemia, Slovakia, Serbia, Montenegro, Croatia and the remaining Balkan states, Bulgaria, Moravia, Ruthenia, Galicia, Trentino, and many more territories, villages, and towns with ever-changing names and borders. These were all part of the extended imperial family—its rebellious children incessantly defying Austria's *patria potestas*. In *The Man without Qualities*—the famous novel set at the end of Emperor Franz Josef's reign and just before World War I—Robert Musil erected a nonpareil monument to the decrepitude—moral and political, social and historical—of the Austro-Hungarian dual monarchy, comically referred to as the Land of Kakania from the abbreviation *k. und k.*, for *kaiserlich* (imperial) and *königlich* (royal). *Kakania* was an endless maze of bureaucratic passages, the deterministic yet disconnected algorithm on which each citizen depended and through which each existed. Its center was Vienna: a modern and decadent hub brimming with cafés, operettas, public gardens, private gardens, salons, and royal courts that Sigmund Freud, one of its most famous sons, loved to fiercely hate. Vienna, *à juste titre*, was also the capital station of sordid sexual affairs and suicides.

By the time Ruth Klüger was born in 1931, the whole of Mitteleuropa had imploded, collapsing like a house of cards and leading to a dramatically rearranged geopolitical situation in Europe. Former satellite entities were now independent, self-determining nations experiencing varying degrees of social and political turmoil after the destabilizing earthquake that was World War I. Of course there was still a Central Europe, but the Mitteleuropa of Arthur Schnitzler, Franz Kafka, Gustav Klimt, and Gustav Mahler had disappeared. However, its *mitteleuropäische* atmosphere stubbornly lingered on, especially in Vienna. The Austro-Hungarian Empire died: but not the effervescent culture it had always fostered. Local folklore played an important role in connecting the new cultural climate to the previous era, and such folklore is a particularly vivid element of Klüger's memories of growing up in Austria. The illusory stability created through a folk (or *volkish*) continuity with the past exists as an ironic backdrop to Klüger's recollections: "Vienna was settled early by the Romans and has had a vibrant history, embellished by folklore . . . The Danube, the surrounding mountains, and even ordinary houses in the city . . . are crawling with supernatural creatures, whose stories found their way into our school books."[22] There is no overstating the influence of these children's stories and of the Austro-German folk tradition on a girl born within that Germanic culture that, more than any other, "has incorporated folk and fairy tales in its literary socialization process so that they play a most formative role in cultivating aesthetic taste and value systems."[23] In their nineteenth-century literary incarnations, fairy tales served not only to socialize the young but also to nurture the nation-building ideals of the middle class, especially in Prussia and Austria-Hungary.

Another famous Viennese, the psychiatrist Bruno Bettelheim, had grown up hearing such fantastic stories about his ancestors from his parents that he admitted to having often blurred fantasy and reality. These tales "were significant parts of our family's oral history," he recalled, and "I am sure they made such a deep impression on me at an early age because they contained so many elements of another literary tradition with which I was quite familiar: that of fairy tales . . . For me as a child, it was not their [his grandparents'] true stories which lent veracity to the many fairy tales I knew but the fairy tales that convinced me of the truth of my grandfathers' stories."[24]

In her memoir, Milena Roth recalls two separate introductions to the world of fairy tales: first, the German tradition passed on by her mother while Milena was growing up in Prague; and second, a British tradition she encountered once she arrived in England with a few thousand other Jewish children from the Kindertransport rescue operation. Roth suggests that the children's books she was exposed to in the two countries seeded in her young subconscious two very different imaginative fields. The Grimm brothers wrote eerie and uncanny stories, but the English tales—about Peter Rabbit, Mr. Bultitude and his son Dick's comical exchange of bodies, and the anti-Napoleonic adventures of Marryat's retired Royal Navy captain—were far less burdened by dark undertones and sinister imagery.[25] In Klüger's tragic biography, there is room only for the Germanic folk tales of her Austrian childhood. By the time she reached safety in America, she was too old for the cheerier Anglo-Saxon tales: Auschwitz, which only a few years earlier had imprisoned a child, had released a broken individual who was chronologically still very young but who had none of her childhood innocence left.

About her early years spent in Vienna, Klüger says: "I had been very receptive to a nascent patriotism, and I loved all of my city's old stories. There was the river nymph in the Danube and the monstrous Viennese basilisk, which could kill you with a glance. There was the defeat of the Turks" (Still Alive, 41). Alongside these mythical creatures were quasi-superhuman figures such as Johann Wolfgang von Goethe, not only "Germany's greatest poet but also . . . traditionally invoked as a role model for all kinds of conduct" (Still Alive, 56). Less worthy personages also ascended to a grandiose status, as in the case of the authoritarian interwar chancellor Engelbert Dollfuss, father of Austrian Fascism and the Ständestaat regime: "We were meant to become good, patriotic little Austrians, and so in first grade we learned a song celebrating the martyr-dom of Chancellor Dollfuss . . . murdered by a Nazi, one fascist in effect killing another fascist" (Still Alive, 40). The border between legend and history blurs in the mind of a child, and it takes later revisions to dismantle the mythology these men had created about themselves. In hindsight, the Shoah throws a deforming or reinforming shadow over everything Klüger knew from before Auschwitz, and only from the distance afforded to her by time is the adult narrator able to reassign new meaning to old, crystallized tales: "Even better was the story about Drunken August, who lived at the time of the Great Plague and wasn't scared but got drunk every night after entertaining the crowd with his bagpipe. One night when he was tumbling home, he fell into an open grave, full of corpses. He slept until morning and crawled out of this deadly ditch bright-eyed and not infected. A possible patron saint of the deported who returned, indestructible, lovable, and a little contemptible in the view of those who never got close to the plague of our time. But Jews have no patron saints" (Still Alive, 41–42). Unlike the battle for Vienna in 1683, whose ferocity was quickly buried under a blanket of triumphalism for the victory of the cross over the crescent, and whose token was the recipe of the delicious croissant taken from the Turks just before they were repelled from the gates of Christian Europe, the Jewish war story has no fairy-tale twist, no feel-good ending, no monumental pastry. And yet despite its utter sterility and hopelessness, it compels those who returned from the living graveyards of the Konzentrationslager to speak. The same hindsight that allows Klüger to look on those formative Austrian mythologies with new eyes also allows her to reevaluate those family values that were so fundamental in the national self-understanding and society-building process of the prewar era. Despite the frivolity and coquettishness with which the Belle Époque had spiced lifestyles and culture in the big cities, the bourgeoisie was still clinging to an idyllic, sober, corseted idea of itself. And at the very center of this unrealistic ideal was a family model that required homogeneity and internal coherence, stable gender roles and rigidly defined hierarchies. Yet Klüger's text gives us a more complex, and subversive, picture of turn-of-the-century family life—not homogeneous, coherent, or stable, and with gender roles sometimes reversed and hierarchies ignored whenever possible.

The Klügers belonged to the Viennese upper middle class. Unlike Edith Bruck and Sarah Kofman, who hailed from poor Jewish Orthodox environments, Klüger came from an assimilated Mitteleuropean family that, blessed by the Haskalah and Viennese cultural and social enlightenment, comfortably lived by the *maskil* poet Judah Leib Gordon's motto: "Be a man in the streets and a Jew at home."[26] A closer look into their household reveals a not entirely *gemütlich* family style. Ruth Klüger's mother, Alma, the figure around which *Still Alive* revolves, had been divorced. She had always wanted to live in Vienna, the great capital that was less provincial than her native Prague. She took the initiative of moving there, divorcing her husband and taking with her Schorschi, her only son. In Vienna, Alma married Viktor Klüger, a well-known and respected gynecologist, with whom she had one child, Ruth.[27] During a summer vacation, Schorschi was sent to visit his father, who—taking advantage of this opportunity—obtained custody of the child and refused to return him to his mother. The two never saw each other again. During the war, Schorschi was deported and murdered in Riga.

After the *Anschluss*, which incorporated a willing Austria into the quickly forming Hitlerian empire, and the *Kristallnacht* pogroms of 1938, which in turn were followed by massive arrests of Jewish men, it was concluded that it would be best for Viktor to flee Austria and organize his family's rescue once he was in a safer place.[28] Tragically, the plan failed. Viktor first crossed the border into Italy, and from there he passed into southern France, where he was captured and sent east to his death. Based on Viktor's strategy, we learn that in the early days of the genocide, people still thought it reasonable to assume that women, children, and the elderly would remain unharmed: "Because the Jews believed that only men were in real danger, they responded with gender-specific plans to protect and save their men."[29] Marion Kaplan points out that following the "November Pogrom, in a strange twist of fortune, the men interred in concentration camps were released only upon showing proof of their ability to leave Germany immediately. Families—mostly wives and mothers—strained every resource to provide the documentation to free these men and send them on their way while some of the women remained behind . . . Even as women feared for their men, they believed that they themselves would be spared serious harm by the Nazis."[30] As a consequence of such miscalculations, Alma was left alone in Vienna to care for her daughter, aged mother-in-law, and other elderly family members (who did not survive the war). Eventually, Klüger and her mother were arrested and taken to Theresienstadt; they were later sent to Auschwitz and then other camps, which they survived. While they were in Christianstadt, an orphaned girl, Susi, became Ruth's best friend and a permanent member of the family ("whom I still call my sister," Klüger says [*Still Alive*, 123]). Thanks to Klüger's courage and initiative, the three of them were able to escape from Gross-Rosen in February 1945. Sustained and guided by Alma's strength and resourcefulness, they all managed to reach New York and build new lives. Alma remarried several times, and she helped her two daughters get the all-important academic degrees necessary in postwar America to have careers, attain independence, and achieve integration.

*Still Alive* opens with these words: "Their secret was death, not sex. That's what the grown-ups were talking about, sitting up late around the table" (15). Interestingly, these two concepts, sex and death—the very muses of human outer (art) and inner (subconscious) worlds for Freud—are recognized by Bettelheim, Carl Jung, Erich Fromm, and Mercea Eliade as the underlying psychological concerns allegorically imbedded in and metaphorically thematized by all folk tales and myths. Klüger's autobiography marshals these two opposite yet complementary concepts to tell the story of a daughter and her mother, a story of sex (and the larger gender systems it reflects) and death (loss, abjection, and victimization). Bettelheim, who often wrote about his hometown, psychoanalyzing its nature as if it were an ailing patient on his couch, observed: "In this unique Viennese culture, the strongest inner powers were thanatos and eros, death and sex . . . Viennese culture liked to explore these psychological complexities and embodied them in its creations."[31] Klüger's *Still Alive* is here to tell us about this culture's creative and destructive tendencies.

## THE WICKED (JEWISH) MOTHER

Traditional fairy tales are articulated around fixed structures. They often start by succinctly describing the setting of the story and then quickly transition to the conflict that will sustain the plot's momentum through trials and perils to a resolution and a moral. Similarly, *Still Alive* opens by setting up the scene for the reader and then abruptly turns to the conflict that forms the core of the story. Contrary to expectations, this conflict is not the deportation to or arrival at a concentration camp; rather, it occurs before Auschwitz in the life of a girl in Vienna in the late 1930s. The opening conflict is shaped by the presence of the Nazis but centers on the mother and affects the girl's early perception of maternal figures. Now eight years old, Ruth has one wish: to see *Snow White*.[32] But the Nuremberg Laws banned Jews from all public spaces, including movie theaters, so the girl kvetches about the unfairness of anti-Jewish legislations until, exasperated by her complaints, her mother suggests that she ignore the laws and simply go see the film:

[My] mother proposed that I should leave her alone and just go and forget about what was permitted and what wasn't.

I hesitated a bit at this unexpected go-ahead, for it was a Sunday, we were known in the neighborhood, and to go to a movie right there in broad daylight was a kind of dare. My mother couldn't accept the absurdity of blatant discrimination. She assured me that no one would care who sat in an audience of children. I shouldn't think I was that important, and I should stop being a coward, because she [mother] was never a coward, not even when she was my age. So of course I went, not only for the movie, but to prove myself. (Still Alive, 46)

The challenge the mother throws out to her daughter pushes the girl into action. Little does she know that Ruth is about to learn her own lesson from the Snow White story.

The cinema is full of enemies, both on-screen and off. Ruth shrewdly purchases a ticket for one of the best loge seats, hoping not to meet anybody she knows there and perhaps thinking that the sophisticated people in the loge would not make a fuss over her being in the theater. The scheme fails: a nineteen-year-old girl and her enthusiastically Nazified siblings immediately spot the Jew in the audience. This mob is only referred to as "the children of the local baker," and their anonymity produces both an oddly humorous effect and a fairy-tale-like atmosphere. In fairy tales, the characters' namelessness points to the general validity of the experience undergone by the hero and integrates their presence into the mythical story of good versus evil. As Bettelheim notes, anonymity is of great importance in fairy tales because it makes "clear that [the story] tells about everyman, people very much like us . . . If names appear [in fairy tales], it is quite clear that these are not proper names, but general or descriptive ones."[33] For over an hour, Klüger tells us, she could focus only on the threatening presence of the baker's children and the power they held over her life. In agony, her mind begins to confuse the movie with her own nightmarish reality: "The wicked queen of the film merged with my neighbor, her fairy-tale malice a poor imitation of the real thing, and it was I, and no innocent princess, who was lost in the woods, offered poisoned apples, and in fear of glass coffins" (Still Alive, 46). Her guilt doubly exposed—for having broken a law and for being Jewish—the girl makes sense of the inexplicable events by projecting the movie's plot onto her reality. Like Snow White, who had unwittingly defied the queen by surpassing her in beauty, this Viennese girl had also broken an unfair law (the prohibition) and defied her enemies. In addition, she was Other—Jewish—and would be condemned to death. An interesting subconscious manipulation makes the writer assign to the narrated girl a fear of glass coffins that Snow White cannot have.

Although a sophisticated cultural capital like Vienna is far removed from the world of fairy tales, the absurdity of a world that fashions itself according to an unbending, willful morality that is in fact immoral reveals surprising similarities with those magical realms. In order to get across the uncanniness of a reality that seems to have lost all sense, Klüger ingeniously returns to a childhood memory that involves a fairy tale. The feeling of total disbelief in the horror that was slowly unfolding is often mentioned by Holocaust victims, who look back at the years before the outbreak of war and report a continued inability to understand not so much why (an unanswerable question) but how it could have happened, and specifically how it could have happened to them. It is as if the victims fell into a gap between objective and subjective reality, a horrendous vacuum we could think of as *skepsis*: an abyss in which all assumptions about oneself vis-à-vis the outside world are no longer viable. The prewar years—with their growing restrictions on people's lives, the worsening of antisemitic threats, the bellicose public speeches of various dictators, and so on—were ones of total madness, yet people lived through them under the pretense of sanity. The Jews, even those as young as Klüger, had to relearn how to live; they had to adapt to their suddenly shifted place in the world and quickly understand the new rules to play by. The changes were implemented steadily yet in a piecemeal fashion over the course of a year and a half; they were incremental and unpredictable, not to mention totally nonsensical. One could be shopping at a jeweler's on Kärtnerstrasse (Vienna's most chic boulevard) on Monday but find oneself banned from it on Tuesday. One day, a Jewish child could go to school and expect to sing the national anthem and Christmas carols with other children in class; the following day, those same Christian friends would stop talking to the child, refuse to come to his or her birthday party, and yell anti-Jewish epithets on the street. This was particularly confusing and shocking for two categories of people: utterly assimilated Jews in sophisticated urban settings and children. In *My Knees Were Jumping*, a documentary film about the Kindertransport rescue operation,[34] Erika Estis, one of the interviewees, talks about an antisemitic jingle that children sang on the street when she passed by. After flawlessly reciting it by heart in German, Estis lowers her voice, looks down, and pensively says, almost as if to herself: "These were my friends." After over half a century, it is still incomprehensible to her how the same kids who played with her the day before the *Anschluss* could despise her and publicly harass her the day after it.

The new logic to which the victims were forced to quickly adjust created a schizophrenic split between personal and public reality and between subjective and objective truth. To a certain extent, violence always infantilizes its victims: it is possible, therefore, to turn to certain aspects of child psychology to uncover the effects of abuse and trauma on the adults. The adult whose daily reality has undergone drastic and life-threatening changes must learn to renegotiate his or her position in the larger social universe. In a way, the adult becomes a childlike figure, afraid of committing a mistake in a game whose rules are not entirely revealed to him or her and whose logic is impossible to understand. Klüger consciously labors to define and represent this *skepsis*: the impossibility a child faces in grasping his or her revolutionized circumstances. Survivors-witnesses experienced this split not only during the events but also when they revisit those days of impotence and ignorance. "Why didn't I get up and walk out?" Klüger retrospectively wonders about the incident in the movie theater, and answers herself: "Perhaps in order not to face my mother, or because any move might attract attention" (*Still Alive*, 46). The psyche of the young girl naturally draws a connection between the evil characters in the *Snow White* film and the evil characters in Nazi Vienna, but on further reflection, she also begins to see that the narcissistic queen of the movie and her mother might have something in common, too. The wicked queen who lures Snow White into eating the poisoned apple merges with the narrator's mother, who had dared the young child to defy laws that even adults felt compelled to obey. A child might learn a positive lesson about friendship (through the seven dwarves), love (through the valiant prince) or triumph (through the revenge against the stepmother) from Snow White, but Ruth leaves the movie theater having learned only what it means to be rejected as Other and to mistrust her mother—two lessons also discreetly woven into the fabric of the story. The girl is thus initiated into the tragedy that often arises when private life and history collide. A chasm has opened up, and the girl has learned to recognize how things stand for the Jews in the real world and how things stand for her in relation to her mother, the "wicked queen"— who, in telling her to defy the law and enter the cinema, put her in harm's way. If every fairy tale represents a rite of passage, as Mercea Eliade suggests,[35] then the afternoon at the movie theater represents for the little girl an initiatory scenario, one quickly transferred from the imaginative plane of the film onto the historical plane: "I had found out, for myself and by myself, how things stood between us and the Nazis and had paid for knowledge with the coin of pain . . . I had had the feeling of deadly danger, and this feeling didn't leave me but escalated until it was justified. Without having to think it through, from now on I was ahead of the grown-ups" (*Still Alive*, 47).

The enabler of this terrifying rite of passage is the mother: "I got the impression that I shouldn't trust my mother, that she had only bad advice for me" (*Still*

*Alive*, 48). Folk tales often turn mother figures into stepmothers who impede the full realization of the fair heroine and provide the plot with its necessary peripeteia and conflict. The young girl must feel unjustly treated, misunderstood, or unappreciated by her mother. Mirroring a child's psychic life, fairy tales often hinge on the development and resolution of conflicts between the young and their parents—between sons and fathers or daughters and mothers. A child has to escape the family and explore the relational dynamics of the outside world (in school with friends, in a sympathetic adult world separate from the home). Social adjustment and individuation, according to this arc, would therefore be the positive outcome of the conflict with the mother. The assumption that a war with the mother is necessary for the daughter to reach her potential is of course extremely problematic, and the case in question is rendered even more complex because of the historical circumstances. The child of our story runs away from a wicked mother only to encounter a far more wicked world outside the house. Everything, from possessions to psyches and lives, is destroyed in genocide: childhood itself is shattered. Geoffrey Hartman's statement that "before Auschwitz we were children in our imagination of evil; after Auschwitz we are no longer children"[36] is valid for the survivors as well as for the subsequent generations of this story's listeners. J. R. R. Tolkien assigned to fantasy three positive functions, recovery, escape, and consolation; Bettelheim added a fourth and negative one, threat.[37] The automatic behaviors that sustain a child's imaginative and psychic world, and that are echoed by folk tales, are short-circuited by the Shoah circumstances. There is a concrete, not imaginary, threat imperiling the physical life of the Shoah child, and the anxiety that arises from the clash between inner psychic conflicts and outside material threats plants seeds of resentment toward humanity (in Klüger's case, toward the mother), leading to feelings of anger, confusion, depression, and frailty. The child's world is regulated by a basic principle of justice: good is rewarded, evil punished. G. K. Chesterton idealistically said that "children are innocent and love justice, while most of us are wicked and naturally prefer mercy."[38] But what if justice is turned on its head? What if the child inhabits a reality in which any logical connection between crime and punishment is lost; in which one is punished for no comprehensible reason; and in which, apart from the historical cataclysms, one must also deal with a domestic reality that appears to defy the comforting assumptions that mothers are good, the home is a haven, fathers are protective and strong, and adults know best?

In revisiting the years that preceded Auschwitz, Klüger depicts a mother who is absent and dismissive of many of the child's concerns and fears, which makes her, to the daughter's eye, a kind of wicked queen. The "familiar look" in her mother's eyes, we are told, is "rigid, vacuous," and heralds an impending explosion of "accumulated anxiety and rage" (*Still Alive*, 49–50). The daughter feels lost, alone, and helpless when confronted by this gaze. The psychoanalyst Caroline Eliacheff and the sociologist Nathalie Heinich describe this type of mother as "more woman than mother," one who feels the urge to compete with her daughter and whose commitment to her own life outweighs her commitment to her offspring: "The 'more woman' type figures as the 'bad mother': she is mostly absent, indifferent, and loves poorly. The girl can . . . love herself in her mother's stead, but at least she will be able to complain about it and even turn her impossible love into hate."[39] *Still Alive* spews forth a good measure of this daughterly hate. An unexpressed accusation seems to linger in the air: my mother didn't care about my survival. Can the subconscious desire of such a "more woman than mother" to kill the daughter spill over into conscious reality? The grown-up narrator knows the answer to this question, but the child's sense of self, as well as her perception of the world and her mother, was marred by painful doubt. The adult narrator's knowledge is juxtaposed against the young girl's (Oedipal) blindness.

The girl also believes that the wicked mother has maliciously schemed to separate her from her father (who, as we recall, left her behind in his escape from Austria):

There had been talk that he [father] could take me on his passport. I had forgotten or repressed that idea, but decades later my mother confirmed it. "Viktor had you on his passport and wanted to take you." So why didn't he? Either she didn't want to let me go, or he didn't want to have me along . . . And then I wasn't even permitted to come along to the station . . . Maybe my mother was afraid he and I would leave together at the last moment. Instead I was in bed . . . where one had to go if anything exciting happened. And I thought with tears of resentment how they'd refused all my wishes—even simple, modest wishes they had rejected—and I never knew beforehand when they'd say no. (*Still Alive*, 37)

Unlike the adult narrator who knows she is in the dark as far as her ability to make sense of other people's decisions from over half a century earlier, the narrated child has no doubt about her interpretation of the facts: to the child it is incontrovertible that her father must have wanted to take her along, but the mother must have forbidden it. Indeed, as Bettelheim has pointed out in another context, "this is what the oedipal and adolescent girl wishes to believe about her father: that even though he does as the mother bids him, he would side with his daughter if he were free to, tricking the mother as he did so."[40] The narrator and the reader understand this abandonment scene differently from its protagonist because they are endowed with a historical hindsight that looks back on events and demystifies them. As Nancy K. Miller points out about such autobiographical demystification, the reader is "a partner in crime" of the auto-biographical subject;[41] the reader is the necessary Other whose detached presence helps effect a synthesis among the various historical and compositional truths of the text. Alma, not the "wicked mother" but the loving and clever one, did not want to let go of her daughter: she already made the mistake once of letting a child, Schorschi, slip out from under her control, and as a consequence she lost him forever. This time she made sure that her daughter remained alive, under her protection.

Both the mother and the outside world wear a two-sided mask, and it is impossible for the child to predict which face—the good one or the evil one— she is going to see from one moment to the next. One day Klüger is riding the subway alone, and a man offers an orange to the little Jewish girl with the yellow star sewn on her coat: a small act of compassion by yet another nameless character. But if anonymity in fairy tales serves a universalizing purpose, here it produces the opposite effect. This stranger is not everyman: kindness toward a Jew is the exception, not the rule, in Nazified Vienna. Furthermore, this stranger's kindness elicits an outraged reaction from Alma. When she hears of the incident, she accuses her daughter of being a shameless beggar, of having no dignity, and she feels only disdain, and no sympathy, for the difficult position in which Klüger had found herself. By accepting the gift, she debased herself in the mother's eyes, but had she refused it and thus made a fuss over the man's unsolicited charity, she would have risked condemning him to arrest for breaking the law that forbade Aryans from interacting with a Jew: "I was helpless before this moral double bind: my mother's disapproval, the stranger's goodwill" (Still Alive, 50).

Another conflict between mother and daughter arises from Alma's disapproval of Klüger's love of poetry. The mother repeatedly discourages Ruth's artistic ambitions, and even after Klüger becomes a professor and a writer, she is acutely aware that her mother "considered my career an embarrassment" (Still Alive, 210). Klüger is not alone among the girls of her generation to report that a daughter's artistic ambitions were likely to be thwarted by tyrannical parents, other family members, or someone else wielding influence in their lives. This resistance is a recurring theme in all the texts examined in Holocaust Mothers and Daughters, and it is widespread in the literature and experience of young women from that era in general.[42] For instance, in her multilayered memoir, Sophie Freud (Sigmund Freud's granddaughter) repeatedly highlights the sad stories of women such as her maternal grandmother, Ida Drucker, a phenomenally talented performer whose singing career was never allowed to take off because of her father's stern opposition to it.[43] Apparently critics raved about her public performances, and the prestigious Staatsoper in Berlin was ready to welcome her. Ida's father, however, devised a plan that would thwart his daughter's artistic ambition; he married her off to the first Jewish suitor who came along, Leopold Drucker—who followed in his father-in-law's footsteps and forbade his talented and beautiful wife to ever pursue a singing career. Ida died in a concentration camp. Just as her grandmother's singing career had been cut short by an unfeeling father and husband, so Sophie's desire to pursue an academic career in the humanities was unbendingly opposed by her own mother, who used a variety of tactics—such as vetoing the idea, fainting, and becoming hysterical—to prevent it and ultimately succeeded.

Alma Klüger also shows characteristics of another "mother typology," or what Eliacheff and Heinich define as the "failing mother" (mère défaillante),[44] who alternates among various personae: guardian angel (whose presence ensures that as long as she is around, her daughter shall never fear for her life), girlfriend and accomplice, or irresponsible little girl (who provokes a response of exaggerated seriousness and responsibility on the part of the daughter, who suddenly sees herself as her mother's mother or protector). In discussing what Heinz Kohut calls "the injured self,"[45] Jerrold Post explains that often the rejection "by cold and ungiving mothers" is one of the causes of the "injury" that damages the child's sense of self. He adds: "A special form of rejection is overprotection by the intrusive narcissistic mother. She cannot let her child individuate because she sees him as an extension of herself. Her own sense of perfection seems to depend on her child's perfection."[46] To the various forms that the "bad mother" type can take, Alma adds the extra pungent shibboleth of the "Jewish mother" archetype: a paranoid, jealous, and intrusive mother who cripples her children's psyche and whose mothering is smothering. Klüger sketches a portrait of a Jewish mother that is in keeping with the stereotypical image evoked in so much of Jewish comedy: "[She] tortured me with her anxieties. She alluded to the suicide attempts of unnamed women; she talked about fatal illnesses and the imagined destination of the ever more frequent transports of deportees . . . When I came home to our cramped quarters from a rare outing with other Jewish kids, happy and exhausted from running around in the open air, she'd paint the specter of deadly pneumonia, which I was very likely to have caught, she said. She persuaded me that I had flat feet (I don't) . . ." (Still Alive, 54). But the one time Klüger becomes seriously ill, Alma doesn't pay any attention to her daughter's agony (Still Alive, 56). In addition, Alma responds to the crazy historical circumstances in a curious way: "My mother turned superstitious and regularly frequented a fortune-teller . . . She talked about a miracle-working rabbi who had been an ancestor of hers and whose spirit protected the family in times of need" (*Still Alive*, 56). Odd though her strategy may have been, it's not altogether inexplicable that for Alma, magic, superstition, and mysticism begin to look like perfectly reasonable options once reality becomes so irrational. Many European Jews such as Alma were the neurotic products of a millennia-long oppression, and to them the Holocaust provided not a motivation for, but a confirmation of, their worst fears. On the one hand, the narrator sees herself as the product of this crippling Jewish psychic genealogy, thus inserting herself, her mother, and her whole family into the larger discourse on the European Jew as endemically sick, inadequate, agonizing, and thus partly responsible for his or her tragic fate. On the other hand, she challenges this view by providing a broader context. Melanie Kaye/Kantrowitz hits on an important issue when she points out that "fuzzy boundaries between the self, family and community can be a sign of Jewish health."[47] Paradoxically, the mother's paranoid mistrust, fearful guardedness, and invasive possessiveness prove to be a healthy answer amid the unhealthiest of historical circumstances.

Riffing on Lessing's phrase, "there are things which must cause you to lose your reason or you have none to lose,"[48] the Viennese existential psychoanalyst and Holocaust survivor Viktor Frankl illustrates the surprisingly self-preserving powers of the human mind vis-à-vis the unexpected and the unbearable: "An abnormal reaction to an abnormal situation *is* normal behavior."[49] This is clarified once Klüger and her mother arrive in Auschwitz: the Jewish mother's disturbed ego turns out to be quite an asset in the disturbing reality of the death camps because the troubling surroundings now reflect the mother's troubled mind, which had handicapped her in the "normal" circumstances before Auschwitz. Once in the camps, the young daughter finally sees the world through her mother's eyes. When the disturbed outside matches the mother's disturbed inside, the daughter realizes that her mother, constantly fearing the arrival of some imminent threat, had been right all along. That is, it is the adult, writing daughter who realizes this; the young girl could not have possibily arrived at any such illuminating insight amid the all-obscuring horror of Auschwitz. Auschwitz was no location for enlightenment, *Bildung*, or self-improvement.

Not much is revealed about the torments of their months in the camps.[50] What Klüger chooses to describe instead are touching flashbacks of a network of nurturing female support and an astounding motherly heroism that preserves her daughter's life and that of Susi, the orphaned girl. In the camps, the mother applies the same technique she had used in Vienna to push her daughter to go to the movie theater, daring her to defy the terrifying Nazi authorities. But now, the "wicked queen" does so to save "Snow White," not to put her in harm's way. When faced with the last, fatal *Selektion*, the mother's unsentimental reaction, triggered by desperation, saves the girl's life. Not without a touch of Jewish humor, the tragic moment is described as follows:

> Two ss men conducted the selection . . . He condemned me as if I had stolen my life and had no right to keep it . . . We [mother and I] stood on the street between the two rows of barracks and argued. She tried to persuade me that I should try a second time, with the other ss man in the other line, and claim that I was fifteen . . . "You are a coward," she said half desperately, half contemptuously, and added, "I wasn't ever a coward." So what could I do but go in a second time . . . I had proved to my mother that I wasn't chicken . . . I had won an extension on life. (*Still Alive*, 104–8)

The patches of memory sewn together by the daughter compose a portrait of a mother who is both victim and victimizer, innocent and guilty. Alma's presence in her daughter's life is both life-saving and life-threatening, salvific and condemnatory. Made abnormally harsh, paranoid, and tyrannical by the school of life, this mother is also logical, loving, and eager to defy the odds which oppressive sociopolitical systems set against women, and against this mother and daughter specifically.

In Kafka's short masterpiece *In the Penal Colony*, an utterly unjust justice system delivers its sentence by writing it on the flesh of the condemned citizen, who eventually dies under the torture of this etching. In a way, Alma is a mother whose mind and body bear the marks, like the prisoner in Kafka's story, of the sentence that patriarchal society has carved on her. However, as I hope to show, although patriarchy's text is being written over the female experience, and although patriarchal violence scars the female body, Klüger and her mother cooperate to weave their own alternative, intersubjective story, of which *Still Alive* is one expression.

## FAILING FATHERS

In the dominant tradition of Western fairy tales, fathers are more weak than wicked, and children must contend instead with malicious older women (usually stepmothers or witches). In his remarkable study of French baroque *contes de fées*, Lewis Seifert notices that "most fathers play only a marginal role at best" and that "the marginality and, even, absence of fathers is in sharp contrast, and perhaps inversely proportional to their symbolic importance."[51] Moreover, fathers in *contes de fées* are rarely classified as either "good" or "bad" as mothers regularly are, and, most important, "wayward fathers come around in the end whereas 'evil' stepmothers can never be redeemed."[52] Klüger, Kofman, Bruck, and Frank all seem to confirm that in the child's understanding of reality, the idyllic love between her and her father is disrupted and imperiled by the appearance of the mother, who figures as a stepmother or intruder. In Klüger's case, the mother intrudes upon her daughter's relationship with her German nanny in Vienna, with her girlfriends once they are in America, and, crucially, with her father as well: "My father came home with the new currency [the German one that replaced the Austrian currency] and showed it to me . . . My father explained the value of the new money and imitated the weird pronunciation of the invaders. In brief, we had fun. My mother indicated that this was scandalously childish behavior in desperate times. I didn't understand what she meant and wondered if she was right . . . or if she was being a spoilsport" (Still Alive, 29).

Not unlike the "failing father" we encountered in the childhood story of Edith Bruck, Viktor Klüger is also depicted as powerless in the world—albeit tyrannical at home—and as the object of the daughter's complete adoration. Klüger describes him as "a person of absolute and yet phony authority, a tyrant with great charisma who was no last resort, for he didn't return" (Still Alive, 37). Klüger can find no resolution to her doubts stemming from the ambivalence of a father who, to her younger self, seemed to oscillate between obeying the mother's law and defying it: to help her "kill" the rival daughter or save her. Her relationship with her father is an unfinished and unresolved business, as she explains (Still Alive, 33). The following passage describes a central episode that captures the ambivalence and sorrow that still surround the daughter's memory of her father:

> There was a big luncheon, lots of family, and I had been allowed to invite my best friend to show her my newly released father [he had just returned from a temporary internment in Buchenwald]. He was talking, and everyone was listening to him; he was the center of attention, and I wanted to be noticed by him, contact him, probably be reassured about the abrupt changes in our lives. All it got me was a thrashing such as I had never had before, in front of my wide-eyed friend—the humiliation of it!—and being banished from the family table. To this day I don't know why or how I made him so mad, and to this day I would like to know and make up for it. But that was not to be: it's my last impression of him, forever connected with terror, violence, injustice, and the deep regret of having been misunderstood. Again these incorrigible memories. (Still Alive, 36)

The child could not understand what happened, and the adult writer could find it out only through her mother's help; Klüger needs parental validation of her own memories. However, experience seems to have taught Klüger that people can't be always trusted ("they themselves [the adults] lied without batting an eyelash, even about drastic matters" [(Still Alive, 36)] and that her mother in particular uses "language for manipulation, not to express an opinion or state a fact. What sounded like a fact might be a lie" (Still Alive, 197). Klüger's motto becomes "honor the dead, but mistrust the living" (Still Alive, 151).

Without further help from the outside world to correct or adjust the unreliable (as much as "incorrigible") memories she has of her father, Klüger is left with the picture of a fun yet unjust father, a powerful head of the family yet a powerless father without good choices (leave the daughter behind or drag her with him to their death?). In fact, she realizes how little she knows of her father. One day, the adult daughter discovers the details of how men in the gas chambers were found dead lying on top of the weakest victims, women and children who didn't have enough strength to crawl upward for a last breath of air. Klüger succinctly distills her traumatic discovery in this vision: "I see my father as an authoritative figure in the life of a small girl. That he ended up in a cramped room, naked, swallowing poison gas . . . makes all these memories singularly insignificant . . . There is a gap between knowledge and memory, and I can't bridge it" (Still Alive, 33). This passage was already used in Klüger's reflections on her father's life and death in weiter leben: Eine Jugend, originally published in Germany in 1992 (see the introduction) and from which Still Alive derives. As Klüger was translating this particular section into English for Still Alive, she received an e-mail message from a Frenchwoman who had read weiter leben and wanted to inform her that she had the list of deportees' names for Transport 73, the one that had carried Viktor Klüger out of Drancy to his death. It turned out that, contrary to what Klüger had believed all her life, her father did not die in Auschwitz's gas chambers but on that transport headed to the Baltic States. She reacts to this new knowledge thusly: "Now my mental furniture has to be rearranged . . . How did he die then? I know so little about who he was, and now I don't even know this final, inalterable fact. These stories have no end" (Still Alive, 40). The survivor's crammed mind has to rearrange its contents time and again, and even after such labor, certain images will never fit together. There are only composite truths, the narrated self and the narrator each composing its own arrangement.

Interestingly, while mothers are either good or wicked in fairy tales, fathers are frequently presented as either good or simply unsuccessful. Bettelheim describes the latter type as "weak" and therefore useless to his children.[53] His psychoanalytical interpretation matches up almost too neatly with his analysis of other weak fathers from the historical (specifically Jewish) context, on whom he delivers an infamously severe judgment. He sees the (male) European Jew as having internalized the surrounding antisemitic hatred, which, according to him, explains the Jew's failure to survive Auschwitz and to save his family. At one point the target of Bettelheim's fiery darts is Otto Frank, whom he faults for the family's demise.[54] In doing so, Bettelheim, like others before him, dangerously categorizes the Jewish male as being either good (the resistance fighter) or bad (the sheepish father).[55] In summarizing Bettelheim's move, which ultimately works to discredit Anne Frank's legacy in view of her father's guilt, Sander Gilman remarks that the bad Jew (Otto Frank) invalidates all testimony and condemns "the speaking witness as the lying witness."[56] Bettelheim's accusation is constantly challenged and refuted by memoirs such as Klüger's that force us to confront the full complexity of what we call identity (and the way oppression affects this identity). These memoirs reexamine the role of personal agency in the worst of circumstances—an agency that Bettelheim's concept of the completely dehumanized victim rules out—and the concrete obstacles of the early twentieth-century patriarchal world that foreclosed chances of success, especially for women.

Writing from postwar America, Bettelheim was nostalgic for the notion of the father as absolute and uncontested master of the home (or castle) and as the victorious hero of history. As we will see, this vision predictably affected Bettelheim's reading of fairy tales as well. He considered the modern father's ego to have been mortally wounded by contemporary culture. Unfortunately, in his idealized tale of a phallocratic *domus*, Bettelheim disregarded history. If successful fathers are those who guarantee a "family's physical existence and . . . its emotional well-being,"[57] what of those fathers who failed at this task when confronted by a well-organized war waged against them by a perfectly civilized, patriarchal society of which they themselves had been a part? And what of those other men, Nazis and victimizers, who were excellent fathers and husbands in their own homes?

Bettelheim claims that a child's sense of "greatness" derives exclusively from the example provided by the father: a father who toils, who is in charge, who reads Scripture to an enthralled family. Daydreaming, the expression of a child's playful psyche, is spurred on by what the child sees his father doing, according to Bettelheim: "The ideal 'doing together' shows the child the validity of his daydreams of future greatness because, while he dreamed them, something real was achieved by his father."[58] Needless to say, Bettelheim's daydreaming child is a boy. Although the role of the mother is that of an emotional nurturer, the role of the father, according to this vision, remains "to protect against the outside world and to teach how to meet this world successfully . . . We all need both: someone [the mother] who always takes our side and sees things our way, no matter what: and also someone [the father] who, though definitely on our side, can be relied on to give us sound advice even if it goes against our wishes, who responds to our needs by seeing them in a broader perspective."[59] The women writers I consider in the present book did not experience such universal fathers in their lives—no fairy-tale king, no righteous knight, and no infallible God the Father.

This vein of masculinist rhetoric used by Bettelheim was still predominant in the 1940s and 1950s, and it was the kind of rhetoric that Klüger and her mother encountered in America after they left Europe. Some Jews like Bettelheim, who had made it to the United States before the war or in time not to witness the worst, patronized these newcomers[60] and tried to push them back into roles that had lost all credibility, to push them into a social identity ("to play lady" as Klüger puts it [Still Alive, 141]) that had proved useless if not deleterious just a few years earlier and whose pernicious vacuity had been revealed. Once in New York, Klüger and her mother had to face the petty pretentiousness and the emotional, as well as economic, stinginess of those family members and friends who had made it to America before the war. These earlier immigrants dreaded their female relatives' presence because it was a reminder of their own guilt and responsibility toward those left behind to die. Because in her family "the women had survived, not the men," Klüger explains, those who made it through were not worth enough to repay the Jewish world for its immeasurable loss, and "that meant that the more valuable human beings [men] had lost their lives" (Still Alive, 184).

The young immigrant girl, Ruth, seeks traces of her father in all the men from the Old World she encounters in America; she thinks that they all have his voice. "Viennese male voices resemble each other," Klüger writes (Still Alive, 201). Their Austrian accent is Klüger's version of the Proustian madeleines. But the Austrian-German accent of her father that she initially hears everywhere will gradually be forgotten. What finally pushes the father's "voice" out of the girl's head is not the passage of time but the association she quickly draws between that idealized paternal voice of her childhood and the disheartening behavior of the surrounding male world. Klüger cannot find any warmth or support from the male world before or after the war, and she clearly associates the violence of the Shoah with male power.[61] Furthermore, to trace in another man's voice the lost presence of the dead father would be a sentimental act, and in her *Weltan-schauung*, the sentimental is a lie and thus banned from Klüger's remembrance of things past. Like Bruck, Klüger refuses to sentimentalize life, that of the living or the dead. She refuses to fit the role of the good Jewish girl for the sake of

America's optimistic, future-oriented society, or for the past-oriented Jewish world "which reduces its daughters to helpmeets of men and circumscribes their spiritual life within the confines of domestic functions" (*Still Alive*, 30), or for a religion that forbids a woman—that forbids her—to say kaddish for her father.

The end of the Holocaust does not mark the end of her suffering; *Still Alive* forcefully reminds us of the cost of survival. Klüger experiences tremendously painful feelings of rejection in America from those whom she thought would be able to take the place of her father: "Today I understand (though still not fully) that these men [Jewish male refugees who had spent the war years in America] had their own agenda . . . the Jewish catastrophe was mainly and merely a re-sounding humiliation to them" (*Still Alive*, 187). Through the nexus between death and gender systems that underpins the structure of her narrative, Klüger reveals the double bind in which female survivors found themselves, guilty for having survived yet still struggling against an oppressive gender system.

It is not surprising, therefore, that Klüger entertains thoughts of suicide. "I wondered whether I could make myself drown in a river like the Hudson . . . And so I stumbled through days of psychic imbalance with suicidal thoughts, talking to my ghosts" (*Still Alive*, 191), writes Klüger about her safe days in America, where death, like a mythical siren, enticed her more than once. The annals of twentieth-century Jewish history are full of people who chose suicide as a remedy for a psychically (if not physically) intolerable life: Walter Benjamin, Paul Celan, Jean Améry, Robert Maxwell, Stefan Zweig and his wife Lotte, Arthur Koestler and his wife Cynthia, Jerzy Kosinski, Piotr Rawicz, Primo Levi, the "assisted" death of Sigmund Freud in London, and Sarah Kofman. Even Alma Klüger attempted, unsuccessfully, to take her life while in New York. The list is long, and I will end here with one last significant name: Bruno Bettelheim, who asphyxiated himself with a plastic bag in 1990.

## BROTHERS AND SISTERS : THE UGLY DUCKLING SYNDROME

There are several sets of motifs regarding siblings in the folk-tale tradition. For instance, sisters often figure as wicked stepsisters, and brothers often figure as the (incestuous) allies of younger sisters. Sibling rivalry is a recurrent theme, in which the "lesser" (usually youngest) child—who symbolizes the successful integration of id, ego, and superego—triumphs in the end. This is the so-called ugly-duckling scenario and is often imbedded in the bildungsroman narrative (which *Still Alive* partially adopts). Bettelheim interprets this scenario as follows: "A small child, bright though he may be, feels himself stupid and inadequate when confronted with the complexity of the world which surrounds him. Everybody seems to know so much more than he, and to be so much more capable."[62] Is such an arc applicable to Still Alive? Klüger had a half-brother, Schorschi, to whom she was very attached—a "first role model," she calls him (Still Alive, 28). Although brief, her acquaintance with this older role model left a lasting impression on her. Yet in the reconstruction of her family picture, Klüger does not fail to include the book-perfect scenario of sibling rivalry played out around her relationship with Schorschi—not the real brother brutally murdered by the Nazis, but his ghost. At one point, Klüger asks her mother, "Whom do you like better, him [Schorschi] or me?" and suffers the consequences of such puerile curiosity when, in response, Alma blatantly voices her preference: "Schorschi, because I have known him longer." Klüger laments that "sixty years later . . . I still hear her say it" (Still Alive, 29). The unspeakable way in which Schorschi's life ended leaves a deep wound on both Alma's and Klüger's psyches. Once again, this memoir highlights how the Shoah experience twists the meaning of every archetypal situation for the child who triumphs over genocide. Implicitly, Still Alive seems to ask how one can reconcile one's rivalry with a sibling for the mother's love when the sibling in question was murdered in a concentration camp. Not surprisingly, this issue often comes up in the autobiographical works of second-generation authors. In his graphic postwar memoir, Maus, Art Spiegelman talks about his brother, whom he never knew: Richieu was killed by the Nazis at the age of six. His photograph hangs in their parents' bedroom, and Artie, the narrator, says: "The photo never threw tantrums or got in any kind of trouble . . . it was an ideal kid, and I was a pain in the ass. I couldn't compete."[63] Like Vladek and Anja, Spiegelman's parents, Klüger's mother mourned the loss of her son all her life: "And suddenly she'd say to me: 'You can't know this, but I think of him [Schorschi] every day.' She never asked whether I thought of him, whether he meant something to me. And I confess, I was so suspicious that I mistrusted the full extent of her grief and speculated to what extent she was playacting. Perhaps I was simply jealous of her greater right to mourn him" (Still Alive, 80). Long after the war, Alma keeps bringing up Schorschi's memory as a devastatingly effective way to hurt her daughter: "If it hadn't been for you, I would have saved him [Schorschi]" (Still Alive, 29). We are faced with the perfect archetype of the wicked queen tormenting a Snow White–like daughter. However, we must ask ourselves whether this is the child's or the adult's perspective that has disturbingly cast the story in these fabulistic terms.

Another fairy-tale motif operative in Still Alive is that of the mother who favors her legitimate children over her stepchildren. This plays out through Alma's relation to Susi, the daughter she had "adopted" at Christianstadt but whom, after the war, she treated with some cruelty. Klüger tells us: "Susi always thought that my mother saved her life . . . For us, Susi [during the internment days] was not only a presence, she was important . . . Without us she would have remained isolated; with us she was part of a family, and thus valuable . . ." But Klüger then punctures this feel-good story. "Dear reader," she warns us, "don't wax sentimental. We are a family, which means we are like other families, only perhaps a bit worse. In later years my mother often rejected the woman [Susi] whom she had once treated as her own child," to the point where she wouldn't allow Susi to enter her home (Still Alive, 123). Alma, as paranoid as ever, was apparently terrified that Susi, who by then was an accomplished psychiatric nurse, was scheming to have her institutionalized. But this fear passed with time, and in old age Alma became reconciled with Susi (who had patiently waited for Alma's fear of her to fade) and accepted her again. However, Alma's panic-stricken and irrational reactions at the mention or sight of Susi had a terrible emotional effect on Klüger, who considered Susi an older sister and found herself caught between love and loyalty toward Susi and the insane demands of her psychologically damaged mother. In the world of fairy tales, the wicked queen's presence brings about a trial that leads the child to self-confidence, differentiation, and a discovery of her or his independence and strength, but the archetype kick starts no such journey for the girl in Still Alive. The child and young adult reconstructed in the text might have found solace and pleasure in the fairy tales she read, but their allegedly universal lessons, the adult author tells us, do not apply to her particular story, at times even clash with lessons she learns from her own tragic history. Schorschi's story resists being reduced to a category of the imagination; Susi was not a wicked stepsister, but a beloved one with whom Klüger shared a terrible past in which they had united to defeat death. In reworking the sibling-rivalry scenario, Klüger does not allow us to take our attention away from the tyranny of patriarchal hegemonic structures. The fairy tale's principle is that an a priori combination of biological and divine design has chosen some people to emerge, survive, and triumph over everyone else. In Still Alive, the narrated self is well aware of her "ugly duckling" status, both in her own family and in the broader society. "Therefore," explains Klüger, "this is not the story of a Holocaust victim, and becomes less and less so as it nears the end. I was with them [the murdered ones, her brother among them] when they were alive, but now we are separated. I write in their memory, and yet my account unavoidably turns into some kind of triumph of life" (Still Alive, 138).

Bettelheim reproaches Hans Christian Andersen for the pessimism of his classic story The Ugly Duckling. Bettelheim objects to the undeserving character of the hero in Andersen's story, who relies on fate and a measure of predestination for redemption or salvation. What bothers Bettelheim is that the ugly duckling will turn into a majestic swan without having had to accomplish anything. Calling this a "depressive world-view," he claims that a child's "chance for success in life is not to grow into a being of a different nature as the duckling grows into a swan, but to acquire better qualities and to do better than others expect, being of the same nature as his parents and siblings . . . that he must do something to achieve his superiority."[64] Despite Bettelheim's objections to the tale, its nontriumphalist tone offers a suitable model for a Shoah child's desires and expectations. For a child whose survival or triumph owes so much to chance and indeed fate—as a Shoah child would know—the tale's "depressive world-view" resonates strongly. Bettelheim also underestimates a child's desire to grow into a different breed—or to be born under the star of a less threatening identity, for instance. Klüger's narrated self fantasizes about escaping her sense of smallness through an ugly duckling–like transformation. Referring to her first years in America, she writes: "I felt inferior, saw myself through the eyes of others, and there were times when it seemed that instead of having been liberated, I had crawled away like a cockroach from the exterminator . . . I would have liked to be a man, and preferably not a Jew" (Still Alive, 185). This wish projects a metaphorical desire for individuation and separation as much as the desire to escape from a culture that is oppressive and repressive. For her younger self, indeed, it would have been providential to morph into a royal swan, as happens to the ugly duckling in Andersen's story.

Far from feeling victorious (or "superior") for having survived when her brother did not, Klüger makes two things clear. First, her survival cannot be equated to a fairy-tale triumph because the deaths of millions, including her brother, afflicted the survivors with a sense of guilt or muteness, opening an unbridgeable gulf that will forever prevent the successful integration of the individual and collective id, ego, and superego. And second, her feelings of inadequacy were neither natural or neutral: they were caused by people who refused to sympathize with her situation, take her pain seriously, or simply listen to her. One of these people, Klüger explains, is Dr. Lazi Fessler, an old friend of her father in Vienna who resumed practicing psychiatry in New York after escaping, and whom Alma had secretly hoped to marry. Klüger is brought to Fessler by her mother, who hopes to get expert help for her difficult daughter. During the first visit "he had snapped at me," Klüger remembers, "perhaps because I had tried to take part in the conversation instead of just smiling sweetly" (Still Alive, 186). Fessler takes every chance to reprimand the girl, we are told, and keeps addressing her with the distancing Sie, the formal address in German, rather than du, the informal "you," which Klüger "would have taken . . . as a sign of goodwill to the sixteen-year-old daughter of his murdered friend" (Still Alive,

187). Fessler apparently did not particularly believe in post-traumatic disorders and was therefore of no help to the girl. Klüger traces her feelings of inadequacy back to other people as well. For instance, there is her rich Austrian uncle, the new American living on Long Island, who looks down on her and her mother as the needy, broken relatives from the Old World. Furthermore, back in Vienna there is a great-uncle who, had Ruth been a boy, "would have treated me differently, that I was sure of. Boys had to study . . . But girls did not need that" (Still Alive, 50). Klüger also remarks that these people are products of a society and culture that values the male child over the female, but she finds Americans no different: "Our circle [of American friends and family] took due notice [of my behavior] and disapproved . . . Had I been a boy, no one would have minded my long, lonely, nightly walks through Manhattan or the fact that a couple of years later I hitch-hiked with a few other girls to Canada . . . In a girl such self-assertive conduct was unforgivable" (Still Alive, 175–76).

Klüger has many memories of gender-specific double standards on which to draw. For example, she remembers how the wonderful Jewish holidays, which one is supposed to look back on nostalgically, in fact segregate rather than include women: "Passover is an imaginative feast and appealed to a little girl who loved poetry . . . But in truth, it is all these good things for men and children, and scarcely for women" (Still Alive, 44). Even the visionary father of Israel, a son of fin de siècle Vienna, did not have a broad enough vision to include women in his otherwise accurate predictions of the Jewish future: "Even Theodor Herzl, the founder of political Zionism and our hero and guru, who hailed from my part of the world, believed that it was the duty of Jewish wives to be especially supportive of their husbands, because only men had to put up with anti-Semitism" (Still Alive, 72). And in the family, the son is the ultimate Jewish boon: her father "aborted a child of his own, which would have been a boy, my mother says, and he was 'sad for days'" (Still Alive, 35). Of course, had there been such a small baby in the family, even a boy, none of them would have survived their arrival in Auschwitz, because Mengele had specifically ordered that pregnant women and women with small children be gassed right away.

The narrator of this memoir leads us through her dystopian fairy tale, delivering unexpected twists to various archetypal staples. Bacchilega warns us that a fairy tale "reflects and conforms to the way things 'truly' are, the way our lives are 'truly' lived. As with all mirrors, though, refraction and the shaping presence of a frame mediate the fairy tale's reflection."[65] So Klüger's story—bounded by death, the Shoah, and patriarchal gender roles—reflects the true state of things while opening up the narrative to the possibility of revolt and gender disidentification. By recognizing and showcasing the process of identity production through the speaking mirror of her memoir, Klüger uncovers the forces that mold identity and impel agency. As Judith Butler puts it, understanding identity as an effect "means that it is neither fatally determined nor fully artificial and arbitrary."[66] Klüger seems to embrace this same understanding. She conceives of identity as arising from the compulsive reflection of mother and daughter. But because the reflection is also controlled and regulated by the forces of patriarchy, she reframes her story so as to reflect what the archetypal universals fail to show. The artifice behind identity making, gender systems, familial dynamics, and intrafamilial power structures reveals itself in the mirror of this reflective autobiography, and no one is exonerated for his or her contribution to the injurious effects of these processes and structures.

## CONCLUSIONS : DISENCHANTING THE MIRROR, DISPELLING THE MOTHER

Bettelheim fabricates an unconvincing explanation for the rare appearance of bad fathers in fairy tales, arguing that because the father is not as present as the mother in the home, the boy's imagination can minimize the father's importance in its psychic struggles. Hence, Bettelheim deduces, "the father who blocks the boy's oedipal desires is not seen as an evil figure within the home or split into two figures, one good and one bad, as the mother often is. Instead, the oedipal boy projects his frustrations and anxieties onto a giant, monster, or dragon."[67] However, Bettelheim claims that a girl's imagination takes a different route, splitting the mother into two competing forces (good and bad) and thus allowing her to save the father, whose ineffectuality can be blamed not on him but on higher powers—such as the stepmother's influence or dark magic. Thus, I conclude, the boy, by recasting his Oedipal grudge onto ogres and monsters, can save the real father while the girl is incapable of saving the mother through such imaginative rerouting; instead, she sacrifices the mother and still manages to free the father from all responsibility. Bettelheim, who misses this central implication, goes on to optimistically report that "both oedipal girls and boys, thanks to the fairy tale, can have the best of two worlds: they can fully enjoy oedipal satisfactions in fantasy and keep good relations to both parents in reality."[68] But this is not the case. The boy is able to have the best of both worlds because by projecting his hatred for the father onto external forces, he secures the domestic world in which he will be king. However, the girl shatters the domestic idyll, is deprived of the good mother, and fights for the love of an ineffectual father against the powers of an evil woman. The girl has no place to stay or go back to.

"A girl can love her mother more," Bettelheim postulates, "because she puts out all her anger at the mother-competitor, who gets what she deserves—as Snow White's step-mother is forced to put on 'red-hot shoes, and dance until she dropped dead' . . . The boy can love his real father even better after having gotten out all his anger at him through a fantasy of destroying the dragon or the bad giant."[69] Yet, in truth, fairy tales produce a less joyous aftermath: a scene emptied of the mother's presence. Bad fathers either don't exist or are redeemed, but mothers are lost for good; the bad mother is slain, and the good mother is already dead before the story begins. Exeunt mothers. The girl remains alone with her prince, or a king, or maybe a brother: does she no longer need women, then? Not surprisingly, female bonding is rarely the stuff of traditional fairy tales.[70] On the contrary. *Still Alive*, which I have been arguing reworks the fairy-tale pattern to retell the most unfairy-tale-like story, casts female friendship as the most important factor in the narrator's life and survival. The mother's influence and the bonds of female friendships are what made this heroine's triumph possible. Klüger concludes: "I had spent my life among women, and this didn't change in New York. In my family, in the camps, and even after the war, men had been at the periphery of my life. It was true that from that periphery they called the shots because they had the power, and my mother never ceased to assure me that a woman needed to marry someone who'd provide for her. But her own example was different" (*Still Alive*, 179). This inflexible, paranoid, and difficult ("bad") mother, so concerned with pleasing male expectations, had extricated herself from an unfulfilling marriage, left her hometown, "a rather unusual step in those days" (*Still Alive*, 27), and aborted an unwanted pregnancy. On the one hand, Klüger emphasizes the crippling faults of her mother; on the other hand, she admits that her own strength, subversiveness, and feminism were inspired by her mother's example.

Because Klüger recognizes all of these complex aspects that make up her and her mother's past, a past extending well beyond the frame of Auschwitz, the end of the war does not signal the end of her book. Only one of the text's four sections concerns itself strictly with the experience in the camps. Klüger's war with her mother continues beyond Auschwitz, and so does her war with a world that wants to forget the atrocity and imposes its own dastardly denial on the survivors as well. The moral core of fairy tales, myths, and even biblical stories is found in the final administration of justice (be it *redde rationem* or *lex talionis*). But this reckoning had to be brushed aside in Klüger's tale of survival because of the demands of postwar realpolitik. Survivors could not hope for justice—how could justice be measured or delivered? Instead, they had to content themselves with having a new chance at reentering society, often one that had not particularly objected to seeing them disappear en masse. America promised a future, though only in exchange for deleting the past. Klüger's Long Island parvenu aunt advises the young girl to "erase from [her] memory everything that happened in Europe," an absurd proposition for a camp survivor: "I thought, she wants me to get rid of the only thing that I own for sure: my life, that is, the years I have lived" (*Still Alive*, 177). Although Alma edits her birth record to take six years off her life and erase a period she refuses to recognize as hers, her daughter, for whom those six years represented a third of her life, refuses to disown that experience. Klüger writes: "She [mother] forced me into little girl dresses for which I was too grown-up and too plump . . . My mother consistently pretended to be six years younger than she really was. Six years is the length of World War II. Perhaps she didn't want to have aged in those years. She pretended that the Nazi years had washed over me, as if, being a child, I hadn't been quite conscious of what was happening" (*Still Alive*, 180).

In America, Klüger's conflicts with her mother reemerge. The larger human narrative of which the two of them are constructed discourses slowly forms again after the war, as the world tries to reestablish its old hierarchal structures. On the one hand, the postwar world demands amnesia as much as universal amnesty (so that the victimizers as well as the victims can be reintegrated into the normal flow of life, and all wrongs can expediently be set aside); it is imperative to rebuild and move on. On the other hand, in an attempt to find a mental (national, historical) place for the victims, the collective imaginary quickly devises a stock image by which to categorize the six million dead, rendering them a depersonalized group. Many war memoirs by Jewish women seem to indicate this same resistance on the part of the first-person narrator to being lumped into the ossifying, one-dimensional role of victim, the innocent persecuted heroine who is frozen in time. Such unidimensionality serves the interests of a society that strenuously resists complexity, and subsuming women into larger undifferentiated categories makes them magically disappear. Klüger recognizes that despite her mother's courage and intermittent defiance of cultural and societal demands, Alma's transformative power is constantly checked by pre- and post-Shoah society, a society of totalizing categories that holds onto its masculine language, that puts "the shame of the victim into the service of the victimizer" (*Still Alive*, 159), and whose standards of normality have been unmasked as a fraud by Auschwitz. Once in America, Alma, a woman who had taught her daughter to fiercely reject "the role of passive victim who could be comforted with small demonstrations of kindness" (*Still Alive*, 49), assumes that very role. Her priority is now to survive in her new reality, put herself under the protection of a husband, and guarantee a future to her daughter—and these goals require that she play along with a new (or, rather, quite old) set of rules.

It is impossible for Klüger, or for the reader of the retrospective analysis of her life, to miss the extent to which this mother is framed by the patriarchal context. As Bacchilega observes, every magic mirror is always framed. The frame of our text's mirror is that of patriarchy: a patriarchal *Kultur* that gestated and unleashed an evil progeny, that of the Nazis and their antihuman ideology. To transpose this in the Snow White context, this frame limits what the mother in the patriarchal mirror says and does; in fact, as we know from the fairy tale, the mirror even commands mother and daughter to rival each other. The stepmother and Snow White keep seeing each other as rivals, though as allies they'd be capable of surviving the worst the male-dominated world could throw at them.

As psychoanalysis reveals and fairy tales illustrate, a daughter's path to adulthood requires the sacrifice of a/the mother. This model apparently leaves no room for the mother in the postchildhood life story (or survival story) of a daughter. It is a model in stark contrast to the experience of Klüger and many other female survivors. Borrowing from Bacchilega's poignant observation regarding the mirroring effects in Snow White,[71] I argue that an autobiography's traditional narrative strategy of mirroring—in particular of mirroring its relation to truth and personal or collective history—freezes the heroine looking into this mirror (and being seen through it) and turns her in a permanently one-sided, immobile image. Klüger ingeniously devises a way to thaw the frozen image in the picture and expose the artifice of memoir writing. Memoirs dramatize the construction of the self, even when the Shoah has a large role in this construction. "Construction is not opposed to agency," Butler explains. "It is the necessary scene of agency, the very terms in which agency is articulated and becomes culturally intelligible. The critical task for feminism is not to establish a point of view outside of constructed identities . . . The critical task is, rather, to locate strategies of subversive repetition enabled by those constructions, to affirm the local possibilities of intervention through participating in precisely those practices of repetition that constitute identity and, therefore, present the immanent possibility of contesting them."[72] *Still Alive*'s task seems to be to show the life of this particular survivor in the mirror, while working to expose its mechanisms from within. The unification of the child's self, Lacan teaches us, happens through a mirror,[73] but that unified self is undone when it searches for its reflection in the distorting mirror of Klüger's text.

The shattering of glass mirrors and crystal coffins that we find in fairy tales translates to a renunciation of wholeness, a choice of fragmentation and multi-layeredness, and to a breaking of the spell under which women, as well as survivors, are paralyzed. This sense of breaking free is evident not only in *Still Alive* but also in Klüger's first memoir, *weiter leben*. Pascale Bos comments on Klüger's choice to return to Germany and use its language for her memoir: "By writing in German and publishing in German," Klüger reveals in the first memoir "the subversive function of its critical discourse as it seeks to undo the repetitive patterns of reification that Klüger experienced as a Jewish woman both during and after the war."[74]

Klüger strategically constructs a narrative that makes safe the importance of what is told while at the same time disintegrating the frames within which the truth about the Shoah, gender, and power relations is generally held or reflected. And what better way to exemplify this reflection than by metaphorically turning her memoir into a talking mirror that can both reveal and distort the truth? Klüger uses her narrative as a mirror that forces her as well as the reader to ask personal and historical questions. What comes back in answer is the process of mirroring itself. Contrary to what the wicked queen in Snow White believes, the enchanted mirror does not always tell the truth. Or better yet, there is never just one single truth emerging from the mirror's reflections, and it is precisely this multiplicity of reflections that ends up shattering the mirror's authority. As in Greek tragedy, the speaking chorus shatters the power of the oracle. Klüger inserts her own version of such a disruptive choral voice into her text as well: she uses (and, when necessary, questions) the point of view of her mother, her friends (who intervene through e-mail messages, phone calls, conversations, and so forth) and the *auctoritas* of history books. We can think of these voices as the kind of chorality that Hélène Cixous calls "*peuplement*" (peopling).[75] In interrogating the mirror of memory, Klüger is never in thrall to one single voice. The symbolic order of the father (the voice of history) is disordered by the appearance of the unrepressed and heterogeneous utterances of a woman's memory, utterances that refuse to provide univocal and homogeneous answers to her questions. Her strategy of *peuplement*, which allows her to marshal history without "abandoning all authority to history," reveals, as Michael Rothberg points out in his compelling analysis of Klüger's German memoir, "the necessary heterogeneity of both experiences and the modes or sources through which they come to be represented."[76] Paraphrasing Bacchilega on postmodern fairy tales,[77] I claim that postmodern autobiography—with its multiplicity of contrapuntal voices—holds its own mirror up to the sanitizing mirror of history (personal and communal) and, in so doing, shatters it and exposes its duplicity. The autobiography as mirror does not remain unchanged. Bacchilega writes that "while this play of reflection, refraction, and framing might produce ideologically 'destructive,' 'constructive' and 'subversive' effects, the self-reflexive mirrors are themselves questioned and transformed."[78] The fairy tale of the wicked queen thus emerges as a far more complex, differentiated, and ambiguous story than the one shaped by the univocal voice of patriarchy. The Snow White–type mirror speaks with the voice of patriarchy, and its truth is a lie rooted in its failure to incorporate otherness.

Indeed, it is the patriarchal mirror itself that shows the queen her murderous path. Bettelheim's reading of Snow White places the spotlight on the girl, the maiden in distress who is not necessarily the central figure of the tale. On the contrary, the central figure appears to be Snow White's antagonist, the queen, who is more than merely a foil who allows the protagonist to reveal her heroic nature. After all, it is the queen who has power, narrative centrality, and—most important—a defined quest. She is threatened, and she reacts to the threat by setting in motion the plot of the story. But it is in the mirror that this threat is formulated; moreover, the threat is formulated in language. In fact, the particular mirror the queen interrogates is blind, not reflecting images, but—like an oracle—answering questions. A message is conveyed to the queen through the voice of the mirror, which is masculine. Bettelheim's analysis of Snow White suggests that the mirror "seems to speak the voice of a daughter rather than that of a mother."[79] This is arguable. In the German tale, it is syntax itself that forces the teller to use the masculine personal pronoun to refer to the mirror, because in German the word *Spiegel* (mirror) is masculine. Disney's animated film gives the mirror a male voice, though whether this stemmed from its creator's knowledge of German grammar or a sense that the mirror represented a patriarchal voice is anyone's guess. Cleverly, Zipes's masterful translation of the Grimm brothers' text avoids the use of any pronoun at all for the mirror, repeating the noun "mirror" throughout the story.[80]

In addition to the complicated roles of the queen and the mirror, the dwarves are also used to interrogate gender in this fairy tale. *Pace* Bettelheim, the dwarves do not so much represent a failed sexuality as indispensable tools in the mechanics of gendering. During the latency years of Snow White's adolescence, they represent and support the sexual order that she is being prepared to enter. In return for their protection, the dwarves ask Snow White to clean, cook, and tidy the house for them. Gilbert and Gubar point out that "her life with them is an important part of her education in submissive femininity."[81] She is being domesticated and readied for her subservient role to her savior, the prince. The message? A girl who is obedient and domestic is also safe. The mirror and the dwarves work for the same masculine order.

This is how Bettelheim explains the opening of the Grimm brothers' tale: "Snow White's mother pricking her finger so that three drops of red blood fall upon the snow" means that "sexual innocence, whiteness, is contrasted with sexual desire, symbolized by the red blood," and in this way, the story "prepare[s] the child to accept what is otherwise a most upsetting event: sexual bleeding, as in menstruation and later in intercourse when the hymen is broken. Listening to the first few sentences of 'Snow White,' the child learns that a small amount of bleeding . . . is a precondition for conception, because only after this bleeding is the child born."[82] What the child instinctively learns instead, I believe, is that her birth demands the blood of her mother—in fact, her mother's death. Furthermore, I want to stress that the purity in question is not only Snow White's; the snow's whiteness reflects the purity of the unborn child's mother, too. At this prematernal stage, the mother is still the good mother. And good mothers are pure (virginal, "white") and without daughters yet. Metaphorically, the daughter in this story is created out of the mother's spilled blood (possibly a Christian metaphor for maternal self-sacrifice), and this image is quickly literalized by the death of the good mother. This tangential reading allows us to glimpse the frame through which the story of Snow White must be read. Bettelheim omits to mention the third element in the constitution of Snow White: the black frame. The Grimms' story explains that the good queen wishes her child to display the whiteness of the snow, the redness of her blood, and also the blackness of the window frame in her chamber. The wish is granted: Snow White has black hair, and her story is framed before she is even born.

After she is born, her mother dies—a history Snow White shares with the most illustrious daughters of fairy tales. Because they are born, their biological mothers, who are good mothers, die, to be replaced by new (bad) mothers. The wicked queen has no room to evolve. The good one will never disappoint or worsen; the bad one will never better or redeem herself. The world of fairy tales does not allow for ambiguities. When a story centers on the battle between women (fair young maidens and wicked older female figures), only men, particularly fathers, are allowed to be ambiguous characters. A king who rules unobstructed over the immense fairy tale kingdom is no match for his wife's unalloyed evil and her desire to annihilate another woman—or is he?

Feminist readings of the story of Snow White particularly condemn the ending, in which the heroine is asleep and must wait for a man to come along and awaken her. But, I ask, what does she learn on awakening? That as long as the queen is alive, she—Snow White—is not safe? That a mirror has been speaking her name? That a mirror has marked her for death? Shouldn't she shatter the mirror, rather than kill the queen, for the plot to be resolved successfully? Snow White can not see that the wicked stepmother is also in a kind of sleep from which she needs be awaken. Mirrors, Bacchilega observes, are "desire containers," and "folk and fairy tales are ideologically variable desire machines"; breaking their spell means exposing "that magic which seeks to conceal the struggling interests which produce it."[83] Klüger's autobiographical text produces its particular effect by thematizing the conflict between the normative function of the Shoah autobiography and the subversive function of woman's autobiography.[84] The way in which Klüger makes sure not to reproduce any magic is to expose the mechanics of textual production. "*Weiter leben*'s unique quality," writes Bos, "lies precisely in the fact that the narrative turns a critical eye toward itself. It self-consciously deconstructs its own testimony and the psychological, historical, and literary discourses that have surrounded this kind of literature for the last twenty-five years."[85] The same is applicable to *Still Alive*, which furthers *weiter leben*'s deconstruction of memory by referring to and even amending the previous memoir, creating a parallel version of it.

Klüger's uses of narrative enchantments help deconstruct the mirror's frame by critically focusing on it; thus, as the reader progresses through the text, she encounters a constantly shifting portrait and is made aware of the mirroring process at work in this text. Klüger's understanding of Snow White hits on an important point: the queen and Snow White both fight for their right to remain in the king's castle.[86] The king's presence is no longer necessary to the development of the fairy tale's plot. The mirror, I believe, can be understood as a reflection of the king's phallic desire, which causes the queen to panic because she knows that such a narrative necessitates her death.

In *Still Alive*, mother and daughter each see themselves mirrored in the other's life: entangled in a common trauma, with each one's story incomplete without the other's. "I was a stage prop, her property, at most a minor figure in her drama," says the daughter (*Still Alive*, 180), while the mother's counteraccusation reveals a different perspective: "You have always run away from me" (*Still Alive*, 181). The dialogue between mother and daughter is like a threaded needle piercing a cloth and forming different patterns on both sides. Throughout their fraught life together, both the mother and the daughter prevail at different times. For instance, the mother determines that they will go to America rather than Palestine; the daughter decides for everybody that it is time to escape the labor camp, and later she decides to go to graduate school in California, as far as possible from New York and her mother. *Still Alive* tries to mend the injured self by allowing it to recover the moments in the text of the daughter's prepubertal, teenage, and adult resistance to her mother and to patriarchal society at large, which is there to frame and limit the possibilities of a different mother-daughter encounter.

Klüger's memoir is always open to the possibility of variants, not only in the multiplicity of voices that join the narrator's *I* but also in its double ending. The memoir could have easily been concluded with the scene that describes Ruth leaving New York and her distraught mother behind:

> When I left New York, everything was in a heap and a jumble at my mother's place . . . It was late summer, and the heat was something, the external disorder a mirror image of inner chaos. I hardly knew what to take along. My friends were there and helped me pack, and my mother was desperate. She was aware that I wouldn't come back.
>
> So this is the end of the story, the hit-and-run end, the living room with my stuff on the floor, my bad conscience . . . and the disappointment of my mother . . . After I left, she read my papers, discarded my correspondence, got rid of my books. At the end of the story there was a vacuum, in the rooms, in the people. At the end there was my betrayal: I had become Shylock's Jessica, abandoning an unloved parent. (*Still Alive*, 202)

Klüger's betrayal finds its antecedent in the betrayal of another girl: Shylock's Jessica, the daughter of the maligned Jew. Luce Irigaray asks her own mother, "And when I leave, is it not the perpetuation of your exile?"[87] Does Jessica's betrayal of Shylock perpetuate his exile? Shylock had naively thought that he had found a new home and stability, a safe place where his power could be restored; he demanded justice and what was due to him; instead, the daughter, in league with his enemies, snatched all his certainties away from him. Klüger's mother, perhaps feeling similarly betrayed, reacts to this loss, to the new chaos of her daughterless life, with a suicide attempt.

By the time she is composing *Still Alive*, however, Klüger knows that this is not the end of her story. After all, a daughter can return to her mother, and a mother doesn't have to simply vanish. Klüger adds a different epilogue to her new memoir, devoted to the story of Alma's death. Oddly, it is with this epilogue that Klüger finally allows a note of triumph to enter her autobiography, a triumph that she locates not in having survived Auschwitz but rather in the peaceful, civilized death of her mother far from Auschwitz. Alma's last gift to her daughter is exactly this sense of victory over the annihilating degradation of genocide. "I felt a sense of triumph," Klüger writes, "because this [mother's] had been a human death, because she had survived and outlived the evil times" (*Still Alive*, 211). As in so many myths and tales, victory goes hand in hand with death.

Alma's slide toward death begins with a worsening psychological illness (her paranoia), followed by senile dementia that makes the now aged lady regress into her Czech youth. Paradoxically, in the end Alma turns into a child herself, and Klüger looks after her like a mother; their roles have been reversed. By the end of her almost century-long life, Alma's face—as Klüger points out in a nod, perhaps, to the fairy tales that play so central a role in her memoir—is as wrinkled as that of a witch (Still Alive, 213), and her eyes are greatly weakened, perhaps like those of the wicked lady in the tale of Hansel and Gretel. Yet Alma has one last love in her life: Klüger's granddaughter, Isabela, who in return is very attached to her wizened great-grandmother. Every time Alma sees Isabela, she enthusiastically and proudly exclaims "Ein Wunderkind!" (a wonder child) (Still Alive, 213). The text opens as a young girl, Ruth, experiences the death of her grandmother's parrot in Vienna, the prelude to a childhood full of tragic deaths. It ends with a four-year-old girl in America, Isabela, facing her first encounter with death when her great-grandmother's cat dies and preparing to lose her great-grandmother, too. The story comes full circle.

By the last page of her memoir, Klüger has succeeded in redefining the "latency period" in the life of a Shoah survivor: the Auschwitz parenthesis. But Auschwitz, Klüger's work implies, is no latency period: the concentration camp is not a kind of glass coffin in which life is frozen until the spell is broken, the coffin cracks, and a few lucky ones are allowed to return home. This representation would lead us to the triumphalist deduction that those who made it back were rewarded—with life—for qualities others lacked. Klüger doesn't deny that after Auschwitz, the girl represented in her memoir was necessarily a different human being than the one who entered Auschwitz. Klüger admits that when she wants to say something noticeable about herself she says she was in Auschwitz, despite being all too aware that she is not "from" Auschwitz, she is from Vienna.[88] Auschwitz profoundly and irrevocably affected her, but it did not make her—because genocide is a force of distruction, and it births nothing positive; it only creates death and trauma. The sections of the memoir that follow its treatment of the death camps are there to warn us against the sentimental notion that Auschwitz has any transformative power, that one enters it a child and emerges from its horrors a grown-up who has learned some of life's fundamental lessons, like in a Dickensian coming-of-age novel. Still Alive does not allow for this sort of developmental arc, or indeed any kind of soothing catharsis. Its epilogue thus allows the memoirist to push her biography far beyond the hellish gates of Auschwitz. After recording the catastrophe, she concludes with the memory of her mother dying in her bed, surrounded by the love of a great-granddaughter and her own daughter, signs of a rehumanized life now visible in this female family chain.

The image of this life-affirming bond is best exemplified by a photograph Klüger finds in her mother's house the day of her burial. It is a happy photograph of Alma gleefully rubbing noses with the four-year-old Isabela. Photographs are frozen images of time and space. But unlike the Auschwitz glass coffin, the photograph Klüger holds in her hands is a safe place of suspension, one that does not undercut sanity and humanity but rather restores both.

Holding this photograph, which frames and fixes in time and space the physical and spiritual connection between great-granddaughter and great-grandmother, the narrator stands between two generations of women and witnesses their reciprocal recognition: "On one side, the child whose mind hadn't reached maturity, on the other, the old adult who had once lost a teenage son to *anonymous* murderers" (*Still Alive*, 214; emphasis added to stress that "anonymity," discussed above, comes back in the end). Presence seems to have triumphed over absence, but presence, like memory, can be illusory (if consoling). It can never quite be pinned down. In the end, life is translated into a series of losses and growing emptiness: the autobiographical *I* undoes life as it pronounces it. Isabela and her great-grandmother are each other's asymmetrical replication, each knowing only the here and now in the artifice of the photograph's reflection. Affinity, not identity, connects them. And Klüger, the seasoned professor of Germanic philology, knows that "affinity," in the elective culture of Goethe, still magically conjures up echoes of passionate resistance and great rebellions to come.

Klüger looks at this image of two women, one born at the beginning of the twentieth century and the other born at its end, and concludes her memoir by noticing that in the photograph, the "present . . . miraculously stood still for [Alma and Isabela], time frozen in space and space made human. Perhaps redeemed"(*Still Alive*, 214). Then, contrary to what fairy tales teach us, wicked mothers are redeemable too.

The scripted phrase that ends all fairy tales and that children know by heart in their native tongues ("And they lived happily ever after") in German is: "Und wenn sie nicht gestorben sind, so leben sie noch heute" (and if they haven't died, they are still living today)—or if they survive, they get to tell their story and proclaim that they are "still alive."

For every image of the past that is not recognized by the present as one of its own concerns threatens to disappear irretrievably.

—⚬⚬ **WALTER BENJAMIN**, *Illuminations*

# CHAPTER 3

# AUTO DA FÉ
## Sarah Kofman's Totemic Memoir

At the time of the shortest, sleepy winter days, edged on both sides with the furry
dusk of mornings and evenings, when the city reached out deeper and deeper into
the labyrinth of winter nights, and was shaken reluctantly into consciousness by the
short dawn, my father was already lost, sold and surrendered to the other sphere.

BRUNO SCHULZ, *Cinnamon Shops*

In the present work on Holocaust mothers and daughters, Sarah Kofman's biography offers perhaps the most complex variant. Hers is not only a life devastated by the impact of the war she survived in hiding with her mother, but also a life torn between two mothers who remained symbolically irreconcilable for this daughter: the Jewish victim mother, whom the child eventually rejected, and a Christian mother figure, her wartime savior, who "colonized" the Jewish girl's identity, won her over, and separated her from her biological mother, her family, and her past.

Born in 1934, Kofman was one of six children of a Polish Orthodox rabbi, Berek Kofman, who had emigrated with his wife to France in 1929. For the first years of Kofman's life, the family lived in a house on Rue Ordener in Paris, where her father was the leader and *shokhet* (ritual slaughterer) of a small Jewish community. During the Nazi occupation, Berek Kofman was arrested and deported to Auschwitz, where another prisoner beat him and buried him alive because he refused to work on the holy day of Shabbat.

Sarah and her siblings remained under the sole care of their mother (Fineza Kofman, née Koenig) who lacked money and connections in her adoptive country and spoke very little French. Despite these obstacles, Fineza Kofman, helped by anti-Vichy underground partisans, managed to save her children by placing them with various protectors in the French countryside. However, Sarah, then eight years old, refused to be separated from her, and the two hid together in the apartment of a Christian acquaintance, on rue Labat, in the very heart of occupied Paris. Claire Chemitre, or Mémé (grandma) as she is referred to by Sarah Kofman, treated the girl as her own daughter and occasionally passed her off as such. The girl discovers herself to be no longer emotionally attached to her biological mother (the rebbetzin from Poland, the foreigner with an accent, alone in a world inimical to her as foreigner, Jew, and woman). Instead, Sarah finds her love is deeper for Mémé, who—in the act of saving her—condemns her to a new exile that begins with her abandonment of the paternal territory and continues with her banishment of the maternal one. In twenty-three short chapters, Kofman's memoir *Rue Ordener, Rue Labat* tells the story of a girl's strong initial attachment to a father who disappears forever from her life and to a mother who is forcibly eclipsed by the presence of the new mother; finally, the book recounts the girl's detachment from both mothers as she becomes a woman and an artist whose numerous works (both texts and artworks) were, as she herself declared, an indirect way of working through this traumatic childhood.[1]

There are very clear boundaries between the different geographical, historical, and psychological spaces revisited in *Rue Ordener, Rue Labat*. The title itself indicates no diaporesis as to which street to choose: there's no "and" or "or," just one joint street name, the literal and symbolic location of the lost childhood on one side of the comma, the site of life beyond or in spite of the Shoah on the other side. Because this text inhabits a child's perspective, it maintains from the very start a radical separation between spheres (paternal and maternal, Jewish and non-Jewish, adulthood and childhood, truth and fiction), a separation that reflects, in part, the child's unambiguous and compartmental way of understanding the world. The comma between the names of the two streets in the book's title is like the thin rim of a coin with two faces: on one side, Rue Ordener; on the other, Rue Labat. The two sides of the coin coexist but never face each other, although neither can be read without the other. The logic of the bildungsroman or *Künstlerroman* would have produced a title like "From Rue Ordener to Rue Labat," but this true coming-of-age story does not follow such developmental trajectories. The painful path from Rue Ordener, (Judaism, the father, mother-daughter unity) to Rue Labat (Frenchness, de-Judaization, symbolic matricide) passes through two metro stops, two homes, two mothers, and many deaths. Rue Ordener and Rue Labat are the two faces of the currency of a childhood bearing the imprimatur of two mothers, and in Kofman's identity these two aspects are not separable. She does not really move from one to the other; she owns them both but can face only one at a time.

Before *Rue Ordener, Rue Labat*, Kofman had only sporadically written about her private life. A collection of her personal essays was published in English in the journal *Sub-Stance* as "Autobiographical Writings" (1986) and later in the volume *Selected Writings*, while an earlier book, *Paroles suffoquées* (*Smothered Words*) grafted the autobiographical (the story of her father's murder) onto an analysis of the writings of Maurice Blanchot and Robert Antelme on the Shoah. Kofman theorized about the genre of autobiography in two works—*Autobiogriffures* and *Explosion I: De l'"Ecce Homo" de Nietzsche*. Finally, in *Rue Ordener, Rue Labat* she applied all the philosophical, psychoanalytical, and feminist tools she had used as a scholar in the composition of her own autobiography—and with it, Kofman ended her writing career.[2]

This memoir about mothers is quite anomalous for a writer like Kofman, whose entire career centered on the interpretation, albeit through a feminist lens, of the great "fathers" of Western civilization (Plato, Rousseau, Kant, Lacan, Derrida, Nietzsche, and so on). In particular, she had an intellectual fixation on Sigmund Freud, to whom her most influential works were devoted, and in his eulogy for Kofman, Jacques Derrida rightly pointed out that she had understood Freud and interpreted him for us all as no one else in the twentieth century had done.[3]

In the opening lines of *Rue Ordener, Rue Labat*, Kofman declares that her personal experience—as a Jewish war survivor whose life was saved and shaped by two mothers, and whose universe remained tainted by the death of her father—influenced everything she ever wrote. Therefore, I will look at *Rue Ordener, Rue Labat* as a piece of a larger autobiographical project Kofman was writing throughout her intellectual career, in which she tried to reconcile herself to the past and make sense of the complex relational dynamics between a child and the adult world around her, between conflicting identities and an entire nation's dark past. In analyzing the ambiguity of the mother-daughter story depicted in her autobiography, I discuss how Kofman applies to the writing of her memoir various analytical tools that she had already tested in her dissections of other authors' texts, tools that derived from the critical language of philosophy, literary theory, or psychoanalysis. The resulting book is an unexampled mixture of real and screen memories, full of deceptive pitfalls and hidden clues that Kofman tacitly invites the reader to sort out. She once said that all readers are *lecteurs policiers* (text detectives), who like to discover who has committed the crime before the plot reveals it.[4] I offer an interpretation of *Rue Ordener, Rue Labat* as a confession, a book of public penance and intimate sacrifice(s): Kofman's auto da fé.

I borrow this term from Kofman herself, who entitled a chapter "Auto-da-fé" in *Pourquoi rit-on?*, which was devoted to Freud's *Jokes and Their Relation to the Unconscious* and in which she declared that this text was the son's (Freud's) self-defensive way of reenacting the father's murder.[5] In her very first book, *L'Enfance de l'art*, Kofman called Freud the "new iconoclast" because of his innovative idea of linking the problem of art to that of the father and of recasting the artist as a parricidal son.[6] In *Totem and Taboo*, Freud had conceived of the totem as the monument erected by the parricidal sons to the dead father, whose power was thus symbolically reinstated. He postulated that the first poet was a hero who distanced himself from the community of men and took upon himself the collective murder of the father. Furthermore, Freud argued, the main factor determining our aesthetic pleasure in the artistic product is its enactment of our own subconscious dream, one we share with the rest of the audience, to be ourselves the father's murderer. Far from being a gift from the gods, the artist's genius is thus a curse arising from the artist's past. By replacing religion, art repeatedly performs the primal totemic rite of parricide, which, in eliminating the father, sacralizes him at the same time.[7] The questions that Kofman's work raises and that this chapter addresses are the following: What does it mean for a Shoah daughter to be an artist? If we believe in the patricidal drive of art, can a Jewish survivor and daughter of a Shoah victim be an artist? Can the collective guilt for the father's murder be lifted by an artist such as Kofman, whose father had been literally murdered in a collective crime that went grossly unpunished? Since the symbolic collective murder of the father has been made real by the Shoah, is it possible, if even only theoretically, for the daughter of the Shoah victim to conceive of another, ritual killing of this father? I will argue that Kofman imagines a memoir that, although "totemic," must avoid performing the symbolic murder of the father. The question, then, is how to eschew this ritualistic task? The answer appears to be by killing the mother (two mothers) instead. The memoir is thus a "totemic memoir" in a way that only a daughter could conceive of it. If patricide is followed by the erection of a totem, so is matricide for Kofman: like the primal son for his father, this daughter erects a monument to the murdered mother, and by doing so she acknowledges the maternal power and her personal debt to the disappeared woman. (And as Nietzsche reminds us, there are no *Schulden* [debts] without *Schuld* [guilt].)[8] Ultimately, the artist herself pays the highest price for the act of making art: Kofman took her life on October 15, 1994, shortly after the publication of *Rue Ordener, Rue Labat*.

### WRITING ÇA : WITH AND AGAINST THE MOTHER

The opening of *Rue Ordener, Rue Labat* reveals an important truth about the genesis of the text we hold in our hands. Simultaneously it obscures a relevant side of this truth, leaving us face to face with an insoluble enigma, the enigma of life—or, better yet, the enigma of death, since as Derrida has shown us, when we talk of life "the trait that relates to the graphical must also be working between the biological and biographical, the thanatological and the thanatographical."[9] Here is the opening:

A fountain pen, that's all I have left of him. One day I took it from my mother's purse, where she kept it together with other mementos of my father. It's the kind of fountain pen they don't make any more and that you had to keep filling with ink . . . I still have it, all patched up with Scotch tape; it lies on my desk before my eyes, it compels me to write, to write.

My many books, perhaps, were all indirect routes necessary to get me to tell about "this" [ça].[10]

Kofman puts the important word—ça (this)—in quotation marks. To what does "this" refer? And why bracket it off that way? Grammatical and syntactic logic indicates that "this" refers to everything that has been said thus far, which is very little considering that we are on the first page of the book. And yet in the eyes of the narrator, this short chapter constitutes the essence of all she had to write, and in fact of all she ever wrote. That is, what has compelled her to live so far has been to fill the void between presence and absence (of the father), between desire and death, through words.

Could ça also refer to a crime to which she is confessing? All that is left of her father (the pen) is being guarded by the mother, and the daughter reaches into her mother's forbidden place and steals a piece of her father away from her. The pen is a paternal relic and a phallic symbol: it ejects ink (its semen) onto the page, making it pregnant with the daughter's art; however, it is also an old pen, which continuously dries up (or dies) as it creates and needs to be refilled (fed) by the daughter. Lastly, the father's pen allows the daughter to birth books with and about him. The old pen is a transversal voice, a voice that Kofman uses to speak of her father in an attempt to repossess him—to possess, in other words, the impossessible: both the father (precluded to the daughter by the Oedipal prohibition) and writing (precluded to the woman by male culture). Ça is, among other things, this act of rebellion against culture (a woman who dares to write), nature (Oedipal incest), and the mother (deprived by the daughter of the last remnant of her husband). In order to salvage the father, the daughter must commit a crime against the mother, who is the custodian of the pen, the symbolic phallus.

*Rue Ordener, Rue Labat* is the memory of this crime. The daughter-artist-murderer first replaces the father with a surrogate, Mémé, the Christian savior of Rue Labat; then Mémé, like the patriarchal Father she symbolically represents, overpowers the mother and annuls her. The mother is thus twice sacrificed for the sake of keeping the father symbolically alive. In spite of herself, the daughter kills the father as well through turning to Mémé. The girl sides with Mémé against her biological mother, assuaging the unbearable pain of losing her father in the loving embrace of a woman who represents everything the girl's family is not: French, Christian, alive. She subconsciously casts Mémé as her new father, the person who leads her to triumph (survival) and who is the bearer of a culture not threatened by annihilation. However, Mémé, though symbolically a father, is literally a new mother figure: she wants to have Sarah all for herself, to the point that after the war, she obtains legal custody of her.[11] As a mother, Mémé will also have to be rejected, but rejecting Mémé means killing once again the father she symbolically has resuscitated. A true double bind: Kofman resolves it by eventually substituting for the maternal world of her childhood the paternal and patriarchal world of her academic life. After high school, she enters a university and binds her professional life to the life and thought of a set of symbolic fathers, the subjects of her vast scholarly production, by way of offering to them her artistic and analytical gifts—that is, her art—to expiate her guilt.

If *Rue Ordener, Rue Labat* is Kofman's auto da fé, then *ça* is the incriminating, if maddeningly indeterminate, evidence: *ça* cannot simply refer to the father or the father's story, as the opening chapter seems to imply. Rather, it refers to Kofman's coming to terms with the victimhood of everybody involved, herself included. *Ça* is the psychological burden the guilty daughter has to live with, the multiple losses and betrayals. *Ça* is trauma, one in need of a willing audience. After decades of psychoanalysis, Kofman realized that her story had not been heard in the way she needed it to be heard. "I've always wanted to tell about my life," she wrote in an essay, but the analyst to whom she told her story remained quiet, indifferent to her telling.[12] As she explained in an interview, "I turned the corner in my analysis when I ceased to talk, to tell my story in a rational and sustained fashion; when it became possible for me to talk without expecting a reply from the analyst; when I stopped trying to communicate a meaning, expecting to get one by means of frenetic demand. In short, when I became able to just speak; in other words, when I gave myself up to the play of language, that is, writing."[13] *Rue Ordener, Rue Labat* is the result of Kofman's newfound way of "speaking."

The free-associative style in which the war memories are reconstructed in *Rue Ordener, Rue Labat* keeps the paternal and maternal realms starkly separated. The father and his surroundings conjure up the romantic atmosphere of Hasidic *maysele*. Once he vanishes, the world takes on all its usual prosaic qualities, and the mother's realpolitik and resourcefulness hold no charm or poetry for the daughter. The father's office is described as bathed in an aura of sacredness. The mother's kitchen, where meats are left to bleed in the sink according to Jewish laws, makes the girl sick to her stomach. The father prays, leading the family in Shabbat and Havdalah songs, and his only vice, smoking cigarettes, is remembered by the daughter tenderly and indulgently. The same indulgence, however, is not granted to the mother. The first description of her is offered in relation to the story of the father's capture. According to the daughter's version, a round of arrests had been announced for July 16, 1942, and Rabbi Kofman had hoped that by giving himself up to the authorities, his family would be spared. He thus stayed in Paris and warned as many Jews in his community as possible about the imminent danger so that they could flee, while he sat at home waiting for the ominous knock on the door that would signal his arrest: "He waited and prayed to God that they may come to take him but save his wife and children" (RO/RL, 11). The image of the praying father, Kofman tells us, resembled the *Akedah*, the binding of Isaac, which she had encountered in her Hebrew Bible. When the French policeman finally does arrive, the mother opens the door:

> "Rabbi Berek Kofman?"
> "He's not here," says my mother. "He's at the synagogue."
> The policeman does not insist. He is about to leave. But my father comes out of his room . . . and says:
> "Yes, here I am. Take me!"
> "But this is impossible, the baby I'm holding is not two yet!" says my mother pointing at my brother Isaac, and adds: "I'm pregnant with another child!" . . .
> My mother lies! (RO/RL, 12)

"Here I am," says the father—the same words (in Hebrew, *hineni*) with which another father, Abraham, always answers God's call.

On one side is a father who insists on immolating himself even though his wife's strategy might have gained him time to work out a plan to save himself and his family. On the other side is a mother who outsmarts the policeman and could have saved her husband were it not for the latter's intervention, which annuls her courageous act. She succeeds instead only at embarrassing her daughter, who is appalled by the discovery that her mother is capable of lying (and willing to do so). That was the last day Kofman saw her father; his family heard from him again only once more in a postcard from Drancy written in French (therefore not in the father's handwriting, but dictated by him to a native speaker), in which he requested cigarettes and sent his love to everybody. Apparently, the mother kept that card safe through the years, but "when my mother died it was impossible to find anywhere that postcard which I had re-read so many times and which I myself wanted to keep now. It was as if I had lost my father a second time. From then on there was nothing left of him, not even that lone postcard which he hadn't even written himself" (RO/RL, 16). The daughter's only words about the death of her mother are thus overshadowed by the more important loss (for the "second time") of the father. We are not told anything else about the mother's death. Kofman seems to be able or willing to mourn only the loss of the father. Probably it did not escape Kofman that the lost postcard figures in her story as the mother's subconscious revenge for the pen the daughter had stolen for herself.

We are not told when or how Kofman's mother dies, but we do receive the story of Rabbi Kofman's death in at least two of his daughter's texts: *Paroles suffoquées* and *Rue Ordener, Rue Labat*. "They beat him with a pickax and buried him alive one day because he had refused to work," Kofman writes in her memoir. "It was Shabbat: he had done no harm . . . he was simply praying to God for them all, victims and victimizers alike" (RO/RL, 16). In *Paroles suffoquées*, we read: "One must talk about it, *sans pouvoir* [literally, "without power"; without being able to] . . . And how can one not talk about it, when all those who returned—and he did not return—vowed to tell, to tell endlessly, as if only an 'infinite conversation' could equal out the infinite *dénouement*?" Kofman goes on to ask herself: "To speak in order to witness, but how? How can witnessing escape the idyllic law of storytelling? How can one speak of the 'unimaginable' . . . without the help of imagination?"[14]

The storytelling of her father's life is indeed idyllic. The father emerges from the daughter's pages as an allegorical model of righteousness and justice, the perfect mixture of the divine and the human. Ancient mythology teaches us that when the divine is grafted onto the human, the resulting character always ends up feeding some tragic plot. These characters, be it Prometheus or Jesus, are not fit for life—they are usually destined for an exemplary, if tragic, end that turns them from personal and familiar figures into transpersonal and universal ones. Kofman negotiates the story of her father in her texts in just such a mythical mode. He becomes not only the paradigm of victimhood, but also the embodiment of that place (Auschwitz, *sensu stricto* and *largo*) about which the "powerless" daughter (*sans pouvoir*) is compelled to write without any experience of it except through the untellable and unknowable experience of her father. The memoir seemingly starts out as a book about the father: the father's pen and its injunction to write; the father's marvelous study, the site of great mysteries (marriages, circumcisions, and ritual killings); the story of the father's arrest and his heroic self-sacrifice (*kadosh haShem*); the father whose smallest gestures are the object of the daughter's undivided fascination ("I observed his every move in awe" [RO/RL, 12]). But amid this "infinite conversation," where does the rest of the story—the traumatic survival of the mother and daughter—fit? *Rue Ordener, Rue Labat* grapples with precisely this conundrum: how to integrate a finite story into the infinite story, what can be said into what can't be said, and a daughter's biography into a father's thanatography.

Michael Stanislawski poignantly remarks that apart from the question of "whether or not it is credible that a rabbi at Auschwitz would pray to God on behalf of the Nazis . . . [Rabbi Kofman's] self-sacrifice was . . . in a profound sense transgressive of his faith rather than demanded by it" because it disregarded the duty of *pikuah nefesh*, the obligation to suspend the observance of a mitzvah when one's life or someone else's may depend on it.[15] It is obvious then, that in this story, which Kofman took so long to express, the father's two acts of self-sacrifice—one of which defies logic and the other religious law—need to be retold not in the rational language of history but in the creative and imaginative language of literature:

> In the house, there reigned a religious and sacred atmosphere. My father was a rabbi and we maintained the strictest observance of the dietary laws . . . On Rosh Hashanah . . . we listened to father blow the shofar. Mother was very proud of him . . . He practiced at home and I observed him take the shofar out and then put it back in its drawer next to his *tallis*, his teffilin, and the knife with which he slit the chickens' throats according to the ritual. Every Friday evening, women stood in our foyer, carrying one or two chickens in their shopping bags . . . All this was full of mystery and filled me with fear. I associated the razor of the *shokhet* with the knife of Abraham and the guttural sounds of the shofar with the cries of the slaughtered chickens . . . I also loved . . . the holiday of Simchat Torah when I saw my father dance in the synagogue with the other Hasidim lifting up in the air the Torah scrolls which we all kissed. (RO/RL, 19–21)

Is it due to a Freudian slip that some of the terminology related to Jewish practice and traditions (well known to a girl raised in strict orthodoxy) are either spelled incorrectly or mistakenly referred to by the author? Stanislawski points out that "she refers to the Havdalah prayer on Saturday night as 'kiddush,' refers to Sukkot as 'Shoukkott,' and even more curiously, recalls only 'seven plagues' at the Passover seder."[16] Are these due to a *lapsus linguae* or perhaps a *lapsus calami*—a slip of the pen, the father's pen?

Through the eyes of the child, the father is powerful, presiding over mysterious ceremonies in his mysterious study, where magic things happen and secret rites are performed. Does this idealized life of ritual constitute the *ça*? Or does *ça* refer to something more than this enchanted paternal space?

The real autobiography, the story of one's history, cannot remain in the ahistorical or antihistorical atmosphere of magic and mysticism: it is not there that ça takes place. Rather, ça is to be found beyond what remains of Kofman's childhood illusions and daydreams; it is rooted in what happens once the daydreams are shattered, once repression erects barriers against memory. Once the father is forever removed from the child's life, the historical takes the place of the mythological, and *Rue Ordener, Rue Labat* is consequently taken over by the two mothers.

At first, we experience this memoir as a book about the father: a phantasmic, incomplete mosaic, as the talking of analysis that operates by free association: a pen that demands a flow of ink (blood or semen) in order to work, the blood of the father about to be spilled, the blood of the animals killed according to the rules of kashrut, the blood of the son Isaac *in extremis* replaced by the blood of a lamb. Then, slowly, the whirlwind of images takes a more organized form as history forces its way into the narration and a new story emerges: the story of the mother. The rest of the book will be devoted to the syncretic, equivocal, duplicitous maternal presence in a daughter's life. Understanding the ambiguity of the mother-daughter relationship is the key to the complex space of *Rue Ordener, Rue Labat*.

## TO EAT OR NOT TO EAT

In 1987 Kofman published a short autobiographical essay titled "Sacrée nourriture"[17] (translated into English as "Damned Food")[18] in which she sketched the triangular relationship among mother, father, and child in connection to food, which functions as the force that both holds the triangle together and simultaneously tears it apart. In that essay, Kofman recalls the origins of her own rather unhealthy relationship with food as influenced by ancient Jewish dietary laws.

Because of its subject and the extremely poetic quality of the prose, this brief essay could easily have been incorporated into *Rue Ordener, Rue Labat*; in any case, it can be read as utterly complementary to the book. The essay is a compact yet complete summary of Kofman's early life. *Rue Ordener, Rue Labat* could almost be seen as an expansion of this original kernel.

"Sacrée nourriture! Et deux fois sacrée!" ("Damned food! And twice so!")— the essay opens with these sibylline exclamations. This overture sets the tone for the entire piece, which is full of puns and subconscious parapraxes. The English translation ("Damned Food!") of this opening sentence fails to capture the double-entendre of the original French: idiomatically, *sacrée* means "damned," but its literal meaning is the exact opposite: "sacred." Interestingly, we also find this meaningful play, or play on meaning, in the all-important Hebrew *qadosh*, as Stanislawski notes.[19] Is the food to which she refers in her essay sacred or damned? It is both: and it is so twice over (*deux fois*). The text announces:

Damned food! And twice damned.
—You must eat, my mother used to say . . .
—You mustn't eat everything, my father used to say.[20]

The food is sacred in that it is Jewish food, permitted (kosher) and therefore implicitly blessed by divine law. In this Jewish household, the food's sacredness is guaranteed by both mother and father. It is prepared by the Jewish mother in the kitchen according to the laws of kashrut, but the father—a rabbi and *shokhet*—must perform the ritual killing (sacred blood) and recite prayers for the food to become sacred. "Sacrée nourriture" is also partly about the Kofman family's wartime experience, and therefore the food is also in a sense damned, the food of trauma and death.

The first part of the essay sketches a portrait of the prewar Kofman family's dynamics through its relationship to food. Kofman stages the house as the temple where, as she reminds us in *Rue Ordener, Rue Labat*, everything is made sacred by the presence of a holy father. In this temple, mother and father share the priestly functions related to the administration of food. The father makes sure that only permitted foods are admitted to the table; he ensures that plates for dairy foods and meats are kept separate, and that they are properly purified "once a year for Passover, in the eventuality that some mistake was committed inadvertently (*par mégarde*)."[21] "Sacrée nourriture" is the most Jewish of Kofman's writings: the memories of these domestic scenes, full of commands and interdictions, are suffused in a *Yiddishkeit*-colored atmosphere. Kofman even uses the proper terminology from the *mameloshen* of her childhood for unmixable foods—milchig (dairy) and *fleishig* (meats)—as she recalls how her father and mother both obsessed over keeping them apart. She reports that her father incessantly repeated that one is not allowed to eat just any kind of meat, or eat on just any plate, or use the same silverware with all the dishes. The mother is in charge of the process of kosherization itself and the preparation of food: "My mother, high priestess, officiated in the kitchen, where not infrequently one would see a cut of salted beef left bleeding for hours or a carp wiggling in a basin while my father, rabbi and *shokhet*, slaughtered chickens in his den according to the law." The ritual food processing that goes on in the mother's kitchen kills the little girl's appetite and makes her stomach queasy. In "Sacrée nourriture," the mother is typecast as the *yiddishe mame*, the obsessive feeder, the persistent nagger, a relentless source of annoyance: "And she stuffed us and stuffed us. No risk of being deprived of dessert with her." The daughter's sarcasm turns the nurturing and loving mother into an overprotective and anxious Jewish mother. Arising either from the fear of transgressing a religious prohibition or from the mother's overfeeding, the girl stops being hungry and "resisted with all [her] forces the maternal categorical imperative." If one could, *par mégarde*, commit sacrilege and contravene the laws of kashrut, one can hardly escape the *garde* of the mother who hovers over her children, making sure they eat more than enough of the permitted foods. The mother cannot be accused of *mégarde*—the failure to guard over those in her charge. Since Sarah refused to eat, we are told, the mother would run after her all the way to her school's gate holding a bowl of café au lait. Then she would animatedly declare to the teacher, "She has not eaten this morning!!!"[22] The comedy of this scene is evident, and thus satirized, the mother is kept at an emotional distance by the narrator's irony.

Were we to translate the title of this essay into English (translations are unfortunately always treacherous), we could call it "Bloody Food" rather than "Damned Food" because the former reminds us of the blood drained out in the kosherization process, of the blood left in by the nonkosher preparations of Mémé and, perhaps more important, of the blood lines that exist between those who give food and those who receive it. *Sacrée nourriture*: the father makes the food *sacré* (sacred) and the mother makes it *sacré* (damned)—or is it the other way around? The father also makes it bloody (he slits the chickens' throat according to the ritual), and so does the mother (she leaves pieces of beef bleeding in the kitchen). The prohibitions against food are the way in which the father puts himself between the bodies of the child and the mother. "Thus, the maternal body is used in the service of a paternal law," postulates Kelly Oliver, "that outlaws the very body whose authority is invoked in order to enforce the law."[23] Therefore the maternal body must be rejected as well.

Kofman ties her nausea and eating problems to her mother's suffocating solicitousness. The fact that the entire essay is devoted to food clearly underscores the role of eating (and the mouth) as a place of discomfort (the sight of blood), ambivalence (mother or father), nonnegotiable rules (kashrut), and the fear of transgression and of breaking a taboo. Food also connects the body to society and is a metaphor for a psychological desire (drive) and its sublimated fulfillment. In women's literature, particularly women's autobiographies, the girl or woman often negotiates her identity vis-à-vis the surrounding world and her family through her relationship to food (see also chapter 5). The subject of food often inspires metaphors connected to ingestion, penetration, and invasion: from the outside, food carries something inside the body of the eater and lodges it there. Here, it is a Jewish identity that is being forged through the act of eating. Consequently, as soon as the task of feeding Sarah is taken over by Mémé, the girl absorbs a new identity, a French one. The child described by Kofman often demonstrates her resistance to threats from the outside world by rejecting food (either refusing to eat or vomiting up what she is forced to eat); alternatively, at times she welcomes the outside world by accepting its alimentary offerings (Mémé's French cuisine).

One wartime episode illustrates Kofman's complex and highly symbolic relationship with food. Between July 1942 and February 1943, after Kofman's father had been deported, her mother took on the dangerous enterprise of hiding her many children among various protectors inside and outside of Paris (RO/RL, 29). Kofman's brothers Isaac, whose name was Francophonized to Jacquot, and Joseph (the youngest) were put in a nursery in northern France; her sister Annette was left in Nonancourt with a Jewish communist married to a non-Jew; Rachel (renamed Jacqueline), Aaron (now Henri), and Sarah are hidden in Merville, where these city children are happily exposed to the beauty of the countryside. Ironically, the name of this safe and salvific town is one letter short of the French word *merveille* (marvel or wonder)—and is pronounced as if it were written *mère ville* (mother town). In Merville, Sarah makes new friends and enjoys the farm animals, nature, and the novelty of walking to school in her heavy sabots. But her fraught relationship to food intervenes to spoil the idyllic picture. Wonderfully fresh produce abounds, but unfortunately for her, so do a lot of pork-based dishes. Only pork is mentioned as a problematic food, though of course even without pork, practically all of the foods in the French, nonkosher farm kitchen would have violated Jewish dietary rules. "School was the only place where I felt 'well' or where I was able to bear the separation from my mother a little better," Kofman recalls. The rest of the time, she would cry and refuse to eat what "had always been forbidden to me" (RO/RL, 30). Is it the nonkosher diet or the separation from her mother that makes the girl miserable? Regardless, it is through her resistance to this new food that she effects a reunion with her mother. Her refusal to eat nonkosher foods is a mortally dangerous behavior that risks betraying her, her siblings, and their protectors to the unsympathetic local collaborators, so dangerous that her sister Rachel asks their mother to take Sarah back. Sarah's method proves successful: her obedience to the father's law allows her to return home, to Paris, with her mother. Parenthetically, by abiding by Jewish law at a time when doing so might cost her and other people's life mirrors the father's supererogatory self-sacrifice.

In Kofman's case, therefore, rejecting her mother's food offerings cannot be interpreted simply as a rejection of the mother but rather as a complex strategy for expelling those fears that her mother has instilled in her: fear of starvation, sickness, and de-Judaization. The maternal categorical imperative that the girl tries to resist is *Eat!*—that is, *Live! Be healthy! Be Jewish!* However, it would be misleading to read this act of resistance as carried out solely against the mother, as Tina Chanter seems to do.[24] The categorical imperative of the mother is only one aspect of the Jewish categorical imperative, whose holder is always and ultimately the father. After all, it is the father who decrees the Jewish law and the way in which kashrut marks each Jew by controlling what he can introduce inside his body and what he can't. Sarah realizes as soon as she starts living in the French world that kashrut is also a set of laws that, by delimiting what a Jew should and should not eat, further separates the Jews from their surrounding society. The Jews obey 613 commandments, 248 of which are positive (mitzvot aseh) and 365 of which are prohibitory (mitzvot taaseh): "do" and "do not" mingle together in the legal code. Understood this way, the opening paragraph of Kofman's alimentary essay does not simply demonstrate the author's rejection of the mother as much as confirms the author's inability to explicitly articulate her rejection of the father. Kelly Oliver asks: "Might the rejection of the mother cover up the rejection of the paternal law?"[25] I argue that it does.

Il faut manger (one must eat) and il ne faut pas tout manger (one cannot eat everything) are part of one single order: be Jewish. The privileged altar on which the ceremony of Judaism is performed in the house is the table. Around the table, there is a perfect convergence of the maternal and paternal roles in the nourishing rituals: the mother serves and the father blesses the foods. But first, the mother officiates in the kitchen, the father in his den. The priest and the priestess work in unison, yet the priestess is more of a vestal, an executioner of the priest's commands; and it is the latter whose order, as I'm about to show, reigns supreme for the entire family.

This paternal, priestly power becomes evident in the second part of the essay, in which we witness an unexpected reversal of roles (or rules). The war has already begun, and during their "exodus" (Kofman's word) to Brittany, the family runs into Red Cross volunteers who are distributing ham and butter sandwiches to the famished French population at the train station; the mother instinctively says to her children, "Don't take them." Surprisingly, the father intervenes and nullifies her order. "Let the children eat," he says, "it's the war." Not only milchig and fleishig together, but what fleishig!—Of all meats, ham is the most impure, the most abominable. Kofman remembers how much she enjoyed the taste of the prohibited food, surmising that that pleasure derived not so much from the actual flavor of the treyf itself as from the victory of the father's word over the mother's: "I found that ham-and-butter sandwich, which until then had been decreed impure, to be delicious: purified by circumstances and paternal authority."[26] Suddenly, the priest and the priestess switch roles: she who used to say "do" now says "don't," and he who used to say "don't" now says "do." By narrating this reversal, is Kofman implying that the kosherization of food is nothing but an act of permission? That behind Jewishness—as defined by what a Jew does or does not do—there is no transcendental truth or justice, but only the exercising of masculine power (its immanence)? The father's privilege to verbally impose or lift a ban? That kashrut, and perhaps Judaism itself, rests on the arbitrariness of the father's word? The father's power always wins out inside and even outside of his domestic temple. We could thus read Kofman's essay as a feminist midrash that questions the very logic of Jewish identity.

Furthermore, we must ponder the disquieting nature of Kofman's statement that the sandwich is "purified by circumstances and paternal authority" and its implication that father and war can purify impure food. Father and Nazism purify pork, expand the range of the edible beyond the confines of Jewish law. Is this same man who applies *pikuah nefesh* when completely unnecessary? The same Rabbi Kofman who, as a prisoner in Auschwitz, goes beyond the call of religious duty to observe the Shabbat and pays for it with his life? Therefore his act is again transgressive rather than respective of his own law. Kofman seems to be suppressing a subconscious knowledge that the father's authority is a dangerous delusion.

Though the war is initially described as a positive circumstance because it lets her father overrule the mother's uncharacteristic order not to eat, it eventually changes everything for the worse. "A few years later," Kofman understatedly remarks, "my father was deported." And at that point "we couldn't find anything to eat anymore."[27] The ham sandwich, though it made no difference between life and death, did open a breach in Sarah's sense of herself as a Jew. Furthermore, after her father is gone, the mother's word never regains its former authority. While hiding in the apartment of the Christian savior, the mother will have to yield to Mémé, who feeds Sarah her *treyf* in order to save her, to make her healthy in body and spirit—that is, to de-Judaize her by depriving her of Jewish traditions, of which food is a central one. In a way, Mémé mirrors the well-meaning Red Cross nurses who could save children only if they are willing to eat ham and butter. "After countless turns of fortune, I was 'saved' just in time by a woman who kept me with her, in the very heart of Paris, until the end of the war," writes Kofman, surprisingly editing out of this recollection her mother, who, as we know, was also saved by Mémé.[28] And why does she put "saved" in quotation marks? Perhaps it is to highlight the fact that something else was sacrificed. If Mémé's heroism in saving the Jewish girl and her mother is undeniable, it is also true that her intervention caused a rift not only between the two victims but also between the girl and her Jewish identity. Mémé saved the girl, but not the Jew.

There exists a close connection between food (nurture) and the maternal (be it biological or symbolic). The moment Mémé replaces Jewish food with non-

Jewish food, Sarah's mother is also replaced by Mémé, and the former's defeat is completed:

> At the same time as she [Mémé] was teaching me what we mean by "having a Jewish nose," she also submitted me to a completely different diet (*régime*): she declared the food of my childhood harmful to my health . . . red meat cooked rare (like raw horsemeat in broth) was supposed to "restore me to health" . . . From then on, this was my daily ration (until the day when we finally had nothing left to eat and had to go begging at the soup kitchen for a canteen cup of macaroni or beans).
>
> Put in a real "double bind," I couldn't swallow anything anymore and I vomited after each meal.[29]

Is the daughter's persistent vomiting the somatization of her subconscious recognition of the mother's victimhood? Is the daughter subconsciously enacting through her body the rejection (vomiting out) of a state of things, or a circumstance, that does not make the accessible world delicious (like the ham-and-butter sandwich) but unbearable and deadly?

Mémé changes the girl's diet as a way of saving her: the Nazi occupation and the final solution require a change of identity that Mémé interprets very literally. Similarly, the father on the train had interpreted the change in circumstances (the war) to require that the children be now allowed to eat pork. For Mémé, it is not enough to give shelter to the Jewish girl; she must also de-Judaize her. Kofman talks about her change of diet as a new *régime*, a word that carries a political undercurrent. A change of regime certainly occurs alongside the new diet, not only in the larger sense of the Nazi occupation but also with Mémé taking over the father's role, his priestly officiating over foods and the stewardship of the family. Thus Kofman refers back not only to the *régime* of Mémé, or the previous one of her mother and father, but also to an entire life of having food forced on her. The girl must submit to each dietary regime, but she responds to it with vomiting: her body rejects what her voice cannot refuse. "Sacrée nourriture! Et deux fois sacrée," exclaims Kofman. The food of her memory is twice sacred (or bloody) because it is associated with two victims (her mother and father) as well as two saviors (her two mothers), and because there are two ways of conceiving food and nutrition (Christian and Jewish, maternal and paternal or legal). Finally, food is twice damned because of its constantly duplicitous role. Before the war, food had been a problem in that one had to master the dietary laws in order not to break any taboo. But during and immediately after the war, food had turned into a different problem due to the fact that there was none left for anybody; around food there occurred a split between paternal and maternal control; and food was the backdrop against which the maternal rivalry for Sarah's affections took place.

Here's another pivotal scene that connects food with death as well as with life. One night, after the father's deportation, an unknown man knocks at the door and warns Madame Kofman to run away because a roundup has been scheduled for their building. "Without finishing our vegetable soup, and without fully comprehending what the stranger had just told us, we went to [Mémé's] house . . . I threw up all along the way," Kofman recalls in her memoir (RO/RL, 40). The escape from the certain to the uncertain is marked by a painful somatization of fear by vomiting. However, as soon as they reach safety in the apartment on Rue Labat, the French lady has a calming effect on the terrified child: "I found her very beautiful, sweet and affectionate. I almost forgot what had brought us there that night" (RO/RL, 40). So reassuring is Mémé that despite her upset stomach, Sarah manages to eat the rich dessert, *oeufs à la neige*, that this stranger prepares for them. This marks their entrance into Rue Labat: from this moment on, Kofman will revisit the apartment on Rue Ordener only in her dreams—or rather in her nightmares, she tells us.

Once settled in Rue Labat, Kofman's mother looks powerlessly on as her daughter is fed nonkosher foods and exposed to the licentious behavior of Mémé, who once a week receives a nighttime visit from her boyfriend. She feels that the affection Mémé shows the girl is immoderate (RO/RL, 49). Kofman confesses: "My mother suffered in silence . . . no news from my father, no way of going to see my brothers and sisters, no power to stop Mémé from transforming me, from detaching me from her and from Judaism. I had, it would seem, buried my entire past: I had begun to adore those beefsteaks cooked rare with butter and parsley" (RO/RL, 67).

The scene describing Sarah's tonsillectomy, in chapter 12 of *Rue Ordener, Rue Labat*, dramatizes the symbolic detachment from one food turned indigestible (mother, Judaism) to another source of food now desirable (Mémé, Frenchness): "When I was ill, unlike my mother, Mémé did not panic . . . I cry and scream in pain. My mother starts speaking louder, pitying me in Yiddish and wants to alert the doctor. Mémé stays very calm, smiles and says: 'It's nothing, and you're going to eat a lot of ice cream!' I immediately stop crying. That day I vaguely began to realize that I was detaching myself from my mother and attaching myself more and more to the other woman" (RO/RL, 52–53). The girl leaves behind the *yiddishe mame* and her smothering apprehension and embraces the French mother and her promises of self-fulfillment and happiness. Yet despite her ecstatic acceptance of the French lady, Kofman also recalls that Mémé is neurasthenic (RO/RL, 48) and obsessed with her own stomach and digestion problems (RO/RL, 52). And despite Mémé's excellent cooking, the girl "frequently vomited and Mémé would get angry . . . my body in its own way was refusing this diet that was foreign to me and a source of anxiety" (RO/RL, 51).

Throughout *Rue Ordener, Rue Labat*, Kofman associates the goodness displayed by maternal figures with the bitterness of her childhood memories. For example, she adored her elementary school teacher, Madame Fagnard, who vocally resisted the Vichy regime, taught her students to give to the poor and feed the hungry, and took care of Sarah and her siblings in various occasions. Sarah had a true veneration for Madame Fagnard, her first surrogate mother (RO/RL, 25). The teacher grew so close to the girl that Sarah chose to call herself by the surname Fagnard on the fake Aryan documents the resistance fighters provided to her, her siblings, and her mother. Yet even a person as good as Madame Fagnard risks imposing her alterity on Sarah; this danger arrives, not surprisingly, in the form of food, through the mouth, reaching deep into her body, which promptly somatizes the frightening alterity and spits it out: "In the school courtyard, when she distributed dietetic cakes and skim milk, [Madame Fagnard] always overserved me, well beyond the allotted portions. One day . . . I had drunk so much milk during recess that I threw up in the middle of class: I was sent to the corner and made to kneel. I was all the more upset by this incident because my family had always forbidden Christian-style genuflections, which were way too Christian" (RO/RL, 28). Madame Fagnard has pushed too far, and the girl's adoration of this teacher suddenly dries up. "What can be more maternal an image than feeding a child milk," asks Stanislawski.[30] Yet the girl had overfed on this maternal figure to the point of self-endangerment. The law of the father forbids such acts of worship of pagan idols, and going against this law means pain and death. Again, food and the mother are connected, one leading to (or away from) the other. The girl's subconscious works out a strategy (the refusal or acceptance of food) to negotiate the boundaries with the people around her and to exercise power. Kofman, certainly conscious of their significance, works her memories about food and vomit into oral metaphors that become key to her formulations on the impotence of witnessing.

## BETWEEN SEDUCTION AND CONVERSION, KOFMAN'S *MORTE BLANCHE*

An expert on Lacan, Kofman knew the psychoanalytical meaning of ça, and Lacan's definition of "it" (Ça, Es, id) can be extremely helpful to us in understanding Kofman's as well:

Let us think of a mailbox and of the inner cavity of some Baal-like idol; let us now think of the *bocca di leone* which, in combining them, acquired its fearsome function in Venice. A reservoir, yes, as it were, that is what the id [Ça] is, and even a reserve; but what is produced in it, missives of prayer or denunciation, comes from the outside, and if it accumulates inside, it is in order to sleep there. The opacity of the text stating that silence reigns in the id [Ça] is thereby dispelled: the silence is not metaphorical, but relates to an antithesis that must be pursued in the subject's relation to the signifier, which is expressly designated to us as the death drive.[31]

Lacan's *bocca di leone* and Kofman's own formulation, *bocca della verità*—by which she means her mouth—are significant images. *Bocca della verità* is connected not only to truth but also to prophecy. By contrast, Lacan's *bocca di leone* conflates two central concepts: truth (the act of denouncing) and guilt (the exposure of the person who is being denounced). In Venice, the *bocche di leone* were special mailboxes marked with the effigy of the lion of Saint Mark, the symbol of *la Serenissima* (the Republic of Venice), and were scattered all over the city. Passers-by could drop in anonymous denunciations to which only the magistrates had access. However, the lion, with its wide-open mouth, is also a symbol of voracity; therefore, a link between eating (devouring, or being devoured) and guilt (of the accuser and of the denounced) is created in Kofman's subconscious topography.[32] In her obsession with psychoanalysis, Kofman would position the mouth (a biological cavity and repository of dark drives) at the center of many associations. In talking about her psychoanalytical experience, Kofman describes the process of telling as a linear, uninterrupted flow that passes through her mouth and is released and expelled out of this orifice: a cavern of darkness and knowledge not unlike Plato's cave. This knowledge, however, emerges only through the encounter with the Other's ear. "Everything 'started' when I had nothing to say anymore," Kofman declares. She describes her disappointment in the analytical process: "The first period of my analysis was me reciting my long story. A linear, uninterrupted story . . . never the slightest rupture, the slightest gap, the slightest mistake . . . From the other side of the couch, nothing. 'My life' was met with indifference."[33] In the psychoanalytical encounter, the therapy works when the patient becomes her own witness, when she hears her own story in a different way, through (and thanks to) the ear of the Other. "So my mouth," writes Kofman, "stopped being a place from which a reassuring discourse was being emitted—*bocca della verità*—and turned into the cave from where there burst forth cries, more or less articulate, more or less intelligible words, whose tone, extremely variable (thunderous, evanescent, hardly audible, jerky, melodious, etc.), shocked even me."[34] We think immediately of Kafka's *Die Verwandlung* (*The Metamorphosis*)[35] and the moment when, awakening from his unsettling dreams, the protagonist Gregor Samsa's terrifying transformation is revealed to his family—who is attempting to talk to him through his closed door—through the loss of his human voice. I'll return to Kofman's connection with Kafka shortly, but for the moment I wish to point out that in Kofman's conception of analysis, a new person is speaking, in words that are at once foreign and recognizable, through a new mouth: "My mouth, enclosed, sewn, tight-lipped, shut (*fermée*). Constipated."[36] The mouth is the metaphor for all orifices, genital ("generous mouth that dispenses its . . . semen") and anal (it is a constipated mouth):

> I knew for example that if I was constipated on a given day I wouldn't be able to "talk" on the couch either, that *ça* would not dispense anything, that nothing would pass through . . . What passes through my mouth, during analysis, has nothing to do, then, with either truth or meaning. It emerges from my guts to be offered as a gift (*cadeau*) for the other to appreciate. Hence, the silence of the analyst is intolerable. It is a sign not of indifference to the events of my life but of a depreciation of my most intimate possession. A refusal . . . of my presents, of what comes out of my womb, of what I produce: my merchandise, then, is shit! I might as well not give anything, not tell anything. At least silence is golden. But this silence, too, is intolerable for me, from which comes the driving need to hear my words . . . not in order for them to be given meaning or be interpreted, but in order for an exchange to subsist, one that transmutes "poop" ("*caca*") into gold.[37]

When the Other (the analyst here) refuses the gift (*cadeau*) the analysand is dispensing—out of her entrails—this gift, her "baby," becomes *caca*. However, as Kofman has already said on various occasions, silence is not an option. In truth, silence is not golden but intolerable. If we follow her metaphor, gold is synonymous with sperm, the fluid endowed with life that also comes through the speaking mouth when it (*Es, ça*) is properly being heard.

In her book *Conversions*, Kofman analyzes in depth the theme of the three caskets in *The Merchant of Venice*, starting with the premise that Freud had only partially understood or had only been partially willing to hear that drama's powerful implications. Kofman criticizes Freud for confining his analysis of the choice of the three caskets to a discussion of love and for not pushing the discussion further, as she does, to account for temporal ambivalence: "the duplicitousness (*double face*) of time, premise of all conversions and of all reversals."[38] The transformation of gold into *caca*, of good into bad and vice versa, is the central concern of Kofman's *Conversions*, and, as I discuss later in this section, this fascination for doubles and duplicitousness will come up explicitly in *Rue Ordener, Rue Labat* in a discussion of her favorite Hitchcock movie, *The Lady Vanishes*. Time itself, Kofman hypothesizes, is ambivalent because it has two faces, like Janus Bifrons (the ancient god who guarded the entrance to Roman homes; the god of transitions, beginnings, and endings): one face is melancholic-depressive, the other manic. The face looking toward the future smiles, the face looking backward frowns. Ambivalence leads to conversion (reversal), which in turn is governed by time. And what purpose, Kofman asks, does ambivalence serve? Ambivalence, she answers, is at the service of desire. "The only thing that matters to us, in the end, is the ambivalence of love (its identification with death)," she concludes.[39] The heart of the matter is not Shylock's forced conversion but the fluidity of ambivalent things; the conversion that interests Kofman is that of lead (a vulgar metal, a symbolic excrement) into gold (the noble metal that hides its base origins), "the transmutation of something base into something perfect" and, ultimately, the conversion of life into death.[40]

"The theme of the choice among three metals, in fact, cannot be replaced by the theme of the choice among three women," writes Kofman, "because the three metals are not constitutive only of the caskets, which are the alleged symbols of the women; each one of them, with its ambivalence, embodies one of the three main characters: Antonio, Bassanio, Shylock . . . and because one of them, Shylock the Jew, like lead (despite the fact that Shylock represents silver [money]), the true scapegoat, is accused of all sorts of crimes."[41] Could Kofman be identifying her mother with Shylock in *Rue Ordener, Rue Labat*, her own conversion of theory into memoir?

The problems of false appearances, transmutability (of bad into good and vice versa), and the ambivalence at the root of love—which is one with death and means both exaltation and despair—become the main theme of one of two important entr'actes nested within *Rue Ordener, Rue Labat*. After the plot reaches a tragic climax in a chapter titled "Liberations" (note the plural), the narration comes to a sudden halt. Kofman has just told us that after the war, her mother brought a suit against Mémé in order to separate Sarah from the Frenchwoman for good. "Mémé was accused in court," Kofman recalls, "of having 'taken advantage' of me and of having mistreated my mother. I did not quite understand what she [mother] meant by 'taking advantage,' but I was convinced that she was lying. I was outraged to see her falsely accuse the person to whom we owed the fact that we weren't dead and whom I loved so much! So, in turn, I accused my mother" (RO/RL, 70). The mother's plan backfires as the daughter betrays her (again). She is yet another Jessica, another Shylock's daughter, who—as

Ruth Klüger does in *Still Alive*—carries the guilt of having betrayed her parent. Thanks to Sarah's testimony against her own mother, the tribunal (improvised in a school courtyard by the Forces Françaises de l'Intérieur) decides in favor of Mémé. For the second time, the mother loses the daughter's respect because of her lies, although the girl does not even fully understand what these lies are, and the adult narrator does not intervene to clarify this crucial issue: the truth about whether the mother lies or not—was the girl sexually abused by Mémé?—remains inaccessible to us. From the daughter's perspective, whenever the mother attempts to save someone, she lies. Although the mother had to resign herself to her husband's capture, she combats her daughter's capture by Mémé; she kidnaps her back after the trial, hitting her and screaming in Yiddish: "I am your mother! I am your mother! . . . you belong to me!" Kofman remembers trying "to wiggle free. I cried and sobbed. Deep down, I was relieved" (RO/RL, 71). Here is the maternal "sentence"—as opposed to the French (patriarchal) one of the tribunal—and it's delivered in Yiddish. The buried language has reemerged. The past returns via the mother, who tries to bring Sarah back into the Jewish fold. (Later in the memoir, we learn that during the postwar years, when she was living again with her mother, Sarah returns to Judaism, relearning Hebrew and observing all the laws and interdictions of her childhood before once again leaving all of it behind once she finishes school.)

Before Kofman resumes the childhood memoir proper with a few anticlimactic chapters, she composes two anomalous entr'actes: one devoted almost entirely to a quote from Freud on Leonardo da Vinci's *The Virgin and Child with Saint Anne and St. John* (titled "Leonardo's Two Mothers"), and another centered on *The Lady Vanishes*. It is as if a hole opens up in the middle of the text after the traumatic trial and has to be filled with artistic meditations rather than childhood memories. I have analyzed elsewhere the entr'acte about Freud and Leonardo,[42] so here I will devote my attention exclusively to the one about Hitchcock. The Polish writer, painter, and Shoah victim Bruno Schulz once wrote the following in a letter to his friend Ignacy Witkiewicz:

I do not know just how in childhood we arrive at certain images, images of crucial significance to us. They are like filaments in a solution around which the sense of the world crystallizes for us . . . They are meanings that seem predestined for us, ready and waiting at the very entrance of our life . . . It seems to me that the rest of our life passes in the interpretation of those insights . . . These early images mark the boundaries of an artist's creativity . . . But art will never unravel that secret completely. The secret remains insoluble. The knot in which the soul was bound is no trick knot, coming apart with a tug at its end. On the contrary, it grows tighter and tighter. We work at it, untying, tracing the path of the string, seeking the end, and out of this manipulating comes art.[43]

The Hitchcock entr'acte in Kofman's memoir contains one such tightly knotted string that, following Schulz's insight, we can see that Kofman worked at untying all her life and out of which not a solution but only more art comes forth.

Hitchcock's movie is a classic of the switched identity plot, or as Slavoj Žižek describes it, "the most beautiful and effective variation on the theme of the 'disappearance that everybody denies.'"[44] On a train, the heroine of the film (Iris) meets a lovely old governess (Miss Froy) with a maternal face and with whom she happily shares the compartment; when Iris dozes off momentarily, the place of the old lady is taken over by another woman dressed exactly like Miss Froy, who in the meantime has disappeared. But this "new" Miss Froy has a disagreeable face, and Iris is sure this is not the same kind lady she had been traveling with. The protagonist goes on a frantic search for the disappeared lady with the likable face and refuses to believe that she never existed, as a series of people on the train insist. Undeterred by the conspiratorial coverup, Iris looks for the vanished lady everywhere. The replacement of the real Miss Froy causes Kofman great anxiety when she watches the film: "It is always unbearable for me when brutally in place of the benevolent, 'maternal' face of the old lady . . . suddenly I see the face of her replacement . . . a face frightfully harsh, fake, shifty, menacing, in place of the sweet and smiling good lady, just when one was expecting to see that one again" (RO/RL, 76–77). The uncanny effect in the movie is produced precisely by this substitution of the motherly figure with the uncanny figure, "the one perfectly separate from the other, the one morphing into the other" (RO/RL, 77). But how do we know that the good lady is in fact good? Not surprisingly, the answer brings us back to the issue of food: "she [the maternal lady in the film] always has food provisions" (RO/RL, 77), writes Kofman. Just like in her life, good maternal figures are connected with food, but a shift in their attitude might turn them into unpleasant figures and make their food intolerable to her.

Hitchcock's film returns in the "Angoisse et Catharsis" chapter of Kofman's L'Imposture de la beauté, published posthumously: "In fact, Miss Froy is not as 'good' or perfect as she appears."[45] The vanished lady is a British secret agent (espionne) working against the Nazis. She is thus not that "good" because she has lied about her identity, and this moral contamination is reflected in her replacement, the bad lady. Purity and contamination are two central leitmotifs of Kofman's texts. We think back to the scene in "Sacrée nourriture" (which also takes place on a train) when her father allows the children to eat pork, thus "purifying" what had been previously been impure—or, to put it differently, contaminating what had previously been sacred. We also think back to the scene in *Rue Ordener, Rue Labat* in which the mother's lie (an attempt to save her husband from deportation) contaminates the perfection of the father's world. Kofman sees the same contamination at work in Hitchcock's film: "She [Miss Froy] does not have any more the purity of the ideal or its perfection." According to Kofman, "it had been necessary for her to die, and, in the course of the journey, she loses her protective power. On the contrary, it's the young woman [Iris] who saves her from the hands of the *comploteurs*."[46] If *maman* is Shylock, is Mémé a *comploteur*?

In Kofman's childhood, in order for Mémé to keep being good, the mother has to keep being bad; the biological mother has to pay the price of the daughter's need for disambiguation by maintaining the plausibility of her hallucination. Kofman sees the same premise at work in *The Lady Vanishes*: "turning 'badness' into the generalized feature of all the faces [that Iris sees on the train] is a 'ruse' of the film director and of the heroine's psyche in order to convince her that the original good image was . . . exclusively of a hallucinatory type." Kofman raises a central question about Hitchcock's film, one that we can redirect toward our analysis of *Rue Ordener, Rue Labat*: "Isn't the young woman involved . . . in the disappearance of the 'good' lady and in her transformation?" The subconscious guilt of Iris and Sarah is the unifying thread running through these two narratives. In both stories the heroine is as duplicitous as the ladies or mothers on whom her life depends and whom she alternately loves and hates; moreover, she displays a good side as well as a bad one. In the film, Iris at first behaves unpleasantly; she is unreasonable, unkind, and difficult, and thus not *sans tache* (free of stain or fault): "On the eve of the trip . . . [Iris] was detestable, intolerant . . . She bribed the maître at the hotel . . . behaving like a rich 'spoiled' brat who always gets her way."[47] Sarah too (the daughter who rejects her mother, who accuses her in front of the tribunal) is far from angelic (*sans tache*).

Kofman's analysis of Hitchcock provides interesting clues to help the reader understand her own text: "Her [Iris's] death drive, projected onto the outside world, makes the other travelers in the train compartment appear to her as threatening persecutors, plotting against her well-being. This projection is responsible for the transformation of the 'good' lady into the 'bad' mother, an imagined metamorphosis that is sanctioned by reality, for Miss Froy is not perfect."[48] However, unlike in the classic tragic or comedic plots of fiction, in *Rue Ordener, Rue Labat* anagnorisis does not fundamentally alter the course of the text. It is in the nature of a memoir that the heroine's blindness remains unaffected by the awareness the narrator gains of her situation and of other characters in her story.

In Hitchcock's film, the heroine meets a bohemian musicologist who initially seems to be her antagonist but who ends up becoming her ally and guardian angel. In fact, the two fall in love and, it is implied, will marry. Kofman finds the equivalent of Iris's helpful paramour in the guardian fathers of Western culture through whom—via rewriting them, de- and reconstructing their thought—she searches for the good mother who has vanished. Applying Žižek's interpretation of *The Lady Vanishes* to Kofman, we can say that through *Rue Ordener, Rue Labat* and all her writings, she affirms that Woman—who, according to Lacan, does not exist—in fact exists. But despite this affirmation, there is no happy ending to the story. As Žižek writes of all stories, "The happy ending is never pure, it always implies a kind of renunciation—an acceptance of the fact that the woman with whom we live is never Woman, that there is a permanent threat of disharmony, that at any moment another woman might appear who will embody what seems to be lacking the marital [maternal, in our case] relation."[49] Kofman's many "fathers" (Freud, Nietzsche, Rousseau, and so on—the cultural substitutes for the biological father) are like oracles: she interrogates them in order to solve the enigma of the disappearance of the good face of motherhood. All she receives in return are more enigmas, riddles, and paradoxes along with clues that are impossible to decipher. Male patriarchal culture is ill equipped to address the blind spot that it has assigned to woman, to the mother.

Nonetheless, Kofman loved riddles and knew that the pleasure (*jouissance*) is in discovering, and not in solving, an impenetrable conundrum. Her dreams provided her with plenty of interesting riddles. She once woke up from an anxiety dream and jotted it down on a piece of paper, which was later found and published in the journal *Fusée* in 2009. In this dream, she saw herself on a country road surrounded by mountains: a landscape that infused her with "absolute joy" (*jouissance*).[50] However, in order to contemplate the splendor of this landscape, the dreamer has to climb a winding ladder, at the top of which she sees an enormous wave full of white foam, which turns into an angel robed in white holding a scythe. Grabbing her from behind, the angel starts scratching her with the scythe and knocks her dead: "Awakened by the anxiety, not at all sure that it was just a dream, I whisper: 'my death milk [*lait de ma mort*].'" A milk of death like that of Madame Fagnard or Mémé, or a milk of life turned deathly like that of Kofman's father and mother? Kofman decides that the title for this dream should be *la mort blanche* (white death).[51] The death she dreams of might be white or innocent (*morte blanche* can refer either to the death of infants in their sleep or to death by lack of oxygen), but the death milk is probably not white but black, like the Shoah milk that Paul Celan writes about in his famous poem "Deathfugue" ("Todesfuge"): "Black milk of daybreak we drink it at evening / we drink it at midday and morning we drink it at night / we drink and we drink."[52]

Another dream that Kofman, at once a Freudian and an anti-Freudian reader, interprets for us deals with her Jewish identity through the metamorphosis of a name. This dream reinforces Chanter's suggestion that Kofman strongly identified with Freud not only because they both had a conflicted relationship to Jewishness but also because they both had humble origins.[53] In the essay "Tombeau pour un nom propre," we read:

> Dream: on a book cover, 'I' read:
> Kafka
> translated by
> Sar . . . Ko(a)f . . .[54]

Kofman tries to interpret this enigmatic dream by digging into the origins of her own family name, which was the result of a bureaucratic mistake by an unknown city employee who had Gallicized the German Ashkenazi original, Kaufmann, "which cannot but evoke commerce, money, caca [kaka], the Jew."[55] Kofman interprets this as a guilt dream because she links her name with the anal orifice, claiming that this connection between name and anus is guilt ridden (culpabilisant) or at least points to a guilt. Standing between Ka(f)ka and Kaufmann (equally synonymous with poop) in her cryptic dream is Kofman. The dream is doubly cryptic: kryptos in Greek means cavern or grotto—here, that inner cavern in which the caca is stored and expelled, as well as sperm, and words (of memory):

> Isn't though the severing "elision" the equivalent of a double castration, chastisement of she who meant to deny her blood, erase her lowly origins, to hold her head high?
> Sar . . . Kof . . . Sarkof?
> (S)he gets mutilated of two sexes, cat-rat (chat-rat), I devour my own flesh: sarcophagus.[56]

The spelling "mistake" restores her "head" (Kof—Kopf means head in German) and allows her to hold it high. She signs this dream "Sar . . . Ko(a)f . . ." and points out that in Hebrew, the "a" elided from her first name in the dream indicates the feminine gender of a noun, while the German suffix "Man(n)" in her family name reestablishes the male presence. Hence sarcophagus becomes sar-kof-phagus, or she who feeds on Sarah's head.

And how can one ignore that, as Kofman must have known, *kof* is also the name of the Hebrew letter k and that the bad lady in Hitchcock's movie, Miss Kummer, has a name also starting with *kof* and it contains the letter *mem* (m) (like Kofman, but also twice like *maman* and Mémé). It also contains one of two important Indo-European lexemes (*mer* and *mar*) to which Kofman attaches great importance in another dream-related essay, titled "Cauchemar" ("Nightmare"),[57] a lexeme that is an utterance of misfortune and whose traces are still found in a few modern words of common usage—such as *cauchemar*.

Kofman is the autophagous woman with an obsession for the mouth, the organ Lacan identified as "l'objet primitif par excellence" (the primitive object par excellence).[58] There is a *régime* (both dietary and political) that is ruled through the mouth and that rules the mouth, and at the head of this *régime* are the father and the patriarchal mother. The idea of the mouth from which words, vomit, sperm, and *caca* can erupt connects Kofman the Freudian scholar to another famous woman whose therapy (like Kofman's) also failed: Irma—who like Sarah, had a propensity to vomit. As Freud notes about Irma's case, "the first organ to emerge as an erotogenic zone and to make libidinal demands on the mind is, from the time of birth onwards, the mouth."[59] The mouth was at the very center of Freud's famous dream about Irma—a semi-successful (and thus also semi-failed) psychoanalytical case of a woman who had refused his prescriptions. "A large hall—numerous guests . . . Among them was Irma," Freud writes about his dream. The woman complains of pain in her throat, stomach, and abdomen, lamenting that the pain is choking her. Freud continues: "I took her to the window and looked down her throat, and she showed signs of recalcitrance, like women with artificial dentures . . . She then opened her mouth properly . . . I at once called in Dr. M., and he repeated the examination . . . My friend Otto was now standing beside her as well, and my friend Leopold was percussing her through her bodice."[60] The men proceed to give Irma an injection with an infected syringe. This dream, one that in my opinion hints at a group rape fantasy, may be even more unsettling for those who read it now than it was for Freud, who dreamed it. It is, as Lacan points out, a terrifying image that turns Irma into a Medusa, one who holds in the depth of her oral cavity, hidden or stuck in her throat, something unnamable, unpronounceable. The mouth is a symbol of the female sexual organ but also, as Lacan says, "the gulf . . . in which everything gets swallowed . . . the image of death where everything ends."[61] Behind the composite imago of Irma are three men (either Breuer, Fleischl, and Emanuel or Otto, Leopold, and Fliess),[62] but also three women (Irma, the patient Freud fails to cure, Irma's friend that Freud would like to have as a patient, and Freud's wife, Martha). Chanter has written of Freud that he "is working through his relation to his father's death at the same time as he confronts his incestuous desire for his mother. Death and female sexuality have in common the fact that neither of them 'can be faced directly.'"[63] The symbol that conflates Death and Woman and that makes it impossible to face either of them directly, lest one dies, is the head of Medusa (which Ovid had already understood as a sexual symbol). The Gorgon Medusa was one of three chthonic sisters, whose effigy was used on shields and amulets for protection—female protection: although the Medusa herself is mortal to man, her double or effigy can be vital, a good-luck charm. This means that Medusa can be looked at only as reflection, as double. Kofman tells us that she has a special apotropaic amulet thanks to which her writing and her life were safe: the father's pen. Hence, the father's pen is cast in *Rue Ordener, Rue Labat* as the double or reflection of the deadly face of the mother or Medusa. Although facing the mother(s) is deadly to the daughter, using the mother(s)' double, the pen, is life saving. I will show in a moment, though, how the ambiguity of the double spoils this otherwise straightforward postulate.

Kofman draws an important distinction between ambiguity, which is equivocal, pointing to one thing or another, and ambivalence, which affirms simultaneously two opposing things, "sense and nonsense."[64] She stipulates that ambivalence is a maternal figure, with its roots not in the Oedipus myth but in the original connection of Love and Death, their convertibility.[65] Death can never be figured, says Kofman, other than as its double (Love). She goes on to explain that "despite appearances, gold . . . is not the opposite of lead"; in other words, "ambivalence is the condition . . . of [these metals'] convertibility or transmutability."[66] Kofman places this same ambivalence at the heart of the mother-daughter bond, noting: "At a certain point in [the daughter's] development there occurs a double transformation . . . the daughter goes from loving to hating [the mother]. On the other hand, she also changes the love object: she goes from a fixation for the mother to a fixation for the father."[67] I will venture to say that Mother is Medusa and Father is Janus. Kofman writes about Janus, whose effigy the Romans imprinted on their coins, that he is the "emblem, in virtue of his double face, of vigilance as well as of a limitless imperialism: essentially, he is the god of entries and exits, who guards the inside as attentively as he guards the outside, the right and the left, front and back, above and below . . . he is the god of transitions and passages: from a state to another, from the past to the future, from one vision to the next, from one universe to a different one."[68] We must therefore conclude that Medusa, the face that one cannot love without dying, is to Janus, the face that does not exist because it is always double, what ambiguity is to ambivalence. In Marcia Ian's compelling study of literary modernism and its relation to language, at whose center she positions the powerful image or fetish of the "phallic mother," we read the following paragraph which provides further support to my reading of the character of Mémé in Kofman as phallic mother: "The phallic mother, seemingly all productivity and reproductivity, flows with milk and semen, and yet stands like a screen between us and our prehistory as 'inanimate things'; she stands at the beginning of our psychic, cultural, and specific history as Death's mirror image as well as death's symbolic negation."[69] As Rome defeats Jerusalem in the ancient world, so in Kofman's story a Christian substitute, Mémé, replaces the Jewish father: the double devours its matrix. In *Rue Ordener, Rue Labat* Mémé is the passageway to French culture for the small girl: she introduces Sarah to books, crossword puzzles, dictionaries and encyclopedias, "la grande musique" (in particular Beethoven), and charming *chansonniers*—as well as the geniuses of Western civilization such as Spinoza, Marx, Bergson, and Einstein, whom she uses as paradigms of Jewish people's exceptional intelligence. However, she also undermines Jewish people's worth by describing the entire race as stingy, pushy, physically ugly deicides. Mémé embodies the promise of life, of a future, while the mother embodies a past lost for good—a past that the memoirist cannot look straight in the eyes (like Medusa) lest she be petrified.

## WRITING LIKE A CAT : KOFMAN'S IDENTIFICATION WITH E. T. A. HOFFMANN'S MURR

*Rue Ordener, Rue Labat* is Kofman's last text of and on ambivalence—a theme that preoccupied her all her life. In the memoir, she borrows from a famous Prussian writer—E. T. A. Hoffmann—the idea of doubling a text and the metaphor of writing as a scratching that leaves profound, devastating marks on the page. Kofman deeply identified with Hoffmann's bizarre *The Life and Opinions of the Tomcat Murr*. Hoffmann's novel deals with a pompous, self-taught tomcat who writes his autobiography by scratching the page with his claws, using as blotting paper the biography of a hypochondriac, grumpy, antisocial musician, Johannes Kreisler (Hoffmann in *fabula*). By mistake the two texts get spliced together, and out of this error—committed by a painter—is born an uncanny (though highly humorous) double narrative. Based on this fantastic double text, Kofman draws a general rule, according to which there is not only internal heterogeneity in a text, an inner *griffure* (scratch) proper to each book, but different books end up scratching one another, altering reciprocally every text.[70] Kofman loved Hoffmann's fantasy about a cat who writes his autobiography. According to her, Cat Murr's writing is a "double writing . . . one contradicting the other, in a complex way: at times the scratching of the cat tears to pieces the book of man; at times, on the contrary, it creates a book . . . more 'human' than the one written by Kreisler's biographer . . . Double writing, double biography—at the very least."[71] This "double writing" speaks to a more general truth about autobiography: these texts are internally heterogeneous and texts reciprocally mark each other with their *griffures* (scratches).

I am aware that I am splicing together Kofman-the-scholar with Kofman-the-autobiographer, but I believe that as her readers and interpreters, we have Kofman's tacit permission to do so. In using Kofman's own reading method to read Kofman, I therefore return to what she wrote about Cat Murr to shed light on her autobiographical project: "The text . . . had to be for Murr a way to be loved, to obtain the recognition of the superiority of his nature, to showcase his genius . . . If on the one hand writing is supposed to 'elevate' the cat to the level of humanity, on the other, it also runs the risk of leading him to 'madness': a double madness, inscribed into the text . . . the first one written into Murr's text, the second into the text of Kreisler's biographer."[72] Is Kofman guilty, as Cat Murr is, of being a "plagiarizer," of using the intellectual property of others for her own profit? "The plagiarisms of the cat turn the cat's writing into a text of quotations," says Kofman; these quotations "underline, through parody, the quotability of all texts and the absence of paternity."[73] The cat represents Woman for Kofman. She reads the story of Tomcat Murr through the (scratchy) irony of a feminist lens and concludes: "Almost unanimous incredulity surrounds the idea that a cat should write. Indeed, hostility: to write means to claim a human privilege, it means to deal a hard blow to man's narcissism and dethrone his kingship over the universe. To allow a cat to write means to inscribe writing into life itself and it means . . . to condemn the Cartesian principle by taking a position different from that of intellect and science."[74] In Kofman's essay, Hoffmann loses paternity over his text,[75] which is grafted on the older and illustrious cat story by Ludwig Tieck, *Puss in Boots*. By the same token, does Kofman in a sense lose maternity over her memoir? After all, hers is a story that must take the form of a well-established genre (subvert that genre though she does), and that uses multiple quotes from a lifetime's accumulation of intellectual knowledge from Western culture as a whole. Moreover, her memoir splices together her personal history and the historical events of the Shoah. Is *Rue Ordener, Rue Labat*, then, an impostor text like Hoffmann's? Again, as we have seen with Ruth Klüger (chapter 2), the Shoah memoirist finds herself questioning the viability of the mirror of memory. To what extent can the truth be represented, and can the author profess to know this truth? Klüger draws into her text the at times contradictory voices of other protagonists, witnesses, and historical experts; Kofman refers to the entire corpus of Western thought, literature, and art. These postmodern Shoah autobiographers choose hybridity as the only reliable way of speaking (*sans pouvoir*). And Kofman has learned the power of hybridity from an ingenious, postmodern work *avant la lettre* such as Hofmann's Cat Murr: a "hybrid text . . . effaces ownership . . . through authorial pluralism . . . annuls any effort to guarantee *maîtrise* [ownership; literally, mastery] of it. A writing that freezes like Medusa."[76] As a result, Kofman's book of memory is no longer autobiography but *auto-bio-griffure*, a text not peacefully inked onto the page but scratched into it, a book full of quotations and a representation of life borrowed from various sources and one that "is no longer a complete object peacefully resting in the closed space of a library." She adds: "The cat—a bookworm (*rat de bibliothèque*)—gnaws at the volumes, undoes their enclosures, and . . . becomes the murderer of the author as father of an *oeuvre*."[77] Thus to replace paternity with maternity means to become mother to the son or text that, in turn, will become matricidal—out of love and in self-defense—when it turns on its creator.

The act of autobiographical writing, notes Kofman, is an act of self-love committed to affirm oneself and be admired.[78] In a letter to Edward Bernays dated August 10, 1929, Freud wrote that an autobiography should meet two conditions: the subject of the autobiography should have participated in some important events and be of some importance for the entire world; and the autobiography should be a psychological study—which, according to Freud, would put at grave risk the autobiographer's relationship with those people close to him or her whose private lives would be exposed to the world. This, Freud explained, is why he refused, despite the endless requests from publishers and friends, to write his autobiography. Of course, he added that "what makes all autobiographies worthless is, after all, their mendacity."[79] Kofman certainly might have agreed, but she found that it is precisely this "mendacity" that makes autobiographies worth our while. And hence the need for the reader to be a *lecteur policier*. In the end, perhaps ironically confirming Freud's fear, Cat Murr's project fails. Are all autobiographical projects ill fated?

Kofman shatters the autobiographical project that traditionally has been predicated on the reader's identification with the great man—the imago of the father, God, the writer.[80] If Hoffmann had already punctured this inflated sense of the autobiographical subject, Kofman emulates him in her traumatic memoir. She writes of Hoffmann's work: "The desire to set oneself up as an example . . . means to deny the bestiality (*animalité*) within humanity . . . to deny the plagiarisms. And yet, whoever mistakes himself for a god cannot succeed except by showing very strong claws. Only these claws can protect from the censorship of the editors, against the rigor of criticisms . . . Behind the apparent sweetness of a cat . . . behind the 'divinity' of genius, hide the animal's claws: the animal will reveal his true nature to whomever will dare to pluck his feathers (*déplumer*), or to dispossess him."[81] Not only does *déplumer* mean to pluck an animal's feathers, but *plume* is also the archaic word for pen, quill pen (*calamus* in Latin); to extend the metaphor, to defeather is to take the pen away from the autobiographer, to dispossess her of her story. Neither Tomcat Murr nor Kofman deny their own animality in protecting their stories.

The frontispiece of Hoffmann's book is a droll picture of a cat holding a quill pen that Hoffmann himself painted. Kofman writes of this drawing that the cat it represents is not Murr but his double, and she compares this double to an intimidating penis: Murr's double has sucked, like a vampire, the soul of Murr, who, therefore, is entitled to steal back the pen (*plume*) in order to recuperate the blood that has been lost. Murr's task is to avenge himself for the blood his double has sucked away from him, to avenge the murder committed at his expense. If, as Kofman affirms, doubles are always vampires, then we must also revise my earlier analysis, according to which her apotropaic amulet (the father's pen)—being the safe projection of the deadly Medusa head, her double—is a salvific force. Ambiguity intervenes to rob us of this hope: instead, the double, which we have presumed saves the daughter's life, is actually a vampire, too, and as such it sucks the daughter's life. Pushing this idea of the deadliness of the double even further, Kofman postulates that in drawing an image of a sweet, friendly cat, Hoffmann is hiding the real, diabolical nature of the memoirist. An autobiography is the portrait of the author that, like the mirror (which always diabolically doubles) held in front of Medusa's face by Perseus, kills the onlooker: who is the onlooker in the mirror of memory if not the author herself? Kofman's double writing does away with the reassuring portrait of greatness we expect to receive from an autobiography. Instead, painted the way Kofman (or Hoffmann) does, the text offers us the unsettling image of a murder. With *Rue Ordener, Rue Labat* Kofman has claimed her right to pen her memoir in a demystifying way by murdering the author and depriving her text of paternity.

Freud himself had recognized in Medusa's head a signifier for the mother's sex.[82] In unpacking Kofman's understanding of Freud's penis envy, Oliver writes: "Freud learns too well the maternal lesson that the gift of life must be repaid with death." In Oedipal terms, since the satisfaction of the forbidden incest with the mother would bring about the mother's death, the son must avoid at all costs this body and this sex and avert his gaze from the petrifying Medusa. "So he [the son, Freud] tries to sublate his incestuous desire into a desire for scientific research on sexuality, which leaves the fundamental riddle of feminine sexuality unanswered . . . [In this way] he repays his mother's gift of life with death; he sacrifices her out of gratitude. He kills her so that she won't die."[83] In

Freudian theory, the woman's lack of phallus guarantees the man's power. So, too, Kofman's repossession of the phallic pen at the beginning of her memoir guarantees the death of the father: it enacts her loving act of patricide. But, paradoxically, it is through this phallus that the mother's story emerges in *Rue Ordener, Rue Labat*. A phallus that does not work any longer: it's a patched-up pen, lacking the lymph (ink) necessary for it to exercise its power. The real (not symbolic) father has been murdered, independently of the daughter's act. The daughter can only hallucinate that she is keeping him alive through her creative act: that she is paying back the gift of death with life. Perhaps Kofman realizes in this last self-analytical memoir that for the father and Mémé (his double) to subsist, the death of the real mother (ça, it) was required. In the same way Freud's science had saved the mother through killing her, out of love, Kofman's feminism had come at the expense of the mother.

This mystifying process takes us back to the equally mystifying subject of Kofman's memoir: ça. Stanislawski contends that "'it,' the ça . . . is clearly the story of her relationship with mémé, not that of her father's death."[84] Oliver reads the "it" at the opening (the mouth?) of *Rue Ordener, Rue Labat* as "the story of her [Kofman] father's death and her relationship with her mother during the war."[85] I argue that ça encompasses all three solutions: it is Kofman's love story with Mémé, and it is the story of the father and the story of the mother. But that ça is first and foremost, I believe, Kofman's realization of how this story had to be retold, of how she had been able to assimilate the (indigestible) story of her father only through the symbolic killing of the mother—only at the price of (s)mothering her. Her "crime" is ça: and ça demanded an auto-da-fé.

In that rarely used room reigned an exemplary order since Father's death . . .
Only a sheaf of peacock's feathers standing in a vase . . . had not submitted to
regimentation. They were a frivolous, dangerous element, untenably revolutionary,
like a class of high-school boys, all devotion in their eyes, but full of unbridled
impertinence behind those looks. Those eyes on the feathers never stopped looking
. . . Even in my mother's presence, while she lied on the sofa . . . "I was not lying,"
my mother said, while her mouth started swelling and at the same time becoming
smaller. I could feel that she was flirting with me, like a woman with a man.
    **BRUNO SCHULZ**, "Cockroaches"

# CHAPTER 4

# MATERIAL MOTHERS
## Milena Roth and the Kindertransport's Legacy, *Objets de Mémoire*

Even Winston [Churchill] had a fault. He was too fond of Jews.

**GENERAL SIR EDWARD LOUIS SPEARS**, quoted in

Martin Gilbert, *Churchill and the Jews*

A two-and-a-half-minute black-and-white film recorded by Julius Jonak immortalizes the departure from Prague of thirty Jewish children between the ages of two and eleven aboard two Dutch Douglas airplanes on January 11, 1939. The planes were headed to London, via Rotterdam. This group was only a portion of the approximately ten thousand Jewish children entering England as refugees before the war erupted, thanks to what is known as the Kindertransport Rescue Operation.[1] In this final farewell, we see children arriving with their families, and rescuers gently separating them from their parents. The adults maintain a dignified comportment, their emotions under control, but their faces are tense. The filmmaker must have cajoled some of the children to laugh and cheer, but when they are not consciously posing for the camera, no one smiles. Adults and children alike have ashen faces, almost deformed by anxiety. The camera sweeps a couple of times over the crowd of parents standing tightly packed on the tarmac, behind a small security fence to keep people at a safe distance from the runaway. Then the camera zeroes in on a few intimate scenes. It captures a mother leaning over the fence to reach for her daughter, who remains behind the group of children being taken aboard the aircraft; the woman kisses her little daughter's face frantically as if to imprint her love on it before letting her go. The skillful filmmaker also picks out from the crowd a distinguished couple, a husband and wife who are exquisitely attired. The mother wears her hat slanted to the side in the fashion of those days, while the father wears an elegant, large-brimmed fedora and a long, square-shouldered woolen coat. The mother's eyes are glued on the child the couple has released: we do not see the child, but it's clear from the mother's face that he or she is looking at them from the spot where the organizers are herding the children onto the plane. From the depths of her shattered being, the mother—visibly trying to control a rising tide of horror—courageously produces something close to a smile aimed, presumably, at encouraging and reassuring the onlooking child. The father is petrified, his right arm slung around his wife's shoulders, possibly to prevent her—or himself—from collapsing. The woman lifts her right arm, and, with perceptible strain, waves it in the air in a last goodbye. Never did anonymity have a more identifiable face. This couple's naked pain is unbearable to watch. Were they among the few adults who eventually joined their children in safety? Were they murdered before they could escape? If so, are we witnessing two parents looking at their child for the last time?

Among the Kinder saved in the unique rescue operation was Milena Roth, born in Prague in October, 1932, the only daughter of Anna Rothová[2] (née Steinová) and Emil Roth. Thanks to her mother's prescience and indefatigable struggles with a labyrinthine bureaucracy, Milena had a berth on the last transport vessel out of Czechoslovakia; her train left for England on July 18, 1939. Four years later (also in July), a different train heading in the opposite direction carried Milena's parents and the other members of their families to Poland, where they were murdered. Nine out of ten children of the Kindertransport never saw their parents again.

One day long after the war, Milena was readying herself to leave the house of Doris Campbell, the Englishwoman who had rescued her many years earlier when, at the age of six, she had arrived in England alone and in tears on that transport from Prague. Doris handed her a large envelope, adding with her typically British "breviloquence": "You'd better have these." The envelope was stuffed with correspondence from before and during the war between Doris and Anna, Milena's mother. Out of this personal treasure, Roth eventually crafted her remarkable Kindertransport memoir, Lifesaving Letters: A Child's Flight from the Holocaust.[3] Of the numerous Kindertransport memoirs available, I chose to focus on Roth's story because of the insight her book gives into the history of the rescue operation as witnessed by both the survivor narrator and the child's mother at the time of the events.[4] Roth adds to this mixture of perspectives her own perceptions, childhood memories, and adult impressions and elaborations. Her book's title reflects the two parts of her memoir: the mother's story (emerging through her letters to Doris Campbell) and the daughter's story (Roth's own memories of growing up in England). Since all Roth was left with from her European past were these letters and a handful of objects her mother had stuffed in her suitcase, I was led to ponder the importance of objects in the reconstruction of Shoah memory. Therefore here I will highlight the way in which Roth's memoir forces us to interpret the historical experience of women through their relationship to the material world that (symbolically, metonymically, and sometimes literally) reflects that experience.

I will also devote part of this chapter to putting the Kindertransport in historical context. An in-depth discussion of Great Britain's historical attitudes toward the Jews (or one of other free Western nations' political stances vis-à-vis Hitler's open aggression against the Jews) falls beyond the scope of this book, but it will be productive to briefly examine the culture into which the child refugees were transplanted and that affected how they reshaped their identities, understood their role in Holocaust history, and both remembered and memorialized their past. Moreover, since *Holocaust Mothers and Daughters* aims to demonstrate the broader oppression and injustice surrounding Jewish women (as women and as Jews), outside of the geographical and chronological boundaries of the genocide, this chapter affords a glimpse of that oppression in a national context unpolluted by the direct threat of Nazism—England was at war with, but not invaded by, Germany. Strictly speaking, the Kindertransport remains outside of the war's chronology because the operation ended the day the war began. The reactions to the Jewish emergency by the non-Fascist world, specifically regarding the fate of Jewish children, illuminate a telling aspect of the world in which the Jews lived that is often underplayed or brushed away from popular memory. Despite the large body of academic work on American and British reactions to Hitler before the war, outside the scholarly world these unflattering aspects of America's and England's national pasts are not well known. With this study, I wish to offer a possible answer to the question of why the story of the Kindertransport rescue operation has gained so little visibility in the Western consciousness. Why, despite much important scholarly work devoted to it, has this aspect of the Holocaust failed to catch on in the public imagination? I suggest that the answer lies in the female inflection of the Kindertransport story. That story is strongly marked by the presence and action of women—a presence, as we have seen, that has traditionally struggled to gain visibility in its own right. Since the story of female-inflected experiences is underrepresented (or even irrepresentable in patriarchal society), it is not surprising that the same fate applies to the story of the Kindertransport, which is rooted in the private domestic realm and the enterprise of mothers. Consequently, this study raises some questions regarding how the Kindertransport tragedy has been memorialized and explores whether the public modes adopted to remember it (mainly local statues at train stations or displays of artifacts in various Holocaust museums) adequately reproduce the feminine character of the event.

In 1938 the *Anschluss*, Germany's annexation of Austria and the Sudetenland; the German invasion of Czechoslovakia; the implementation of "Aryanization" policies in these regions and the increasing restrictions over all aspects of life for Jews wherever the Nazis came to power (imitated by Hitler's ally Benito Mussolini in Italy); and the ghastly riots known as *Kristallnacht* in November of that year were all signals that "life for Jews in Europe, particularly in Central Europe, was becoming more and more difficult."[5] Furthermore, the mounting wave of aggression that characterized 1938 was a symptom of Hitler's growing threat, which only a stronger international pressure could halt.[6] Judging from the way foreign leaders were appeasing the German chancellor while turning a blind eye to his criminal acts, such intervention did not seem to be in the cards, and thus some farsighted anti-Nazi activists thought it wise to help at least a portion of the European Jewish population get out of harm's way. Children, naturally, were a humanitarian priority. In particular, the Quakers were greatly alarmed by the Nazi government's increasing violations of human rights and, in collaboration with some Jewish organizations abroad, they began to mobilize. All eyes turned toward America, Canada, and England, whose outstanding democratic records qualified them as the likely candidates to organize a rescue operation for the Jews under Nazi totalitarianism. All of these nations, however, had just undergone the calamitous economic crash of the late 1920s and 1930s that, among other factors, had increased the opposition of the public and politicians toward interventionism and immigration. The overt antisemitism of some key political players in these countries did not help the Jewish cause.

Canada's immigration laws had always been based on race, and Jews did not qualify as one of Canada's preferred races. In 1938, as the persecution of the Jews in Europe took an unambiguous turn for the worse, Fredrick Blair, Canada's assistant deputy minister of immigration, wrote his counterpart in London: "I suggested recently to three Jewish gentlemen with whom I am well acquainted, that it might be a very good thing if they would call a conference and have a day of humiliation and prayer which might profitably be extended for a week or more where they would honestly try to answer the question of why they are so unpopular almost everywhere . . . If they would divest themselves of certain of their habits I am sure they could be just as popular in Canada as our Scandinavians."[7] Canada also distinguished itself for its callousness in 1939 when—together with Argentina, Cuba, Panama, Paraguay, Uruguay, and, most noticeably, Franklin D. Roosevelt's United States—it refused admission to the 930 Jewish refugees on the St. *Louis* cruise ship, forcing it to return to Europe.[8]

The megalomaniac and politically maladroit US ambassador to England,

Joseph P. Kennedy, at best misunderstood the threat Germany represented to the world and at worst simply approved of the Nazis' *Weltanschauung*. He seemed to have indicated this approval to Herbert von Dirsken, Germany's ambassador to England. After meeting the American, von Dirsken reported to Hitler in 1938 that Kennedy "understood our Jewish policy completely," and, referring to Kennedy's mild criticism of *Kristallnacht*, noted that "it was not so much the fact that we wanted to get rid of the Jews that was so harmful to us but rather the loud clamor with which we accompanied this purpose."[9] Blinded by his well-documented antisemitism, Kennedy once commented to Harvey Klemmer, an aide, that "individual Jews are all right, Harvey, but as a race they stink. They spoil everything they touch. Look what they did to the movies."[10]

Remarkably, Senator Robert F. Wagner (a Democrat from New York) and Representative Edith Rogers (a Republican from Massachusetts) sponsored legislation to increase immigration quotas for Jewish children living in Nazi Germany, allowing more of them to enter the United States. But Congress responded to the Wagner-Rogers Bill and the pressure of prominent political, religious, and intellectual lobbyists with the utmost obstructionism and bigotry. In 1939, the American Legion joined forces with the vociferous Senator Robert Reynolds, a North Carolina Democrat who was fiercely opposed to all immigration, to kill the Wagner-Rogers bill (despite Eleanor Roosevelt's sympathy and support for this cause), "arguing that . . . the admission of 20,000 children without their parents was against the laws of God."[11]

Great Britain, not a prosemitic country by any historical standard, distinguished itself in this case through an enormously ethical act. On the one hand, on a different geopolitical stage, England had firmly refused to allow Jewish refugees to enter Palestine, fearing that the mass arrival of Jews there would strengthen the Zionist cause and threaten Britain's hegemony in the region. On the other hand, the heroic resolve of people like Sir Nicholas Winton (the savior of Czech Jewish children), the Quakers Bertha Bracey and Jean Hoare, Rebecca Sieff, Sir Wyndham Deedes, Viscount Samuel, Rabbi Solomon Schoenfeld (whose prioritization of children from Orthodox families embroiled him in a fiery dispute with Winton and others who did not intend to distinguish among the genocide's targets based on matters of religious observance), and Lord Baldwin (the former prime minister, whose famous appeal to his nation is said to have moved the British conscience) led to the creation of a movement to steer public opinion and push the British government to grant special visas to a group of about ten thousand Jewish children from Germany, Austria, Czechoslovakia, and Poland, with the hope that their parents would follow soon afterward. Half of these children would be housed in hostels, and half of them were to be hosted by temporary foster families, both Jewish and non-Jewish. A network of philanthropists, volunteers, social activists, and religious leaders quickly took action to get the British Parliament to approve of the immigration, establish welcome centers, recruit English foster families, put together the list of young candidates eligible for expatriation, get permits from the Nazi government, arrange for their transport, notify the families, gather the children on the established dates, safely get them to their destination, and oversee their welfare once in England. The sponsors had to pay £50 per child—a considerable sum at the time. Vera Fast describes the time frame originally envisioned for the Jewish children's stay: "According to the Inter-Aid committee agreement with the government, the children were to be in Britain, supported by the Jewish community, for educational purposes for up to two years, by which time they were expected to have re-emigrated."[12] Obviously, England's entry into the war radically changed the terms of this deal. The last transport out of Nazi Europe was fortuitously scheduled for, and dutifully took place on, September 1, 1939, the day Hitler invaded Poland.

### IN THE HOUSE OF STRANGERS

Former Kindertransportees may have shared their survival stories with their close friends and family members, but the tales received scant public attention for fifty years (despite the 1964 publication of Lore Segal's autobiographical Kindertransport novel, *Other People's Houses*).[13] They had been "lucky" children, spared the worst; they were expected to pay back their debt to British society through an uncritical appreciation of and a voluntary submission to its rules and behavioral norms. To make a public display of their pain or remain attached to the tragic past could have been interpreted by their host country as an act of ungratefulness. Thus for a long time, the former Kindertransportees were denied (or did not recognize) their identity as Shoah survivors. They had, after all, "nothing" to complain about: they had been saved, they had had a roof over their heads and food on the table while other Jews were being butchered and starved to death on the Continent. To be guaranteed salvation in England, the Kindertransportees had been instructed, advised, expected, and sometimes forced to be quiet, obedient, inconspicuous children. By war's end, having gone through the traumatic experience of separation, relocation, acculturation, and orphanhood, most of them had naturally become quiet, inconspicuous, and well-behaved adults. They had learned their place. So they stayed to one side while history and a growing Holocaust culture honored, recognized, memorialized, and tended to the "real" victims. As Milena Roth unequivocally remarks, "there was a hierarchy of suffering, and we [Kindertransportees] were at the bottom."[14] Roth is no less sparing in her assessment of the motives behind the rescuers' decision to take in the Jewish children. Her overall judgment is not entirely flattering, even when it involves Doris Campbell, her own savior:

> There were some cases of altruism . . . Others had other motives. Many of the families were religious, and some were doing their good deed. I remember Doris talking about me in whispers at church, where she was admired for having taken me in . . . Some hosts were emotionally disturbed, and many children suffered at their hands. Some hosts took in refugees because we came from middle-class homes, which was thought preferable to being forced to accept evacuees from London after its expected bombing, since those people would come from poor homes, in London's East End perhaps, and cause all sorts of trouble. Some took girls of thirteen, fourteen, and fifteen and used them as servants right away. But some did provide secure loving homes. Interestingly, I have not met many of these.[15]

In her Kindertransport memoir, Eva Figes suggests another possible explanation of why some rescuers were moved by the plight of these particular children: "Whatever their normal prejudices, the English middle class found it easy to feel sorry for refugees whose manners and clothing betrayed a style of living equal or superior to their own, even if they were Jews and had now fallen on hard times."[16]

The Jewish communities in Europe, in collaboration with the Movement for the Care of Refugee Children from Germany (later known as the Refugee Children's Movement) in England and the other rescue parties involved, applied various criteria to choose the "right" children to include in the Kindertransport lists. Of course, the gravity of the risk the Jewish children faced—arising from the imprisonment or death of one or both parents, their financial situation, geographical location, and so on—was a primary factor. But as Claudia Curio has amply illustrated in "'Invisible' Children," when it came to finding the right match between Jewish refugee candidates and prospective foster families in the United Kingdom, more mundane considerations played a role in the selection. The children had to be deserving of saving; they had to have all the qualities the foster parents would have wished for in their own children. Only perfectly normal children, physically and mentally fit, were allowed on the lists. Needless to say, normality, especially under such utterly abnormal circumstances (death threats, military occupation, impending genocide, poverty) is a cruelly capricious formula. Curio recounts several harrowing stories, including the case of a deaf and dumb boy from Vienna, Heinz Gastler, who took the initiative of writing directly to prospective adoptive families in England and pleading his desperate case: "One person who heard from [Heinz], Lord Stead, passed the letter on to the Refugee Children's Movement, which sent the letter back to Vienna with the following note: 'We regret that we cannot do anything for this boy, for within the framework of our organization we can only bring children who are 100 percent healthy, both mentally and physically, to England.'"[17] Consequently, Gastler was denied sponsorship; he was later sent to Theresienstadt and murdered.

"Only those children capable of integrating were to be sent to England, in order to give a positive impression and thus to support further emigration of children," Curio explains.[18] In 1938–39, the children selected had demonstrated the appropriate qualities that allowed them to be among the few saved from the massacre. In order to survive, they learned to be adaptable and inconspicuous, which perhaps explains why their stories remained underreported for so long. In 1988 Bertha Leverton, a former Kind (a child from a Kindertransport) still living in England, noticed that the fiftieth anniversary of her arrival was coming up. She was about to let it pass unnoticed because, as she quickly realized, no one was talking about it. There were no signs of any upcoming commemorations. "I then started to organize a fifty year jubilee reunion," Leverton recalls: "News travelled fast, and shortly I had a world-wide two-day reunion on my hands."[19] Together with Shmuel Lowensohn, Leverton edited the first anthology of stories from former Kinder, I Came Alone.[20]

Starting in the early 1990s, many European nations began creating spaces for Holocaust memorialization—ranging from big institutional ones, such as national museums and cenotaphs, to small-scale works of commemorative art on the streets, in city parks, or in other public spaces. Several memorials were also commissioned in the twenty-first century for the children who escaped death on those trains to England. In 2003 a memorial sculpture by Flor Kent titled Für das Kind—Displaced was installed at the Liverpool Train Station in London, where all the transports arrived.[21] The memorial was meant to symbolically link this point of arrival together with all the Continental points of departure of the transports—at Hlavní Nádraží in Prague, at Westbahnhof in Vienna, at Bahnhof Friedrichstrasse in Berlin, and at Gdańsk Główny in Poland—to commemorate the success of the rescue operation and to mourn the disaster that broke families apart and destroyed lives.

I mention the belated and relatively exiguous attention given to the Kindertransport episode because the characteristics that mark so discreet a commemoration (reservedness, tactfulness, reticence, and so forth) reflect the loneliness, isolation, and forlornness that defined the overall experience of these refugee children. At their young age, they had lacked the perspective to grasp the magnitude of what was happening, and even as adults they were for a long time reluctant to classify themselves as victims alongside the other violated and dispossessed Jews. After the process of relocation, assimilation, and integration was completed, the former refugees ended up seeing themselves mostly as lightweight survivors, so to speak, as if there had been something cowardly and not worth retelling about their escape before having suffered the worst of the Shoah's physical and mental damage. About this feeling of total isolation, Roth recalls: "I didn't know another person in the world to whom this had happened. Absurd as it sounds, I had come off one of those trains, one among 10,000, but had been too young to take in, or to remember later, that there were others who had literally been in the same boat. I had no idea until about 1988 that there *were* 10,000 of us."[22] A sentence from Ruth David's memoir highlights this same isolating effect: "I was confused. One of my suitcases was with me, the other larger one had vanished. Suddenly I saw it standing on a platform, looking as forlorn as I felt."[23] This sense of forlornness is a returning motif in all former Kinder's memoirs.

The youngest of these refugees belong to what Susan Rubin Suleiman calls the "1.5-generation," or "child survivors of the Holocaust, too young to have had an adult understanding of what was happening to them, but old enough to have been there during the Nazi persecution of Jews."[24] The world around the child refugees did not pay much attention to their psychic needs and was not very sensitive about their conflicted identities. The enculturation process was hard, and its success required the victims to dismiss their traumatic upheaval. Curiously, the subtitle of Roth's memoir is *A Child's Flight from the Holocaust* (which is almost identical to the subtitle used by Ruth David, *A Young Girl's Flight from the Holocaust*). It is interesting that both Roth and David use the word "flight" rather than, say, "rescue" or "escape," which are more frequently assumed to relate to war. "Flight" brings to mind the idea of "flight of imagination," the "flights of fantasy" of imaginative children. We could perhaps read this "flight" as the incapacity to face the traumatic past, the need to "look away" from it, that has characterized the Kinder, who felt that their luck somehow stripped them of the right to be counted among the victims and feared that any such claim to victimhood might be taken as an act of ungratefulness by the country that had harbored them. This state of denial may in part be imputable to the host country's unacknowledged vein of antisemitism. The resistance to memorialize the Shoah in Great Britain indicates the persistence of an old enmity.[25] "I was so busy trying to pretend to be British and normal," Roth remembers, "that I couldn't think of Jewishness and refugeedom at the same time." Eventually, she "grew to love the British in spite of everything,"[26] and this feeling of love, gratitude, and belonging is shared by other Kinder alongside an awareness that although they had become British, they never succeeded in becoming English.

The Kindertransport chapter is, like all aspects of this atrocious historical epoch, uniquely tragic from a number of perspectives. The rescue operation itself, the first of its kind, was certainly a grand humanitarian act and an extraordinary testament to national and personal resistance to barbarianism. Though the movement was of course a success—the children were saved, their lives and futures ensured—this triumph ought to remain permanently shrouded in mourning because, as Sue Vice points out, the Kindertransport stories are fundamentally about "the trauma of transplantation rather than the success of rescue."[27] The experience of these children was neither one of traditional emigration nor of adoption. They were exiled refugees, and they had not been abandoned by their biological mothers and fathers or orphaned (yet). Often these Jewish children came from richer, more sophisticated and progressive milieus than those of their new families in England. And not only was British culture and society different from Germany's, but the Jewish culture of the children—no matter how assimilated and secular their backgrounds—created a further degree of differentiation between what the refugees were leaving behind and the new circumstances they encountered. "Despite the best intentions of host families and groups," Phyllis Lassner rightly points out, "because the rescue was predicated on a temporary stay and because of cultural mismatches, misperceptions, and misunderstandings, the establishment of emotionally intimate and secure relations was rare."[28] The quality of the relations the Kinder established with the host families, which many times became their adoptive ones, varies greatly from case to case.

As mentioned earlier, Britain's traditional attitudes toward Otherness in general, and the long-standing English antipathy toward the Jews in particular, contributed to certain difficulties in relating to and accepting these foreigners. The English-Jewish relationship was an old one and had gone awry as early as 1290, when England expelled all its Jews until Oliver Cromwell saw the economic advantages of inviting them back over three centuries later. "Britain was a tolerant society and was thus opposed to the *intolerance* of anti-Semitism," Tony Kushner explains. "The Jew, in return for his total acceptance in Britain, would remove any distinctiveness. The corollary of this, however, was that if anti-Semitism persisted after emancipation then it was the Jew's own responsibility."[29] Jews and liberals in Britain understood antisemitism as a backlash resulting from the widespread socioeconomic conditions of the lower classes: if you cure poverty and ignorance, you cure antisemitism was the naïve adage of the era. However, as Richard Bolchover writes, it turned out that "educating the

Jews against anti-semitism . . . was an easier task than educating the Gentiles."[30] To the English mind, as Kushner penetratingly points out, what was objectionable about Germany's attitude toward the Jews during the Nazi era was not the fundamental racism but the inelegant character and disproportionate magnitude of its expression—that is, the barbaric riots and uncivilized hooliganism. "Nazi anti-Semitism," Kushner argues, "remained a mystery to many in Britain because it could not be justified in terms of a response to Jewish behavior. Social ostracism and 'polite' discrimination were acceptable but mass murder could not be rationalized."[31] To the liberal, civilized Englishman, barbarianism was intolerable, even if directed against the Jews. In the years between the two world wars, there appeared on the prestigious pages of the *Times* a series of articles on the theme of "Alien London." One of them, from November 27, 1924, describes the Jews in these terms: "They stand aloof—not always without a touch of oriental arrogance . . . They look upon us with suspicion and a certain contempt . . . These people remain an alien element in our land."[32]

The idea of the tolerated foreigner as an indebted subject who ought to completely merge with the majority society in order to be accepted or else risk rejection (and thus be responsible for his own fate) was as much alive in the nineteenth century as it was in the mid-twentieth. In fact, as Bolchover suggests, the infamous cowardly behavior of a large section of Anglo-Jewry vis-à-vis their European coreligionists during the Nazi era can be attributed precisely to the persistence (and fear) of Judeophobia in England.[33] Many Anglo-Jews had prioritized "English blending" over "Jewish identification" and had been unwilling to open their doors to refugees. On this topic, Roth rhetorically asks, "where *were* the Jewish homes, and most particularly the Orthodox Jewish homes, when they were needed in 1939? Some Orthodox children lost their lives because such homes were in short supply, and their religious leaders refused to compromise with any other kind of home . . . It was even felt by some Jewish leaders that these Kindertransports should not be encouraged, as they might provoke more anti-Semitism." Roth too fell victim to the dynamics of self-loathing generated by such a homogeneity-obsessed society. "I didn't admit my Jewishness or foreignness to any new acquaintance," Roth remembers of her postwar life, "and many of my friends didn't know about it till years later, because I feared being thought of as dirty and somehow bad, being 'different' or pitied."[34] Of those mid-century years in England, Roth recalls that "the British were very anti-Semitic, in the sense that they regarded Jews as somehow dirty. All foreigners were funny, both ha-ha *and* peculiar funny, but the Jews were beyond funny . . . The subject of Jews was almost taboo in society and in the newspapers. The implication was that they had *almost* brought all their troubles upon themselves." Although she never encountered any hatred or ill treatment in her relationship with local children, apparently adults had no qualms about expressing their displeasure to her. This was the case with the "openly anti-Semitic" family ("uneducated snobs," Roth calls them) of Arthur Campbell, Doris's husband: "When I got married, one of them asked me, 'Does his family mind that you are Jewish?'"[35]

Nowadays, a lot has changed. European countries are dealing with utterly metamorphosed societies, racial and ethnic mosaics that have made these countries begin to rethink their conception of nation. This has in some sense cracked the monolithic, national veneer behind which the Jews (the oldest permanent minority in Europe) had been forced to hide for over two thousand years. As Beate Neumeier remarks, "normative Englishness has only recently given way to an acknowledgement of the plurivocality of Britain as a multicultural society."[36] This changed and improved climate (Europe's newfound willingness to deal with its past and responsibilities) is reflected in the proliferation of memorials, plaques, statues, museums, and other Shoah-related public displays, including the recent Kindertransport monuments. These monumentalizations and memorializations signal the important revision each country has been forced to undergo vis-à-vis its own imbrication and responsibility in the genocide of the Jews during World War II. One particularly significant example is the permanent national Holocaust Exhibition in London, opened by Queen Elizabeth II in 2000 as the latest addition to the prestigious Imperial War Museum (founded in 1917). It was a request from the Imperial Museum that Milena Roth donate a relic of her past as a child refugee in England that gave her the courage to view her private, silenced past as something she might share publicly, something that others might now, at last, want and need to hear. Roth found a few relics to spare, but she also sat down to write her memoir.

## IN THE HANDS OF WOMEN : CONTEXT, MEANING, AND MEANS OF THE KINDERTRANSPORT STORIES

The most powerful parts of Roth's memoir are the letters written in English by Anna Rothová to her friend in England, Doris Campbell.[37] The two had met in 1930 at the International Girls Guides Jamboree in England, to which Anna, then still young and single, had proudly participated as the Czech "ambassador" and leader of her nation's Brownies and Guides troop. Anna established very strong ties with Doris and four other English girls from the Midlands on this occasion. Later, these five women were instrumental in helping to save her child and looking after Milena when Anna could no longer do so herself.

Anna was very good at keeping up the correspondence with her girlfriends across the Channel, a correspondence that also gave her the much-welcomed chance to practice her English. The letters to Doris Campbell are initially light-hearted, cheerful, and full of domestic and pedestrian details about weather, health, family matters, engagements, marriages, and holiday planning. In one, she joyously communicates the birth of her first (and only) child, Milena. The first part of Roth's memoir is composed of these letters; the second half of the book is a reflection on her experience as a transplant in a foreign culture who is aware of the tragedy of which she had been a victim and yet who denies herself—and is denied by the surrounding world—the right to fully mourn. This testimonial memoir enjoys the hindsight perspective of the adult survivor daughter but also speaks in the direct voice of a victim: the murdered mother. By including the letters penned by her mother, Roth allows her to tell at least part of her story in the first person. In this case, the daughter's task is not only to remember her own past but to fill in the blanks of her mother's past as well, to speak for her when the victim's voice ceases. After a final, excruciating missive written by her mother before being deported to Theresienstadt, the daughter takes up the story. Though it purports to tell Roth's own story of Holocaust survival, this unusual memoir is in fact the chronicle of a mother's fight to save her daughter at all costs, as well as an entire family's story of victimhood.

Roth's story presents us with a double-motherhood scenario again. But unlike Kofman's experience with two mothers, this time the daughter's loyalty and attachment to the biological mother remains unchallenged, and her case does not reproduce the old "bad mother supplants good mother" archetypal story. Roth's biological mother is not supplanted in the daughter's affections, and the daughter does not fall under the spell of the new mother. Despite the heroic role played by Doris Campbell in saving Milena, the relationship between the adoptive mother and her accidental daughter remains cold, distant, and impersonal, much like Doris's relationship with her own children—one of whom lost his life defending England in the war. Doris turns out to be a complex female figure, though one with behavioral traits not at all rare for her times. She was quite a typical representative of her class except, it must not be forgotten, that few of her peers voluntarily offered their money, houses, and lives to save other people's children, as she did. Doris belonged to that Anglo-Saxon brand of Puritanism that sometimes jarringly combines good samaritanism with a heart of stone; strict vigilance with a complete lack of interest in people or world affairs; an extreme attention to society's demands with an extreme protectiveness of private boundaries; and, of course, an obsession with appearances with a sense of ethical obligation deriving from one's class.

Roth describes her new guardian thusly: "Doris was a big dominating figure, tall, not thin, with a loud voice, very frightening to me."[38] She adds:

Interaction with her was a one-way street. She talked; others listened and responded to orders. We never did have a conversation in all the years I knew her. She didn't listen, and she never asked questions except about domestic tasks done or not done. I had complete privacy in my head. She never asked me what I had done at school or anywhere else. She had no idea who my friends were. I was a nuisance, even though she had invited me and insisted on keeping me when she knew my parents couldn't reach England . . . She taught me to massage her back, place damp cloths on her head for her migraine, and hold her head when she was sick. And of course I had many domestic tasks, was a good listener, and didn't argue. Her highest compliment was, occasionally, that I had been "useful."

She preferred animals to people and told this to the world, and particularly to me. "Don't you dare ill treat my animals!" . . . "We chose to have them. You were pushed onto us." . . . She said it after we'd learned the fate of my parents.[39]

Such cruelty on the part of the foster parents or hostel matrons was none too rare, but these instances must be partially chalked up to that era's widespread inadequacy in dealing with children and to English child-rearing methods of the day, which were warped by strict, maiming, and often counterintuitive Victorian principles. Roth describes the climate of her English home as follows: "I could feel no fun or laughter in the home; the atmosphere made me tiptoe. Nobody seemed to relax or do anything together, especially not talk. It was a house, not a home."[40] This coldness was perhaps influenced by the specific brand of British antisemitism, which was, as many have argued, a paradoxical product of British liberal culture.[41] As is stressed often in the memoirs of the Kinder, no one asked them anything: these strangers were not seen and were indeed not supposed to be seen. Kushner observes: "There was essentially no educational, cultural or artistic attempt to confront the subject" of the extermination of the Jews in the immediate aftermath of the war, and this "was not simply a case of benign, naïve ignorance, but was part of the informal workings of liberal ideology under the added restraints of an exclusive Englishness. With regard to the Holocaust and pre- (and post-) 1945 British racisms, there has been a conscious desire to remember to forget—a process achieved largely in a voluntary and discreet manner . . . For example, the few Holocaust survivors who were allowed into Britain after the war were told in no uncertain terms to shut up about their particular, un-English experiences."[42] The British had tacitly agreed to save 10,000 Jewish children as long as no one had to confront their messy pasts. Roth became very close to Jane, Doris and Arthur's daughter, yet "despite our longstanding friendship, I've never talked to her about my own family. I feel she would share the general attitude that looking back is futile and insulting, and she's never asked me any questions whatsoever. It's as if my whole background never existed. It was unimportant."[43]

Although grateful for her good fate, Roth caustically writes that Doris "had continued with the mental annihilation where Hitler finished with the physical." Doris's cousin confirms the accuracy of Roth's sense of uneasiness by telling her (many years later) that whenever her name was mentioned, everybody in the family would always add a sympathetic "That poor little Milena, [Doris has] turned her into a servant." More explicitly, another relative of the Campbells tells Roth that Doris "wanted to break you." This particular relative, Doris's sister Kathleen, a missionary, had once tried to convert Milena to Christianity: "She was benevolent, though there was that strange sadistic undertow, the punishing Victorianism, with which they'd all been brought up . . . For instance, when Kathleen explained to me that her sister had wanted to break me, she said it with a certain relish, as if breaking people was quite an acceptable and recognized way of exerting power. Also, quite oblivious to the hurt it might cause, she quoted her mother as saying of me, 'We don't know where she came from'."[44] Implicitly, Roth's memoir is an attempt to answer this question: where did she come from?

## FOREGROUNDING ROOTS

In the 1920s and 1930s Czechoslovakia was an independent republic, and its founder, Tomáš Masaryk, was an enlightened, philosemitic, feminist, and progressive president. After centuries of subjugation to the Austro-Hungarian Empire, after World War I the country's self-respect and economy were on the rise. Regrettably, though, there were unresolved ethnic tensions, as the Slavs (mostly peasants and members of other lower classes) bitterly resented the ethnic Germans (mostly members of the urban upper middle class). The German-speaking minority was not ashamed to flaunt its sense of intellectual and financial superiority in the face of the Slavic majority. Squeezed between the two factions was a sizable Jewish minority that was divided into two subgroups: Jews of Germanic origin who spoke German but felt profoundly connected to the history and political interests of Czechoslovakia (Franz Kafka's family, for instance); and Jews who spoke Czech and had severed all bonds with the Prussian or Austrian world of their forebears.[45] The only thing on which the first two groups, Christian Slavs and Germans, could agree was their common dislike of the third group, the Jews, regardless of which language or customs the latter adopted.

It is hard to detect traces of the Steins' or Roths' Jewish affiliations in Anna's letters to Doris from before 1938, partly because of the outsize role Christmas plays in the correspondence. Anna and Doris sent each other thoughtful cards and Christmas presents every year, and Anna explains in detail the traditional ways in which the holiday is celebrated by the Czechs (and, one can deduce, by her family as well). "You asked me about Xmas," we read in a letter from March 4, 1932: "Yes, we too have turkey, and always fish . . . We haven't got any Xmas pudding, (but Xmas cakes) . . . in most of the families there is a Christmas tree, i.e. a fir tree lovely trimmed with cakes, glittering things and candles . . . We haven't got holly in our country at all, (it does not grow here), and the custom with mistletoe we have adopted from England I think." The following year another happy letter announces: "I have got your present and dutifully have opened it at Xmas Eve (which is the greatest moment of the whole Xmas time in our country.) . . . I must confess that in the first moment I was not quite sure about the ruffles you sent me, what they were for. My husband suggested they might be muffs for the baby. But later all the family came for supper, (Xmas Eve they were all my guests), so we determined with my sisters and sister in law that they were ruffles, so used them for this purpose, and they were perfect for this. So I hope we were right." References to nonkosher foods and more Christmas details abound: "The St Nicholaus brought Milena lovely toys to play with" and "for Xmas we shall have a Xmas tree nicely trimmed with all kinds of glittering and sweet things on it."[46] I want to call attention to the fact that these descriptions are characterized by an overabundance of material things, which in turn signals, as I will show later, Anna's almost overactive consumerism. Specific references to Judaism or Jewish identity, however, remain conspicuously rare. Clearly, Doris was not enquiring about Jewish celebrations, and Anna was not volunteering details that might be unwelcome or alienating. In a letter from 1931, Anna sends photos of her civil wedding ceremony and tells Doris about her new husband, specifying that "he is Jewish as I am." The issue comes up again four years later, around another Christmas time: "We shall have a Xmas tree although we are Jews, and don't keep of course religiously the habits of this feast, but it is such a joy for the children to have a Christmas tree and presents under it."[47] This attitude was predominant in Europe among assimilated Jewish families living in urban settings: Jews in Prague, Vienna, and Berlin adopted the Christmas festivities as a way to bask in a warm, familial atmosphere. Devoid of its spiritual and theological content, a secularized version of Christmas allowed assimilated Jews to be like their neighbors without compromising their own identities as Jews. Sharing in the Christmas celebrations—more specifically, sharing in the holiday's most pagan and consumerist aspects—was a sign of

Jewish willingness to partake in the cyclical rhythms of the Christian world that had only recently allowed them to join in other aspects of civic life. In a way, such celebration can be seen as a token of gratitude on the part of the more secular Jews to the society that had emancipated them. As David writes in her Kindertransport memoir, "my grandmother had belonged to a society in which Jews were integrated and unafraid. They felt they belonged to a cultured, civilized nation, and were proud to be part of it. Indeed many Jews were scarcely aware of their Judaism."[48]

Once again, acting like everybody else was not only the condition tacitly enforced by society but also the tactic that Jews thought to be most effective in preventing the recurrence of old conflicts with the outside world. In an uncannily circular way, Anna Rothová's letters reflect the same uncomfortable self-consciousness about one's Jewishness that her daughter would experience many years later while living in a free, civilized, culturally advanced, and post-Shoah England. After the French Revolution, it had been considered bad taste in Europe to make a show of one's identity when this identity was other than the normative one; during a large portion of the postwar era, Europeans held steadfast to this tradition. Eventually, almost nothing will remain of Roth's ethnic background. A "vestigial Jew," as she calls herself, Roth analyzes her detachment from Judaism in these terms: "I've lived among Christians for the major part of my life and feel more alien among practicing Jews than among foreigners of any kind."[49]

As the situation for the Jews on the Continent worsened considerably, the letters between Anna and Doris include more serious topics, which makes it impossible for either of them to avoid the uncomfortable subject of Anna's Jewishness. "Thank you very much indeed for your kind words," Anna writes on December 18, 1938 (probably in response to sympathy and worry expressed by her English friend after hearing about Germany's claims to the Sudetenland): "I do hope that the time will not be so bad . . . Maybe that you still remember my being of Jewish confession which is a chapter for itself in Central Europe."[50] Despite the fact that news of Kristallnacht had occupied the entire Western world for weeks, Anna's letter indicates that Doris does not make the connection between her Czech friend's Jewishness and the danger Nazism held for her. And despite the turmoil that brings Anna's Jewishness to the fore, Doris keeps sending Christmas cards to her friend year after year, further indicating her detached stance toward the Jewish aspect of her friend's identity.

Anna's letters to Doris become more and more desperate as the noose around the neck of Central and Eastern European Jews tightened and Anna frantically tried to save her daughter, herself, her sister, and her husband by securing all of the adults jobs in England, along with life-saving exit visas. Doris understood the urgency and helped her friend. The Kindertransport rescue operation would not have been as successful as it was without the involvement at all levels of women like Doris. Sybil Oldfield pays tribute to several key figures behind the rescue operation, identifying the centrality of women's role in this movement. Obviously, in a world where so few women held a position of even slight influence, the political and financial backing of a group of influential Englishmen was essential for the start of the enterprise. The stockbroker Otto Schiff, the banking mogul Lionel de Rothschild, the Member of Parliament Philip Noel-Baker, Sir Samuel Hoare, Lord Baldwin, Sir Wyndham Deedes, and Viscount Samuel were among the most notable men who used their political leverage to influence the British government's position on refugees and who initially provided the much-needed financial backing for the rescue operation. But, as Oldfield points out, "it was in the very nature of this particular project, focusing on the care of children and teenagers, that it would be *women* who would have to carry the essential responsibility in ensuring day-to-day success over ten years, or in certain cases bear the responsibility for failure."[51] Oldfield focuses on the indispensable role women played at all levels of the bureaucratic hierarchy to ensure the success of the transports. It is mostly thanks to the former refugee children's testimonies, however, that we can form a more intimate portrait of the individual women involved. The history of the Kindertransport revolves around children, and the traditional association between children and women makes it almost natural that the entire operation would be marked by the presence and involvement of women—biological and foster mothers, their female friends, nurses, schoolteachers, hostel matrons, and so on. These women played an enormous role in the everyday lives of the children, as well as in the decision making and implementation of the rescue operation. Reading Kindertransport memoirs and listening to the testimonies, one gets the impression that fathers were more reluctant to emigrate or to let their children—especially their daughters—travel alone, while mothers took an active role in organizing their children's departure. "[Father] too knew that we must emigrate," writes David in recalling the swelling antisemitism in the Germany of her childhood, "but he felt daunted by the enormity of such an undertaking. He knew no language but German, he had spent most of his working life on one project, the factory [in remote Fränkisch-Crumbach]. It was Mother who saw the urgency more clearly and who, 14 years younger than her husband, was more prepared to face a new and probably very hard life."[52] Eventually, it was David's mother who got a place for her on the Kindertransport, while both mother and father were murdered at Auschwitz after a long series of deportations from camp to camp. The father of another Kind, Ursula Rosenfeld, was beaten to death in Buchenwald, where he had been imprisoned in 1938 with hundreds of Jewish men and boys after Kristallnacht. Therefore, Ursula's escape was organized by her mother, who accompanied her to the train station the day she left for England. The last glimpse she had of her mother is an image Ursula would have gladly done without: "it was terrifying, . . . [her] contorted face, full of agony, very sad."[53]

There are exceptions, of course, to this tendency for mothers to take the lead, such as the case of Miriam Darvas. Darvas's father was an intellectual, a journalist in Berlin, a debunker of Nazi propaganda, and he was very much aware of the dangers of the situation. He was quick to realize that Jews had to get out of Europe as speedily as possible.[54] By and large, however, it appears that fathers had a particularly hard time accepting a separation from their children, probably because, consciously or unconsciously, this was also an acceptance of their incapacity to protect their own family. To send a child away was to delegate the paternal role to others. It is easy to imagine how reluctant a father would be to make so emotional a break. I suspect that viewers of the documentary *Into the Arms of Strangers* will find it as hard as I did to forget the tragic story of Lori Cahn. The only daughter of adoring parents, Lori boarded one of the lifesaving Kindertransports along with dozens of other children. As the train was leaving the station, Lori leaned out of the window to take the hand of her father who, running after the train, desperately called out, "I don't want you to go!" Locking hands, the father pulled the girl out of the large train window. Lori landed on the platform, "devastated," as she recalls, but her father "was in seventh heaven [because] he had his *puppele*, his little girl, back." As a result, Lori spent the war not in England but in Auschwitz, where she was sent with her parents—who didn't return.

In England it was often the lady of the house who took the lead in helping the refugee children. These women read or heard about the humanitarian emergency in Europe, mobilized themselves, convinced their husbands, and completed the necessary paperwork to apply as foster families. It is sadly true that not all rescuers had the noblest of intentions in inviting young Jewish girls into their homes; some English families hoped to turn the refugees into cheap (because they received no wages) domestic servants.[55] Nevertheless, the positive stories outnumber the negative ones, and in any case, one cannot ignore the involvement of women in the rescue. *Lifesaving Letters* testifies not only to the resourcefulness and ingenuity of Anna Rothová but also to the activities of the network of women that made Roth's rescue possible. Even if this account can be taken as only a partial reflection of what must have been going on in thousands of other households—both the Jewish ones in Europe and the rescuers' in England—it nevertheless becomes apparent that (often unheralded) female volunteers were the engine behind the Kindertransport's success.

In Roth's family, all plans to obtain the exit visas were clearly made by Anna, not by her husband, for whom she is also responsible. "Only with my husband I have great sorrows," she confesses to Doris, adding: "Would you by any chance know of some kind of post in business or factory . . . I really have no idea up to now what to do with him." Anna mentions in several letters that, were she single, she would be able to get to England, but that she will not leave her husband behind.[56] Of her husband, Emil, there exists only one written memento: a short, loving note to his daughter in 1940 that was attached to one of his wife's many letters. Emil resisted his wife's plan to send his daughter abroad, only reluctantly consenting in June 1939—almost too late.

In the meantime, Doris was appealing to aristocratic and well-connected families in an attempt to rescue the Roths and their closest relatives and find jobs for the adults. This attempt is also documented in a separate bunch of letters that Milena Roth inherited from her adoptive mother. As Anna, Doris, Elsie (another former Girl Guide from England), and other women were exploring all paths and exploiting all of their social connections for a solution, the responses they got were "benevolent if not actively helpful." One notable exception among the generally positive responses to Doris's appeal came from a certain Mr. I. T. In 1939 Doris had the idea of calling in a favor she had done for a family three years earlier. She had arranged for the Campbells to host this family's daughter, Ela, in their home for an extended holiday period. Roth publishes the letter Doris received in 1936 from Ela's mother (Mrs. H. T.), which is full of gratitude and expresses her joy in knowing that her daughter is happy and safe with these good people: "It certainly is most kind of you to come to the rescue so promptly and I can never thank you enough for having accepted Ela into your home."[57] The choice of the word "rescue" is painfully ironic in hindsight, since only a few years later, Ela's parents have apparently forgotten their gratitude when faced with a situation in which a child actually needed rescue. Doris had contacted Mr. I. T. (Ela's father) to ask him for help in speeding the Roths' escape. It seems that Mr. I. T. worked in some administrative post (at an embassy or consulate), and that he was probably Czech; Doris pleaded with him for assistance in getting exit visas for the Roths. I will let his hostile response speak for itself:

Dear Mrs. Campbell,
I am afraid I can be of no help to your friend here in Prague . . . Whilst I fully appreciate your kindness and generosity in trying to help your Jewish friends, I should advise you not to get unduly worried: the Jews here are no

worth [sic] off then the rest of the nation. There is no Jew baiting and not likely to be [any]. Of course they are not a very brave race, and it's them who come squealing to the Legation, and they all want to leave the country . . . But apparently, to get sympathy nowadays you must be a Jew. The Czech Jews in particular are in no danger whatsoever . . . most of them have always been disloyal to the Republic . . .

I do not think you will be doing your country a very good service in the long run in taking all these people in. It's true they offer now to go to domestic service and work, but they won't stay there long . . . as the richest and most influential race in the world, [they] never do any manual work, but soon obtain control of commerce, finance, and all the more profitable trades . . . I certainly do not approve of the persecution in any form, and the brutal manner in which some policies are at present enforced in some parts of the world . . .

My daughter is still at boarding school in England as you know, and I have to thank you for all the kindness you have ever showed her . . . My job I expect will go west soon, and not being Jews, we have little hope of finding benefactors or refuge in your beautiful country.[58]

Contrary to what this bureaucrat had written to Doris—who, to her great honor, not only ignored him but never mentioned his name again, Roth says— many Jews in Europe were prepared to accept any kind of menial jobs should they make it to England or America on an exit visa. "When not sitting in the waiting rooms of consulates and embassies," Segal writes in her memoir, "everybody was going to the classes that had sprung up all over the city [Vienna]. Jewish professionals were scurrying to learn hand skills . . . My father . . . learned machine knitting and leatherwork . . . My mother learned large-quantity cooking. She took a course in massage, too."[59] Anna Rothová herself, as if anticipating Mr. I. T.'s hostile reaction, had written to Doris explaining that "I can just as well, for a week or two, work for a smaller wage or for nothing. I shall be happy to find a home, and am no 'grand lady' who would be afraid of work or consider one work better than the other." And the inaccuracy of Mr. I. T's slander about the Czech Jews' disloyalty toward their country is clear in an incident that has become one of the best-known Auschwitz anecdotes, of which we also read in a letter from Heda Kaufmanová, Anna's best friend, to Roth written in 1960: "One day, it was on March 7th, Ela [an old friend who was in Auschwitz with Anna Rothová] told me, in 1944 if I am not mistaken, the whole transport with which she [Anna] came from Terezin to Osvecim [Oświęcim/Auschwitz], was taken to the gas-room. They knew where they were going to. While they marched in, they were all singing Kde Domov Muj, — 'Where is my home' — the Czech National Anthem." [60]

Despite the unpleasantness exhibited by figures like Mr. I. T., Roth's book abounds with tales of women who were pivotal in providing help, advice, and sometimes even just moral support to Anna, Doris, and Milena: Mrs. Mathewson, Miss Wellington, Miss Wilson, Heda Kaufmanová (who eventually committed suicide), and the indefatigable Elsie, "who finally persuaded your parents," Heda writes in her letter to Roth, "to send you abroad after the Nazi invasion. And she was pulling strings and moving mountains to get your parents abroad too." [61]

## MATERIAL MOTHERS

The material world enters Roth's memoir with a force that is not found in other Shoah texts examined in this book. When we read the personal stories of refugee children who arrived in England, one of the elements that jumps out at us is the conspicuous presence in these survivors' lives of things. This presence is not usual in memoirs of concentration camp survivors, whose experiences of complete dispossession seem to be reflected in their distance from the material world (apart from references to functional things such as food or clothing that made their survival possible). *Lifesaving Letters* allows us to consider the identity of women, the strength of female resistance to oppression, and the female technologies of memory making through the lens of the materiality of the surrounding world, particularly at a moment in history where, together with millions of people, every thing they had was also to be lost forever.

The Kinder were given objects by their parents to keep as souvenirs of their families, and their memoirs display a profound awareness of the relevance of these objects in their past and present lives. They are both objects of childhood (the authors') and adulthood (their parents'), of survival and victimhood, of life and death. They are the children's connection to a death they were destined for but did not experience.

Objects are not passive in the identity-making process. "Objects . . . participate in the formation of identities and the constitution of embodied subjectivities," Beth Fowkes Tobin writes. She explains that "subjects can endow objects with subjectivity, and furthermore, objects can act with a kind of agency we tend to think should be reserved for human subjects." They participate in the making of meaning and can become "a 'mechanism' or a 'technology' for producing specific identities and kinds of social interactions," as anthropological scholars have recently argued. [62] Not surprisingly, the colonization of the Kinder's Jewish identities often began by confiscating the objects they had brought with them from Europe. "Often, during the transformation of these suspicious exotics into 'nice English girls and boys,'" Mona Körte points out, "the clothing from home ended up in the oven. Clothing always carries a high symbolic value in life as in narration."[63] In the past two decades, scholars have begun to tackle the question of whether objects, and our relation to them, are gendered. For instance, the respected hobby of collecting, traditionally a male privilege, is antipodal to shopping, the unproductive (when not morally suspect) occupation of women. When women collect—and, historically, they have—they usurp an important power of the patriarchal and capitalist vision in which men are owners and women are consumers. Paradoxically, if women's consumerism is culturally seen as (moral) weakness, it has also assumed an incredible relevance in the capitalist world since the middle of the nineteenth century—a world that thrives on the consumeristic drives of women and, indeed, largely caters to those desires. Culturally, women are thus condemned for something that, economically, they can be exploited for. Yet the capitalist economic apparatus is mostly in the hands of men. In the late nineteenth century, shopping had become an activity central to the construction of the identity of the urban woman.[64] I intend to show how both Anna and Doris reflect this new urban, empowered, materialist identity.

I will consider three ways in which the object functions in Roth's text. First, Anna and Doris used their objects to organize the material world around them. Their possessions thus allowed their identities (national, ethnic, and maternal) to emerge. Second, objects are the palpable repositories of memory through which Roth connects to both mothers and works through her Shoah trauma. What I call "memory objects" (*objets de mémoire*, to borrow and build on the French historian Pierre Nora's idea of "sites of memory," *lieux de mémoire*) are of supreme importance in the Kindertransport stories.[65] Third, it is through objects that we reconstruct history and form a collective memory of the past. To state the obvious, museums cannot display people, only their things. Therefore, in a museum's retelling of the phases and technologies of the Holocaust, objects are vital—so vital, in fact, that they are organized by museum curators in specific, well-studied ways in order to tell more than just their objective and immediate story and become symbols of a larger, cumulative history. For example, the collection of shoes at the museum installation in Auschwitz—some improvised out of the simplest materials, some brand-new, others patched up or soleless, some unpaired heaped together with girls' and baby shoes—tells the story of millions, of the guilt of millions, of the silence of millions, and of the millions silenced. Often, the objects displayed in such museums were found after the liberation and were bought or received from private collectors or donors. Museums are collections of things on a grand scale, and they underline the connection, obviously not a superficial one, between our culture and objects. From the private, intimate world of the house to the public world of museum exhibits, our history is full of and told by the things we leave behind.

Objects are links to a disappeared past, and we read and re-collect that past through its objects. Our museum culture is perhaps the best proof of the collective use of objects we have adopted in order to both remember and construct anew our national or international pasts. Once donated to a museum, the objects salvaged from destruction or the survivors' heirlooms become part of a collection (and a collective one at that). It is worth remembering that museums' collecting practices are part of a specifically masculine way of constructing and maintaining history born out of the nineteenth century's love of display, accumulation, and ownership. A traditional historical museum is a collection of objects, and it is important to keep in mind, as Constance Classen and David Howes point out, that "collecting is a form of conquest and collected artifacts are material signs of victory over their former owners and places of origin."[66] Collecting is colonial, part of an imperialistic project. Given that Hitler's project was also imperialistic, collecting (through looting, dispossessing, hoarding, otherwise improperly acquiring, amassing, and relocating) was one of the Nazi regime's prominent (and destructive) features. In fact, ironically, as Jeffrey Feldman reminds us, our Holocaust museums today owe their mountains of human artifacts to the Nazis' hoarding practices.[67] The Nazis did not destroy their victims' belongings because they were supposed to be sent to the motherland for redistribution among the German population (victims' clothes and shoes), for national or private cultural consumption (looted art), or for recycling (victims' hair, prosthetic limbs, metal braces, gold teeth, and so forth). Interestingly, the perpetrators planned to leave no trace of their crime. The idea was that after finishing their ethnic cleansing, they would tidy up the mess that had temporarily arisen from the industrial elimination of millions of people, and everything would return to a sanitized Germanic order. Instead, history thwarted Hitler's imperialist utopia, and, contrary to his plans, the traces of the disaster remained visible everywhere. In fact, traces were all that was left behind.

In the remainder of this chapter, I propose that we follow the path of these objects of Shoah memory from their domestic incarnation, when they resided in the hands of their victimized owners, to their universalization in the collective space of the museums, where the Kindertransport's traces are now amassed, categorized, displayed, and explained. By asking what happens to these traces once they are translated from the private to the public sphere, I seek to answer the question of why the Kindertransport has stimulated the collective imaginary less than other aspects of the Holocaust drama.

## ANNA

Roth's memory of packing with her mother before leaving for England captures some important details of her experience:

> I perfectly remember us packing two suitcases together. My mother filled one with all the family linens—many . . . were embroidered with her maiden initials, A.S.—and the lace tablecloths made by her mother. She also packed the dark-red silk with the cream-colored bird and my hand-embroidered Czech peasant outfit in dark lovely colors, with its many petticoats, puffed sleeves, and richly embroidered apron and headband. There was a doll in a matching outfit. Last but not least, she included her two diaries, written in Czech, which she had started when I was born, describing every bit of my progress until I was four. My own suitcase was filled with clothes, books, toys. I can see us both bent over the suitcases on the floor at the dining end of our living room. We are discussing what I should take. I see myself moving my arms and talking, but I don't know what I said. I know I was left with the uneasy feeling that I had somehow made the wrong choices. As to what I felt, it's a blank. I see myself like a moving doll who is dumb but wants to speak.[68]

One of these suitcases, with Roth's exit number painted on it in green, became a Kindertransport artifact at the Imperial War Museum in London.

After losing her mother, Roth struggled to anchor herself emotionally in the surrounding world, a world that turned colder and more distant after her departure from home and was incapable of giving her, as a child or an adult, the sense of warmth and safety she had briefly known in Prague with her parents. The presence of these objects, however, allow the daughter and mother to connect, albeit only in memory. Marianne Hirsch calls this kind of material remnants of the past "testimonial objects" and points out that they "carry memory traces from the past, to be sure, but they also embody the very process of its transmission."[69]

Anna and Doris are also linked by their relationship to objects. As I have already noted, it is obvious from Anna's letters that the material world was extremely important for both women, regardless of the impending war and the destruction the future threatened for Anna. In a letter sent to another British Girl Guide, Mildred, Anna writes: "It is now quiet here, but things have got a new feature. A funny thing. The same object, and it has changed its feature, the same man [person] and he has changed his view to look at things."[70] She is referring to the shift in the political circumstances in the autumn of 1938, and she conceives of this shift in terms of how she views the objects around her. In trying to convey a picture of her life to Doris and her other friends, Anna continuously refers to the material world: the things she buys or plans to buy, the loving memories of things she has seen during her stay in England and that she imagines her daughter will soon see, the burden of things that must be transferred from one place to another as the Roths move from Prague to the countryside and then back to Prague.

In late August 1939, just days before the war would destroy all hopes of escape, Anna was still frantically working on her and her husband's emigration. It is impossible to tell if she knew how slim their chances were and was merely trying to keep hope alive, but her letters express the faith that a "miracle" (as Anna refers to the possibility of securing an exit visa and joining their daughter in England) would happen.[71] Between the lines, however, one senses a desperate panic and a loss of hope:

> Tuesday 22nd August 1939
> Dear Mrs Campbell,
> I have been so glad to have got your very nice letter of the 17th, by which you have told me that you want to wait for me and that you apply for the double Permit . . . Thank you also for the snap[shot]s, and also very much for the plan and suggestions of what I have to take.
> If only I could distinguish words like dresser, sideboard, cupboard, wardrobe, I should be glad . . . Well the main thing is, that you suggest me to bring a sideboard. Please could you tell me what it is for and how it looks like in England. Is it not something similar as the dresser? . . . And what is a dresser for? Where do you put food, flour, stores of marmalades etc? I have a small laundry room for it.
> This I intend to bring, and if possible the piano, wireless, gramophone, and sewing machine. Two armchairs, table and small chairs . . . Have I well understood that in case I should not bring a bed for Milena, you would lend yours? Thank you very much indeed.[72]

From these lines, it appears that Anna was trying to mitigate the terror of her present situation through the fantasy of preserving a middle-class lifestyle in England and the attendant material comforts. The concern over furniture and other such objects perhaps allowed her to avoid thinking about the threat of losing everything (including life), which loomed large. The original of this letter is reproduced in Roth's book, and it even includes a drawing Anna made of the cabinet she would have liked to bring but for which she lacked a word in English; therefore, she drew a picture in the letter to show it to Doris. Anna had asked her friend to give her a specific description of the lodgings she and her husband (who would have been employed as a gardener at the Campbells' home) were to occupy. This allowed her to fantasize about furnishing it and making it cozy for her family. Through this fantasy, Anna was able to hold onto her role of mother and wife and project herself into a future of normalcy.

Both mothers highlight a very specific and feminine relationship to objects and consumption, one that somewhat clarifies how Anna and Doris could have become friends in the first place. The pleasure with which each talks and cares about the things they owned or wished to acquire expresses a sense of empowerment and identity. Although these women were from different national, religious, linguistic, and social backgrounds, they were able to connect at such a deep level that one friend offered to protect the most prized possession of the other: her only daughter. Roth inherits the attachment her mother felt to her possessions, as shown in the former refugee's memories of the objects from Doris's world and those she acquires for herself as an adult—including her own first child. "Along with my intense fear of never having a family again," Roth confesses, "I had a huge fear of losing my first baby; this would be the very first flesh and blood after all the losses [in the Shoah]. The first true physical belonging."[73] This fear illustrates how for the victims of genocide, particularly female victims, to be violently separated from the material world violates their sense of self. And as the quote from Roth indicates, children are sensorial, physical, and material possessions in their own right. Having a child becomes for the survivors a form of reconstituting a lost attachment to the world and to life: "I had a tremendous craving for 'normality.' This to me meant being ordinary, having an actual, real family and a 'place' where I belonged without question," Roth writes: "To see others lead what looked like normal lives was really hard. They were so relaxed, so apparently complacent. They had a *cushion* of care under them,"[74] It is fitting that the metaphor Roth uses relies on a household object: a cushion. Like her mother in the letter quoted above, she can only fantasize about such objects of comfort.

The connection between memory and objects is subtle yet powerful; even the young Roth's preference for certain children's books is subconsciously determined by a link between their content and her personal attachment to them as objects of her past. For example, once in England, she becomes a great fan of Beatrix Potter's books, among which her favorite was *The Tailor of Gloucester* "for the beauty of the fabric and embroidery and the pathos of the story." The way in which she recalls the beauty of those books is tactile and reminiscent of the embroidered pillowcases her mother packed in her suitcase. It is perhaps because of her intensely tactile memories of her Prague past that Roth's first days in England were so unpleasant: "I embarked on a week of non-stop crying for my parents, day and night. Doris complained that it was very inconvenient

. . . I remember playing a primitive game of mud pies in the garden . . . About fifty years later, Doris told me that I had written to my mother saying that I was mad with longing for her. From then on, I was crippled with homesickness at every move. I could not stay away from my new home for even a week without getting ill with it."[75] Given Doris's cold personality, it is clear that "home" here must be understood as the physical house: its objects, rooms, and the human figures populating it. Since Roth had not found a home in the sentimental sense of the word (the loss of that kind of home in fact was the root of the child's inconsolable suffering), she formed an intense attachment to the safety of the physical place. In its materiality, the new house filled the void left by the absence of her mother.

In Muriel Dimen's study of the gendered character of "want" and "need," we learn that these are inseparable in infancy but grow apart as one develops into adulthood: "Wanting, associated with adulthood, active will, and masculinity, is better than need, lined to infancy, passive dependency, and femininity . . . These patriarchal judgments fuse with unconscious forces and political exigencies to make need alarming." Dimen brings up a paradox in our cultural representations of subjectivity: "The subject, 'Man,' desires and represents authorship, agency, and adulthood. But women are adults and as such are expected to be subjects, too. However, at the same time, through conjoined psychic and cultural splitting, women are also expected to be objects."[76] However, this expected passivity clashes with the inducement of women (from the nineteenth century on) to be consumers in the capitalist world. On the one hand, women are encouraged to go out and acquire things that will increase their desirability for men; on the other hand, it is imperative to limit women's desires so that they do not compete or interfere with what men wish themselves to obtain, including an education and a high-status profession. Both Doris and Anna are women caught in this paradoxical predicament. Both were denied opportunities, and many of the girls brought to England on the Kindertransports were denied (by historical and personal circumstances, but also by tacit societal restrictions on their desires) high-powered careers and the education necessary to pursue them. For instance, when Ruth David was taken under the protection of two English female teachers who saw her intellectual potential, she was made to feel ungrateful and disloyal by the hostel's matrons for having such ambitions. Similarly, Doris's emotional stinginess damaged Roth's sense of self-worth and dampened her enthusiasm to pursue a "serious" profession. Roth declares: "I feel a sense of outrage for all those generations (including my own) that were denied proper and adequate schooling . . . This happened again and again in my own and many other families . . . [And when competing with boys for opportunities, g]irls, of course, were the second ones to get a chance."[77]

To be sure, material objects in Roth's memoir signal both an abundance and a lack. Anna tries to make sure that her daughter will have enough clothes and possessions while in England so as to be comfortable and so as not to be a burden on the Campbells. "Milena will have sufficient dresses I think for this and the coming year," she writes to Doris. What Anna most tragically cannot supply Roth with is the memory of who she is and where she comes from. For this she must rely on Doris, but the English woman will fail to comprehend the urgency of helping the girl remain connected to her roots and disregards Anna's plea. Anna hopes to preserve Roth's attachment to her Czech origins through books, important connective objects in their own right: "I want to send also Czech books with her things, Fairy Tales etc. because I should like her to have something of her own language near her and not to feel quite lonely. And then I should not like her to forget quite her mother tongue."[78] However, her daughter, unassisted by Doris and the surrounding world, cannot fulfill her mother's wish: she forgets Czech. Anna had tried to save not only her daughter's life but also her daughter's identity. Yet somehow Anna's objects do succeed in keeping Milena attached to her roots and to her vanished mother. Furthermore, Anna's choice of the Czech books demonstrates how objects—even nontextual ones—are intertwined with the mother tongue, both literally and symbolically, in Roth's memoir. Together with her mother's letters—a material cache—Roth has also inherited Anna's two diaries, both written in Czech, a language she can no longer read.

Despite her limited contact with Doris over the years, Anna perfectly understood the risks of dealing with a peculiar woman like her. She was terrified that Doris would change her mind and put Roth out on the street, and thus her letters gingerly communicate her family's dire situation without debasing herself. She reassures Doris that Roth will not be a problem, and that she and her husband will make excellent, loyal workers. She repeats to Doris several times that "if there would be again something you would like me to tell Milena, please do it . . . I can help you a little bit with this."[79] In this way, Anna retains something of her role as mother, acting as her daughter's protector by offering to mediate between her and her new foster parents, conciliating Doris so that her daughter won't be suddenly rejected or made to suffer. It will take the young girl years to figure out empirically what Anna intuitively grasped about Doris's tetchy character.

"She is a very good child with very much good will," Anna writes Doris just days before Roth would reach England on the Transport. She continues:

And she always tries to do so as it is right. But of course as with all children one must know the right way to treat her. She can dress and undress herself, brush her teeth and wash herself. She is a very good eater and eats everything. She does not like fish. She loves milk. Raw fruit and raw carrots etc she is very much fond of. If you still would like something that would be good to teach her, please tell it to me. Her supper consists of bread and butter and milk, or bread and butter and an egg, boiled or fried, or some ham, and so on. I don't think she will much like porridge in the beginning . . . I think it will be easy to accustom her to the English time of meals and to the English food . . . But maybe in the beginning she would be hungry if she would get the last meal at 4.30 p.m. Although I know your tea is such a big meal that it would be perfectly sufficient.[80]

But the tea wasn't sufficient, and Roth recalls her nighttime hunger pangs quite well, along with Doris's inflexibility in changing the meal schedule. In a significant chapter devoted to family correspondence among Jews just before and during the war, Alexandra Garbarini remarks that "writing was parents' only means of communicating specific information as well as affection and support to their children" once the young had been sent abroad, either to relatives across the Channel or in Palestine, on the Kindertransports, or through other means, and Garbarini incisively defines this as a form of "parenting at a distance."[81] Anna presents a particularly interesting case of such parenting because she is indeed a mother trying to instruct another mother on how to bring her daughter up. She is kind of a translator in that she is trying to explain her daughter's nascent character to a stranger, while trying to prevent as many conflicts as she can that might be caused by the clash between the two cultures, the two languages, and the two maternal models that her young daughter will not be able to navigate, interpret, and negotiate for herself.

In spite of Anna's best efforts, Doris completely changes Roth's sense of self. Through Doris's reeducation, the good girl Roth's mother had made her believe she was becomes a bad girl, worthless and a nuisance to everybody. "Was I as good as my parents felt, or as bad as Doris said," Roth wonders. She continues: "I lived in an atmosphere that told me I was a bad person, a disgrace . . . Doris actually wished me to fail and forecast my downfall daily . . . 'You'll never pass your exams, you have no friends, you can't achieve anything, you have no money, have you?' Also, no one would ever want to marry me, what with my Jewish looks and my general badness . . . She never learned what my eventual profession was . . . To this day I don't know what my crime was, except that I existed."[82]

In Prague, Roth had clearly been accustomed to a loving family atmosphere. Her mother's tenderness and sweetness come through quite clearly in her letters. "The other day we were busy with Daddy a whole afternoon sticking some of the snap[shot]s of you into an album," writes Anna to her daughter. "It will be a nice souvenir for you one day when you are grown up." In a footnote, Roth informs us that the photo album did not survive. Anna's own love for material things made her particularly sensitive to their broader importance. Perhaps she had already realized that whatever she could deliver safely to her daughter in England would one day be the only connection between them. She was right: in Roth's relationship with her absent mother, objects became connective and supportive tools for personal psychic survival, and they also made memory possible. Even the objects that disappeared or were never sent are present in their radical absence: a void that reflects their owners' loss. "I wanted to send Milena a parcel with the rest of the things," Anna writes Doris on August 12, 1939, "but now I shall wait and take them with me"[83] Neither the parcel nor the mother ever made it to Roth.

What does survive, however, is a final handwritten letter to her in Czech, signed with a moving "Tvoje mamínka" (your mommy), in which Anna anxiously imparts an important lesson to Roth about manners, diet, and, not surprisingly, objects. Now that her daughter is a disadvantaged immigrant child (and soon to be an orphan), she instructs Roth not to touch things that she is not allowed to have ("You can't have everything you see . . . You can listen to Jane playing [her violin] but you mustn't want it"), not to refuse foods that taste funny to her ("don't ever say, Milena, 'This is not good'"), and to "be good, so they continue to like you."[84]

## DORIS

Doris is an extraordinarily complex character, the only one of the three women at the center of this memoir who does not have a voice of her own. As previously mentioned, her role can be read through the archetypal motif of the bad mother replacing the good mother, but Roth twists this expected development into a more interesting and complex articulation. In this case, before her death, the good mother leaves her daughter (and us) an alternative interpretation of the Doris character, by whom she is to be replaced. Interestingly, her abdication is implicitly signaled in one of the later exchange of letters. Anna had always called her various English friends by their first names, except for her most important friend, whom she always addressed as "Dear Mrs. Campbell." That is, until September 9, 1939, six days after the United Kingdom declared war on Germany, when all borders were shut and all her hopes of escape shattered. Then, finally, Anna addressed her friend in a new way: "My dear Doris." This shift is enormously tragic, indicating as it does that Anna had a clear sense of what the changed circumstances meant for her and her family. Irrevocably trapped on the Continent, she could now talk to Doris, who was to become her daughter's new mother, on an informal, equal footing—from woman to woman, friend to friend, mother to mother. Mrs. Campbell was no longer going to be her employer; Doris was going to be her daughter's only hope. Thus by addressing the letter to "My dear Doris," Anna acknowledges the women's newfound intimacy and her own abdication.

Anna was Doris's friend; she was very fond of her and obviously trusted her greatly. Thus Doris is perceived differently by the reader depending on whether we reconstruct her through Anna's words or through Roth's. Anna admired Doris and flattered her Englishness, drawing comparisons between her own Czech culture and Doris's British world and enthusiastically commenting on all the things she had seen, tasted, and learned while she was in England. Anna, who loved the English language, also relied on Doris to teach her all the words she did not know or couldn't find in her treasured Czech-English dictionary, which she sent to Roth once she realized she wouldn't be able to make much use of it anymore, with the war having started and the dream of getting to England about to die with her. In contrast to her mother, who paints an encomiastic portrait of Doris, Roth makes fun of Doris's ungenteel South London accent, which very clearly identifies her as a woman who has risen to a higher social standing from a lower one: "Doris did not speak or act like a lady." Doris's accent inspires Roth to imitate the more refined accents of her ladylike teachers, which, in turn, irritates Doris, who accuses Roth of not knowing her place. Roth takes this rebuke to mean one thing: "I should be servile in my attitude because my parents would have been her servants."[85]

Though this may paint an unflattering portrait of Doris, we should note that despite Doris's self-serving plans to get good use out of her refugees if they were brought to safety to her house in England, Roth's parents were in fact grateful for the chance of work, no matter how hard or lowly, if it meant being reunited with their daughter in a safe place. Aside from all practical considerations, Anna was eager to earn her keep because she had a highly developed sense of her own productivity. As a young girl, she had fought with her father over pursuing her studies, which was her dream, but being the oldest child, she had been chosen to take over the father's business the way an oldest son would have. Anna "was the one that got the raw deal and was denied the higher education she desperately wanted."[86] Her mother—Roth's grandmother Marie—had also been taken out of school, in her case to learn the craft of dressmaking, while her brother—Roth's great-uncle—had been pushed onto the education track and became a doctor.

Anna and Doris had experienced the same gender imbalances in their youth; Doris was "another woman who had wanted an education and been denied it." She had married up, and her in-laws did not let her forget it. However, she fully embraced her newly elevated status: "She had a lot of good clothes," Roth recalls, "in spite of clothes rationing . . . Her shoes were fine leather, in elegant styles and with high heels. Doris loved clothes." Growing up in England in the early 1900s, Doris had had own soul crushed, her own aspirations checked, by hearing the same disparaging comments that she would later use to criticize Roth. "Who do you think is going to look at *you*?" her parents would tell Doris, placing her in the same lowly, unwanted position she later would cruelly force Roth into.[87]

Despite these various character flaws, Doris came into her own during the war. Roth's and Kofman's memoirs delineate interesting portraits of two women during World War II, Doris and Mémé, who were defiant and challenged the societal norms of their time. Mémé braved the terrible dangers associated with harboring Jews in occupied Paris; Doris opened her house to a child who could (and did) become a permanent burden against the advice of some acquaintances, such as the odious Mr. I. T., who warned her about taking up the cause of ungrateful refugees. Mémé had the audaciousness to have a lover; Doris was married, and although her husband had been most useful in securing a higher social status for her, his lethargic nature allowed her to take charge of the home and all practical matters. The war had reduced the people of Europe to an unprecedented state of need. Shortages and rationings meant that the vast majority of people were subsisting on minimal resources. Yet Mémé and Doris lacked for nothing, and the people in their care were also better off than many of their compatriots. Kofman recalls: "Despite the rationing, and thanks to the black market and the packages of eggs and butter sent regularly by her cousin from Saint-Lô, she [Mémé] was able to prepare exquisite dishes, and I had never eaten so 'well'" (RO/RL, 51). And Roth writes:

> [Doris] was most unusually lucky in having a car of her own . . . She and Arthur gained all sorts of privileges for themselves, for petrol because he was a doctor and made house calls, and to produce food in the country . . . There were hens and ducks for eggs and meat, goats for milk, rabbits, honey, vegetables, and fruit. Even walnuts and chestnuts from their own trees, and sugar to give to the bees. But there was never enough to eat, especially for children. Not even for her own children . . . She managed to employ servants

even during the war . . . Sometimes we did have a chicken or a rabbit from the country. The majority of people at that time were slim [but Doris was always heavy].[88]

The fact that Roth and the other children in the household were always hungry was not for lack of food but because of Doris's bad temper and harsh discipline, which contributed to that "atmosphere of sin and punishment [that] did seem to haunt their backgrounds" and makes Roth wonder if Doris "must have caught the tail end of the Victorian era."[89]

And yet Doris's prosperity manifested itself in the home. Roth describes in detail the rooms of the house and the objects that she distinctly remembers in them. This material abundance paints an image of women who not only were heroes because of their ethical choices but who also subverted masculine visions of appropriate female behavior despite their conformity in areas like social snobbery and antisemitism. In a compelling essay, Andrea Adolph examines the intersection between austerity in times of national hardship and women's agency over desire. "Wanting," she writes, "is perceived as purposeful, willful, and masculine; the desire that arises from wartime scarcity pushes the limits that have traditionally defined women as needy, and thus as passive."[90] Britain at war asked of its citizens great sacrifices and self-restraint. On the one hand, it asked women to get out of the house and become active players in the war effort, as nurses, volunteers, makers of goods to be sent to the front, relief workers on the Continent at the war's end, and so on. But on the other hand, it emphasized a conception of femaleness that was quite archaic. The proper consuming habits that had been enforced on women for centuries became a central issue again during the war, when food shortages and rationing made women's self-sacrifice a matter of patriotism and national safety.[91] Women were expected to put their desires on the back burner and make the good of others a higher priority. Adolph sees this call for self-denial, especially vis-à-vis food, as one explicitly aimed at women, since "the mouth and the vaginal cavity are linked as twin creatures of transgressive desire—one for gluttony, the other for lust—and this conflation of female desires results in a policing of what enters the mouth as a way to proactively defend the genitals, that biological center of femaleness . . . The ongoing equation of lust with hunger has resulted in what is now considered a normative, 'feminine' interest in self-denial—of food, of sex, of embodiment . . . The World War II era in Britain presented no exception to this rule; indeed the fact of scarcity only increased the ways in which women were figured as icons of self-denial."[92]

At a time when women's practices of consumption were under particular scrutiny, people like Doris and Mémé took the meaning of their affiliation (or loyalty) to the nation into their own hands and resignified it: they actively and ethically defied the enemy by defending those whom the Germans had decided to annihilate. This was their heroism and their way of honoring their nations. In this light, Mémé's act of defiance in particular becomes exemplary: her act was one of disloyalty to the nation in 1942, because Pétain's France was allied with the Germans in the genocidal project, but it became an act of true heroism in the Gaullist France of 1945. These heroic women helped Jews survive, and they also made sure to procure for themselves and those in their care the food and necessary comforts to live adequately, at least in the circumstances in which they found themselves—which speaks to their incredible resourcefulness, cleverness, and industriousness. In a paradoxical way, then, these women (to whom we can also add Anna, with her love for material goods) gave a subversive spin to the long-held idea of women as passive and idly consuming. Their consumption was itself an act of resistance, self-assertion, and activism in its most literal political sense: these were resistance women who reacted against a male-dominated totalitarianism and imperialism to which they independently responded by choosing their loyalties, saving Jews while not submitting to the widespread policing of desire that Adolph identifies during World War II. These women made themselves survive when history had set them first in line to die (the self-sacrificing mothers of nations at war)—together with their heroic sons and brothers, the nation's soldiers. It is important to remember that Doris had also given a son to the nation.

Anna and Doris both saw the material world as a canvas on which to create a representation of their identities. They defined themselves as middle class, independent, and self-supporting through their ownership, while they also inscribed themselves into history through heroic and self-sacrificing acts of resistance to domination, imperialism, and the genocidal fury of their time. This is also true of Mémé who exposed herself and her extended family to retaliation, possibly even death, for harboring two Jews in her apartment in occupied France.

Throughout the decades, Roth made ample use of her mother's things. In fact, it is through using these objects that a contact point can be established between Roth and Anna, daughter and mother, survivor and victim. The term "contact point," a concept to which I will return in a moment, is used by Feldman to refer to the interaction between body and object and what remains of this interaction after the disappearance of the body.[93] Roth laments: "I wish I'd known my mother's mother, Marie . . . I have so many of the lovely things she made. Lace tablecloths, seven of them, and in particular the 'special' cloth, which she made for each of her three daughters, possibly intended for the wedding dowry and breakfast. That is what we have used it for, for my own and my elder daughter's weddings, and I expect my mother put it to the same use . . . These material things become so important, perhaps too important, because the people themselves are missing." Later, she writes: "I use this furniture every day and feel a satisfying sense of connection with her [Anna]. The desk in particular is in front of me now . . . [the desk] has been used for the whole of my life, and this matters when all else has been broken . . . And, on further reflection, I realize that such objects were seen as somehow more 'permanent' in those days." Roth ultimately realizes the precious contact points these objects represent: "Thus my mother's preoccupation with these belongings was not so futile. They did form a very real thread of continuity between us."[94]

## MEMORY OBJECTS : EXHIBITING WOMEN'S EXPERIENCE

The same year that Roth's memoir was published, the American scholar Alison Landsberg released an important book in which she argues that "modernity makes possible and necessary a new form of public cultural memory," which she labels "prosthetic memory." According to Landsberg, prosthetic memory "emerges at the interface between a person and a historical narrative about the past, at an experiential site such as a movie theater or museum. In this moment of contact, an experience occurs through which the person sutures himself or herself into a larger history . . . the person does not simply apprehend a historical narrative but takes on a more personal, deeply felt memory of a past event through which he or she did not live."[95] Almost a quarter-century earlier, Nora had coined another term, *lieux de mémoire*, to define the sites "where consciousness of a break with the past is bound up with the sense that memory has been torn—but torn in such a way as to pose the problem of the embodiment of memory in certain sites where a sense of historical continuity persists. There are *lieux de mémoire*, sites of memory, because there are no longer *milieux de mémoire*, real environments of memory."[96] Using this concept to guide his three-volume work on the national memories of France (*Les lieux de mémoire*, published in English as *Realms of Memory*),[97] Nora bemoaned the defeat of real memory, which is "life" in his terminology, at the hands of "history," which to him is an artificial reconstruction of life—or, better yet, of its absence. As Michael Rothberg, Deberati Sanyal, and Max Silverman point out, it is quite ironic that the monumental *Les lieux de mémoire*, a *lieu de mémoire* itself, "helped stimulate a boom in the study of memory [and yet it] is premised on the demise of memory!"[98] In this closing section of the chapter, I want to focus attention on the roles of mnemonic objects salvaged from genocide and how they are used to reconnect past with present, surviving victims with their lost lives, and the victims with us. And I intend to reiterate the importance of women's memoirs and the centrality they often assign to objects in the reconstruction of these pasts and relationships. When some of these objects pass from the hands of their direct inheritors to the public space of museum collections or various mausoleums (as was the case with Roth's luggage, pillowcase, and her mother's letters), an important shift occurs in the psychic charge of the given object. This shift has the potential to confine Shoah memory to a new hegemonic and curatorial domain, which might obscure the traces that some of these objects carry of the historical experience of women. In this light, I hope to reinforce the importance of women's writing as an act of resistance against the hegemonic modes of the making of history or memory that often trample the gendered character of human experience. In the heterodox space of women's memoirs, the difficult equilibrium between private sentimental memory (*milieux de mémoire*) and communal or universal memory (prosthetic memory, or *lieux de mémoire*) can be successfully reached.

In the service of representing a lost past, objects become precious mnemonic prostheses, endowed with the power to hold and call forth a memory that is otherwise intangible, indescribable, or perhaps not even fully formed (as is the case with memories inherited by the second generation or those of early childhood). Building on Landsberg's idea, I argue that objects and the memories they carry are prosthetic even before they end up behind museum doors and are exposed to the eyes and interpretation of the world. I am interested in the prosthetic power of objects in the private sphere, where they still belong to people directly touched by the traumatic events. In other words, I use Landsberg's idea of prosthetic memory to signify not only the ethical act of taking on another group's traumatic memory by people utterly detached from the events involved, but also the process by which someone personally related to the past that the object refers to is able to keep connected to it. I also suggest that objects are prostheses of memory, as much as people are prostheses to the memory objects: it is our effort to recollect, to provide contexts and stories for each object, that symbolically animates these things and empowers them with a prosthetic function for future generations and for people culturally, geographically, or historically removed from them. We have seen (in chapter 1) how writing books about the Shoah was a way for Edith Bruck to call the dead back into the traumatized present. In Roth's case, it is her mother's letters that summon the living to remember. The many objects the former Kindertransport refugees mention so often in their memoirs, and that many of them have donated to the London museum, perform the same call to remember. These objects summon the living to the dead. As Landsberg explains in her chapter on the Holocaust, these objects create a transferential space where a mixture of cognitive and processual (or sensual) approaches to knowledge allows the public to "adopt" the position of inheritors of someone else's past.[99] Memory objects enable identification and empathy.

Prosthetic objects replace absence with presence. Landsberg's prosthetic memory, *de novo* (or even ex nihilo), can transmit the knowledge of an event to people who are unconnected to that event.[100] So too the prosthetic objects of memory can, in the hands of their direct inheritors (such as a former Kindertransport refugee, a genocide survivor, or a daughter of a survivor) act as a psychological life support, as necessary and as intimate a part of one's being as a bodily limb. They are the phantom limbs of many a survivor's life. However, as we know, a prosthesis is an artificial part that functions similarly to the one it replaced, yet it is also only a fiction. The memories and the objects that contain them are felt as real and present by the first- and second-generation survivors who cling to them, but they are not an organic part of the remembering I. It is in the crevices of this unbridgeable chasm—between what remains and what is radically absent—that the texts of the Jewish women this book examines reside.

Landsberg sees in these prosthetic connections a positive way for people to know and empathize with the histories of others, but Nora regrets the loss of what he calls "real memory" at the hand of the *lieux* (or institutions) of memory, which in his view are like prostheses or signifiers empied out of the signified. "*Lieux de mémoire*," Nora explains, "arise out of a sense that there is no such thing as spontaneous memory . . . without commemorative vigilance, history would soon sweep [all preserves of memory] away."[101] The use Roth personally makes of her mother's objects seems to work as an antidote to the anxiety Nora expresses about memory's succumbing to history under the pressure of the modern era. With each point of contact between the survivor and her mother's objects, the Holocaust is made present and the mother is intimately remembered; her letters speak in the present, not in a fossilized past. This living memory happens without the dispossession that public ceremonies, official celebrations, and monumental displays often effect. Adapting Nora's terminology, I call the objects still in the hands of individual survivors *objets de mémoire*, or memory objects, intelligible and perceptible by both mind and body. In a literal sense, they are objects of memory in that they are the focus of memory, but they are also objects in the grammatical sense because they are just as much affected by the action of the subject as they affect that action—while being the goal of the subject's action as well. It is their actuality that makes them potential sites for the transferability and transmittability of history, while their psychological impact far outweighs their material value or any practical use they might have. Given the Shoah context I am dealing with here, I am wary of using the word "sacred," but such objects can be read as totemic (in that they stand in for a sacrifice), ritualistic (in that they signify a rite of passage and perpetuate the repetitious timelessness of trauma), magical (in that they symbolically corporealize something that no longer exists), and—most of all—unalterable yet shifting (in that they are subject to the dialectics of remembering and forgetting). Either in the private environments of their owners or in museum installations, these memory objects are memory sites, and the same definition that Nora supplies for *lieux de mémoire* applies to them: "simple and ambiguous, natural and artificial, at once immediately available in concrete sensual experience and susceptible to the most abstract elaboration. Indeed, they are *lieux* in three senses of the word—material, symbolic, and functional."[102] Yet, unlike Nora, I invest the idea of memory objects with a positive valance: these memory objects are not without real environments of memory. Although Nora's treatment of *milieux* subsumes the feminine under hegemonic, phallocentric discourses (history and memory are implicitly male in his discourse), the objects I explore here are bonded to the domestic world and the intimacy that women derive from using, owning, and sharing them. Paying attention to the domestic quality of these *objets de mémoire* allows women's histories and memories to emerge.

Before I continue with my analysis, a word of clarification is in order. Although I am appropriating those valuable concepts from Nora that help support my hypotheses regarding the material objects that are instrumental agents between the vanished past and its posthumous reconstructions, I am troubled by Nora's formulations about what constitutes real memory and his problematic nostalgia for the lost (premodern) community. Nora's basic idea is that memory (as we "once" knew it) is dead, but a new memory—a modern one—has formed and is made omnipresent by innumerable locations (*lieux*) of memory. In our age, Nora proposes, the past has been irrecoverably disconnected from the present because of the disappearance of a real, "lived," intimately experienced memory. All the memorial apparatuses (monuments, museums, works of art, texts, films, and so forth) that we put in place in order to represent the past and hence to produce memory in fact end up killing it: monuments in particular, in his view, destroy memory's spontaneity by making remembering a hyper-self-conscious act. I agree with him on this particular point: a monument or a museum risks subsuming other types of memory by cementing its own version of the past. These polymorphous apparatuses are the *lieux de mémoire*, whose signified isn't "real memory"—yet it is the only memory available to us nowadays, in Nora's view. The disappeared "real memory" used to be spontaneous, intimate, practically unmediated memory, chronologically nestled in the premodern era. But, most important, Nora's "real memory" is synonymous with good memory—that is, *la vie paysanne* (the rural life of the peasants) and the village communities of the provinces, animated by figures such as the schoolteacher and the postman. Of course, it is not clear that such a good simple life (especially for the peasants, even the French ones) ever existed. In any case, Nora postulates that these *milieux de mémoire* have been erased twice: first by modernity's vision of nationhood (whose institutions—such as family, school, and church—overpowered the close-knit intimacy of old communities) and second by postmodernity's stress on minorities, plurivocality,[103] democratization (Nora's word), mass culture on a global scale, and its hypermediated way of experiencing history. Nora nostalgically gloats: "Through the past we venerated ourselves" (I find that "we" in his work profoundly disquieting). And he laments: "Now that we no longer have a single explanatory principle, we find ourselves in a fragmented universe . . . When we look at the past . . . we know [it] is no longer ours."[104] Nora charges a number of minority communities with the responsibility of having "cracked" the internal coherence of the nation with their claims to particularism: Jews, royalists, Bretons, Corsicans, women, workers, and other provincials.[105] The conservative, if not reactionary, tone underscoring Nora's nostalgic idea of real memory and national past renders his work on the subject not entirely persuasive to me, but I intend to tap into and resignify some of the most valuable propositions he offers: by creating the concept of memory objects (*objets de mémoire*), I hope to take the most usable aspect of Nora's idea of *lieux de mémoire* and inject it with a positive, generative, and feminist edge. The memory objects I talk about are *lieux de mémoire* in that they are prosthetic, but they also retain a connection to the domestic, intimate, lived experience that Nora sees as the lost *milieu*. In the context I highlight here, these *lieux* are not devoid of mnemonic *milieux*, thanks to the living relationship established with them by either the surviving refugees or the following generations.

In the hands of the (direct or indirect) survivors, memorial or prosthetic objects inhabit a space between their direct connection to the places, times, and events of the past and their future position in the collective culture as metonymies of an entire historical chapter to which they refer and for which they are prostheses. The survivors, who also inhabit this middle space, are not erased or replaced by the objects. "Memory," explains Nora, "is rooted in the concrete: in space, gesture, image and object."[106] But how, I wonder, can these *lieux de mémoire* make memory manifest? It is not through their mere existence; it is not their intrinsic, essential power, but their ethical encounter with the human that allows them to bear witness, to speak a story (history) with authority. The personal relation between survivors and these prostheses of memory is ongoing and can illuminate complex aspects of the past that we risk losing in our historical reconstructions (in museums, films, and so forth). The Kindertransport chapter of history is profoundly marked not only by the proactive presence and mobilization of women and the centrality of children (a category always assimilated to that of women) but also by the objects brought to safety that constitute the only bridge remaining between the vanished lives from a vanished continent these refugees left behind as children and their present identities. As I've argued, these objects are strongly rooted in the gendered space of the domestic world, a world that is always a challenge for the phallocentric culture to represent.

The lucky children who made it onto the Kindertransports were allowed only one or two small pieces of luggage each: a cargo no larger than what a child could carry alone. How to pack your child's life in one suitcase, a suitcase small enough for the child to handle but complete enough to anticipate the needs of an uncertain future? Together with the indispensable, mothers and fathers managed to smuggle into those bags a little special something that they knew would become the only simulacrum of their previous lives together that their children would have left: a photograph, a teddy bear, an embroidered towel, a special blanket, a family Bible, a piece of jewelry (which could also come in handy in case of financial need), sometimes even a piece of perishable food to bring to mind the memory of a family meal in happier times. As previously noted, nine out of ten children of the Kindertransport never saw their parents again.

These objects, brought to safety to England in a suitcase, were all that most Kinder possessed after the war. Some kept going back to them incessantly throughout their lives; some put them away and rediscovered them only much later, when, as adults, something in their psyches finally allowed them to face the past and recognize themselves as victims, therefore beginning the long-delayed process of mourning for their lost families and lives by reconnecting with these little material things. Regardless, as Körte points out in her article on the metaphorical and literal value of these mementos, "the object not only presents a connection to childhood experience, but it also forms a link to the parents, later becoming a support for memory and still later, with greater distance from events, functioning as a bridge to memory or a bracket for an event."[107]

Lee Edwards, a former Kind, writes about her special object: "It has nine pearls and twenty-six little diamonds. I know, because I just looked at it again. I can't say I look at it very often—maybe once or twice a year, and I NEVER WEAR IT, but just looking at it brings back all the memories; some sad, some bitter-sweet; some joyful."[108] Despite the danger of being caught by the Nazis on guard at the station, Edwards's mother managed to quickly hide a precious necklace under a blanket in the child's suitcase: "My mother achieved her wish on that gray March morning at the Frankfurt railway station in 1939: I could not treasure her; I never saw her again, but I treasure her necklace for ever."[109] Another object was a tapestry woven by the mother of Kindertransport refugee Ester Friedman. The mother had started the project once she and her husband were deprived of the right to work in 1940 and evicted from their Viennese apartment. A non-Jewish woman, a neighbor, kept the tapestry until she was able, after the war, to locate Ester and give it to her. Ester asks: "The Tapestry? What has a tapestry got to do with the death of my father, mother, sister, uncles, aunts, cousins and six million Jews?" She answers her own question this way: "What is there of greater value to me than this heirloom worked in times of happiness with love and in utter despair. The only thing that escaped destruction — the only thing left of them except their ashes in a mass grave in Auschwitz."[110] In Segal's memoir, the packing scene offers very moving family vignettes: "'She can take my best crocodile belt,' said my father, wanting to give me something." As her frantic mother searches the kitchen for foods to pack that will last until their daughter reaches England, the girl, more to calm them down than anything, suggests knackwurst. "'Not without bread,' said my father. '*Knackwurst*,' said my mother. 'You like that? I'll go down this minute and get you one.'"[111] And so it comes to pass that Segal escapes Germany with a sausage in her suitcase. Not surprisingly, it very quickly begins to stink and, discovered by the supervisors and the other children in the hostel, it causes an embarrassing scene for Lore. In the textual space of her memoir, the unpreserved sausage found posthumous life: the family love it represents has outlived and certainly outweighed the temporary pain of being made fun of by other children. In one final anecdote about these objects, Ruth David inherits from her aunt Liese, a survivor, a few pieces of silverware that her family's neighbors in Germany had kept safe for her during the war. This cutlery is jokingly referred to by David and her siblings as the Rheingold (the mythical treasure of the saga of the Nibelungen) — though irony aside, she appreciates its true value: "She left this cutlery to my brother Michael and me. I treasure my share of it. It is a constant reminder and a witness to the potential of goodness in humans."[112]

One could argue that both Roth's memoir and her Shoah memory took shape in 1999, when she was contacted by the Imperial War Museum, as mentioned above. Her memory was thus triggered by the reestablishment of a connection to the objects of those days. She chose a pillowcase and the suitcase she and her mother packed together, which by 2000 was battered, rusty, and missing a handle but still had the green exit number assigned to her painted on its back.

When viewed behind glass in the museum, these objects are the prostheses that Landsberg writes about. The pillowcase, which for Roth functions as a metonymy for her lost mother, functions as a metonymy for the whole Shoah in the public context of the museum (a "devotional institution"[113]). The object now connects the visitors to the larger Kindertransport story and to the broader Holocaust tragedy. Interestingly, Landsberg does not find this transition or translation problematic. Although philosophers and intellectuals have always been deeply concerned about the disenfranchising powers of mass culture and the ever-present risks of the modern spectacle, Landsberg seems to have overcome this anxiety by having located even in our culture, with its omnipresent mass-media, the opportunity for ethical encounters and intercultural empathic sharing. On the one hand, Landsberg points out how memories of the Holocaust have been created by films (such as *Schindler's List*) and museums (such as the US Holocaust Memorial Museum, in Washington, D.C.) to the point where the Holocaust has become an "American memory" grafted onto the consciousness of people racially, religiously, politically, geographically, and chronologically removed from the events of the Shoah. On the other hand, Landsberg describes the object-related experience that visitors are invited—in fact, forced—to have on the second floor of the US Holocaust Memorial Museum and concludes that the objects' "very materiality . . . their seductive tangibility, draws you into a lived relationship with them."[114] And for her, it is precisely this relationship that makes the all-important ethical transference possible. I find her argument compelling and convincing.

Whether or not a relationship can actually be established with and through the materiality of the objects exhibited in a museum raises another question: are museums able to make apparent the gendered complexities of each object? Some of these complexities, as we have seen, refer to a very specific and uniquely female experience of history, family life, emigration, and acculturation. Museums (such as Holocaust museums that deal with events on a massive geographical and historical scale) strive for maximum historical precision, yet this precision necessarily tramples on historical details. The enormous number of victims makes the task of zeroing in on the life of each one impossible. In the last two decades, memory artists have attempted to establish a meaningful contact point between the present and the radical absence of the past. Antimuseums, invisible museums, post-traditional museums, and a *Gesamtkunstwerk* approach to memory that involves mixtures of media and genres are all postmodern answers to the question of how to reshape memory to better capture the Jewish experience. James Young writes: "Rather than a singular master narrative of memory—that which has been traditionally recited as liturgy—there are now many forms of memory, each owing a debt to the particular Jewish community doing the memory-work."[115] However, as it turns out, architectural or visual postmodernism has not necessarily provided the antidote to a gender-essentialized vision of the Shoah. The canonic museums are still heavily imbricated with the masculine and patriarchal culture that birthed them in the first place over a hundred years ago; these institutions are often one more cultural technology that normalizes history as paradigmatically male. Anna Reading pertinently asks: "Are artefacts [sic], films and photographs in Holocaust museums shorn or attached to the gendered stories that may explain their provenance or inclusion?"[116]

After carefully examining how the specificity of gendered experiences is represented in some of the most renowned Shoah memorial sites (the Auschwitz-Birkenau camp in Poland, the Imperial War Museum, the US Holocaust Memorial Museum, and the Jewish Heritage Museum in New York), Reading concludes that "while the dominant narratives of men tend to confirm and reinforce each other in different national museum contexts, the stories of women remain somewhat disjointed and discontinuous."[117] She finds the Imperial War Museum to be most successful in terms of including women and their war or genocide stories, while the US Holocaust Memorial Museum is the least successful. The field of museum studies has produced extensive and high-quality scholarship over the last two decades. Its important critique of museum culture has highlighted both the positive impact of these sites of cross-cultural contact as well as the old and new pitfalls associated with how these sites exercise hegemonic control over the telling of a past or a culture to the subjects who enter the complex space of the museum. In the twenty-first century, research in the field has turned from the content of the museum to the context of the museum. As Anna Conlan and Amy Levin explain, the musem is now a place not only in which but also on which to conduct research: "This self-reflexive framework departs from traditional museum concerns of collections and classification and emphasizes social relations embedded and enacted in the museum."[118] Much work needs still be done, however, in terms of feminist readings of the museum locus, discourse, and praxis.

In this era of excessive and spectacular memorialization, we risk a new memorial colonialism through the institutionalization of memory—that is, the claim of control over personal and collective memories by national or international bureaucracies, not to mention the warranted and unwarranted spinoffs of the mass-mediatic productions and the way they shape our social reality. Is there a difference—or a différance, that Derridean idea of an epistemological "spacing"—between the embroidered pillowcase from Prague that Roth used and preserved in her linen chest for fifty years and the embroidered pillowcase we look at in a display at the Imperial War Museum? Can we establish what Feldman calls a "contact point" with it? Feldman has illustrated the idea of "contact points" in his study of relational dynamics within the contact site of museums (or what Mary Louise Pratt named, borrowing from linguistics, "contact zones"[119]). Feldman supplies an intriguing example of his own personal contact point with the Shoah.

One day, as Feldman stood in front of the pile of thousands of camp prisoners' shoes displayed at the US Holocaust Memorial Museum, he became nauseated by the stench emanating from the old leather, the mildewed fabric, and perhaps (in such places our imagination runs wild) remnants of human skin. This powerful reaction helps illuminate one of the flaws of all traditional museum systems: although traditional museums do not completely suppress all sensory experiences, they are unprepared to work with them, to combine other sensory experiences with those of sight, and to engage the other senses in ways that can enhance and complicate the impact of the visitor's encounter with an object.[120]

Western tradition has decreed that the experience of women is grounded in the material, physical, and sensory, thus by design museums are engineered to exclude women in their exclusion of that material, physical, and sensory experience. Most traditional Holocaust museums are ultimately sites of visual experiencing. Images, relics, and objects are there to be seen and absorbed through the overfocused, overstretched sense of sight. Since the social world, in contrast, is shaped by the experience of the body,[121] and this particular level of experience is usually connected to the feminine, excluding the sensory experience from the historical reconstruction that goes on in museums is to undercut the possibility of female experiential modes manifesting themselves, or "speaking." Of course, this exclusion also affects the museum visitors' contact with the objects they encounter there: some of their senses are restrained and put under surveillance. "The sensory approach to objects . . . positions them as integral to human behavior," write Elizabeth Edwards, Chris Gosden, and Ruth Phillips. "It accentuates the relational qualities of objects as 'categories' (e.g. subject/object) or entities (e.g. person/thing) which work in relation to one another to produce further sets of relationships or understandings that, at their broadest, might be termed 'culture,' 'society' or 'locality.'"[122] As noted by Feldman and others, the centrality of seeing (versus feeling or perceiving) privileges a patriarchal, rationalist (Western) approach to knowledge over alternative methods of access.

In the Western mind, sensuousness used to be considered the prerogative of so-called primitives but was also typically associated with women. Around the beginning of the twentieth century, museums arose as public places in which to display collections of various kinds, and as such, they had to exercise extreme control over their audiences, which were now pulled from the masses rather than from a restricted pool of elitist connoisseurs. Museums "reflected many of the visualizing trends of the day . . . They were major sites of display: wealthy capitalist nations needed showcases of cultural capital. Museums were also sites of surveillance and public order. Strict bodily discipline was required from museum visitors who were expected to become as close to pure spectators as possible: not to touch, not to eat, not to speak loudly."[123] Building her argument around the 1950 term "proxemics," coined by the anthropologist Edward T. Hall, Beverly Gordon reminds us that "the male-formulated ideal [in traditional Western aesthetics, is] related to the abstraction and depersonalization of the far distances. The tangible, sensory qualities of the near distances [are] considered suspect." Proxemics, or "the use of space as an elaboration of culture," was used by Hall in the middle of last century to study and measure the way in which people interact when set against an intercultural background: "Culture permeates and colors perception, and if men and women live in overlapping but different cultures, they perceive and experience the world somewhat differently. Given the masculine bias of the dominant culture in the West . . . women's perceptions and experiences have been devalued."[124] This bias forces us to ask whether the patriarchal hegemony that sustains the way we experience culture also permeates the way in which Holocaust museums are conceived of and received.[125] Feldman thinks that it does, writing that "museum displays risk reinscribing the silences and eliminations that gave rise to the contact point in the first place."[126] In other words, this devaluation of women's experience risks colonizing again that to which it had meant to give agency and authority.[127] Similarly, Classen and Howes argue that museums are sites for cross-cultural consumption that upset the sensory order that every society has developed (and that is part of every society's DNA) precisely by ignoring that sensory order in their exhibits.[128] Museums still largely operate on the old Western dichotomy between the world of the body (which is feminine and suspect) and the world of the mind (masculine and privileged). We know that these dichotomies and categories subordinate the feminine to the masculine. Given that the concept of the modern museum as public space originated in the strongly patriarchal and imperialist society of the nineteenth century, the museum risks reproducing systems of ethnic, racial, class, sexual, and gender oppression, despite its best curatorial efforts to balance gender in its contents.

As Reading's study highlights, significant strides have been made toward a more inclusive view of women's presence in museum reconstructions and representations of history. Women have begun to be included in the creation, conceptualization, and design of Holocaust museums, which is a first step toward constructing a more balanced discourse on gender. For example, the feminist scholars Joan Ringelheim and Marion Kaplan lent their expertise to the US Holocaust Memorial Museum and the Museum of Jewish Heritage, respectively.[129] Yet despite this female participation, there are more essential ways in which museums, themselves the product of a European patriarchal culture, are intrinsically ill suited to accommodate female experiential modes—including the social, historical, and personal. On the most basic level, traditional museums reflect the patriarchal order in that they derive their modus operandi from two activities deeply connected with masculinity: collecting and historiography. What happens to the gender-specific experience of women in a homogenizing site such as a Holocaust museum? And what happens to experiences (of both men and women) that are rooted in the feminine or the maternal, such as the many stories from the Kindertransport—whose ultimate success, as we have seen, depended on the actions, connections, resourcefulness, and resistance of women?

Earlier in this chapter, I pointed out that the Kindertransport rescue operation is a less well known aspect of the Nazi genocide (not for scholars, but for the broader public), and that the episode is shrouded in a forlornness that somehow mirrors the abandonment and loneliness of its protagonists, as well as the things they carried with them. The forlorn objects from the Kindertransport may be just what is required to highlight the difficulty of finding a space for women in museums and history. In the communal history of the Jewish genocide that is still largely told from a male perspective (characters in this awful drama are still understood as paradigmatically male unless specifically identified as female), the appearance of the Kindertransport rescue operation on the margins creates a small yet permanent rupture. It forces us to confront the role of women as protagonists and agents of history; the overlooked, gendered aspects of survival techniques; and, most important, female modes of memory making. As I've stated repeatedly, the Kindertransport movement was defined by the actions of women. These refugees' stories did not take place in the dehumanizing spaces of concentration camps and ghettos but were contained and experienced inside the domestic borders of people's homes. They are profoundly connected to the house, the domestic world, and what is traditionally categorized as the female sphere. Therefore, the appearance of these stories within the overarching story of the Holocaust—defined by the eruption of an imperialistic (and hypermasculine) war—disrupts the expectations and modes of retelling or reconstructing the past to which traditional historiography has accustomed us.

Reading the Shoah through a feminine lens also heightens our attention to issues such as the effects of genocide on the body. I use the body here not only to mean the corpses left behind by the genocide but also to refer to the living record on which the Shoah has inscribed its passage: the tattoos on the arms, the shaved heads, the destruction of physiological functions (amenorrhea, digestion problems, and excretion inhibition), and, more abstractly, a kind of amputation from or impaired physical connection to the material world. The objects that were preserved by the survivors and their relatives and that resurface in the memoirs of Shoah writers (Kofman's fountain pen, Bruck's photographs, Roth's tablecloth and pillowcases) are captured in these women's texts in all of their fragile individuality and specificity. Such objects come from the domestic world of the victims, a world whose material demolition was an integral part of the perpetrators' plan to annihilate human lives. These objects used to be part of the daily landscapes of the living. And because the domestic sphere (the place from which the objects were expunged) is where the presence of women is traditionally charted, scrutinizing the material world and the relation that survivor writers have with these salvaged objects can allow the specificity of gendered experiences of violence and genocide to emerge more distinctly. Furthermore, as Marion Kaplan remarks, violence against objects is a symbolic act aimed at violating the owners of those objects: "A powerful image," Kaplan writes, "mentioned often in Jewish women's memoirs, is that of flying feathers—feathers covering the internal space of the home, hallway, and front yard or courtyard. As in Russian pogroms at the turn of the century, the mobs tore up feather blankets and pillows, shaking them into the rooms, out the windows, and down the stairways. Jews were deprived of their bedding and the physical and psychological sense of well-being it represented. Broken glass [after Kristallnacht] in public and strewn feathers in private spelled the end of Jewish security in Germany."[130] Objects become invaluable memory sites that are capable of restoring women's historical voices. As illustrated in this chapter, the material and the narrative are interwoven in Roth's memoir. On the one hand, the narrative becomes material (through the donations of objects and letters to a museum); on the other hand, the material (letters, her mother's two diaries in Czech, Roth's heirlooms) is the narrative.

The relationship established in the private domestic sphere between survivors and objects disrupts—or counteracts—the colonizing forces of museums, which tend to separate the body from the material world to which it belongs. Objects are thus made into historical relics by the decontextualization they undergo in the passage from their original environments to the recontextualizing environment of a museum. In a Marcusean or Durkheimean sense, these objects end up losing their inherent everyday functional purpose and become somewhat sacred, and hence museums risk becoming reliquaries. The once vital objects become, as Nora would lugubriously point out, history. In the literary space of memoirs, in contrast, these objects maintain a connective role. Language re-presents them as mothers' ways of saving and bonding with daughters across space and time. Furthermore, before the war and before they were passed on to the next generation, these objects were in many instances an expression of women's agency and power as consumers, urban subjects, and independent daughters or wives. In short, they were meaningful objects before becoming Shoah relics, material traces of a connective sensory chain that enables remembrance. They are not fossils but very much part of the survivors' living landscape and as such they change according to the shifting perspective of the owner (or writer). For instance, Roth's relationship to the things salvaged from the catastrophe has gradually evolved from denial to acceptance and even closure. She admits that she has not always been psychologically capable of looking at them and acknowledging their meaning, but nevertheless they are "the background wallpaper of my life." [131]

Although I agree with Nora's idea that "modern memory is, above all, archival," [132] I also believe in the productive power of the archive—in the constructive force of a text (especially a memoir) to function as a *lieu de mémoire*, and one in which other *lieux de mémoire* can be deposited and held, like the example Nora cites of the French revolutionary calendar of 1789. Nora includes memoirs as possible *lieux de mémoire* only when they do not simply present memory but interrogate it. [133]

An example of a memory object that needs literature in order not to disappear (because it couldn't easily be assimilated into the traditional storytelling space of a Shoah museum) is Kofman's fountain pen (chapter 3). It is so intensely an object of her memory that, as she declares, it alone allowed her to write all that she did during her career. To put it another way, everything she wrote was indirectly about it. What would it mean to exhibit such a pen in a glass case of a museum? The mausoleum of Rabbi Kofman's pen is his daughter's text—that is, all of her texts.

The fountain pen, Roth's letters, Bruck's photos, and even the original copy of Anne Frank's orange-checked diary do not merely delegate memory, they are memory. And to use Nora's wording, they interrogate memory, not merely display it. The maternal and feminine legacy that defines the specific objects I have discussed here makes them especially valuable to the historical record because women's activities are difficult to represent and therefore remain largely unillustrated in the documentary archives. [134] The Kindertransport, the maternal objects that the refugee children contribute to our prosthetic memory of the Holocaust, and the women's memoirs that embrace the material world and invest objects with specific narratives subvert established expectations about Shoah representation and Shoah memory making. Writing memoirs, as well as writing their mothers and the mothers' materiality in those memoirs, is a compelling site of appearance for women survivors: a comfortably furnished room, or a highly sensory archive, of their own.

[English workingmen] are not so selfish as to be unsympathetic towards the victims of circumstances or oppression. They do not respond in any marked degree to the anti-Semitism which has darkened recent Continental history, and I for one believe that they disavow an attempt to shut out the stranger from our land because he is poor or in trouble, and will resent a measure which, without any proved necessity, smirches those ancient traditions of freedom and hospitality for which Britain has been so long renowned.

**WINSTON CHURCHILL**, quoted in Martin Gilbert, *Churchill and the Jews*

# CHAPTER 5

# FROM THE THIRD DIASPORA
## Helena Janeczek and the Shoah
## Second Generation's Disorders

So far this book has focused on mothers and daughters who experienced the Holocaust firsthand. But the vortex of pain does not end there, and we can follow its spiraling effects through the complicated relation that postwar children had with their Shoah parents.[1] Although existential, historical, psychological, and geographical rupture is the predicament of the Shoah survivor, the last two and a half decades of work on second-generation testimonies have clearly shown that the children of Shoah victims are not immune to the aftershocks of the trauma experienced by their parents. In fact, it is tempting to say that they are predisposed to an array of symptoms that show the devastating repercussions of genocide. Therefore, this work cannot consider only those women who stared at the abyss of the Holocaust themselves and who testified to the life-affirming bond with their mothers, after surviving the unsurvivable (the Shoah is an experience that one never really "goes beyond," to return to the meaning of *supervivere*, from which the word "survive" is derived). It must also consider the way in which daughters born in the second half of the twentieth century had to "survive," to combat not the threat of death but the psychological threat that the Holocaust projected into their lives through their damaged, tormented Shoah mothers. These sons' and daughters' psyches show signs of traumatic lesions as well.

The body of autobiographical works by children of Holocaust survivors, especially in the United States, is astonishingly large. The narratives of the postwar generation (whose members have found expression not only in literature but through a wide range of media) stage the persistent problem of how to represent the genocide, as well as implicitly or explicitly articulate the question of how its memory will be preserved in the future, after the few generations chronologically close to it will have disappeared. Once the living connection with the historical experience thins with the passing of time, and eventually vanishes, under whose custody will this story be preserved and how?[2] It is an anxiety-ridden question, and an urgent one too. "At stake is precisely the 'guardianship' of a traumatic personal and generational past with which some of us have a 'living connection,' and that past's passing into history or myth," writes Marianne Hirsch.[3] The issue of the Holocaust's aftereffects and representation after the fact generated a rich and influential branch of studies in what Hirsch famously labels "postmemory,"[4] a new term describing "the relationship that the 'generation after' bears to the personal, collective, and cultural trauma of those who came before—to experiences they 'remember' only by means of the stories, images, and behaviors among which they grew up. But these experiences were transmitted to them so deeply, and affectively as to *seem* to constitute memories in their own right."[5] Postmemory is not the direct memory represented in survivors' narratives and testimonies after the war, but the secondhand memory the children of the firsthand witnesses inherited from their parents and their parents' generation: a mediated memory ("mediated not by recall but by imaginative investment, projection, and creation"[6]); a mosaic memory to which many voices, inputs, and filters must contribute. In other words, the second generation narrates memories that are not entirely theirs and that yet are entirely part of their memory.

As Hirsch explains, she arrived at the "postmemory" neologism when she was trying to define a memory she could not have of a past she did not herself experience, but that she knew so well it was imprinted in her mind as if it belonged to her:

> Strangely, the streets, buildings, and natural surroundings of Czernowitz [her family's hometown]—its theaters, restaurants, parks, rivers, and domestic settings, none of which I had ever myself seen, heard, or smelled—figure more strongly in my own childhood memories and imagination than do the sites and scenes of Timisoara, Romania, where I was born, or Bucharest, where I spent my childhood.
>
> Some of these same places, however, were also the sites of my childhood nightmares of persecution, deportation, and terror. When I began to write about my own early memories . . . I needed a special term to refer to the secondary, belated quality of my relationship with times and places that I had never experienced or seen, but which are vivid enough that I feel as though I remember them. My "memory" of Czernowitz, I concluded, is a "postmemory." Mediated by the stories, images, and behaviors among which I

grew up, it never added up to a complete picture or linear tale. Its power to overshadow my own memories derives precisely from the layers—both positive and negative—that have been passed down to me unintegrated, conflicting, fragmented, dispersed.[7]

Postmemory and its literary derivate, postmemoirs, are concepts that do not exclusively encompass the experience of Holocaust survivors' children. This is clearly laid out in Leslie Morris's essay "Postmemory, Postmemoir," which illustrates how a memory of the Holocaust has ended up permeating the collective imaginary and now "circulates beyond the actual bounds of lived, remembered experience (and beyond the geographical where the 'real' took place), [and] . . . seeps into the imaginary of other cultures (and other geographical spaces) as postmemory and as postmemoir."[8] Morris offers a comparative examination of a diverse group of authors that includes the Shoah victim Sarah Kofman; the German author Wolfgang Koeppen, who is not Jewish; Helen Fremont, who was born in the United States and discovered only in her thirties that her parents (whom she had always known as Catholics) were Jewish Holocaust survivors; the survivor impersonator Binjamin Wilkomirski; and others. Unlike Morris, however, I subsume under the rubrics of postmemory and postmemoir only the mnemonic works of Holocaust-related experiences by authors directly connected to the survivors. In other words, in my work, I refer to postmemory not as the representation of a memory of the Holocaust that springs up through education, cultural awareness, entertainment, and so forth, but rather as the representation of memories directly affected by the Holocaust but after the Holocaust ended: the memory that the postmemoirists have of themselves growing up as children of survivors or young refugees. Postmemory to me is thus full of direct points of contact (including absence) with the Ur-event. Therefore, the resulting postmemoir is a hybrid genre at the interface between a narrator's memory and the Holocaust memories of that narrator's family. Nevertheless, even in my more limited application of the concept, Morris's definition still applies: postmemory is a "memory that cannot be traced back to the Urtext of experience, but rather unfolds as part of an ongoing process of intertextuality, translation, metonymic substitution, and a constant interrogation of the nature of the original."[9] In a way, therefore, postmemoirs are postmodern works par excellence because their modes are predicated on many of the tenets and concerns of the postmodern project: hybridity that works against authorship, uprootedness, meta-identity, narrative pastiche, and so forth. Post-Holocaust, postmodernism, postmemory: they all share a prefix that paradoxically means to stress the beginning of a new historical or intellectual stage rather than the eclipse of an old one. As Hirsch remarks, "post" never signals the end of the phenomena it modifies by way of prefixing them but, on the contrary, signals (Derrida would probably say "it posts") their "troubling continuity."[10] In this chapter, I want to propose an exemplary case of postmemoir: Helena Janeczek's *Lezioni di tenebra* (Lessons of darkness),[11] a story of exile that exemplifies some of the complexities of second-generation inherited trauma via the projection of the author's innermost psychological disorders onto the main themes of her memoir, food and language.

Janeczek is the only daughter of Holocaust survivors from Poland. After the war they moved to Germany, where Janeczek was born in 1964. In 1983 she moved to Italy to distance herself from a Shoah mother, whose lingering, ineradicable fear of the Nazis was not eased by her living in Munich, where she felt she was surrounded by enemies. Only from her self-imposed exile in a new country could Janeczek find the words to narrate the story of her German Jewish postwar upbringing, and she did so not in German but in Italian. Janeczek's memoir forces us to think about a host of issues: the global (diasporic) subject, the Jewish diaspora, feminine dislocations of identity through mother-daughter stories of survival and escape, and eating disorders as displaced symptoms of traumatic Shoah memory or postmemory. Morris points out: "While there are still memoirs being published that seek to capture history 'wie es eigentlich gewesen ist,' there is now a corpus of texts that challenge the very undertaking of writing history (personal and political) and that highlight the difficulties inherent in any attempt at representation of the Holocaust. Thus the discursive space of 'the Holocaust' now encompasses texts that explore the uncertainty of authorship, experience, and identity and the slippage not only between national and ethnic identities, but also between fact and fiction, between trauma and recovery, between Jew and non-Jew, and between victim and perpetrator."[12] Janeczek's is one of these texts.

Marianne Hirsch and Nancy K. Miller write that "mutual imbrication rather than clear opposition between a desire for roots and an embrace of diasporic existence is symptomatic of our post-millennial moment."[13] However, we must also consider that for the children of Holocaust survivors, and certainly for their parents, diaspora is far more than an intellectual (or bourgeois) posture or theoretical approach. Feelings of alienation from one's nation, God, and patriarchal authority are intellectual pangs not exclusive to the Jews, and they have emerged as the *forma mentis* of post-Holocaust existence. Indeed, exile could be considered the crux of the postmodern condition. But although our newly acquired transnational sensibility allows us to stake a romantic claim on a piece of the diasporic dream, when the term "diaspora" is applied to communities like the Jews, the Armenians, or the Palestinians that have experienced diaspora in concretely devastating ways, the concept of exile and diaspora become noticeably less vague and negotiable. There is the existential diaspora that Jews share with the rest of the human community, and there is the diaspora that Jews (and many other dispossessed groups) have known in history and that has forced them in a position of inequality and vulnerability vis-à-vis their surrounding communities.

Exile and diaspora were old tropes in Jewish identity long before Jacques Derrida or Edward Said appropriated and refreshed them in order to critique the insidious ethnocentric discourses of the postwar era (with their corollaries of chauvinism, racism, bellicism, and so forth), thus making these terms universal. Exile happens to single individuals, whereas diasporas happen to entire peoples or communities. Israel—which can designate either one symbolic man (the Jew) and the collectivity (the Jewish people)—is sentenced to both. Diaspora presupposes exile, but the reverse is not necessarily true. Maybe there is a bit of Jewish humor in the fact that the Hebrew term for diaspora, *galut*, originally "referred to the setting of colonies of Jews outside Palestine after the Babylonian exile."[14] It appears that the original diaspora for the Jews was less focused on wandering than on settling, less on searching for a new home than longing for the old. On the one hand, there is exile—around which the Jewish spirit has constructed a complex and lyrical myth about itself and its cosmic purpose, over which Jews like to brood but on which their national pride as a people stands firmly; on the other hand, there is diaspora, which is chained not to the soul but the soil and is historical, not spiritual, and inflicted politically, not divinely.

Jews have suffered two diasporas in their history, and I claim that the post-Holocaust era can be considered their third and that the authors treated in this book belong to it. Janeczek's text, and the works of the other women studied here (with the exception of Anne Frank), all speak from this exilic position, first and foremost because none of their parents or they themselves live in Israel but also because of the antisemitic violence and the Nazi eradication of Jews in their home countries that made it impossible for them and their families to "return."[15] Although far removed from biblical Palestine, the European world had gained for the Jews the status of homeland during the two thousand years that they had been there. Then, in the middle of the so-called progressive twentieth century, Jews found themselves expropriated, their belongings and often their entire villages destroyed, and their families annihilated. They were dispersed once again, and for most of them, there was no hope of ever returning to these scenes. This time they faced a diaspora without return, without messianic hopes—they were no longer anchored anywhere. Obviously, the third diaspora has very different characteristics from the previous ones which, with the fall of the First and Second Temple, inaugurated a history of stateless wanderings for the Jews. The importance of the events of 586 BCE and 70 CE, when the Babylonians and the Romans, respectively, fought the Israelites, destroyed Jerusalem and its kingdoms, and scattered the Jewish people to the four corners of the Mediterranean world, lies in the fact that the sacred Jewish roots put down in a land divinely sanctioned as their own had been torn up. *Galut* is as much a religious (or mystical) exile as a historical exile from Israel. Despite the lack of comparable spiritual covenants, however, two thousand years of life on the European continent cannot be dismissed as inconsequential. Throughout the centuries, Jews forged deep connections with the various lands of Europe. Although France, Poland, Germany, Hungary, and Italy certainly did not have the same importance as Jerusalem did on the spiritual plane, for many European Jews to lose Paris, Vienna, or Vilna must have been no less painful than bidding farewell to his home for a Judean. However, as we will see with Janeczek's mother, the dream of going back to such prewar cities—especially Eastern European ones like Warsaw—was as unrealistic as a return to the Temple days. The third diaspora reshuffled Jewish geography, and the new dispersion brought many European Jews back to, among other places, Palestine. But however welcome the homecoming, the Shoah survivors' return to Israel is a much less triumphalist narrative than the one imagined by the prophet Ezekiel when he dreamed of God announcing to him that "I will now restore the fortunes of Jacob and take the whole House of Israel back in love . . . I have brought them back from among the peoples . . . They shall know that I the Lord am their God when, having exiled them among the nations, I gather them back into their land" (39:25).

After the war, not all Jews left Europe, although most of those who stayed moved to different towns or countries. And even the few who had not lost their physical homes had nonetheless lost the secure sense of what being home means. According to Pascale Bos, "the Holocaust ended the life of European Jews as it had existed for centuries." She points out that the cataclysm "brought about [together with the physical destruction of everything] a traumatic *shift in identity* for surviving European Jews. Particularly the assimilated, middle-class Jews of Western and Central Europe had to confront and redefine their sense of belonging in Europe after 1945 as Jews and citizens."[16] The manipulation of Holocaust memory that allowed the United States to foster a new brand of communal identity after the war (the American Jew), and which is analyzed by Peter Novick in his controversial *The Holocaust in American Life*,[17] has no equivalent in Europe. The bleak post-Holocaust reconstruction era includes the notorious Kielce pogrom of 1946, various other postwar antisemitic riots in Eastern Europe, Stalin's antisemitic purges, the "informal" expulsions of the Jews from Soviet Russia, their formal expulsion from Egypt in 1956, the Arab nations' coordinated attack against Israel in 1967, the massacre at the 1972 Munich Olympics, the fatal shooting of adults and children in a Hebrew school in Toulouse in 2012, terroristic attacks on synagogues, and so on. But despite the persistently recurring tragedies, the humanscape of Europe has changed enormously in the last few decades, and diversity is, with great effort, winning out over hostile national impermeability. This transnational reality is Europe's new identity, and in this transformed landscape, the Jews are gaining greater visibility and a voice that is more audible than ever before. The Kindertransport escapee Edith Milton assesses this disparity between the insular world she grew up in and the global society of today, noting that the twenty-first century comfortably inhabits a sort of terra incognita "which is perhaps the New World of our age, the place in which a greater and greater number of us seem to live and to which more and more of us think about moving. With luck, by the next millennium, we will all be there."[18] We could consider ourselves truly lucky if no apocalyptic political event shakes the stability we seem to be achieving, with various hiccups along the way. As Andreas Huyssen remarks about the infinitely more contentious human scenario left behind by 9/11, "when civilizations clash, the space for diasporic thinking, transnational exchange, and cultural hybridity shrinks. Orientalist and occidentalist tropes have a field day, banal anti-American and anti-European stereotypes abound on both sides of the Atlantic, and the metaphysics of civilizations, cultures, and nations takes over yet again."[19]

Edmond Jabès has beautifully written: "Exile had so changed my features . . . that none of my community / Would take me under his roof. For all of them, I was already dead."[20] This lyrical statement painfully yet precisely highlights the two great losses of exile: recognizability and language. Janeczek, the other Jewish memoirists considered in this book, and the many survivors scattered all over the world would probably share Jabès's mournful realization. Quoting "Ashkenazia," a short story by Clive Sinclair, Bryan Cheyette notes that "for the post-Holocaust writer . . . an 'imaginary homeland' can not merely be constituted by words alone as Europe is littered with 'fields of wooden skeletons.'"[21] As I hope to show in the following pages, the post-Holocaust writer in Europe no longer owns even a language she can call home.

A theme that often characterizes postmnemonic narratives is that of the trip of return, the second-generational desire, acted on or simply fantasized about, to return to the place of origins—a place that no longer exists. Or rather, the place exists only in memory, where—freed from the imagination's bounds of lived experience—it is construed, embellished, destroyed, and transformed. The impossibility to satisfy this desire of return opens up an irreparable wound, which stands as the event horizon beyond the emptiness left behind by the Holocaust, a sort of black hole—both a liminal point of no return and the orbit of Holocaust trauma. Hirsch and Miller indicate the drawbacks of projecting oneself into such an irrecoverable past: "While the idea of postmemory can account for the lure of second-generation 'return,' it also underscores the radical distance that separates the past from the present and the risks of projection, appropriation, and over-identification occasioned by second- and third-generation desires and needs."[22] Janeczek's Lezioni deals with this "radical distance" in surprising ways. As I will show, Janeczek also embarks on a trip of return, not one she initiates but one organized entirely by her mother. As a writer strongly influenced by the postmodern spirit that was so important in Europe in the 1990s, Janeczek ends up using her diasporic condition in generative ways to question her nation's past, her own present relation with a new country, and her Jewish identity in order to provide a safe space (her heterotopic postmemoir) in which her mother's suffering and pain can finally be expressed. In the end, Janeczek concludes that any search for home is senseless. Her text is diasporic not because it longs for a home but because it can exist only in a position of homelessness. The text is possible because this daughter has abandoned all illusions of unambiguously belonging, of unambiguous (national, ethnic, or linguistic) identification—including with her mother.

Lezioni showcases the situation of foreignness and uprootedness of the Shoah second generation from the perspective of a woman who has chosen emigration not for economic reasons or to flee political oppression, but as the only possible route to witnessing and writing. Like the texts examined previously in this work, Lezioni is a double memoir that tells the story of both a daughter's and a mother's life. It uses the daughter's experience as a kind of magic lantern to project the tragic past and psychotic present of an exceptional, though also half-crazed, Holocaust mother. At the center of this memoir lies the story of the two women's journey back to Auschwitz in 1995, for the fiftieth anniversary of the liberation. Generally, the second-generation children begin to seek out their origins only once they are older and settled in their lives, with careers, families, and defined identities of their own; by then, their Shoah parents are usually already dead. Janeczek's case is out of the ordinary in that her mother is not only alive but travels with her on this journey of discovery. The trip to Poland sustains the entire text at a narrative, thematic, and structural level. It is both a literal and a metaphorical conduit. It ties the mother and daughter to each other's past while moving the story and the characters along a trajectory that is both vertical (in time and traumatic memory) and horizontal (in space, passing through actual nations and their borders). The metaphorical and literal presence of borders is accompanied by two other central motifs, food and language, through which Shoah memory is channeled in this text. Food and language are used by Janeczek to explore her relation to her Holocaust mother, her Jewish ancestry, and her identity—or rather her "identity disorder," which is what Jacques Derrida calls the effect of losing one's clear sense of origins.[23] By focusing on Janeczek's pathogenic relationship with food and on the inability of any single language to denote her identity, I use *Lezioni* and other postmemoirs to explore the uneasy and perplexing exilic state foisted on the members of the Shoah second generation by their parents' experience. It is only in the exilic space of her postmemoir that Janeczek is able to map her identity outside the limiting boundaries of family, nation, and language. The story of this mother and daughter—their ferocious arguments, their painful trip to Poland, and the daughter's retreat to Italy—maps a journey into the depths of each one's dark past in search of unattainable knowledge. It is ultimately also the story of the daughter's successful escape from the past that, growing up, haunted her through the accented voice of a foreign mother who had been made a permanent stranger (both to her daughter and to the surrounding world) by the unknowable Holocaust and the reconfigurations of the third diaspora.

### *KATABATIC* JOURNEY: THE TRAUMATIC DESCENT

Helena Janeczek's mother, née Nina Franziska Lis, was born in 1923 in an assimilated, bourgeois Polish-speaking family. Nina and her family were transferred to the Warsaw Ghetto from Zawiercie, but Nina sensed the mortal danger that lay in wait for those entrapped there and ran away—leaving behind her mother, who was later murdered. Eventually, she was captured and sent to Auschwitz, while her husband managed to survive in hiding, carrying false identity papers, until the end of the war. She and her husband were reunited in 1945, the only survivors from their respective families. At that point, their plan had been to emigrate to the United States, but because the husband had contracted tuberculosis, he was not eligible for a visa. They were already in Germany, in a displaced persons' camp in Bavaria, when they attempted to get their passes to leave Europe, and when their emigration plan failed, they decided to stay put. In Munich, Helena's mother opened a successful Italian-style shoe store called *Italy Ninetta* and passed off her otherwise "suspect" accent as Italian. Necessity had turned this woman into a chameleon capable of adjusting to any situation that life would throw at her, always attempting to be a few steps ahead of an invisible enemy. A woman constantly on edge, she did not hesitate to lie or deceive in order to insulate herself from danger. It was this paranoia, her fear of being caught or betraying herself—a tragically permanent effect of the war years—that would characterize and damage her relationship with her only daughter, Helena, on whom she tirelessly imposes her impossibly strict lessons for an impossible survival: "you are safe only if you do not commit a mistake."[24] Eva Hoffman too remembers the "hampering insistence on perfectionism and impeccably correct behavior" hammered into the psyches of survivors' children by their parents, because "if one wants to survive, one must make no mistakes!"[25] But one never finds out precisely what constitutes a mistake. And as we shall see, Janeczek learns to navigate the mother's dark labyrinth of dangers, fatal errors, and invisible traps and as a result suffers from post-traumatic symptoms of her own: nightmares, guilt, low self-esteem, depressive states, hyperprotectiveness toward her parents, and recurrent panic attacks. It is at the fringes of this dark maternal territory, one shaped by atrocious memories and a terrifyingly unforeseeable future, that the daughter's text situates itself.

In 1995 the world paused to commemorate the fiftieth anniversary of the liberation of Auschwitz and the end of World War II. Along with politicians, academics, and other dignitaries—all of whom were spouting grandiose rhetoric—Janeczek's mother, by then a widow, also decided to mourn the event, although in a less public fashion. She organized a trip back to Poland with a few other survivors who were her friends, and she asked Janeczek to accompany her. For the first time in decades, Nina was to see Poland again: her husband's native village, Warsaw, and the gas chambers where her mother perished. Janeczek, who thus far had only had a basic knowledge of her parents' tragic story and who was living in Italy with her husband, let herself be guided by her mother through this terrible odyssey, which she succinctly explains in these terms: "I don't think my mother ever wanted to entrust me with her story, not even its most bare-boned version. Instead, she decided to go back to Poland, at least once, and I decided to go with her: to see her house, my father's house, the city" (*Lezioni*, 133). Led by the mother, she enters into a hellish time warp that brings together many loose ends relating to her own past and origins, her broken identity, her problematic relationship with an incomprehensible mother, and her parents' lives—especially, as we will see, that of her invisible father. Uncannily, the story of mother and daughter seems to trace a full circle: a daughter, Nina, who had to abandon her mother in order to survive the Nazis' extermination plan, takes a trip with her own daughter, Janeczek, who, in turn, abandons her mother by moving to a different country for the sake of her own psychological survival. Shortly after this trip to Poland, Janeczek felt compelled to write *Lezioni*.

The book's genesis suggests that it will be a sort of travelogue, a genre with a distinguished literary pedigree, but this proves to be only partly true. If anything, it is the book of two journeys taking place on different planes: a geographical visit to Poland occurring on the horizontal plane, and an inner journey into ravaged, excised, and salvaged memories, which we can imagine as following a vertical trajectory into the depths of the mother's and daughter's damaged psyches. This downward trajectory is what connects the text to the eminent literary tradition of the *katabasis*, or journey into the underworld, epitomized by Dante Alighieri's *Divine Comedy*. It may be no accident, then, that Janeczek writes her own contemporary version of a *descensus ad inferos* in Italian, Dante's language. The architecture of her physical voyage is not organized as a vertical subterranean structure (like Piranesi's prison) but takes place horizontally, its plane flat like the Ptolemaic universe, through the charming views of everyday downtown Warsaw and the birch-tree-lined fields of Oświęcim. However, the return to the traumatic memory of the Holocaust is often talked about (not only by the survivors) as if it were a descent into an unworldly—indeed, underworldly—place. Trauma itself could be metaphorically imagined as the permanent hell of the mind (an inner world of despair and suffering). Building on Freud's hypothesis that traumatic experience forms an inaccessible space in the mind, Cathy Caruth adds that the space of trauma and the space of memory are not one and the same. In fact, they interfere with each other. Contrary to what one would expect, trauma causes memory to short-circuit. As Caruth explains, "the vivid and precise return of the [traumatic] event appears, as modern researchers point out, to be accompanied by an *amnesia* for the past, a fact . . . referred to by several major writers as a *paradox*."[26] Nevertheless, I argue that the visitations of one or the other of those spaces (mnemonic and traumatic)—nightmares, flashbacks, and associations both willed or occasioned by unexpected circumstances, conscious or unconscious—can be treated metaphorically as a series of *katabatic* plunges. The injured mind (which, Freud suspected, is probably trying not to think about the injurious events[27]) plummets into those deep inner chambers in search of a lost unity, a pretraumatic wholeness: a wholeness that is possible only in the realm of the comprehensible, and that therefore is shattered by the utter incomprehensibility of what happened, of what the traumatic space has in store. Trauma, thus conceived of as an inner hell—a place of pain and unmitigable fear of death or injury—recurs continuously and continues to produce deleterious effects and symptoms; the Shoah's second-generation children therefore become the inheritors of the survivors' *etterno dolore*. As Rachel Falconer points out in her extraordinary work on postwar descent narratives, "it is easy to go to Hades by dying, but difficult to cross over when alive."[28] The necessity and unbearable difficulty of this continuous crossing over into the space of an intolerable memory is both the permanent condition of the traumatized mind and the inextricable Gordian knot of the second generation's relationship with the Shoah parents.

Primo Levi famously brought Dante's *Inferno* to Auschwitz. During his detention in that place of horror, Levi recited, taught, and translated cantos from the poem in order to keep himself from turning into a *Muselmann*—a prisoner who had given up on surviving, the camp's most horrific figure.[29] Other victims had also drawn this allegorical parallel during their captivity. For example, Etty Hillesum writes in her Westerbork diary: "Really, Dante's *Inferno* is a comic opera by comparison. 'Ours is the real hell,' S. said recently, very simply and drily.'"[30] In her journal, Hélène Berr reports a similar allusion made by a friend of hers: "News from dad. He talks of heart-wrenching, unthinkable scenes [in Drancy] ... Paul says it is Dante's hell."[31] Not by chance, the title of Eugen Kogon's classic report on the daily life of prisoners in Buchenwald is *The Theory and Practice of Hell*, an allusion that recurs repeatedly in the descriptions of the Shoah and its death apparatuses.[32] "The space of the camp ... can be effectively represented as a series of concentric circles that, like waves, uninterruptedly touch a central nonplace, inhabited by the *Muselmann*," Giorgio Agamben writes in *Quel che resta di Auschwitz* (Remnants of Auschwitz), a philosophical disquisition on the spatial and mental hell into which Levi was dragged, along with millions of others. The concentric circles, we know, also characterize the structure of Dante's Inferno. "The farthest border of this nonplace is called in the camp jargon *Selektion*," according to Agamben, but its epicenter is death, the head of the Gorgon no one can face without becoming petrified.[33] The *Muselmann*, Agamben postulates, is the prisoner who has had the misfortune of staring straight into the face of horror and has thus became the most abject of humans.

I would like to highlight this compelling intellection of an architecture of hell and add to it another component: the movement toward this hell that defines the *katabatic* experience. As noted above, in classical narratives, either tragic or comic, *katabasis* is a journey into the underworld. It is undertaken by a protagonist to fulfill a quest, and its characteristic sequence is "a descent, an inversion or turning upside down at a zero point and a return to the surface of some kind."[34] Classically, one descends into hell; Hades is the underworld, and the Western imaginary can conceive of a journey to it only as a downward movement, a movement that carries the unlucky soul or the heroic explorer in the opposite direction and as far as is imaginable, from heaven. However, twentieth-century hell is no longer the sunken realm traveled to by Dante, Ulysses, Aeneas, or Orpheus; rather, it has eerily moved to the upper world and is irrevocably among us. Shoah stories of survival, rediscoveries of the past, and trips of return to the places of horror (in second-generation literature, for instance) are all *katabatic* narratives in many ways. However, the experience these narratives refer back to, the historical truth they try to make sense of through a posteriori knowledge, belongs very specifically to Europe. Our ultimate ethical fall is not part of an expository and edifying myth but real history that occurred in the world. Janeczek's memoir thus exemplifies the simultaneous journey down through traumatic memory and across historical, geographic space. Her geographic journey with her mother stretches from Warsaw to Oświęcim, while the psychological and traumatic journey runs from the Warsaw Ghetto to Auschwitz and follows a vertical trajectory deep into the darkness of the inferno of the conscious and subconscious mind.

An uncanny coincidence helps me better explain this mystifying aporia (which literally means, as Sarah Kofman reminds us, "without passage")[35] between geographical places and the traumatic power those places hold in the post-Shoah mind. Some of the areas where the genocide was carried out had belonged to the Prussian or Austro-Hungarian Empire, and it is not unusual for towns in eastern Poland, western Ukraine, or the former Czechoslovakia to be known by both Slavic and German names. The first time I went to Poland in 1989, a teenager with a governmental summer scholarship on my own quest for a vanished Jewish past, I ventured all alone to get myself a train ticket from Cracow to the most notorious extermination camp, only forty-one miles outside the glorious royal town. It was a place I had been obsessing about for as long as I could remember and now had the opportunity of seeing with my own eyes for the first time. I was shocked when everybody at the station refused, some even aggressively, to sell me a ticket "to Auschwitz." I ran back to the hostel in tears and utterly shaken, certain that the angry looks and the rude responses were signs of the locals' unvarnished antisemitism. I was young, inexperienced, and facing a nation that was old and inured to the cruelties of history. It turned out that I had inadvertently offended my interlocutors as much as they had offended me. I should have asked for a ticket to Oświęcim. Technically speaking, there is no such town as Auschwitz in Poland. And to most Poles, especially in those days, Auschwitz did not exist.[36]

Oświęcim and Auschwitz are forever separate despite their sameness. The journey into Auschwitz does not happen in Oświęcim, and yet Oświęcim is, geographically and lastingly, where Auschwitz happened. One is in constant danger of getting lost in the labyrinth of these complex personal, national, and universal pasts, and postmemoirs perfectly articulate this danger. All *katabatic* voyagers, Janeczek among them, therefore need a guide who guarantees that the traveler won't get lost in the unfamiliar map of Hades and, more important, will make it out alive. Janeczek is led through the inferno of her mother's memory by the mother herself. In this case, as I will show, the guide (her mother) is not only the entranceway to the inferno but the inferno itself, its human embodiment. The mother is the territory of trauma, the epicenter of the Shoah's impact and the expression of its lingering aftershocks.

Marianne Hirsch and Leo Spitzer have written compelling works on memorial prostheses and testimonial objects for the Shoah's second generation.[37] As we saw in the case of the former Kindertransport refugees (chapter 4), these relics and photos are important to the Shoah children, who lack any other link to the disappeared past when they undertake their return. Interestingly, in Janeczek's case, the presence of the mother seems to render all these testimonial objects irrelevant. In fact, Janeczek does not talk about photographs or any other concrete object as helping her to conjure up images of her mother's past.[38] The mother herself is the prosthesis of the daughter's postmemory: the daughter's gaze at the traumatic sites aligns itself with the gaze of the mother, not merely in a symbolic sense but in a very literal sense because Nina is there with Janeczek, leading her, interpreting things for her, pointing, explaining, and guiding her vision.

The trip to Poland constitutes the core of this text, yet *Lezioni* is more crucially the story of the impossibility of narrating this journey. This seems to subvert the expectations of the traditional *katabatic* narrative. Falconer lists sixteen recurring features of *katabatic* narratives,[39] whose point of departure is a quest for knowledge, which ultimately is always self-knowledge:

> In classical katabasis, the descent to Dis or Hades is about coming to know the self, regaining something or someone lost, or acquiring superhuman powers or knowledge. The descent requires the hero to undergo a series of tests and degradations, culminating in the collapse or dissolution of the hero's sense of selfhood. In the midst of this dissolution comes the infernal revelation, or the sought after power, or the spectre of the beloved. The hero then returns to the overworld, in some cases succeeding, in other cases failing to bring back this buried wisdom, love or power from the underworld . . . In katabatic narratives written after 1945, while the descent to Hell still functions as a quest for knowledge . . . the descent occurs within a context which, unlike their classical predecessors, is already understood to be infernal.[40]

Shoah narratives (fictional or autobiographical), as Falconer explains, can be taken as the modern equivalent of the ancient *katabatic* journeys. However, I want to offer the idea that second-generation journeys of discovery (as exemplified in the works by Janeczek, Paula Fass, Eva Hoffman, Anne Karpf, Lisa Appignanesi, Martin Lemelman, and many others)[41] fit better than the first generation's narratives in this rubric of modern-day *katabasis*. The metaphor of the survivors fall into the depths of hell when they enter Auschwitz is useful because our language is not equipped to describe such an event and must appeal to the reservoir of words and images that literature has made understandable and familiar to us. However, I suggest that the second generation's exploratory journeys into their parents' past provide an even more exact equivalent of the ancient genre of *katabasis* than do the stories of the firsthand victims. The immediate victims did not voluntarily go on an epistemological journey; rather, it is the survivors' children who, digging into their past, willingly undertake the quest for knowledge. First-generation victims were all alone in navigating everyday uncertainties and horrors; the second-generation travelers always have a guide who will lead them on their journey. They are directed by a parent, they interrogate old relatives, or they travel back to Europe and find guidance from history keepers, curators of Jewish museums, or archivists in the ghostly remnants of once-thriving Jewish communities; they track down elderly survivors in their parents' hometowns; and there are always plenty of Judaica hobbyists to be found in the non-Jewish world. The travelers must rely on helpers to lead them through the maze of fragmentary information, broken links, and insufficient evidence. Most important, unlike the firsthand victims, these second-generation archeologists are guaranteed to return from their journey. In light of all this, I can confidently claim that all second-generation narratives of exploration are indeed *katabatic* in nature, structure, and mode.

The journey on which Janeczek's narrated I embarks is also literal, though it has symbolically *katabatic* undertones. Her quest seeks to answer the question, "Who is my mother?"—a question whose answer is the solution to many other riddles, including the riddle of her own identity:

> My mother, who reads through to the last page of a Scandinavian novel even when she finds it incredibly boring . . . who could never stand fat people or ugly people, who was always an aesthete, this is the mother I know, the opposite of me, the one who irritates me because I want to be her opposite. But the one who with no money in her pocket fled the ghetto . . . telling her mother, "I'm leaving, I don't want to burn in the ovens!" Who is that one? (*Lezioni*, 13)

Clearly, this particular explorer is on a quest for the truth about her mother, knowing all too well that what she will find could be unbearable. Of the truths sought after by Shoah narratives, Falconer asks: "How do we access this hugely destructive, underworldly truth? Do we descend to it, and if so, how do we return?

Do we return? Or alternatively, does it come to us; are we dragged down unwillingly?"[42] To enter the inferno, Dante has to pass through a gate displaying an ominous admonition: "Abandon all hope ye who enter here."[43] As we all know, a gate with a message also marked the entrance into the Auschwitz hell—this one cruelly exhorting its damned to work for their freedom. Hovering between allegory (Dante) and literality (Auschwitz) is Janeczek's personal entryway into the knowledge of her infernal past, her mother. The portal through which she begins her descent into hell is a terrifying scream in Polish emitted by Nina, who breaks down at the sight of the barracks and crematoria she brought herself and her daughter to: "She cries, fifty years later, in Poland," Janeczek writes:

> She screams of having left "my mother, my mother" alone. She is screaming like an eagle at the museum installation in Auschwitz . . . in front of a display case that exhibits a sample of Zyklon B, she is again a little girl screaming "Mama, Mama!" I loved her then fully and proudly because of that public scene. I love the mother who survived more . . . than the other one who weighs herself on the scale every morning, and I can't reconcile them. And I know I am dealing with an insoluble mystery; I am aware that I will never know my mother, and that at the same time I know her too well. (*Lezioni*, 13–14)

Because the victim mother does not threaten the daughter, the daughter can love her fully and proudly. The other mother—the survivor who is not dead but present and alive—represents a different, inaccessible, and even hostile territory to the daughter. I will show how this impenetrability is symptomatized in the daughter's eating disorders and most forcefully expressed in the abusive language that characterizes their bond.

### INHERITING AN "OBSCENE GIFT" :
### A MOTHER'S LESSONS OF DARKNESS

Janeczek concedes: "I am grateful to my parents for having spared me their reminiscences; I think they were right not to tell anything" (*Lezioni*, 101). However, what Fass, a historian, wrote—"I cannot remember a time when I did not know that my mother and father were survivors"[44]—sounds quite true for Janeczek as well. Fass, seventeen years older than Janeczek, was also born in Germany, and her parents also were Polish camp survivors; in Fass's case, the parents succeeded in emigrating to the United States. The fathers of these two post-Shoah daughters were both quiet men who didn't talk about their pasts, a symptom not uncommon in survivors' households (mothers seem more likely to share their war and prewar memories with their children). However, it is one thing not to be told details about the Shoah past and quite another not to know about it at all. "The survivor's child may be intuitively sensitive to the parents' secrets which are never talked about and yet are somehow sensed," the British psychoanalyst Dinora Pines points out.[45] Janeczek, for example, says that all her life she had a clear sense of being Jewish and "not quite" German, despite the complete assimilation and secularism of her family. There are two forces pulling the children of the survivors in directions that are overwhelmingly difficult to negotiate, especially when one is young. Although the second-generation child does not know the secrets that shroud the parents' identity and past, she (or he) does know that every move she makes will be read through that mysterious past: Is she as worthy as the other children who were lost? Is she honoring with her behavior the memory and traditions of multiple lines of victimized relatives she never met? Is she adding more pain to the already martyred souls of her father or mother? Then there is another dilemma that makes it hard for many second-generation children to ever fully possess a home country: on the one hand, all survivors want is for their children to be happy, safe, and prosperous in the free society where they have rebuilt their lives; on the other, because the parents themselves strain to fully belong to these new nations—where they arrived as adults with a heavy burden of pain and with accents, traditions, and social behaviors they retain—their children like them may end up feeling split between fully belonging (a healthy inclusiveness mostly enabled by the school systems) and being foreigners in their country of birth. Appignanesi's postmemoir records this condition splendidly:

> I longed to bury the past and its traces. Above all, I longed to be as ordinary as all my suburban [Canadian] friends. They had nice, bland, bridge-playing, club-going parents. Parents who could speak English in full unaccented sentences. Parents who talked of mundane things, and not of concentration camps and ghettos and anti-Semitic laws and the dead and the missing. Their mothers baked cookies and cakes . . . Their fathers only read the Montréal papers and *Time* magazine and not on top of these a slew of newspapers in strange Hebrew script . . . I rarely brought any friends home and if I did, I made sure they left before my parents returned.[46]

Janeczek sensed that there was something extraordinary in her parents' past. They were foreigners, while she was a native; they spoke differently from other children's parents and had different friends. She knew she was Jewish, but that remained more of a veneer than a fully formed identity because the family didn't practice the religion. It was important for her mother that Janeczek fully belong and "pass" as German, and that she have access to all the advantages the postwar life offered her generation. However, the mother also instilled in the daughter a contradictory sense of identity. Janeczek was never really free to feel 100 percent German. In fact, when she turned thirteen, her parents began a small-scale Judaization campaign in the hope of steering her away from German boys and encouraging her to embrace her Jewish identity, despite having raised her in a secular, Germanic environment. This is how Janeczek ventriloquizes her mother imparting one of her lessons about "they" and "us":

> We offer coffee at the café; we don't just pay for our own, because we are not Germans. We are hospitable and invite friends to our house and cook an overly abundant meal because we are not Germans. We don't give a monthly allowance to you . . . we do not distinguish between what is "mine" and what is "yours" because we are not Germans. We do not believe that a child who turns eighteen is suddenly an adult. Children are always children, and that's because we are not Germans. (Lezioni, 29)

But whether the "we" in the refrain "we are not Germans" includes Janeczek remains an open question. Is "we" the Jews, the Janeczeks, the Polish mother and father? Is the daughter, who was born in Munich and whose first language is German, part of this non-German community of Germans? This scene perfectly stages what Dan Diner famously dubbed the German-Jewish "negative symbiosis," according to whose sad irony "for both Jews and Germans, whether they like it or not, the aftermath of mass murder has been the starting point for self-understanding—a kind of communality of opposites."[47] Janeczek's mother and father live in Germany as if in passing—especially Nina, who is a master of camouflage. The basic awareness of where one belongs, an awareness that comes to children through their childhood homes, is missing in Janeczek because her parents are new Germans, old Poles, and fractured Jews; they had lost their families, language, and names before settling in the new nation, and they were already foreigners at home before becoming foreigners in a foreign land. Eventually, the postwar daughter, the Shoah survivors' loyal inheritor, is pushed to make an impossible choice: "I didn't want to become German either. Therefore, I didn't" (Lezioni, 31).

Nina is an overbearing mother whose one task is to instill in her only child the ultimate lesson: survive! Trick life (and death), implores Nina, at all costs, even when you think you are not in danger, because danger will come sooner or later. Nina demonstrates an unflagging capacity for transformation and adaptation under which lurks the terror of death, a paranoid fear of being discovered or singled out. In the constant grip of unmitigable fear, Janeczek's mother tries to train her daughter so that she'll always be prepared to resist, and even predict, the blows of chance: "It is fear that teaches you to adapt, to slip away, to avoid attracting attention" (*Lezioni*, 91). Although Janeczek does not inherit her mother's uncanny ability to "slip away," she undoubtedly learns what fear is. The daughter's paralyzing fears have nothing to do with escaping the burning Warsaw Ghetto, avoiding the selection in Auschwitz, or passing under the radar of an ss officer on the street. Rather, they derive from her mother's withering gaze, from the anxiety to succeed in passing for the ideal survivor's daughter her mother would like her to be. It is from the mother, not the Nazis, that Helena inherits her fears and panic: "I was afraid only of her: of her capacity to root out my flaws, to discover the few forbidden transgressions, the rare lies. I feared her giving me the third degree, her questionings, her control over me, and of course her screaming, those words she would throw at me and her guilty verdicts delivered against me . . . Out of all this came a fear of something without precise contours, a fear of being unworthy of the task of living, the fear of being exactly the vermin she said I was" (*Lezioni*, 110). Following the strategy of the legendary King Mithridates, who took small doses of poison to build up a resistance to it, Nina tries to inoculate her daughter by administering ever-increasing doses of the Shoah venom, but the intended antidote turns out to be as lethal as the fate it attempts to immunize against. Janeczek ends up absorbing the poison and ingesting the unmanageable trauma of her mother.

It is this poisonous relationship with the omnipotent mother that the daughter is trying to work through in her text. This relationship takes place over shifting territories: geographic (Italy, Germany, and Poland); chronologic (past and present); linguistic (Italian, German, Polish, Yiddish, and Hebrew); psychic (trauma and memory); and that of identity (Jewish, German, mother, daughter). The mother is the meta-territory that encapsulates all others: she is the past and present; she is every language spoken; and she is trauma (both its victim and its source for the daughter). The mother affects the daughter from all these different angles; at the same time, the daughter has access to these various loci only through the mother. Hirsch hints at the sense of separation such a limited access implies when she writes that "Holocaust postmemory . . . attempts to bridge more than just a temporal divide. The children of exiled survivors, although they have not themselves lived through the trauma of banishment and the destruction of home, remain always marginal or exiled, always in the diaspora."[48] Melvin Jules Bukiet, a second-generation writer, declares: "We have been given an obscene gift . . . It's our job to tell the story, to cry, 'Never Forget!' despite the fact that we can't remember a thing."[49] In Janeczek's case, her mother's obsession is not merely that her daughter remember but also that she foresee the unforeseeable, as impossible a demand as remember what you don't.

We have seen how for Sarah Kofman the direct traumatic experience of the genocide left traces of itself not only in the difficult relationship she had with food but also in the lingering associations she frequently construed (in her writings and psychoanalytical sessions) between her bodily orifices, together with what came in and out of them, and Shoah witnessing. Something very similar happens to Janeczek, who, particularly in her youth, suffers from eating disorders. The connection between childhood victimization and eating disorders has been long established by the psychiatric community. Yet relatively little work has been done in terms of the connection between Shoah-related trauma and food-related pathologies, either in survivors or in the victims' and perpetrators' offspring. One of the few studies on this topic was conducted by a team of Israeli scientists on fifty-five survivors and a matched control group of forty-three other people; the researchers detected no relevant deviations in the eating patterns of the survivors' group.[50] Oddly, Shoah literature seems to present a different picture. Could a relationship exist among Shoah trauma, eating disorders, *and* writing? Eating—either as underfeeding or overfeeding, as lack or overabundance of food—is a frequent subject of war memoirs and postmemoirs. With war comes hunger. And hunger in World War II killed twenty million people. Most of Europe was famished during those interminable war years. The infamous Hunger Plan, developed by the Reich Minister of Food and Agriculture Herbert Backe, had been put in place in order to guarantee sufficient food supplies for Germany at the expense of the occupied lands, whose residents were to be starved into extinction. As Lizzie Collingham brilliantly illustrates, food was a part of military strategy during the war.[51] Think, for example, of how the effects of the ominously worsening shortage of food permeates every page of Dawid Sierakowiak's desperate Łódź Ghetto diary.[52] On August 8, 1943, Sierakowiak died, probably of tuberculosis, at the age of nineteen. Three months and a half earlier, in his last diary entry, he had written with hope that a friend might procure a job for him at the ghetto's bakery. We don't know whether he ever got that much sought-after job, but by that entry he was already starving, feverish, and so weak that he could hardly stand. Levi said of his days in Auschwitz that they made it impossible to imagine not being hungry: "the *Lager* is hunger: we ourselves are hunger, living hunger."[53] The memories of those who survived (in the concentration camps, in hiding, and in occupied towns) are filled with recollections of desperate hunger that often pushed people to act recklessly to find something to eat for themselves or others in their care. As a reaction, those who came out of the war alive made sure to construct a world of plenty, especially for their children. Second-generation memoirs often touch on the issue of food:

they talk of parents who overfeed children or are overprotective of them, always scared a child might get sick, run into some unpredictable danger outside the home, and so forth. But before I explore further the impact of war deprivation on the way the survivors' generation later obsessed over their children's well-being, safety, and satiation, I want to show how Janeczek herself connects her struggle with her own identity to food, nutrition, and Shoah survival. This is how her postmemoir Lezioni begins:

> The other night on TV, a woman claimed to be the reincarnation of a girl murdered in a death camp . . . Then an older Jewish lady . . . talked about the concentration camp as an "elevated experience" . . . What I've been wanting to know for a while though is whether one can transmit knowledge and experiences not just through the maternal milk but earlier still, through the amniotic fluid or something similar, since my mother, for instance, did not breast-feed me, yet I carry around an ancestral hunger, the hunger of starved people, a hunger she herself doesn't have anymore . . . When she was little my mother never ate as much as me; she didn't like anything . . . She says that only the war cured her lack of appetite, and on hearing this, people from her generation who remember the heroism of that hunger give her a look of mutual understanding. She does not specify to them, however, what kind of hunger she suffered, and the sentence "there was no food" can mean different things to different people. She doesn't tell them that it was by sheer chance or by miracle that she did not starve to death, that she was not killed by asthenia from malnutrition, or murdered by gas. (Lezioni, 9–11)

The TV program on reincarnation with which the memoir opens strikes at the heart of Janeczek's complicated psychological experience. To reincarnate means "to make flesh," to embody. Hence Janeczek is not only the regeneration of a mother's life, but she also strives to reincarnate through her self-destructive eating habits (binging) the fleshless (gaunt) body of the Auschwitz survivor, who—like Tantalus in Hades—experiences the torment of eternally inaccessible satisfaction. The mother's body has come to be inhabited by an insatiable vacuum. The mother's body is accessible to the child as a source of food, and thus it is no surprise that this particular daughter's relation to food is a pathological one. It is a long-standing truism that we relate to our mothers through food, and that food has the arcane power of connecting us to our mothers, to carry forth our memory of them. Sadly, this is not true for Holocaust mothers like Nina, who cannot be accessed through food because their own relationship to it has degenerated, has been maimed by experiences of starvation, debasement, and sickness. Hence it is not surprising that we often find illustrations, at least in Shoah literature, of daughters' pathological relations to both food and mothers.

Janeczek repeatedly makes unambiguous associations between Shoah and eating. She tells us about how she uncontrollably eats any food lying around, good or bad, a practice to which she ascribes her corpulence and that is the target of her mother's harshest criticism. Nina's signals to her daughter are always mixed: she overfeeds Janeczek while also chastising her for being overweight; she dreads persecution while constantly monitoring her daughter to catch her in errors. This alienating confusion is the bread of affliction with which this Holocaust mother nourishes her daughter. In *Lezioni*, food rarely gives satisfaction; rather, it often provokes dissatisfaction and is connected to a negative self-image. The indestructible mother's lingering hunger for life is passed on to the vulnerable daughter in a literalized form: hyperphagia. Janeczek's disorders are tied to her mother's eating dysfunctions. Nina is fixated on thinness and measures every intake very carefully to preserve her refined Old World figure. Her obsession with her own and her daughter's appearance suggests an incurable nostalgia for her prewar life, when social superiority was also showcased through looking and behaving impeccably at all times, both in private and in public. Janeczek writes:

> Now that she is old . . . she has regained a strict control over her nutrition . . . She begrudges me the fact that I automatically chow down every piece of bread around even as she pours half of her portion onto my plate . . . We are complete opposites, I think with a mixture of satisfaction and shame for my body and my hunger. All I want to know is whether it's possible that she passed this hunger onto me, her own hunger. So, just as to this day she still gives me half of her schnitzels, her mashed potatoes, half of her pasta entrée—although she often calls me "my butterball"—perhaps she has also passed along the hunger from when she was half-dead in order to overcome that half-death and regain the character, personality, and individual psychology of her prestarvation years. (*Lezioni*, 11–12)

Unlike the Israeli researchers mentioned above, other researchers observed that many survivors do share certain food-related traits and eating habits.[54] One team notes:

> Survivors reported that "food controls their lives" . . . This item probably reflects the most characteristic eating problem that survivors still have. During the interview, in fact, many of them told us about persistent and specific thoughts about food and eating. Their most common characteristic was the

position of defence of their food during meals (both arms around the plate and the head lowered). Some described their incapacity to allow someone else, even their partner, to eat something from their plate . . . These attitudes have generally persisted throughout the 51 years since liberation. They do not seem to constitute a problem for survivors; rather, they are a characteristic to which they have adapted and sometimes a form of comfort from bad memories."[55]

In *Lezioni*, however, it is the daughter who is affected by the insatiable hunger "from" Auschwitz, and her yearning for comfort can find no satisfaction. The mother's dictatorial management of all aspects of their lives—a side effect of the Shoah terror—extends over food and nutrition; she controls her own and her daughter's eating habits with austerity, both inflexible and contradictory.

Overeating and overprotectiveness are recurrent symptoms in the households of Shoah survivors and frequent themes of second-generation writers. "My parents experienced the post-war world as cold, both in their bodies and their minds," writes Karpf. She remembers being permanently swathed in layers as a child due to her parents' preoccupation with her catching cold: "Cold for them was life outside the home."[56] This overprotectiveness can cut both ways if the children of vulnerable parents reverse the traditional roles and attempt (or hope) to become their parents' parents. The post-Shoah children often feel that they are replacing their parents' murdered parents—replacing the lost love with a new one; sometimes they anxiously try to shelter their parents from any further pain or disappointment in life. Helen Epstein, a post-Shoah daughter, is a prime example of this latter phenomenon. Her mother saw her parents taken to Auschwitz, from which they never returned; she survived labor camps and death camps; and she dealt with the ailments and illnesses that survivors contracted in such places for the rest of her life. As the mother lies dying in a hospital room, Epstein is tormented by irrational thoughts of guilt and remorse: "That night, I lay in my mother's bed feeling that I had failed to protect her just as she had failed to protect her parents."[57] Fass reflects: "My childhood was a bed of anxieties, a diet of anxieties, a wardrobe of anxieties. Today, as I worry about my own children, I realize how much of this is a continuation of my upbringing."[58]

In Janeczek's memoir, overeating is a sign of the daughter's desire to penetrate the mother's past and rectify it; it is the expression of the daughter's wish to end the mother's starvation and heal the victim's pain. If the victim sadistically projects onto her daughter the traumatizing degradation she was subjected to, then the daughter works through this traumatizing abuse by symbolically sacrificing herself (through binge eating) to vindicate the mother. The daughter's body thus becomes the martyred place where the Shoah comes to life again. Auschwitz happens again on her body: the girl wishes to modify the past by changing her mother's starvation into her satiation—a transformation that should, in Janeczek's mind, restore order to the Shoah chaos. But of course the past cannot be changed, and Janeczek is ridiculed for her weight by the very mother she subconsciously seeks to help by overeating. The Shoah chaos is not dispelled but passed on to the daughter.

Janeczek is helpless in the face of her mother's trauma, and such feelings of impotence are common in members of the Shoah second generation. Karpf explains: "I would have gladly taken over some of my parents' bodily functions—eaten for them, breathed for them. Or, failing this, suffered for them. (But, even here, it wasn't enough: I would never be able to match them in suffering)."[59] Karpf continued to variously somatize her postmnemonic anxieties throughout her childhood and adulthood; as a result, she suffered from neurotic post-traumatic disorders. Tellingly, she once developed eczema that flared up most intensely on the part of her arm that would have been branded by a concentration camp number.

Judith Kestenberg remarks that "parents who had survived starvation continued to worry about feeding their children as if it were a matter of life and death,"[60] which may explain food's central role in second-generation memoirs. Food remains one of the oldest Jewish romanticized tropes, a metaphor for a lost paradise of domestic order and ancestral fixity. Yet second-generation women often use food in their writings in strategically antipatriarchal and subversive ways. In women's memoirs, food is the battleground on which young girls fight in their struggle for self-affirmation. We observed this in Edith Bruck's treatment of food in relation to the memory of her dejected mother, and I have expounded above on Sarah Kofman's "queasy stomach," as Kelly Oliver calls it.[61] Another classic example is the Italian Jewish writer, postwar child, and leftist politician Clara Sereni, famous for the way in which she reinterpreted the food trope in *Casalinghitudine* (*Keeping House*).[62] *Casalinghitudine* is a memoir in recipes written by a woman who was anorexic in her youth and who, as a mother, must depend on her own culinary inventiveness to feed her gravely handicapped son, Matteo, who has a very complex relationship with her, the outside world, and food.

Growing up, Sereni found herself reacting to her family's pressures (she is the offspring of a long line of pedigreed Italian Jews) and the masculinist oppression of the outside world (although she was eventually elected to the Italian Parliament, she struggled all her life to be heard as a woman politician) by either refusing or overindulging in food. Her life was marked by a long series of negotiations pertaining to food: she constantly struggled to reconcile her family's food, regional food, kosher food, Christian food, the kosherized meats of her grandmother, the regional pork sausages and overly fatty condiments of her Christian in-laws, the foods she had to prepare for the political meetings at her house, and the concoctions she had to invent so that her handicapped baby would not suffocate or die of starvation. Yet Sereni unambiguously locates the source of her eating disorders in her relationship with her very famous, powerful, and controlling father, Emilio—specifically, his almost ascetic approach to eating. During the war, Emilio Sereni was tortured by the Nazis, while his brother died in a heroic action against them. In his youth, he had flirted with Jewish mysticism and had, to everybody's shock, turned into a Hasid before becoming an atheist Marxist, embracing politics, and leaving his mark as one of the most important leaders of the Italian Communist Party. When he died, he was buried in the Jewish cemetery of Rome. *Casalinghitudine* does not explicitly mention the members of the Sereni family deported to Auschwitz, the resistance fighters tortured by the Nazi and Fascist police, or the heroism of an aunt who smuggled Jewish survivors into Palestine at war's end. On the contrary, this second-generation daughter chooses to travel back into her past (personal, familial, communal, and national) not through these historical personages' dramatic actions but via the literal and metaphorical vehicle of food. She thus structures her memoir as a recipe journal with everyday female experiences—public and domestic—sprinkled throughout.

Food permeates post-Holocaust children's lives, either as a memory of past starvation or present oversatiation. Appignanesi remembers that when she was a child growing up in Quebec, her survivor parents' friends—escapees and survivors themselves—spent leisurely afternoons in the Old European way: eating, drinking tea, discussing politics, gossiping, talking business, and all in sentences that "would begin in Polish, merge into Yiddish, migrate into French or stumbling English and go back again with no pause for breath."[63] She describes this unusual group of émigrés as characters out of a Peter Greenaway or Federico Fellini movie:

There were tailors and furriers and accountants and one-time doctors and almost dentists. There was a man with a lined, ugly, pallid face in which intense eyes burned between red rims. There was a tiny woman with pink cherub cheeks and a giggling laugh. There was another with long hair and limbs and languid gestures. She wore rings . . . There was a gnome of a man with a dark mop of hair. When his head was bent next to my father's shiny pate, the thatch looked so like a wig, that it felt as if one quick gesture could achieve a desired transposition. There was a man with twinkling eyes married to a plump woman who never spoke, but ate unceasingly. Everyone ate—fragrant chicken soup with barley, sour-cream-flecked borscht with a hot potato at its centre, pickled herring buried in onion rings, slabs of boiled beef as thick as the moist bread, pastries filled with cinnamon and raisins or a sugary goo of apple. The ardour with which they ate spoke of an unstoppable hunger as if food were a novelty which might disappear at any moment. So they ate and told stories.[64]

To remind himself of the novelty of their comfort, Appignanesi's father kept a photograph of a woman dying of starvation in the Warsaw Ghetto, where he had also been imprisoned before being deported to even more malign destinations. She reports that from time to time, he would look at the photograph of this anonymous creature, lying down on the ground with enormous eyes, but he never told her who she was: "She was, simply, 'the Ghetto.'"[65] Hunger too can call forth the Ghetto in the same way that the image of the anonymous woman can. Food has the magic power to conjure up lean, tragic days and at the same time ward them off.

If food can act as a powerful apotropaic magic for the survivors, so can children: "There is sometimes a parent-child dynamic at work in which a messianic hope is attached to the child who must enact great deeds to justify prior loss."[66] As if this pressure to restore a past purity to their psychologically ravaged parents were not overwhelming enough, the second-generation Shoah children can also let their parents' trauma negatively affect their relationship with their own children. When Karpf (who, we recall, suffered from various psychosomatic postgenerational symptoms as a child) became a mother, she began to fear that she would pass on to her daughter her sanguinary Shoah inheritance along with her maternal milk. Here is how she recalls the birth of her first baby:

> Our baby was due on 1 September 1989—fifty years after the Nazi invasion of Poland. A close friend declared with absolute certainty that it would be born either then or on 3 September (fifty years after the start of World War II) . . . B was duly born on 3 September. Her first weeks dashed each comforting habit and anchor, leaving instead a dark dis-order . . . The split between good and bad was made flesh, in nipples so cracked that a ravine ran through them . . . Yes, there was a physiological cause . . . but also a failure of trust in my ability to mother. When B sicked up milk, there were traces of my blood in it, and I read them as my badness. I couldn't even say the word "milk": whenever it cropped up in a sentence, it amazingly came out as "blood." B cried incessantly—she was hungry—and I fed her incessantly, in pain and flinching . . . In those early months, motherhood struck me as almost wholly a matter of loss.[67]

As diverse as these cases of second-generation daughters' writings are, they all have in common the interweaving of stories of suffering with the literal or symbolic presence of food. One unexpectedly comic and self-deprecating example is the memoir of the television personality S. Hanala Stadner, about overcoming an impossible childhood in the household of two Auschwitz survivors. Issues related to food, bulimia, and self-image distortion abound. "One night Ma's at work and Daddy tries to make me eat a bowl of lima beans. Beans are old-man food, not child chow. But Daddy says I can't leave the table until I finish the bowl. Even for an adult, it's a huge bowl," Stadner remembers. "It's a Jethro Bodine bowl . . . Daddy hands me a spoon big enough to shovel snow and leaves the kitchen . . . The beans sit in the bowl and I sit at the table staring at them. The beans have become the enemy." In Stadner's experience, each of her parents can change from extremely loving to extremely cruel in the blink of an eye, though her mother's transformation is the more terrifying of the two: "Daddy shifting into Monster Man is bad, but not as bad as when Ma morphs." Her mother unthinkingly pours the undiluted poison of her war memories into her daughter's ears; and again, consciously or not, Stadner associates these unpleasant stories with food. As Stadner recalls with black humor (perhaps as a defense against the traumatic experiences described by her mother), "sometimes late at night after Ma comes home from the bakery, we sit at the kitchen table sharing a Danish. I listen to her relive one shocker after another. A Yiddish *Twilight Zone*. Tonight's episode: 'Ma's Choice.'" Stadner's reaction to the violent "Monster Ma," the psychologically unbalanced "Survivor Ma," and "Foreigner Ma"—altogether unfit for the real world—is predictably conflicted: "Oooh, I just hate Ma! But I *can't* hate her, she's a Holocaust survivor. I must be very bad to be mad at a *Holocaust* survivor. I bury my fury with food. But salami, saltines and social tea biscuits can't keep the anguish down. I'm getting fat. I'm so disgusted with myself, I eat more. I get fatter and madder."[68]

In migrant narratives, food traditionally fosters bonding and healing. In Janeczek's experience, however, food stands for violence (against oneself and others) rather than mourning, revolt rather than nostalgia.[69] In *Lezioni* food is used to wage an alternately masochistic and sadistic war against the daughter's body. The only exception occurs when mother and daughter travel together through Poland, when food unexpectedly sparks positive (that is, prewar) memories in the mother, who recollects—and the daughter imagines—the tastes of the antebellum order, and peace is momentarily restored. In this episode, food and language come together to recreate a lost history. The Polish names of flavorful dishes, which the daughter connects to the mother's culture and past, separate food from its traumatic associations and allow Janeczek to finally locate her lost mother. Through those foreign names and flavors, the German-born daughter is able to see a version of her mother that finally makes sense. The myriad fragments of a puzzle that she had never been capable of fitting together now make up a coherent figure: a woman momentarily at home in a country and in a language from which genocide and exile had brutally separated her. Through food and language, the German-born daughter crosses the invisible bridge that leads to her mother: "In her native language, my mother ordered two beers and pieroẓki [pierogi] filled with cabbage and dry mushroom . . . and when I tasted [them] I rediscovered a flavor from far away, familiar to me . . . [through] the sound of my mother's language, the taste of those homemade dishes received . . . a deeper truth . . . : here is my mother who speaks Polish to a Polish waiter, who eats pieroẓki" (Lezioni, 134–35). However, these foods and language are still foreign to her—the inherited objects of secondhand mourning and nostalgia, an intangible dowry. Through them, the daughter is able to pierce the curtain of darkness that had always shrouded her mother's secret past, but this revelation is short-lived and only partially illuminating. Despite everything, her mother remains a dark and unknowable territory. As Janeczek explores her parents' birth places in Poland, she comments: "I can't even begin to pretend I know my mother" (Lezioni, 129).

How can this daughter retrace her origins if she can't even rely on a clear picture of her parents' past? Ephraim Sicher has remarked that by identifying with the victims, second-generation authors symbolically rescue their family members while "also telling the story of their own origins and identity, literally writing themselves into history."[70] But how can Janeczek "rescue" her mother if she can't identify with her because her truest identity is buried so deep that it takes a trip to Poland, a once-in-a-lifetime occasion, to get even a glimpse of it? This process of sharing the past between members of the second generation and their parents is what Kestenberg calls "transposition," a mechanism "used by a person living in the present and in the past."[71] But I would argue that because that past is only imagined by the second generation, the actual sharing fails, and the children are left with only the symptomatology caused by the parents' past. Postmemory, therefore, is this symptomatology: a shadow signifier.

In her psychoanalytical practice, Pines once treated a second-generation patient who—identifying completely with her father's sister, who had been murdered in a concentration camp—revealed to her analyst the following secret about herself: "although she [the patient, Jenny] was living in a student hostel where adequate meals were provided, she crept downstairs every night after lights were out to an outside yard where the dustbins were kept. She rummaged through them for scraps of food, salvaged half-eaten pieces of bread and other bits which she ate equally stealthily, hidden in the dark."[72] Jenny's middle name was her aunt's, Ilse, and she had been told by her mother about this relative who didn't make it out of Europe alive; her father had always been completely silent about this and similar Shoah stories. Jenny had moved to Europe at nineteen, the same age when Ilse had been killed, and thus, concludes Pine, Jenny subconsciously and symbolically fulfilled the wish of so many second-generation victims: to pick up their family histories just where they had been brutally interrupted and fantasize the fiction of a continuation. "The second generation's return to Europe," Pines comments, "seemed to bring to light aspects of identity that had been previously hidden."[73] Previously hidden aspects of Janeczek's problematic, multifaceted identity are indeed revealed during her *katabatic* trip, and she most clearly articulates them through the cardinal tropes of food and language. Food becomes all-important in the memory of the traveler, functioning as a vehicle between outer and inner worlds. It is the various meals, dishes, and flavors tested, more than tasted, in her mother's company that Janeczek seems most willing and able to focus on as she experiences this tragic and painful journey. She clings to the names of the foods and remembers those foreign, pleasant-sounding words in Polish, Yiddish, or German, turning language and the flavors it evokes into the only safe place from which to weave her tale.

### *MEIN BARBAR* : SPEAKING AFTER THE HOLOCAUST

Janeczek knows the litany of her mother's directives by heart: she "still tells me what to wear, how much weight I should lose, that I should quit smoking to have a child; she wants to know where I've been and with whom, she instructs me on everything and, speaking about things that concern me, she still says 'we'" (*Lezioni*, 189–90). Kestenberg's psychoanalytical data show that a level of sadism or cruelty can tragically be injected into the relationship between children and parents who suffered from a heightened form of this same cruelty while in the concentration camps.[74] Indeed, Nina's attacks on her daughter exceed the bounds of normal parental criticism: "someone like you," she unflatteringly tells Janeczek, "so messy, won't keep a husband . . . if you keep gorging on bread . . . you'll look like that 220-pound friend of yours . . . you can't wear this kind of skirt because it accentuates your giant ass, your '*yiddisher toches*' . . . don't dye your hair . . . don't talk about those things . . . don't trust those people" (*Lezioni*, 56).

When Nina is not attacking her daughter's physique, she is demeaningly criticizing her manners and behavior: "*Where did you learn to hold the fork that way? . . . Do you realize that at the table you use your hands instead of a knife . . . ? Mein Barbar*" (*Lezioni*, 190).[75] The phrase *Mein Barbar* (my barbarian) betrays the mother's psychological and linguistic background. An assimilated, nonobservant, urban Jew—not a Yiddish-speaking *Ostjude* (the implicitly derogatory term for Eastern European Jews)—Nina still holds onto prewar societal and aesthetic codes. The irony here cannot be missed; this accusation comes from someone who personally witnessed how the impeccable use of fork and knife, as well as an appreciation of Chopin's music and other fine arts, did not prevent even the most cultured of people from turning into barbarians. Even after the war, it was impossible for a certain class of Jews (Janeczek's mother among them) to rid themselves of their profound trust and belief in the bourgeois conception of *Kultur*, grounded in the principles of *Bildung* (self-edification through learning and acculturation) and of the Enlightenment, and under whose aegis they had grown up. It was *Bildung* and French rationalism that had promised the Jews a future without ghettos. The fact that the extermination of the Jews was a product of the same urban bourgeois, Illuministic high culture that Jews had waited so long to be admitted into, and to which they rushed to contribute, was an insoluble riddle for post-Shoah Jews. The Jews had to reconstruct a place for themselves within society even after the Shoah. What was the alternative? To surrender the dignity that the perpetrators had either believed was lacking in the Jews or had tried to deprive them of? The fact that the center of Western civilization—Europe—had quickly turned into the center of barbarism was only one absurdity among the many that permeated the genocidal and wartime enterprise. The oppressive nature of society might not have come as an utter surprise to those who were already on its bottom rung: the Eastern European *shtetl* Jews, who lived among peasants who were equally oppressed and powerless. But it did shock many urban Jews, many of whom—utterly assimilated even if not converted to Christianity—looked at their religious heritage as a remnant of old superstitions they were anxious to shed in order to move on (and up) toward a promising future. The second generation's testimonies help illustrate the different cultural outlooks in the Jewish world before the war. Post-Shoah children inherit impressions of Europe shaped by what their parents told them about it, and these visions vary depending on whether the survivors grew up in large urban settings or in the countryside of Central or Eastern Europe. The survivors from the cities passed on to their children a vision of life in the Old World that was better than what they found in their new environments after emigrating. Those children have been brought up hearing about higher cultural standards and proper behavior that the parents expected their American children to absorb and maintain. The children of rural European Jews have usually heard more negative stories about Europe, including Europe before the war.[76] For many of these children's parents (although certainly not for everybody), the

Old World was already hellish, and its hardships only peaked during the war years: it was a place where they and generations before them had often known much misery, subjugation, hatred, violence, and persistent inequality. Janeczek, Epstein, and Hoffman belong to the first group—those with survivor parents from cities rather than *shtetlach*. Epstein painstakingly researched her genealogy back to her European great-grandmother, and she was able to discover many particulars that allowed her to connect in a profoundly spiritual way to the Bohemian family's matriarch, Theresa. However, Epstein was disturbed to learn about the stubbornness and blindness of her grandfather, Emil Rabinek, who was unable to get rid of "the Vienna in him, his snobbery, his entitlement and self-centeredness . . . his dismissal of Czech culture and his misreading of his German environment." Despite the worsening conditions for all Jews in the Czech lands during the 1930s, he "continued to believe he was German" and therefore superior (to other Jews) and untouchable.[77] Emil was a convert to Christianity who insisted on baptizing his only daughter, Franci, at birth. He and his wife, a woman from the old ghetto (as he often disparagingly remarked), were gassed immediately after they arrived at Auschwitz.

Janeczek's mother perceptively picks up class distinctions, especially among certain types of Jews. She never gives up the haughtiness of someone who (according to her categorization) comes from a good family. And as she teaches her daughter, you can tell who is from a good family by these clues: "Those who go to Chopin concerts, those who still speak Polish and use it instead of Hebrew or Yiddish, those who do not push their way ahead . . . those who don't raise their voices, those who at the breakfast buffet don't pile up jam, eggs, bacon, desserts and sausages on the same plate until they roll off of it . . . those are from a good family" (*Lezioni*, 138). Epstein recounts an episode that reveals a similar preoccupation with class. After her mother's death, she was invited to give a lecture at the only remaining Jewish Czech organization in the United States. She agonizes over what to wear and what impression she will make on her penetratingly analytical, hyperopinionated listeners—who stand in for her critical mother. When she approaches the podium and looks at the audience, it is as if the whole scene is happening not in New York City but somewhere far away and in a different time:

> With their carefully coiffed white and gray hair, in their modest but spotless clothes, the surviving members of the Joseph Popper Lodge looked, in my mother's approving phrase, very "well put together" . . . They wore good but sensible shoes, good but unobtrusive jewelry, little makeup. No flamboyant Zsa Zsas here, no garish redheads . . . These elders of my tribe displayed the

same understated style everywhere their diaspora took them, replicating in California, England, Israel, and Australia the tidy lives they were raised to live in Prague even as they lost their place in its social hierarchy . . . Their intellectual and cultural lives, however, were unaffected by emigration. They . . . made up a loyal audience for piano recitals, chamber music, and symphony concerts, the opera, museums, and lectures.[78]

Second-generation children are frequently anxious about struggling to fit into a picture that no longer exists. It is as if one were to photoshop oneself into a daguerreotype from a century ago. How does one live up to such antiquated, indeed extinct models? Or live up to such heroic parents? "How dare I suffer?" ask the survivors' children. "What claim do I have to Holocaust pain if I was born after the war? Am I an impostor?" There is no room for these children in Holocaust history, and yet it is profoundly their history, too. They are the belated generation—born late enough not to witness the camps but also too late to save the dead. They have also been called a sandwich generation—that is, they are squeezed between the survivors and the new generation, whose members are completely untouched by the events that now seem to have happened so long ago. (I sometimes wonder whether for my undergraduate students born after 1990, a class on World War II is only as emotionally involving as a course on the Napoleonic campaigns would have been to my generation.) Meanwhile, the suvivors' generation never forgets or lets the second generation forget; for that first generation, the past is not only very near but happening again in little fragments, in sudden little apparitions, every day. Daniel Vogelman, an Italian Jew from Florence, once simply yet eloquently described the psychological torment of his sandwich-generation position. His Polish refugee father, despite having escaped from Galicia and reached the Swiss border with his first family, did not succeed in avoiding capture and was sent to Auschwitz, where his wife and child were immediately gassed: "My father said little about his camp experience, perhaps to not upset me. And yet something entered silently within me: fear of others? a sense of the absurd? the capriciousness of fate? In a word: from the moment that, in the normal course of events, I should not have been born, what sense did my life make, what should I do to justify it, and, above all, what ought I do to live up to such a father?"[79]

In Janeczek's case in particular, the demands of the Shoah mother become unendurable precisely because of their absurd premise: Janeczek will inevitably fail to heal her mother's wounds or to fill the space left open by the absence of all those murdered people in her family. Janeczek ends up accepting the irreversibility of her mother's loss by escaping to Italy. Finally separated from her mother, she is able to perform small acts of resistance against the injunction to pass by simply ceasing to try. She stops trying to be free of errors or aristocratic in her comportment; over the phone (and from a safe geographical distance), she yells at her mother that there are no Nazis around now and assures her that even if she forgets to run errands, stays on the couch the whole day in her pajamas smoking cigarettes and eating junk food, she is going to survive. Refusing her mother's obsessive injunction to pass, the daughter struggles painfully not to buckle under the weight of victimhood. The daughter's text is ultimately the device that best resists the impulse to pass. Looking back at herself as a young girl who had not yet mustered the strength to move away, Janeczek confesses to having been defenseless against her mother's verbal abuses: "At that age the idea of doing anything that would displease her was unbearable to me . . . I succumbed to her attacks castigating some sin of mine . . . and that invariably ended with the accusation that I was selfish, a verdict which I usually accepted while begging for forgiveness and crying. But in this manner, I would obtain neither forgiveness nor an end to our quarrel; on the contrary, her violence would increase. It seemed to grow with every word I said and with each tear I cried" (*Lezioni*, 17). The Holocaust has turned the mother's language into an instrument to be used not for communication, but for passing, strategizing one's survival, and controlling one's visibility or invisibility according to necessity. Janeczek's memoir raises the question of whether it is possible to ever escape the language of the mother. The second-generation child is stuck between the revelatory allure of her mother's prewar language—"the sound of my mother's language, the taste of those homemade dishes revealed . . . a deeper truth" (*Lezioni*, 134)—and the horror of her mother's Shoah language—*Mein Barbar!*

The mother uses her multilingual repertoire to constantly either relate to or distance herself from her daughter and the inimical world around her. It is a kind of linguistic shtick—as Janeczek calls it—that both of her parents had to quickly learn for themselves in order to survive and adapt during and after the war: "My mother becomes extraordinarily elegant and Italian, imperturbably answering 'sississississì,' yesyesyesyes, to her clients" (*Lezioni*, 24). Thus in Italy, her business associates think she's German, but in Munich she is assumed to be Italian. (Her real nationality is revealed only in the late 1970s, when she testifies in a war crimes trial against a former ss officer from her hometown of Zawiercie.) She also takes pain to erase nonlinguistic markers of identity: even the Auschwitz number on Nina's arm must go, and she has it removed "as one removes any common tattoo" (*Lezioni*, 25).

Because of the Shoah, the mother is in large part unknowable. Even in moments of mother-daughter intimacy, Janeczek experiences a constant shifting in this obscure maternal realm that she can't always keep up with. The skill to pass from one accent to another, from one attitude to the next, and between identities is her mother's defining ability—one that results, sadly, in her daughter's confusion, unbearable anxiety, and loss of confidence in herself and the surrounding world. The mother demands an impossible assimilation. "She gets so mad at me. She cannot accept that I won't change, that I wouldn't adapt to her instructions," Janeczek laments (Lezioni, 88).

The mother's language is no maternal language to Janeczek; rather, it is an arsenal that Nina uses to launch merciless attacks against Janeczek or gain further leverage over her. "My mother is not satisfied by simply calling me bungler, 'bałaganiasz,' in Polish, or in Yiddish 'schnorrer,' beggar, because of the way I dress, or 'Dreckspatz' and 'Fressack' in German when she wants to point out my questionable hygienic standards and excessive appetite, or, with Teutonic solemnity, 'mein Naturkind,' my little savage; she does not simply warn me against the danger that 'man wird dich ausnehmen wie eine Weichnachtsgans,' 'they'll cook your goose,' but she also elaborates on these terms with further commentaries and explanations" (Lezioni, 55–56). Depending on the mood of the conversation, the mother may refer to herself as "deine Mutter" (a severe "your mother") or "deine mame" (a sweet "your mom") (Lezioni, 56).

Nevertheless, Nina's foreignness is also capable of infusing the daughter's native German with a tender and charming coloratura. After decades in Munich, Nina still mispronounces vowels such as ö and ü so that the German word for breakfast, "Frühstück," becomes in the mouth of the Polish Jewish mother "Fristick" (frishtick), and the preposition "für" (for) is gauchely pronounced "fir." Janeczek writes about these mispronunciations quite movingly: "I remembered that when I was a child in first grade, the teacher explained to me that we write 'für' not 'fir,' and although I had assimilated that lesson, I kept dedicating my drawings for my mother with a 'fir meine Mamma'—with that i in homage to her" (Lezioni, 71).

In most postmemoirs, when language comes up (as it regularly does), it is in connection to the multilingualism of the parents, a fluency that might either be inaccessible to the children (the "secret" language of the adults) or that, if the children share it, creates a split between the foreign languages one speaks at home and the one spoken with monolingual friends outside the home. In both cases, there is often an element of embarrassment on the part of the post-Shoah generation in its relationship to language(s). Lezioni highlights yet another role of language in these memoirs, as the mother's language not only sounds foreign—indeed, comically strange—but also expresses the survivor's frustration, fears, paranoia, and incontrollable cruelty. It is not only how the mother says things that Janeczek insists on but what the mother says, and in which language she chooses to say it. The survivor's utterances, which are in no way free of the shackles of the past, constitute a language born out of Shoah memories and indelible impressions.

Mother and daughter fight in German when they are in Italy, and they fight in Italian if they are speaking over the phone between Milan and Munich. During their multilingual logomachy, the mother calls the daughter "Hélena," stressing the first syllable in a menacing Teutonic fashion rather than using the softer Slavic variant, which shifts the emphasis onto the second syllable. The mother also sometimes refers to her daughter in the third person, as if she were absent, by saying "'meine Tochter' doesn't listen to me, my daughter loses everything, my daughter doesn't take care of her mother" (Lezioni, 72). However, their tender moments call for a host of pet names: Maus (German: mouse), Spatz (German: sparrow), along with their respective diminutives Mausl (little mouse) and Spatzl (fledgling sparrow); along with roisele (Yiddish: little rose), ketzele (Yiddish: kitten), złota rybka (Polish: little golden fish, or goldfish), ptaszek (Polish: little bird), and lalka (Polish: doll). The better the two get along, the larger is the daughter's repertoire of loving appellatives as well: mom, mommy, mamma, mame, mamele, maminka, mameshi, mameshi kroin, matka, matusia, matuśka, mamusia, mamuniu—a colorful gradation from English to German to Polish, passing through Italian and lots of Yiddish in between.

The daughter's list, one notes, is marked by the conspicuous absence of the German Mutti or Mutter. Although German is Janeczek's first language, Polish is her mother tongue, the one that vibrates in her like a familiar lullaby every time she hears those sibilant Slavic words, which she intuitively understands without knowing their meaning. Even Yiddish is a kind of maternal language to her, despite the fact that it was not spoken at home and she knows only certain idiomatic phrases and a few words here and there. Counterintuitively, her most fragile linguistic connection is to German: the language and the country instill in her only a weak heimat, partly because of her parents' history. "We are not Germans," says her mother. "Don't date German boys!," Janeczek is told, "because she [her mother] wouldn't have been able to bear it" (Lezioni, 28). And "the utmost reproach, the unappealable verdict from my Judge Mother: 'You behave like a German,' like a 'yecke' [Yekke] . . . Or even 'you talk like a German' and 'you think like a German'" (Lezioni, 30).

Negotiating and rethinking one's relation to the outside non-Jewish world is an ongoing process in the lives of the survivors who did not leave Europe. Settled in the safe, democratic, and rich new Germany, Janeczek's parents struggled with how to let their daughter live a full life that exploited all the advantages available to her generation, while at the same time alerting her to dangers of her identity that should not be forgotten. Assuaging this tension was probably easier for Shoah parents who brought up their children in North America, and it is understandable that many of them resisted their children's propensity to explore the family's past via a return trip to Europe. Such was the case with Fass, who as a young college graduate won a Fulbright Fellowship to study for a year in Germany and was just about to leave when, paying a visit to her parents, she found her father in a terrible state of emotional disarray. Her strong camp survivor father was suddenly a broken man. "I became aware that my father was withdrawn and seemed to have lost weight and energy. He was clearly deeply troubled," Fass remembers. "I asked my mother if it was related to my plans to spend the year away in Germany. 'Of course,' she said, 'he has been sick about it.' . . . 'Of all places you could have chosen,' my father said, 'why Germany?' He said this calmly and sadly, not in a fit of passion or pique."[80] Fass changed her plans and did not go to Germany at that time.

Delaying, as Fass did, the confrontation with the places of horror, with a country in which echoes of the past could still be heard, is a luxury not available to Janeczek. Her entire childhood took place in Germany. Her parents' decision not to sever all ties to the site of the tragedy by emigrating had an enormous impact on their daughter's life, condemning her to a limbo state in which she was constantly reminded of the past while being unable to redeem it. Therefore, language for Janeczek is yet another exilic space in which she is forever foreign, an impermanent territory, another utopia in which she lacks full citizenship. Hirsch writes that "European Jews of the postwar generation . . . can never catch up with the past; inasmuch as we remember, we remain in a perpetual temporal and spatial exile."[81] To the temporal and spatial ones, the third diaspora adds a linguistic exile as well, and Janeczek powerfully reflects this dislocated language in her text. Beginning with her choice to write in Italian—a foreign language—Janeczek uproots herself by abandoning the original mother tongue and inhabiting the insecurity and susceptibility of borrowed languages.

It is worth taking a longer view and remembering that language has played a large role in the history of Jewish exile. In nineteenth-century antisemitic fantasies, the Germans imagined the Jew to be the supreme corrupter of their language. They created a verb for the "sick" way in which the Jews spoke: *mauscheln*. It was their disagreeable *mauscheln* (according to composer Richard Wagner, a "peculiar 'blubber'") that hindered any attempt of the Jews to pass as authentic Germans.[82] In the post-Shoah dispersion, most of the survivors abandoned their fatherlands and mother tongues and migrated to new countries, carrying with them their "strange" accents, which branded them as foreigners. And thus what had been a malicious paranoia about the assimilated Jews' inability to speak their mother tongue became the matter-of-fact condition for those who late in life had to adopt a new language. Second-generation Jews often respond to this particular predicament of their parents not with venom but with humor. Art Spiegelman makes sure to reproduce his father's English in a way that captures his quirky mistakes and funny mispronunciations.[83] Stadner transcribes her parents' dialogues in a heavily accented and Yiddish-flavored English that mixes the comic into even the most tragic of tales. "Oy . . . Hanala," begins a typical conversation between young Stadner and her mother, "you know da vay you love babies? Vell . . . I loved my brodder's children like dey vere my own, and because I couldn't save dem, dey got chopped up mit an ax, what can I tell you?"[84]

Without the help of onomatopoeias (a recurrent and accepted tool only in American Jewish humor—though recently it has begun to creep into European humor as well), Janeczek still makes the unspeakability of the Shoah identity appear through the insertion of a multiplicity of tongues, all equally hers and all equally foreign. As Appignanesi beautifully says, "I am all too aware that my parents' past is a narrative in a foreign and forgotten language."[85] Janeczek also has a mother language she doesn't know, and this paradox has no language of its own to be explained to others (Lezioni, 76). Her real language, German, offers no asylum; her true mother tongue is one she doesn't speak, and from which she is exiled. She maintains an almost vestigial sense of this language, but because of its origins in the Shoah mother, it is also a language of darkness: poisoned and rooted in death.

According to Sophia Lehmann, "disparate diasporic communities are now faced with the shared struggle of articulating a cultural identity in which history and home reside in language, rather than nation, and in which language itself must be recreated so as to bespeak the specificity of cultural experience."[86] But is language truly a viable possibility for achieving such rootedness? Or does Janeczek persuasively show just how illusory this hope is? Is she hinting at the impossibility of rooting her history and home in either nation or language? Lezioni raises the question of what happens when we don't speak the language we are rerooting into? (A concomitant problem is expressed by the question of which home are we to return to if home is lost?) Lezioni raises crucial questions about the definition of the mother language or the mother tongue. Polish and Yiddish are merely emotional sounds coming to Janeczek from a lost past, a past that can't be spoken because it is the fundamental experience that erases all experience. The traces of Polish and Yiddish symbolize the desolate territory of the parents' exile: physically expatriated to new countries, the survivors are exiled from their linguistic homeland as well. Very often, the native languages of survivors are not spoken by their children, and the survivors' multilingualism betrays an enforced nomadism whose linguistic and emotional effects linger. Furthermore, Janeczek's text also seems to suggest that any effort on the part of post-Shoah children to rebuild that linguistic territory is just a lenitive fiction. To hope to leave German in order to migrate to Yiddish or Polish or Hebrew is only to embrace another diasporic state. At the same time, her text alerts us to the fact that we inhabit a linguistic space as if it were a country, and therefore the rupture of exile is experienced in this space as well. Janeczek ends up verbalizing all this in a language (Italian) that is in no way related to her roots: she herself becomes a narrator with a foreign accent.

Furthermore, experience teaches us, we best tell our most intimate stories in the language in which they happened. The stories of Nina's Polish past inhabit the Polish language and can be expressed only through its sounds and words. Therefore, it is not unreasonable that Janeczek equates her inaccessibility to Polish to her inaccessibility to her mother's past. At first the chaos of history seemed to become reified in the chaos of languages heard in Auschwitz. Tadeusz Borowski memorably defined the resulting linguistic bedlam "the crematorium Esperanto."[87] Then, as survivors tell their stories of those years, they are often compelled to repeat words they learned or heard for the first time in the camps in the language in which they were spoken. For Levi, *Wstawać!* (Wake up!) famously became the linguistic equivalent of torture, the call in Polish at dawn that would force the prisoners out of the barracks and back to their pointless, consuming work. For the Italian survivor Liana Millu, the *Lagersprache*, the parlance of the camp, includes the terrifying words *stubowa* (the all-powerful block senior) and *Strafkommando* (or "penal Kommando," perhaps the worst job a prisoner could be sentenced to in the camp): these terms recur almost obsessively in Millu's memoir, and the survivor is compelled to use them in German, never in their Italian translation.[88] But there are also gentle, love-infused words remembered from the prewar years. The survivors' children often pick up some expressions or words from the dead vocabulary of their parents. For example, Epstein was always particularly enthralled with the foreign words that, not incidentally, the mother used to describe herself and her beloved prewar job as a famous dressmaker: *švadlena* (the "common" Czech word for fashion designer, for when business was bad) and *couturière* (the "sophisticated" French version for the same concept, when things looked up).[89]

A shocking revelation for Janeczek in regards to language and its hidden, exiling truths is the discovery that her family name is not, in fact, the name of her family. Janeczek was the Polish name used by her father on his war *Kennkarte*, the fake Aryan I D under which he hid and which he kept ever after, perhaps for good luck. Her name, then, is another foreign territory onto which she was arbitrarily cast by the shipwreck of history. Eventually she discovers her father's real surname, but her mother, directly intruding on the daughter's text, forbids her from mentioning it in her memoir: "*Don't write your father's name! . . . Delete it*" (*Lezioni*, 69). The mother is omnipresent in this text—including her reactions to the text itself, which Janeczek faithfully reproduces in italics. However, the father is a discreet presence, a shadow, practically absent. His invisibility reflects Janeczek's ignorance of his life and story. Moreover, discovering anything about him after his death makes her feel all the more cheated, powerless, and hurt. The real date of her father's birth, together with his real name, has been obscured. Apart from calling him by his fake name, she had celebrated her father's birthday on the wrong date, and throughout his life, he had patiently let her read him the wrong horoscope every week. Because she discovers these facts the day after his funeral, they remain unreal to her, and this belated truth is now unserviceable. She is unable or unwilling to memorize the new information, and she doesn't know which name to pass on to her son. Her mother's surname, Lis, has also been lost, removed from the records by the rigid German laws according to which a woman must take the husband's family name. Ironically, then, in changing from Lis to Janeczek, her mother was forced once again into a fake identity, another camouflage.

The family life of so many children of survivors is characterized by the presence of secrets. For example, Fass's father also lied all his life about his age. Only on his deathbed he confessed his real date of birth, so that it would be marked correctly on his tombstone. He was six years older than his daughter thought. Had he lied about his age in Chelmno or Auschwitz in order not to be selected for the gas chamber and merely kept up the pretense? His daughter, another second-generation "archeologist," never found out. But when she finally traveled to Europe, she discovered that in the official registers of her father's native city, Łódź, it was recorded that he was born on yet a third date: Had he ended up completely forgetting who he was? Another puzzle, another secret, another area of darkness on which no light would shine. "Of course, his age was only the simplest of his secrets. Much deeper secrets troubled him," Fass writes. "As a child, privy to his business, I thought I knew them all, and as a child with whom they shared their memories, I thought I also shared their past. In fact, all along my relationship with my father was based on subtle deceptions . . . And my knowledge of their past was feeble and incomplete."[90] Fass's father lost his parents, his first wife, and four children in Auschwitz and never recovered from it.

Holocaust fathers are often quiet and more reserved than Holocaust mothers, reclusive, out of reach. Janeczek imputes her father's sad aloofness to the emasculating experience of surviving in hiding rather than encountering, as his wife did, the very worst the Shoah had to offer: Auschwitz. Here is a rare sketch of this shadowy figure:

> Sometimes I think that my father is the one less capable of being well . . . not my mother. When I think about it, this idea seems to be confirmed by his total lack of initiative in every aspect of life: it was not he who made friends, or developed the business, or bought the house, or decided to leave Poland. It was my mother who was the engine of their lives . . . Upon returning home late with mom after a day at the store, my father would flip on the TV to watch the news after dinner, and then he would retire to his favorite couch, an old one in a small room . . . to read the newspaper . . . On that couch with his newspaper, my father was happy . . . For sure, he had a more complex nature than my mother . . . However, I also understand that it was he who did not get over the persecutions . . . he got away too easily . . . For someone like him, proud, combative, it must have been terrible to accept both his good fortune and his impotence . . . I think that it had been worse for the men: failure on top of the catastrophe, their disgrace. (Lezioni, 126–28)

From his guilt-ridden perspective, this nameless man suffered from an unjustified inferiority complex for not having seen enough of the Shoah, so he needed to know and hear what had happened to those who faced the catastrophe head-on. Her mother confirms as much: "'Your father as well' she told me 'was always asking me to tell him about the concentration camps, but I always refused to'" (Lezioni, 127).

It will take the journey to Poland for Janeczek to discover that Helena was the name of her mother's mother, the woman left behind in the ghetto by her daughter and gassed in Auschwitz. Janeczek's numerous middle names all belong to murdered women in her family as well. We encounter again the reincarnation metaphor—the narrator embodying all the past lives of her deceased relatives. Second-generation children often feel that they host Shoah martyrs in their bodies and in their identities.[91] For the survivors, naming children after the Shoah victims was, as Ruth Wajnryb explains, a ritual of "enormous significance. Children were named for dear ones lost. They were born to replace beings who to them were just names."[92] About the discovery of her name's origin, Janeczek painfully concludes: "By the time I learned the 'historical truth' about that grandmother . . . it was too late for me to be able to connect myself to my mother and to her mother through my name" (Lezioni, 21). Once in Poland, the daughter does not see the mother's past; what she faces is the loss of the mother.

## CONCLUSIONS : LESSONS TO UNLEARN

All returns to the homeland of their parents by members of the second generation are journeys back to the site of acquired memories, where the images,
sounds, and landscapes that one has only imagined and conjured up throughout the years finally materialize. Often, to the travelers' surprise, these places
do not fit the mental picture they have carried the way a tourist would bring a
city map—the contents of the travelers' maps have vanished. No matter how
uncannily familiar, these are unknown landscapes. We must ask ourselves how
deep can the connection be to such places that, although still physically present,
have had the signs of their human past eradicated? Janeczek's trip to Poland is
a trip without a fixed point of arrival. For both the mother and the daughter,
geographical specificity offers no remedy to their exiles; the landscape they find
only echoes the emptiness left behind by history.

Language itself fails to capture the past because, after all, this is a story
(trauma) that cannot find its shape in words, because it resists comprehension.
For example, the mother's traumatic experience resurfaces with an explosion
of pain that is expressed not in words but in sound. The first night at the hotel
in Warsaw, Nina begins to scream, an uninterrupted, inconsolable wail (*Lezioni*,
133). Janeczek thus discovers that the transmission of memory is achieved
through neither a geographical nor a verbal journey. This elastic tension between memory and geography, language and silence, presence and absence is
the most distinguishing trait of her text and constitutes her ultimate discovery.

Maria Mauceri proposes that Janeczek's writing represents a symbolic return
to the country of origin and to the mother.[93] Contrary to Mauceri's analysis,
I believe that instead it represents the safe territory from which this severely
traumatized and scarred daughter can protect herself from both the threatening
Holocaust mother and a nation tainted by its past. We are confronted with a
literature that stares directly into its own void. It is a memoir without memory,
in that the kind of memory the narrator is after—knowledge of her mother's
history—is irrecoverable; it is a travelogue without a journey to recount, in that
Helena's odyssey is more psychological than physical. Even the memories in this
text are only partially the author's, as attested to by the mother's interjections
and contributions. Since Janeczek is the rootless daughter who has no recourse
to the territoriality of her homeland or her mother language, she settles instead
in the exilic space of her writing, much as George Steiner did when he famously
claimed the text to be the Jew's—and, by extension, his—true homeland.[94] In
his study of the ancient Jewish dispersals, which offers a refreshing portrait of
Jews as active participants in and not simply passive victims of the foreign communities in which they lived, Erich Gruen writes:

Diaspora lies deeply rooted in Jewish consciousness . . . At a theoretical level, that experience has been deconstructed from two quite divergent angles. The gloomy approach holds primacy. On this view, diaspora dissolves into *galut,* exile, a bitter and doleful image, offering a bleak vision that leads either to despair or to a remote reverie of restoration. The negative image dominates modern interpretations of the Jewish psyche. Realization of the people's destiny rests in achieving the "Return," the acquisition of a real or mythical homeland. The alternative approach takes a very different route. It seeks refuge in a comforting concept: that Jews require no territorial sanctuary or legitimation. They are "the people of the Book." Their homeland resides in the text.[95]

By text, Gruen means not only the Bible but the entire canon of Jewish cultural production, a "portable Temple," as he calls the heavy yet splendid baggage that Jews carry through history. From the perspective of women, both alternatives—the pessimistic and the optimistic—are fantasies to which they have no recourse: both exclude women. If wandering fathers carry the Torah scrolls on their backs, what do wandering mothers carry? In this "portable Temple," do women, who have greatly contributed to its maintenance and survival, still have to sit apart, far in the back? It would appear that some of the daughters of Israel, such as Janeczek, Klüger, Bruck, and Kofman, have stepped forward from behind the *mechitza,* not to elbow their way toward the center where their brothers and fathers have always stood but rather to leave the temple altogether. "The Book" is a homeland not promised to Janeczek or any other Jewish daughter; in contrast, their own writing and art are the alternative spaces, the no man's land that welcomes these strangers' presence.

Janeczek is finally able to write this liberating text when—in her late twenties and after the journey to Poland—she stops living in the constant survival mode that her Holocaust mother required her to adopt. Writing is where survival is assured, despite the fact that writing emerges from the dark territory of death and defeat, from the Shoah in which no survival is possible. Performing a constant mobility of identity, memory, and narrative diction, *Lezioni* allows no stability, no planting of firm roots. Paradoxically, this diasporic text's (a text properly belonging to the third diaspora) refusal of territoriality is freeing and welcomed rather than estranging. It demands to be left in its exilic state, its sine qua non. The Holocaust mother and daughter are located at the extremes of a history of violence that cannot be overcome or mastered through the clarity of language or the comfort of food. Mother and daughter are conjoined at the crossroads of silence, and *Lezioni* attempts a journey into the utopia of preverbal communication. Janeczek wonders if a mother can pass along her fears "through the amniotic fluid." It might be true, as Mauceri suggests, that Janeczek intends to connect to her mother through writing her postmemoir, but I believe that she is instead trying to explore whether it is possible to disconnect from a Holocaust mother whose trauma she has been feeding on since the womb.

Consider the case of Eva Hoffman. She faced the challenge of finding a language that could translate her into visibility so that she would be accepted into her new North American environment and by her new friends without erasing the traces of her past: "A true translation proceeds by the motions of understanding and sympathy; it happens by slow increments, sentence by sentence, phrase by phrase."[96] Hoffman declares: "I am the sum of my languages—the language of my family and childhood, and education and friendship, and love, and the larger, changing world."[97] Born in 1945 in Poland, she was transplanted to North America when she was old enough in 1959 to remember each moment of the boat trip that brought her family to Canada and away from the country of her happy childhood and trustworthy identity (where she knew who she was and what behavior was expected of her; where she had friends, piano lessons, and familiar streets to walk on). Despite her enormous success in the English-speaking academic and publishing world, and despite her exquisite mastery of written English, Hoffman never quite recovered from the emotional trauma of exile and complete uprooting. She was left with a sad *tęsknota*, a nostalgia steeped in mourning for the lost object, the womb of her origins, the comforting site of her early life. Hoffman's parents had survived the war in hiding and had lost their families and friends; they were still in Poland when Eva and her sister were born. In those early years of her childhood in Cracow, she didn't realize that that soil was saturated in the blood of a poisonous past. "It is Cracow, 1949, I'm four years old, and I don't know that this happiness is taking place in a country recently destroyed by war, a place where my father has to hustle to get us a bit more than our meager ration of meat and sugar," Hoffman recalls.[98] It is only later that the knowledge of her family's past and the shock of exile will evoke in her an inconsolable *tęsknota*. At least Hoffman has this untranslatable Polish word to express her feeling of uprooted longing. In contrast, Janeczek has lost something that had already disappeared before she could utter it or forge her own relationship to it: her mother's language and culture. As an adult, Janeczek made an effort to study Polish, approaching Poland and its history the way a scientist looks at a fossil, with love and interest but also from an unbridgeable distance.

Mauceri argues that "as suggested by the word *lezioni* . . . Janeczek's book is a *Bildungsroman*, in which the story of the development of the daughter interweaves with that of her mother."[99] On the contrary, I believe the title to be purposely misleading. Let us not forget that these are lessons both of and in darkness (*di tenebra*). The trauma-based *lezioni* dispensed by this mother must be resisted, not absorbed; Janeczek struggles to purge herself of the internalized voice of the Holocaust mother who, though intending to save her daughter, ends up almost asphyxiating her. The ultimate lesson of trauma is one of constant unlearning. The victim's strategies destroy the normalcy of daily behavior. Janeczek's mother demonstrates an unwearied capacity for transformation and adaptation spurred on by her paranoid fear of the unforeseeable. Trauma forces the victim to live according to a logic outside of logic, a logic of the underground that is not applicable to the postwar world and whose unintended consequence is to perpetuate the nightmare. The mother survives Auschwitz, and the daughter grows up to be a self-fulfilled, moral, and successful woman not because of but in spite of the Shoah lessons. "The experience of the concentration camps," Janeczek reiterates "is no experience at all, nothing is learned from it" (*Lezioni*, 12–13). This goes for the firsthand victims as well as for their inheritors. The Shoah, Epstein notes, forced a new identity on both survivors and their children, and yet the "trouble was that while it conferred an identity, it provided no structure, no clue to a way of life."[100]

*Lezioni* is no *Künstlerroman* either. There is no point of enlightened arrival, no epitasis in this plot, no constructive revelation; any newly acquired knowledge only adds to the picture of darkness and past annihilation. The becoming of the artist, writing itself, is a symptom of the inherited illness that is Shoah memory.

### AN AFTERTHOUGHT : A SECOND MOTHER

There is one secret corner that represents the closest approximation to what Janeczek might call home. This special place is nested within the marginal story of Cilly, the daughter of a Wehrmacht pilot killed in action in World War II. Cilly (Cäcile Lahrs) is the Christian German nanny from Bremen introduced at the very end of *Lezioni*. Janeczek surprises the reader by affirming in the final pages of her book that "it was not my mother who brought me up" (*Lezioni*, 191) but the simple, uneducated Cilly, who loves the girl, changes her diapers, gives her milk, and puts her to bed—until Nina dismisses her when Janeczek turns sixteen. In this memoir, Cilly stands as a metonymic figure for Germany and the narrator's relationship with her native country. To the confused Jewish girl, something about her love for the German nanny feels wrong and fraught with guilt. Only as a mature Jewish woman returning from the Auschwitz tour does Janeczek understand that one can only write, not rewrite, history. At that point, it becomes possible for her to unearth from her own story the figure of another mother and talk about this alternative figure in a way that will no longer feel like a betrayal of her Holocaust mother.

Janeczek's mother accuses her of having picked up her plodding way of walking from Cilly. "Cilly spoiled you," she claims (Lezioni, 194), referring to her daughter's inelegant carriage. But despite Cilly's childlike handwriting with big, round letters, it was she who corrected Janeczek's homework because "she was the only one who knew German" in the house (Lezioni, 193). Helena received a precious gift from Cilly that more than made up for the latter's clumsiness: "German, her language" (Lezioni, 202).

During their lengthy annual trips to visit friends in Italy, the Janeczeks would bring Cilly along. Although she was always treated as a member of the family by their Italian hosts, and though she eventually began to learn some Italian, Janeczek remembers that Cilly never stopped feeling out of place when she was away from her country: "I think indeed that sometimes she did mention she missed Germany and hinted at the fact that it made her happy to return home" (Lezioni, 195). Unlike the Jewish family that easily adapts and blends in, at home everywhere and therefore nowhere, Cilly has a place in Germany that is unnegotiably her home. She simply belongs. She doesn't need to pass. Her capacity for camouflage is nonexistent; neither her language nor her home harbor ambiguities. "Speak German when Cilly is around [and not Polish]" (Lezioni, 199), Janeczek's parents would remind each other. When Cilly was present, they would also all stand in front of the Christmas tree singing "Stille Nacht" ("Silent Night") and exchange presents "fir mama," "fir papa," and "für Cilly": "We were not Germans, but this could not be said or stressed before Cilly, who, instead, was German" (Lezioni, 199).

When Helena turned sixteen, Cilly was sent away, and the teenager, we are told, very quickly forgets all about this crucial maternal figure from her childhood: "I am not sure whether my erasing all memory of Cilly, which mirrored the erasure of the Jewish victims by the Germans, was somehow the execution of a small collective wish . . . Today I know that I did not forgive Cilly for leaving without ever keeping in touch, and I did not forgive myself for not having been capable of restoring the bond between us, and shame grows side by side with oblivion" (Lezioni, 200). At the fringes of her memoir—that is, only in the closing chapter and last few pages of Lezioni—Janeczek reverses oblivion and pays tribute to Cilly, to whom the most touching words of this text are devoted. These final paragraphs are perhaps the closest thing she has to a homecoming, one that brings her back to the only home available to her: the loving and unthreatening Cilly.

A dark history has put too heavy a burden on the shoulders of second-generation children, setting them up for failure when faced with the impossible psychic demands of an inherited, secondhand trauma. Janeczek grew up with the tormenting notion that she had failed both mothers. She couldn't save her own mother from the past, and to please her she learned to be disloyal to the nanny who loved her, who brought her up like a substitute mother, and to whom she owes her native language, German.

"The second generation is intimately connected to the Holocaust by both a physical and psychic umbilical cord," note Alan and Naomi Berger.[101] And through this impalpable connection, according to Dori Laub and Nanette C. Auerhahn, the second-generation "child echoes what exists in his parents' inner world; his inner reality thereby reveals the indelible marks left by the events of our time. The particular style the child adopts—whether it be acting out, neurotic symptomatology, character traits, artistic expression, or occupational endeavors—is subtly and complexly determined by a myriad of psychological and reality factors."[102] As Irene Kacandes points out, in "no small measure . . . [second-generation writers] become the enabler-cowitnesses for parts of their parents' stories, stories that may or may not have been told in verbal language and yet were nonetheless communicated—some have said 'transmitted'—to the next generation."[103] The work of the survivors' children is therefore fundamental in keeping alive the contours of an absence, in keeping in session an ongoing trial in which the victims' silence must be heard and accepted as damning evidence against injustice. Alan Berger remarks that since second-generation children speak and write as natives, they "make themselves understood in a way unavailable to most of their parents."[104] The case of a writer like Janeczek is all the more interesting because she chooses a language secondary to all parties involved, perhaps because the particularities of language are irrelevant when speaking the translinguistic experience of the Shoah. In If This Is a Man Levi attempted to describe the linguistic pandemonium of Auschwitz. In that infernal Babel, all European languages had been stripped of their cultural, humanistic, aesthetic, poetic, and relational content, and what remained was merely a tool for survival. No meaning could be produced out of these languages any longer—only a purely utilitarian tool to steal scraps of time from the clutches of death.[105]

Regarding the rarely discussed role of the reader in shaping Shoah memory, Kacandes writes: "the fact that we readers hold in our hands [a second-generation Shoah book] . . . constitutes proof that, even if they could not undo it, these displaced women eventually displaced trauma with writing, writing from which we can learn if we cowitness to it."[106] Although I agree with Janeczek that the Shoah is not an educational experience and that these are lessons of darkness,

I also agree with Kacandes that the sharing of these traumatic texts can foster cowitnessing and establish co-humanity, a term I am borrowing from Levi. This is how Levi memorably describes the dejected Other, whom we refuse to see for so long until, suddenly, he is clearly delineated in front of our astonished eyes in his full, frail, imperfect, yet undeniable humanity: "a human being in flesh and blood who stands before us, within reach of our providentially myopic senses." Levi speaks of a providential myopia, meaning that "only saints [are] granted the dreadful gift of pitying the multitudes . . . The rest of us, at best, are left with enough sporadic pity for the single individual, the Mitmensch, the co-human."[107] Yet the primal ethical scene occurs exactly in this encounter with the radical and (Lacan would say) traumatizing face-to-face encounter with the Other. Or, as Emmanuel Lévinas magnificently put it, "the epiphany of face qua face opens humanity."[108] If Levi speaks of a real visage, a face of flesh and blood, Lévinas's philosophy places the primordial call of ethics in a disembodied face that is not necessarily a temporal presence but rather the mere evidence, the trace, of something irrepresentable. The cardinal call to ethical responsibility and responsiveness for Lévinas comes from somewhere beyond sheer intersubjective identification. In his face, the Other is disincarnate.[109] It is this encounter with the Other's face, Lévinas argues, that "opens a primordial discourse whose first word is obligation."[110] For this creature, this timeless face, with whom we are called to inextricably engage, Levi, the Italian survivor of Auschwitz, coined the term Mitmensch (co-human), fittingly drawing on the language of the past enemy to point the way to a future ethics.

My guide and I crossed over and began
. . .
To ascend into the shining world again.
He first, I second, without thought of rest
we climbed the dark until we reached the point
where a round opening brought in sight the blest
and beauteous shining of the Heavenly cars.
And we walked out once more beneath the Stars.

 **DANTE ALIGHIERI**, Inferno, Canto XXXIV

# CHAPTER 6

# "I HAVE TO SAVE MYSELF WITH A JOKE"
## Anne Frank and the Survival of Humor

The diary is a gem. Never before, I believe, has anything been written enabling us to see so clearly into the soul of a young girl ... during the years of puberal [sic] development. We are shown how the sentiments pass from the simple egoism of childhood to attain maturity; how the relationships to parents ... first shape themselves ... how friendships are formed and broken. We are shown the dawn of love ... so that the child suffers under the load of secret knowledge but gradually becomes enabled to shoulder the burden. Of all these things we have a description at once so charming, so serious, and so artless, that it cannot fail to be of supreme interest to educationists and psychologists.

SIGMUND FREUD, preface to *A Young Girl's Diary*

On the dreary morning of April 15, 1947, a man about to be hanged asked for four wishes to be granted. The first was for a cup of coffee, quite a luxury in those hard times. The war having recently ended, Europe was a pile of rubble, and economic (as well as spiritual) recovery was still out of most people's reach. As word of the request spread from the gallows, the crowd exchanged ideas about how to respect that highly honorable tradition in Western culture: the fulfillment of a condemned prisoner's last wishes. Eventually, a woman came forward and, in an act of mercy, admitted to having a little bit of coffee at home (possibly an implicit confession of black marketeering). She agreed to prepare some for the prisoner. It was thus that Rudolph Franz Ferdinand Höss, the Kommandant of Auschwitz-Birkenau, its creator and absolute ruler, sipped his last cup of coffee as the sun rose over the slightly frosted fields and meadows lined in the distance with old, lanky birch trees. Despite the sizable crowd that had spontaneously gathered at the execution site, all was quiet and still at the inoperative Auschwitz camp. For his second and third wishes, Höss asked for a priest and for a message to be delivered to his wife and children. Finally, he expressed his fourth and last desire: "I ask for the Polish people to forgive me for all I have done to them."[1]

Thus disappeared, contrite for his sins, one of the most murderous figures of the twentieth century. Among those sins, Höss understood his gravest to be "that I believed everything faithfully which came from the top," as he put it in his last letter to his family from prison, a day after his death sentence was pronounced. The Polish people undoubtedly had much to forgive the Germans for, after the devastating war waged on them by their insatiable Teutonic neighbors. But what of the Jews? In Höss's missives from prison to his wife and children, he expresses repentance and a newly acquired understanding of how misspent his life had been. However, he makes no mention of the Jews. Here is a typical formulation that elides the ethnic component of his crimes: "It is tragic that, although I was by nature gentle, good-natured, and very helpful, I became the greatest destroyer of human beings who carried out every order to exterminate people no matter what."[2] Yet despite his professed gentle nature, Höss had murdered before the Holocaust; he and a group of comrades who "had come back from World War I and couldn't fit into civilian life anymore"[3] demonstrated their passion for their homeland through the illegal and violent bravado of the paramilitary Free Corps (an organization opposed by the government). In one episode, they beat to death a man who had allegedly betrayed a German friend of Höss to the French. Höss was arrested for this crime in 1923, accused of being the ringleader of the attacking group, found guilty, and sentenced to ten years in prison. After that conviction, he proudly admitted to having committed the crime, claiming that the victim, named Parchimer, was a traitor and deserved no better. However, Höss complained of having been unjustly labeled the Führer of the group: "Then and even now, I am still firmly convinced that this traitor deserved to die. Since in all probability no German court would have sentenced him, we passed judgment on him by an unwritten law which we had instituted ourselves because of the need of the times."[4] Tough times, Höss suggests, call for tough measures. Yet what times could possibly call for the murder of 1.5 million children and millions of adults? At his Nuremberg trial, Höss was interrogated about the severity of the Nazis' measures. "So a child of three or four years old was dangerous to the German people? . . . The German people could not rise at all because of the four-year-old Jewish children?" a lawyer asked him.[5] Höss simply replied, "Yes," an answer that most of us find fathomless to this day.

The truth is that tough times elicit different reactions from different people. In the harsh conditions and shifting moral climate of wartime Europe, some Christians responded heroically rather than immorally. More than 20,000 people in Holland, for example, hid Jews at the risk of their own lives. Perhaps the most famous among them was an expatriate from Vienna living in Amsterdam.

Her name was Hermine Santrouschitz, whose married name was Gies, but we all know her as simply Miep. Over the course of twenty-five months between 1942 and 1944, Miep was instrumental to the survival of three families in hiding and one memorable girl: Anne Frank. Miep writes: "I willingly did what I could to help. My husband did as well. It was not enough. There is nothing special about me . . . I was only willing to do what was asked of me and what seemed necessary at the time . . . My story is a story of very ordinary people during extraordinarily terrible times. Times the like of which I hope with all my heart will never, never come again. It is for all of us ordinary people all over the world to see to it that they do not."[6] Through her selfless, heroic, independent, and loyal behavior, Miep greatly impressed Anne Frank and won her deep affection and admiration. She was one of the many positive models through whom Frank had come to appreciate the better side of humanity. When she famously wrote in her diary that she believed "people are truly good at heart,"[7] she probably had in mind people like Miep and her husband, Jan; her father's other employees Johannes Kleiman, Victor Kugler, and Bep Voskuijl; the Dutch resistance fighters; or people like their neighbors who knew there were Jews hiding under the roof at 263 Prinsengracht but chose not to denounce them. Bruno Bettelheim skeptically responded to Frank's optimism by noting that "if all men are good, there was never an Auschwitz."[8] Yet there was a Miep, and there was an Auschwitz. And Frank's diary clearly reflects an awareness of this irreconcilable paradox.

Auschwitz has been the pervasive shadow that each memoir and life examined in this book has struggled to escape. "Auschwitz" is both the label of a literal place and the metonymy for the Shoah—the symbol of an event that far exceeds what went on within the 15.5 square miles of that infamous, barbed-wired camp next to the otherwise unknown town of Oświęcim. This book has explored the relationship between daughters and mothers, and between young girls and the female world around them, from the perspective of stories built around the legacy of Auschwitz. Within the plethora of possible variants—we have seen girls who witnessed their mothers' murder, mothers and daughters surviving the camps together, mothers hiding with their daughters, Kindertransport orphans displaced forever in a new country, and Shoah second-generation women working through their parents' trauma—there is at least one more case that needs to be acknowledged and without which this volume could not conclude. This last variant encapsulates and exemplifies the Shoah tragedy and is itself a synthesis of ultimate horror: it is the story of a girl who dies in the Shoah with her mother.

I have already explored the evocative, as well as invocative, power of the epistolary genre, particularly when imbedded in war memoirs (chapter 1). With Frank's diary, we return to this genre and further illustrate its complexity. There are several reasons why this diary has enthralled the hearts and minds of millions of people all over the world since its publication.[9] I believe that, at least in part, the secret of its uninterrupted success and immediacy arises precisely from that epistolary apostrophe, "Dearest Kitty." Letters have been an important presence in this book: they are part of the fictional conversation between Edith Bruck and her Auschwitz victim mother; and Milena Roth's polymorphous text, as we saw, owes its unique witnessing power to the inclusion of her mother's letters. As I argued in regard to Bruck, the apostrophe creates an ethics of presence by which we, the called-on, become responsible for preserving the memory of the past. In her diary, I argue, Frank deploys the epistolary genre as a fictional decoy through which the author (and victim) shapes her story into a work of art that, thanks to the power of her apostrophe to the outside world, incontrovertibly records for posterity the brutality of history and forces the addressees of her letters to reckon with the burden of this dreadful past.

The choice of the imbedded fictional correspondence turns the traditional diary into a more creative work of writing, a girl's autobiographical epistolary production. Anne could not send letters or receive them while in hiding. Therefore, when she pretends to write to real people (such as her friend Jacqueline) and to have heard back from them, it is just a fiction within her diary. Frank's stroke of literary genius is to invent an imaginary addressee for her book who is neither her actual best friend nor a projection of herself. At first, Frank had addressed her entries to various imaginary characters (one of whom was named Kitty) borrowed from a famous storybook from those days, *Joop ter Heul*, by Cissy van Marxveldt.[10] However, after hearing the announcement of Gerrit Bolkestein, the Dutch Minister (in exile) of Education, Art, and Science, on Radio Oranje that after the war, the government planned to collect diaries, letters, sermons, and other documents from the occupation years to paint a "picture of our struggle for freedom . . . in its full depth and glory,"[11] Frank immediately sensed that her diary, in which she had so passionately and tirelessly recorded her wartime story, would be her special contribution to this national effort. Nigel Caplan writes that she "began to consider writing . . . a 'romance of the "Secret Annexe"' . . . However, the original Dutch word *roman* is a 'romance' only in the sense of an imaginative prose narrative: that is, a novel."[12] Once she decided to turn her journal into a book (she promptly undertook an impassioned revision of her notes), Frank chose a single fictional addressee, Kitty, for the narrator's letters and treated her with coherence and consistency as a person totally separate from the speaker—someone capable of being surprised, entertained, amused, informed, and even bored by her correspondent.[13] Kitty is not Jewish; most important, she is not in Europe.[14] The fact that Kitty is constructed as inhabiting a position outside of the catastrophe fully effectuates the fiction of the epistolary correspondence: Anne's letters survive because the fictional Kitty survives; Kitty's "answers" do not exist because Anne and all that belonged to her no longer exist. Kitty gives Frank an eternal, symbolic survival because she is a stranger: an addressee foreign to and detached from what her interlocutor, the real girl, the historical victim, is enduring.

In a compelling article that systematically compares the existing versions of the diary, Caplan writes: "The interactive style . . . distances the reader into the spectator role, by making the referent of the 'you' a figure from Anne's own fiction. Each entry thus begins with a salutation, which reminds us that we cannot participate in the relationship between the constructed letter writer and her fictitious correspondent."[15] This is certainly the case with the epistolary genre used in utterly fictional works (such as Mary Shelley's *Frankenstein*). But the historicity of the actual diary (which frames the fictional correspondence), combined with the reader's awareness of the intricate relationship between content and context, radically change the effect Frank's apostrophe has on the reader. On the one hand, Kitty's survival aligns us with her—all the time, with every reading, generation after generation. On the other hand, Kitty's sheer nominality, her lack of historical referent, allows Frank's apostrophe to turn "her" into a version of us all—those who, like Kitty, pick up Frank's diary anywhere in the world and at any time. Kitty is the cumulative name for those outside of the catastrophe. The reader might not have identified as intensely with the receiver of these messages had they been addressed to, for instance, Hanneli Goslar, Anne's real best friend and an Auschwitz survivor. By the time Frank chooses Kitty, the fictional addressee has become an allegorical figure for the outside world that the condemned fourteen-year-old desperately misses and to which she is trying to reconnect. "Dearest Kitty" is the empty place that waits to be filled by each reader. "Dearest Kitty" both lets us be present at the tragedy and distances us from it and its victim; it positions us, through the rhetorical figure of the apostrophe, in front of a terrible truth that unfolds before our eyes.

Rachel Brenner claims that "Frank's intention to share her experience with an addressee-outsider approximates the intent of Holocaust survivors-writers—for instance, Elie Wiesel, Pelagia Lewinska, Primo Levi, and others . . . Like them, she writes for a distant reader who is unfamiliar with the situation."[16] Unlike Brenner, however, I believe that Frank's mode of address starkly differentiates her text from the works of survivor writers. Wiesel, Levi, and other postwar authors write from a position of hindsight to a public often unaware of the events, or else they address an audience that knows, at least on the basic historical level, as much as the writer knows. In part, the irresistible attraction of Frank's diary is the perfect tragic irony that sustains it. Frank does not know what everybody else (we, "Kitty") knows: none of her hopes will be realized; she will see her mother starve to death, her sister die, and other innocent people murdered; and she will die herself of scabies, typhus, and malnutrition in Bergen-Belsen.

There is the diary and there is Anne Frank. For some, the story of the author is what legitimizes the significance of the diary; for others, it is the diary that posthumously calls attention to the significance of the writer's life and suffering. A certain tension persists in the evaluation of the diary as a literary product in its own right and in the debate over Frank's role as a Holocaust writer. For many critics and scholars, Frank's is the canonical voice of the Holocaust, more in a religious sense of the word (she has been canonized—that is, sanctified—through her martyrdom) than as part of an intellectually sanctioned group of Shoah witnesses, of which Wiesel, Levi, and Tadeusz Borowski form the core. The world has embraced Anne Frank and turned her into an immortal cultural icon. Audiences have often fallen in love with her symbolic character while overlooking or underplaying her ultimate credibility as a Shoah witness and the literary quality of her writing. The intellectual and academic world has chosen more often than not to ignore, minimize, marginalize, and diminish her contribution. Indeed, for some scholars, as Christopher Bigsby points out, it would have been better if the diary had never existed.[17] Catherine Bernard insightfully writes: "The diary [as genre], after all, seems to be a perfect expression of the role to which women have been relegated time and time again: it is personal, emotional, unobtrusive, spontaneous, and without 'serious' literary pretensions. The idealizations of Anne Frank as a symbol of gentle forgiveness or as a touchstone for identification with the oppressed of the world do not challenge this role. Anne Frank herself ventured far outside these guidelines, but she was posthumously forced back into them." And more stringently she points out: "Ultimately, there is no room in the world for a living Anne Frank: the uses to which her diary and her persona have been put require her to be dead."[18]

The resistance to a reading of Anne Frank qua artist points us toward the difficult question at the very core of this book: how are we to read the testimony of women? I have worked to establish women's acts of witnessing on an equal footing with those of men, who are still posited as standard or universal speakers, and few works of literature can help us understand these ideologically oppressive dynamics better than Anne Frank's diary. Only since the 1990s have feminist approaches to Frank's legacy finally begun to challenge the vision of male scholars such as Harold Bloom, who argued that the diary "is more of a historical emblem than a literary work";[19] Edward T. Sullivan, who wrote that the diary is "more a coming of age story of a precocious young adolescent than an insightful look into the horrors of the Holocaust";[20] and Lawrence Langer, who claimed that "wisdom and spiritual insight rarely fall from the lips of a . . . fourteen-year-old girl."[21] In addition, Bettelheim and others have denied Frank's literary importance, resented her utterly assimilated Jewish identity, suggested that her work does not belong under the rubric of Holocaust literature, or, more disturbingly, denied this young woman her role as a speaker and Shoah witness.[22] As Caplan reminds us, it took the US Holocaust Memorial Museum ten years before acknowledging Frank's diary as one of its Holocaust artifacts, and only in 2003 did it finally devote an exhibition to it.[23] However, in recent years and especially from a feminist perspective, a new generation of scholars has engaged with Frank's legacy, producing a much-needed vindication of her paramount importance in the Jewish literary canon, not only as Shoah victim but also as a legitimate witness, speaker, and female artist. Two outstanding works in this new vein are *Writing as Resistance*, by Rachel Feldhay Brenner, in which the author comparatively examines Anne Frank, Edith Stein, Simone Weil, and Etty Hillesum, reclaiming for these women's intimate writings (their journals, diaries, and letters) a historical and intellectual weight as subversive female resistance to Fascism, genocide, and patriarchy; and Denise De Costa's *Anne Frank and Etty Hillesum*, a compelling reading of Frank's diary through Julia Kristeva's psychoanalytical theories on the mother-child bond.[24]

My original plan was to open this volume with the chapter on Anne Frank. But as I struggled for a long time to organize the book around her, it seemed to me that her difficult presence stopped every other treatment from developing. It was as if writing about Anne Frank meant writing about the end of the story. The chapter on her refused to work as a beginning, partly because it—like its text— is sui generis in *Holocaust Mothers and Daughters*. Frank writes about a mother who is alive and being persecuted, but who is not yet a victim of the genocide. Furthermore, in contrast to the other texts examined here, the diary is not a *post factum* elaboration on events, yet the fact remains that Frank composes the diary as a literary creation. Her entries are not simply daily notations (as is the case, for instance, with the Łódź Ghetto diary of Dawid Sierakowiak,[25] which more closely reflects the traditional form of the genre). Instead, Frank consciously develops her narrative, using dialogue and carefully constructing interesting characters; she edits, rewrites, and cleans up her drafts to produce a good prose.

Moreover, the entries, in keeping with the fiction of the ongoing correspondence with Kitty, have a formal beginning and end, whereas a diarist might merely jot down a few haphazard lines one day, leave off an entry midsentence another day, repeat pieces of information that had been previously offered, and so on. Lastly, opening this book with a story of complete annihilation in Auschwitz and closing it with the chapter about life after Auschwitz in second-generation stories risked reproducing that dangerous hopeful vision (the clichéd light at the end of the tunnel) of the inevitable triumph of will and endurance over the murderous forces of human immorality: a vision that I worked hard not only at avoiding but at dismantling with this book.

Let's return briefly to the uniqueness of Frank's diary. As mentioned above, the fact that it is instrumentally and artificially constructed by Frank as a dialogue in letters with an imaginary friend points to its intentional literariness. Frank was consciously engaging in the practice of writing a book; she intended to publish it as a memoir of her war experience in hiding. Had she lived but failed to complete this particular project, she intended to write other books once the war's end would have returned life to normality. She tells Kitty that "to become a journalist . . . that's what I want! I *know* I can write. A few of my stories are good, my descriptions of the Secret Annex are humorous, much of my diary is vivid and alive, but . . . it remains to be seen whether I really have talent . . . But, and that's a big question, will I ever be able to write something great, will I ever become a journalist or a writer? I hope so, oh, I hope so very much" (*The Diary of a Young Girl*, 250–51). She developed a passion for writing and on various occasions expressed a desire to achieve fame from her craft. As she composed and revised her diary, Frank was exercising her literary and narrative skills with great craft and concentration, reediting, proofing, and constantly polishing her manuscript. This authorial effort is significant because, as Brenner points out, the act of diary writing in times of life-threatening hardship is a sure sign of psychological, ideological, moral, and even physical resistance to annihilation. Brenner wonders about Frank's and Hillesum's obsession with recording the horror rather than trying to keep their minds off of it for the sake of maintaining their sanity, especially given the claustrophobic (Frank) and overwhelmingly violent (Hillesum) circumstances they were forced to endure daily. "As a consciously made choice," Brenner proposes, "writing thus becomes a sign of vitality that counteracts the inertia of fatalism and fear . . . The diaries of the victims of the Jewish genocide present the 'improbable possibility' of art-as-life in the death-in-life reality of the implacable decree of the Final Solution."[26]

As Brenner explains, resistance, especially by women, can occur in less obvious ways than armed fighting; resistance to mental annihilation can also take the form of a victim's concentrating on remembering a poem (as when Levi recited Dante's *Divine Comedy* in Auschwitz and taught it to others). Drawing on and cultivating one's intellectual sophistication is one strategy for resisting morally bankrupt surroundings, in the same way that eating a piece of bread can stave off physical decline in the extreme circumstances of camp imprisonment. Holding onto any vestige of civilization was many victims' answer to the widespread savagery and immorality of surrounding societies. And the private daily act of writing (in hiding, in the camps, in Nazi-occupied Paris, and so on), of producing art, must be understood as a potent strategy of defiance on the part of Frank and other men and women of whom all that remained after the war were only their recordings of the injustice and atrocities, artifacts of their will to witness horrendous events as they were unfolding. "I note down the facts . . . in order not to forget them, because one *must not* forget," writes twenty-three-year-old Hélène Berr, a French university student and violinist, in her war journal.[27] Imbedded within each artistic, combative, and self-affirming act of testimony are multiple strategies of resistance. I will focus on one in particular that is often overlooked yet that is as ancient as the human community, one that is usually associated with men rather than women, a strategy that so obviously characterizes Frank's diary that critics' failure to appreciate it is ironically comical: the text's humor.

## THE LAUGHING GIRL IN THE ATTIC : ANNE FRANK'S HUMOR

The topic of laughter and the Holocaust has been examined before. Usually, though, the focus is on the legitimacy of playing Holocaust situations for laughs,[28] as in the endless debate surrounding the 1997 film *La vita è bella* by Roberto Benigni. Much less attention has been paid to the survival of laughter during the Holocaust—in other words, to the power of laughter as an extraordinarily subversive technique of resistance against moral, psychic, and civic annihilation. An important exception is Steve Lipman's study of the uses of humor during the Holocaust. "Wit produced on the precipice of hell was not frivolity," Lipman writes, "but psychological necessity."[29] Like Lipman, I am not interested in the meaning and uses of Holocaust humor after the Holocaust; instead, I focus on the importance of laughter, the sophistication of humor, as a potent tool for self-preservation and as an ethical agent in response to mass-murderous hatred. Producing art—and laughter—during the war was a way for the victims to array creativity, civilization, and pacifism against the brutality of genocide. Therefore, humor can not be equated with "frivolity," as Lipman rightly points out; rather, it must be seen as a courageous protest against contemporary barbarism. The victims' recourse to humor should not be taken lightly (as humor often is). John

Morreall writes: "In this period [the Holocaust], humor had three main benefits. First was its critical function: humor focused attention on what was wrong and sparked resistance to it. Second was its cohesive function: it created solidarity in those laughing together at the oppressors. And third was its coping function: it helped the oppressed get through their suffering without going insane."[30] The Nazis sensed the threat to their power that humor represented. Although private engagement with the arts was not expressly forbidden—Jews were allowed to play chamber music at home, write diaries and personal letters, and paint, before the deportations interrupted this appearance of normalcy—humor was officially censored and outlawed. Antonin Obrdlik remembers that during the occupation in Czechoslovakia, anti-German ridicule was met with "new waves of mass arrests" because "evidently this kind of humor was not very humorous to the Nazis."[31] In keeping with a long tradition of tyrants who dread humor more than revolt, Hitler immediately forbade political jokes against himself as soon as he gained power.[32] Morreall writes:

> One of the first actions of the new Nazi government in 1933 was the creation of a "Law against treacherous attacks on the state and party and for the protection of the party uniform." As Hermann Goering reminded the Academy of German Law, telling a joke could be an act against the Führer and the state. Under this law, circulating and listening to anti-Nazi jokes were acts of treason. Several people were even put on trial for naming dogs and horses "Adolf." Between 1933 and 1945, 5,000 death sentences were handed down by the "People's Court" for treason, a large number of them for anti-Nazi humor.[33]

Yet humor has a long-standing tradition of its own: not to let itself be silenced. Under Nazism, wit remained an annoying "cultured insolence," to use Aristotle's definition.[34] Not surprisingly, it is Sigmund Freud, a master of irony, who left us the most memorable jibe at the expense of the murderous and obtuse bullies ruling Europe. When the Germans annexed Austria, they arrested the internationally famous doctor and then released him, allowing him to leave the country as long as he signed a statement confirming that no harm had been done to him. So Freud wrote them the following note:

> To Whom It May Concern:
> I can heartily recommend the Gestapo to anyone.
> Sigmund Freud[35]

There's no stopping political jokes, especially under tyranny. Even if political jokes are forbidden in the newspapers and editors, writers, and comedians are exemplarily sacked, imprisoned, exiled, or shot, jokes nevertheless survive them and keep cropping up in pubs, university corridors, and people's living rooms. If there is no other space for them to circulate, they're whispered in prison cells and on the gallows. Nazi-occupied Europe was no exception. Anti-Fascist activists, resistance fighters, and the victims themselves produced a vast repertoire of disobedient humor—a type of humor that breaks the law—in many forms and genres. Of course, "whether we, who did not share the victims' pain, can fully share their laughter is another question."[36]

I use the term "humor" here in its broadest sense, referring not merely to jokes or scripted slapstick but also to the capacity of the humorist to relieve her or his sense of oppression and anxiety—as well as the audience's—by employing irony, wit, and even mere cheerful optimism. Humor is one of "the great series of methods which the human mind has constructed in order to evade the compulsion to suffer," Freud wrote.[37] "And what would be the point," after all, Frank asks herself, "of turning the Secret Annex into a Melancholy Annex?" (The Diary of a Young Girl, 70). Frank's diary is, in its humorous turn away from melancholy, a true masterpiece of rebellion and disobedience to a law that demanded her silence, suffering, and, eventually, death.

In July 1944, when a secret plot failed to free the world of Hitler, Frank reports: "An assassination attempt has been made on Hitler's life, and for once not by Jewish Communists or English capitalists, but by a German general . . . The Führer owes his life to 'Divine Providence': he escaped, unfortunately . . . Perhaps Providence is deliberately biding its time getting rid of Hitler, since it's much easier, and cheaper, for the Allies to let the impeccable Germans kill each other off" (The Diary of a Young Girl, 335). She proceeds to make a joke out of Hitler's order that whoever in the army knows of a superior involved in the assassination must execute the "coward" on the spot:

> A fine kettle of fish that will be. Little Johnny's feet are sore after a long march and his commanding officer bawls him out. Johnny grabs his rifle, shouts, "You, you tried to kill the Führer. Take that!" One shot, and the snooty officer who dared to reprimand him passes into eternal life . . . Eventually, every time an officer sees a soldier or gives an order, he'll be practically wetting his pants . . . (The Diary of a Young Girl, 335)

Frank's fun at Hitler's expense is an effective way to highlight the baseness of the enemy (that "hideous puppet show," as she calls the Führer and his propaganda [The Diary of a Young Girl, 90]).

It would be unrealistic to think that Jewish victims never cracked a joke or made a funny remark, a smug comment, or a sarcastic criticism that elicited a smile from a listener, especially considering that the Jews' famous brand of humor was born precisely to alleviate the strains of persecution. Jewish humor has always been an analgesic for the pain arising from antisemitism and violent oppression. Jewish fatalism has birthed a famous brand of irony that works as a moral balm on the scars created by centuries of injustice and sufferance. For example, even in his apocalyptic journal that faithfully records the hopeless fate of hundreds of thousands of Jews trapped in the deathly Warsaw Ghetto, Emanuel Ringelblum weaves together tragedy and humor. On May 8, 1942, he writes: "They say that Churchill invited the rabbi of Góra Kalwaria over and consulted him on how to defeat the Germans. The rabbi gave him the following answer: There are only two possibilities: either by natural means or by miracle. The natural way: a million angels with flaming swords descend on Germany and annihilate it. The miracle: a million Brits fall on Germany and crush it."[38] The *chassidish rebbe* of this story forgets that where there are only two possibilities, the Jews will find a third: the Warsaw Ghetto prisoners took their fate into their own hands and fought the Germans on April 19, 1943, in what is famously known as the Ghetto Uprising. Alas, aided neither by God nor the Brits, they were defeated.[39]

In Theresienstadt the Nazis had created a special center, the *Technische Abteilung*, to exploit Jewish artistic talent for the benefit of German propaganda, which the inmates were ordered to produce. This turned out to be a chance for scores of Jewish artists to use the resources willingly put at their disposal by the Nazis to make art (at the risk of being discovered and consequently tortured and killed) that would surreptitiously bear witness to the atrocities committed against them. The Czech caricaturist Bedřich Fritta was the central figure in the artistic life of Theresienstadt and director of the *Technische Abteilung*. This was a poor choice from the invaders' point of view, considering that Fritta had ended up in Theresienstadt (along with his wife and his three-year-old son, who were both later killed in Auschwitz) for having spread "horror propaganda" against the Nazis. Given this opportunity, Fritta could not resist, even under threat of death, the temptation to satirically denounce the oppressors. One particularly powerful piece of work that he produced testifies to the horrors of the camp and hurls the victim's accusatory laughter at the perpetrators. The work, in black chalk, pen, and ink wash (on abraded paper), is titled *Deluge* (1943–44). In this painting, Fritta stages a theater of the grotesque rife with bitter satire: against the backdrop of the concentration camp's brick walls and barbed wire, a saucy demoiselle toasts the crowds, lifting her flute of champagne in the air while mimicking the military salute with her right hand. Her public is a macabre crowd of skeletons, the zombies of Terezín, among whom a Nazi guard in uniform and carrying a rifle conspicuously stands out. The stage is painted in an expressionist style, and on close inspection the soubrette turns out to be a one-eyed marionette. Her monocle is attached by a string to a saber, and, in an additional symbol of bourgeois masculinity and war, a medal is pinned on her naked breast over her nipple. She wears an exaggerated Tarbucket-style helmet with a Parisian flair. I see Brechtian cabaret where other commentators have seen cinema. "In *Deluge*," writes Glenn Sujo, "the astounding contrast between the crowd of bedraggled, skeletal figures (film extras) and the hallucinatory vision of a svelte, fair-skinned doll, a poor relative of the silver-screen idols, bestows a dream-like intensity and unreality on the work."[40] Regardless, black humor is the scene's indelible feature. Using ridicule, Fritta attacks the pretence of normality and *Kultur* the Germans thought they could maintain while, out of sight, millions were being murdered. By incongruously bringing the city cabaret and the extravagance of civilized life (reduced to a grotesque mannequin) into the concentration camp, an accusatory satire is born. Fritta was murdered in Auschwitz in 1944.

Another example comes from Hillesum's diary from the transit camp of Westerbork: "There are moments when my head spins with the wailing and the howling and the screeching all around . . . And yet now and then that bright and bubbling good humour of mine rises to the surface again, . . . and it isn't gallows humor either."[41] If humor must have now and again inadvertently surfaced to bring some solace to those lucky enough to share in it, it is all the more extraordinary that some made a conscious effort to keep their comic sense alive in the face of tragedy and to incorporate it into their art. Some people wrote cabaret entertainment, composed irreverent anti-Nazi songs, or put on carnivalesque shows even in the concentration camps, thus hyperbolizing the grotesque reality of those places through caricature. Some, like Frank, wrote exquisitely funny short stories—in Frank's case, to be read out loud for the benefit of the inhabitants of the Secret Annex, stories written in elegant, literary Dutch that, at times and not so subtly, parodied the people in the audience. And the German artist Charlotte Salomon composed the first Jewish graphic autobiography, in which art, music, and text were woven together in the author's gently sarcastic style.[42] To give another example, Berr attempted to maintain the illusion of normalcy for as long as possible by enjoying her days with a defiant insouciance and finding something comical to laugh about with friends and family despite the Nazi occupation of Paris. Indeed, a portion of her war journal—the only thing that remains of her—is infused with this lightness and *joie de vivre*.[43]

Hillesum, Frank, Salomon, and Berr did not return from Auschwitz. Like many others, they left behind signs of resistance to its annihilating force, not only in their acts of courageous recording (be it in writing, painting, or music) but also in leaving behind the image of a victim capable of laughing and making others laugh. Humor is a highly complex expression of the human mind, one that indicates the capacity to synthesize and transform and whose goal is to bond, commune, and—via the momentary relief that comedy affords—heal. Henri Bergson wrote: "We could not enjoy the comic if one felt isolated from others. Laughter seems to stand in need of an echo . . . Our laughter is always the laughter of a group."[44] I am not talking about the smug laughter or the gallows humor of a condemned person, a guilty defendant who has lost his moral bearings and gives the world one last, spiteful kick before leaving it. Frank's humor is self-preserving and stands on a solid ethical foundation: it is optimism's answer to pessimistic circumstances; it originates from a world where laws and logic have been turned upside down, but it speaks for the rational vision of the humorist, who has kept her coherence and moral system in place and, through jesting, tries to make order out of chaos and brutality. In Frank's diary, we witness Enlightenment humor with a distinctively female twist.

Some of the humor in the diary comes from the conversations and attitudes expressed by the adults around Frank. One can imagine that her quip about the "German wonder weapon" turning out to be "little firecrackers" (The Diary of a Young Girl, 322)—referring to the Nazi army's disintegration in the face of the Allied Forces' attack—was probably born around the table, where everybody would gather once a day to listen to the BBC radio broadcasts with an almost religious concentration. Frank had grown up in a cheerful atmosphere of serenity and good humor. Ironically, her life had started with a bit of a joke, too: in the hospital files from the morning of June 12, 1929, "the birth of a male child" is recorded.[45] Edith Frank had had a difficult delivery, and in the commotion of that day, the doctor had simply made a mistake. Yet there was a touch of irony in the error: Kati, the Franks' maid at the time, remembered that "after all there was something of the boy about Anne."[46]

One important distinction needs to be made. Humor in Auschwitz is not freeing for us, those who are after and outside of Auschwitz. Freud made us aware that a speaker uses humor to enlist his or her audience as an ally against a third party, but this dynamic is predicated on the notion that speaker and audience are contemporaneous—they share space and time. This dynamic fails to work here. The delay between the utterance of the Shoah performer and our receiving the message creates a vacuum of death and absence that can generate only horror in the receiver. It neither frees nor exculpates us; it is not cathartic. The laugh we hear from the Shoah past freezes the audience by revealing its truth, because its truth is death. It creates embarrassment, not relief. As we are readying ourselves to be cathartically purged, these works suddenly break the illusion of art. Kafka's magnificent short story, "An Imperial Message"[47] (see chapter 1), comes to mind once again. That tale forces us to stare into an un-bridgeable gap in communication: the addresser (the deceased emperor) is no longer there, the message is not interpretable or knowable, and the addressee is too far removed to attempt to understand it. Humor, an act of resistance and an expression of moral and intellectual superiority to the raw brutality of murder-ous hatred, reaches us long after its performers have been annihilated. It ends up horrifying, not amusing, by carrying to us the traces of humanity's horrible legacy: this genocide. Laughter from the dead, in such context, is therefore as distant and as unrecoverable as the emperor's last words.

When editing his daughter's manuscript for its first printing, Otto Frank censored some passages to make it less shocking to the public. He could not have guessed that what would have made the audiences uncomfortable in his daughter's diary were not the explicit references to her blossoming sexuality but her humor.

When we encounter a humorous passage in Anne Frank's diary, our aware-ness of the impenetrable and unbridgeable distance that separates us from the performer and her utterance is heightened. This distance is not emotional sepa-ration but an empathic awareness of Otherness. I consciously become aware of the radical Otherness of the victim: my distance from her does not leave me indifferent, but rather opens me up to bear witness to the crime committed against her. I form an active alliance with a subject that remains Other to me: I empathize (in German, *einfühlen*, to project oneself into the other's position), but with a movement toward the Other that requires an intellectual effort, a will to know and learn the pain of the Other. I am a bystander. I cannot overcome my position, but I choose to activate this position in the only way available to me: through intellectual and emotional engagement. "Empathy and reciprocity," Martin Hoffman notes in his study of the congruity of empathy with morality, "are orthogonal . . . they may combine to produce a powerful justice motive."[48] And Alison Landsberg observes: "Empathy recognizes the alterity of identifica-tion and the necessity of negotiating distances and is therefore essential to any ethical relation to the other."[49] By acknowledging the victim's act of resistance through the recognition of all its expressions, I am thus responding to the ethical imperative to hear and remember. Therefore, in hearing the victim's laughter, I become more aware of what was lost. Yet, despite ourselves, a smile emerges that reaffirms life against annihilation, even as it simultaneously reveals the obscenity of our being able to derive enjoyment after Auschwitz, or to be alive. But that is our conundrum, not the victims'. Even if only to take their minds off the surrounding apocalypse for an instant, they were entitled to laugh. We are not.

## FAMILY PORTRAITS

Before we can interpret Frank's humor and its function, we must situate it in the context of her family's dynamics both before and during the Holocaust. We must also consider the influence that the memories of those who knew the Franks and who after the war helped us construct a picture of their characters and lives has had on our understanding of Frank's diary and its humor.

The focus of *Holocaust Mothers and Daughters* is the mother-daughter relationship, and in Frank's case, I believe that the literary choice to portray her world humorously affects the way this relationship is constructed on the page. If the mother's negative portraiture is partly due, as others have argued, to the Oedipal crisis the teenage daughter experienced during her years in hiding, it also owes a lot to the artistic creativity of the daughter, who knew how to manipulate her dramatis personae in order to enrich her literary world. Humor plays a central role in the way this manipulation occurs and in the way the relationship with the mother (and the rest of the world) is eventually resolved. Therefore, to deliver Edith from the either negative or invisible position to which she has often been relegated, I want to open a parenthesis in this chapter in order to sketch a new identy for this Holocaust mother. We should not forget that it is in the nature of Anne Frank's journal (written with an eye toward future publication) to interweave real-life characters and literary characters—or, rather, to illuminate the characters in the diary in both a historical and literary light. A fair treatment of Frank's humor must take into account the textual people, whom this humor textually shapes, as well as the historical people to whom, as I will show, this humor binds and allies the writer.

Like all the other memoirs of war childhoods examined so far, Frank's diary testifies to a young woman's struggle to survive in two senses. On the one hand, the Jewish writer is doing her best to survive the Nazis; on the other hand, a girl is deploying, through her writing, psychological defenses and offenses aimed at surviving her mother—or, better, at surviving the passage from childhood to adulthood, a struggle that is played out against the often turbulent background of a daughter's relationship with her parental figures. One aspect of Frank's diary that has hardly escaped anybody's notice is the author's conspicuously harsh judgment of her mother. This would appear to be a classic case of the daughter-father idyll ruined by the interference of the "bad mother." We have already seen this dynamic (and its literary resolutions) in the memoirs of Ruth Klüger, Edith Bruck, Sarah Kofman, and Helena Janeczek (though less explicitly in the latter's case). However, as demonstrated in these works, a girl's personal psychic drama is more complex than the Oedipal story rigidly formatted by traditional psychology. Like all the others, Frank's case is exceptional. It is surprising that virtually no attention has been devoted to the fact that the family triangle in her diary is complicated by the appearance, and quite literal interference, of another mother: Mrs. van Daan. To be clear, Mrs. van Daan is not a mother figure to Anne. But she is a mother (her son, Peter, is also one of the Annex characters), and as such she is compared and contrasted to Edith, and the two mothers compete against each other. As we have seen, Kofman lived in hiding with two mothers, and the child narrated in *Rue Ordener, Rue Labat* ends up rejecting her own *maman* and replacing her with the uncanny double of *Mémé* (chapter 2). Similarly, Roth was brought up by two different mothers, but unlike her French peer, she never quite emotionally united with her adoptive one (her Christian savior), while she remained very faithful to the loving memory of her biological mother. Frank introduces yet another variant: this time we have two mothers of two different sets of children, simultaneously present on the scene, both of whom are Jewish and both of whom are harshly criticized by the narrator. However, as soon as the second mother makes her entrance, she allows the writer to redirect the anger, anxieties, and frustrations previously channeled toward the biological mother to her instead. In a way, then, the appearance of the worse mother makes the bad mother look better.

Another exceptionality of Frank's diary is that the father figure in it is a significant presence, the all-important emotional north in the psychic and life compass of the daughter and, it would appear, of everybody else who came in contact with this extraordinary man. None of the fathers of the other authors we've examined were alive by the time the daughters were writing their memoirs, and with one exception (Janeczek's father), all of them perished in the Holocaust. Otto Frank was the only one of the eight people in the Secret Annex to return from Auschwitz.

Otto Frank adored his family, and his sweet temperament and love for people made him a paternal figure to all who knew him: even in the concentration camp, he showed kindness to others. One of the younger inmates even took to calling him *papa Frank* and did so for the rest of Otto's life.[50] In reading the diary for the first time after returning from internment, Otto was quite struck by his daughter's antipathy for her mother, and he initially thought it wiser and more respectful of the memory of the dead to omit those parts from the diary (along with the explicit bits about sex) when he edited it for publication in 1947. Critics have noted how Anne had started to censor herself on the subject of her mother about halfway through the diary by writing less about her; one explanation is that, having decided to publish it one day, she began to think it would be inappropriate or uninteresting for such antimaternal rants to be made public. However, a more plausible explanation is provided by Dalsimer's psychoanalytical reading of the text, according to which, in the final entries of the diary, Anne "has less need to rail against her [mother], less need to repudiate her because their bond is now less frightening."[51] According to this reading, Anne successfully concluded her passage from childhood through adolescence to the dawn of adulthood during her two years in hiding (which coincided with the two years of the composition of the diary). At this stage, the child grows to recognize her complete autonomy from her father and mother, who can now be safely seen as a (sexual) couple in their own right.

What interests me, however, is how the negative commentaries on the mother in Anne's diary shaped the way in which Edith has been understood by other people. This is apparent in the way in which the person of Edith is posthumously reconstructed by those who knew her. In the documentary film *Anne Frank Remembered*, one of Anne's childhood acquaintances tells the interviewer about a piece of gossip that bowls over all the adults in Frank's circle: "I remember very strongly that Mr. Frank was seen as an ideal daddy. That he was *the* daddy, because he was so much involved in his girls' education and then there was this story that he fixed his wife breakfast on Sunday mornings and brought it to her bedside which was unheard of in our circles! So the news made the round 'Oh, Mr. Frank does this for his wife! How great!'" Henk van Beersekamp, an employee of Otto Frank at the Dutch Opekta Company who was a young man at the time, remembers that "Mrs. Frank was different from Otto Frank. Otto Frank was a familiar, friendly man, who treated me as an equal, and with kindness. Mrs. Frank was a bit [here Beersekamp is stumped for words and begins to mimic through body language what he finds too difficult to verbalize; he stiffens up his body and pulls back from the interlocutor, signaling distance and haughtiness] . . . well, maybe she had been accustomed to better things in life in Germany, I don't know." The way this opinion is stated leaves the audience with the distinct impression that Edith Frank thought of herself as superior and belonging to a different—that is, better—category of people. "Margot was a bit subdued . . . but Anna was a dear," Beersekamp continues, and he tells the story of a game he used to play with Anne that amused her tremendously. "She was a great girl," he concludes, speaking much more tenderly than he had in recalling Edith or Margot.[52]

The film *Anne Frank Remembered* is a phenomenally successful attempt at reconstructing the lives and deaths of the eight people in the Secret Annex of Anne Frank's childhood, as well as the world of those around her—children, adults, friends of the family, employees of Otto Frank, fellow prisoners in Westerbork, Auschwitz, and Bergen Belsen. The documentary is based on the homonymous memoir by Miep Gies, who is the main narrator of the events in the film. Miep was the person who most often saw and interacted with the Franks in the last miserable years of their lives. She was the one in charge of bringing Margot to the hiding place where her parents and Anne were waiting for her: Miep rode her bike together with Margot to the designated place (taking a different route than the rest of the family did) and made sure to keep the girl safe from arrest. This is how Miep describes for Blair the Frank family's first day in the small and messy warehouse that was to become their home for twenty-five excruciating months: "Mrs. Frank and Margot were sitting down on the bed. They could not do anything. They could not accept this situation. But Anne and Mr. Frank were busy, very busy . . . The next day when I came, all was OK . . . Anne and Mr. Frank were busy the whole day!" The interviewer interjects: "Was this typical of the family?" to which Miep replies, without hesitation and with an insinuating smile, "Yes, that was typical for the family." Of that first day, Frank notes down in the diary: "Mother and Margot were unable to move a muscle. They lay down on their bare mattresses, tired, miserable and I don't know what else. But Father and I, the two cleaner-uppers in the family, started in right away" (The Diary of a Young Girl, 25). Despite the shock that, according to these reports, left the mother and older sister paralyzed before the enormity of the circumstances, that same day (July 10, 1942), Edith found the strength to cook split-pea soup, even if, in the surrounding chaos, she ended up burning it so irrecoverably that "no amount of scraping could get [the peas] out of the pan" (27). Yet, successful or not, she did do something. The following day, both Edith and Margot had "recovered somewhat." and when Anne grew frightened of sitting downstairs with the rest of her family listening to the British broadcasts on the radio, "Mother understood my anxiety and went with me [back upstairs]" (27). If one depiction ("Mother and Margot were unable to move a muscle . . . they [were] . . . miserable") tries to conjure up the state of shock felt by her mother and sister in reaction to an objectively terrifying situation, other details ("mother felt well enough to cook split-pea soup"; "We started off immediately the first day sewing curtains" [27]) construct a realistic scene where everybody busily did what they could to organize the place to make it suitable as a long-term dwelling. The writer accepts her membership as part of the group of scared women from which she had made a point to initially distance herself. But this balanced portrayal is obscured in Miep's memory.

In the first few days in their new hiding place, the Franks were alone. Soon, however, the van Pels were scheduled to join them, and Anne hoped their arrival would bring joy and "much more fun" (*The Diary of a Young Girl*, 27). The annex ended up hosting quite a diverse, and at times comedic, cast of characters. Miep describes the group of escapees thusly: "Margot and Peter were quite withdrawn . . . Mrs. van Daan was temperamental, flirty, chatty. Mrs. Frank, kind and orderly, very quiet but aware of everything that went on around her. Mr. van Daan was the joke teller, something of a pessimist, always smoking, and somewhat restless. Mr. Frank was the calm one . . . the most logical, the one who balanced everyone out. He was the leader, the one in charge. When a decision had to be made, all eyes turned to Mr. Frank."[53]

Subtly, Miep and others hint that Edith was something of a "Jewish princess," a woman with feeble nerves, slow to react (even lazy), and certainly not a cutup like the others around her. However, two words that appear in many descriptions of her are "kind" and "quiet." In the 1950s Schnabel interviewed forty-two people who had known the Franks to get as much information about their lives and deaths as possible. During her interview with Schnabel, Miep concedes that Mrs. Frank was the only person besides Mrs. van Daan to have a very clear premonition of how it would all end, although, as Schnabel paraphrases Miep's testimony, Mrs. Frank, unlike Mrs. van Daan, "was not at all anxious, rather humorous and kindly, often very quiet. The great love Margot always displayed toward her would be proof that Anne was also unjust in her description of her mother."[54] Miep eventually amends this statement to Schnabel in Anne's favor. "Perhaps I ought not to talk about justice," Miep tells Schnabel. "In her own way she [Anne] was just. You see, she was uncompromising . . . Still, she was the happiest of all of them. For the others, those twenty-five months were nothing but misery. Margot, *too*, was sometimes terribly depressed."[55] We can infer that the "too" refers to Edith's depression: mother and older daughter apparently were the least cheerful people in the hiding place. However, as we will see, various entries in the diary prove that Anne was not exactly "the happiest of all of them" either, in spite of Miep's description. Nevertheless, the nobility of spirit and good cheer with which everybody tried to keep their chins up, especially in the presence of their Christian visitors from the outside, seem to have been traits common to everybody in the hiding place.

In the film *Anne Frank Remembered*, Miep sketches another singular scene for us, this one contradicting what she had reported to Schnabel decades earlier: "Mrs. Frank was the most depressed of all people. Sometimes . . . she went with me till the door—I did not understand . . . what did she want of me? And once again I go with her in her sleeping room and she closed the door and she said to me 'Miep, I am so afraid . . .' She told me all her troubles. But what could I do? I did not say anything, because I was in the same position as she."[56] The same scene is explained in much more detail in Miep's memoir. Edith was desperate for a confidante, someone on whom she could unload her worries:

> As winter approached, Mrs. Frank began to act oddly. When I left the hiding place, she would follow me downstairs just as far as she could go . . . but then, rather than bid me goodbye, she'd just stand there and look at me, with an expression of wanting in her eyes. I'd stand and wait for her to say what it was that she wanted of me, but she wouldn't say a word, just stand there awkwardly. I began to feel very uncomfortable, standing face to face with her . . . It took a while, but finally I realized that what she wanted was to be able to talk with me in a confidential way.[57]

Although Miep's partiality to Anne—to whose memory and legacy she devoted, like a priestess, her entire life—and to Otto (whom she thought of as her boss but "also [as] our father"[58]) is deeply touching, her coldness toward Edith's despair as a woman and mother is somewhat puzzling.

Is it possible that people's testimonies about Anne Frank's world have been affected by the published diary? Could the witnesses' memories have been subconsciously manipulated by the writer's perspective on her mother? Anne saw herself in quite romantic and heroic terms as an objective, rational, and scientific observer of people and life. She was proud of her criticisms, which of course, given her age, were not always mitigated by tolerance or flexibility. However, one ought not to overlook the fact that her impatience with her mother is only one component of their relationship, which oscillates between frustration and admiration. At one moment Anne asserts: "I can't stand mother. It's obvious that I'm a stranger to her" (The Diary of a Young Girl, 41). Yet in the same day's entry she also writes: "Father and Mother always defend me fiercely" (42). "I have loving parents" (6), she explains to Kitty, and proudly introduces her mother as "Mama Frank, the children's advocate!" (88).

Elli, Anne's friend and real-life confidant, tells Schnabel: "It was only natural for Anne to be most closely attached to her father . . . The two of them were alike. Mr. Frank, too, . . . is a person with the kind of understanding one mostly finds only in writers. He too, could be as affectionate as Anne, and he, too, was unsparing with himself."[59] Yet Anne also had some of her mother's traits, and certainly much of her appearance, too. In a photo from May 1941 in which the whole family poses in the sun in front of their apartment at Merwedeplein, the mother-daughter resemblance is particularly noticeable. Equally noticeable is the emotional closeness of the four Franks: Anne is squeezed between father and mother; Edith holds her daughter's left hand very tightly; Anne's right arm is wrapped around her father, who in turn holds Anne under his right arm and

Margot under his left. However, despite this warmth, it is not an altogether happy picture. By then the Nazis had already been in Holland for a year, and the pressure shows on everybody's face: Otto and Margot try to smile, but Anne and Edith remain serious.[60] Another photo from happier days in 1936 shows Edith with her two daughters sitting on the grass and enjoying a sunny day in the park. The three of them radiate joy, their smiles hinting at traces of laughter lingering in the air. Although Edith sits between her two daughters, with her hands folded impartially on her lap, her body leans sideways toward Anne, which produces a sense of closeness and intimacy.[61] In another photograph, a summer day at the beach in 1934 is immortalized in a beautiful shot that portrays Margot, slightly apart from the other women, voraciously enjoying an ice cream while Anne contemplates the stump of her cone with a delighted smile as she stretches her left arm to pull affectionately on her mother's right shoulder. Edith looks straight at the camera with an amused smile that is a faithful reproduction of the one on Anne's lips.[62] Anne's gestures in these photos are very natural, not the product of the photographer's stage directions. The physical fluidity between Anne and the world around her, particularly between her and her mother, reflects a portrait of her confirmed throughout her diary and in the testimonies of those who knew her. She was extroverted, profusely affectionate, and not at all afraid of expressing her feelings through speech and body language—that is, she was the opposite of her reserved, shy, and very composed sister. But Edith appears in all of these photos to be comfortable in her surroundings as well; she is not caught looking away from the camera, she smiles elegantly but not stiffly, she holds her daughter by the hand, and she does not stand away from her husband or show any other body language that might indicate an off-putting, unsociable person.

Something about Edith apparently struck the family's new friends in Holland as unpleasant or diffident. However, she was obviously an open-minded, modern woman who, together with her husband, had opted more leading-edge child-rearing methods for the girls—reflected, perhaps, in the warm family photographs capturing the two happy daughters. The girls were much loved (Anne would have said "spoiled rotten" [The Diary of a Young Girl, 208]), and their parents had also created around them a healthy family environment in which laughter and good humor were the norm even when times turned for the worst. Hanneli Goslar—Anne's closest friend, to whom one of the most touching and almost mystical pages of her diary is devoted—tells about the time when her father had the silly idea of masquerading as Hitler, his pomaded hair combed stiff to one side, a Führer moustache, and so forth, and went next door to the Franks' as a joke. The impersonation was perfect, and "everybody was so scared at first!" Goslar laughs at the memory of the prank and at the absurd idea behind it, that Hitler himself could knock at the Franks' door.[63] However, her anecdote also indirectly confirms the importance for the persecuted to joke and laugh even as the circumstances clearly caused most serious apprehension. The stunt apotropaically warded off for a moment the serious threat looming larger every day by diminishing and ridiculing it. But not forever: Goslar's father was murdered in Bergen-Belsen.

Growing up, Frank breathed in this atmosphere of good-humoredness and love, which makes one struggle to explain her later rants against her mother, the harshest of which is the following:

> And yet Mother, with all her shortcomings, is tougher for me to deal with . . . I can't very well confront her with her carelessness, her sarcasm and her hard-heartedness, yet I can't continue to take the blame for everything. I'm the opposite of Mother, so of course we clash . . . She's not a mother to me—I have to mother myself. I've cut myself adrift from them . . . I have no choice, because I can picture what a mother and a wife should be and can't seem to find anything of the sort in the woman I'm supposed to call "Mother" . . . But . . . the worst part is that Father and Mother don't realize their own inadequacies and how much they let me down. Are there any parents who can make their children completely happy? (The Diary of a Young Girl, 141)

It is important to notice that the girl slowly closes the gap she had set between her parents (a wide gap that separated the wonderful father from the terrible mother), and even Otto ("the most adorable father I've ever seen" [The Diary of a Young Girl, 7]) ends up falling off the pedestal on which the daughter had placed him. In one entry, surprisingly, we read: "This is a point I think about quite often: why is it that Pim [Otto] annoys me so much sometimes?" (331).[64]

Written on October 30, 1943, the above entry about Edith is positioned in the middle of the diary, in the middle of the Franks' stay in the annex. As such, it depicts the climax of Anne's Oedipal drama just before it begins to be successfully resolved, and it unfolds in a denouement during the second half of the book. By January 2, 1944, Anne is ready to reassess the situation: "I tried to understand the Anne of last year and make apologies for her . . . I was furious at mother (and still am a lot of the time). It's true, she didn't understand me, but I didn't understand her either. Because she loved me, she was tender and affectionate, but because of the difficult situations I put her in, and the sad circumstances in which she found herself, she was nervous and irritable, so I can understand why she was often short with me. I . . . was insolent and beastly to her . . . We were caught in a vicious circle of unpleasantness and sorrow. Not a very happy period for either of us, but at least it's coming to an end" (*The Diary of a Young Girl*, 158–59). Other outbursts occur, but they are farther apart, and the tension between Anne and her mother begins to be mitigated by the maturation of the daughter, who has come to better grasp the situation (both the interpersonal situation with her mother and the historical circumstances of the Shoah they all shared).

Throughout the diary, there are frequent swings between love and hate for the mother, between anger at her and admiration for her. Anne's own ambivalence certainly owed a lot, as Dalsimer explains, to the psychological metamorphosis she was experiencing as a teenager. However, Blair's documentary ends up highlighting only Anne's adoration for Otto and enmity toward Edith, despite the fact that this dichotomy was not that unambiguously delineated but full of gray areas. The writer of this diary was more complex than that.

In spite of its less than subtle take, Blair's film does thoroughly examine this mother-daughter conflict and tries to find out how the pair withstood the test of Auschwitz. Bloeme Evers-Emden, one of the survivors who knew the Franks before the war (she was a teenager at that time) and who was with them in the *Lager*, talked to both Blair and the writer Willy Lindwer about those days, highlighting the closeness and love among the three Frank women. They were together all the time, and they supported and gave strength to one another to the point that when a chance arrived for Edith and Margot to be transferred out of Auschwitz to a more benign camp without gas chambers, they decided unanimously, and without hesitation, to remain in Auschwitz with Anne, who had developed a terrible rash and was not selected for this lucky transport. Thus, Anne's mother and sister may have lost their only chance of surviving. Evers-Emden also explains that "they were always together—mother and daughters. Whatever discord you might infer from the diary was swept away now by existential need. They were always together. It is certain that they gave each other a great deal of support. All the things that a teenager might think of her mother were no longer of any significance."[65]

To illustrate Anne's ability to transform the people around her to meet her narrative and literary goals, it suffices to consider a hilarious episode that occurred in school and that is reported in the entry for June 21, 1942.[66] Punished by her math teacher, Mr. Keesing, for talking too much in class, Anne is ordered to write an essay at home entitled "A Chatterbox." She turns this into an opportunity to compose a wonderfully self-referential (and also very funny) bit of storytelling. "I began thinking about the subject while chewing the tip of my fountain pen. Anyone could ramble on and leave big spaces between the words, but the trick was to come up with convincing arguments to prove the necessity of talking" (*The Diary of a Young Girl*, 11). Wittily finding her way out of trouble, the writer comes up with a solution: "I argued that talking is a female trait . . . but that I would never be able to break myself of the habit, since my mother talked as much as I did, if not more, and that there's not much you can do about inherited traits" (11). Anne gets around a second "punitive" assignment from Mr. Keesing who, clearly tickled by his student's brilliance, further puts her to the test by ordering her to write a new essay, "Quack, Quack, Quack, Said Mistress Chatterback." Anne's reply is a most imaginative poem—"it was beautiful!" she assures us (11–12)—that wins her the permission to talk as much as she wants. I want to stop and consider for a moment what the girl said in the first essay: Was Edith a quiet woman or the chatterbox her daughter made her out to be? Could it be that the writer, in order to win her argument with the math teacher, needed a talkative mother and created one on the page, just as the witnesses describing Edith as quiet needed her to be a haughty, disdainfully aloof person in order to make their impressions align with Anne's negative portrayal of her mother? Were they, in their unsympathetic descriptions, subconsciously trying to match their idea of Jewish woman, or perhaps align their memories with the impressions Anne left us of her mother without factoring in their literarity?

I am not suggesting that we dismiss the reality of the conflict between the daughter and her mother. Matching what Dalsimer has clarified for us in her study on female adolescence, the diary records the step-by-step developmental stages, over a two-year period, of the teenage girl from a pre-Oedipal union with the parents, to complete Oedipal rejection of the mother and love for the father, and finally to a disengagement from both, achieving autonomy and getting to see (and accept) the parents as a couple formed of separate, independent beings. In the 1990s feminist scholarship began to consider the mother-child bond not as the root of a rigid principle of separation and individuation, but rather as the fundamental relationship from which is born our ability to commune with the Other, to recognize the Other's otherness and empathize with the Other. "The caretaker [of the child] is not only an 'object' to which the infant attaches," writes the clinical psychologist Janet Surrey, "but a subject with her or his own qualities that immediately begin to influence the relationship and determine its course. They *both* will proceed to become further defined as people as they change *because of* the relationship. Optimally, they both will grow toward more relatedness, not less; toward better relatedness, not separation." Surrey's definition of a relationship, "an experience of emotional and cognitive *intersubjectivity*," is different from what is commonly referred to as an "attachment."[67] What I am proposing is that even understanding Frank's criticism of the mother as part of a psychological and self-individuating process of subconscious rejection, we should not disregard her authorial agency, the artistic and literary constitution of her diary. In this view, we must take into account the fact that Frank chose humor as a crucial vehicle of literary and intersubjective expressiveness. Relatedly, we must remember that two of the privileged devices of humor are exaggeration and hyperbole—both of which she amply applies to the way she portrays everybody, including her mother, her favorite character.

## USES AND ABUSES OF THE COMIC MOTHERS

Anne's opinions about her mother change for the better when the figure of Auguste van Pels appears. Mrs. van Pels immediately receives a droll pseudonym: Petronella van Daan. Most of the Secret Annex's characters are referred to by nicknames, which accentuate each persona's comic function: Fritz Pfeffer becomes Dussel, the van Pels are all renamed van Daan, she usually refers to her father as Pim and to Miep's husband as Henk, and the Opetka's employees are also all rechristened. The arrival of Petronella van Daan, also sarcastically referred to as Madame van D., allows the young author to shift her attention to a new comedic character and thus takes some of the pressure off her intense relationship with her mother. In fact, I argue that the new woman's arrival even allows Anne to ally herself with her mother.

When judging her mother against the rival figure of Mrs. van Daan, Anne can't resist taking her mother's side. "'You must have a strange outlook on life to be able to say that to Anne,'" (The Diary of a Young Girl, 45) Mrs. van Daan is reported as saying to the Franks in a pretentious tone after one of those famous discussions on the subject of Anne, the naughty child. She goes on: "'Things were different when I was growing up. Though they probably haven't changed much since then, except in your modern household!'" (45). Anne takes this to be an unsubtle swipe at her parents', particularly her mother's, modern child-rearing style. Her unruffled mother, Anne writes with evident pride, slashes back at Mrs. van Daan, and the following comedic, and highly theatrical, scene ensues:

> "Well, Mrs. van Daan, I agree that it's much better if a person isn't over-modest. My husband, Margot and Peter are all exceptionally modest. Your husband, Anne and I, though not exactly the opposite, don't let ourselves be pushed around."
>
> Mrs. van Daan: "Oh, but Mrs. Frank, I don't understand what you mean! Honestly, I'm extremely modest and retiring. How can you say that I'm pushy?"

Mother: "I didn't say you were pushy, but no one would describe you as having a retiring disposition."

Mrs. van D.: "I'd like to know in what way I'm pushy! If I didn't look out for myself here, no one else would, and I'd soon starve, but that doesn't mean I'm not as modest and retiring as your husband."

Mother had no choice but to laugh at this ridiculous self-defense, which irritated Mrs. van Daan. Not exactly a born debater, she continued her magnificent account in a mixture of German and Dutch, until she got so tangled up in her own words that she finally rose from her chair and was just about to leave the room when her eye fell on me . . . Mrs. van D. wheeled around and gave me a tongue-lashing: hard, Germanic, mean and vulgar, exactly like some fat, red-faced fishwife. It was a joy to behold . . . She struck me as so comical . . . I've learned one thing: you only really get to know a person after a fight. (The Diary of a Young Girl, 46)

Mrs. van Daan is described as a truculent matron, pushy, unintelligent, a perfect yenta, and a masterpiece of *yiddishe mamehood* doting over her Jewish boy (Peter). Edith responds to her with moments of comedic Jewish-motherly kvelling: "'You see, Mrs. van Daan,' Mother said, 'there's a big difference between Margot and Peter. To begin with, Margot's a girl, and girls are more mature than boys. Second, she's already read many serious books and doesn't go looking for those which are no longer forbidden. Third, Margot's much more sensible and intellectually advanced, as a result of her four years at an excellent school'" (The Diary of a Young Girl, 35). By using the comic mode, Anne is able to recast her mother in a more heroic light.

Aside from the diary, Anne also filled several notebooks with fictional and autobiographical stories. Published under the title Tales from the Secret Annex, these represent an important archive of finished and unfinished attempts at creative writing in which she tried her hand at dramatic stories focused on the war; some short fantasies, quite imaginative and intricate, almost dreamlike; and of course some excellent spin-offs on the domestic comedic sketches described in her diary. Most important, variations on the figure of the mother are found throughout the Tales. Frank demonstrates an ability to imagine different versions of maternal figures, but in those fictional experiments, fathers and fatherly figures remain conspicuously absent or secondary. In her notebook of short writings, for example, Frank describes her mother this way: "Mama: has a hearty appetite, but doesn't live up to her potential. I always have the idea that people forget she's there, since she's off in the corner. Whenever the conversation turns to literature, you can learn a lot. She has a vast knowledge and is well read. No one has the impression, as they do with Mrs. van Daan, that she's a housewife."[68] This brief portrait reveals Edith as modest and reserved but also as an intellectually rich woman. She is someone Anne clearly admires, although she can only admit this admiration through a humorous comment. In contrast, "Mrs. van D. . . . [is] known to be exceedingly pushy, empty-headed and perpetually dissatisfied. Add to that, vanity and coquettishness . . . I could write an entire book about Madame van Daan, and who knows, maybe sometime I will."[69] The narrator then proceeds to find allies in support of her opinion: "Mother thinks that Mrs. van D. is too stupid for words, Margot that she's too unimportant, Pim that she's too ugly (literally and figuratively!) . . . *Will the reader please take into consideration that this story was written before the writer's fury had cooled?*"[70]

Although Edith's frustration earned Anne's respect, it did raise eyebrows with other acquaintances. Miep recalls being somewhat scandalized by Edith's breach of decorum when, in one of those moments when Edith tried to unburden her heart, she confessed that she couldn't stand Mrs. van Pels because of the way she kept putting Margot and Anne down, which she found utterly unjust. "Sometimes," Miep writes, "she [Edith Frank] would complain about Mrs. van Daan—something no one else had ever done about anyone in the Annex for my ears . . . She'd complain that Mrs. van Daan was always impatient with her girls, especially Anne, complaining that the Frank girls were too free for her. It seemed that Mrs. van Daan was always bringing up her feelings about Anne and Margot at the dinner table . . . This criticizing of Anne and Margot upset Mrs. Frank very much."[71] The fact that the van Pels and Pfeffer often criticized the Frank girls is confirmed in Anne's diary and *Tales from the Secret Annex*. Interestingly, most of this criticism refers to the unusual upbringing the girls had received from their lenient and modern parents. According to the van Pels and Pfeffer, the disciplinarian, Margot and Anne were allowed to read books inappropriate for their ages and gender; the very fact that they were allowed to spend so much time reading often provoked harsh censure. When Anne and Margot were thus attacked, it was almost always Edith who became heated and fiercely defended them. During one of the scenes in which Edith challenged the criticisms of the other refugees, "Mr. van D. yelped, Mrs. van D. yipped, Dussel shushed and Mother shouted. It was a hellish scene . . . The words flew thick and fast." As always, Anne was amused by the spectacle of adults fighting. She reports that Mr. van Daan insisted that "'It'd be better for the children [Anne and Margot] if they helped out . . . instead of sitting around all day with their noses in a book. Girls don't need that much education anyway!'" Anne continues: "'You're crazy!' Mother suddenly exclaimed. I was actually pretty startled. I didn't think she'd dare."[72] She did dare on more than one occasion, and despite the fact that such scenes are portrayed humorously by Anne, who takes a keen pleasure in the domestic comedy unfolding around her, they also indirectly sketch out the patriarchal context in which women had to battle for their right to intellectual and social freedom and show that this context is the same as it was before the war. The genocide that had forced the refugees into hiding had not broken the loyalty of some of them to old methods of oppression of women and girls. Anne responds to these patriarchal expectations characteristically, by cracking a joke: "Margot and I were supposed to be pressed into maid service in Villa Annex."[73] Moreover, she unequivocally sides with her mother and turns her into a paladin of women's rights: Edith is obviously the one who reacts the most strongly to people's reactionary visions of femininity. Anne connects this ludicrous moment (in which her right to read is questioned) to what has become of the national and domestic patriarchal order that the captive van Pels and Dussel keep defending: "it would be better to remind them [van Pels and Dussel] in no uncertain terms that without us [the Franks] and the others they'd be facing death, in the truest sense of the word. In a labor camp you have to do a whole lot more than peel potatoes . . . or look for cat fleas!"[74]

Also in *Tales from the Secret Annex* is a remarkable skit called "Evenings and Nights in the Annex," in which Frank artfully blends the romantic, the comic, and the tragic. It begins with a jolly atmosphere: "It's my turn for the bathroom. I wash myself from head to toe . . . I brush my teeth, curl my hair, manicure my nails and dab peroxide on my upper lip." However, humor soon breaks the illusion of idyllic normality: "I wash myself from head to toe, and more often than not I find a tiny flea floating in the sink (only during the hot months, weeks or days) . . . The next [person] in line invariably calls me back to remove the gracefully curved but unsightly hairs that I've left in the sink." To these two tones—idyllic and comic—a third one, the tragic, is added: *Ten o'clock*: Time to put up the blackout screen . . . For the next fifteen minutes . . . the house is filled with creaking of beds and the sigh of broken springs, and then, provided our upstairs neighbors aren't having a marital spat in bed, all is quiet . . . Sometimes the guns go off during the night . . . all of a sudden I find myself standing beside my bed, out of sheer habit." Fear has become as much a resident of the annex as the Jews hiding there, but because months of similar scenes have accustomed the fugitives to their situation, the comic aspect creeps in again: "This is no fun, especially when it concerns a roommate named Dr. Dussel [with whom Anne had to share her sleeping quarters]. First, I hear the sound of a fish gasping for air, and this is repeated nine or ten times. Then, the lips are moistened profusely. This is alternated with little smacking sounds, followed by a long period of tossing and turning and rearranging the pillows. After five minutes of perfect quiet, the same sequence repeats"[75]

Though the situation in the annex was utterly miserable, Otto had made sure that the hiding place would have the minimum features required to guarantee its inhabitants the basics of dignified life—a way to wash, a table on which to eat properly, beds, a library in order to keep the children up to speed with schoolwork, and so forth. Keeping up with civilized modes of living may be incongruous in so uncivilized a context, yet it is also essential; this incongruity is highlighted by Anne's humor, which—being a sign of a civilized life of intellectual refinement, critical observation, and objective criticism—ironically turns into something incongruous itself. The narrator of this sketch asserts the importance of aesthetics (through her hygiene and beauty routine) and humor as a way of showcasing human dignity in a crisis; by the same token, however, the tragic element she weaves into the piece undermines the power of her defensive strategies. Therefore, although humor is a way to momentarily take her mind off the tragedy or make the pain more bearable, her awareness of humor's limitations never allows her to forget her objective circumstances.

Frank was able to locate the ridiculous in the frightful conditions of hiding and turn it to her own personal, psychic advantage: that is, by satirizing the adults around her and capturing the tragic absurdity of the situation in a way that did not diminish its seriousness but allowed the humorist to withstand it. For example, the eight refugees' worst fear was of dying in the aerial bombardments, trapped and unable to run outside in case of fire. Notice how Frank recounts one such night of intense ground and air fighting when everybody was convinced the annex would burst into flame any minute:

> We all rushed upstairs to see what was going on. Mr. and Mrs. van D. had seen a red glow through the open window . . . she was certain our house was ablaze. Mrs. van D. was already standing beside her bed with her knees knocking when the boom came. Dussel stayed upstairs to smoke a cigarette, and we crawled back into bed. Less than fifteen minutes later the shooting started again. Mrs. van D. sprang out of bed and went downstairs to Dussel's room to seek the comfort she was unable to find with her spouse. Dussel welcomed her with the words "Come into my bed, child!" We burst into peals of laughter, and the roar of the guns bothered us no more; our fears had all been swept away. (The Diary of a Young Girl, 102–3)

On other occasions, the teenage girl gets angry at the adult world for making her the center of their evening discussions. Yet she is still able to muster enough aplomb to report everybody's poor opinion of her in quite hilarious terms: "We all decided I [am] an ignoramus . . . Then we discussed my ignorance of philosophy, psychology and physiology (I immediately looked up these big words in the dictionary!)" (*The Diary of a Young Girl*, 39). Frank cagily turns these criticisms of her into an opportunity for a joke at the expense of the critics (what she calls "giv[ing] them a taste of their medicine" [44]): "I should be used to the fact that these squabbles are daily occurrences, but I'm not and never will be as long as I'm the subject of nearly every discussion. (*They refer to these as 'discussions' instead of 'quarrels,' but Germans don't know the difference!*)" (43–44, emphasis added).

Parenthetically, it is worth noting how language itself becomes a subject of humor. No one in the annex was a native Dutch speaker, and although the adults tried hard, their repeated mistakes and gaffes were still made fun of by the children. Miep writes: "The new language had come hardest for Mrs. Frank, probably because she was at home so much. It had been much easier for Mr. Frank, out in the world of Amsterdam all the time, and the children had taken to it like ducks to water."[76] In contrast, Anne's diary suggests that Mrs. van D.'s Dutch was equally bad (and even that Mrs. van D. spoke the worst Dutch of them all). More interestingly still, the *Critical Edition* offers a different take on the men's Dutch fluency: "Please bear in mind, dear Kitty, that the two ladies here speak terrible Dutch. (I daren't say anything about the gentlemen, because they would be very offended.) If you could hear their bickerings you would burst out laughing: we don't pay attention to it any more, it's no good correcting them either" (*Critical Edition*, 253). Is this another case in which the writer manipulates her characters to make them fit her narrative? Or another case in which the memory of a witness (Miep, in this case) is subconsciously readjusted to fit a story that needs be repeated consistently—a story that demands that the real Edith Frank be as faulty as the textual Edith Frank?

To return to the issue of humor in tragic times, it seems clear that Anne is consciously using humor as a genre within her narrative, as a coping strategy that works on several levels. I must stress that by coping strategy I do not mean a form of denial that obscures the reality in which she lived. Rather, she is very much aware of the situation in which the Jews of the Secret Annex, Holland, and the rest of Europe find themselves; yet she composes her diary in a way that both honors the tragedy and uses irony and humor to narrate her situation effectively. Hers is neither gallows humor proper nor jejune insouciance. As Brenner points out, "in her 'good'—that is, hopeful—moments, Frank realizes that a representation of such a terrible reality requires a rhetoric appropriate for the 'uninitiated' person."[77]

As late as the middle of June 1944 (two months before the eight refugees were arrested), when everybody's threshold of tolerance for the conditions was about to be crossed, Frank chooses to make light of the situation rather than give in to it: "Peter's becoming insolent, Mr. van Daan irritable and Mother cynical. Yes, everyone's in quite a state! There's only one rule you need to remember: laugh at everything and forget everybody else! It sounds egotistical, but it's actually the only cure for those suffering from self-pity" (*The Diary of a Young Girl*, 321). Mrs. van Daan is predictably the most agitated: "Mrs. van D. is at her wits' end. She's talking about getting shot, being thrown in prison, being hanged and suicide. She's jealous that Peter confides in me and not in her, offended that Dussel doesn't respond sufficiently to her flirtations and afraid her husband's going to squander all the fur-coat money on tobacco. She quarrels, curses, cries, feels sorry for herself, laughs and starts all over again" (321).[78] This sketch of the hysterical bourgeois woman—which has illustrious fictional predecessors in Nicolai Gogol's Russian matrons, Franz Kafka's bossy inn proprietresses, and Robert Musil's opulent Viennese ladies—is in this context both funny and extremely tragic. Mrs. van Daan's fears are far from exaggerated. Auguste van Pels will be murdered in a concentration camp (which one and on which date is not yet known). Hermann van Pels, her husband, "melted away right away [in Auschwitz], two days and he was gone, he gave up" according to an eyewitness.[79] Peter van Pels, their eighteen-year-old son, died in Mauthausen.

Although by the middle of 1944, it was quite clear that the war was not going well for Germany and that the end was near, the danger faced by Jews in Europe had not abated; in fact, the implementation of the Final Solution had intensified. Trapped in a small space, without privacy, in conditions of forced gregariousness, deprived of all rights, aware that their fate as Jews and Europe's fate were not necessarily aligned, everyone in the Secret Annex was on the verge of losing their minds, the youngest among them included. "Let something happen soon," Frank prays in desperation one day, "even an air raid. Nothing can be more crushing than this anxiety. Let the end come, however cruel" (*The Diary of a Young Girl*, 308). Evidently, among other things, Anne had also inherited from her mother a profoundly sensitive and, at bottom, pessimistic streak.

I want to offer two final anecdotes to highlight how strangely conflicting the testimonies about Edith Frank's character can be—as opposed to the uniform image of Anne preserved in the mind of everyone who knew her. A woman who was with the Franks in Westerbork confirms the portrait of Edith as an uncommunicative woman, and of Anne as "lovely, so radiant." She continues: "You ask me what Anne's mother was like? There in Westerbork she was quiet; she seemed numbed all the time . . . She no longer talked very much . . . She said nothing at work, and in the evenings she was always washing underclothing.

The water was murky and there was no soap, but she went on washing, all the time."[80] Again, a quiet woman who, we're given to understand, likes to keep to herself. How can we blame her? Admittedly, there must have been little to say in those circumstances, in Westerbork, out of one trap (the Secret Annex) and into another (a transit *Lager*). Contrary to what Schnabel's interviewee seems to suggest, Edith still had a voice. Another woman, a Mrs. de Wiek, remembers her using it at the most heart-rending moment imaginable: "On October 30 there was another 'selection.' There stood the doctor, and we had to step into the light ... Then came Mrs. Frank—and she, too, joined our group at once. Then it was the turn of the two girls, Anne and Margot. Even under the glare of that searchlight Anne still had her face, and she encouraged Margot, and Margot walked erect into the light. There they stood for a moment, naked and shaven-headed, and Anne looked over at us with her unclouded face, looked straight and stood straight, and then they went on. We could not see what was on the other side of the searchlight. Mrs. Frank *screamed*: 'The children! Oh God.'"[81]

### BONDING HUMOR

Anne Frank's diary is characterized by extreme sadness and anxiety. Unexpectedly, humor goes hand in hand with this profound desolation. Humor is a literary choice as much as a spiritual one—a conscious effort on Frank's part to keep her spirits up even when she wasn't writing. Shoah scholars and theorists have often feared that the lightheartedness of the comedic scenes in her journal could mislead readers or later interpreters to underestimate the terror in which she and the people around her lived. Lawrence Langer remains one of the most conscientious defenders against abuses of the diary and Holocaust representation in general. We must guard against approaching the diary through the lense of our feel-good Hollywood culture or the myth of the triumph of the unique individual so deeply engrained in the American ethos. The fourteen-year-old heroine of this story understood herself as neither unique nor alone; most of all, she was well aware of the tragedy of her circumstances, since in such conditions of constant proximity, the adults could not talk secretly and keep their worries hidden from children. Miep explains that during her daily visits, Anne would overwhelm her with questions, and that she did not keep anything from the child; rather, she informed her in detail about what was happening outside of the hiding place. Moreover, as soon as the van Pels arrived, they brought into the annex horrid reports about the *razias* (roundups) and deportations. "The Van Daans," writes Miep, "told harrowing tales of how streetcar line number 8 had been used to transport Jews to the Centraal Station. Anne, Margot, and Mrs. Frank went gray as they listened. Some of the Jews sitting side by side on these transports had been their own friends and neighbors."[82] On October 7, 1942, Anne writes: "We assume that most of them are being murdered. The English radio says they're being gassed. Perhaps that's the quickest way to die" (*The Diary of a Young Girl*, 54). The arrival of Pfeffer brings fresh, grisly news from the outside: "We don't really know how to react. Up to now very little news about the Jews had reached us here, and we thought it best to stay as cheerful as possible. Every now and then Miep used to mention what had happened to a friend, and Mother or Mrs. van Daan would start to cry, so she decided it was better not to say any more. But we bombarded Mr. Dussel with questions, and the stories he had to tell were so gruesome and dreadful that we can't get them out of our heads. Once we've had time to digest the news, we'll probably go back to our usual joking and teasing. It won't do us or those outside any good if we continue to be as gloomy as we are now" (70). And yet the tone of her previous entry is far from upbeat: "I get frightened myself when I think of close friends who are now at the mercy of the cruelest monsters ever to stalk the earth. And all because they're Jews" (70). Many such starkly realistic passages show that the witty and funny sections are not part of an escapist strategy, and that humor is a psychological tactic that allows the writer to connect to, not disconnect from, the world. The intention of being entertaining feeds the artistic necessity of providing a range of emotions (surprise, suspense, tears, and laughter) to her audience—both the contemporary one made of herself, the other refugees to whom she read her stories and on whom she practiced her entertaining skills and the future readers of her book, whom she didn't wish to bore with endless brooding. The presence of the comedic van Daans and Dussel characters in the diary is fundamental to this end.

Humor in the diary fulfills three fundamental tasks: to reconnect Anne to her parents, in particular to bridge the distance that separates her from the mother; to allow her to begin to see herself as part of the larger world (that is, beyond the family circle) and to learn to both forge bonds in and erect boundaries within that world (functions fundamental to Freud's model of joking); and last, to hold onto a humanist conception of society and history, one that, as Langer has cynically though correctly pointed out,[83] did not save her, but without which, I argue, life would have been inconceivable for her.

First, then, at a time when Anne feels as if she is being pulled away from her parents, humor allows her to reenter their camp, to reconstitute the secure nucleus in which she feels safer and in her own element, protected, and in a position of strength vis-à-vis the surrounding world, which is made to look comically small. "Thus," Freud writes, "the humorist would acquire his superiority by assuming the role of the grown-up and identifying himself to some extent with his father, and reducing the other people to being children."[84] As I pointed out above, when compared to Mrs. van Daan, Edith Frank becomes an ally and no longer an enemy: Anne sees her family forming a separate camp (of *superior* people) from those *fools* with whom they must associate for the moment but who are also a key source of material for her storytelling. In her humorous sketches, we find the mother, father, and daughter on the same side of the good versus evil divide (within the limited annex universe), bonding and poking fun at the unreasonable and nonsensical other side. Her humor is a vehicle, not a screen. Humor allows for a reprieve in the conflict between the writer (the young teenager misunderstood by the grown-ups) and the adult world, between the youngest daughter and the mother, who—thanks to her own witticisms and the writer's sense of humor—passes (if only temporarily) from *bad* to *good*. The first function of this humor, therefore, is to reconnect the humorist to her mother and father, to inscribe Anne into the Frank family circle from which she had begun to feel separated in her adolescence. In a way, it is her brilliant sense of humor (albeit at the expense of Mrs. van Daan) that allows Anne to forge a rapprochement and new identification with her mother.

Second, humor allows Frank to inscribe herself within the circle of a larger community, the human one from which she has been exiled. At this level, those who were previously vilified as separate (in order to strengthen the Frank clan's cohesiveness) are now included in this larger human family. The writer broadens her circle of affiliation, and it is no longer the Franks against the other four people in the annex, but everybody in the annex (and in the world) against the oppressor, the Nazis. Frank was able and willing to look beyond her family boundaries and incorporate more members into her community of laughter. When she writes funny stories that she reads out loud to entertain the other refugees at night, or when she cracks jokes to lift up the sinking spirits of the adults around her, she is giving up her position of exclusivity with her mother, father, and sister to compose a larger resistance group against the ever-worsening situation. Take, for example, one classic *trait d'esprit*: "Fine specimens of humanity, those Germans, and to think I'm actually one of them! No, that's not true, Hitler took away our nationality long ago" (*The Diary of a Young Girl*, 55). She manages both to hold onto her national identity (she *is* German) and at the same time dissociate herself from the nation's current regime thus indirectly assert its absurdity. "Hitler took away our nationality" is the truth, but it is also absurd, and in a world of sanity and justice it shouldn't be possible—the factuality of where one is born being inalienable. Furthermore, by referring to the Nazi standards for judging who can claim German identity and who cannot (and considering that Hitler was not German-born himself), another absurdity in an irrational reality, she indirectly states that not all Germans are "Germans"—which is to say that not all Germans are Nazis. These ironic lines provide a good example of how the author is able to pull herself away from any association with the barbaric Germans and implicitly associate herself not only with the Jews but also with all the victims and opponents of Nazism and Fascism. At this level, the van Daans and Dussel are included in her expanded group of allies: they become fellow victims and friends.

And last, by translating laughter into literature, Frank attains a twofold goal. First, she reinserts herself into the flow of civilized life, into a world outside the annex but unlike the contemporary historical one—a place without Nazis and gas chambers, where laughter reinstates human bonding, empathy, life-affirming principles, and ethical values. Through humor, she regenerates an ideal world in which everything once again makes sense, an ideal that affirms equality (she is particularly sensitive about gender issues),[85] freedom, and rebellion against the Nazi order. Second, she also incorporates us, the readers of her book, into her circle of like-minded citizens who, while forced to take the Nazi threat seriously, also protest the obscenity of war, cruelty, and genocide through her resisting and ridiculing laughter. We cannot turn the Holocaust into a joke, but we can share her perspective. After sixth grade, Anne was moved to the Jewish Lyceum, where her sister had also been a student. Perhaps there she had internalized one of the most profound lessons in Jewish ethics: *tikkun olam*, the mending of the world—an operation that demands everybody's ethical engagement to heal and transform the future, one act of lovingkindness at a time.

Humor, in the sense I have explored it here, is not so much a tool with which to create pleasure in the midst of pain, but rather what Warren Poland calls the "gift of laughter," which is the "capacity for sympathetic laughter at oneself and one's place in the world . . . a regard for oneself and one's limits *despite* pain." We can identify Frank's humor as "mature humor," according to Poland's definition: a humor that "exposes a mature capacity to acknowledge inner conflict and yet accept oneself with that knowledge, even when it is the knowledge of one's narcissistic limits. Such humor, often linked to an appreciation of irony, requires a self-respecting modesty based on underlying self strength and simultaneous recognition of and regard for others."[86] When considered in this light, the seemingly self-aggrandizing statements Frank makes to compare herself and her parents to the petty van Daans–Dussel group turn out to be moments of humorous reflection on her circumstances and the world inside and around her.

We must also consider the role that writing a diary plays in the psychological life of a teenager. In reference to the diary's role as an interlocutor, Dalsimer writes that by "creating an imaginary being into whom she breathes life, the adolescent attempts to fill the void left when the parents no longer hold the place they held in childhood, but new bonds have not yet been consolidated." As for the strategy of writing a diary, Dalsimer observes: "Indeed, the diary is ideally suited to the narcissism and compensatory grandiosity of this phase . . . It is a literary mode whose legitimate subject is the self. It reflects the fluidity of self-esteem in adolescence—the vacillation between self-disparagement and self-aggrandizement—that the diary is valued both because it will guard one's shameful secrets and also because it may one day be published. The imagined 'other' brought to life in the pages of the diary helps to ward off the depression associated with loss."[87] The young girl "loses" her parents, who are about to be substituted (according to the Freudian and, in general, the patriarchal script) with a man, the love interest who will eventually come to dominate the adult woman's life (her husband). Anne is in a transitional stage: the diary-writing time coincides with the psychological time at which a teenage girl returns to the narcissistic stage left behind in infancy and turns her libido toward herself exclusively, withdrawing it from other people and external things. The girl's turning back into herself, according to Freud, is the important intermediary step that will force the boy or man to pursue her sexually—for he, the male, is capable of overcoming his narcissism and searching for a love object outside of himself.

Freud distinguished between two types of narcissism: a healthy one (primary narcissism, which responds to an impulse for self-preservation) and a pathological one (secondary narcissism). Polemically taking on Carl Jung and Sándor Ferenczi, Freud wrote in "On Narcissism" that women have an enviable capacity for narcissism. Although men are destined to love women—for a "man loves a woman as his infant self loved his mother"[88]—women are programmed to continue to love themselves, a self-love especially strong in adolescence. Interestingly, Freud's group of born narcissists includes, along with women, animals (cats, in particular), criminals, and humorists. And, mind you, not just any criminal or humorist, but "great criminals and humorists." Narcissism in women, according to Freud's analysis, is a sign of health: women are no longer defined by a void (the lack of a penis) but rather through a compensatory mechanism that becomes a positive attribute in its own right. Women will never grow a penis, but they can still love themselves. A primary narcissism maintained in adulthood is what allows women (only "the most beautiful," Freud notes) to attract men: "Strictly speaking it is only themselves that such women love with an intensity equal to that of the man's love for them. Nor does their need lie in the direction of loving, but in being loved."[89] But Freud makes sure to throw in a corrective statement that counterbalances women's fortunes so that they do not threaten or overwhelm men's: once a child arrives, (even) the woman finally breaks the resistance of narcissism and pours her love onto an external object. As far as my analysis is concerned, the interesting question is why Freud would associate women and humorists in his discussion of narcissism. Is it because, like narcissism, humor seeks love and wants approval from an audience (the humorist's superego)? We should also consider another parallel between the humorist and women: the second wave of narcissism in the girl arises in puberty with the "loss" of the parents, and humor is also described as a tonic against the pain of something lost—control over a reality that has turned too painful. Thus both narcissism and humor are defense mechanisms against loss, and both rely on the capacity of the superego not only to punish but also to reward with a feeling of well-being.

The humorist wants to be loved, wants an alliance with the audience. Many people who knew her refer to Frank's clownish streak and recount that she loved to make people laugh, to be the center of attention in class, and to perform pantomimes arousing admiration and mirth in adults. Frank was a born spinner of tales and had a tremendous imagination. For example, it is reported that when she was invited to spend the night at the house of her friend Jopie, who lived a stone's throw from the Franks, she always brought a suitcase with her: "The suitcase was empty of course, but Anne insisted on it, because only with the suitcase did she feel as if she were really traveling."[90] Miep fondly remembers how great a mimic Anne was and her ability to make everybody laugh when she reproduced "the cat's meow, her friend's voice, her teacher's authoritative tone ... Anne loved having an attentive audience, and loved to hear us respond to her skits and clowning."[91] We know that humor pleases both the self and others, but its workings are too elusive and subtle to be comprehensively theorized, as are the workings of narcissism—which remained for Freud the least clear of the mind's mechanisms. By 1927, therefore, Freud decided to put the two together, and in his conclusive work on humor he wrote: "Like jokes and the comic, humour has something liberating about it; but it also has something of grandeur and elevation ... The grandeur in it clearly lies in the triumph of narcissism, the victorious assertion of the ego's invulnerability. The ego refuses to be distressed by the provocations of reality, to let itself be compelled to suffer. It insists that it cannot be affected by the traumas of the external world; it shows, in fact, that such traumas are no more than occasions for it to gain pleasure. This last feature is a quite essential element of humour."[92] Frank's humor is particularly complex because it follows two different trajectories at once, unlike, say, the more clear-cut political satire that a professional humorist might produce against a regime. Her humor allows her both to stand up against (which is the literal meaning of the Latin *re-sistere*) public antisemitism and to fight the inner battle for self-definition waged in a private, familial setting. Through humor, she rebels against the patriarchal Father, whose oppressive rule is allegorized in the figures of Mrs. and Mr. van Daan and Dussel and their antiquated ideas about women and child rearing. Anne rightly understands them as part and parcel of a patriarchal conception of femaleness and family that she has decided to reject even at such a young age. Furthermore, her humor allows her to rebel against the broader symbol of paternity, which is the nation—the world of the Nazis, warmongers, pogromists, and all the "cruelest monsters ever to stalk the earth."

However, as Freud demonstrates, humor is not born out of an appraisal of reality (that would be wisdom) but out of an appraisal directly counter to reality, a "rejection of the claims of reality."[93] Thus in the old joke about the criminal who, being led out of his cell on the Monday of his execution, looks outside and says, "Well, the week's starting nicely," the humor comes, Freud explains, from the person's incongruous assessment of his position in reality. He might be right that the week is going to be a good one, but it is certainly not going to be good for him. "Humour," Freud says, "is not resigned; it is rebellious. It signifies not only the triumph of the ego but also the pleasure principle, which is able . . . to assert itself against the unkindness of the real circumstances."[94]

As we have seen, in writing about narcissism, Freud associated this special, healthy gift with women, humorists, and criminals. And we have seen how women's humor is itself tied to criminality in that it breaks the law of the Father and, in our case, of the Nazis. We may perhaps dare add to Freud's eccentric list the only type he left out: Jews—who have been traditionally enlisted as members of all the above categories. Jews are effeminate (women); they are immoral, and they are lecherous violators of Aryan women's purity (criminal); and they are like rats (in that they overreproduce and carry infections fatal to the wholeness of nations)—these are some of the most common clichés of antisemitic propaganda. Freud himself, with *Jokes and Their Relation to the Unconscious*, his masterpiece on (Jewish) *Witz*, opened the twentieth century with his own reactive, subversive, and resisting stance against antisemitism.[95] Frank, as a woman, humorist, Jew, and "criminal," establishes herself as a militant agent against an antisemitism that feminizes the Jew, criminalizes him, and takes away the Jew's humor—replacing it with its own crass and hateful verbal injuries in order, as Kofman wrote, to dismember the Jew's identity so that he should never recompose himself as a whole, never conceive of himself as an organic corpus.[96] Therefore Frank—again, as Jew, woman, and "criminal"—turned to the most adequate tool to disrupt further a law (the Nazi order) that has condemned her, in order to elevate herself above it.

Ultimately, by connecting humor to narcissism, Freud's system places the (symbolic) father at the origin of humor. "And finally, if the super-ego," he concludes, "tries, by means of humour, to console the ego and protect it from suffering, this does not contradict its origin in the parental [Freud undoubtedly means "paternal"] agency."[97] The superego thus engenders humor as a paternal way to soothe the ego: "The main thing is the intention which humour carries out, whether it is acting in relation to the self or other people. It means: 'Look! here is the world, which seems so dangerous! It is nothing but a game for children—just worth making a jest about!'"[98] According to this logic, Frank's humor might be read as a subconscious way through which the humorist attempts to become her own father, to tell herself those words of comfort that, given the unbearably fearful situation, she needs to hear so badly.

We saw how Otto Frank was the only one in the annex not to get himself involved in the daily quarrels between the other adults. He was the peacemaker while the mother was the fighter, the paladin of the children. Could it be possible, then, that instead of identifying with the father, Anne was taking over the role she would have liked him to play more actively—that is, fending off the attacks of the other adults as her mother was doing? What if the daughter were using humor to indirectly join forces with her mother by imitating Edith's resistance, a resistance Otto avoided? In this case, the mother and humorist would not be joining forces to win the love and attention of the man but rather to achieve their own mutual recognition.

Such female recognition is at the heart of Frank's diary. "There is a fiction," Dalsimer hypothesizes, "fervently maintained, that the diary is another person; yet this other person, like the mother of infancy, is continuous with the self."[99] According to De Costa, "in more than one way, Anne Frank's oeuvre can be interpreted as her attempt to position herself in a symbolic order in which exclusion mechanisms are at work . . . [H]er texts can be read as a representation of a mother-daughter dynamic in a patriarchal society that insists on a radical break between them."[100] By writing, and specifically by writing to Kitty, Frank fulfills Hélène Cixous's feminist vision: "It is by writing, from and toward women, and by taking up the challenge of speech which has been governed by the phallus, that women will confirm women in a place other than that which is reserved in and by the symbolic, that is, in a place other than silence."[101] I hope to have supplemented the conclusions of feminist scholars like Dalsimer, De Costa, Brenner, and others by adding the overlooked, forgotten, or underestimated mechanics of humor in Frank's understanding of herself, her mother, and their contemporary world. As De Costa observes, "the act of writing is in itself a way of maintaining contact with the semiotic [mother] while occupying the symbolic order [father]."[102] More subversively, I would add, this female author consciously repossesses a tradition of humor that has consistently posited woman as its object, not its agent, and from which women (with a superego feebler than that of man, according to Freud) had been altogether excluded.

In conclusion, I claim that Frank's humor strives to seduce and attract the father, but she also succeeds in creating the conditions in which to identify with her mother. At the same time, she overcomes the adolescent impulse to isolate herself from the rest of the world and instead rationally faces her historical circumstances and preserves her bond with the human community inside and outside of the hiding place. And all of this happens in the diary, through writing, and with a feminine smile of recognition and defiance.

## THE HIDING PLACE

This chapter opened with the death of Rudolf Höss. Höss spent his last days before his execution in captivity, and he devoted those days to writing. Höss had been totally free as he ruled and disseminated death and terror over his Nazi realm, yet his memoirs reveal that he had been a prisoner all his life in the rigid cage of a hateful worldview. In his last thoughts, Höss conspicuously avoided the Jewish question, except for saying the following: "Today I realize that the extermination of the Jews was wrong, absolutely wrong . . . The cause of anti-Semitism was not served by this act at all, in fact, just the opposite. The Jews have come much closer to their final goal."[103] In brief, he was unrepentant. In a claustrophobic, mice-infested warehouse in Amsterdam that had been turned into a hiding place, a fourteen-year-old girl of boundless creative energy was able to transcend her limited experience and limiting circumstances and keep intact her moral values, a desire for self-improvement, and a vision of humanity still worth engaging. Two different deaths, two different faces of humankind. As Höss and the procession of defendants at the Nuremberg trials prove, the portrait of Nazism, and of any murderous totalitarianism, often features the vacant eyes and dimwitted expression of bureaucracy. The Nazi extermination plan was carried out efficiently by diligent citizens who did their jobs exceedingly well. Sometimes they were people who simply followed orders, with all the moral apathy required to liquidate millions of people without blinking.

Inspektor Karl Silberbauer, a former Nazi from Austria, kept working into the 1960s in the Viennese police force until Simon Wiesenthal uncovered him as the Gestapo man who had arrested the Franks in Amsterdam in August 1944. A reporter asked him, "What about Anne Frank? Have you read her diary?" The petty bureaucrat answered in a deadly serious tone: "Bought the little book last week to see whether I'm in it. But I am not." When the interviewer asked him about possible feelings of regret now that he had been suspended from his post and an investigation of his past loomed over him, Silberbauer's answer was: "Sure I feel sorry. Sometimes I feel downright humiliated. Now each time I take a streetcar I have to buy a ticket, just like everyone else. I can no longer show my service pass."[104] Dostoyevsky himself could not have written this script better. Here is a masterpiece of the bureaucratic mind, the unthinking official, a resident of that land where the light of wit cannot penetrate, where there is no autonomous observation and no will to commune with the human spirit, where the forgiving laughter of acceptance and inclusion has no oxygen to ignite.

Because of Silberbauer's diligence, the end of Frank's diary is not the happy one its author had so vehemently hoped for. Fate has it that the very last entry in the diary produced a passage of wrenching tragedy whose irony can hardly leave us untouched. As in the best comedic tradition, humor conveys profoundly sad thoughts about the human condition: "I'm what a romantic movie is to a profound thinker—a mere diversion, a comic interlude, something that is soon forgotten: not bad, but not particularly good either" (The Diary of a Young Girl, 336). The closing paragraph of her journal rehearses that funny Jewish family shtick we have come to recognize from decades of sitcoms and Hollywood movies, but with a last sentence that leaves us no choice but to laugh and cry:

> If I'm quiet and serious, everyone thinks I'm putting on a new act and I have to save myself with a joke, and then I'm not even talking about my own family, who assume I must be sick, stuff me with aspirins and sedatives, feel my neck and forehead to see if I have a temperature, ask about my bowel movements and berate me for being in a bad mood, until I . . . get cross, then sad, and finally end up turning my heart inside out, the bad part on the outside and the good part on the inside, and keep trying to find a way to become what I'd like to be and what I could be if . . . if only there were no other people in the world.
>
> Yours, Anne M. Frank (The Diary of a Young Girl, 336)

Anne was teased in the annex for being so obsessed with writing. The others used to jokingly ask her "What do you have so much to write about?,"[105] and she would defend herself with quick but mordant answers, blushing a little. When not laboring over it, she jealously hid her diary in her father's leather briefcase. When the Nazis arrested them and searched the annex for valuables, somone— who knows, perhaps it was Silberbauer himself—opened Otto Frank's old briefcase and shook its contents on the floor, hoping something worth looting would fall out. When the briefcase produced only a bunch of handwritten and typed pages, school notepads, and a girlish journal bound in a reddish orange, checkered fabric, the Nazis left everything on the ground, looked elsewhere, and eventually left the scene. They were there to take lives and trample into oblivion all traces of their existence. Miep and the other Opetka employees had tried to save these eight lives. Failing everything else, they rushed to the hiding place once the SS men had gone to collect the few pieces of their friends' existence left behind and preserve them for when they would come back, or as an indicting record of their not coming back. In her quick-witted wisdom, Anne did not bring the diary with her but left it in the Secret Annex, where she used her creativity, her humor, and her tragedy to craft a literary work that still compels her addressee, Kitty—us—never to look away.

To end this hodgepodge of news, a particularly amusing joke told by Mr. van Daan:

"What goes click ninety-nine times and clack once? A centipede with a clubfoot."

— ANNE FRANK, *The Diary of a Young Girl*

# EPILOGUE
## Remember What Zeus Did to You

*Holocaust Mothers and Daughters* has surveyed only six of the numerous mother-daughter plots originated by the drama of the Holocaust. Before I can end this work, however, I feel compelled to pay tribute to one last woman, a young German painter who created art as a daughter and died in Auschwitz as a mother: Charlotte Salomon. From southern France, where she had emigrated in the hope of escaping her terrible fate, Salomon was deported to Auschwitz in 1943 at the age of twenty-six. She was gassed on arrival because she was five months pregnant. Her condition made her so inconsequential to the Nazis that they neither used her for work nor wasted the ink necessary to tattoo her arm or register her in their records. Yet if her passage through Auschwitz was too irrelevant to be recorded anywhere by the camp's fastidious bureaucracy, her passage through life and the twentieth century is indelibly marked by her work: the first Holocaust graphic autobiography, *Life? or Theatre?*[1]

We owe the most comprehensive and illuminating understanding of Salomon's life and artistic legacy to the outstanding research of Mary Felstiner. In this epilogue, I intend to zoom in on only one aspect of Salomon's work: the importance she attached to her female genealogy, and specifically how she understood her art (and, indeed, her destiny) as deriving from this genealogy. She wrote: "I was my mother my grandmother, yet, I was all the people in my play. I learned to walk all paths and I became myself."[2]

In 1939 her father (Albert Salomon, a respected surgeon) and stepmother (Paula Salomon-Lindberg, a famous opera singer) had thought it best for Charlotte to leave Berlin and find safety in Villefranche-sur-Mer on the Côte d'Azur, where her maternal grandparents had already emigrated as soon as Hitler had come to power. Salomon's life in France was safe for a period, but it was certainly not peaceful. The frightful news about Nazi abuses against the Jews in Germany made her old grandmother extremely anxious, and, desperate with fear and impotence, she took her own life. At this point, deprived of his wife, alone with his granddaughter in a foreign country, and cut off from the rest of the family by the war, her grandfather, Ludwig Grunwald, decides to initiate

Charlotte into the dramatic story of her maternal genealogy: "This is the fifth time I've gone through this," he blurts out, "Your mother tried it with poison, then she threw herself out of the window."[3] Salomon, who had been eight years old at the time and had blocked out all memories of her mother, had always been told that she had died of flu. Together with the traumatic loss of her grandmother and this shocking revelation about her own mother's death, Salomon also discovers that her great-uncle had killed himself; her uncle Schneider had drowned himself in front of Charlotte's grandmother, his own mother; her great-aunt and her husband had taken their own lives; her aunt Lottie (after whom Charlotte was named) drowned herself at the age of eighteen, a tragedy followed by the suicide of her younger sister Franziska (Charlotte's mother); her great-grandmother, after many attempts, had succeeded in taking her life; her second cousin, her grandmother's nephew, had also committed suicide; and finally so had her grandmother. This time, Salomon had witnessed the event.

Was Charlotte to be next in line? Caught between suicide (seemingly destined for her by genetic derangement) and Auschwitz (destined for her by national derangement), what was she to choose? To make reality even more unendurable, Charlotte and her grandfather were deported to the Gurs concentration camp in the Pyrenees in 1940. They were both released after two months, at which point they returned to the Riviera, where Charlotte suffered a severe nervous breakdown. This was attributable both to the historical circumstances and to personal tensions between the two family members. "One year later [in 1941]," writes Salomon about those days (speaking of herself in the third person), "during which the world fell ever more apart, the spirit of this strangely twin-natured creature [Charlotte] was ever more crushed by the proximity of her grandfather, tragically hounded as he was by Fate."[4] Salomon found a way out of this crisis. She left her grandfather, moved to Nice, and plunged herself undividedly into the composition of a graphic autobiography whose genesis is explained by its protagonist in these words: "Despite her utter weakness, however, she [Charlotte] refused to be drawn into the circle of the straw-graspers . . . and remained alone with her experiences and her paint brush . . . And she found herself facing the question of whether to commit suicide or to undertake something wildly eccentric."[5] Often refusing to eat or sleep, Salomon began to work feverishly on her magnum opus and finished it in 1942.

As she writes and illustrates her life story, she is aware of the suicidal streak running through her matrilineal history, and she now places herself within it too. Although the represented self in Life? or Theatre? is blind to this truth, the representing painter drops clues about those suicidal tendencies in her depiction of the protagonist's past. Salomon is also aware of the murderous streak that has pervaded contemporary society and that is about to catch up with her. Between suicide and Auschwitz, then, she chooses painting. Salomon's, like Frank's, is another emblematic case of victims' intellectual resistance to annihilation, and particularly of a woman's artistic act of defiance vis-à-vis impending catastrophe.

Life? or Theatre? both puts to the test and parodies the Wagnerian concept of Gesamtkunstwerk, a total artwork. It is composed of 769 gouaches accompanied by text, is organized like a musical composition, and contains stage directions like a play or operetta; it blends together images, texts, lyrics, and music. Its originality makes this artwork hard to classify[6]—and perhaps this partly explains why it is often overlooked or forgotten. Like Frank, Salomon infused her work with caricatures, irony, and humor. She responded to her frightful historical circumstances by depicting her life, the central people in it, and the historical context—Germany in the interwar period; Berlin's bourgeoisie and its mannerisms; the rise of Nazism and its ideological, social, ethical, and aesthetic barbarism—through a satirical lens. For instance, when the Jews are expelled from all sectors of life by the Nuremberg Laws, Salomon shows the dangerous imbecility of the German antisemites in a gouache that portrays the Jewish musician Kurt Singer (renamed Dr. Singsong) at the Cultural Ministry appealing for the permission to create a Jewish theater. He finds himself in the waiting room with a large crowd of Nazified Germans (whose looks recall those of Jaroslav Hašek's Good Soldier Švejk) who declare "At last one can breathe again—the air is not polluted by Jews," while a Jew is standing right in their midst. The scene continues with Dr. Singsong being admitted to the "Ministah for Propagandah," who likes the maestro's project and thinks to himself, "Yes, this is a good project . . . A pity he's a Jew—must see if I can't make him an honorary Aryan."[7] All the illustrations to this story are set to a mocking tune: "I am the Ministah for Propagandah! I'm busy night and day, no time for rest or play."

In another example of her sly humor, Salomon paints the swastikas in scenes of Nazi rallies and parades rotated 180 degrees, a purposeful inaccuracy that derides Nazism by manipulating its symbol. Her swastikas recall somewhat stylized dragons, and they replace the symbol of Nazism as Germany's rising sun with a symbol that reveals the monster Nazism actually was. "For all its tragic content," Griselda Pollock poignantly remarks, "Charlotte Salomon's Life? or Theater? deploys exactly the kind of deadly irony and perverse flippancy that catches the insanity of the era she was forced to live in and to become its artistic witness."[8] Like Frank, Salomon chooses parodic pseudonyms for her characters while referring to herself in the third person. Her father becomes Dr. Kann and his only daughter, Charlotte Kann; her stepmother, the daughter of a rabbi, becomes Paulinka Bimbam (bim-bam recalls the opening lyrics of a traditional Shabbat tune); her maternal grandparents are renamed Dr. and Mrs. Knarre; Alfred Wolfsohn, Paula's protégé and singing teacher, becomes Amadeus Daberlohn; the famous Berlin composer and conductor Siegfried Ochs appears as Professor Klingklang, and so on. Although the pseudonyms separate the persons from their names, these performers' identities are the opposite of hidden. Perhaps she chooses this humorous masquerade because, as Michael Steinberg has written, this memoir is not about recuperating any one memory but about reframing one's identity and past once the artist has discovered her family's secrets, in ignorance of which she had unknowingly formed a false sense of self. "As a work of recovery, *Life? Or Theater?* is not in any straightforward way a work of recovered memory, or indeed of memory at all," says Steinberg. "On the contrary, it is a massive and thorough regrounding of a life, and thereby a correction of a pattern of memory that was formed by other people's narratives and quite literally by other people's lies . . . It is a work of history as the production of differentiation, and therefore a correction to that aspect of memory which desires immediacy and identification with its objects and object-worlds."[9]

In her reconstruction of the last moments of her grandmother's life—that is, after her first failed suicide attempt—Salomon depicts herself trying to motivate Mrs. Knarre to live, and it is clear that the words addressed to the grandmother, whom the painter knows did not survive, are equally addressed to the living artist, who is struggling to keep herself from committing suicide by writing her book of life. "So I'll make you the following proposition," Charlotte tells her grandmother, "instead of taking your own life in such a horrible way why don't you make use of the same powers to describe your life? I am sure there must be some interesting material that weighs on you, and by writing it down you will liberate yourself and perhaps perform a service to the world."[10] While Charlotte tries to preserve life via her art, the grandfather has a way of insidiously pushing everybody to a breaking point. "You know, Grandpa," she tells him, "I have a feeling the whole world has to be put together again." To which he brusquely responds, "Oh, go ahead and kill yourself and put an end to all this babble!"[11] As in Frank's work, here—whether intended or coincidental it's hard to tell—we find a trace of the Jewish mystical idea of *tikkun olam*, the repairing of the world, in Salomon's feeling that the world ought to be mended. However, for Salomon, the possibility, or necessity, of mending the world occurs not through mitzvoth but through art—or, perhaps, an art turned into a mitzvah.

If art is a necessary and even life-saving force, Salomon's grandfather Ludwig persistently turns a blind eye to it and to his granddaughter's need for art.[12]

However, Ludwig Grunwald, overall portrayed as a negative character, remains a marginal figure, as is Albert, Charlotte's father. Instead, Salomon centers the emotional axis of her life around two important female characters: her grandmother and, most of all, her stepmother Paula Salomon-Lindberg (Paulinka) with whom she developed a strong mother-daughter bond. Salomon-Lindberg was internationally renowned (until the Nazis banned her from performing in public), incredibly well-connected within the high society of her day, and full of charm; she also had a very strong and courageous character. She had been indefatigable in her effort to free her husband from Sachsenhausen, the concentration camp ruled for some time by Rudolf Höss, where Albert had been imprisoned following *Kristallnacht*. Paula had pulled all possible strings and used her fame—"What's the use of my charm if I can't win over anyone I like?"[13]—and eventually won Albert's release. He was forced to walk fifteen miles back home with another prisoner, who did not survive the march.

As she was rediscovering her own place within the story of her matrilineal family, while also framing it within the turpitude of Germany's ideological turn, Salomon found a muse in her substitute mother, to whom she paid an indelible tribute. Paulinka is depicted as strong, decisive, intelligent, and generous. Charlotte clearly loved her dearly. However, we can't but notice that the main and longest section of *Life? or Theatre?* is devoted to the figure of Daberlohn (Alfred Wolfsohn), Paula's protégé. A shell-shocked veteran of World War I and a penniless, brooding musician, Wolfsohn was unlucky and disturbed in equal measure. By hiring Wolfsohn and granting him the essential work papers, Paula had saved his life. Daberlohn is depicted as an adulator of his famous benefactress, as someone who is quite self-centered, with an exalted Christ-like vision of himself and a yearning for other people's admiration, particularly for the worship of young women. Salomon reveals that there had probably been a love affair between Paula and her poor, dejected voice coach. Charlotte found herself "caught between watching them have each other and wanting to have them both."[14] Inevitably, the young Charlotte falls in love with the bohemian artist; he pays attention to her, but his attitude is also ambiguously portrayed as both supportive and mischievously critical of Charlotte's work. Eventually, Daberlohn does seduce the teenage stepdaughter of his benefactor, whose husband was also Daberlohn's patron. However, I believe that the episode of the protagonist's infatuation with the mature man of genius (certainly significant in the life of the teenage girl), an episode depicted years after the affair occurred, is more revealing of a sublimated (and taboo) desire for Paula.[15] Felstiner writes: "Without [Wolfsohn] Lotte Salomon would surely have been a painter, but not of *Life? or Theater?*"[16] And yet the adult artist painting her memory of

Wolfsohn as Daberlohn is paying a tribute to him only in part, as her sarcastic and not entirely positive portrayal of him aligns her with Paula, who did her best to help him but never completely fell under the spell of his tortured charm. Wolfsohn had predicted that Charlotte would soar above mediocrity when he had first seen one of her early works, "Death and the Maiden," from 1937–1938. Salomon's "Death and the Maiden," as Felstiner informs us, owed its origins not to the Schubert Lied of the same title but rather to Charlotte's ecstatic joy at hearing Paula sing it while she syncopated it at the piano for her.[17] That first drawing, like her only complete and final work, *Life? or Theatre?*, sprung from maternal bonds and not from her adolescent infatuation for Wolfsohn. When the struggling artist—with the ego of a Nietzschean Prometheus and the fiber of a schlemiel—enters the scene, he breaks up the harmonious relationship that Paula and Charlotte enjoyed. It is his ambiguous presence that creates tension between the women and turns them into rivals. Therefore, I would argue that the dramatis persona of Daberlohn, apart from enflaming the young girl's desire to emerge as an artist, illuminates the problematic and complex relationship between mother and daughter (or between women) and also illustrates the danger a female artist faces of falling victim to the domination of over-controlling male mentors or self-appointed guardians and other Faustian figures, such as Daberlohn.

Ultimately, whatever the truth may be behind this romantic ménage (possibly à trois),[18] Charlotte links her own appreciation for the arts, and everything she knew about navigating contemporary society as a woman, to Paula, not to her first lover. It is in fact through Paulinka, not Daberlohn, that Charlotte had received her passion for music from a very young age, and music penetrates and inhabits every single visual trait of Salomon's work. Marthe Pécher, the owner of La Belle Aurore, where Salomon was staying while composing her work, reports that while the young artist drew night and day, one could hear her sing and hum incessantly.[19] For the upper middle class to which Salomon belonged, music was far more than a simple form of entertainment: it was the aesthetic language that allowed an expanding civilization to express its utopian dream of transcendence, the dream that worldly ugliness (of which antisemitism was a major component) could be sublimated, and thus overcome, through the salvific beauty of art. This civilization, which seemed to be at its glorious height as Europe ushered in the twentieth century and its promises of prodigious progress, was brought to a halt by the brutality of World War I before descending into total barbarism with the crimes of World War II. In Salomon's life, music was linked to the figure of Paula, a loving mother and mentor, whose affection Charlotte returned with (almost incestuous) passion, devotion, and admiration.

Felstiner notes that "Paula Salomon-Lindberg's voice must have moved Lotte's brush, for most of the work's several dozen melodies flow straight from a German singer's repertoire. A number of scenes are accompanied by Bach's 'Bist Du Bei Mir,' a song Paula recorded before the Nazis ended her career."[20] As Salomon painted her life story in the shadow of the collapse of Western civilization, she was thus listening to this sublime aria whose lyrics, sung by Paula into her ears, declare: "Be thou with me, and I'll go with joy toward death and to my rest."

Inspired by the voice of her stepmother, Salomon paints her life under the shadow of her unknown mother and of several women's suicides, as well as under the threat of a world dominated by violence. She strives to combine, and perhaps reconcile, art (a life force) and her maternal genealogy (a deadly force). Christine Conley writes that Salomon's struggle is to "[imagine] and [represent] a female subject position that could redeem her maternal genealogy without succumbing to its self-destructive legacy." Conley goes on to ask poignantly: "How to love and identify with the mother while averting her fate? How to represent a relation of sameness *and* difference within the economy of the same? This is a dilemma of biographical circumstance that registers most acutely the very terms of woman's alienation within a patriarchal symbolic, the lack of representational support for the daughter's desire for the mother and for her mourning of her loss as a loss of self."[21] Relatedly, the way in which daughters are programmed to rival and distance themselves from their mothers is rooted in the formational myths of matricide—a product of the symbolic order of the father that requires that a daughter (or a son as well) escape (reject, abandon, or kill) the mother. Julia Kristeva seems to accept this scenario unproblematically when she writes: "For man and for woman, the loss of the mother is a biological and psychic necessity, the first step on the way to becoming autonomous. Matricide is our vital necessity, the *sine qua non* condition of our individuation . . . The lesser or greater violence of matricidal drive, depending on individuals and the milieu's tolerance, entails, when it is hindered, its inversion on the self; the maternal object having been introjected, the depressive or melancholic putting to death of the self is what follows, instead of matricide."[22] Again, as we saw with Klüger read through the mirror of Snow White, there is no room for mother and daughter together, only an either/or choice between them. This leaves the daughter helpless; once the mother is lost, the daughter has no recourse against this radical alienation from the self because, unlike her brother, she cannot become the father but only speak and act on his behalf. If, as Freud posited, patricide leads to becoming a subject, where does matricide lead? The loss of the mother can only be incorporated but never introjected—and where introjection ("the work of mourning," in Freudian terms) fails, the process of mourning cannot take place. Mourning the mother would mean to give symbolic expression to our bond with her, and "so long as there is no possibility of giving symbolic expression to the mother-daughter relation, the latter will inevitably remain an area of pathology."[23] Furthermore, as Marcia Ian remarks in her compelling text on the phallic mother, "insofar as human history is the history of men, and insofar as Freud is a man in fear of shrinking, it is no wonder that he obsessively prevents Mother from moving about either the psychological or the cultural landscape with subjectivity and sadness of her own."[24]

Luce Irigaray paved the way for generations of feminist scholars toward a deeper understanding of the implications for our sociocultural situation of the annihilation of the maternal generative power through the fantasy of matricide. The myth that is commonly taken as paradigmatic of the loss of the mother, her exile from culture, and the triumph of the symbolic order is the story of the murder of Clytemnestra as transmitted to us, in its most popular versions, through Aeschylus's *Oresteia* and Euripides's *Electra*. Clytemnestra, wife of Agamemnon, king of Mycenae, bears him four children: Electra, Orestes, Iphigenia, and Chrysothemis. During the war with Troy, Agamemnon is challenged by the goddess Artemis, who promises to deliver him victory against the enemy (by putting favorable winds in the sails of Agamemnon's fleet) if he kills his daughter, Iphigenia—which the king proceeds to do, in an act of blind vanity, pushing his hubris beyond forbidden limits. He returns home victorious (accompanied by his mistress, Cassandra), but when Clytemnestra learns what he has done to her daughter, she murders him. Spurred on by his sister Electra, who hates her mother, Orestes revenges his father by killing the queen.[25] Orestes is tried for his crime in Athens and, thanks to Athena's intercession in his favor, is set free. How could Athena (the motherless goddess) condone so vehemently Orestes's murder of his mother?

The famous story of the cursed House of Atreus has been the subject of innumerable commentaries, revisions, and studies throughout the centuries. Looking with a fresh new eye at its symbolic significance for the child-mother story in Western culture, Amber Jacobs has argued that the Oresteia is but the manifestation of our patriarchal socioculture's deep-seated desire to do away with the mother. However, the latent primal scene that the story of Clytemnestra covers like a screen is, according to Jacobs, really buried in a much older, and conveniently forgotten myth, one that if uncovered would allow us to understand the root of Athena's insensitivity toward Clytemnestra's motives and her exculpation of the matricidal son, Orestes. Jacobs locates the root of our cultural crime against the mother not in the Oresteia but in the much older myth of Metis, the Titaness. The melancholy story of Metis reminds us that Athena was not in fact motherless; on the contrary, she was denied the possibility of introjecting the loss of the mother she once had and thus lost all ties to her maternal genealogy. The myth of Metis, as Jacobs demonstrates, reminds us of what has been forgotten time and again: that the mother has been violently eradicated from our cultural, personal, and collective experience. By tying it to the foundational myth of Metis, Jacobs's interpretation of the Oresteia allows her "to rethink the cultural problem concerning the impossibility of knowing the mother and of the mother knowing herself as a subject with an unconscious, a subject of history, desire, ethics, and genealogy."[26]

Let us briefly rehearse the story. Zeus, father of all fathers, covets Metis, the priestess of wisdom and knowledge who, after trying to escape him by transforming herself into various shapes, succumbs to his violence and is made pregnant.[27] Fearing that Metis might have a son who would one day overthrow him, Zeus cajoles Metis into showing him her famous transformative powers and, as soon as she turns into a fly he swallows her whole. From his belly, Metis, still pregnant, directs Zeus with her knowledge and wisdom. When it's time for Metis to give birth, Zeus's head splits open, and out of it emerges his daughter —his brainchild—perfectly formed, fully armed, and fierce like a warrior: steely Athena, the virgin goddess, loveless and childless. Athena does not know her own origins; the traces of her mother's existence are completely lost. In fact, Metis is never heard of again; her loss is mourned by no one. Zeus has thus triumphantly replaced our connection to that lost generative navel with his narrative of paternal parthenogenesis. Yet every time we look at a representation of Athena, we unknowingly stare at a trace of that lost mother's presence. Athena's armor had been crafted by Metis; it was the mother's gift to her, including the famous shield that bears the effigy of the Medusa. Jacobs writes:

> Metis, the pregnant, swallowed mother who is not lost or mourned vanishes to the invisible inside. Her incorporation means that there will be no gap, no void into which a stream of symbolic products can flow, to stand in for and master her absence. Instead, this incorporated mother becomes irreplaceable: no substitute is possible. In this way, she will constitute the resistance to representation, to interpretation, to theory—eradicated from memory and history—the mute grounding from which the paternal metaphor with its sole claim on meaning takes off in all its (defensive) grandiosity.[28]

Jacobs attempts to unearth a generative matricide that could counter the dominant narrative of the Oedipal myth and castration anxiety. She calls for a "new set of unconscious laws" that "will necessarily create a different organization of culture. . . . [and the resulting unconscious structure] can lead to the possibility of the representation and symbolization of heterogeneous diverse structuring of the mother-daughter relation(s)."[29] It is thanks to Jacobs's groundbreaking work that I now possess a structure and a language to understand the implicit act of rebellion that the art by the daughters presented in this book embodies and signifies. It is precisely through the staging of the mother-daughter plot (one that is traditionally caged in the binaries of fusion/rejection, love/hate) that these daughters witness not only "what Amalek did to them" (as proposed in the introduction) but also "what Zeus did to them." They bring attention to two parallel yet profoundly interconnected threads: the story of the Holocaust (Jewish) and the story of the unmourned loss of the mother (universal). In other words, they bring attention to the removal of the mother (the absence of a mother's law, the unlegislated matricidal prohibition) in the patriarchal historical and socio-symbolic systems.

By acknowledging their matricidal drive in the retelling of their paths to adulthood, Bruck, Klüger, Kofman, Roth, Janeczek, and Frank implicitly acknowledge the absence of the mother in the cultural discourse to which they belong, a mother they are not equipped to represent other than in the process of "killing" her. The mother that the daughter is "programmed" to hate and separate herself from is a simulacrum, the external projection of a voiceless core, concealed in the belly of the speaking Father. These women's personal narratives struggle to distinguish from among the utterances of the Father what can be traced to the maternal wisdom and knowledge of Metis. Therefore, these daughters' creative acts attempt the impossible (or, rather, the forbidden): to introject the mother in order to mourn her—and mourning is the healthy response to loss, in psychology. Their creations also contribute to the rebellious attempt to deliver her out of Zeus's belly, from which there is no escape other than through the mediation of the Father (culture).

Remembering or surviving the Shoah becomes secondary to remembering or surviving the mother in the generative space of these women's texts. Through remembering the vital navel imprisoned in the belly of the deadly violator, through focusing on the maternal connection, these artists—despite the pressures of male-dominated cultural discourse—set their origins in the generative soil of female genealogy rather than in the degenerate paternity of the Holocaust. Only in reconnecting with their mothers can they grasp the implications of what was done to them, personally and communally; hold onto roots that were brutally severed; and bear witness to what defies the act of witnessing itself—the Shoah.

If God the Father orders the Jews to remember what Amalek did to them, the concealed Mother compels the daughters to remember what Zeus has done to them as well. Thus, the daughters presented here resisted becoming part of patriarchy's symbolic concealments and affirmed themselves and their mothers as battling, complex, morphing characters (like Metis, who changes her shape in order to save herself) who strategized their own survival and safeguarded their own creations despite the overwhelming forces (of history or society, community or family) that worked to erase them. As I hope to have demonstrated, these women were able to do so through art, through their relationship to psychically charged objects, or simply through humor.

Salomon's operetta ends with these words: "And with dream-awakened eyes she saw all the beauty around her, saw the sea, felt the sun, and knew: she had to vanish for a while from the human plane and make every sacrifice in order to create her world anew out of the depths."[30] And the closing canvas reads: "And from that came: Life or Theatre?"[31]

Not long before she was murdered in Auschwitz, Salomon discovered hidden truths about her mother and embarked on an artistic journey to let not only her voice but the voices of Paulinka and her grandmother emerge "out of the depths" too. In the space of her art, she succeeded in creating the world anew: a new world in which the story of her mother's death is no longer a shameful secret and will not be ignored or forgotten; a world in which the strength of her second mother, Paula, is also honored; and a world in which the loss of her grandmother (no longer explained in terms of matrilineal or female derangement, but of national, ideological, or masculine derangement)[32] can be mourned properly.

Charlotte did not kill herself. But she did kill her grandfather, by serving him a veranol omelette. As Ludwig Grunwald lay in bed, slipping deeper and deeper into death, Charlotte painted the likeness of this man she had once referred to as an "actor," because of the falsehood and hypocrisy that played such a big role in his life and family; as she thus witnessed his passing, Charlotte heard a voice in her head say, "The theater is dead."[33] Charlotte Salomon therefore is not only the artist who creates as a daughter and dies in Auschwitz as a mother, but she is also the only woman, certainly unique among the many we have encountered in this study, who defeats the symbolic Father by the literal killing of the grandfather—the patriarchal figure that haunts her, clips her wings, endangers her life and art with his obsessive, incestuous, tyrannical demands.

Like the other works explored in this book, *Life? or Theatre?* is a book of mothers; they are all present at once, all saved from oblivion, and all saviors of or inspirations for their daughters' art and sense of self. This is especially true of Salomon's biological mother—whose story, having been rewritten, had been made to disappear. Symbolically, Salomon's work represents the most emblematic attempt to make the vanished mother reappear, and with her the artist herself. The last image of Salomon's masterpiece is a self-portrait of the artist sitting on the beach, facing the sea with her back to the viewer, her expression concealed from us, holding a sketch pad of which only the outline is visible. The words "Leben oder Theater" are painted along the shoulders and back of the subject, whose body is thus turned into a human billboard. The surface of the sketch pad is transparent, and therefore the plane of the seawater and that of the invisible page coincide, blending into one. Water, the symbol of the universal mother[34]—archetypal of the creative potential of the subconscious—is a pervasive presence, especially in the first and last section of Salomon's three-part graphic autobiography. In this last image, the work of art (the sketch pad) and the mother (symbolically represented by the seascape that the artist is capturing) organically penetrate each other: the work of art is the mother as much as it reveals the mother. However, the concealed mother is also present as an infinite unknown, and because the viewer's gaze and the painted subject's gaze are aligned along the same trajectory, Salomon forces us to stare with her into the immensity of this perturbing secret: our mothers.

# NOTES

## INTRODUCTION : REMEMBER WHAT AMALEK DID TO YOU

1. David G. Roskies, *Against the Apocalypse: Responses to Catastrophe in Modern Jewish Culture* (Syracuse, NY: Syracuse University Press, 1999), 10.

2. The law says: "The firstborn whom she [the widow] bears shall be established in the name of his dead brother, that his name be not wiped out from Israel" (Deuteronomy 25:6–7).

3. Judith Tydor Baumel, *Double Jeopardy: Gender and the Holocaust* (London: Vallentine Mitchell, 1998), ix.

4. Ibid., xiii.

5. Rochelle G. Saidel, *The Jewish Women of Ravensbrück Concentration Camp* (Madison: University of Wisconsin Press, 2004), 3. See also 109–20.

6. Ringelheim, Joan. "The Split between Gender and the Holocaust," in *Women in the Holocaust*, ed. Dalia Ofer and Lenore J. Weitzman (New Haven: Yale University Press, 1998), 344. See also 340–41.

7. Carol Rittner and John K. Roth, *Different Voices: Women and the Holocaust* (St. Paul, MN: Paragon, 1993); Vera Laska, ed., *Women in the Resistance and in the Holocaust: The Voices of Eyewitnesses* (Westport, CT: Greenwood, 1983); Marion A. Kaplan, *Between Dignity and Despair: Jewish Life in Nazi Germany* (New York: Oxford University Press, 1998); Nechama Tec, *Resilience and Courage: Women, Men, and the Holocaust* (New Haven: Yale University Press, 2003); Elizabeth R. Baer and Myrna Goldenberg, *Experience and Expression: Women, the Nazis, and the Holocaust* (Detroit: Wayne State University Press, 2003); Sara R. Horowitz, "Women in Holocaust Literature: Engendering Trauma Memory," in *Women in the Holocaust*, ed. Dalia Ofer and Lenore J. Weitzman (New Haven: Yale University Press, 1998), 364–77; Phyllis Lassner, *Anglo-Jewish Women Writing the Holocaust: Displaced Witnesses* (New York: Palgrave Macmillan, 2008); Anna Reading, *The Social Inheritance of the Holocaust: Gender, Culture, and Memory* (New York: Palgrave Macmillan, 2002).

8. Lenore J. Weitzman and Dalia Ofer, "Introduction: The Role of Gender in the Holocaust," in *Women in the Holocaust*, ed. Dalia Ofer and Lenore J. Weitzman (New Haven: Yale University Press, 1998), 14.

9. S. Lillian Kremer, *Women's Holocaust Writing: Memory and Imagination* (Lincoln: University of Nebraska Press, 2001), 14.

10. Primo Levi's *Se questo è un uomo* was first published in 1947 by De Silva. In 1959 it was translated and distributed in English as *Survival in Auschwitz*, a title completely different from the original Italian. Only in 1986 was the book published in English with the title *If This Is a Man*, which more exactly reflects the Italian title.

11. Natalia Ginzburg, *Lessico famigliare* (Turin, Italy: Einaudi, 1963), translated as *Family Sayings* in 1967.

12. Zoë Vania Waxman, *Writing the Holocaust: Identity, Testimony, Representation* (New York: Oxford University Press, 2006), 120.

13. This connection between the intimate lingo of family's daily life and identity is evident in the original Italian title, *Lessico famigliare*, which means both "a family's language" and "familiar language" or lingo.

14. Alexandra Garbarini, *Numbered Days: Diaries and the Holocaust* (New Haven: Yale University Press, 2006), xii.

15. For more on the Oyneg Shabes archive, see Samuel D. Kassow, *Who Will Write Our History? Emanuel Ringelblum, the Warsaw Ghetto, and the Oyneg Shabes Archive* (Bloomington: Indiana University Press, 2007); Robert Moses Shapiro and Tadeusz Epsztein, eds., *The Warsaw Ghetto Oyneg Shabes—Ringelblum Archive: Catalog and Guide* (Bloomington: Indiana University Press, 2009).

16. Emanuel Ringelblum, *Kronika Getta Warszawskiego* (Warsaw: Czytelnik, 1983), 394 (my translation).

17. Hélène Berr, *Journal 1942–1944* (Paris: Éditions Tallandier, 2008).

18. Ibid., 106 (my translation).

19. Hélène Berr, surviving witnesses tell us, was beaten to death on her bunk in a barrack in Bergen-Belsen one morning because she was too weak to move and get up for work. This happened five days before the British soldiers entered the camp and liberated it. I must thank Theodore Rosengarten for providing me with the details about the last moments of Berr's life.

20. Kassow, *Who Will Write Our History?*, 15.

21. See Samuel D. Kassow, introduction to *The Warsaw Ghetto Oyneg Shabes—Ringelblum Archive: Catalog and Guide*, ed. Robert Moses Shapiro and Tadeusz Epstein, trans. Robert Moses Shapiro (Bloomington: Indiana University Press, 2009; xv–xxiv).

22. Kassow, *Who Will Write Our History?*, 14.

23. In his powerful study of Ringelblum's life, work, and personality, Kassow notes that by the summer of 1942 the indefatigable chronicler's disjointed and fragmentary writing style of his daily journal entries "betray[s] Ringelblum's anxiety and confusion as the world around him disintegrated, and as his comrades and friends disappeared, one by one, into the boxcars. The notes were also a reminder that he was human" (ibid., 334). Kassow traces various points throughout the letters, diary entries, and other writings by Ringelblum that signal his "inner turmoil and grief" and his growing dissatisfaction and pessimism, justified by the gravely worsening situation. But, Kassow points out, "ultimately [Ringelblum] rose above his feelings and continued to fulfill his mission" (347).

24. Paula E. Hyman, "Gender and the Immigrant Jewish Experience in the United States," in *Jewish Women in Historical Perspective*, ed. Judith Reesa Baskin (Detroit: Wayne State University Press, 1998), 312.

25. Marlene Heinemann, *Gender and Destiny: Women Writers and the Holocaust* (New York: Greenwood, 1986), 2–3. In the specific case of Jewish women, when we talk about the selective transmission of memory, as Sarah Silberstein Swartz and Margie Wolfe write, "what has been neglected may be as critical as what has been passed down" (*From Memory to Transformation: Jewish Women's Voices* [Toronto: Second Story, 1998], 9).

26. Lawrence L. Langer, ed., *Art from the Ashes: A Holocaust Anthology* (Oxford: Oxford University Press, 1995).

27. Caroline Eliacheff and Nathalie Heinich, *Mères-filles: une relation à trois* (Paris: Albin Michel, 2002), 385 (my translation).

28. Joyce Antler, *You Never Call! You Never Write! A History of the Jewish Mother* (Oxford: Oxford University Press, 2007); Sylvia Barak Fishman, *Follow My Footprints: Changing Images of Women in American Jewish Fiction* (Hanover, NH: Brandeis University Press, 1992); Donna Bassin, Margaret Honey, and Meryle Mahrer Kaplan, eds., *Representations of Motherhood* (New Haven: Yale University Press, 1994); Janet Handler Burstein, *Writing Mothers, Writing Daughters: Tracing the Maternal in Stories of American Jewish Women* (Urbana: University of Illinois Press, 1996); Adalgisa Giorgio, *Writing Mothers and Daughters* (New York: Berghahn, 2002); Marianne Hirsch, *The Mother/Daughter Plot: Narrative, Psychoanalysis, Feminism* (Bloomington: Indiana University Press, 1989).

29. Mary Lowenthal Felstiner, *To Paint Her Life: Charlotte Salomon in the Nazi Era* (Berkeley: University of California Press, 1997), 208.

30. Quoted in Kremer, *Women's Holocaust Writing*, 14.

31. Elie Wiesel, *Night*, trans. Marion Wiesel (New York: Farrar, Straus and Giroux, 2006), 8, 11.

32. Ibid., 29.

33. Horowitz, "Women in Holocaust Literature," 367 (emphasis added). In October 2011, Spiegelman released the volume *Meta Maus*, which included a CD-ROM that devotes a section to recovering memories of Anja through the recollections of women who had known her—women interviewed by Speigelman.

34. Anne Karpf, *The War After* (London: Minerva, 1997), 249.

35. The way we can make sense of this attitude is that, unconsciously, through the one-dimensional depiction of a world in which evil—and thus good, too—is absolutely recognizable, in which "figures are ferocity incarnate or unselfish benevolence" (Bruno Bettelheim, *The Uses of Enchantment* [New York: Vintage, 1989], 74), the canonical Shoah writer strives to bring the reader (the nonwitness or judge) to a more direct understanding of the writer's actions and reactions at the time. See Giorgio Agamben, *Il linguaggio e la morte* (Turin, Italy: Einaudi, 2008) and *Quel che resta di Auschwitz* (Turin, Italy: Bollati Boringhieri, 1998); Hannah Arendt, *Essays in Understanding, 1930–1954*, ed. Jerome Kohn (New York: Harcourt, Brace, 1994); Bruno Bettelheim, *The Informed Heart* (New York: Avon, 1971).

36. Tellingly, the film does include a couple of unlikable Jews—profiteers, black marketeers and corruptible *kapos*—one of whom showcases the physiognomy of the ugly and dangerous Jew typical of antisemitic propaganda (a lanky man who moves nervously, with kinky hair, a hooked nose, a giant upper lip, and shifty eyes). But these types do not end up on the list of "Schindler's Jews"—the ones who are saved—nor do we witness their fate. They are not good Jews, so presumably they are not saved.

37. Ruth Klüger, *Still Alive: A Holocaust Girlhood Remembered* (New York: Feminist, 2003), 90.

38. The primary texts of the first five chapters in *Holocaust Mothers and Daughters* are autobiographical works and war memoirs. The sixth chapter, on Anne Frank, deals with the diaristic genre—although Frank's work could also be categorized as an autobiographical epistolary. When discussing, as I do in this introduction, the relevance of women's literary contributions, I use the terms "autobiography," "memoirs," "journals," and "art" quite broadly. In doing so, I aim to highlight the importance of the broader range of women's cultural production, particularly in the field of life memory.

39. Amber Jacobs, *On Matricide: Myth, Psychoanalysis, and the Law of the Mother* (New York: Columbia University Press, 2007), 24.

40. Ibid., 25.

41. Sue Vice, *Children Writing the Holocaust* (New York: Palgrave Macmillan, 2004), 2.

42. Aliki Barnstone and Willis Barnstone, eds., *A Book of Women Poets from Antiquity to Now* (New York: Schocken, 1992)

43. Adalgisa Giorgio, "Dall'autobiografia al romanzo. La rappresentazione della *Shoah* nell'opera di Edith Bruck," in *Le Donne delle minoranze*, ed. Claire E. Honess and Verina R. Jones (Turin, Italy: Claudiana, 1999), 297–307, and "Strategies for Remembering: Auschwitz, Mother and Writing in Edith Bruck," in *European Memories of the Second World War*, ed. Helmut Peitsch, Charles Burdett, and Claire Gorrara (New York: Berghahn, 1999), 247–55.

44. Edith Bruck, *Lettera alla madre* (Milan: Garzanti, 1988), *Lettera da Francoforte* (Milan: Mondadori, 2004), and *Signora Auschwitz: Il dono della parola* (Venice: Marsilio, 1999).

45. Irene Kacandes, *Talk Fiction: Literature and the Talk Explosion* (Lincoln: University of Nebraska Press, 2001), 146, 147.

46. Ruth Klüger, *weiter leben: Eine Jugend* (Göttingen, Germany: Wallstein Verlag, 1992), and *Still Alive: A Holocaust Girlhood Remembered* (New York: Feminist, 2003).

47. Michael Rothberg, *Traumatic Realism: The Demands of Holocaust Representation* (Minneapolis: University of Minnesota Press, 2000).

48. Pascale R. Bos, *German-Jewish Literature in the Wake of the Holocaust: Grete Weil, Ruth Klüger, and the Politics of Address* (New York: Palgrave Macmillan, 2005), 4.

49. Jerry Schuchalter, *Poetry and Truth: Variations on Holocaust Testimony* (Bern, Switzerland: Peter Lang AG International Academic, 2009).

50. Klüger, *Still Alive*, 206.

51. Ibid.

52. Ibid., 210.

53. Caroline Schaumann, "From 'weiter leben' (1992) to 'Still Alive' (2001): Ruth Klüger's Cultural Translation of Her 'German Book' for an American Audience," *German Quarterly* 77, no. 3 (2004): 328.

54. Ibid., 325.

55. Schuchalter, *Poetry and Truth*, 76.

56. Schaumann, "From 'weiter leben' (1992) to 'Still Alive' (2001)," 326. This softness of voice is even more remarkable in Klüger's latest autobiographical text, *unterwegs verloren: Erinnerungen* (Vienna: Paul Zsolnay Verlag, 2008).

57. Sarah Kofman, *Rue Ordener, rue Labat* (Paris: Galilée, 1994).

58. Kathryn Robson, *Writing Wounds: The Inscription of Trauma in Post-1968 French Women's Life-Writing* (New York: Rodopi, 2004), 135.

59. Alice A. Jardine, "Sarah Kofman," in *Shifting Scenes: Interviews on Women, Writing, and Politics in Post-68 France*, ed. Alice A. Jardine and Anne M. Menke, trans. Janice Orion (New York: Columbia University Press, 1991), 104–12.

60. Kelly Oliver, "Sarah Kofman's Queasy Stomach and the Riddle of the Paternal Law," in *Enigmas: Essays on Sarah Kofman*, ed. Penelope Deutscher and Kelly Oliver (Ithaca: Cornell University Press, 1999), 174–88; Tina Chanter, "Playing with Fire: Kofman and Freud on Being Feminine, Jewish, and Homosexual," in *Sarah Kofman's Corpus*, ed. Tina Chanter and Pleshette DeArmitt (Albany: State University of New York Press, 2008), 91–121, and "Eating Words: Antigone as Kofman's Proper Name," in *Enigmas: Essays on Sarah Kofman*, ed. Penelope Deutscher and Kelly Oliver (Ithaca: Cornell University Press, 1999), 189–204; Jean-Luc Nancy, "Cours, Sarah!" in *Les Cahiers du Grif No. 3: Sarah Kofman*, ed. Françoise Collin and Françoise Proust (Paris: Éditions Descartes, 1997), 29–37.

61. Sarah Kofman, *Selected Writings*, ed. Thomas Albrecht, Georgia Albert, and Elizabeth G. Rottenberg (Stanford: Stanford University Press, 2007).

62. Milena Roth, *Lifesaving Letters: A Child's Flight from the Holocaust* (Seattle: University of Washington Press, 2004).

63. Lore Segal, *Other People's Houses* (London: Victor Gollancz, 1965).

64. Tony Kushner, "Remembering to Forget: Racism and Anti-Racism in Postwar Britain," in *Modernity, Culture and "The Jew,"* ed. Bryan Cheyette and Laura Marcus (Stanford: Stanford University Press, 1998), 226–41, "Beyond the Pale? British Reactions to Nazi Anti-Semitism, 1933–39," in *The Politics of Marginality: Race, the Radical Right and Minorities in Twentieth Century Britain*, ed. Tony Kushner and Kenneth Lunn (London: Frank Cass, 1990), 143–60; Tony Kushner and Ken Lunn, eds., *Traditions of Intolerance: Historical Perspectives on Fascism and Race Discourse in British Society* (Manchester, UK: Manchester University Press, 1989); Bryan Cheyette, *Constructions of "The Jew" in English Literature and Society: Racial Representations, 1875–1945* (Cambridge: Cambridge University Press, 1993), "Moroseness and Englishness: The Rise of British-Jewish Literature," *Jewish Quarterly* 42, no. 1 (1995), 22–26; David Cesarani, "Joynson-Hicks and the Radical Right in England after the First World War," in *Traditions of Intolerance*, 118–39; Phyllis Lassner and Lara Trubowitz, eds., *Anti-Semitism and Philosemitism in the Twentieth and Twenty-First Centuries: Representing Jews, Jewishness, and Modern Culture* (Newark: University of Delaware Press, 2008); Richard Bolchover, *British Jewry and the Holocaust* (Cambridge: Cambridge University Press, 1993).

65. Pierre Nora, "Between Memory and History: Les Lieux de Mémoire," trans. Marc Roudebush, *Representations* 26 (Spring 1989): 7–24, and "General Introduction: Between Memory and History," in *Realms of Memory: Rethinking the French Past*, under the direction of Pierre Nora, English-language edition edited and with a foreword by Lawrence D. Kritzman, translated by Arthur Goldhammer (New York: Columbia University Press, 1996), 1:1–20.

66. Reading, *The Social Inheritance of the Holocaust*.

67. Roth, *Lifesaving Letters*, 115.

68. Wolfgang Benz, Claudia Curio, Andrea Hammel, and Toby Axelrod, eds., *Shofar* 23, no. 1 (2004); Lassner, *Anglo-Jewish Women Writing the Holocaust*, 19–102; Iris Guske, *Trauma and Attachment in the Kindertransport Context: German-Jewish Child Refugees' Accounts of Displacement and Acculturation in Britain* (Newcastle upon Tyne, UK: Cambridge Scholars, 2009); Vera K. Fast, *Children's Exodus: A History of the Kindertransport* (London: I. B. Tauris, 2011); Ann Byers, *Saving Children from the Holocaust: The Kindertransport* (Berkeley Heights, NJ: Enslow, 2012).

69. Helena Janeczek, *Lezioni di tenebra* (Milan: Mondadori, 1997).

70. Marianne Hirsch, *The Generation of Postmemory: Writing and Visual Culture after the Holocaust* (New York: Columbia University Press, 2012), 5. Furthermore, feminist approaches to memory and postmemory bring to the fore the fact that, as Hirsch and Nancy K. Miller emphasize, these "legacies of the past, transmitted powerfully from parent to child within the family, are always already inflected by broader public and generational stories, images, artifacts, and understandings that together shape identity and identification" (introduction to *Rites of Return: Diaspora Poetics and the Politics of Memory*, ed. Marianne Hirsch and Nancy K. Miller [New York: Columbia University Press, 2011], 4).

71. See, for example, Dina Wardi, *Memorial Candles: Children of the Holocaust*, trans. Naomi Goldblum (London: Routledge, 1992).

72. Alan L. Berger, *Children of Job: American Second-Generation Witnesses to the Holocaust* (Albany: State University Press of New York, 1997). The expression comes to literary studies from psycho-

analysis. In my work, I use the term "second generation" to signify exclusively the generation of the survivors' children.

73. See, for example, Erin McGlothlin, *Second-Generation Holocaust Literature: Legacies of Survival and Perpetration* (Rochester, NY: Camden House, 2006). Starting in Germany in the 1970s, a new term, *Väterliteratur* (fathers' literature) has come to label the vast category of novels that question the German national past—the past of the fathers—and, more specifically, the autobiographical texts of perpetrators' children that deal with their identity crises. On *Väterliteratur*, see Anne Fuchs, Mary Cosgrove, and Georg Grote, eds., *German Memory Contests: The Quest for Identity in Literature, Film, and Discourse since 1990* (Rochester, NY: Camden House, 2006); Laurel Cohen-Pfister and Susanne Vees-Gulani, eds., *Generational Shifts in Contemporary German Culture* (Rochester, NY: Camden House, 2010).

74. See, for example, Efraim Sicher, *The Holocaust Novel* (New York: Routledge, 2005); Dan Bar-On, *Legacy of Silence: Encounters with Children of the Third Reich* (Cambridge: Harvard University Press, 1989), *Fear and Hope: Three Generations of Holocaust Survivors' Families* (Cambridge: Harvard University Press, 1995), and *The Indescribable and the Undiscussable: Reconstructing Human Discourse after Trauma* (Budapest: Central European University Press, 1999); Helen Epstein, *Children of the Holocaust: Conversations with Sons and Daughters of Survivors* (New York: Putnam, 1979); Geoffrey Hartman, *The Longest Shadow: In the Aftermath of the Holocaust* (Bloomington: Indiana University Press, 1996).

75. Anne Frank, *The Diary of a Young Girl* (New York: Anchor, 1996) and *Tales from the Secret Annex*, trans. Susan Massotty (New York: Bantam, 2003).

76. Rachel Feldhay Brenner, *Writing as Resistance: Four Women Confronting the Holocaust: Edith Stein, Simone Weil, Anne Frank, Etty Hillesum* (University Park: Pennsylvania State University Press, 1997); Denise De Costa, *Anne Frank and Etty Hillesum: Inscribing Spirituality and Sexuality* (New Brunswick, NJ: Rutgers University Press, 1998).

77. Katherine Dalsimer, *Female Adolescence: Psychoanalytic Reflections on Literature* (New Haven: Yale University Press, 1986).

78. Aristotle, *On Rhetoric: A Theory of Civic Discourse*, trans. George A. Kennedy, 2nd ed. (New York: Oxford University Press, 2007), 151.

79. Sigmund Freud, "On Narcissism: An Introduction," in *The Standard Edition of the Complete Psychological Works of Sigmund Freud*, ed. and trans. James Strachey (London: Hogarth, 1973), 14:67–102; "Humour," in ibid., 21:159–66.

80. In particular, I am referring to the essay "Cultural Resistance to Genocide" (in Lawrence L. Langer, *Admitting the Holocaust: Collected Essays* [Oxford: Oxford University Press, 1995]), where Langer raises important questions about the legitimacy of using a term such as "resistance" to qualify the artistic works produced by Jews during the Holocaust: artifacts that, at the end of the day, did not injure the enemy (an enemy "scornful of the very idea of Jewish culture") and did not "save Jewish lives" (52).

81. Gill Plain, *Women's Fiction of the Second World War: Gender, Power, Resistance* (Edinburgh: Edinburgh University Press, 1996), 22.

82. I am aware that I am using the terms "patriarchy" and "women" as if they were self-evident, undivided categories, thereby disregarding the antihumanist, postmodern challenges that feminists have rightly raised against the use of a terminology that reproduces the same colonizing dynamics it tries to break. For my present analysis, rooted as it is in literary criticism, I find that, as long as we remain aware of this shortcut's pitfalls and imprecisions, it can in

this introduction lead me more directly to a discussion of what will be later treated in a more nuanced way that takes into account different locations from which these subjectivities express themselves—Jewish, poor, bourgeois, young, old, Ashkenazi, orthodox, secular, and so forth.

83. Klüger, *Still Alive*, 56.

84. Kaplan, *Between Dignity and Despair*, 8.

85. Baumel, *Double Jeopardy*, 7. Kaplan suggests that, generally, women were more likely to lobby for a departure long before their husbands concluded that that would be the best course of action; however, Kaplan postulates that ultimately "*decisions* regarding emigration seem to have been made by husbands. Despite important role reversals, both men and women generally held fast to traditional gender roles in responding to the political situation—unless they were overwhelmed by events" (*Between Dignity and Despair*, 67).

86. Quoted in Ernst Schnabel, *Anne Frank: A Portrait in Courage*, trans. Richard Winston and Clara Winston (New York: Harcourt, Brace, 1958), 30.

87. Baumel, *Double Jeopardy*, 9.

88. Klüger, *Still Alive*, 29.

89. In fact, one of the tools at the disposal of antisemitic discourse is that of "feminizing" Jewish men: the hysterical, unheroic coward is a staple of anti-Jewish propaganda. When in 1942 news of Hitler's plan for the Final Solution reached the free world, through Eduard Schulte (a German anti-Nazi industrialist) and Gerhart Riegner (a representative of the World Jewish Congress in Geneva), it was at first perceived as an expression of Jewish fear and panic (Richard Breitman and Alan M. Kraut, *American Refugee Policy and European Jewry, 1933–1945* [Bloomington: Indiana University Press, 1988], 149).

90. Charlotte Salomon, *Life? or Theatre?*, trans. Leila Vennewitz (Zwolle, Holland: Waanders, 1998), 677, 678–79.

91. Ibid., 733.

92. Ibid., 746.

93. Quoted in Jardine, "Sarah Kofman," 107.

94. Ibid., note 5 (by Kofman).

95. In a telephone conversation in May 2010, Jean-Luc Nancy shared with me disheartening anecdotes regarding Kofman's anger and sense of humiliation at feeling unappreciated by her colleagues.

96. See for example, Ruth Klüger, *unterwegs verloren*.

97. I had the opportunity to ask Bruck about *Lettera alla madre* and its relation to the real-life events the author experienced in her youth. Bruck confirmed that this novel is profoundly autobiographical, like most of her writings, and she said: "I write about the things I know and saw with my own eyes." Adalgisa Giorgio incisively wrote in this regard: "The power of Edith Bruck's writing comes from her ability to recognize the narrative potential in some of the circumstances of her own life and of life in general and to utilize them in order to represent the conditions of the [Holocaust] survivors in today's world" ("Dall'autobiografia al romanzo," 300).

98. Klüger, *Still Alive*, 30.

99. Ibid., 185.

100. Ibid., 162.

101. Sheila Meintjes, Meredeth Turshen, and Anu Pillay, *The Aftermath: Women in Post-Conflict Transformation* (London: Zed, 2001), 100.

102. Plain, *Women's Fiction of the Second World War*, 28–29.

103. Klüger, *Still Alive*, 179.

104. I purposely forgo a discussion of those who took the side of heinous criminality and choose to focus exclusively on the victims and those who stood against the wave of violence.

105. Baumel, *Double Jeopardy*, 15.

106. Gerda Lerner, *The Creation of Patriarchy* (Oxford: Oxford University Press, 1986), 80.

107. The fact that Anne had been able to develop such a strong sense of self was undoubtedly the result of Otto and Edith Frank's modern child-rearing methods and progressive mentality, of which Anne speaks in her journal and that has been confirmed by many people who knew the family well.

108. Frank, *The Diary of a Young Girl*, 116.

109. Ibid., 319.

110. Frank, *Tales from the Secret Annex*, 20.

111. Klüger, *Still Alive*, 210, 31.

112. Roth, *Lifesaving Letters*, 120 (emphasis added).

113. Suzette Henke, *Shattered Subjects: Trauma and Testimony in Women's Life-Writing* (New York: St. Martin's, 2000), xvi.

114. Ibid., xii.

115. Garbarini, *Numbered Days*, 131–32.

116. Roskies, *Against the Apocalypse*, 10.

117. Bella Brodzki, "Mothers, Displacement, and Language," in *Women, Autobiography, Theory: A Reader*, ed. Sidonie Smith and Julia Watson (Madison: University of Wisconsin Press, 1998), 156.

118. Kofman, *Rue Ordener, rue Labat*, 9, my translation.

119. Frank, *The Diary of a Young Girl*, 145.

120. Ibid., 147.

121. Amos Funkenstein, *Perceptions of Jewish History* (Berkeley: University of California Press, 1993), 6, 7.

122. Carmel Finnan, "Autobiography, Memory and the Shoah: German-Jewish Identity in Autobiographical Writings by Ruth Klüger, Cordelia Edvardson and Laura Waco," in *German Monitor: Jews in German Literature since 1945—German-Jewish Literature?*, ed. Pol O'Dochartaigh (Amsterdam: Editions Rodopi B.V., 2000), 448.

123. David N. Myers, preface to *Jewish History and Jewish Memory: Essays in Honor of Yosef Hayim Yerushalmi*, ed. Elisheva Carlebach, John M. Efron, and David N. Myers (Hanover, NH: University Press of New England, 1998), xiii.

124. Rothberg, *Traumatic Realism*, 133.

## 1. EDITH BRUCK'S DEAD LETTERS

1. Samuel Taylor Coleridge, "The Rime of the Ancient Mariner," in *English Romantic Verse*, ed. David Wright (London: Penguin, 1986), 155.

2. Primo Levi, *Il Sistema periodico*, in *Opere*, ed. Cesare Cases (Turin, Italy: Einaudi, 1987), 1:570. All translations from the Italian texts in this chapter are my own.

3. Edith Bruck, *Signora Auschwitz: Il dono della parola* (Venice: Marsilio, 1999), 14.

4. Edith Bruck, *Chi ti ama così* (Venice: Marsilio, 1997), 25.

5. Edith Bruck, *Lettera alla madre* (Milan: Garzanti, 1988), 8. In an interview I conducted with Bruck in the summer of 2007, I asked her about the discrepancy between the two *Selektion*

scenes, and she explained that the facts occurred as she told them in Chi ti ama così. However, after a brief pause, she looked at me and added, "But the other is true too."

6. Manuela Consonni, "The Written Memoir: Italy 1945–1947," in The Jews Are Coming Back: The Return of the Jews to Their Countries of Origin after WWII, ed. David Bankier (Jerusalem: Yad Vashem and Berghahn, 2005), 173.

7. As Consonni reveals in her research, many camps memoirs were written by Italian Jewish women survivors, and this may further explain these texts' invisibility. In the specific context of Italian postwar political discourses of group and party ideology, there was no room left for woman's subjectivity—let alone Jewish woman's subjectivity. Marxist theory unambiguously casts a negative light on women's autobiographies and fictions (Carol Lazzaro-Weis, From Margins to Mainstream: Feminism and Fictional Modes in Italian Women's Writing, 1968–1990 [Philadelphia: University of Pennsylvania Press, 1993], 94–116), while a combination of the totalizing patriarchal logic and party politics (dominated by Marxist orthodoxy) in postwar Italy precluded the possibility of including Jewish identity, gender concerns, and other peripheral accents in the public discourse. As Thomas Nolden correctly points out, "the initial wave of politicization in the late 1960s and the 1970s [in Italy, France, and West Germany] left little space for the exploration of ethnic, religious, regional, and cultural differences. After all, Marxism insisted that any affiliation other than solidarity with the working class was tantamount to false consciousness, a remnant of bourgeois ideology" (introduction to Voices of the Diaspora: Jewish Women Writing in Contemporary Europe, ed. Thomas Nolden and Frances Malino [Evanston, IL: Northwestern University Press, 2005], xvi–xvii).

8. Bruck writes of her novel Il silenzio degli amanti: "While I was writing it I knew all too well that I was delivering a bastard child, which would probably be rejected by the readers who were going to push me back inside my tattooed skin; but I tried nevertheless and I will do so again" (Signora Auschwitz, 17).

9. Adalgisa Giorgio, "Dall'autobiografia al romanzo. La rappresentazione della Shoah nell'opera di Edith Bruck," in Le donne delle minoranze, ed. Claire E. Honess and Verina R. Jones (Turin, Italy: Claudiana, 1999), 300. My translation.

10. Edith Bruck, Lettera alla madre, Lettera da Francoforte (Milan: Mondadori, 2004), and Signora Auschwitz.

11. Jonathan Culler, The Pursuit of Signs: Semiotics, Literature, Deconstruction (Ithaca: Cornell University Press, 1981), 139.

12. Paul de Man, The Rhetoric of Romanticism (New York: Columbia University Press, 1984), 69.

13. Ibid., 97, 75.

14. Ibid., 75–76.

15. For an analysis of de Man's manipulations of Wordsworth's text, see Don H. Bialostosky, Wordsworth, Dialogics, and the Practice of Criticism (Cambridge: Cambridge University Press, 1992), 152–99.

16. William Wordsworth, The Prose Works of William Wordsworth, ed. Alexander B. Grosart (London: Edward Moxon, 1876), 2:41.

17. Bruck, Lettera alla madre (hereafter Lettera in the text), 59, 62.

18. Bruck, Chi ti ama così, 8.

19. Bruck, Signora Auschwitz, 36.

20. Giorgio, "Dall'autobiografia al romanzo," 300.

21. Bruck, Chi ti ama così, 21.

22. Adalgisa Giorgio, "Strategies for Remembering: Auschwitz, Mother and Writing in Edith Bruck," in *European Memories of the Second World War*, ed. Helmut Peitsch, Charles Burdett, and Claire Gorrara (New York: Berghahn, 1999), 252.

23. Bruck, *Chi ti ama così*, 23.

24. Bruck, *Lettera da Francoforte*, 93.

25. Edith Bruck, *Itinerario/Útirány* (Rome: Quasar, 1998), 49.

26. Bruck, *Signora Auschwitz*, 18.

27. Ibid., 26–27.

28. Bruck, *Itinerario/Útirány*, 67.

29. Julia Kristeva, *Black Sun: Depression and Melancholia*, trans. Leon S. Roudiez (New York: Columbia University Press, 1989), 3.

30. Bruck, *Signora Auschwitz*, 16.

31. Barbara Johnson, "Apostrophe, Animation, and Abortion," *Diacritics* 16, no. 1 (1986): 36.

32. Ibid., 32.

33. Jacques Derrida, *The Post Card: From Socrates to Freud and Beyond*, trans. Alan Bass (Chicago: University of Chicago Press, 1987), 104.

34. "Envois" is positioned as a mere preamble to three main essays on psychoanalysis, "To Speculate: On Freud," "Le facteur de la vérité," and "Du tout"—but, by overturning the hierarchy of the book, Derrida makes "Envois" the longest section of *The Post Card* and lets the sketchy messages "posted" in the opening part of the book be the true pre-face, the leading commentary of everything that follows.

35. Derrida describes the event at the Bodleian Library in Oxford this way: "Yesterday, then, Jonathan [Culler] and Cynthia [Chase, who later became Culler's wife] guide [sic] me through the city. I like them, he is working on a poetics of the apostrophe . . . They themselves knew the *carte* . . . They had already seen it, and could easily foresee the impression it would make on me" (*The Post Card*, 15).

36. Peggy Kamuf, ed., *A Derrida Reader: Between the Blinds* (New York: Columbia University Press, 1991), 485.

37. Derrida, *The Post Card*, 143–44.

38. Ibid., 52.

39. Ibid., 12.

40. Ibid.

41. Ibid., 15.

42. Ibid.

43. Ibid., 29.

44. Bruck writes: "When I used to tell you that I would not have the life you had, you would once again stop answering or saying hello to me when I came back from school . . . you wouldn't talk to me. You didn't notice me, you looked past me, like Mengele the Selector" (*Lettera*, 36).

45. Giorgio Agamben, *Quel che resta di Auschwitz* (Turin, Italy: Bollati Boringhieri, 1998), 48–49.

46. Martin Buber, *I and Thou*, trans. Ronald Gregor Smith (New York: Scribner Classics, 2000), 19.

47. Ibid., 24.

48. Ibid., 20.

49. Ibid., 25.

50. Ibid.

51. Martin Buber, *Israel and the World: Essays in a Time of Crisis*, trans. Olga Marx and Greta Hort (Syracuse, NY: Syracuse University Press, 1997), 94.

52. Culler, *The Pursuit of Signs*, 150.

53. Bruck, *Itinerario/Útirány*, 19.

54. Ibid., 20.

55. Ibid., 31.

56. Ibid., 47.

57. Ibid., 25.

58. Kai Erikson, "Notes on Trauma and Community," in *Trauma: Explorations in Memory*, ed. Cathy Caruth (Baltimore: Johns Hopkins University Press, 1995), 183.

59. W. H. Auden, *Collected Poems*, ed. Edward Mendelson (New York: Vintage, 1991), 248.

60. Buber, *I and Thou*, 30.

61. Paul de Man, "Shelley Disfigured," in *Deconstruction and Criticism*, ed. Harold Bloom (New York: Continuum, 1979), 39–73, and "Autobiography as De-Facement," *MLN* 94, no. 5 (1979): 919–30. "Autobiography," de Man famously writes, "is not a genre or a mode, but a figure of reading or of understanding that occurs, to some degree, in all texts" (*The Rhetoric of Romanticism*, 70).

62. De Man, *The Rhetoric of Romanticism*, 75–76.

63. Ibid., 76.

64. Susan Gubar, "Prosopopoeia and Holocaust Poetry in English: Sylvia Plath and Her Contemporaries," *Yale Journal of Criticism* 14, no. 1 (2001): 191–215. In her article, Gubar rehabilitates Plath, who had been severely attacked for her 1962 poems "Daddy" and "Lady Lazarus," which compared the suffering of womanhood with that of Holocaust victims.

65. Ibid., 192.

66. Ibid.

67. Ibid., 196–97.

68. De Man, *The Rhetoric of Romanticism*, 78.

69. Kaja Silverman, *The Threshold of the Visible World* (New York: Routledge, 1996).

70. Although cinema and photography are media central to the stimulation of this kind of ethical encounter, I believe that the mental envisioning produced by literature is just as powerful and allows for the same strong cosentiment that Silverman hypothesizes as heteropathic identification.

71. De Man, *The Rhetoric of Romanticism*, 74.

72. Kristeva, *Black Sun*, 42.

73. Ibid., 13.

74. Giorgio, "Strategies for Remembering," 253.

75. Ibid.

76. Kristeva, *Black Sun*, 200.

77. Ibid., 4.

78. De Man, *The Rhetoric of Romanticism*, 3.

79. Ibid., 6.

80. Kristeva, *Black Sun*, 33.

81. De Man, *The Rhetoric of Romanticism*, 7.

82. Ibid., 78.

83. Culler, *The Pursuit of Signs*, 135.

84. Derrida, *The Post Card*, 112.

85. De Man, *The Rhetoric of Romanticism*, 77.

86. Johnson, "Apostrophe, Animation, and Abortion," 30.

87. Irene Kacandes, *Talk Fiction: Literature and the Talk Explosion* (Lincoln: University of Nebraska Press, 2001), 147.

88. Ibid., 146.

89. Ibid., 144, 145.

90. Ibid., 154.

91. Quintilian, *The Institutio Oratoria of Quintilian*, trans. H. E. Butler (London: William Heinemann, 1921–36), 3:397.

92. Ruth Klüger, *Still Alive: A Holocaust Girlhood Remembered* (New York: Feminist, 2003), 30.

93. Quoted in Teddi Chichester Bonca, *Shelley's Mirrors of Love: Narcissism, Sacrifice, and Sorority* (Albany: State University of New York Press, 1999), 92.

94. Kristeva, *Black Sun*, 14.

95. Ibid., 41, 43.

96. Ibid., 43–44.

97. Franz Kafka, *Letter to His Father. Brief an den Vater*, trans. Ernst Kaiser and Eithne Wilkins (New York: Schocken, 1966), 53.

98. Ibid., 7.

99. A fuller version is: "If you had listened to me to the end only once, maybe I wouldn't be writing to you now, maybe I wouldn't have written any of my books; I owe this literary desease of mine to you, and to Auschwitz" (*Lettera*, 78).

100. Kamuf, ed., *A Derrida Reader*, 485.

101. Franz Kafka, "An Imperial Message," in *Kafka: Selected Stories*, trans. Ian Johnston (West Valley City, UT: Waking Lion, 2008), 96.

102. Ibid.

103. Ibid.

104. Charlotte Delbo, *Auschwitz and After*, trans. Rosette C. Lamont (New Haven: Yale University Press, 1995), 4.

105. Kafka, "An Imperial Message," 96.

## 2. *LUPUS IN FABULA* : THE END OF THE FAIRY TALE IN RUTH KLÜGER'S MOTHER-DAUGHTER SHOAH PLOT

1. Etty Hillesum, *An Interrupted Life and Letters from Westerbork*, trans. Arnold J. Pomerans (New York: Henry Holt, 1996), 305.

2. Ibid.

3. I am using the term "fairy tale" in the broad and most common sense of the word, without distinguishing among the numerous and complex genres of myth, legend or folklore, classical fables, and so forth.

4. Jack Zipes, *When Dreams Come True: Classical Fairy Tales and Their Tradition* (New York: Routledge, 1999), 34.

5. Walter Benjamin, *Illuminations: Essays and Reflections*, ed. Hannah Arendt, trans. Harry Zohn (New York: Schocken, 1968), 87.

6. Elie Wiesel, *Night* (New York: Farrar, Straus and Giroux, 2006), 8, 10.

7. Ibid., 12.

8. Ibid., 24.

9. Dan Miron, *The Image of the Shtetl and Other Studies of Modern Jewish Literary Imagination* (Syracuse, NY: Syracuse University Press, 2000),

10. Cristina Bacchilega, *Postmodern Fairy Tales: Gender and Narrative Strategies* (Philadelphia: University of Pennsylvania Press, 1997), 28.

11. Vladimir Propp, *Morphology of the Folktale*, ed. Louis A. Wagner, trans. Laurence Scott (Austin: University of Texas Press, 1968).

12. Northrop Frye, *Fables of Identity: Studies in Poetic Mythology* (New York: Harcourt, Brace, and World, 1963), 31.

13. Ruth Klüger, *Still Alive: A Holocaust Girlhood Remembered* (New York: Feminist, 2001). On the genealogy of this text and my rationale for working with the English rather than the German version of Klüger's life story, see the introduction.

14. Bruno Bettelheim, *The Uses of Enchantment* (New York: Vintage, 1989), 214.

15. Sidonie Smith, *A Poetics of Women's Autobiography: Marginality and the Fictions of Self-Representation* (Bloomington: Indiana University Press, 1987), 26.

16. Bella Brodzki and Celeste Schenck, introduction to *Life/Lines: Theorizing Women's Autobiography*, ed. Bella Brodzki and Celeste Schenck (Ithaca: Cornell University Press, 1988), 1.

17. I am indebted to Alexandra Garbarini for this particular formulation of this concept.

18. The story of Snow White has numerous incarnations in many languages and cultures all over Europe, and not all of them have the queen interrogate a talking mirror. My references to Snow White in this chapter refer to the Grimm brothers' version of the story.

19. Sandra M. Gilbert and Susan Gubar, *The Madwoman in the Attic: The Woman Writer and the Nineteenth-Century Literary Imagination* (New Haven: Yale University Press, 1979), 36.

20. Bacchilega, *Postmodern Fairly Tales*, 9.

21. Ibid., 22.

22. Klüger, *Still Alive*, 40 (hereafter *Still Alive* in the text).

23. Jack Zipes, *Fairy Tales and the Art of Subversion: The Classical Genre for Children and the Process of Civilization* (New York: Methuen, 1988), 134.

24. Bruno Bettelheim, *Freud's Vienna and Other Essays* (New York: Alfred A. Knopf, 1990), 132.

25. Milena Roth, *Lifesaving Letters: A Child's Flight from the Holocaust* (Seattle: University of Washington Press, 2004), 102.

26. Gordon's Hebrew poem "Awake, My People!" (1866) contains the line "Be a man in your going out and a Jew in your tents," which—loosely translated as "be a man in the streets and a Jew at home"—became a famous Haskalah motto, embraced by scores of Jews all over Europe (quoted in Michael Stanislawski, *For Whom Do I Toil? Judah Leib Gordon and the Crisis of Russian Jewry* [New York: Oxford University Press, 1988], 50).

27. Interestingly, for the first seven years of her life, Klüger had been called Susi, short for Susanna—although Ruth was her first Hebrew name. At the time, the girl did not know that Susanna (Shoshanna in Hebrew) was also a Jewish name, and therefore she made a point of demanding that everybody start calling her only Ruth in honor of a Jewish identity she embraced in response to the fact that the Nazis were set on separating her from her countrymen based on that identity: "Now that my tentative faith in my homeland was being damaged by daily increments beyond repair, I became Jewish in defense. Shortly before I turned seven years old . . . I changed my first name. I had been called Susi, a middle name, but now I wanted the other name, my first name, the Biblical name . . . I tenaciously corrected the grown-ups when they used

my old name, and miraculously they gave in . . . I got my proper name not even knowing then how right it was for me, that it means 'friend' and belonged to the woman who left her country because friendship meant more to her than kinship" (*Still Alive*, 42).

28. After the *Anschluss*, Jews were not allowed to practice their professions. Viktor kept working secretly and was denounced and arrested for practicing illegal abortions.

29. Lenore J. Weitzman and Dalia Ofer, "Introduction: The Role of Gender in the Holocaust," in *Women in the Holocaust*, ed. Dalia Ofer and Lenore J. Weitzman (New Haven: Yale University Press, 1998), 5.

30. Marion A. Kaplan, *Between Dignity and Despair: Jewish Life in Nazi Germany* (New York: Oxford University Press, 1998), 140.

31. Bettelheim, *Freud's Vienna and Other Essays*, 12–13.

32. Even before watching the Disney film, the Viennese girl certainly knew the original story, in its German version by the Grimm brothers. For a discussion of the Disney-fication of folk stories, see Kay F. Stone, "Fairy Tales for Adults: Walt Disney's Americanization of the Märchen," in *Folklore on Two Continents: Essays in Honor of Linda Dégh*, ed. Nikolai Burlakoff and Carl Lindahl (Bloomington, IN: Trickster, 1980), 40–48.

33. Bettelheim, *The Uses of Enchantment*, 40.

34. Melissa Hacker, director, *My Knees Were Jumping: Remembering the Kindertransports* (New York: New Video Group, 2003), DVD. The documentary was made in 1995 and released in DVD format eight years later.

35. Mercea Eliade, *Myth and Reality* (New York: Harper and Row, 1963). Also see Mircea Eliade, *The Two and the One* (Chicago: University of Chicago Press, 1965) and *Cosmos and History: The Myth of the Eternal Return* (Princeton: Princeton University Press, 1954).

36. Geoffrey Hartman, *The Longest Shadow: In the Aftermath of the Holocaust* (Bloomington: Indiana University Press, 1996), 130.

37. J. R. R. Tolkien, *Tree and Leaf* (Boston: Houghton Mifflin, 1965); Bettelheim, *The Uses of Enchantment*).

38. G. K. Chesterton, *Brave New Family: G. K. Chesterton on Men and Women, Children, Sex, Divorce, Marriage and the Family*, ed. Alvaro de Silva (San Francisco: Ignatius, 1990), 80.

39. Caroline Eliacheff and Nathalie Heinich, *Mères-filles: une relation à trois* (Paris: Albin Michel, 2002), 102. All translations from this work are my own.

40. Bettelheim, *The Uses of Enchantment*, 205.

41. Nancy K. Miller, *But Enough about Me: Why We Read Other People's Lives* (New York: Columbia University Press, 2002), 2–3.

42. In the previous chapter we saw how Edith Bruck's mother harshly disparaged her daughter's attempts at poetry. Sarah Kofman's mother (see chapter 3) forbade her to use electricity at night to read or write. We will also see (in chapter 5) that Helena Janeczek's identity, behavior, and choices constantly met with maternal disapproval. Anne Frank's parents seem to be an exception; however, although they were supportive of the creative inclinations of their youngest daughter, the people in hiding with them disapproved of the girl's activity because they thought a girl should devote more of her time to domestic chores.

43. Sophie Freud, *Living in the Shadow of the Freud Family* (London: Praeger, 2007), 8.

44. Eliacheff and Heinich, *Mères-filles*, 203–26.

45. Heinz Kohut, *The Analysis of the Self: A Systematic Approach to the Psychoanalytic Treatment of Narcissistic Personality Disorders* (New York: International Universities Press, 1971).

46. Jerrold M. Post, "Current Concepts of the Narcissistic Personality: Implications for Political Psychology," *Political Psychology* 14, no. 1 (1993): 107.

47. Melanie Kaye/Kantrowitz, "The Issue Is Power: Some Notes on Jewish Women and Therapy," in *Jewish Women in Therapy: Seen but Not Heard*, ed. Rachel Josefowitz Siegel and Ellen Cole (Binghamton, NY: Haworth, 1991), 13.

48. Quoted in Viktor E. Frankl, *Man's Search for Meaning: An Introduction to Logotherapy*, part 1, trans. Ilse Lasch, 3rd ed. (New York: Simon and Schuster, 1984), 38.

49. Ibid. (emphasis added).

50. One significant memory, however, concerns their arrival in Auschwitz: "The same evening . . . my mother explained to me that the electric barbed wire outside was lethal and proposed that she and I should get up and walk into that wire . . . I was twelve years old, and the thought of dying, now, without delay, in contortions, by running into electrically charged metal on the advice of my very own mother, whom God had created to protect me, was simply beyond my comprehension. The idea of it! . . . My mother accepted my refusal nonchalantly, as if she had merely offered me a walk in the country in peacetime" (Klüger, *Still Alive*, 96–97).

51. Lewis C. Seifert, *Fairy Tales, Sexuality, and Gender in France: 1690–1715* (Cambridge: Cambridge University Press, 1996), 156.

52. Ibid., 159.

53. Bettelheim explains that "a weak father"—that is, a father like those of Snow White and of Hansel and Gretel, is of no use to his children. Yet these types of fathers appear frequently in fairy tales, suggesting "that wife-dominated husbands are not exactly new to this world. More to the point, it is such fathers [weak fathers] who either create unmanageable difficulties in the child or else fail to help him solve them" (*The Uses of Enchantment*, 206). The only way for the child to successfully integrate Oedipal conflicts, according to Bettelheim, is through a balanced combination of maternal care and paternal protection (strength). Bettelheim postulates: "If a girl cannot form a positive identification with her mother, not only does she get stuck in oedipal conflicts, but regression sets in, as it always does when the child fails to attain the next higher stage of development for which she is chronologically ready" (ibid.). However, it was the Nazis, not her own or her parents' inadequacies or failings, that had endangered this developmental stage for Klüger.

54. Bruno Bettelheim, *Surviving and Other Essays* (New York: Vintage, 1980), 246–57.

55. Sander L. Gilman, *Jewish Self-Hatred: Anti-Semitism and the Hidden Language of the Jews* (Baltimore: Johns Hopkins University Press, 1986), 350–51.

56. Ibid., 351.

57. Bruno Bettelheim, "Fathers Shouldn't Try to Be Mothers," *Parents' Magazine*, October 1956, 40.

58. Ibid., 127.

59. Ibid., 129.

60. On Bettelheim's emigration and his attitude toward Judaism and European Jews, see Richard Pollak, *The Creation of Dr. B: A Biography of Bruno Bettelheim* (New York: Simon and Schuster, 1998).

61. Pascale R. Bos, *German-Jewish Literature in the Wake of the Holocaust: Grete Weil, Ruth Klüger, and the Politics of Address* (New York: Palgrave Macmillan, 2005), 86.

62. Bettelheim, *The Uses of Enchantment*, 103.

63. Art Spiegelman, *Maus: A Survivor's Tale* (New York: Pantheon, 1996), 175.

64. Bettelheim, *The Uses of Enchantment*, 105.

65. Bacchilega, *Postmodern Fairy Tales*, 28.

66. Judith Butler, *Gender Trouble: Feminism and the Subversion of Identity* (New York: Routledge, 1999), 187.

67. Bettelheim, *The Uses of Enchantment*, 114.

68. Ibid.

69. Ibid., 115.

70. I am talking about friendship among peers. Usually, if a heroine is helped by a female figure the helper is either older, has magical powers, or is not human—in sum, the helper belongs to a different hierarchy than the heroine.

71. Bacchilega, *Postmodern Fairy Tales*, 35.

72. Butler, *Gender Trouble*, 187–88.

73. Jacques Lacan, *Écrits I* (Paris: Editions du Seuil, 1999), 92–99.

74. Bos, *German-Jewish Literature in the Wake of the Holocaust*, 85.

75. Hélène Cixous, *La jeune née* (Paris: Union Générale d'Edition, 1975), 158–59.

76. Michael Rothberg, *Traumatic Realism: The Demands of Holocaust Representation* (Minneapolis: University of Minnesota Press, 2000), 133.

77. Bacchilega, *Postmodern Fairy Tales*, 23.

78. Ibid., 24.

79. Bettelheim, *The Uses of Enchantment*, 207.

80. Jack Zipes, trans. and ed., *The Complete Fairy Tales of the Brothers Grimm* (New York: Bantam, 1987), 196–204.

81. Gilbert and Gubar, *Madwoman in the Attic*, 40.

82. Bettelheim, *The Uses of Enchantment*, 202. Clearly, Bettelheim's analysis takes for granted that the audience for the tale of Snow White is exclusively female.

83. Bacchilega, *Postmodern Fairy Tales*, 7.

84. This is what Bacchilega rightly recognizes as being the workings of a folk tale, which thus are able to generate magic, or wonder (ibid.).

85. Bos, *German-Jewish Literature in the Wake of the Holocaust*, 80.

86. Klüger writes: "The story of Snow White can be reduced to one question: who is entitled to live in the king's palace and who is the outsider" (*Still Alive*, 47).

87. Luce Irigaray, "And the One Doesn't Stir without the Other," trans. Helene Vivienne Wenzel, *Signs* 7 (1981): 66.

88. Klüger says: "Ich komm' nicht von Auschwitz her, ich stamm' aus Wien" (quoted in Renata Schmidtkunz, *Im Gespräch: Ruth Klüger* [Vienna: Mandelbaum Verlag, 2008]), 5.

### 3. AUTO DA FÉ : SARAH KOFMAN'S TOTEMIC MEMOIR

1. Sarah Kofman, *Rue Ordener, rue Labat* (Paris: Galilée, 1994), 9.

2. Sarah Kofman, *Selected Writings*, ed. Thomas Albrecht, Georgia Albert, and Elizabeth G. Rottenberg (Stanford: Stanford University Press, 2007); *Paroles suffoquées* (Paris: Galilée, 1987); *Smothered Words*, translated with an introduction by Madeleine Dobie (Evanston, IL: Northwestern University Press, 1998); *Autobiogriffures. Du chat Murr d'Hoffmann* (Paris: Galilée, 1984); *Explosion I: De l'"Ecce Homo" de Nietzsche* (Paris: Galilée, 1992).

3. Jacques Derrida, "Sarah Kofman (1934–94): . . . . . . . ," in *The Work of Mourning*, ed. and trans. Pascale-Anne Brault and Michael Naas (Chicago: University of Chicago Press, 2003), 173.

4. Kofman, *Autobiogriffures*, 98.

5. Sarah Kofman, *Pourquoi rit-on? Freud et le mot d'esprit* (Paris: Galilée, 1986), 17.

6. Sarah Kofman, *L'Enfance de l'art: Une interprétation de l'esthétique freudienne* (Paris: Payot, 1970), 35.

7. Sarah Kofman, *La Mélancolie de l'Art* (Paris: Galilée, 1985), 32.

8. Friederich Nietzsche, *On the Genealogy of Morals and Ecce Homo*, ed. and trans. Walter Kaufmann and R. J. Hollingdale (New York: Random House, 1967), 62–63.

9. Jacques Derrida, *The Ear of the Other: Otobiography, Transference, Translation: Texts and Discussions with Jacques Derrida*, ed. Christie V. McDonald, trans. Peggy Kamuf (New York: Schocken, 1985), 5.

10. Kofman, *Rue Ordener, rue Labat*, 9 (hereafter RO/RL in the text). All translations from this work and other French editions of Kofman's writings are my own.

11. After the war, Sarah's mother had taken Mémé to court, accusing her of improper behavior toward the child. The French court not only dismissed the Jewish mother's claim but assigned custody of the girl to Mémé—thanks to the girl's testimony against her own mother.

12. Sarah Kofman, "'Ma vie' et la psychanalyse," in *Les Cahiers du Grif No. 3: Sarah Kofman*, ed. Françoise Collin and Françoise Proust (Paris: Éditions Descartes, 1997), 171. This was translated into English as "'My Life' and Psychoanalysis" and published in Kofman, *Selected Writings*, 250–51.

13. Alice A. Jardine, "Sarah Kofman," in *Shifting Scenes: Interviews on Women, Writing, and Politics in Post-68 France*, ed. Alice A. Jardine and Anne M. Menke, trans. Janice Orion (New York: Columbia University Press, 1991), 105.

14. Kofman, *Paroles suffoquées*, 16, 43.

15. Michael Stanislawski, *Autobiographical Jews: Essays in Jewish Self-Fashioning* (Seattle: University of Washington Press, 2004), 157.

16. Ibid. To this list I would add the use of "Simhatorah" instead of Simchat or Simhat Torah.

17. Sarah Kofman, "Sacrée nourriture," in *Les Cahiers du Grif No. 3: Sarah Kofman*, ed. Françoise Collin and Françoise Proust (Paris: Éditions Descartes, 1997), 167–68.

18. Kofman, *Selected Writings*, 247–48.

19. Stanislawski, *Autobiographical Jews*, 141.

20. Kofman, "Sacrée nourriture," 167.

21. Ibid.

22. Ibid.

23. Kelly Oliver, "Sarah Kofman's Queasy Stomach and the Riddle of the Paternal Law," in *Enigmas: Essays on Sarah Kofman*, ed. Penelope Deutscher and Kelly Oliver (Ithaca: Cornell University Press, 1999), 188.

24. Tina Chanter, "Eating Words: Antigone as Kofman's Proper Name," in *Enigmas*, 189–204.

25. Oliver, "Sarah Kofman's Queasy Stomach and the Riddle of the Paternal Law," 182.

26. Kofman, "Sacrée nourriture," 168.

27. Ibid.

28. Ibid.

29. Ibid.

30. Stanislawski, *Autobiographical Jews*, 159. He also points out: "Only later in the autobiography will Kofman reveal to us, if in a highly muted way, that her own hysterical vomiting was indeed coupled first with thumb-sucking and then with homosexual attraction to her surrogate Christian mothers" (ibid.).

31. Jacques Lacan, Écrits, The First Complete Edition in English, trans. Bruce Fink (New York: W. W. Norton, 2006), 552.

32. Leone is also the root of the name Leonardo—the great artist with whom Freud had deeply identified and whose proverbial "smile" Kofman dissected in L'Enfance de l'art and uncovered as the ultimate expression of motherhood, a smile that is pure fiction and disquiets us so profoundly because "it never existed" (109). On Kofman's interpretations of the Leonardian smile, see Federica K. Clementi, "Nightbirds, Nightmares and the Mothers' Smile: Art and Psychoanalysis in Sarah Kofman's Life-Writing," Women in French Studies 19 (2011): 67–84.

33. Kofman, "'Ma vie' et la psychanalyse," 171.

34. Ibid., 171–72.

35. Franz Kafka, Die Verwandlung, ed. Heribert Kuhn (Frankfurt: Suhrkamp, 1999).

36. Kofman, "'Ma vie' et la psychanalyse," 172.

37. Ibid.

38. Sarah Kofman, Conversions: Le Marchand de Venise—Sous le signe de Saturne (Paris: Galilée, 1987), 68.

39. Ibid., 69.

40. Ibid., 42.

41. Ibid., 47.

42. Clementi, "Nightbirds, Nightmares and the Mothers' Smile."

43. Quoted in Jerzy Ficowski, introduction, trans. Michael Kandel, to Bruno Schultz, The Street of Crocodiles, trans. Celina Wieniewska (New York: Penguin, 1977), 19–20.

44. Slavoj Žižek, Looking Awry: An Introduction to Jacques Lacan through Popular Culture (Cambridge: MIT Press, 1992), 79.

45. Sarah Kofman, L'Imposture de la beauté (Paris: Galilée, 1995), 142.

46. Ibid.

47. Ibid., 143.

48. Ibid., 144.

49. Žižek, Looking Awry, 82.

50. Lacan worked all his career at refining his concept of jouissance—a term that in French has a sexual connotation and is linked to the idea of orgasm, and that Lacan recasts as a climax of emotions and excitement so strong as to be almost intolerable to the subject that experiences it. Lacan defined jouissance not in sexual terms but in relation to the speaking subject and the gap that opens between the tellable and untellable, which always produces lack, failure, and loss. Jouissance occurs in this space beyond language and is therefore always bonded to pain, absence, or death, and its place is language (see, in particular, Écrits, The First Complete Edition in English, 671–702). In the 1970s, Lacan applied the term to the realm of the Other (Woman) and developed the influential concept for subsequent feminist theorists of feminine jouissance (Encore: Séminaire, livre XX, ed. Jacques-Alain Miller [Paris: Éditions du Seuil, 1975]). Jouissance is Lacan's elaboration on what Freud had already located in the pull between the opposite drives of sex (life) and death: Lacan hypothesizes that jouissance is harmful to the subject because the attainment of satisfaction also entails its opposite—acute suffering—which annuls the effects that pleasure produces.

51. Sarah Kofman, "La mort blanche," Fusées, no. 16 (2009): 7.

52. Paul Celan, Selected Poems and Prose of Paul Celan, trans. John Felstiner (New York: W. W. Norton, 2001), 31.

53. Tina Chanter, "Playing with Fire, " in *Sarah Kofman's Corpus*, ed. Tina Chanter and Pleshette DeArmitt (Albany: State University of New York Press, 2008), 95.

54. Sarah Kofman, "Tombeau pour un nom propre," in *Les Cahiers du Grif No. 3: Sarah Kofman*, ed. Françoise Collin and Françoise Proust (Paris: Éditions Descartes, 1997) 169–70.

55. Ibid.

56. Ibid., 170.

57. "Cauchemar" appears in Sarah Kofman, *Comment s'en sortir?* (Paris: Galilée, 1983). It was published in English as "Nightmare: At the Margins of Medieval Studies" in Kofman, *Selected Writings*.

58. Jacques Lacan, *Le moi dans la théorie de Freud et dans la technique de la psychanalyse: Séminaire, livre II*, ed. Jacques-Alain Miller (Paris: Editions du Seuil, 1978), 196.

59. Sigmund Freud, *An Outline of Psychoanalysis*, ed. and trans. James Strachey (New York: W. W. Norton, 1989), 24.

60. Sigmund Freud, *The Interpretation of Dreams*, vol. 4 of *The Standard Edition of the Complete Psychological Works of Sigmund Freud*, ed. and trans. James Strachey (London: Hogarth, 1973), 107.

61. Lacan, *Le moi dans la théorie de Freud*, 196.

62. See Shoshana Felman, *What Does a Woman Want? Reading and Sexual Difference* (Baltimore: Johns Hopkins University Press, 1993), 68–120; Marilyn Migiel, "Faltering on Demand: Readings of Freud's Dream of Irma," *Diacritics* 20, no. 2 (1990): 20–39; Madelon Sprengnether, "Mouth to Mouth: Freud, Irma, and the Dream of Psychoanalysis," *American Imago* 60, no. 3 (2003): 259–84.

63. Chanter, "Playing with Fire," 92.

64. Kofman, *Conversions*, 28.

65. Ibid., 26.

66. Ibid., 41.

67. Sarah Kofman, *L'Énigme de la femme: la femme dans les textes de Freud* (Paris: Galilée, 1983), 194.

68. Kofman, *Pourquoi rit-on?*, 42.

69. Marcia Ian, *Remembering the Phallic Mother: Psychoanalysis, Modernism, and the Fetish* (Ithaca: Cornell University Press, 1993), 13.

70. Kofman, *Autobiogriffures*, 83.

71. Ibid., 18.

72. Ibid., 139–40.

73. Ibid., 130.

74. Ibid., 60–61.

75. Ibid., 131.

76. Ibid., 152.

77. Ibid., 131.

78. Ibid., 143.

79. Sigmund Freud, *Letters of Sigmund Freud*, ed. Ernst L. Freud, trans. Tania and James Stern (New York: Dover, 1992), 391. In another letter, this time to Arnold Zweig (May 31, 1936), Freud elaborates on the issue of biographical writing: "Anyone turning biographer commits himself to lies . . . for biographical truth is not to be had . . . Truth is unobtainable" (ibid., 430).

80. Kofman, *Autobiogriffures*, 146.

81. Ibid., 147.

82. Oliver, "Sarah Kofman's Queasy Stomach and the Riddle of the Paternal Law," 176.

83. Ibid., 177.

84. Stanislawski, *Autobiographical Jews*, 161.

85. Oliver, "Sarah Kofman's Queasy Stomach and the Riddle of the Paternal Law," 183.

## 4. MATERIAL MOTHERS : MILENA ROTH AND THE KINDERTRANSPORT'S LEGACY, *OBJETS DE MÉMOIRE*

1. *Kindertransporte* (*Kinder* means children in German) was the word used by the German rail authorities to diligently record the transportation of these children (Vera K. Fast, *Children's Exodus: A History of the Kindertransport* [London: I. B. Tauris, 2011], 21). The term "Kindertransport" quickly entered the English language and is still the universal signifier for this complex chapter in twentieth-century Jewish history. I am greatly indebted to the US Holocaust Memorial Museum, in Washington, D.C., for having made available to me the remaining footage of the children's evacuation operation.

2. Milena Roth westernized her family name, getting rid of the Slavic female suffix "ová" at the end of a woman's surname.

3. Milena Roth, *Lifesaving Letters: A Child's Flight from the Holocaust* (Seattle: University of Washington Press, 2004).

4. Another important text that features the heartbreaking correspondence between parents trapped in wartime Germany and a child safe in England is Anne L. Fox, *Between the Lines: Letters from the Holocaust* (Margate, NJ: ComteQ, 2005).

5. Jürgen Matthäus and Mark Roseman, *Jewish Responses to Persecution* (Lanham, MD: Alta-Mira, 2010), 286.

6. As Giles MacDonogh remarks, in 1938 Hitler "was probably simply hoping to get as much as he could without fighting the great powers" (*1938: Hitler's Gamble* [New York: Basic, 2009], x). Hitler might have made up his mind by then about his "solution" to the Jewish question, MacDonogh observes, but he had not shared his plans with other political leaders at that time, nor had an active annihilation machine been put in place yet.

7. Quoted in Franca Iacovetta, Paula Jean Draper, and Robert Ventresca, *A Nation of Immigrants: Women, Workers, and Communities in Canadian History, 1840s-1960s* (Toronto: University of Toronto Press, 2002), 418.

8. Cuba had initially promised entry to the refugees, who therefore left Hamburg aboard the St. Louis in May 1939, many hoping to emigrate to the United States from Cuba. But by the time the ship reached Havana, changes in the Cuban government's immigration laws blocked the passengers from being granted permission to disembark. President Roosevelt refused to put pressure on Cuba or to allow the refugees to land on US territory, thus washing his hands of their fate. Eventually the cruise ship was left with only one option: return to Europe. Three-quarters of its Jewish passengers, readmitted into European countries soon to be invaded by Germany, did not survive the Holocaust (Louise London, *Whitehall and the Jews 1933–1948: British Immigration Policy and the Holocaust* [Cambridge: Cambridge University Press, 2003]).

9. Quoted in Seymour M. Hersh, *The Dark Side of Camelot* (Boston: Little, Brown, 1997), 64.

10. Quoted in ibid., 63.

11. Jeffrey S. Gurock, *America, American Jews, and the Holocaust* (New York: Routledge 1998), 227.

12. Fast, *Children's Exodus*, 21.

13. Lore Segal, *Other People's Houses* (London: Victor Gollancz, 1965).

14. Roth, *Lifesaving Letters*, 168.

15. Ibid., 133–34.

16. Eva Figes, *Little Eden: A Child at War* (London: Faber and Faber, 1978), 12.

17. Claudia Curio, "'Invisible' Children: The Selection and Integration Strategies of Relief Organizations," trans. Toby Axelrod, *Shofar* 23, no. 1 (2004): 51.

18. Ibid., 48.

19. Bertha Leverton, "Dear Friends and Readers," in *I Came Alone: The Stories of the Kindertransports*, ed. Bertha Leverton and Shmuel Lowensohn (Lewes, UK: Book Guild, 1990), 8.

20. Bertha Leverton and Shmuel Lowensohn, eds. *I Came Alone*. Since 1989 the former Kinder have done a lot to inscribe themselves into history, while scholars have seemed very slow to catch up. The former refugees established a Kindertransport Association, organized international meetings, and involved their children in the remembering process. Over the last two decades, a considerable number of Kindertransport memoirs has been published. Two remarkable documentaries have been released on the subject: *My Knees Were Jumping: Remembering the Kindertransports* (New York: New Video Group, 2003), directed by Melissa Hacker, whose mother arrived in England on a Kindertransport from Vienna and to whom Hacker dedicated her masterpiece, which is both biographical and autobiographical; and the Oscar-winning *Into the Arms of Strangers: Stories of the Kindertransport* (Los Angeles: Warner Brothers, 2001), directed by Mark Jonathan Harris and produced by Deborah Oppenheimer, whose mother was also one of the Kinder saved on a transport out of Germany. In 1996 the playwright Diane Samuels wrote the theatrical work *Kindertransport*, inspired by a documentary film about the refugees' stories she had seen on TV in the late 1980s. The academic world has only recently begun to produce much-needed research on this historical episode. Some seminal contributions are Nicholas Stargardt, *Witnesses of War: Children's Lives under the Nazis* (New York: Alfred A. Knopf, 2005); Phyllis Lassner, *Anglo-Jewish Women Writing the Holocaust: Displaced Witnesses* (New York: Palgrave Macmillan, 2008), which includes an examination of the Kindertransport literature; and the 2004 special issue of the journal *Shofar*, which was devoted entirely to the Kindertransport. Three recent monographs about the rescue operation are Iris Guske, *Trauma and Attachment in the Kindertransport Context: German-Jewish Child Refugees' Accounts of Displacement and Acculturation in Britain* (Newcastle upon Tyne, UK: Cambridge Scholars, 2009); Fast, *Children's Exodus*; and Ann Byers, *Saving Children from the Holocaust: The Kindertransport* (Berkeley Heights, NJ: Enslow, 2012). Also relevant is Richard Bolchover, *British Jewry and the Holocaust* (Cambridge: Cambridge University Press, 1993).

21. This memorial was later relocated and replaced by a different memorial sculpture by the Israeli artist and former Kind Frank Meisler. Flor Kent's Kindertransport sculptures in London, Vienna, and Prague are titled, respectively, "Für Das Kind—Displaced," "Für Das Kind" (For the child), and "Pro Dítě" (For the child). Frank Meisler's sculptures in London, Berlin, and Gdansk are titled, respectively, "Children of the Kindertransport," "Züge ins Leben—Züge in den Tod: 1938–1939" (Trains to life—trains to death: 1938–1939), and "Pociągi Życia—Pociągi Śmierci (Life trains—death trains).

22. Roth, *Lifesaving Letters*, 123.

23. Ruth David, *Child of Our Time: A Young Girl's Flight from the Holocaust* (London: I. B. Tauris, 2003), 53.

24. Susan Rubin Suleiman, "The 1.5 Generation: Thinking about Child Survivors and the Holocaust," *American Imago* 59, no. 3 (2002): 277.

25. Tony Kushner, "Remembering to Forget: Racism and Anti-Racism in Postwar Britain," in *Modernity, Culture and "The Jew,"* ed. Bryan Cheyette and Laura Marcus (Cambridge: Polity, 1998), 226–41.

26. Roth, *Lifesaving Letters*, 132, 117–18.

27. Sue Vice, *Children Writing the Holocaust* (New York: Palgrave Macmillan, 2004), 45.

28. Lassner, *Anglo-Jewish Women Writing the Holocaust*, 7.

29. Tony Kushner, "Beyond the Pale? British Reactions to Nazi Anti-Semitism, 1933–39," in *The Politics of Marginality: Race, the Radical Right and Minorities in Twentieth Century Britain*, ed. Tony Kushner and Kenneth Lunn (London: Frank Cass, 1990), 145.

30. Bolchover, *British Jewry and the Holocaust*, 47.

31. Kushner, "Beyond the Pale?," 149.

32. Quoted in David Cesarani, "Joynson-Hicks and the Radical Right in England after the First World War," in *Traditions of Intolerance: Historical Perspectives on Fascism and Race Discourse in Britain*, ed. Tony Kushner and Kenneth Lunn (Manchester, UK: Manchester University Press, 1989), 128.

33. Bolchover, *British Jewry and the Holocaust*, 52.

34. Roth, *Lifesaving Letters*, 103, 137.

35. Ibid., 121, 122.

36. Beate Neumeier, "Kindertransport: Memory, Identity and the British-Jewish Diaspora," in *Diaspora and Multiculturalism: Common Traditions and New Developments*, ed. Monika Fludernik (New York: Rodopi, 2003), 88–89.

37. The surviving correspondence also includes letters and notes to her daughter.

38. Roth, *Lifesaving Letters*, 112.

39. Ibid., 112–13.

40. Ibid., 105.

41. For some of the most relevant scholarly contributions to the study of this particular topic, see Tony Kushner, "Remembering to Forget: Racism and Anti-Racism in Postwar Britain," in *Modernity, Culture and "The Jew,"* ed. Bryan Cheyette and Laura Marcus (Stanford: Stanford University Press, 1998), 226–41; Tony Kushner and Kenneth Lunn, eds., *Traditions of Intolerance: Historical Perspectives on Fascism and Race Discourse in British Society* (Manchester, UK: Manchester University Press, 1989); Bryan Cheyette, *Constructions of "The Jew" in English Literature and Society: Racial Representations, 1875–1945* (Cambridge: Cambridge University Press, 1993); Cesarani, "Joynson-Hicks and the Radical Right in England after the First World War"; Bolchover, *British Jewry and the Holocaust*; Bill Williams, "The Anti-Semitism of Tolerance: Middle-Class Manchester and the Jews 1870–1900," in *City, Class and Culture: Studies of Social Policy and Cultural Production in Victorian Manchester*, ed. Alan J. Kidd and Kenneth W. Roberts (Manchester, UK: Manchester University Press, 1985), 74–102.

42. Kushner, "Remembering to Forget," 228.

43. Roth, *Lifesaving Letters*, 117.

44. Ibid., 115, 116.

45. See Tara Zahra's *Kidnapped Souls: National Indifference and the Battle for Children in the Bohemian Lands, 1900–1948* (Ithaca: Cornell University Press, 2008) for an interesting discussion of the way in which children became the center of nationalistic discourses in Czechoslovakia from the end of the nineteenth century through World War II and how Czech nationalists and German loyalists used this particular demographic group as an important element in their political

and ideological war. Of particular interest and value is the way in which Zahra's work ultimately contributes to an understanding of national identity (in the Czech lands but also in a broader sense) as a very complex phenomenon: although nationalist movements and political parties needed to paint an image of nationality and nationalistic feelings as very clear, in reality the everyday picture of the relations among ethnic groups in Europe was much more equivocal, and the sense of identity of each group and subgroup was far more porous than we are generally given to believe. Zahra talks therefore of a "long history of national indeterminacy in East Central Europe" (272) rather than a simplistic dichotomy along ethnic lines.

46. Quoted in Roth, *Lifesaving Letters*, 34, 37, 42.

47. Quoted in ibid., 29, 44.

48. David, *Child of Our Time*, 13–14.

49. Roth, *Lifesaving Letters*, 180.

50. Quoted in ibid., 49.

51. Sybil Oldfield, "'It Is Usually She': The Role of British Women in the Rescue and Care of the Kindertransport Kinder," *Shofar* 23, no. 1 (2004): 57.

52. David, *Child of Our Time*, 30.

53. Harris, *Into the Arms of Strangers*.

54. Miriam Darvas, *Farewell to Prague* (San Francisco: MacAdam/Cage, 2001).

55. Astonishingly, there are no statistics available today that categorize the 10,000 rescued children by gender, origin, and age. However, a 2005 survey conducted by the Association of Jewish Refugees in Britain was able to provide statistical data on 1,025 former Kindertransportees still alive in the country. It was ascertained that 43.6 percent of the refugees in the sample were boys and 56.4 percent were girls. If this is a representative sample of the entire group of rescued children, it is safe to assume that the majority of all of the Kinderransportees were also girls.

56. Quoted in Roth, *Lifesaving Letters*, 61. It is possible that Doris's husband's foreignness (Emil Roth was born in Alexandria, Egypt, but his family had moved to Europe many years earlier) might have been why he had to make himself particularly inconspicuous.

57. Ibid., 53, 54.

58. Quoted in ibid., 55–56.

59. Segal, *Other People's Houses*, 22.

60. Quoted in Roth, *Lifesaving Letters*, 57, 145.

61. Quoted in ibid., 152.

62. Beth Fowkes Tobin, "Introduction: Consumption as a Gendered Social Practice," in *Material Women, 1750–1950: Consuming Desires and Collecting Practices*, ed. Maureen Daly Goggin and Beth Fowkes Tobin (Burlington, VT: Ashgate, 2009), 2.

63. Mona Körte, "Bracelet, Hand Towel, Pocket Watch: Objects of the Last Moment in Memory and Narration," *Shofar* 23, no. 1 (2004): 114.

64. Tobin, "Introduction," 8.

65. Pierre Nora, "Between Memory and History: Les Lieux de Mémoire," trans. Marc Roudebush, *Representations* 26 (Spring 1989): 7–24, and "General Introduction: Between Memory and History," in *Realms of Memory: Rethinking the French Past*, under the direction of Pierre Nora, English-language edition edited and with a foreword by Lawrence D. Kritzman, translated by Arthur Goldhammer (New York: Columbia University Press, 1996), 1:1–20.

66. Constance Classen and David Howes, "The Museum as Sensescape: Western Sensibili-

ties and Indigenous Artifacts," in *Sensible Objects: Colonialism, Museums, and Material Culture*, ed. Elizabeth Edwards, Chris Gosden, and Ruth B. Phillips (Oxford: Berg, 2006), 209.

67. Jeffrey David Feldman, "Contact Points: Museums and the Lost Body Problem," in *Sensible Objects*, 245–67.

68. Roth, *Lifesaving Letters*, 64.

69. Marianne Hirsch, *The Generation of Postmemory: Writing and Visual Culture after the Holocaust* (New York: Columbia University Press, 2012), 178 (the chapter in question was written by Hirsch and Leo Spitzer).

70. Quoted in Roth, *Lifesaving Letters*, 48.

71. Ibid., 74.

72. Quoted in ibid., 76–78.

73. Ibid., 135.

74. Ibid., 136 (emphasis added).

75. Ibid., 81.

76. Muriel Dimen, *Sexuality, Intimacy, Power* (London: Analytic, 2003), 212, 188.

77. Roth, *Lifesaving Letters*, 82, 13.

78. Quoted in ibid., 68, 66–67.

79. Quoted in ibid., 73.

80. Quoted in ibid., 66.

81. Alexandra Garbarini, *Numbered Days: Diaries and the Holocaust* (New Haven: Yale University Press, 2006), 103.

82. Roth, *Lifesaving Letters*, 120.

83. Quoted in ibid., 92, 73.

84. Quoted in ibid., 94.

85. Ibid., 105.

86. Ibid., 17.

87. Ibid., 105, 109.

88. Ibid., 110–11.

89. Ibid., 115.

90. Andrea Adolph, "Nostalgic Appetites: Female Desire and Wartime Rationing in Virginia Woolf's *Between the Acts* and Noel Streatfeild's *Saplings*," in *Material Women*, 56.

91. Ibid.

92. Ibid., 56–57.

93. Feldman, "Contact Points," 245.

94. Roth, *Lifesaving Letters*, 12, 84, 83.

95. Alison Landsberg, *Prosthetic Memory: The Transformation of American Remembrance in the Age of Mass Culture* (New York: Columbia University Press, 2004), 2.

96. Nora, "Between Memory and History," 7.

97. Nora, director, *Realms of Memory*.

98. Michael Rothberg, Deberati Sanyal, and Max Silverman, *Noeuds de Mémoire: Multidirectional Memory in Postwar French and Francophone Culture* (New Haven: Yale University Press, 2010), 4.

99. Landsberg, *Prosthetic Memory*, 113.

100. It is important to note that Landsberg's prosthetic memory does not erase difference or artificially construct an inauthentic sense of common origins: "People who acquire these memories are led to feel a connection to the past but, all the while, to remember their position in

the contemporary moment" (ibid., 9). By respecting their position of difference (not of likeness or identification) they can achieve empathy, "not an emotional self-pitying identification with victims but a way of both feeling for and feeling different from the subject of inquiry" (ibid., 135).

101. Nora, "General Introduction," 7.

102. Nora, "Between Memory and History," 18–19.

103. Ironically, *Realms of Memory* is rather polyphonic itself, being the product of the collaboration of numerous scholars.

104. Nora, "General Introduction," 12–13.

105. Ibid., 11, and Pierre Nora, "Preface to the English-Language Edition," in *Realms of Memory*, 1:xxii.

106. Nora, "General Introduction," 3.

107. Körte, "Bracelet, Hand Towel, Pocket Watch," 110.

108. Lee Edwards, "The Necklace," in *I Came Alone*, 79.

109. Ibid., 80.

110. Ester Friedman, "The Tapestry," in *I Came Alone*, 99, 101.

111. Segal, *Other People's Houses*, 26, 27.

112. David, *Child of Our Time*, 27.

113. Nora, "Between Memory and History," 12.

114. Landsberg, *Prosthetic Memory*, 132.

115. James E. Young, "Jewish Memory in a Postmodern Age," in *Modernity, Culture and "The Jew,"* 214.

116. Anna Reading, *The Social Inheritance of the Holocaust: Gender, Culture, and Memory* (New York: Palgrave Macmillan, 2002), 105.

117. Ibid., 141.

118. Anna Conlan and Amy K. Levin, "Museum Studies Text and Museum Subtexts," in *Gender, Sexuality and Museums: A Routledge Reader*, ed. Amy K. Levin (New York: Routledge, 2010), 299–300.

119. Mary Louise Pratt, *Imperial Eyes: Travel Writing and Transculturation* (New York: Routledge, 2008), 8.

120. Feldman, "Contact Points," 247.

121. Ibid., 255.

122. Elizabeth Edwards, Chris Gosden, and Ruth B. Phillips, introduction to *Sensible Objects*, 12. The authors are quoting from Haidy Geismar and Heather A. Horst, "Introduction: Materializing Ethnography," *Journal of Material Culture* 9, no. 1 (2004): 5–9.

123. Classen and Howes, "The Museum as Sensescape," 208.

124. Beverly Gordon, "Intimacy and Objects: A Proxemic Analysis of Gender-Based Response to the Material World," in *The Material Culture of Gender, The Gender of Material Culture*, ed. Katharine Martinez and Kenneth L. Ames (Winterthur, DE: Henry Francis du Pont Winterthur Museum, 1997), 243, 238.

125. Landsberg observes that contemporary audiences, especially in America, have begun to expect (or demand) a more experiential approach to historical knowledge, which can be provided through the help of complex mass-mediatic technologies (in museums, for instance) in order to supplement, not erase, more traditional cognitive approaches (*Prosthetic Memory*, 130).

126. Feldman, "Contact Points," 247.

127. After all, as Jacques Derrida reminds us, the word "archive" comes from *arkhē*, "the principle according to nature or history, *there* where things *commence* . . . but also the principle according to the law, *there* where men and gods *command*, *there* where authority, social order are exercised" (*Archive Fever: A Freudian Impression*, trans. Eric Prenowitz [Chicago: University of Chicago Press, 1996], 1).

128. Classen and Howes, "The Museum as Sensescape," 212.

129. Both failed and successful attempts to include gender diversity within Holocaust memorial discourses are examined in depth in Reading, *The Social Inheritance of the Holocaust*, particularly chapter 5.

130. Marion A. Kaplan, *Between Dignity and Despair: Jewish Life in Nazi Germany* (New York: Oxford University Press, 1998), 125.

131. Roth, *Lifesaving Letters*, 89.

132. Nora, "Between Memory and History," 13.

133. Nora, "General Introduction," 15, 17.

134. Rickie Bruman, "Jewish Women and the Household Economy in Manchester, c. 1890–1920," in *The Making of Modern Anglo-Jewry*, ed. David Cesarani (Oxford: Basil Blackwell, 1990), 56.

### 5. FROM THE THIRD DIASPORA : HELENA JANECZEK
### AND THE SHOAH SECOND GENERATION'S DISORDERS

1. A reduced and modified version of this chapter was published as Federica K. Clementi, "Helena Janeczek's Lessons of Darkness: Uncharted Paths to Shoah Memory through Food and Language," *Contemporary Women's Writing* 6, no. 1 (2012): 1–19; reproducd with permission.

2. I am borrowing the term "living connection" directly from Eva Hoffman and Marianne Hirsch, *The Generation of Postmemory: Writing and Visual Culture after the Holocaust* (New York: Columbia University Press, 2012), introduction, 1.

3. Ibid., 1.

4. Marianne Hirsch, *Family Frames: Photography Narrative and Postmemory* (Cambridge: Harvard University Press, 1997).

5. Hirsch, *The Generation of Postmemory*, 5.

6. Ibid.

7. Marianne Hirsch, *Ghosts of Home: The Afterlife of Czernowitz in Jewish Memory* (Berkeley: University of California Press, 2010), 9.

8. Leslie Morris, "Postmemory, Postmemoir," in *Unlikely History: The Changing German-Jewish Symbiosis, 1945–2000*, ed. Leslie Morris and Jack Zipes (New York: Palgrave Macmillan, 2002), 291.

9. Ibid., 293.

10. Hirsch, *The Generation of Postmemory*, 5.

11. Helena Janeczek, *Lezioni di tenebra* (Milan: Mondadori, 1997).

12. Morris, "Postmemory, Postmemoir," 294.

13. Marianne Hirsch and Nancy K. Miller, introduction to *Rites of Return: Diaspora Poetics and the Politics of Memory*, ed. Marianne Hirsch and Nancy K. Miller (New York: Columbia University Press, 2011), 2.

14. Judith Shuval, "Diaspora Migration: Definitional Ambiguities and a Theoretical Paradigm," *International Migration Quarterly Review* 38, no. 5 (2000): 42.

15. Even Sarah Kofman—who, born in Paris, survived the war there—was in fact separated from her geographical and cultural roots, the Poland that her parents had emigrated from and the Yiddish-speaking world of her hasidic father and mother.

16. Pascale R. Bos, "Return to Germany: German-Jewish Authors Seeking Address," in *Unlikely History*, 203.

17. Peter Novick, *The Holocaust in American Life* (Boston: Houghton Mifflin, 1999).

18. Edith Milton, *The Tiger in the Attic: Memories of the Kindertransport and Growing Up English* (Chicago: University of Chicago Press, 2005), 53.

19. Andreas Huyssen, "Diaspora and Nation: Migration into Other Pasts," *New German Critique* 88 (2003): 149.

20. Edmond Jabès, *The Book of Resemblances*, trans. Rosmarie Waldrop (Hanover, NH: University Press of New England, 1990), 56.

21. Bryan Cheyette, "Moroseness and Englishness," *Jewish Quarterly* 42, no. 1 (1995): 25.

22. Hirsch and Miller, introduction, 4–5.

23. Jacques Derrida, *Monolingualism of the Other—Or the Prosthesis of Origin*, trans. Patrick Mensah (Stanford: Stanford University Press, 1998), 16.

24. Janeczek, *Lezioni di tenebra*, 87 (hereafter *Lezioni* in the text). All translations from this work are my own.

25. Eva Hoffman, *After Such Knowledge: Memory, History and the Legacy of the Holocaust* (New York: Public Affairs, 2004), 70.

26. Cathy Caruth, "Recapturing the Past: Introduction," in *Trauma: Explorations in Memory* (Baltimore: Johns Hopkins University Press, 1995), 152.

27. Ibid.

28. Rachel Falconer, *Hell in Contemporary Literature: Western Descent Narratives since 1945* (Edinburgh: Edinburgh University Press, 2005), 43.

29. Primo Levi, *Se questo è un uomo* (Turin, Italy: Einaudi, 1986).

30. Etty Hillesum, *An Interrupted Life and Letters from Westerbork*, trans. Arnold J. Pomerans (New York: Henry Holt, 1996), 183.

31. Hélène Berr, *Journal 1942–1944* (Paris: Éditions Tallandier, 2008), 119 (my translation).

32. Eugen Kogon, *The Theory and Practice of Hell: The German Concentration Camps and the System behind Them*, trans. Heinz Norden (New York: Farrar, Straus and Giroux, 2006). However, in principle, this metonymy is objectionable because hell is a religiously charged concept, the place where guilty people are sent and where divine punishment is delivered. Nonetheless, for lack of more apt metaphors, "hell" is often used (and I am guilty of doing so myself repeatedly in this volume) to give a sense to the living of the unimaginable tortures inflicted on the dead in that place.

33. Giorgio Agamben's *Quel che resta di Auschwitz* (Turin, Italy: Bollati Boringhieri, 1998), 46–47. All translations from this work are my own.

34. Falconer, *Hell in Contemporary Literature*, 45.

35. Sarah Kofman, *Comment s'en sortir?* (Paris: Galilée, 1983).

36. Through the years I never stopped wondering why people had reacted so antagonistically to my indelicate yet relatively innocuous mistake. Had I been Polish, I wouldn't have made that mistake. The fact that I was not Polish could mean only one thing to them: I was Jewish. Poles have long resented the world's association of Auschwitz with the victimization of the Jews when, from the Polish perspective, Poles were martyred there too. What bothered them most

that day at the train station? My being a Westerner, a Western Jew, or a (Western Jewish) woman? My Polish friends suspect one thing, my Jewish friends another, and ultimately we keep rehashing our own biases in answering this question.

37. Hirsch, *The Generation of Postmemory*, 177–99 (the chapter in question was written by Hirsch and Leo Spitzer); Marianne Hirsch and Leo Spitzer, "The Tile Stove," *Women Studies Quarterly* 36, nos. 1–2 (2008): 141–50, and *Ghosts of Home: The Afterlife of Czernowitz in Jewish Memory* (Berkeley: University of California Press, 2010).

38. However, the mother is pathologically attached to such remnants and to the objects she owns, like her elegant antique rugs.

39. Falconer, *Hell in Contemporary Literature*, 42–43.

40. Ibid., 3–4.

41. Paula S. Fass, *Inheriting the Holocaust: A Second-Generation Memoir* (New Brunswick, NJ: Rutgers University Press, 2009); E. Hoffman, *After Such Knowledge*; Anne Karpf, *The War After* (London: Minerva, 1997); Lisa Appignanesi, *Losing the Dead* (Toronto: McArthur, 2001); Martin Lemelman, *Mendel's Daughter: A Memoir* (New York: Free Press, 2006).

42. Falconer, *Hell in Contemporary Literature*, 31.

43. Dante Alighieri, *The Inferno*, trans. John Ciardi (New York: Signet, 1982), 42.

44. Fass, *Inheriting the Holocaust*, 2

45. Dinora Pines, "The Impact of the Holocaust on the Second Generation," in *Holocaust Trauma: Transgenerational Transmission to the Second Generation; Psychoanalytic, Psychosocial, and Object Relational Perspectives*, ed. Moshe Halevi Spero (Ramat-Gan, Israel: Bar-Ilan University Press, 1992), 87.

46. Appignanesi, *Losing the Dead*, 61.

47. Dan Diner, "Negative Symbiosis: German and Jews after Auschwitz," in *The Holocaust: Theoretical Readings*, ed. Neil Levi and Michael Rothberg (Edinburgh: Edinburgh University Press, 2003), 423.

48. Marianne Hirsch, "Past Lives: Postmemories in Exile," *Poetics Today* 17, no. 4 (1996): 662.

49. Melvin Jules Bukiet, *Nothing Makes You Free: Writing by Descendants of Jewish Holocaust Survivors* (New York: W. W. Norton, 2003), 16.

50. Etyan Bachar, Laura Canetti, and Elliot M. Berry, "Lack of Long-Lasting Consequences of Starvation on Eating Pathology in Jewish Holocaust Survivors of Nazi Concentration Camps," *Journal of Abnormal Psychology* 114, no. 1 (2005): 165–69.

51. Lizzie Collingham, *The Taste of War: World War II and the Battle for Food* (London: Penguin, 2011).

52. Dawid Sierakowiak, *The Diary of Dawid Sierakowiak: Five Notebooks from the Łódź Ghetto* (New York: Oxford University Press, 1996).

53. Levi, *Se questo è un uomo*, 101 (my translation).

54. Angela Favaro, F. C. Rodella, and Paolo Santonastaso, "Binge Eating and Eating Attitudes among Nazi Concentration Camp Survivors," *Psychological Medicine* 30, no. 2 (2000): 463–66; Ada H. Zohar, Lotem Giladi, and Timor Givati, "Holocaust Exposure and Disordered Eating: A Study of Multi-Generational Transmission," *European Eating Disorders Review* 15, no. 1 (2007): 50–57.

55. Favaro, Rodella, and Santonastaso, "Binge Eating and Eating Attitudes among Nazi Concentration Camp Survivors," 465.

56. Karpf, *The War After*, 4.

57. Epstein, *Where She Came From: A Daughter's Search for Her Mother's History* (New York: Penguin Putnam, 1998), 7.

58. Fass, *Inheriting the Holocaust*, 149.

59. Karpf, *The War After*, 53.

60. Judith S. Kestenberg, "Psychoanalyses of Children of Survivors from the Holocaust: Case Presentations and Assessment," *Journal of the American Psychoanalytic Association* 28, no. 4 (1980): 781.

61. Kelly Oliver, "Sarah Kofman's Queasy Stomach and the Riddle of the Paternal Law," in *Enigmas: Essays on Sarah Kofman*, ed. Penelope Deutscher and Kelly Oliver (Ithaca: Cornell University Press, 1999), 174–88.

62. Clara Sereni, *Casalinghitudine* (Turin, Italy: Einaudi, 1987). The work has been published in English as *Keeping House: A Novel in Recipes*, trans. Giovanni Micieli Jeffries and Susan Briziarelli (Albany: State University of New York Press, 2005).

63. Appignanesi, *Losing the Dead*, 18.

64. Ibid., 19.

65. Ibid., 151.

66. Ibid., 220.

67. Karpf, *The War After*, 256.

68. Suzan Hanala Stadner, *My Parents Went through the Holocaust and All I Got Was This Lousy T-Shirt* (Santa Ana, CA: Seven Locks, 2006), 13, 36, 17, 37.

69. Interestingly, in 2002, Janeczek published a second book, with a telling title: *Cibo* (Food). The book is a roman à clef about a German woman in Italy whose entire network of friends and family is interconnected through the love, anxiety, and memories that food can call up. In *Cibo's* complicated portrait of food's role in contemporary life, painful experiences from the past are compounded by the demands of an image-obsessed society (see Helena Janeczek, *Cibo* [Milan: Mondadori, 2002]).

70. Efraim Sicher, *The Holocaust Novel* (New York: Routledge, 2005), 144.

71. Judith S. Kestenberg, "Transposition Revisited: Clinical, Therapeutic, and Developmental Considerations," in *Healing Their Wounds: Psychotherapy with Holocaust Survivors and Their Families*, ed. Paul Marcus and Alan Rosenberg (Santa Barbara, CA: Praeger, 1989), 70.

72. Pines, "The Impact of the Holocaust on the Second Generation," 91.

73. Ibid., 92.

74. Kestenberg, "Psychoanalyses of Children of Survivors from the Holocaust," 781.

75. All of the quoted material here is italicized in the original. *Lezioni* is interspersed with bits and pieces of conversations between mother and daughter (which Janeczek transcribes without further elaborations) and interventions, almost intrusions, by the mother (who speaks directly in the first person) on various topics, including her opinions of the draft of the manuscript that Janeczek lets her read as she is working on it. These parts, which constitute an interruption of the narrative and of the memoir proper, are italicized in *Lezioni*.

76. For a revealing analysis of how different and fraught the memories of Jews and Christians are in regard to the prewar and Holocaust years in Poland, for instance, see the groundbreaking volume edited by Joshua D. Zimmerman, *Contested Memories: Poles and Jews during the Holocaust and Its Aftermath* (New Brunswick, NJ: Rutgers University Press, 2003).

77. Epstein, *Where She Came From*, 143.

78. Ibid., 133.

79. Daniel Vogelman, "My Share of the Pain," in *Second Generation Voices: Reflections by Children of Holocaust Survivors and Perpetrators*, ed. Naomi Berger and Alan L. Berger (Syracuse, NY: Syracuse University Press, 2001), 73.

80. Fass, *Inheriting the Holocaust*, 157–58.

81. Hirsch, *Family Frames*, 244.

82. Richard Wagner, *Judaism in Music and Other Essays*, trans. Ashton Ellis (Lincoln: University of Nebraska Press, 1995), 85. Wagner remarks: "The Jew speaks the language of the nation in whose midst he dwells from generation to generation, but he speaks it always as an alien" (ibid., 84). And then Wagner describes the Jews' alleged way of speaking thus: "In particular does the purely physical aspect of the Jewish mode of speech repel us . . . The first thing that strikes our ear as quite outlandish and unpleasant, in the Jew's production of the voice-sounds, is a creaking, squeaking, buzzing snuffle" (85). See also Sander L. Gilman, *Jewish Self-Hatred: Anti-Semitism and the Hidden Language of the Jews* (Baltimore: Johns Hopkins University Press, 1986).

83. Art Spiegelman, *Maus: A Survivor's Tale* (New York: Pantheon, 1996). Parenthetically, I have always wondered about the unusual names of Spiegelman's parents and his brother in the book. For example, Anja is a very old-fashioned form of the more common Ania; Vladek, although a Slavic name, is not spelled this way in Polish (Władek would be the diminutive of the name Władysław, and Włodek would be the diminutive of Włodzimierz). Most puzzling is the brother's name, Richieu—a name that does not exist in Polish, or, as far as I can tell, in any other Slavic language. My guess is that it is the transcription of Rysiek, the diminutive of Ryszard (Richard). But why wouldn't this have been made clear to Spiegelman by his father or family friends? Again, language is one of the numerous mysteries surrrounding the Shoah parents, mysteries to which second-generation children have no access.

84. Stadner, *My Parents Went through the Holocaust and All I Got Was This Lousy T-Shirt*, 16.

85. Appignanesi, *Losing the Dead*, 81.

86. Sophia Lehmann, "In Search of a Mother Tongue: Locating Home in Diaspora," MELUS 23, no. 4 (1998): 101.

87. Tadeusz Borowski, *Opowiadania Wybrane* (Warsaw: Państwowy Instytut Wydawniczy, 1971), 122 (my translation).

88. Liana Millu, *Il fumo di Birkenau* (Florence: Giuntina, 2008).

89. Epstein, *Where She Came From*, 7–8.

90. Fass, *Inheriting the Holocaust*, 148.

91. Kestenberg, "Psychoanalyses of Children of Survivors from the Holocaust." See especially 787–88.

92. Ruth Wajnryb, *Silence: How Tragedy Shapes Talk* (Crows Nest, Australia: Allen and Unwin, 2001), 148–49.

93. Maria Cristina Mauceri, "Writing outside the Borders: Personal Experience and History in the Works of Helga Schneider and Helena Janeczek," in *Across Genres, Generations and Borders: Italian Women Writing Lives*, ed. Susanna Scarparo and Rita Wilson (Newark: University of Delaware Press, 2004), 141.

94. George Steiner, "Our Homeland, The Text," *Salmagundi*, no. 66 (1985): 4–25. See also George Steiner, *After Babel: Aspects of Language and Translation* (Oxford: Oxford University Press, 1998).

95. Erich S. Gruen, *Diaspora: Jews amidst Greeks and Romans* (Cambridge: Harvard University Press, 2002), 232.

96. Eva Hoffman, *Lost in Translation: A Life in a New Language* (New York: Penguin, 1990), 211.

97. Ibid., 273.

98. Ibid., 5.

99. Mauceri, "Writing outside the Borders," 142.

100. Helen Epstein, *Children of the Holocaust: Conversations with Sons and Daughters of Survivors* (New York: Putnam, 1979), 260.

101. Alan L. Berger and Naomi Berger, introduction to *Second Generation Voices*, 3.

102. Dori Laub and Nanette C. Auerhahn, "Reverberations of Genocide: Its Expression in the Conscious and Unconscious of Post-Holocaust Generations," in *Psychoanalytic Reflections on the Holocaust: Selected Essays*, ed. Steven A. Luel and Paul Marcus (New York: Ktav, 1984), 155.

103. Irene Kacandes, "Displacement, Trauma, Language, Identity," in *Femmes écrivains à la croisée des langues, 1700–2000/Women Writers at the Crossroads of Languages, 1700–2000*, ed. Agnese Fidecaro, Henriette Partzsch, Suzan van Dijk, and Valérie Cossy (Geneva: MētisPresses, 2009), 225.

104. Alan L. Berger, *Children of Job: American Second-Generation Witnesses to the Holocaust* (Albany: State University Press of New York, 1997), 187.

105. Levi, *Se questo è un uomo*.

106. Kacandes, "Displacement, Trauma, Language, Identity," 227.

107. Primo Levi, *I sommersi e i salvati*, in *Opere*, ed. Cesare Cases (Turin, Italy: Einaudi, 1987), 1:692 (my translation).

108. Emmanuel Lévinas, *Totality and Infinity: An Essay on Exteriority*, trans. Alphonso Lingis (Pittsburgh: Duquesne University Press, 1969), 213.

109. Ibid., 79.

110. Ibid., 201.

## 6. "I HAVE TO SAVE MYSELF WITH A JOKE": ANNE FRANK AND THE SURVIVAL OF HUMOR

1. Steven Paskuly, epilogue to Rudolph Höss, *Death Dealer: The Memoirs of the SS Kommandant at Auschwitz*, ed. Steven Paskuly, trans. Andrew Pollinger (Buffalo, NY: Prometheus, 1992), 197.

2. Rudolph Höss, *Death Dealer*, 189.

3. Ibid., 61.

4. Ibid., 62.

5. Quoted in Mary Lowenthal Felstiner, *To Paint Her Life: Charlotte Salomon in the Nazi Era* (Berkeley: University of California Press, 1997), 207–8.

6. Miep Gies with Alison Leslie Gold, *Anne Frank Remembered: The Story of the Woman Who Helped to Hide the Frank Family* (New York: Simon and Schuster, 1987), 11–12.

7. Anne Frank, *The Diary of a Young Girl* (New York: Anchor, 1996), 333.

8. Bruno Bettelheim, *The Informed Heart* (New York: Avon, 1971), 249.

9. The diary appeared first in Dutch in 1947, followed by French and German editions in 1950, an English-language edition in 1952, an American stage adaptation in 1955, and a film version in 1957 (Gerrold van der Stroom, "The Diaries, *Het Achterhuis* and the Translations," in Anne Frank, *The Diary of Anne Frank: The Revised Critical Edition*, ed. David Barnouw and Gerrold

van der Stroom, trans. Arnold J. Pomerans, B. M. Mooyaart-Doubleday, and Susan Massotty [New York: Doubleday, 2003], 66, 74; hereafter *Critical Edition* in the text).

10. David Barnouw, "Anne Frank and Academia," in *Critical Edition*, 104–5.

11. Quoted in van der Stroom, "The Diaries, *Het Achterhuis* and the Translations," 59.

12. Nigel A. Caplan, "Revisiting the Diary: Rereading Anne Frank's Rewriting," *Lion and the Unicorn* 28, no. 1 (2004): 79.

13. Katherine Dalsimer, *Female Adolescence: Psychoanalytic Reflections on Literature* (New Haven: Yale University Press, 1986), 72.

14. See Rachel Feldhay Brenner, *Writing as Resistance: Four Women Confronting the Holocaust: Edith Stein, Simone Weil, Anne Frank, Etty Hillesum* (University Park: Pennsylvania State University Press, 1997), 140.

15. Caplan, "Revisiting the Diary," 89.

16. Brenner, *Writing as Resistance*, 140–41.

17. Christopher Bigsby, *Remembering and Imagining the Holocaust: The Chain of Memory* (Cambridge: Cambridge University Press, 2006), 220.

18. Catherine A. Bernard, "Anne Frank: The Cultivation of the Inspirational Victim," in *Experience and Expression: Women, the Nazis, and the Holocaust*, ed. Elizabeth R. Baer and Myrna Goldenberg (Detroit: Wayne State University Press, 2003), 220, 219. Bernard's point is, in my opinion, confirmed time and again by the distasteful reincarnations of a fictional Anne Frank in literary works (most by male authors), the most famous of which is Philip Roth's *The Ghost Writer* (New York: Library of America, 2007). A more recent male fantasy (a particularly violent, masculine, and unsettling one) on the "return" of Anne Frank is Shalom Auslander's *Hope: A Tragedy* (New York: Riverhead, 2012), a sad case of a good sense of humor meeting bad taste.

19. Harold Bloom, "Editor's Note," in *A Scholarly Look at The Diary of Anne Frank*, ed. Harold Bloom (Philadelphia: Chelsea House, 1999), vii.

20. Quoted in Caplan, "Revisiting the Diary," 77.

21. Lawrence L. Langer, "The Uses—and Misuses—of a Young Girl's Diary: 'If Anne Frank Could Return from among the Murdered, She Would Be Appalled,'" in *Anne Frank: Reflections on Her Life and Legacy*, ed. Hyman Aaron Enzer and Sandra Solotaroff-Enzer (Urbana: University of Illinois Press, 2000), 205.

22. Bettelheim's essay on the diary has been appositely criticized by Bigsby (*Remembering and Imagining the Holocaust*, 219–57).

23. Caplan, "Revisiting the Diary," 77–78.

24. Brenner, *Writing as Resistance*; Denise De Costa, *Anne Frank and Etty Hillesum: Inscribing Spirituality and Sexuality* (New Brunswick, NJ: Rutgers University Press, 1998).

25. Dawid Sierakowiak, *The Diary of Dawid Sierakowiak: Five Notebooks from the Łódź Ghetto* (New York: Oxford University Press, 1996).

26. Brenner, *Writing as Resistance*, 135.

27. Hélène Berr, *Journal 1942–1944* (Paris: Éditions Tallandier, 2008), 106 (my translation).

28. See, for example, Terrence Des Pres, "Holocaust Laughter?," in *Writing and the Holocaust*, ed. Berel Lang (New York: Holmes and Meier, 1988), 216–33.

29. Steve Lipman, *Laughter in Hell: The Use of Humor during the Holocaust* (Northvale, NJ: Jason Aronson, 1991), 8.

30. John Morreall, *Comic Relief: A Comprehensive Philosophy of Humor* (Oxford: Wiley-Blackwell, 2009), 119.

31. Antonin J. Obrdlik, "Gallows Humor: A Sociological Phenomenon," *American Journal of Sociology* 47, no. 5 (1942): 713.

32. Lipman, *Laughter in Hell*, 25.

33. Morreall, *Comic Relief*, 120.

34. Aristotle, *On Rhetoric: A Theory of Civic Discourse*, trans. George A. Kennedy, 2nd ed. (Oxford: Oxford University Press, 2007), 151.

35. Quoted in Morreall, *Comic Relief*, 121.

36. Lipman, *Laughter in Hell*, 9.

37. Sigmund Freud, "Humour," in *The Standard Edition of the Complete Psychological Works of Sigmund Freud*, ed. and trans. James Strachey (London: Hogarth, 1973), 21: 163.

38. Emanuel Ringelblum, *Kronika Getta Warszawskiego* (Warsaw: Czytelnik, 1983), 369 (my translation).

39. The population of the Warsaw Ghetto had officially been liquidated between July 22 and September 12, 1942, almost a year before the uprising. Over 400,000 Jews are estimated to have been imprisoned within the ghetto, an area of about 1.3 square miles. Most of them died there; the rest were deported to extermination camps.

40. Glenn Sujo, *Legacies of Silence: The Visual Arts and Holocaust Memory* (London: Philip Wilson, 2001), 61.

41. Etty Hillesum, *An Interrupted Life and Letters from Westerbork*, trans. Arnold J. Pomerans (New York: Henry Holt, 1996), 183.

42. Charlotte Salomon, *Life? or Theatre?*, trans. Leila Vennewitz (Zwolle, Holland: Waanders, 1998.)

43. Berr, *Journal 1942–1944*.

44. Henri Bergson, *Le Rire: Essai sur la signification du comique* (Paris: Presses Universitaires de France, 1962), 4–5 (my translation).

45. Ernst Schnabel, *Anne Frank: A Portrait in Courage*, trans. Richard Winston and Clara Winston (New York: Harcourt, Brace, 1958), 24.

46. Ibid., 24–25.

47. Franz Kafka, "An Imperial Message," in *Kafka: Selected Stories*, trans. Ian Johnston (West Valley City, UT: Waking Lion, 2008), 96.

48. Martin L. Hoffman, *Empathy and Moral Development: Implications for Caring and Justice* (Cambridge: Cambridge University Press, 2000), 221.

49. Alison Landsberg, *Prosthetic Memory: The Transformation of American Remembrance in the Age of Mass Culture* (New York: Columbia University Press, 2004), 24.

50. Jon Blair, director, *Anne Frank Remembered* (Los Angeles: Sony Pictures Classics, 1995), DVD.

51. Dalsimer, *Female Adolescence*, 70.

52. Blair, *Anne Frank Remembered*.

53. Gies, *Anne Frank Remembered*, 114–15.

54. Schnabel, *Anne Frank: A Portrait in Courage*, 106.

55. Ibid. (emphasis added).

56. Blair, *Anne Frank Remembered*.

57. Gies, *Anne Frank Remembered*, 165.

58. Blair, *Anne Frank Remembered*.

59. Schnabel, *Anne Frank: A Portrait in Courage*, 107.

60. Menno Metselaar and Ruud van der Rol, *Anne Frank: Her Life in Words and Pictures*, trans. Arnold J. Pomerans (New York: Roaring Brook, 2009), 66.

61. Ibid., 51.

62. Ibid., 42.

63. Blair, *Anne Frank Remembered*.

64. The frustrated Oedipal desire for the father is also perfectly exemplified in these lines: "I long for something from Father that he's incapable of giving . . . It's just that I'd like to feel that Father really loves me, not because I'm his child, but because I'm me, Anne" (*The Diary of a Young Girl*, 141).

65. Willy Lindwer, *The Last Seven Months of Anne Frank* (New York: Anchor, 1992), 129.

66. This episode is retold in an even more detailed and literary fashion in Anne Frank, *Tales from the Secret Annex*, trans. Susan Massotty (New York: Bantam, 2003), 56–58.

67. Janet L. Surrey, "The 'Self-in-Relation': A Theory of Women's Development," in *Women's Growth in Connection: Writings from the Stone Center*, ed. Judith V. Jordan et al. (New York: Guilford, 1991), 61–62.

68. Frank, *Tales from the Secret Annex*, 30.

69. Ibid., 17.

70. Ibid., 18.

71. Gies, *Anne Frank Remembered*, 165–66.

72. Frank, *Tales from the Secret Annex*, 20.

73. Ibid.

74. Ibid., 21.

75. Ibid., 24.

76. Gies, *Anne Frank Remembered*, 56.

77. Brenner, *Writing as Resistance*, 141.

78. Miep offers a slightly different version: "The one most affected by bad news was Mrs. Frank. Slowly . . . her attitude was becoming more and more dismal. All the rest of us were encouraged by the rumor that perhaps the *razias* were finished . . . But none of [the hopeful news] seemed to hearten Mrs. Frank . . . As much as all of us argued against her view, she saw no light at the end of the tunnel" (*Anne Frank Remembered*, 132–33).

79. Blair, *Anne Frank Remembered*.

80. Schnabel, *Anne Frank: A Portrait in Courage*, 158, 159.

81. Ibid., 169–170 (emphasis added).

82. Gies, *Anne Frank Remembered*, 108.

83. In particular, I am referring to Lawrence L. Langer, *Admitting the Holocaust: Collected Essays* (Oxford: Oxford University Press, 1995). In "Cultural Resistance to Genocide" in that volume, Langer questions the legitimacy of using a term such as "resistance" to qualify the artistic works produced by Jews during the Holocaust—artifacts that, at the end of the day, did not injure the enemy (an enemy "scornful of the very idea of Jewish culture") and did not "save Jewish lives" (52).

84. Freud, "Humour," 163.

85. For example, in one of her reflections on the subject, Frank writes: "I don't mean to imply that women should stop having children . . . What I condemn are our system of values and the men who don't acknowledge how great, difficult, but ultimately beautiful women's share in society is" (*The Diary of a Young Girl*, 320).

86. Warren S. Poland,"The Gift of Laughter: On the Development of a Sense of Humor in Clinical Analysis," *Psychoanalytic Quarterly* 59, no. 2 (1990): 198 (emphasis added).

87. Dalsimer, *Female Adolescence*, 73.

88. Quoted in Philip Crockatt, "Freud's 'On Narcissism: An Introduction,'" *Journal of Child Psychotherapy* 32, no. 1 (2006): 11.

89. Sigmund Freud, "On Narcissism: An Introduction," trans. James Strachey, in *The Standard Edition of the Complete Psychological Works of Sigmund Freud* (London: Hogarth, 1973), 14: 88, 89.

90. Schnabel, *Anne Frank: A Portrait in Courage*, 49.

91. Gies, *Anne Frank Remembered*, 56.

92. Freud, "Humour," 162.

93. Ibid., 163.

94. Ibid.

95. Sigmund Freud, *Jokes and Their Relation to the Unconscious*, trans. James Strachey (New York: W.W. Norton, 1989).

96. Sarah Kofman, *Pourquoi rit-on? Freud et le mot d'esprit* (Paris: Galilée, 1986), 28.

97. Freud, "Humour," 166.

98. Ibid.

99. Dalsimer, *Female Adolescence*, 75.

100. De Costa, *Anne Frank and Etty Hillesum*, 122.

101. Hélène Cixous, "The Laugh of the Medusa," trans. Keith Cohen and Paula Cohen, *Signs* 1, no. 4 (1976): 881.

102. De Costa, *Anne Frank and Etty Hillesum*, 122.

103. Höss, *Death Dealer*, 183.

104. Simon Wiesenthal, "Epilogue to the Diary of Anne Frank," in *Anne Frank: Reflections on Her Life and Legacy*, 67.

105. Gies, *Anne Frank Remembered*, 122.

### EPILOGUE : REMEMBER WHAT ZEUS DID TO YOU

1. Charlotte Salomon, *Life? or Theatre?*, trans. Leila Vennewitz (Zwolle, Holland: Waanders, 1998). The German title is *Leben? Oder Theater? Ein Singespiel.*

2. Quoted in Mary Lowenthal Felstiner, *To Paint Her Life: Charlotte Salomon in the Nazi Era* (Berkeley: University of California Press, 1997), 109–10.

3. Salomon, *Life? or Theatre?*, 747.

4. Ibid., 815.

5. Ibid., 816–17.

6. Norman Rosenthal writes in his introduction to *Life? or Theatre?*: "The name Charlotte Salomon occurs in few, if any, general histories of 20th-century art and culture—not even those devoted to Germany . . . Its very singularity has stood in the way of its recognition" ("Charlotte Salomon's *Life? or Theatre?* A 20th-Century Song of Innocence and Experience," in Charlotte Salomon, *Life? or Theatre?*, 10).

7. Salomon, *Life? or Theatre?*, 202.

8. Griselda Pollock, "Theater of Memory: Trauma and Cure in Charlotte Salomon's Modernist Fairytale," in *Reading Charlotte Salomon*, ed. Michael P. Steinberg and Monica Bohm-Duchen (Ithaca: Cornell University Press, 2006), 54.

9. Michael P. Steinberg, "Reading Charlotte Salomon: History, Memory, Modernism," in *Reading Charlotte Salomon*, 3.

10. Salomon, *Life? or Theatre?*, 762–63.

11. Ibid., 814.

12. One day, Mr. and Mrs. Knarre and Lotte are enjoying a blissful lunch in the garden overlooking the splendid Riviera. The grandmother asks Charlotte: "Are you here in the world only to paint?" But before she can answer, the grandfather jumps in and scolds his wife: "You are too lenient with her [Charlotte]. Why shouldn't she work as a housemaid, like all the others?" (ibid., 723).

13. Ibid., 655.

14. Festiner, *To Paint Her Life*, 47.

15. For an in-depth discussion, and a slightly different interpretation, of Wolfsohn's figure in Salomon's life and art, see the important chapter devoted to this aspect in ibid., 40–61.

16. Ibid., 61.

17. Ibid., 60.

18. Felstiner reports part of an interview that Paula Salomon-Lindberg gave half a century after the war, in which she casts Charlotte's love affair with Wolfsohn as a mere fantasy of the artist—who, according to Paula, had hardly been alone with him more than three times. The interviewer presses her: "You think the paintings are a fantasy"—to which Paula responds with a terse: "Dreaming. She is dreaming" (quoted in ibid., 53).

19. Ibid., 141–42.

20. Ibid., 143.

21. Christine Conley, "Memory and *Trauerspiel*: Charlotte Salomon's *Life? or Theater?* and the Angel of History," in *Reading Charlotte Salomon*, ed. Michael P. Steinberg and Monica Bohm-Duchen (Ithaca: Cornell University Press, 2006), 99.

22. Julia Kristeva, *Black Sun: Depression and Melancholia*, trans. Leon S. Roudiez (New York: Columbia University Press, 1989), 27–28.

23. Amber Jacobs, *On Matricide: Myth, Psychoanalysis, and the Law of the Mother* (New York: Columbia University Press, 2007), 25.

24. Marcia Ian, *Remembering the Phallic Mother: Psychoanalysis, Modernism, and the Fetish* (Ithaca: Cornell University Press, 1993), 13.

25. As Marianne Hirsch has written, Electra "[identifies] completely with her father's discourse . . . [and] underwrites paternal law and male supremacy, as well as female antagonism, competition, and powerlessness" (*The Mother/Daughter Plot: Narrative, Psychoanalysis, Feminism* [Bloomington: Indiana University Press, 1989], 31). Luce Irigaray points out that it is the oracle of Apollo, son of Zeus, that inspires Orestes to kill his mother: "Orestes kills his mother because the empire of the God-Father [Zeus], who has seized and taken for his own the ancient powers (*puissances*) of the earth-mother, demands it. He kills his mother and is driven mad, as is his sister Electra. Electra, the daughter, will remain mad. The matricidal son, on the other hand, must be saved from madness so that he can found the patriarchal order" (*Sexes and Genealogies*, trans. Gillian C. Gill [New York: Columbia University Press, 1993], 12).

26. Jacobs, *On Matricide*, 69.

27. We shouldn't forget that Zeus himself had been helped by his mother to supplant his father, the Titan Cronus. Cronus, in turn, had castrated his father and replaced him as ruler of the universe. Then, fearing that his offspring might one day overthrow him, he began to

devour them (the baby Zeus escaped this terrible fate thanks to his mother's astuteness and later revenged himself on Cronus).

28. Jacobs, *On Matricide*, 67.

29. Ibid., 72.

30. Salomon, *Life? or Theatre?*, 822.

31. Ibid., 823.

32. As Conley points out, "the ironic commentary of CS [Charlotte Salomon, the persona of the artist who signs the overlays only by her initials] undermines the family patriarchs and the expert opinions of psychiatrists to suggest sources of culpability beyond the presumed degeneracy of the maternal line, most accurately in the veiled accusation of incest in the final scenes . . . where grandfather admonishes Charlotte for refusing to share his bed" ("Memory and *Trauerspiel*," 99).

33. I am indebted for these details about Ludwig Grunwald's death to the revealing documentary film *Leven? of Theater?* directed by Frans Weisz (Amsterdam: Homescreen, 2012), DVD.

34. Robert D. Baird, *Category Formation and the History of Religions* (Berlin: Mouton de Gruyter, 1991), 75.

# BIBLIOGRAPHY

Adolph, Andrea. "Nostalgic Appetites: Female Desire and Wartime Rationing in Virginia Woolf's *Between the Acts* and Noel Streatfeild's *Saplings*." In *Material Women, 1750–1950: Consuming Desires and Collecting Practices*, edited by Maureen Daly Goggin and Beth Fowkes Tobin, 56–72. Burlington, VT: Ashgate, 2009.

Aeschylus. *The Oresteia*. Translated by Douglas Young. Norman: University of Oklahoma Press, 1974.

Agamben, Giorgio. *Il linguaggio e la morte*. Turin, Italy: Einaudi, 2008.

———. *Quel che resta di Auschwitz*. Turin, Italy: Bollati Boringhieri, 1998.

Alighieri, Dante. *The Inferno*. Translated by John Ciardi. New York: Signet, 1982.

Antler, Joyce. *You Never Call! You Never Write! A History of the Jewish Mother*. Oxford: Oxford University Press, 2007.

Appignanesi, Lisa. *Losing the Dead*. Toronto: McArthur, 2001.

Arendt, Hannah. *Essays in Understanding, 1930–1954*. Edited by Jerome Kohn. New York: Harcourt, Brace, 1994.

Aristotle. *On Rhetoric: A Theory of Civic Discourse*. Translated by George A. Kennedy. 2nd ed. Oxford: Oxford University Press, 2007.

Auden, W. H. *Collected Poems*, edited by Edward Mendelson. New York: Vintage, 1991.

Auslander, Shalom. *Hope: A Tragedy*. New York: Riverhead, 2012.

Bacchilega, Cristina. *Postmodern Fairy Tales: Gender and Narrative Strategies*. Philadelphia: University of Pennsylvania Press, 1997.

Bachar, Etyan, Laura Canetti, and Elliot M. Berry. "Lack of Long-Lasting Consequences of Starvation on Eating Pathology in Jewish Holocaust Survivors of Nazi Concentration Camps." *Journal of Abnormal Psychology* 114, no. 1 (2005): 165–69.

Baer, Elizabeth R., and Myrna Goldenberg. *Experience and Expression: Women, the Nazis, and the Holocaust*. Detroit: Wayne State University Press, 2003.

Baird, Robert D. *Category Formation and the History of Religions*. Berlin: Mouton de Gruyter, 1991.

Barnouw, David. "Anne Frank and Academia." In Anne Frank, *The Diary of Anne Frank: The Revised Critical Edition*, edited by David Barnouw and Gerrold van der Stroom, translated by Arnold J. Pomerans, B. M. Mooyaart-Doubleday, and Susan Massotty, 103–8. New York: Doubleday, 2003.

Barnstone, Aliki, and Willis Barnstone, eds. *A Book of Women Poets from Antiquity to Now*. New York: Schocken, 1992.

Bar-On, Dan. *Fear and Hope: Three Generations of Holocaust Survivors' Families*. Cambridge: Harvard University Press, 1995.

———. *The Indescribable and the Undiscussable: Reconstructing Human Discourse after Trauma*. Budapest: Central European University Press, 1999.

———. *Legacy of Silence: Encounters with Children of the Third Reich*. Cambridge: Harvard University Press, 1989.

Bassin, Donna, Margaret Honey, and Meryle Mahrer Kaplan eds. *Representations of Motherhood*. New Haven: Yale University Press, 1994.

Baum, Alwin L. "Parable as Paradox in Kafka's Erzählungen." *MLN* 91, no. 6 (1976): 1327–47.

Bauman, Zygmund. "Assimilation into Exile: The Jew as a Polish Writer." In *Exile and Creativity*, edited by Susan Rubin Suleiman, 321–52. Durham: Duke University Press, 1998.

Baumel, Judith Tydor. *Double Jeopardy: Gender and the Holocaust*. London: Vallentine Mitchell, 1998.

Benjamin, Walter. *Illuminations: Essays and Reflections*. Edited by Hannah Arendt. Translated by Harry Zohn. New York: Schocken, 1968.

Benz, Wolfgang, Claudia Curio, Andrea Hammel, and Toby Axelrod, eds. *Shofar* 23, no. 1 (2004).

Berger, Alan L. *Children of Job: American Second-Generation Witnesses to the Holocaust*. Albany: State University Press of New York, 1997.

———. and Naomi Berger. Introduction to *Second Generation Voices: Reflections by Children of Holocaust Survivors and Perpetrators*, edited by Alan L. Berger and Naomi Berger, 1–12. Syracuse, NY: Syracuse University Press, 2001.

Bergson, Henri. *Le Rire: Essai sur la signification du comique*. Paris: Presses Universitaires de France, 1962.

Bernard, Catherine A. "Anne Frank: The Cultivation of the Inspirational Victim." In *Experience and Expression: Women, the Nazis, and the Holocaust*, edited by Elizabeth R. Baer and Myrna Goldenberg, 201–25. Detroit: Wayne State University Press, 2003.

Berr, Hélène. *Journal 1942–1944*. Paris: Éditions Tallandier, 2008.

Bettelheim, Bruno. "Fathers Shouldn't Try to Be Mothers." *Parents' Magazine*, October 1956, 40, 125–29.

———. *Freud's Vienna and Other Essays*. New York: Alfred A. Knopf, 1990.

———. *The Informed Heart*. New York: Avon, 1971.

———. *Surviving and Other Essays*. New York: Vintage, 1980.

———. *The Uses of Enchantment*. New York: Vintage, 1989.

Bialostosky, Don H. *Wordsworth, Dialogics, and the Practice of Criticism*. Cambridge: Cambridge University Press, 1992.

Bigsby, Christopher. *Remembering and Imagining the Holocaust: The Chain of Memory*. Cambridge: Cambridge University Press, 2006.

Blair, Jon, director. *Anne Frank Remembered*. Los Angeles: Sony Pictures Classics, 1995. DVD.

Bloom, Harold. "Editor's Note." In *A Scholarly Look at The Diary of Anne Frank*, edited by Harold Bloom, vii. Philadelphia: Chelsea House, 1999.

Bolchover, Richard. *British Jewry and the Holocaust*. Cambridge: Cambridge University Press, 1993.

Borowski, Tadeusz. *Opowiadania Wybrane*. Warsaw: Państwowy Instytut Wydawniczy, 1971.

———. *This Way for the Gas, Ladies and Gentlemen*. Translated by Barbara Vedder. New York: Penguin, 1976.

Bos, Pascale R. *German-Jewish Literature in the Wake of the Holocaust: Grete Weil, Ruth Klüger, and the Politics of Address*. New York: Palgrave Macmillan, 2005.

————. "Return to Germany: German-Jewish Authors Seeking Address." In *Unlikely History: The Changing German-Jewish Symbiosis, 1945–2000*, edited by Leslie Morris and Jack Zipes, 203–32. New York: Palgrave Macmillan, 2002.

Breitman, Richard, and Alan M. Kraut. *American Refugee Policy and European Jewry, 1933–1945*. Bloomington: Indiana University Press, 1988.

Brenner, Rachel Feldhay. *Writing as Resistance: Four Women Confronting the Holocaust: Edith Stein, Simone Weil, Anne Frank, Etty Hillesum*. University Park: Pennsylvania State University Press, 1997.

Brodzki, Bella. "Mothers, Displacement, and Language." In *Women, Autobiography, Theory: A Reader*, edited by Sidonie Smith and Julia Watson, 156–59. Madison: University of Wisconsin Press, 1998.

———— and Celeste Schenck. Introduction to *Life/Lines: Theorizing Women's Autobiography*, edited by Bella Brodzki and Celeste Schenck, 1–15. Ithaca: Cornell University Press, 1988.

Bruck, Edith. *Chi ti ama così*. Venice: Marsilio, 1994.

————. *Il silenzio degli amanti*. Venice: Marsilio, 1997.

————. *Itinerario/Útirány: poesie scelte*. Rome: Quasar, 1998.

————. *Letter to My Mother*. Translated by Brenda S. Webster and Garbiella Romani. New York: Modern Language Association of America, 2006.

————. *Lettera alla madre*. Milan: Garzanti, 1988.

————. *Lettera da Francoforte*. Milan: Mondadori, 2004.

————. *Signora Auschwitz: Il dono della parola*. Venice: Marsilio, 1999.

————. *Who Loves You Like This*. Translated by Thomas Kelso. Philadelphia: Paul Dry, 2001.

Bruman, Rickie. "Jewish Women and the Household Economy in Manchester, c. 1890–1920." In *The Making of Modern Anglo-Jewry*, edited by David Cesarani, 55–75. Oxford: Basil Blackwell, 1990.

Buber, Martin. *I and Thou*. Translated by Ronald Gregor Smith. New York: Scribner Classics, 2000.

————. *Israel and the World: Essays in a Time of Crisis*. Translated by Olga Marx and Greta Hort. Syracuse, NY: Syracuse University Press, 1997.

Bukiet, Melvin Jules. *Nothing Makes You Free: Writing by Descendants of Jewish Holocaust Survivors*. New York: W. W. Norton, 2003.

Burstein, Janet Handler. *Writing Mothers, Writing Daughters: Tracing the Maternal in Stories of American Jewish Women*. Urbana: University of Illinois Press, 1996.

Butler, Judith. *Gender Trouble: Feminism and the Subversion of Identity*. New York: Routledge, 1999.

Byers, Ann. *Saving Children from the Holocaust: The Kindertransport*. Berkeley Heights, NJ: Enslow, 2012.

Caplan, Nigel A. "Revisiting the Diary: Rereading Anne Frank's Rewriting." *Lion and the Unicorn* 28, no. 1 (2004): 77–95.

Caruth, Cathy. *Trauma: Explorations in Memory*. Baltimore: Johns Hopkins University Press, 1995.

Celan, Paul. *Selected Poems and Prose of Paul Celan*. Translated by John Felstiner. New York: W. W. Norton, 2001.

Cesarani, David. "Joynson-Hicks and the Radical Right in England after the First World War." In *Traditions of Intolerance: Historical Perspectives on Fascism and Race Discourse in British Society*, edited by Tony Kushner and Ken Lunn, 118–39. Manchester, UK: Manchester University Press, 1989.

Chanter, Tina. "Eating Words: Antigone as Kofman's Proper Name." In *Enigmas: Essays on Sarah Kofman*, edited by Penelope Deutscher and Kelly Oliver, 189–204. Ithaca: Cornell University Press, 1999.

———. "Playing with Fire: Kofman and Freud on Being Feminine, Jewish, and Homosexual." In *Sarah Kofman's Corpus*, edited by Tina Chanter and Pleshette DeArmitt, 91–121. Albany: State University of New York Press, 2008.

Chesterton, G. K. *Brave New Family: G. K. Chesterton on Men and Women, Children, Sex, Divorce, Marriage and the Family*. Edited by Alvaro de Silva. San Francisco: Ignatius, 1990.

Cheyette, Bryan. *Constructions of "The Jew" in English Literature and Society: Racial Representations, 1875–1945*. Cambridge: Cambridge University Press, 1993.

———. "Moroseness and Englishness: The Rise of British-Jewish Literature." *Jewish Quarterly* 42, no. 1 (1995): 22–26.

——— and Laura Marcus, eds. *Modernity, Culture and "The Jew."* Edited by Bryan Cheyette and Laura Marcus, 211–25. Stanford: Stanford University Press, 1998.

Chichester Bonca, Teddi. *Shelley's Mirrors of Love: Narcissism, Sacrifice, and Sorority*. Albany: State University of New York Press, 1999.

Cixous, Hélène. *La jeune née*. Paris: Union Générale d'Edition, 1975.

———. "The Laugh of the Medusa." Translated by Keith Cohen and Paula Cohen. *Signs* 1, no. 4 (1976): 875–93.

Classen, Constance, and David Howes. "The Museum as Sensescape: Western Sensibilities and Indigenous Artifacts." In *Sensible Objects: Colonialism, Museums, and Material Culture*, edited by Elizabeth Edwards, Chris Gosden, and Ruth B. Phillips, 199–222. Oxford: Berg, 2006.

Clementi, Federica K. "Helena Janeczek's Lessons of Darkness: Uncharted Paths to Shoah Memory through Food and Language." *Contemporary Women's Writing* 6, no. 1 (2012): 1–19.

———. "Nightbirds, Nightmares and the Mothers' Smile: Art and Psychoanalysis in Sarah Kofman's Life-Writing." *Women in French Studies* 19 (2011): 67–84.

Cohen-Pfister, Laurel, and Susanne Vees-Gulani, eds. *Generational Shifts in Contemporary German Culture*. Rochester, NY: Camden House, 2010.

Coleridge, Samuel Taylor. "The Rime of the Ancient Mariner." In *English Romantic Verse*, edited by David Wright, 155–75. London: Penguin, 1986.

Collin, Françoise, and Françoise Proust, eds. *Les Cahiers du Grif No. 3: Sarah Kofman*. Paris: Éditions Descartes, 1997.

Collingham, Lizzie. *The Taste of War: World War II and the Battle for Food*. London: Penguin, 2011.

Conlan, Anna, and Amy K. Levin. "Museum Studies Text and Museum Subtexts." In *Gender, Sexuality and Museums: A Routledge Reader*, edited by Amy K. Levin, 299–309. New York: Routledge, 2010.

Conley, Christine. "Memory and Trauerspiel: Charlotte Salomon's *Life? or Theater?* and the Angel of History." In *Reading Charlotte Salomon*, edited by Michael P. Steinberg and Monica Bohm-Duchen, 88–104. Ithaca: Cornell University Press, 2006.

Consonni, Manuela. "The Written Memoir: Italy 1945–1947." In *The Jews Are Coming Back: The Return of the Jews to Their Countries of Origin after WWII*, edited by David Bankier, 169–85. Jerusalem: Yad Vashem and Berghahn, 2005.

Crockatt, Philip. "Freud's 'On Narcissism: An Introduction.'" *Journal of Child Psychotherapy* 32, no. 1 (2006): 4–20.

Culler, Jonathan. *The Pursuit of Signs: Semiotics, Literature, Deconstruction*. Ithaca: Cornell University Press, 1981.

Curio, Claudia. "'Invisible' Children: The Selection and Integration Strategies of Relief Organizations." Translated by Toby Axelrod. *Shofar* 23, no. 1 (2004): 41–56.

Dalsimer, Katherine. *Female Adolescence: Psychoanalytic Reflections on Literature*. New Haven: Yale University Press, 1986.

Darvas, Miriam. *Farewell to Prague*. San Francisco: MacAdam/Cage, 2001.

David, Ruth. *Child of Our Time: A Young Girl's Flight from the Holocaust*. London: I. B. Tauris, 2003.

De Costa, Denise. *Anne Frank and Etty Hillesum: Inscribing Spirituality and Sexuality*. New Brunswick, NJ: Rutgers University Press, 1998.

De Man, Paul. "Autobiography as De-facement." *MLN* 94, no. 5 (1979): 919–30.

———. *The Rhetoric of Romanticism*. New York: Columbia University Press, 1984.

———. "Shelley Disfigured." In *Deconstruction and Criticism*, edited by Harold Bloom, 39–73. New York: Continuum, 1979.

Delbo, Charlotte. *Auschwitz and After*. Translated by Rosette C. Lamont. New Haven: Yale University Press, 1995.

Derrida, Jacques. *Archive Fever: A Freudian Impression*. Translated by Eric Prenowitz. Chicago: University of Chicago Press, 1996.

———. *The Ear of the Other: Otobiography, Transference, Translation: Texts and Discussions with Jacques Derrida*. Edited by Christie V. McDonald. Translated by Peggy Kamuf. New York: Schocken, 1985.

———. *Monolingualism of the Other—Or the Prosthesis of Origin*. Translated by Patrick Mensah. Stanford: Stanford University Press, 1998.

———. *The Post Card: From Socrates to Freud and Beyond*. Translated by Alan Bass. Chicago: University of Chicago Press, 1987.

———. "Sarah Kofman (1934–94): . . . . . . . ." In *The Work of Mourning*. Edited and translated by Pascale-Anne Brault and Michael Naas, 165–88. Chicago: University of Chicago Press, 2003.

Des Pres, Terrence. "Holocaust Laughter?" In *Writing and the Holocaust*, edited by Berel Lang, 216–33. New York: Holmes and Meier, 1988.

Dimen, Muriel. *Sexuality, Intimacy, Power*. London: Analytic, 2003.

Diner, Dan. "Negative Symbiosis: German and Jews after Auschwitz." In *The Holocaust: Theoretical Readings*, edited by Neil Levi and Michael Rothberg, 423–30. Edinburgh: Edinburgh University Press, 2003.

Edwards, Elizabeth, Chris Gosden, and Ruth B. Phillips. Introduction to *Sensible Objects: Colonialism, Museums, and Material Culture*, edited by Elizabeth Edwards, Chris Gosden, and Ruth B. Phillips, 1–31. Oxford: Berg, 2006.

Edwards, Lee. "The Necklace." In *I Came Alone: The Stories of the Kindertransports*, edited by Bertha Leverton and Shmuel Lowensohn, 79–80. Lewes, UK: Book Guild, 1990.

Eliacheff, Caroline, and Nathalie Heinich. *Mères-filles: une relation à trois*. Paris: Albin Michel, 2002.

Eliade, Mircia. *Cosmos and History: The Myth of the Eternal Return*. Princeton: Princeton University Press, 1954.

———. *Myth and Reality*. New York: Harper and Row, 1963.

———. *The Two and the One*. Chicago: University of Chicago Press, 1965.

Enzer, Hyman Aaron, and Sandra Solotaroff-Enzer, eds. *Anne Frank: Reflections on Her Life and Legacy*. Urbana: University of Illinois Press, 2000.

Epstein, Helen. *Children of the Holocaust: Conversations with Sons and Daughters of Survivors*. New York: Putnam, 1979.

———. *Where She Came From: A Daughter's Search for Her Mother's History*. New York: Penguin Putnam, 1998.

Erikson, Kai. "Notes on Trauma and Community." In *Trauma: Explorations in Memory*, edited by Cathy Caruth, 183–99.Baltimore: Johns Hopkins University Press, 1995.

Euripides. *Electra*. In *Ten Plays by Euripides*, translated by Moses Hadas and John McLean, 205–39. New York: Bantam, 1981.

Falconer, Rachel. *Hell in Contemporary Literature: Western Descent Narratives since 1945*. Edinburgh: Edinburgh University Press, 2005.

Fass, Paula S. *Inheriting the Holocaust: A Second-Generation Memoir*. New Brunswick, NJ: Rutgers University Press, 2009.

Fast, Vera K. *Children's Exodus: A History of the Kindertransport*. London: I. B. Tauris, 2011.

Favaro, Angela, F. C. Rodella, and Paolo Santonastaso. "Binge Eating and Eating Attitudes among Nazi Concentration Camp Survivors." *Psychological Medicine* 30, no. 2 (2000): 463–66.

Feldman, Jeffrey David. "Contact Points: Museums and the Lost Body Problem." In *Sensible Objects: Colonialism, Museums, and Material Culture*, edited by Elizabeth Edwards, Chris Gosden, and Ruth B. Phillips, 245–67. Oxford: Berg, 2006.

Felman, Shoshana. *What Does a Woman Want? Reading and Sexual Difference*. Baltimore: Johns Hopkins University Press, 1993.

Felstiner, Mary Lowenthal. "Charlotte Salomon's Inward-Turning Testimony." In *Holocaust Remembrance: The Shapes of Memory*, edited by Geoffrey H. Hartman, 104–16. Cambridge, MA: Blackwell, 1994.

———. "Engendering an Autobiography in Art: Charlotte Salomon's *Life? or Theater?*" In *Revealing Lives: Autobiography, Biography, and Gender*, edited by Susan Groag Bell and Marilyn Yalom, 183–92. Albany: State University of New York Press, 1990.

———. "Taking her Life/History: the Autobiography of Charlotte Salomon." In *Life/Lines: Theorizing Women's Autobiography*, edited by Bella Brodzki and Celeste Schenk, 320–37. Ithaca: Cornell University Press, 1988.

———. *To Paint Her Life: Charlotte Salomon in the Nazi Era*. Berkeley: University of California Press, 1997.

Ficowski, Jerzy. Introduction, translated by Michael Kandel, to Bruno Schulz, *The Street of Crocodiles*, translated by Celina Wieniewska, 13–22. New York: Penguin, 1977.

Figes, Eva. *Little Eden: A Child at War*. London: Faber and Faber, 1978.

Finnan, Carmel. "Autobiography, Memory and the Shoah: German-Jewish Identity in Autobiographical Writings by Ruth Klüger, Cordelia Edvardson and Laura Waco." In *German Monitor: Jews in German Literature since 1945—German-Jewish Literature?*, edited by Pol O'Dochartaigh, 447–61. Amsterdam: Editions Rodopi B.V., 2000.

Fishman, Sylvia Barak. *Follow My Footprints: Changing Images of Women in American Jewish Fiction*. Hanover, NH: Brandeis University Press, 1992.

Fox, Anne L. *Between the Lines: Letters from the Holocaust*. Margate, NJ: ComteQ, 2005.

Frank, Anne. *The Diary of a Young Girl*. New York: Anchor, 1996.

———. *The Diary of Anne Frank: The Revised Critical Edition*. Edited by David Barnouw and Gerrold van der Stroom, translated by Arnold J. Pomerans, B. M. Mooyaart-Doubleday, and Susan Massotty. New York: Doubleday, 2003.

———. *Tales from the Secret Annex*. Translated by Susan Massotty. New York: Bantam, 2003.

Frankl, Viktor E. *Man's Search for Meaning: An Introduction to Logotherapy*. Part 1 translated by Ilse Lasch. 3rd ed. New York: Simon and Schuster, 1984.

Freud, Sigmund. "Humour." In *The Standard Edition of the Complete Psychological Works of Sigmund Freud*, edited and translated by James Strachey, 21:159–66. London: Hogarth, 1973.

———. *The Interpretation of Dreams*. Vol. 4 of *The Standard Edition of the Complete Psychological Works of Sigmund Freud*. Edited and translated by James Strachey. London: Hogarth, 1973.

———. *Jokes and Their Relation to the Unconscious*. Translated by James Strachey. New York: W.W. Norton, 1989.

———. *Letters of Sigmund Freud*. Edited by Ernst L. Freud. Translated by Tania and James Stern. New York: Dover, 1992.

———. "On Narcissism: An Introduction." In *The Standard Edition of the Complete Psychological Works of Sigmund Freud*, edited and translated by James Strachey , 14:67–102. London: Hogarth, 1973.

———. *An Outline of Psychoanalysis*. Edited and translated by James Strachey. New York: W. W. Norton, 1989.

———. Preface to anonymous, *A Young Girl's Diary*. Translated by Eden Paul and Cedar Paul, 7. New York: Thomas Seltzer, 1921.

———. *Totem and Taboo*. Translated by James Strachey. New York: W. W. Norton, 1990.

Freud, Sophie. *Living in the Shadow of the Freud Family*. London: Praeger, 2007.

Friedman, Ester. "The Tapestry." In *I Came Alone: The Stories of the Kindertransports*, edited by Bertha Leverton and Shmuel Lowensohn, 99–101. Lewes, UK: Book Guild, 1990.

Frye, Northrop. *Fables of Identity: Studies in Poetic Mythology*. New York: Harcourt, Brace, and World, 1963.

Fuchs, Anne, Mary Cosgrove, and Georg Grote, eds. *German Memory Contests: The Quest for Identity in Literature, Film, and Discourse since 1990*. Rochester, NY: Camden House, 2006.

Funkenstein, Amos. *Perceptions of Jewish History*. Berkeley: University of California Press, 1993.

Garbarini, Alexandra. *Numbered Days: Diaries and the Holocaust*. New Haven: Yale University Press, 2006.

Geismar, Haidy, and Heather A. Horst. "Introduction: Materializing Ethnography." *Journal of Material Culture* 9, no. 1 (2004): 5–9.

Gershon, Karen, ed. *We Came as Children: A Collective Autobiography*. New York: Harcourt, 1966.

Gies, Miep, with Alison Leslie Gold. *Anne Frank Remembered: The Story of the Woman Who Helped to Hide the Frank Family*. New York: Simon and Schuster, 1987.

Gilbert, Martin. *Churchill and the Jews: A Lifelong Friendship*. New York: Henry Holt, 2007.

Gilbert, Sandra M., and Susan Gubar. *The Madwoman in the Attic: The Woman Writer and the Nineteenth-Century Literary Imagination*. New Haven: Yale University Press, 1979.

Gilman, Sander L. *Jewish Self-Hatred: Anti-Semitism and the Hidden Language of the Jews*. Baltimore: Johns Hopkins University Press, 1986.

Ginzburg, Natalia. *Lessico famigliare*. Turin, Italy: Einaudi, 1963.

Giorgio, Adalgisa. "Dall'autobiografia al romanzo. La rappresentazione della *Shoah* nell'opera di Edith Bruck." In *Le Donne delle minoranze*, edited by Claire E. Honess and Verina R. Jones, 297–307. Turin, Italy: Claudiana, 1999.

———. "Strategies for Remembering: Auschwitz, Mother and Writing in Edith Bruck." In *European Memories of the Second World War*, edited by Helmut Peitsch, Charles Burdett, and Claire Gorrara, 247–55. New York: Berghahn, 1999.

———. *Writing Mothers and Daughters*. New York: Berghahn, 2002.

Goodenough, Elizabeth, and Andrea Immel, eds. *Under Fire: Childhood in the Shadow of War*. Detroit: Wayne State University Press, 2008.

Gordon, Beverly. "Intimacy and Objects: A Proxemic Analysis of Gender-Based Response to the Material World." In *The Material Culture of Gender, The Gender of Material Culture*, edited by Katharine Martinez and Kenneth L. Ames, 237–52. Winterthur, DE: Henry Francis du Pont Winterthur Museum, 1997.

Gruen, Erich S. *Diaspora: Jews amidst Greeks and Romans*. Cambridge: Harvard University Press, 2002.

Gubar, Susan. "Prosopopoeia and Holocaust Poetry in English: Sylvia Plath and Her Contemporaries." *Yale Journal of Criticism* 14, no. 1 (2001): 191–215.

Gurewitsch, Brana. *Mothers, Sisters, Resisters: Oral Histories of Women Who Survived the Holocaust*. Tuscaloosa: University of Alabama Press, 1998.

Gurock, Jeffrey S. *America, American Jews, and the Holocaust*. New York: Routledge 1998.

Guske, Iris. *Trauma and Attachment in the Kindertransport Context: German-Jewish Child Refugees' Accounts of Displacement and Acculturation in Britain*. Newcastle upon Tyne, UK: Cambridge Scholars, 2009.

Hammel, Andrea. "Representations of Family in Autobiographical Texts of Child Refugees." *Shofar* 23, no. 1 (2004): 121–32.

Hacker, Melissa, director. *My Knees Were Jumping: Remembering the Kindertransports*. New York: New Video Group, 2003. DVD.

Hartman, Geoffrey. *The Longest Shadow: In the Aftermath of the Holocaust*. Bloomington: Indiana University Press, 1996.

Harris, Mark Jonathan, director. *Into the Arms of Strangers: Stories of the Kindertransport*. Los Angeles: Warner Brothers, 2001. DVD.

Heberer, Patricia. *Children during the Holocaust*. Lanham, MD: AltaMira, 2011.

Heinemann, Marlene. *Gender and Destiny: Women Writers and the Holocaust*. New York: Greenwood, 1986.

Henke, Suzette. *Shattered Subjects: Trauma and Testimony in Women's Life-Writing*. New York: St. Martin's, 2000.

Hersh, Seymour M. *The Dark Side of Camelot*. Boston: Little, Brown, 1997.

Herzog, Esther, ed. *Life, Death and Sacrifice: Women and Family in the Holocaust*. Jerusalem: Gefen, 2008.

Hillesum, Etty. *An Interrupted Life and Letters from Westerbork*. Translated by Arnold J. Pomerans. New York: Henry Holt, 1996.

Hirsch, Marianne. *The Familial Gaze*. Hanover, NH: University Press of New England, 1999.

———. *Family Frames: Photography Narrative and Postmemory*. Cambridge: Harvard University Press, 1997.

———. *The Generation of Postmemory: Writing and Visual Culture after the Holocaust*. New York: Columbia University Press, 2012.

———. *The Mother/Daughter Plot: Narrative, Psychoanalysis, Feminism*. Bloomington: Indiana University Press, 1989.

———. "Past Lives: Postmemories in Exile." *Poetics Today* 17, no. 4 (1996): 659–86.

——— and Nancy K. Miller. Introduction to *Rites of Return: Diaspora Poetics and the Politics of Memory*, edited by Marianne Hirsch and Nancy K. Miller, 1–20. New York: Columbia University Press, 2011.

——— and Leo Spitzer. *Ghosts of Home: The Afterlife of Czernowitz in Jewish Memory*. Berkeley: University of California Press, 2010.

———. "The Tile Stove." *Women Studies Quarterly* 36, nos. 1–2 (2008): 141–50.

Hoffman, Eva. *After Such Knowledge: Memory, History and the Legacy of the Holocaust*. New York: Public Affairs, 2004.

———. *Lost in Translation: A Life in a New Language*. New York: Penguin, 1990.

Hoffman, Martin L. *Empathy and Moral Development: Implications for Caring and Justice*. Cambridge: Cambridge University Press, 2000.

Horowitz, Sara R. "Women in Holocaust Literature: Engendering Trauma Memory." In *Women in the Holocaust*, edited by Dalia Ofer and Lenore J. Weitzman, 364–77. New Haven: Yale University Press, 1998.

Höss, Rudolph. *Death Dealer: The Memoirs of the SS Kommandant at Auschwitz*. Edited by Steven Paskuly. Translated by Andrew Pollinger. Buffalo, NY: Prometheus, 1992.

Huyssen, Andreas. "Diaspora and Nation: Migration into Other Pasts." *New German Critique* 88 (2003): 147–64.

Hyman, Paula E. "Gender and the Immigrant Jewish Experience in the United States." In *Jewish Women in Historical Perspective*, edited by Judith Reesa Baskin, 312–36. Detroit: Wayne State University Press, 1998.

Iacovetta, Franca, Paula Jean Draper, and Robert Ventresca. *A Nation of Immigrants: Women, Workers, and Communities in Canadian History, 1840s–1960s*. Toronto: University of Toronto Press, 2002.

Ian, Marcia. *Remembering the Phallic Mother: Psychoanalysis, Modernism, and the Fetish*. Ithaca: Cornell University Press, 1993.

Irigaray, Luce. "And the One Doesn't Stir without the Other." Translated by Helene Vivienne Wenzel. *Signs* 7 (1981): 60–67.

———. *Sexes and Genealogies*. Translated by Gillian C. Gill. New York: Columbia University Press, 1993.

———. *Speculum of the Other Woman*. Translated by Gillian C. Gill. Ithaca: Cornell University Press, 1974.

Jabès, Edmond. *The Book of Resemblances*. Translated by Rosmarie Waldrop. Hanover, NH: University Press of New England, 1990.

Jacobs, Amber. *On Matricide: Myth, Psychoanalysis, and the Law of the Mother*. New York: Columbia University Press, 2007.

Janeczek, Helena. *Cibo*. Milan: Mondadori, 2002.

———. *Lezioni di tenebra*. Milan: Mondadori, 1997.

Jardine, Alice A. "Sarah Kofman." In *Shifting Scenes: Interviews on Women, Writing, and Politics in Post-68 France*, edited by Alice A. Jardine and Anne M. Menke, translated by Janice Orion, 104–12. New York: Columbia University Press, 1991.

Johnson, Barbara. "Apostrophe, Animation, and Abortion." *Diacritics* 16, no. 1 (1986): 28–47.

Kacandes, Irene. "Displacement, Trauma, Language, Identity." In *Femmes écrivains à la croisée des langues, 1700–2000/Women Writers at the Crossroads of Languages, 1700–2000*, edited by

Agnese Fidecaro, Henriette Partzsch, Suzan van Dijk, and Valérie Cossy, 213–28. Geneva: MétisPresses, 2009.

———. *Talk Fiction: Literature and the Talk Explosion*. Lincoln: University of Nebraska Press, 2001.

Kafka, Franz. *Die Verwandlung*. Edited by Heribert Kuhn. Frankfurt: Suhrkamp, 1999.

———. "An Imperial Message." In *Kafka: Selected Stories*, translated by Ian Johnston, 96. West Valley City, UT: Waking Lion, 2008

———. *Letter to His Father. Brief an den Vater*. Translated by Ernst Kaiser and Eithne Wilkins. New York: Schocken, 1966.

Kamuf, Peggy, ed. *A Derrida Reader: Between the Blinds*. New York: Columbia University Press, 1991.

Kaplan, Marion A. *Between Dignity and Despair: Jewish Life in Nazi Germany*. New York: Oxford University Press, 1998.

Karpf, Anne. *The War After*. London: Minerva, 1997.

Kassow, Samuel D. Introduction to *The Warsaw Ghetto Oyneg Shabes—Ringelblum Archive: Catalog and Guide*, edited by Robert Moses Shapiro and Tadeusz Epstein, translated by Robert Moses Shapiro, xv–xxiv. Bloomington: Indiana University Press, 2009.

———. *Who Will Write Our History? Emanuel Ringelblum, the Warsaw Ghetto, and the Oyneg Shabes Archive*. Bloomington: Indiana University Press, 2007.

Kaye/Kantrowitz, Melanie. "The Issue Is Power: Some Notes on Jewish Women and Therapy." In *Jewish Women in Therapy: Seen but Not Heard*, edited by Rachel Josefowitz Siegel and Ellen Cole, 7–18. Binghamton, NY: Haworth, 1991.

Kestenberg, Judith S. "A Metapsychological Assessment Based on an Analysis of a Survivor's Child." In *Generations of the Holocaust*, edited by Martin S. Bergmann and Milton E. Jucovy, 137–44. New York: Basic, 1982.

———. "Psychoanalyses of Children of Survivors from the Holocaust: Case Presentations and Assessment." *Journal of the American Psychoanalytic Association* 28, no. 4 (1980): 775–804.

———. "Transposition Revisited: Clinical, Therapeutic, and Developmental Considerations." In *Healing Their Wounds: Psychotherapy with Holocaust Survivors and Their Families*, edited by Paul Marcus and Alan Rosenberg, 67–82. Santa Barbara, CA: Praeger, 1989.

King, Jeremy. *Budweisers into Czechs and Germans: A Local History of Bohemian Politics, 1848–1948*. Princeton: Princeton University Press, 2002.

Klüger, Ruth. *Still Alive: A Holocaust Girlhood Remembered*. New York: Feminist, 2003.

———. *unterwegs verloren: Erinnerungen*. Vienna: Paul Zsolnay Verlag, 2008.

———. *weiter leben: Eine Jugend*. Göttingen, Germany: Wallstein Verlag, 1992.

Kofman, Sarah. *Autobiogriffures: Du chat Murr d'Hoffmann*. Paris: Galilée, 1984.

———. *Camera Obscura: De l'idéologie*. Paris: Galilée, 1973.

———. *Comment s'en sortir?* Paris: Galilée, 1983.

———. *Conversions: Le Marchand de Venise—Sous le signe de Saturne*. Paris: Galilée, 1987.

———. *L'Enfance de l'art: Une interprétation de l'esthétique freudienne*. Paris: Payot, 1970.

———. *L'Énigme de la femme: la femme dans les textes de Freud*. Paris: Galilée, 1983.

———. *Explosion I: De l'"Ecce Homo" de Nietzsche*. Paris: Galilée, 1992.

———. *L'Imposture de la beauté*. Paris: Galilée, 1995.

———. *La Mélancolie de l'art*. Paris: Galilée, 1985.

———. "La mort blanche." *Fusées*, no. 16 (2009): 7.

———. "'Ma vie' et la psychanalyse." In *Les Cahiers du Grif No. 3: Sarah Kofman*, edited by Françoise Collin and Françoise Proust, 171–72. Paris: Éditions Descartes, 1997.

———. *Paroles suffoquées*. Paris: Galilée, 1987.

———. *Pourquoi rit-on? Freud et le mot d'esprit*. Paris: Galilée, 1986.

———. *Rue Ordener, rue Labat*. Paris: Galilée, 1994.

———. "Sacrée nourriture." In *Les Cahiers du Grif No. 3: Sarah Kofman*, edited by Françoise Collin and Françoise Proust, 167–68. Paris: Éditions Descartes, 1997.

———. *Selected Writings*. Edited by Thomas Albrecht, Georgia Albert, and Elizabeth G. Rottenberg. Stanford: Stanford University Press, 2007.

———. *Smothered Words*. Translated with an introduction by Madeleine Dobie. Evanston, IL: Northwestern University Press, 1998.

———. "Tombeau pour un nom proper." In *Les Cahiers du Grif No. 3: Sarah Kofman*, edited by Françoise Collin and Françoise Proust, 169–70. Paris: Éditions Descartes, 1997.

Kogon, Eugen. *The Theory and Practice of Hell: The German Concentration Camps and the System behind Them*. Translated by Heinz Norden. New York: Farrar, Straus and Giroux, 2006.

Kohut, Heinz. *The Analysis of the Self: A Systematic Approach to the Psychoanalytic Treatment of Narcissistic Personality Disorders*. New York: International Universities Press, 1971.

Körte, Mona. "Bracelet, Hand Towel, Pocket Watch: Objects of the Last Moment in Memory and Narration." *Shofar* 23, no. 1 (2004): 109–20.

Kremer, S. Lillian. *Women's Holocaust Writing: Memory and Imagination*. Lincoln: University of Nebraska Press, 2001.

Kristeva, Julia. *Black Sun: Depression and Melancholia*. Translated by Leon S. Roudiez. New York: Columbia University Press, 1989.

Kushner, Tony. "Beyond the Pale? British Reactions to Nazi Anti-Semitism, 1933–39." In *The Politics of Marginality: Race, the Radical Right and Minorities in Twentieth Century Britain*, edited by Tony Kushner and Kenneth Lunn, 143–60. London: Frank Cass, 1990.

———. "Remembering to Forget: Racism and Anti-Racism in Postwar Britain." In *Modernity, Culture and "The Jew*," edited by Bryan Cheyette and Laura Marcus, 226–41. Stanford: Stanford University Press, 1998.

——— and Ken Lunn, eds. *Traditions of Intolerance: Historical Perspectives on Fascism and Race Discourse in British Society*. Manchester, UK: Manchester University Press, 1989.

Lacan, Jacques. *Écrits I*. Paris: Éditions du Seuil, 1999.

———. *Écrits II*. Paris: Éditions du Seuil, 1999.

———. *Écrits, The First Complete Edition in English*. Translated by Bruce Fink. New York: W. W. Norton, 2006.

———. *Encore: Séminaire, livre XX*. Edited by Jacques-Alain Miller. Paris: Éditions du Seuil, 1975.

———. *Le moi dans la théorie de Freud et dans la technique de la psychanalyse: Séminaire, livre II*. Edited by Jacques-Alain Miller. Paris: Editions du Seuil, 1978.

———. *Les quatre concepts de la psychanalyse: Séminaire, livre XI*. Edited by Jacques-Alain Miller. Paris: Éditions du Seuil, 1973.

Landsberg, Alison. *Prosthetic Memory: The Transformation of American Remembrance in the Age of Mass Culture*. New York: Columbia University Press, 2004.

Langer, Lawrence L. *Admitting the Holocaust: Collected Essays*. Oxford: Oxford University Press, 1995.

———. "The Americanization of the Holocaust on Stage and Screen." In *A Scholarly Look at The Diary of Anne Frank*, edited by Harold Bloom, 15–34. Philadelphia: Chelsea House, 1999.

———, ed. *Art from the Ashes: A Holocaust Anthology*. Oxford: Oxford University Press, 1995.

———. "The Uses—and Misuses—of a Young Girl's Diary: 'If Anne Frank Could Return from among the Murdered, She Would Be Appalled.'" In *Anne Frank: Reflections on Her Life and Legacy*, edited by Hyman Aaron Enzer and Sandra Solotaroff-Enzer, 203–5. Urbana: University of Illinois Press, 2000.

Laska, Vera, ed. *Women in the Resistance and in the Holocaust: The Voices of Eyewitnesses*. Westport, CT: Greenwood, 1983.

Lassner, Phyllis. *Anglo-Jewish Women Writing the Holocaust: Displaced Witnesses*. New York: Palgrave Macmillan, 2008.

——— and Lara Trubowitz, eds. *Anti-Semitism and Philosemitism in the Twentieth and Twenty-First Centuries: Representing Jews, Jewishness, and Modern Culture*. Newark: University of Delaware Press, 2008.

Laub, Dori, and Nanette C. Auerhahn. "Reverberations of Genocide: Its Expression in the Conscious and Unconscious of Post-Holocaust Generations." In *Psychoanalytic Reflections on the Holocaust: Selected Essays*, edited by Steven A. Luel and Paul Marcus, 151–67. New York: Ktav, 1984.

Lazzaro-Weis, Carol. *From Margins to Mainstream: Feminism and Fictional Modes in Italian Women's Writing, 1968–1990*. Philadelphia: University of Pennsylvania Press, 1993.

Lehmann, Sophia. "In Search of a Mother Tongue: Locating Home in Diaspora." MELUS 23, no. 4 (1998): 101–18.

Lemelman, Martin. *Mendel's Daughter: A Memoir*. New York: Free Press, 2006.

Lerner, Gerda. *The Creation of Patriarchy*. Oxford: Oxford University Press, 1986.

Leverton, Bertha. "Dear Friends and Readers." In *I Came Alone: The Stories of the Kindertransports*, edited by Bertha Leverton and Shmuel Lowensohn, 8–9. Lewes, UK: Book Guild, 1990.

Leverton, Bertha, and Shmuel Lowensohn, eds. *I Came Alone: The Stories of the Kindertransports*. Lewes, UK: Book Guild, 1990.

Levi, Primo. *I sommersi e i salvati*. In *Opere*, edited by Cesare Cases, 1:651–822. Turin, Italy: Einaudi, 1987.

———. *Il Sistema periodico*. In *Opere*, edited by Cesare Cases, 1:427–649. Turin, Italy: Einaudi, 1987.

———. *Se questo è un uomo*. Turin, Italy: Einaudi, 1986.

Lévinas, Emmanuel. *Totality and Infinity: An Essay on Exteriority*. Translated by Alphonso Lingis. Pittsburgh: Duquesne University Press, 1969.

Lindwer, Willy. *The Last Seven Months of Anne Frank*. New York: Anchor, 1992.

Lipman, Steve. *Laughter in Hell: The Use of Humor during the Holocaust*. Northvale, NJ: Jason Aronson, 1991.

Liska, Vivian. "Parricidal Autobiographies: Sarah Kofman between Theory and Memory." *European Journal of Women's Studies* 7, no. 1 (2000): 91–101.

Liss, Andrea. *Trespassing through Shadows: Memory, Photography and the Holocaust*. Minneapolis: University of Minnesota Press, 1998.

London, Louise. *Whitehall and the Jews 1933–1948: British Immigration Policy and the Holocaust*. Cambridge: Cambridge University Press, 2003.

MacDonogh, Giles. *1938: Hitler's Gamble*. New York: Basic, 2009.

Marcuse, Herbert. *Eros and Civilization*. New York: Vintage, 1962.

Matthäus, Jürgen, and Mark Roseman. *Jewish Responses to Persecution*. Vol. 1, *1933-1938*. Lanham, MD: AltaMira, 2010.

Mauceri, Maria Cristina. "Writing outside the Borders: Personal Experience and History in the Works of Helga Schneider and Helena Janeczek." In *Across Genres, Generations and Borders: Italian Women Writing Lives*, edited by Susanna Scarparo and Rita Wilson, 140–51. Newark: University of Delaware Press, 2004.

McGlothlin, Erin. *Second-Generation Holocaust Literature: Legacies of Survival and Perpetration*. Rochester, NY: Camden House, 2006.

Meintjes, Sheila, Anu Pillay and Meredeth Turshen. *The Aftermath: Women in Post-Conflict Transformation*. London: Zed, 2001.

Metselaar, Menno, and Ruud van der Rol. *Anne Frank: Her Life in Words and Pictures*. Translated by Arnold J. Pomerans. New York: Roaring Brook, 2009.

Migiel, Marilyn. "Faltering on Demand: Readings of Freud's Dream of Irma." *Diacritics* 20, no. 2 (1990): 20–39.

Miller, Nancy K. *But Enough about Me: Why We Read Other People's Lives*. New York: Columbia University Press, 2002.

Millu, Liana. *Il fumo di Birkenau*. Florence: Giuntina, 2008.

Milton, Edith. *The Tiger in the Attic: Memories of the Kindertransport and Growing Up English*. Chicago: University of Chicago Press, 2005.

Miron, Dan. *The Image of the Shtetl and Other Studies of Modern Jewish Literary Imagination*. Syracuse, NY: Syracuse University Press, 2000.

Morreall, John. *Comic Relief: A Comprehensive Philosophy of Humor*. Oxford: Wiley-Blackwell, 2009.

Morris, Leslie. "Postmemory, Postmemoir." In *Unlikely History: The Changing German-Jewish Symbiosis, 1945–2000*, edited by Leslie Morris and Jack Zipes, 291–306. New York: Palgrave Macmillan, 2002.

Myers, David N. Preface to *Jewish History and Jewish Memory: Essays in Honor of Yosef Hayim Yerushalmi*, edited by Elisheva Carlebach, John M. Efron, and David N. Myers, xiii–xv. Hanover, NH: University Press of New England, 1998.

Nancy, Jean-Luc. "Cours, Sarah!" In *Les Cahiers du Grif No. 3: Sarah Kofman*, edited by Françoise Collin and Françoise Proust, 29–37. Paris: Éditions Descartes, 1997.

Neumeier, Beate. "Kindertransport: Memory, Identity and the British-Jewish Diaspora." In *Diaspora and Multiculturalism: Common Traditions and New Developments*, edited by Monika Fludernik, 83–112. New York: Rodopi, 2003.

Nicholas, Lynn H. *Cruel World: The Children of Europe in the Nazi Web*. New York: Alfred A. Knopf, 2005.

Nietzsche, Friederich. *On the Genealogy of Morals and Ecce Homo*. Edited and translated by Walter Kaufmann and R. J. Hollingdale. New York: Random House, 1967.

Nolden, Thomas. Introduction to *Voices of the Diaspora: Jewish Women Writing in Contemporary Europe*, edited by Thomas Nolden and Frances Malino, ix–xxxvi. Evanston, IL: Northwestern University Press, 2005.

Nora, Pierre. "Between Memory and History: Les Lieux de Mémoire." Translated by Marc Roudebush. *Representations* 26 (Spring 1989): 7–24.

———. "General Introduction: Between Memory and History." In *Realms of Memory: Rethinking the French Past*, under the direction of Pierre Nora, English-language edition edited and with a foreword by Lawrence D. Kritzman, translated by Arthur Goldhammer, 1:1–20. New York: Columbia University Press, 1996.

———. "Preface to the English-Language Edition." In *Realms of Memory: Rethinking the French Past*, under the direction of Pierre Nora, English-language edition edited and with a foreword by Lawrence D. Kritzman, translated by Arthur Goldhammer, 1:xv–xxiv. New York: Columbia University Press, 1996.

———, dir. *Realms of Memory: Rethinking the French Past*, English-language edition edited and with a foreword by Lawrence D. Kritzman. Translated by Arthur Goldhammer. 3 vols. New York: Columbia University Press, 1996–98.

Novick, Peter. *The Holocaust in American Life*. Boston: Houghton Mifflin, 1999.

Obrdlik, Antonin J. "Gallows Humor: A Sociological Phenomenon." *American Journal of Sociology* 47, no. 5 (1942): 709–16.

Ofer, Dalia, and Lenore J. Weitzman, eds. *Women in the Holocaust*. New Haven: Yale University Press, 1998.

Oldfield, Sybil. " 'It Is Usually She': The Role of British Women in the Rescue and Care of the Kindertransport Kinder," *Shofar* 23, no. 1 (2004): 57–70.

Oliver, Kelly. "Sarah Kofman's Queasy Stomach and the Riddle of the Paternal Law." In *Enigmas: Essays on Sarah Kofman*, edited by Penelope Deutscher and Kelly Oliver, 174–88. Ithaca: Cornell University Press, 1999.

Paskuly, Steven. Epilogue to Rudolph Höss, *Death Dealer: The Memoirs of the SS Kommandant at Auschwitz*, edited by Steven Paskuly, translated by Andrew Pollinger, 196–205. Buffalo, NY: Prometheus, 1992.

Pines, Dinora. "The Impact of the Holocaust on the Second Generation." In *Holocaust Trauma: Transgenerational Transmission to the Second Generation; Psychoanalytic, Psychosocial, and Object Relational Perspectives*, edited by Moshe Halevi Spero, 85–105. Ramat-Gan, Israel: Bar-Ilan University Press, 1992.

Plain, Gill. *Women's Fiction of the Second World War: Gender, Power, Resistance*. Edinburgh: Edinburgh University Press, 1996.

Poland, Warren S. "The Gift of Laughter: On the Development of a Sense of Humor in Clinical Analysis." *Psychoanalytic Quarterly* 59, no. 2 (1990): 197–225.

Pollak, Richard. *The Creation of Dr. B: A Biography of Bruno Bettelheim*. New York: Simon and Schuster, 1998.

Pollock, Griselda. "Theater of Memory: Trauma and Cure in Charlotte Salomon's Modernist Fairytale." In *Reading Charlotte Salomon*, edited by Michael P. Steinberg and Monica Bohm-Duchen, 34–72. Ithaca: Cornell University Press, 2006.

Post, Jerrold M. "Current Concepts of the Narcissistic Personality: Implications for Political Psychology." *Political Psychology* 14, no. 1 (1993): 99–121.

Pratt, Mary Louise. *Imperial Eyes: Travel Writing and Transculturation*. New York: Routledge, 2008.

Propp, Vladimir. *Morphology of the Folktale*. Edited by Louis A. Wagner. Translated by Laurence Scott. Austin: University of Texas Press, 1968.

Quintilian. *The Institutio Oratoria of Quintilian*. Translated by H. E. Butler. 4 vols. London: William Heinemann, 1921–36.

Reading, Anna. *The Social Inheritance of the Holocaust: Gender, Culture, and Memory*. New York: Palgrave Macmillan, 2002.

Ringelheim, Joan. "The Split between Gender and the Holocaust." In *Women in the Holocaust*, edited by Dalia Ofer and Lenore J. Weitzman, 340–50. New Haven: Yale University Press, 1998.

Ringelblum, Emanuel. *Kronika Getta Warszawskiego.* Warsaw: Czytelnik, 1983.

Rittner, Carol, ed. *Anne Frank in the World: Essays and Reflections.* New York: M. E. Sharpe, 1998.

———— and John K. Roth. *Different Voices: Women and the Holocaust.* St. Paul, MN: Paragon, 1993.

Robson, Kathryn. *Writing Wounds: The Inscription of Trauma in Post-1968 French Women's Life-Writing.* New York: Rodopi, 2004.

Rosenthal, Norman. "Charlotte Salomon's Life? or Theatre? A 20th-Century Song of Innocence and Experience." In Charlotte Salomon, *Life? or Theatre?,* translated by Leila Vennewitz, 9–13. Zwolle, Holland: Waanders, 1998.

Roskies, David G. *Against the Apocalypse: Responses to Catastrophe in Modern Jewish Culture.* Syracuse, NY: Syracuse University Press, 1999.

Roth, Milena. *Lifesaving Letters: A Child's Flight from the Holocaust.* Seattle: University of Washington Press, 2004.

Roth, Philip. *The Ghost Writer.* New York: Library of America, 2007.

Rothberg, Michael. *Traumatic Realism: The Demands of Holocaust Representation.* Minneapolis: University of Minnesota Press, 2000.

————, Deberati Sanyal, and Max Silverman. *Noeuds de Mémoire: Multidirectional Memory in Postwar French and Francophone Culture.* New Haven: Yale University Press, 2010.

Said, Edward. *Reflections on Exile and Other Essays.* Cambridge: Harvard University Press, 2000.

Saidel, Rochelle G. *The Jewish Women of Ravensbrück Concentration Camp.* Madison: University of Wisconsin Press, 2004.

Salomon, Charlotte. *Life? or Theatre?* Translated by Leila Vennewitz. Zwolle, Holland: Waanders, 1998.

Schaumann, Caroline. "From 'weiter leben' (1992) to 'Still Alive' (2001): Ruth Klüger's Cultural Translation of Her 'German Book' for an American Audience." *German Quarterly* 77, no. 3 (2004): 324–39.

————. *Memory Matters: Generational Responses to Germany's Nazi Past in Recent Women's Literature.* Berlin: Walter de Gruyter, 2008.

Schmidtkunz, Renata. *Im Gespräch: Ruth Klüger.* Vienna: Mandelbaum Verlag, 2008.

Schnabel, Ernst. *Anne Frank: A Portrait in Courage.* Translated by Richard Winston and Clara Winston. New York: Harcourt, Brace, 1958.

Schuchalter, Jerry. *Poetry and Truth: Variations on Holocaust Testimony.* Bern, Switzerland: Peter Lang AG International Academic, 2009.

Schulz, Bruno. *Cinnamon Shops.* In *The Street of Crocodiles,* translated by Celina Wieniewska, 85–98. New York: Penguin, 1977.

————. "Cockroaches." In *The Street of Crocodiles,* translated by Celina Wieniewska, 111-116. London: Penguin, 1977.

Segal, Lore. *Other People's Houses.* London: Victor Gollancz, 1965.

Seidel, Michael. *Exile and Narrative Imagination.* New Haven: Yale University Press, 1986.

Seifert, Lewis C. *Fairy Tales, Sexuality, and Gender in France: 1690–1715.* Cambridge: Cambridge University Press, 1996.

Sereni, Clara. *Casalinghitudine.* Turin, Italy: Einaudi, 1987.

————. *Keeping House: A Novel in Recipes.* Translated by Giovanni Micieli Jeffries and Susan Briziarelli. Albany: State University of New York Press, 2005.

Shapiro, Robert Moses, and Tadeusz Epsztein, eds. *The Warsaw Ghetto Oyneg Shabes—Ringelblum Archive: Catalog and Guide*. Bloomington: Indiana University Press, 2009.

Shuval, Judith. "Diaspora Migration: Definitional Ambiguities and a Theoretical Paradigm." *International Migration Quarterly Review* 38, no. 5 (2000): 41–55.

Sicher, Efraim. *The Holocaust Novel*. New York: Routledge, 2005.

Sierakowiak, Dawid. *The Diary of Dawid Sierakowiak: Five Notebooks from the Łódź Ghetto*. New York: Oxford University Press, 1996.

Silverman, Kaja. *The Acoustic Mirror: The Female Voice in Psychoanalysis and Cinema*. Bloomington: Indiana University Press, 1988.

——. *The Threshold of the Visible World*. New York: Routledge, 1996.

Smith, Sidonie. *A Poetics of Women's Autobiography: Marginality and the Fictions of Self-Representation*. Bloomington: Indiana University Press, 1987.

Spiegelman, Art. *Maus: A Survivor's Tale*. New York: Pantheon, 1996.

Sprengnether, Madelon. "Mouth to Mouth: Freud, Irma, and the Dream of Psychoanalysis." *American Imago* 60, no. 3 (2003): 259–84.

Stadner, Suzan Hanala. *My Parents Went through the Holocaust and All I Got Was This Lousy T-Shirt*. Santa Ana, CA: Seven Locks, 2006.

Stanislawski, Michael. *Autobiographical Jews: Essays in Jewish Self-Fashioning*. Seattle: University of Washington Press, 2004.

——. *For Whom Do I Toil? Judah Leib Gordon and the Crisis of Russian Jewry*. New York: Oxford University Press, 1988.

Stargardt, Nicholas. *Witnesses of War: Children's Lives under the Nazis*. New York: Alfred A. Knopf, 2005.

Steinberg, Michael P. "Reading Charlotte Salomon: History, Memory, Modernism." In *Reading Charlotte Salomon*, edited by Michael P. Steinberg and Monica Bohm-Duchen, 1–20. Ithaca: Cornell University Press, 2006.

Steiner, George. *After Babel: Aspects of Language and Translation*. Oxford: Oxford University Press, 1998.

——. "Our Homeland, The Text." *Salmagundi*, no. 66 (1985): 4–25.

Stone, Kay F. "Fairy Tales for Adults: Walt Disney's Americanization of the Märchen." In *Folklore on Two Continents: Essays in Honor of Linda Dégh*, edited by Nikolai Burlakoff and Carl Lindahl, 40–48. Bloomington, IN: Trickster, 1980.

Sujo, Glenn. *Legacies of Silence: The Visual Arts and Holocaust Memory*. London: Philip Wilson, 2001.

Suleiman, Susan Rubin. "The 1.5 Generation: Thinking about Child Survivors and the Holocaust." *American Imago* 59, no. 3 (2002): 277–95.

Sullivan, Ed. "Beyond Anne Frank: Recent Holocaust Literature for Young People." *New Advocate* 15 (2001): 49–55.

Surrey, Janet L. "The 'Self-in-Relation': A Theory of Women's Development." In *Women's Growth in Connection: Writings from the Stone Center*, edited by Judith V. Jordan et al., 51–66. New York: Guilford, 1991.

Swartz, Sarah Silberstein, and Margie Wolfe. *From Memory to Transformation: Jewish Women's Voices*. Toronto: Second Story, 1998.

Tec, Nechama. *Resilience and Courage: Women, Men, and the Holocaust*. New Haven: Yale University Press, 2003.

Tobin, Beth Fowkes. "Introduction: Consumption as a Gendered Social Practice." In *Material Women, 1750–1950: Consuming Desires and Collecting Practices*, edited by Maureen Daly Goggin and Beth Fowkes Tobin, 1–13. Burlington, VT: Ashgate, 2009.

Tolkien, J. R. R. *Tree and Leaf*. Boston: Houghton Mifflin, 1965.

Van der Stroom, Gerrold. "The Diaries, *Het Achterhuis* and the Translations." In Anne Frank, *The Diary of Anne Frank: The Revised Critical Edition*, edited by David Barnouw and Gerrold van der Stroom, translated by Arnold J. Pomerans, B. M. Mooyaart-Doubleday, and Susan Massotty, 59–77. New York: Doubleday, 2003.

Vice, Sue. *Children Writing the Holocaust*. New York: Palgrave Macmillan, 2004.

Vogelman, Daniel. "My Share of the Pain." In *Second Generation Voices: Reflections by Children of Holocaust Survivors and Perpetrators*, edited by Naomi Berger and Alan L. Berger, 72–76. Syracuse, NY: Syracuse University Press, 2001.

Wagner, Richard. *Judaism in Music and Other Essays*. Translated by Ashton Ellis. Lincoln: University of Nebraska Press, 1995.

Wajnryb, Ruth. *Silence: How Tragedy Shapes Talk*. Crows Nest, Australia: Allen and Unwin, 2001.

Wardi, Dina. *Memorial Candles: Children of the Holocaust*. Translated by Naomi Goldblum. London: Routledge, 1992.

Waxman, Zoë Vania. *Writing the Holocaust: Identity, Testimony, Representation*. New York: Oxford University Press, 2006.

Weisz, Frans, director. *Leven? of Theater?* Amsterdam: Homescreen, 2012. DVD.

Weitzman, Lenore J., and Dalia Ofer. "Introduction: The Role of Gender in the Holocaust." In *Women in the Holocaust*, edited by Dalia Ofer and Lenore J. Weitzman, 1–18. New Haven: Yale University Press, 1998.

Wiesel, Elie. *Night*. Translated by Marion Wiesel. New York: Farrar, Straus and Giroux, 2006.

Wiesenthal, Simon. "Epilogue to the Diary of Anne Frank." In *Anne Frank: Reflections on Her Life and Legacy*, edited by Hyman Aaron Enzer and Sandra Solotaroff-Enzer, 61–68. Urbana: University of Illinois Press, 2000.

Williams, Bill. "The Anti-Semitism of Tolerance: Middle-Class Manchester and the Jews 1870–1900." In *City, Class and Culture: Studies of Social Policy and Cultural Production in Victorian Manchester*, edited by Alan J. Kidd and Kenneth W. Roberts, 74–102. Manchester, UK: Manchester University Press, 1985.

Wordsworth, William. *The Prose Works of William Wordsworth*. Edited by Alexander B. Grosart. 3 vols. London: Edward Moxon, 1876.

Young, James E. "Jewish Memory in a Postmodern Age." In *Modernity, Culture and "The Jew,"* edited by Bryan Cheyette and Laura Marcus, 211–25. Stanford: Stanford University Press, 1998.

Zahra, Tara. *Kidnapped Souls: National Indifference and the Battle for Children in the Bohemian Lands, 1900–1948*. Ithaca: Cornell University Press, 2008.

———. *The Lost Children: Reconstructing Europe's Families after World War II*. Cambridge: Harvard University Press, 2011.

Zimmerman, Joshua D., ed. *Contested Memories: Poles and Jews during the Holocaust and Its Aftermath*. New Brunswick, NJ: Rutgers University Press, 2003.

Zipes, Jack. *Breaking the Magic Spell: Radical Theories of Folk and Fairy Tales*. Austin: University of Texas Press, 1979.

———, trans. and ed. *The Complete Fairy Tales of the Brothers Grimm*. New York: Bantam, 1987.

———. *Fairy Tales and the Art of Subversion: The Classical Genre for Children and the Process of Civilization*. New York: Methuen, 1988.

———. *When Dreams Come True: Classical Fairy Tales and Their Tradition*. New York: Routledge, 1999.

Žižek, Slavoj. *Looking Awry: An Introduction to Jacques Lacan through Popular Culture*. Cambridge: MIT Press, 1992.

Zohar, Ada H., Lotem Giladi, and Timor Givati. "Holocaust Exposure and Disordered Eating: A Study of Multi-Generational Transmission." *European Eating Disorders Review* 15, no. 1 (2007): 50–57.

# INDEX

168–69, 172; memory objects and, 23–25, 174; women's role in Kindertransport and, 171

Lindwer, Willy, 273

Lipman, Steve, 258

literary apostrophe: Bruck and, 46–49, 57–58, 62–66, 70–77; *The Diary of a Young Girl* (Frank) as, 253

Lowensohn, Shmuel, 160

*Man without Qualities, The* (Musil), 86

Masaryk, Tomáš, 167

matricide, 14–15, 299–304

Mauceri, Maria Christina, 243, 245–46

*mauscheln*, 238

*Maus* (Spiegelman), 12, 42, 105

Mauthausen, 281

*Mein barbar*, 231–42

Meintjes, Sheila, 33

Mémé. *See* Chemitre, Claire (Mémé)

memory objects: definition, 24, 175; Kindertransport, personal experiences, 177–83, 185–88; material objects and identity, 174–76; pen imagery and Kofman, 40, 123–24, 147, 151–52, 200, 201; prosthetic memory and, 188–202

Mengele, Josef, 11, 51, 55, 108

*Merchant of Venice, The* (Shakespeare), 117, 139–40, 143

Miller, Nancy K., 96, 206–11, 210

Millu, Liana, 240

Milton, Edith, 209

Mitteleuropa, 86–87

Morreall, John, 258–59

Morris, Leslie, 205–6

*morte blanche*, 137–48

mother-daughter bond: "failing" mother typology, 97 (*See also* Freud, Sigmund); gendered differences in writing and, 5; in Greek mythology, 146–48, 150, 151–52, 300–302; "Jewish mother" archetype, 97; memory objects and, 179; Mengele's order to kill mothers with their children, 11, 108; portrayal of, in literature, 10–16; rejection of mother and, 132–37; wicked

stepmother theme in fairy tales, 90–99; womb metaphor and, 54–55

Movement for the Care of Refugee Children from Germany, 159

Museum of Jewish Heritage, 199

Musil, Robert, 86

Myers, David, 41

*My Knees Were Jumping* (film), 92

Nancy, Jean-Luc, 23, 32

narcissism, 286–87

Nazis: Hitler, 260–61, 284–85; Höss, 250–51, 290, 297; Jewish objects hoarded by, 176; Silberbauer, 290–91. *See also* antisemitism; Holocaust; *individual names of concentration camps*

"negative symbiosis," 220

Neumeier, Beate, 164

Nietzsche, Friedrich, 123

*Night* (Wiesel), 5, 6, 12, 52

Noel-Baker, Philip, 170

Nora, Pierre, 24, 175, 188, 190, 191–92, 201

Novick, Peter, 208–9

Nuremberg Laws, 295

Obrdlik, Antonin, 259

Ochs, Siegfried, 296

Ofer, Dalia, 4

Oldfield, Sybil, 170

Oliver, Kelly, 23, 131, 133, 151–52, 226

Opetka Company, 267, 275

Otherness: in the diary of Anne Frank, 27; empathy and, 264; Kindertransport and, 162–63; Klüger and, 91–92, 93; Kofman and, 138, 139; Lévinas on, 249; reader as Other, and autobiographies, 96

*Other People's House* (Segal), 158

Oyneg Shabes, 6–7, 8–9

Paris, Matthew, 58

*Paroles suffoquées* (Kofman), 121–22, 127

patriarchy: Bruck on, 65; fairy tales and, 99–104; fathers/husbands as Holocaust victims and, 30, 34–35; gendered reaction to Nazism/war, 30–31; Holocaust and